Porn 101

Edited by
James Elias, Ph.D.,
Veronica Diehl Elias, Ph.D.,
Vern L. Bullough, Ph.D., R.N.,
Gwen Brewer, Ph.D.,
Jeffrey J. Douglas, J.D.,
and Will Jarvis

Porn 101

Eroticism,

Pornography, and the

First Amendment

Prometheus Books

59 John Glenn Drive
Amherst, New York 14228-2197

Dedicated to

Stanley Fleishman
1920–1999

Champion of the First Amendment,
the disabled, and civil rights.

Published 1999 by Prometheus Books

Inquiries should be addressed to
Prometheus Books, 59 John Glenn Drive, Amherst, New York 14228-2197.
VOICE: 716–691–0133, ext. 207.
FAX: 716–564–2711.
WWW.PROMETHEUSBOOKS.COM

03 02 01 00 99   5 4 3 2 1

Library of Congress Cataloging-in-Publication Data

Porn 101 : eroticism, pornography, and the First Amendment / edited by James
    Elias ... [et al.].
        p.   cm.
    Includes bibliographical references.
    ISBN 1–57392–750–3 (pbk. : alk. paper)
    1. Pornography–United States. 2. Erotica–United States. 3. Censorship–
United States. 4. Feminism–United States. I. Elias, James.
HQ472.U6P67   1999
363.4'7'0973–dc21   99–046627
                                                                        CIP

Printed in the United States of America on acid-free paper

Contents

Section Eleven: Child Pornography: Forbidden Thoughts and Images in an Erotic Landscape

Section Twelve: Historical Aspects of Pornography

Acknowledgments

THIS BOOK IS BASED ON THE PRESENTATIONS GIVEN AT THE WORLD CONference on Pornography held in Los Angeles in August of 1998 involving the legal community, the academic community, and the adult entertainment industry. Bringing together disparate groups in an attempt to provide an open forum for those who defend, research, and are intimately involved in the field of pornography will always provide an intense, volatile, and highly productive experience. Will Jarvis as an industry representative; Jeffrey J. Douglas from the Free Speech Coalition; James Elias, Vern Bullough, Veronica Elias, and Gwen Brewer from the Center for Sex Research planned, organized, and executed the pornography conference. Will worked tirelessly and enthusiastically on this project. It would not have been possible without the help of a number of other individuals. Mark Roysner provided legal counsel for the conference and shepherded us through the legal mine fields that seemed to be around every corner. Jane Hamilton from VCA Pictures jumped in when asked and made things happen and people appear. Bill Margold was a major source of ideas, people, and information and, when needed, turned up with people to help. Art Taitt, our registrar, has helped to guide us through the complexities of conference finances. Carol, from the Free Speech Coalition, worked quietly behind the scenes running interference for us and putting us in touch with those who could help.

Esau Tovar deserves special recognition as our webmaster and colleague. He filled numerous roles and now heads his own research project. Valdis Volkovskis once again ably handled technical materials and saw that equipment needed was in place, calming upset presenters along the way. Martin Hernandez and Jennifer Goodwin performed security duties throughout the conference. They kept an eye on all presentations and programs and diverted those who tried to crash the conference; we owe them

9

a debt of gratitude. The vital work of processing the registrations, sorting names, handling thousands of pieces of paper and envelopes was done by Manna Mohageg, Michelle Betiong, and Joy Chang who spent hundreds of hours putting together the details. This was a great group of assistants, and we are proud to see them graduate and go on to fulfill their personal and academic goals.

The compiling of this book was a major undertaking as the presentations arrived in every conceivable form and by every medium. Dominic Little and David Goldsobel undertook the task of converting the sixty-odd papers into a single, functional format. Bryan Oey has worked as a key assistant on the book project. Dr. Carmel Rosal undertook the major task of final editing to complete this book.

The editors at Prometheus have been especially helpful and have played a major role in putting this manuscript into final form. We express our profound gratitude to Editor-in-Chief Steven L. Mitchell and Eugene O'Connor of the Prometheus editorial staff, without whose prodding and support this book could not have been completed.

James E. Elias, Ph.D.
Center for Sex Research

Introduction

THE KEYNOTE SPEAKER AT THE WORLD CONFERENCE ON PORNOG-raphy, from which the articles in this book are taken, was Nadine Strossen, President of the American Civil Liberties Union. She said the purpose of her paper was to give a "pep talk" to the participants, a statement for which she was denounced in editorials in two New York City tabloids. The *Daily News* editorial writer said that it is "one thing for the ACLU to defend pornographers on First Amendment grounds, quite another to cheer them on,"[1] while the *Post* said that the Strossen "may believe the Founders intended the U.S. Constitution to defend bestiality videos."[2] Such comments only emphasize how controversial the topic of erotica and pornography remains, and that any serious discussion of it invites such misleading comments as the tabloid press of New York gave it.

Strossen spoke at a luncheon banquet and was introduced by Ramona Ripston, executive director of the ACLU of Southern California. Stanley Fleishman, whose paper is in Section 1, received an award. The ACLU's defense of freedom of expression remains controversial, in spite of its success in the courts. For example, the incumbent governor of Hawaii, Ben Cayetano, was attacked during the November 1998 election campaign by his opponent, Linda Lingle, for being a "card-carrying member" of an organization whose President would dare to address the World Pornography Conference. Governor Cayetano was reelected despite this tactic–or perhaps because of it, but the remark emphasizes that the national debate over pornography and censorship is by no means concluded. Since many of the decisions for free speech have not come from legislation but from court decisions defining free speech as well as the right of privacy, those opposed to free speech have usually not openly attacked it, except in the cases of pornography, but rather have concentrated their attack on the indepen-

11

dence of judges and the courts. Probably this attack on the independence of judges and the courts, which is increasingly nasty but also very effective, is the greatest threat to freedom in the United States which we face since the courts ultimately are the shield for all constitutional rights, including freedom of sexual expression.

NOTES

1. "Biased Judge Tips Justice's Scales," *Daily News*, Aug. 12, 1998, p. 28
2. "More Revolting Academic Behavior," *New York Post*, Aug. 11, 1998, p. 16.

Foreword

In Defense of Pornography

Nadine Strossen

I AM CONSTANTLY ASKED WHY I WROTE A BOOK DEFENDING FREE speech for pornography,[1] and why I continue to defend pornography in so many forums. The answer is that I have to keep *defending* free speech for pornography, because so many *other* people keep *attacking* it–especially here in the U.S., with our Puritanical heritage. This point was effectively made by Garrison Keillor, in his 1990 testimony in defense of the National Endowment for the Arts ("NEA"), which is constantly embattled because of the sexually oriented art it funds. Keillor said: "My ancestors were Puritans from England, who arrived [here] in 1648 in the hopes of finding greater restrictions than were permissible under English law at the time."[2]

In that same testimony, Keillor's wit also barbed the double-edged nature of Americans' traditional love-hate attitudes towards sex and sexual expression. These inconsistent attitudes are at best ambivalent and at worst hypocritical. In Keillor's words:

> [O]ver the years, . . . we Puritans have learned something about repression: man's interest in the forbidden is sharp and constant.[I]f Congress does not do something about obscene art, we will have to build galleries twice as big to hold the people who want to see it. [And] if Congress *does* do something about obscene art, the galleries will need to be even bigger. . . .[3]

The persistent attacks against sexual expression that we have seen throughout American history have extended into current times and into our newest communications medium: cyberspace. I am so proud of the leading role the ACLU has played in defending sexual expression on this newest battleground. We led the successful court challenge to Congress's first attempt to censor cyberspace, through the Communications Decency Act

("CDA").[4] And I am thrilled that the Supreme Court's landmark decision in that case, declaring cyberspace a free speech zone, will go down in history under the name of *Reno* v. *ACLU*.[5] Additionally, we have brought and won all four constitutional challenges that have been launched against state cybercensorship laws.[6]

Most recently among the state cases, we won our lawsuit against New Mexico's law, which made it a crime to disseminate online expression that involved "sexual conduct" or even mere "nudity."[7] One of our clients, who would have faced a one-year prison term under this law, is a San Francisco artist who teaches life drawing online, Rebecca Alzofon.

Even more recently, we were victorious in the first lawsuit challenging a local cybercensorship law, which mandated blocking software on public library computers.[8]

No matter how many victories we win, though, the would-be censors are not deterred. They keep coming up with new laws, which we have to keep fighting in both the legislatures and the courts. For example, continuing with the cybercensorship front as one example, in October 1998, President Clinton signed a new federal cybercensorship law. The ACLU promptly challenged this so-called CDA II in a lawsuit named, appropriately, *ACLU* v. *Reno II*. In response, the federal judge in the case promptly issued a "temporary restraining order" prohibiting the government from enforcing the law.[9] Nonetheless, the U.S. Justice Department continues to defend it.

This new law criminalizes any material that any community might find "harmful to minors." As one of our lawyers commented:

> It's the height of irony that the same Congress that plastered the salacious Starr Report all over the Internet now passes a plainly unconstitutional law to suppress a vaguely defined category of "harmful" material. You would think Congress would have learned that "harmfulness" is in the eye of the beholder.[10]

The pertinence of the Starr Report in this context is underscored by my own personal experience. When the book version of that report was published in September 1998, I happened to be speaking in Missoula, Montana. In a display featured in a local newspaper, one of Missoula's bookstores prominently placed stacks of the Starr Report right next to stacks of my book, *Defending Pornography*!

In the ACLU's new lawsuit against the new federal cybercensorship law, I am actually one of the complainants. That is because I am a monthly columnist for a Webzine, *Intellectual Capital*,[11] and my writings could definitely trigger severe criminal and civil penalties under this law. Not that my columns are in competition with *Screw* magazine—I hate to disappoint you! Rather, the concept of "harmful to minors" is so vague and expansive that it endangers essentially all words and images with any sexual overtones—even about critically important topics, about which I do write, such as abortion, AIDS and other sexually transmitted diseases, censorship of sexual expression, contraception, gender discrimination, lesbian and gay rights, sexual harassment, and sexual violence.[12]

I know that many people consider my writings "harmful to minors"– indeed, in the online discussions that follow each column, many readers tell me so!

And I am in very good company. Let me just cite a few of the other plaintiffs in our new case, whose valuable online expression is now also endangered: The American Booksellers Foundation for Free Expression; Artnet, the leading vendor of fine art on the Web; BlackStripe, an organization for lesbian and gay African-Americans; Condomania, the leading online distributor of safer-sex information and condoms; the poet Lawrence Ferlinghetti; a coalition of online news publications, including MSNBC, *Time* magazine and the *New York Times*; OBGYN.Net, a women's health website; *Philadelphia Gay News*; *RiotGrrl*, a magazine for young feminists; and another popular online magazine, *Salon.*

As if the new federal cybercensorship law were not bad enough, at last count, similar laws were also pending in a couple dozen state legislatures– not to mention countless local government agencies, such as school boards and library boards.[13]

And the ACLU recently had to spring to the defense of cyberporn against yet another censorship tactic. During the summer of 1998, a woman in Livermore, California, sought a court order barring the public library from allowing either adults or minors to access certain online sexual materials. She argued that if the library continued to allow such Internet access, it should be shut down as a "public nuisance."[14]

No wonder the ACLU uses as our motto the line attributed to Thomas Jefferson: "Eternal vigilance is the price of liberty."[15] Actually, this same sentiment was put in even more concrete terms, from my perspective, by Thomas Paine–especially on days like today when I have to take a red-eye flight from here in Los Angeles back to New York so I can preside over an all-day ACLU meeting tomorrow. Paine said: "Those who expect to reap the blessings of freedom must . . . undergo the fatigue of supporting it."[16]

We are now facing innumerable, persistent, and nasty attacks on sexual expression not only in cyberspace, but also in all communications media, all over the country, and from all points on the political spectrum, ranging from the so-called Religious Right to the so-called Radical Feminists.

I would like to cite one particular recent attack on pornography that happens to be on my mind now. This attack would be ridiculous, if it had not had such a devastating impact. It is on my mind because I recently had lunch in San Francisco with James Hormel, the distinguished philanthropist whose nomination to be Ambassador to Luxembourg was stonewalled (pun intended!) by Trent Lott–acting at the behest of the "Religious Right."[17]

The initial concern was that Jim, as an out-of-the-closet gay man, would promote "the gay agenda" in Luxembourg,[18] thereby endangering U.S. interests in foreign policy–or maybe I should say in "foreign affairs"! One of the accusations in the vicious attack against Jim was that he was allegedly a promoter of pornography. This is because Jim gave a generous gift to establish a Gay and Lesbian Center at the new San Francisco Public Library. Right-wing activists apparently camped out at that wing, poring through materials, and compiling a collection of works that they condemned as "pro-pedophilia, anti-Christian, and pornographic."[19]

It would be bad enough to attack the library staff for deciding to acquire these materials. But it is completely bizarre to attack the donor who did not even play any role in the acquisition decision. Still, Jim's well-organized, influential opponents demanded that he explicitly denounce each of the challenged works.

As advocates of Jim's ambassadorial appointment pointed out, these supposedly pornographic, supposedly disqualifying works are all in the Library of Congress as well. But I always get nervous when this kind of comparative argument is offered up in an attempt to placate censors. Chances are, rather than diverting the censors from Target #1, this argument simply *also* channels their suppressive efforts toward Target #2! Sure enough, as a result of the anti-Hormel-inspired inquisition into lesbian- and gay-themed library collections, the Traditional Values Coalition has indicated that it might well launch an investigation into "pornography" that is infecting the Library of Congress's collection![20]

CENSORSHIP OF MY ANTI-CENSORSHIP MESSAGE

To give you a sense of how serious the current attacks on sexual expression are—and therefore how critically important your ongoing defense is—I would like to tell you about a few of my own recent experiences.

The first one occurred in that city many of us think of as "Censor-nati." In the wake of the latest wave of attacks on erotic expression there—triggered by Larry Flynt's recently opened store[21]—in March 1998 the local ACLU chapter and other free speech groups[22] banded together to bring me out to give a public lecture presenting the anti-censorship perspective. They gave the lecture essentially the same title as the organizers of the current conference chose for this talk, which is also the main title of a book I wrote several years ago: "Defending Pornography."

For the Cincinnati event, my hosts rented the lecture hall at the city's Museum Center, which is open to the public on a first-come, first-serve basis. A couple days before my lecture, though, the Museum Center suddenly decided to cancel my appearance, because—and here I am quoting one of the Center's directors from the *Cincinnati Enquirer*'s front-page story about this controversy—my lecture topic was so "distasteful."[23]

I therefore found myself in the somewhat unusual position of becoming an ACLU *client*. Fortunately, some wonderful Cincinnati lawyers,[24] working with the local ACLU, were able to defend my right to speak as scheduled.

Actually, as I said, this situation was only "somewhat" unusual. It was not the first time that local ACLU lawyers had been forced to come to the defense of their national President's free speech rights! And—not coincidentally—the first time that happened also involved a talk I was scheduled to give on this very same topic in another community that is not known for enthusiastically embracing the First Amendment: Ventura, California.

As an aside, it is striking to me that of all the many talks I have given since I became ACLU President almost eight years ago,[25] on so many controversial topics, where feelings run very high—from abortion, to gay rights, to the death penalty, to separation of church and state—the only two times I have ever faced efforts to block my talks have both involved the topic of pornography. Since becoming ACLU President, I have given more than 1500 talks all over the U.S., before extremely diverse audiences, ranging from the most liberal to the most conservative. So I think this experience is a telling indication of the unique, irrational, emotional antipathy to sexual expression in our society.

The Ventura incident took place in the spring of 1995, when I was traveling around the country on book tour for my book, whose full title is *Defending Pornography: Free Speech, Sex, and the Fight for Women's Rights.* One of the places I was scheduled to speak was the Ventura Bookstore. To advertise my talk and booksigning, the bookstore owner, Ed Elrod, simply put a poster-size copy of the book's cover on an easel at his store's entrance. No sooner had he done this, though, than some irate citizens stormed into his store, complaining that the very presence of the sign endangered the safety and welfare of women and children in their community and demanding that he take it down. When he refused, some of them announced that they would organize protests at my reading and boycotts of the bookstore. A number of them also filed complaints with the city government.[26]

In fairness, I must admit that the book's title and cover are rather provocative! Having previously written only academic articles, I was myself quite startled when the publisher first presented the cover design to me. With its flamboyant colors and in-your-face title, it was a far cry in looks from, say, the *Harvard Law Review*. In dismay, I sought the counsel of one of my friends who is a successful professional writer, Claudia Dreifus. Claudia explained that the name of the game in book cover design is to attract readers' attention. As she asked me, "Nadine, if you saw this book in a bookstore, would it leap off the shelves?" My answer: "This book commits sexual harassment against you!"

As for the title, I suppose it is fairly tame when you compare it to, say, the titles of X-rated films! But when your previous experience is with legalistic, scholarly books and articles, the title that the publisher chose for my book is rather startling. This perspective was well-captured by Marjorie Heins, who was then the Director of the ACLU Arts Censorship Project, and who is also speaking at this conference. Her comment upon hearing the title that the publisher had come up with: "Gee, Nadine, couldn't they work the word 'orgasm' into it, too?!"

Well, it is one thing to find the cover arresting, but another altogether to find yourself in danger of being arrested just for displaying it. And that is indeed what faced the Ventura bookstore owner, Ed Elrod. Shortly after he had displayed that cover poster, a local fire department official came into his store and asked him to remove the sign, noting that it had been the target of citizen complaints. While this official cited certain obscure local ordinances with which the sign allegedly did not comply, Ed had routinely used exactly the same type of sign to advertise readings and other events at his bookstore for the previous seventeen years and never once had a city official suggested that there were any legal problems involved.[27]

With the backing of the local ACLU, Ed Elrod stood his ground. I was able to give my talk. And the women and children of Ventura County managed to survive this threatening event!

I really want to praise and thank the Ventura Bookstore owner, Ed Elrod, as well as the Cincinnati citizens who organized my lecture there and likewise stood their ground against enormous pressure. It is one thing for me to come in and give a speech in a hostile atmosphere. I can just pick up and leave in a few hours. But these local free speech champions have to go on living in their communities, and dealing with the ongoing wrath of anti-pornography activists and politicians. For them, it takes real courage to defend pornography. It should not have to, but it does, alas.

And, along with the nationally prominent and justly celebrated defenders of free speech for sexual expression—such as Stanley Fleishman—I also want to salute all of the many unheralded, anonymous defenders at the grassroots level. They are absolutely essential to make the promise of free speech an actual reality in the everyday lives of ordinary people all over the United States. That is because no matter how many constitutional battles Stanley Fleishman or the ACLU may win at the U.S. Supreme Court, free speech still will not exist as a practical, tangible reality unless we have, for example, bookstore owners and librarians and teachers and movie theater owners who are willing to actually implement those abstract constitutional principles in concrete cases, in the face of community hostility.

For instance, as I have already indicated, thanks to my book tour, I developed a special respect and gratitude for the independent bookstore owners who invited me do talks and booksignings in their stores. Before I wrote my book, I could never have appreciated that this should be such a big deal. But no sooner had the book been published than I heard that the managers of a major bookstore chain had made a corporate decision that I would not be permitted to do any readings at any of its stores, anywhere in the country—not even in that den of iniquity where I live, Manhattan!—because the topic was deemed too controversial and provocative.

As I said, I am sharing these personal experiences with you because I want to highlight how very embattled sexual expression continues to be on all fronts. So embattled that not only sexual expression itself, but even such a fairly dry, academic, lawyerly book as mine—which is not at all erotic, but just argues against censorship (that is hardly a great marketing pitch for the book, is it?!)–even that has been subjected to various silencing efforts. And not just in the Censor-natis of this country, but also in New York, and even by directors of lecture halls and bookstores, who should be especially committed to the First Amendment.

THE HELLS OF ACADEME

Worse yet, we are constantly fighting attacks on all manner of sexually oriented expression even in the setting where the Supreme Court has long said that free speech should be especially sacrosanct–namely, the halls of academe.[28] Here, the attacks come largely from the left, reflecting the view that women's rights and safety are undermined by any expression that is sexually explicit–or even just sexually suggestive.

Of course, this worldview has been spearheaded by University of Michigan Law Professor Catharine MacKinnon and New York writer Andrea Dworkin. Fortunately, their model anti-pornography laws–which tried to outlaw sexual expression as a violation of women's civil rights–fortunately, these general laws have been shot down in the courts on First Amendment grounds.[29] Unfortunately, though, the MacDworkinite worldview has prevailed in other important arenas. One is sexual harassment rules, which too often reflect the MacDworkinite creed that *any* sexual expression *is* sexual harassment–in other words, falsely equating sex with sex*ism*.[30]

In the context of government workplaces or public campuses, we can rely on the First Amendment to protect the right to engage in sexually oriented expression for professors, other employees, and students. Indeed, a few years ago, the ACLU of Southern California successfully challenged one of these all-too-typical, sweepingly overbroad, sexual harassment policies. This one had been adopted by the Los Angeles County Fire Department, and it barred firefighters from even bringing to the firehouse any "magazines . . . or . . . other material . . . of a clear sexual connotation."

Likewise, Los Angeles attorney Stephen Rohde successfully represented an English and Film Studies professor at San Bernardino Valley College who was punished for sexual harassment after a student complained because he required his class to write essays defining pornography–yes, that was de*fin*ing pornography–not de*fend*ing it. I was really depressed that the federal trial court actually upheld the college's disciplinary actions against this professor, but fortunately justice was finally done by the Ninth Circuit Court of Appeals.[31]

When you turn from the public sector to the private sector, though, the Constitution is completely unavailable as a source of free speech protection.[32] Therefore, in too many workplaces and on too many campuses, all sexually suggestive words or images are being completely banished, with no legal recourse.[33]

As a law professor, I am particularly heartbroken about situations where professors have faced sexual harassment charges merely for classroom discussions of important legal topics with a sexual dimension. In one recent instance, a law professor was charged with sexual harassment for daring to bring up the topic of false claims of rape. You can imagine the chilling effect. Reports abound of law professors—especially males—being discouraged from even broaching the topic of rape, even in criminal law courses.[34]

It is important to understand that this doubly distorted approach—treating all sex*ual expression* as sex*ist harassment*—is not a misinterpretation of the MacDworkinite philosophy. To the contrary, Catharine MacKinnon has expressly advocated precisely this result.[35]

Daphne Patai, Professor of Women's Studies and Comparative Literature at the University of Massachusetts at Amherst, has recently published a book entitled *Heterophobia: Sexual Harassment and the Future of Feminism*,[36] which is a trenchant criticism of how current harassment law threatens many civil liberties, not to mention male-female relations. Consistent with MacKinnon's false equation between sex and sexism—and, correspondingly, between sexual expression and sexual harassment—Patai makes the following sad observation: "'Harassment' threatens to become the predominant word associated with 'sexual.' "[37]

Far from being criticized by legal academics, MacKinnon's dangerously capacious concept of sexual harassment has instead been almost universally lionized. For example, during the spring of 1998, no less prestigious a law school than Yale hosted a conference on MacKinnon's contributions to sexual harassment law and policy that was essentially a lovefest. Only a few speakers were invited who had anything critical or even skeptical to say about her ideas—and those were, by design, white males.[38]

Not that I have anything against white males—don't get me wrong, I love you guys! But this is consistent with a basic strategy of MacKinnon and her allies; they want to convey the impression that they speak at least for all women, and perhaps even for all members of traditionally disempowered groups, including racial minorities, too. Accordingly, they consistently refuse to debate me or other women who have different perspectives on these issues.[39]

Moreover, MacKinnon and some of her supporters go even further in shirking an exchange of views with other women, or women's rights advocates—refusing even to appear at the same conference, or to participate in the same project, with any women who dare to disagree with them.

Just recently, for example, I happened to learn of yet another such incident. David M. O'Brien, professor of political science at the University of Virginia, was editing a textbook on various civil liberties issues, including the censorship of pornography.[40] He wanted to include excerpts from some of my writings and some of MacKinnon's. When she heard that some of my printed words would be—heaven forbid—included in the same book as some of hers, she had a tantrum and told the publisher that he would have to choose—either her words or mine. He refused to withdraw my piece, so she therefore pulled hers—at the galleys stage!

I initially learned of this incident only coincidentally, through a mutual colleague of Professor O'Brien's, whom I did not know personally, and mine (although I subsequently confirmed these facts by speaking directly to Professor O'Brien himself). So for each incident of this sort that happens to come to my attention, I am sure there are many others that do not. And for each incident where the target of the pressure refuses to cave in to these bullying tactics, I am sure there are many others where the target does give in. My book describes a couple of these.

The most disappointing to me occurred several years ago and involved no less prominent a group—which should know better—than the National Association of Women Judges.[41] That august organization abruptly retracted a speaking engagement I had to address its annual national convention, without explanation. I later discovered it was because MacKinnon had also been invited to speak at the convention. I want to underscore that this was not set to be a debate between the two of us; rather, the "problem," from MacKinnon's perspective, was the mere fact that both of us would be appearing, at different times, before the same convention. As one of the judges who organized the event said to a *New York Times* reporter: "The general feeling was that MacKinnon would be less than pleased to be on the program with Strossen, so we had no choice."[42]

As you can see, then, the recent Yale Law School conference is part of a consistent pattern in including no female, feminist counterweights to the MacDworkinites. Still, as a law professor, I was shocked that such a one-sided forum should be sanctioned at such a prominent law school. And I was especially distressed to read that First Amendment scholars in attendance—who should know better—were so eager to jump on the MacDworkinite bandwagon that they cavalierly dismissed First Amendment concerns.

One example is Frederick Schauer, the Frank Stanton Professor of the First Amendment at Harvard. He brushed aside concerns that harassment law can inhibit free speech as "frivolous."[43] In Professor Schauer's defense, that comment was very thoughtful compared to what Andrea Dworkin said about those who dare to raise First Amendment criticisms of sexual harassment law. She denounced these critics as "millions of men [who] want to have a young woman at work to suck their cock."[44]

By the way, I should underscore that I am not pointing the finger at Yale only because of its traditional rivalry with my alma mater, Harvard! As I have already noted, Harvard University has appointed as the Stanton Professor *of the First Amendment* Fred Schauer. Fred has many outstanding personal qualities and professional qualifications, but he would be the first to say—indeed, I am confident, to *boast*—that these do not include a classic libertarian defense of First Amendment rights, particularly for sexually oriented expression. To the contrary. Based on Fred's distinguished scholarly reputation for explaining why the First Amendment should have a relatively limited scope, and in particular should not encompass pornography, Fred was tapped to write the controversial, censorial report of the Meese Pornography Commission.[45]

Selecting a leading anti-pornography advocate for a prestigious chaired professorship in First Amendment studies is consistent with other steps Harvard has taken to suggest that the First Amendment has nothing to do with sexual expression. For example, in March 1998, Harvard University Press–which had published MacKinnon's last anti-pornography tract in 1993[46]–published yet another anti-pornography manifesto by the MacKinnon-Dworkin duo, entitled *In Harm's Way*. And Harvard University Press's gushing press release about the book showed utter contempt for First Amendment concerns. For example, it poses the following rhetorical question: "Can we sacrifice the lives of women and children to a pornographer's right to free 'speech'? The word "speech" is actually in quotation marks! In the same vein, the press release asks, "Can we allow the First Amendment to shield sexual exploitation and predatory violence?"

Harvard University Press promoted *In Harm's Way* as an authoritative, unabridged record of the hearings that were held in various cities that considered the model MacDworkin anti-pornography law, including Los Angeles. But Wendy McElroy, a writer and anti-censorship activist who was living in Los Angeles at the time and campaigning against that law (along with Ramona Ripston and the ACLU of Southern California), has written a devastating review of *In Harm's Way*, which documents that this so-called accurate record is in fact grossly incomplete and distorted.[47] Among its fundamental flaws, the book purports to include all opposition testimony. In fact, though, it includes not one word of either Ramona's testimony or Wendy's. Repressed memory syndrome?

Significantly, I found out about this glaring distortion not only in the MacKinnon-Dworkin "memoir" but also in Harvard University Press's promotion of it, from Ronald K. L. Collins, a legal writer and commentator who is a self-described admirer of MacKinnon and Dworkin. But after he read Wendy McElroy's review, Ron sent me the following email: "Whatever one makes of MacKinnon & Dworkin (and I do admire them in some ways), . . . it is dishonest to do what McElroy claims they have done, especially when future judges and scholars may refer to their work as a 'complete' record. So I'd welcome any ideas you might have to draw more attention to Wendy's book review."

Again, I want to stress that the incidents I have been describing are just the tip of a very large iceberg–namely, a consistent hostility to sexual expression in some of the very precincts where we would expect it to be most protected, including academia. Some of the incidents are well-publicized. One prominent recent example is the crusade by New York Governor George Pataki and some of his appointees to the New York Board of Regents against the faculty and administration of the State University of New York at New Paltz because of a fall 1997 women's studies conference that included workshops on some sexually oriented themes.[48] Other incidents do not receive much, if any, publicity beyond the campus concerned, thus increasing the chilling effect there.

The general censorial landscape I have surveyed should highlight the importance of this conference. Wonderfully rich and impressive as the current program is, and numerous as our speakers and participants are, you are still, unfortunately, only a minority voice in too many important settings. So you have to continue raising your voices wherever you are—whether pursuing your art or your research or your legal cases. Everyone who cares about free speech depends on your talents and expertise and efforts now more than ever.

SAVING THE FREE SPEECH SAFETY NET: INDEPENDENT JUDGES

Speaking of minority voices brings me to that singularly important issue on the legal and political front for which I would like to mobilize your support, as I said before. Our judicial branch of government is designed to provide a safety net for rights that are not respected by other government officials— to protect rights of individuals and minority group members against what James Madison called "the tyranny of the majority."[49] Therefore, all of us who care about any of these rights must mobilize against the increasingly savage—and effective—attack on what our adversaries condemn as "judicial activism," but what we human rights advocates cherish as "judicial independence."[50]

In 1997, House Majority Whip Tom Delay (R-TX) actually called for the impeachment of federal judges who had had the audacity to enforce the Constitution by striking down laws that violated it.[51] And Congress recently has held many hearings on various measures that would endanger the autonomy of our judges—including by imposing term limits on them. I testified at one such hearing in 1998, and it was frightening.[52]

The critical importance of judicial independence for maintaining freedom of sexual expression is vividly illustrated by our fight for such freedom in cyberspace. As I have already indicated, censorial laws sail through the legislative process—with almost no politician, of either party, daring to openly oppose them. For example, almost no one—on either side of the aisle—voted against the suppressive federal "Communications Decency Act." Out of 535 members of Congress, only 21 voted against it.[53] And that one-sided margin is typical.

In contrast, though, the courts have been equally unified in striking down cybercensorship laws as unconstitutional. So far, the ACLU's challenges to such laws have been ruled on by 19 different federal judges from across a broad ideological spectrum—having been appointed by the last six Presidents, including four Republicans and two Democrats. Yet all of these judges—including the entire U.S. Supreme Court[54]—have upheld the First Amendment and struck down the suppressive laws.

Moreover, many elected officials have told us cyberlibertarians how relieved they were that these cybercensorship laws were invalidated. "I knew the law was unconstitutional," they say. "But I couldn't possibly vote against it—for fear of being called " 'soft on porn.' "

As if it is not bad enough that elected officials pass the Constitutional buck to the courts in these important First Amendment cases, to add insult to injury, the elected officials then attack the very judges who take seriously the oath that the politicians also pledge, but honor only in the breach: to defend and uphold the Constitution. I shudder to think where we would be—more precisely where our free speech rights would be—if we did not have the safety net that our federal courts now provide, thanks to their relative independence from politics.

CONCLUSION

Work on behalf of freedom of sexual expression is incredibly important for the free speech cause. What is at stake is not only freedom of sexual expression, important as that is. Rather, what is at stake is free expression more generally. The reason why the ACLU staunchly defends freedom for all expression, regardless of its subject matter or viewpoint—indeed, the reason why the ACLU staunchly defends *all* fundamental freedoms for everyone, more generally—is because of the indivisibility of all these rights. Once we cede to the government the power to violate one right for one person or group, then no right is safe for any person or group. In the free speech context, once the government is granted the power to censor one unpopular or controversial type of expression, it can and will grab the power to censor another.

So, when we defend sexual expression, we are taking a stand not only against a specific kind of censorship. Indeed, freedom of sexual expression is an essential element not only of freedom of expression more generally; even more broadly, it is an essential element of individual freedom and human rights in general. I would like to close with a statement that eloquently captures this pivotal role of sexual expression. It is from a letter that was published in the ACLU newsletter in 1991, which I saved because I found it so powerful. It was written by Gary Mongiovi, an economist who teaches at St. John's University in New York.

He wrote:

> Suppression of pornography is not just a free-speech issue: Attempts to stifle sexual expression are part of a larger agenda directed at the suppression of human freedom and individuality more generally.
>
> It is no coincidence that one of the first consequences of democratization and political liberalization in the former Soviet Union, Eastern Europe and China was a small explosion of erotic publications.
>
> Sexual expression is perhaps the most fundamental manifestation of human individuality. Erotic material is subversive in the sense that it celebrates, and appeals to, the most uniquely personal aspects of an individual's emotional life. Thus, to allow freedom of expression and freedom of thought in this realm is to . . . promote diversity and non-conformist behavior in general.[55]

NOTES

1. Nadine Strossen, *Defending Pornography: Free Speech, Sex, and the Fight for Women's Rights* (New York: Scribner, 1995).

2. *Hearing on the Reauthorization of the National Foundation on the Arts and Humanities Act Before the Senate Comm. on Labor and Human Resources,* 101 Cong.122 (1990) (Statement of Garrison Keillor).

3. Ibid., pp. 122-23.

4. 47 U.S.C.S. 223.

5. 521 U.S. 844 (1997).

6. See *ACLU* v. *Johnson,* 4 F. Supp. 2d 1029 (D.N.M. 1998); *Urofsky* v. *Allen,* 995 F. Supp. 634 (E.D. Va. 1998); *ACLU* v. *Miller,* 977 F. Supp. 1228 (N.D. Ga. 1997); *ALA* v. *Pataki,* 969 F. Supp. 160 (S.D.N.Y. 1997).

7. *Johnson,* 4 F. Supp. 2d at 1032.

8. See *Mainstream Loudoun* v. *Board of Trustees,* 24 F. Supp. 2d 552 (E.D. Va. 1998).

9. *ACLU* v. *Reno,* 1998 U.S. Dist. LEXIS 18546 (E.D. Pa. 1998). In February 1999, Judge Lowell A. Reed issued a preliminary injunction against enforcement of the law and found that *ACLU* was likely to succeed on its claim that the law "imposes a burden on speech that is protected for adults." See *ACLU* v. *Reno,* 1999 U.S. Dist. Lexis 735, at **66 CE.D Pa. 1999). The Justice Department subsequently appealed Judge Reed's ruling. See "*ACLU* v. *Reno,* Round 2: Internet Censorship Battle Moves to Appeals Court" (April 12, 1999) <http://www.aclu.org/features/f101698a.html>. Immediately before this book went to press, the parties were awaiting in a brief schedule for the appeal. Telephone interview by Amy L. Tenny with J. C. Salyer, ACLU Brennan Fellow, June 5, 1999.

10. American Civil Liberties Union Freedom Network, *Rights Groups Prepare Legal Challenge as Passage of Internet "Indecency" Bill Appears Certain* (visited Jan. 8, 1999) <http://www.aclu.org/news/n101598a.html>.

11. <http://www.intellectualcapital.com>.

12. See, e.g., Nadine Strossen, "An Immoral Affront to Our Democracy," *Intellectual Capital* (Dec. 24, 1998) <http://www.intellectualcapital.com/issues/98/1224/icopinions3.asp> (criticizing anti-sodomy laws); "Why Your Vote Counts," *Intellectual Capital* (Oct. 29, 1998) <http://www.intellectualcapital.com/issues/98/1029/icopinions2.asp> (criticizing "partial-birth abortion" bans); "Schoolgirls, Sex and Speech," *Intellectual Capital* (June 18, 1998) <http://www.intellectualcapital.com/issues/98/0618/icopinions2. asp> (criticizing unconstitutional restrictions on minors' access to sexually oriented material); "The People Versus Larry Flynt, Part II," *Intellectual Capital* (Apr. 23, 1998) <http://www.intellectualcapital.com/issues/98/0423/ icopinions2.asp> (criticizing obscenity laws).

13. See generally ACLU Cyberliberties Update (visited Jan. 5, 1999) <www.aclu.org/issues/cyber/updates.html>.

14. See ACLU Defends California Library Against Internet Censorship (visited Jan. 5, 1999) <http://www.aclu.org/news/n122398b.html> (stating that in October 1998, the Alameda County Superior Court dismissed a complaint by a patron of the Livermore Public Library that the library's policy of providing unfiltered Internet access constituted a public nuisance). The patron has since filed an amended complaint asserting a constitutional right to force the library to install blocking software. In response, the ACLU of Northern California filed a second friend of the court brief in support of the Livermore Public Library's policy of providing uncensored access

to the Internet. The Alameda County Superior Court subsequently dismissed the patron's case for the second time. See "Court Upholds Livermore Library's Uncensored Internet Access Policy" (Jan. 14, 1999) <http://www.aclu.org/news/n011499a.html>.

15. John Bartlett, *Familiar Quotations* 14th ed. (Boston: Little, Brown, 1968), 479b n.2.

16. "The American Crisis IV," in *The Life and Major Writings of Thomas Paine* 102, ed. Philip S. Foner (New York: Carol Publishing Group, 1974).

17. See Nadine Strossen, "James C. Hormel and the Ambassadors of Homophobia," *Intellectual Capital* (Aug. 20, 1998) <http://www.intellectualcapital.com/ issues/98/0820/icopinions2.asp>; see also Philip Shenon, "Gay Philanthropist's Nomination to Become Ambassador to Luxembourg Dies in the Senate," *N.Y. Times*, Oct. 20, 1998, at A12 (noting that Hormel's nomination had officially died). But see Katherine Q. Seelye, "Clinton Appoints Gay Man as Ambassador as Congress Is Away," *N.Y. Times*, June 15, 1999, at A16 (reporting that President Clinton exercised a "rarely used" executive privilege known as a recess appointment to appoint Hormel while Congress was on its 10-day Memorial Day vacation).

18. Frank Rich, "All in the Family," *N.Y. Times*, Apr. 18, 1998, at A13. ("[Hormel's] nomination has been put 'on hold' by three G.O.P. Senators–James Inhofe of Oklahoma, Tim Hutchinson of Arkansas, Robert Smith of New Hampshire–eager to pander to the far-right hysteria about a 'gay agenda' that might cause Judy Garland impersonations to break out in Luxembourg.")

19. See Jonathan Weisman, "Envoy's Nomination Fires Debate Over 'Gay Agenda'; Hormel's Support for Homosexual Causes Attacked in Senate," *Baltimore Sun*, June 23, 1998, at 1A.

20. See Louis Freedberg, "Books Cited by Hormel Foes Found in D.C."; "Gay Material in Library of Congress," *San Francisco Chronicle*, Feb. 27, 1998, at A3.

21. See Kristen Delguzzi, "Flynt Indictment Targets Videos, Obscenity, Corruption, Charges Filed," *Cincinnati Enquirer*, April 8, 1998, at A1 (reporting that Larry Flynt and his brother Jimmy were indicted on fifteen obscenity and corruption charges). See "Flynt in Hospital; Surgery Planned," *Boston Globe*, Jan. 15, 1999, at A13. The two Flynts later pled guilty to two counts of pandering obscenity. On the condition that they would stop selling sexually explicit videos and that Flynt's corporations would pay a $10,000 fine, the court dropped thirteen obscenity charges against them, thereby allowing them to avoid time in prison. See Dirk Johnson, "Flynt Pleads Guilty in Ohio Obscenity Case," *N.Y. Times*, May 13, 1999, at A18.

22. The ACLU of Ohio, Campaign Against Censorship in the Arts, the Free Inquiry Group, and Stonewall Cincinnati.

23. Ben Kaufman, "Censorship Face-off Averted," *Cincinnati Enquirer*, Mar. 19, 1998, at A1.

24. I gratefully acknowledge the excellent work of Scott Greenwood, General Counsel of the ACLU of Ohio, Steven Stuhlbarg, Bernard Wong, and Daniel Zavon. I would also like to acknowledge William Messer, Founder of the Campaign Against Censorship in the Arts, for organizing this event and for resisting the pressure to withdraw it from the Museum Center.

25. I assumed the ACLU Presidency on February 1, 1991.

26. See Robin Abcarian, "Chances Are, Women Can Decide for Themselves," *L.A. Times*, Feb. 15, 1995, at E1; see also Catherine Saillant, "Bookseller Ends Dispute over Sign," *L.A. Times*, Feb. 3, 1995, at B2.

27. See Lisa See, "Ventura Bookstore Fights Censorship," *Publishers Weekly*, Feb. 13, 1995, at 23.

28. See, e.g., *Keyishian* v. *Board of Regents*, 385 U.S. 589, 603 (1967) ("Our Nation is deeply committed to safeguarding academic freedom, which is of transcendent value to all of us and not merely to the teachers concerned. That freedom is therefore a special concern of the First Amendment, which does not tolerate laws that cast a pall of orthodoxy over the classroom."); *Shelton* v. *Tucker*, 364 U.S. 479, 487 (1960) ("The vigilant protection of constitutional freedoms is nowhere more vital than in the community of American schools.").

29. See *American Booksellers Ass'n* v. *Hudnut*, 598 F. Supp. 1316 (D. Ind. 1984), aff'd., 771 F 3d 323 (7th Cir. 1985), aff'd. mem., 475 U.S. 1001 (1986); see also *Village Books* v. *City of Bellingham*, C88-1470D (W.D. Wash. 1989) (granting summary judgment for plaintiffs and invalidating ordinance).

30. See Nadine Strossen, "Defining Sexual Harassment: Sexuality Does Not Equal Sexism," in *Defending Pornography*, ch. 6, pp. 119–140.

31. *Cohen* v. *San Bernardino Valley College*, 883 F. Supp. 1407 (C.D. Ca. 1995); rev'd, 92 F. 3d 968 (9th Cir. 1996).

32. Consistent with the so-called state action doctrine, constitutional constraints—including the First Amendment's prohibition on any "law abridging the freedom of speech"—apply only to government officials or agencies. See generally Erwin Chemerinsky, *Constitutional Law Principles and Policies* (New York: Aspen Law and Business, 1997), pp. 385–414.

33. See Nadine Strossen, "Defining Sexual Harassment: Sexuality Does Not Equal Sexism," in *Defending Pornography*, pp. 119–40. See also pp. 19–29.

34. See Nat Hentoff, "Academies of Fear," *Washington Post*, Dec. 18, 1993, at A25 (noting that law professors who choose to discuss issues of rape in criminal law courses face the possibility of being charged with sexual harassment, while professors who choose to avoid rape law entirely may be subjected to charges of sexism).

35. See, e.g., Catharine A. MacKinnon, *Sexual Harassment of Working Women: A Case of Sex Discrimination*; forword by Thomas I. Emerson (New Haven: Yale University Press, 1979); Introduction to "Comment on Sexual Harassment," 10 *Cap. U. L. Rev.* i (Spring 1981); "Not a Moral Issue," *Yale Law & Policy Review* 2, no. 321 (1984).

36. Daphne Patai, *Heterophobia: Sexual Harassment and the Future of Feminism* (Lanham, Md.: Rowman & Littlefield Publishers, 1998).

37. Ibid., p. 3.

38. Ibid. pp. 4–7 (criticizing the Conference's organizers for failing to include "any divergence of opinion" and noting that the only dissenting opinion was expressed by a white male); Jeffrey Rosen, "In Defense of Gender-Blindness," *The New Republic*, Jun. 29, 1998, p. 39 (noting that the Yale conference failed to include "a critical examination" of the principles of sexual harassment law and their effects on speech and behavior restrictions).

39. See Nadine Strossen, *Defending Pornography*, pp. 85–87.

40. *The Lanahan Readings in Civil Rights and Civil Liberties*, ed. David M. O'Brien (Baltimore, Md.: Lanahan Publishers, 1999).

41. See Nadine Strossen, *Defending Pornography*, pp. 86–87.

42. David Margolick, "Catering to a Feminist Superstar, Judges Find Themselves Tangled in a Free-Speech Debate," *N.Y. Times*, Nov. 5, 1993, at B11.

43. Jeffrey Rosen, "In Defense of Gender-Blindness," p. 39.

44. Patai, *Heterophobia*, p. 6. Patai commented as follows on the audience reaction to this statement:

Did anyone rise to contest such outrageous slander directed at all or most men? On the contrary. As Dworkin made her way back to her seat, Judge Guido Calabresi, a courtly gentleman sixty-six years of age [now a Judge on the U.S. Court of Appeals for the Second Circuit, and former Dean of the Yale Law School] stood up and warmly shook Dworkin's hand. . . . It is hard to imagine any other group of people in the United States today who could be so crassly maligned in a public setting without arousing immediate protest.

Ibid., p. 7.

45. *Department of Justice, Attorney General's Commission on Pornography: Final Report* (1986).

46. Catharine MacKinnon, *Only Words* (Cambridge, Mass.: Harvard University Press, 1993).

47. Wendy McElroy, "The MacKinnon-Dworkin Memory Hole," *Jurist* (July 1998) <http://jurist.law.pitt.edu/lawbooks/revjul98.htm#McElroy>.

48. See, e.g., Catharine Stimpson, "Activist Trustees Wield Power Gone Awry," *Chronicle of Higher Education,* Jan. 16, 1998, at B4; Meredith Tax, "Pataki's Army Goes Onward to SUNY," *N.Y. Times,* Nov. 16, 1998, at A29; Jack Sirica, "Jitters on SUNY Sexuality Forum," *Newsday,* Feb. 8, 1998, at A25.

49. James Madison, *The Federalist No. 10.*

50. See, e.g., <http://www.faircourts.com> (The website for Citizens for Independent Courts, a group that describes its members as believing "that access to impartial, independent courts that are free from political influence forms the bedrock of our constitutional guarantee of individual liberty.").

51. See, e.g., Bonnie Erbé and Josette Shiner, "Rights Before the Bench," *Washington Times,* May 17, 1997, at D3; Anthony Lewis, "Do We Trust Our Liberty to Judges or Delay?" *Houston Chronicle,* Apr. 8, 1997, at A20; Nat Hentoff, "The New Political Correctness," *Washington Post,* Apr. 19, 1997, at A21.

52. See *Congress, the Courts, and the Constitution, Before the Subcomm. on the Constitution of the House Comm. of the Judiciary,* 105th Cong. (1998) (Statement of Nadine Strossen).

53. See *Key Actions of the 104th Congress* (visited Jan. 16, 1999) <http://www. aclu.org/vote-guide/overview.html> ("The final bill . . . passed overwhelmingly with only five senators and 16 representatives registering opposition.").

54. Justice Sandra Day O'Connor wrote a partial dissent, joined by Chief Justice William Rehnquist, maintaining that the CDA should be held constitutional only in the extremely narrow circumstances in which it applied to an online communication that an adult directed to an audience consisting entirely of one or more minors. See *Reno* v. *ACLU,* 521 U.S. 844, 911 (O'Connor, J., dissenting in part) (1997). In all other circumstances–namely, the vast majority of online communications–all nine Justices agreed that the CDA was unconstitutional.

55. Gary Mongiovi, Letter to the Editor, *Civil Liberties,* Spring/Summer 1991, p. 2. Mr. Mongiovi is an economist who teaches at St. John's University.

GREAT WAR STORIES: WARRIORS AND THEIR BATTLES OVER OBSCENITY

E ROTIC IMAGES HAVE BEEN FOUND IN THE EARLY CAVE PAINTINGS, and erotic writing has a history almost as old as writing itself. Sexual images and stories were accepted as part of life. Censorship came after the development of printing in the West, and certain books came to be banned or prohibited, originally by the pope. Some of these books dealt with sex, and in the process, discussion of sex seemed as dangerous as the discussion of forbidden ideas. Since the pope's influence was relatively weak in many parts of Europe, his bans had little effect, and those interested could read books printed elsewhere. Illustrations were a different matter, and for a time there was a major industry in painting over the penises which appeared on many works of art or attaching fig leaves to sculptured pieces. Even this did not take place everywhere and there was considerable opposition to this by the artistic community who got around much of it by painting scenes from classic mythology of goods and goddesses, nymphs and satyrs.

As the ability to read became more common, censorship became more common, particularly about sexual matters, and it came about, at least in the English-speaking world, with a new definition of woman as mother. These definitions, popularly associated with Victorianism, emphasized the special qualities of women, creatures made of finer elements than the male, who therefore needed to be protected, because if they strayed, they so easily became depraved. The good woman was pure and innocent, the bad women were the prostitutes, the camp followers, and not quite suitable for the company of proper society. There were many factors at work in bringing about these changing definitions, so many that a brief introduction such as this cannot do justice. One of the results, however, was the banning of books, expurgation and rewriting of others, including some of the plays of Shakespeare, so that the language would be suitable for women, the delicate creature. Classics such as Boccacio were banned, and in the United States in the post-Civil War period Anthony Comstock became the official censor of printed materials originating in New York City or destined for the U.S. mails. To him, such things as contraceptive information was pornographic and obscene. The United States has spent much of the twentieth century recovering from this wave of sexual prudery. It was not easy and as book censorship waned, the effect of the censor was extended to movies and to comic books, and to radio, and ultimately to television. The new cry of the censors, however, was no longer the need to protect women but rather to preserve the purity of the child from the evils of sex. Generally today, printed materials such as books are not subject to censorship nor banning, neither for that matter are plays on the legitimate stage. Movies are also relatively free but they are classified and certain movies cannot be shown to individuals under eighteen. Television is more subject to censor than movies, and certain hours of viewing are more restricted than others. The Internet has so far escaped censorship, but there are strong pressures to make anything dealing with sex more and more difficult to access.

Few of the changes resulting in more openness about sexual matters in various forms of communication were brought about by legislative action; most resulted from court battles fought to enforce the constitutional guarantees of free speech and to include erotic materials. Undoubtedly the courts extended of the First Amendment's free speech provisions to include erotic and sexual materials. In retrospect, the courts were at least in part reflecting the changing attitudes of Americans, but the fact that the various legislative bodies only rarely acted indicates that a strong vocal minority defending censorship could in effect deny free speech and for that matter invade the privacy of others, which emphasizes how essential the court decisions were.

One of the more important victories was the one known as the *U.S. v. 31 Photographs* in 1957. This grew out of the effort of the Alfred Kinsey to import into the U.S. erotic and pornographic materials for the collection he was building at the University of Indiana. Some of the materials he wanted to import came in easily, since earlier court decisions had allowed some of the literary classics to be imported, but often what was allowed and what was not allowed was dependent on the customs office through which it passed or even the agent who was examining it.

The thirty-one photographs in question show a variety of coital positions that differed from the standard missionary positions and were called "blatant obscenity" by the customs collector who seized them. What makes the case so interesting to a reader at the beginning of the twenty-first century is just how innocuous those included in the illustrations in this book now seem, some indication of the radical changes which have taken place in the United States since the 1950s. Jennifer Yamashiro, the Curator of the Kinsey Institute, summarizes the case and its aftereffects in the following artical.

The second article, by Philip D. Harvey, tells of the firm called Adam and Eve which he and Tim Black founded to sell condoms through the mail and gradually branched out in to selling other sex-related materials, only to be raided for selling pornography as part of Attorney General Edwin Meese's effort in the Reagan administration to selectively prosecute pornography in sympathetic courts with sympathetic district attorneys. As Harvey indicates, it was a very much mismanaged campaign by government attorneys who knew little about what they were doing, and most of the cases were eventually thrown out of court.

At the time a particular court case was taking place, we need to keep in mind that in spite of changing standards, the outcome was uncertain. One of the major pioneer attorneys in changing how the law should be interpreted was Stanley Fleishman, a Los Angeles attorney and civil liberties advocate, who argued his first case on pornography before the Supreme Court of the United States in 1957. He lost this case, or rather the court decided against him, but most of the subsequent ones he won, establishing an American legal tradition as he did so. What makes his account of more than passing interest is the attitudes expressed by the justices themselves who, if they could return, would probably be shocked at the radical change in American attitudes and the courts themselves.

Burton Joseph, another veteran defender of civil liberties, first became involved in censorship issues in the trial of Lenny Bruce, the comedian who shocked many in his audience by his attacks on the prevailing puritanism of the time. He has been involved in many of the major cases since that time and eventually became an attorney for *Playboy*. In that capacity he brought suit against the city of Indianapolis which under the influence of Catharine MacKinnon and Andrea Dworkin passed an ordinance against pornography on the grounds that it was harmful to women, a carry-over from the days when women were regarded as special creatures needing special protection.

Another case involving photographs was the Mapplethorpe case, where the photos of gays in the act of having sex were banned in Cincinnati as pornographic rather than being accepted as art as Mapplethorpe and others thought they should be classified. The case represents still another extension of freedom of expression and the rights of artists to portray the world as they see it. The Mapplethorpe photos were much more sexually explicit and of a much higher quality than those involved in the Kinsey case, and it was not customs involved, but city officials, but the issues were the same.

Currently many of the battles are focused on the Internet, and Steven F. Rohde, currently president of the American Civil Liberties Union of Southern California, examines the issues and cases involved here. One result of Congressional concern over the issues was the passage in 1996 of the Communications Decency Act, and Marjorie Heins, who was involved in the first challenge to the law, *ACLU* v. *Reno*, explains what was involved. She raises an interesting question whether there is a need to prevent children from seeing erotic images, a question no court has yet decided, but one which probably will end up in the courts.

1

In the Realm of the Sciences:
The Kinsey Institute's *31 Photographs*

Jennifer Yamashiro

SINCE THE FOUNDATION OF ALFRED C. KINSEY'S INSTITUTE FOR SEX Research in 1947, inauspicious waves of controversy have threatened its survival. One of the most critical waves was a federal court case that tested the laws prohibiting the importation of obscene materials. Kinsey, determined not to let his academic freedom be impinged upon, solicited legal counsel. With the staunch support of then Indiana University President Herman B. Wells, and fortified by the legal expertise of Harriet Pilpel, Kinsey struggled against the boundaries of federal obscenity laws in the landmark federal court case *U.S.* v. *31 Photographs*, also known simply as *31 Photographs*.[1] On August 1, 1956, the United States Attorney "filed a libel, under the provisions of Sec.305(a) of the Tariff Act of 1930, seeking the forfeiture, confiscation, and destruction of certain photographs, books, and other articles which the claimant, Institute for Sex Research at Indiana University, seeks to import into the United States."[2] On October 31, 1957, over a year after Kinsey's death, the Honorable Edmund L. Palmieri, United States Attorney for the Southern District of New York ruled in favor of the claimant, the Institute for Sex Research. The government accepted the decision on January 2, 1958.

Though initiated amidst the atmosphere of the outset of the Cold War, *U.S.* v. *31 Photographs* was resolved in Kinsey's favor at a time when the courts were poised to eliminate obscenity laws in response to the shifting liberalization of sexual and cultural values in the late 1950s (Heins, 1993, pp. 16-23). *31 Photographs* was one of the early cases challenging the obscenity exception to the First Amendment's guarantee of free speech. Yet, the importance of this case has been somewhat obscured by other rulings, such as *Roth* v. *United States* (1957), which extended beyond the scholarly use of erotica.[3] It seems somewhat ironic that in historical analyses, Kinsey's publications on sexual behavior in the human male and female, rather than the federal court case, are credited with shaping America's legal response to obscenity (D'Emilio and Freedman, 1988, p. 287). While other cases have been heralded for increasing the general public's access to sexually explicit materials, *31 Photographs* made a strong statement on behalf of the academic community. It also had a practical and important impact on the institute. This federal ruling made it legal for the institute to ship and receive sexually explicit materials through U.S. Customs and the U.S. Postal Services. Although this historic ruling also stipulated that the future use of such materials be restricted to qualified scholars,[4] the institute's collections are a far cry from the nineteenth-century invention of "secret museums."[5] In practical terms, the court case provided the legal framework that enabled a small scientific research institute at a Midwestern university to accumulate one of the world's most extensive collections of visual erotica and other sexually explicit materials generated by research scientists, clinicians, historians, social scientists, literary and other humanities scholars.

The importance of the case has been under recognized for decades. Even less attention has been devoted to the thirty-one photographs that made the development of the Kinsey Institute's collections possible. Since the photographs have not been reassembled as a group until very recently, they have been remembered in name only.[6] The images and their content should not be glossed over lightly. Indeed, in the context of substantial scrutiny of and interpretative revisionism about the 1950s in America, it is timely to appraise these photographs and consider their layers of meaning. Of the thirty-one photographs, seven present a range of coital positions, two depict cunnilingus, nine portray fellatio, five suggest "lesbian" activity, three represent female masturbation, three depict group sex, one showcases female genitalia, and one, the innocuous anomaly in the group, presents a fully-clothed woman seated in front of a radio.[7] The poor quality of the photographs as prints and their somewhat haphazard formal compositions spurn even the remote possibility of redemption based on artistic or aesthetic merit for those who make this the threshold for distinguishing erotic art from pornography.[8] Kinsey himself felt that aesthetic considerations were simply not at issue for the visual works he collected. In fact, he remarked: "The values do not depend on the authorship of the material, nor upon its intrinsic worth as art, but upon the fact that the material has wide public distribution. In fact, French postcards and cheap Japanese prints may be more significant in a scientific study of sex than the world's finest art."[9] Kinsey's reasoning was straightforward. In the 1950s the primary audience of the fine arts was elite. Although Kinsey did not attempt to trace the contemporary production, distribution, and sale of pornography (Allyn, 1996, p. 414), his statement implies that he understood that the popularity of certain scenarios in representations pointed to real or imagined acceptance or desire of sexual expression.

Nearly fifty years later, of course, technological changes make much more graphic images of these sexual practices readily available to those who wish to see and use them. For example, media such as videotape, designed for home use, portrays erotic activity of a range of explicitness ratings. These changes in technology and availability make it possible and timely to view these images from the early 1950s, disputed at the height of the Cold War, in a cultural and historical context. Fortunately, we can now view them somewhat dispassionately, mindful of the truism that yesterday's "pornography" may be today's rather tame and unremarkable imagery. Of course, on such matters, we can never expect consensus. There are feminists who regard Nicolas Poussin's 1636 painting *The Rape of the Sabine Women*, based on the tale of Romans forcibly seizing the neighboring women of the Sabine tribe to bear them sons, as inherently and always "pornographic."[10] The fact that some viewers might always regard images such as those in *U.S. v. 31 Photographs* as pornographic is not sufficient reason to exempt them from interrogation. To most contemporary viewers, these photographs appear less explicit or provocative than images in current mainstream adult magazines. The thirty-one photographs are simply not as "glossy," "colorful," or "professional" as the pictures in today's *Playboy, Playgirl, Penthouse*, and *Hustler*. It is precisely this change in perspective that illuminates the historicity of mid-twentieth century sexual discourse on obscenity at issue in *31 Photographs*. The contention over these images also contributes to current historiographical debates on the 1950s in America. Some recent scholarship on the era suggests that it was not a decade of repressive puritanism as it has popularly been portrayed and remembered. A more complex view of the 1950s emerges from the work of many distinguished contributors to cultural studies debates.[11]

Arguably, *U.S. v. 31 Photographs* offers valuable insights into shifting boundaries of public discourse upon sexuality, gender, censorship, obscenity, and acceptable domains of public regulation, already perceptively outlined by Estelle B. Freedman, Andrea Friedman, and John D'Emilio. This case also bears analysis in relation to David Allyn's understanding of Kinsey's publications as fuel which accelerated postwar moves towards the "deregulation" and "privatization" of sexual behavior. In these considerations, the images themselves provide important textual evidence of the conflict at issue, and help to situate the instabilities in public discourse which substantially contributed to the ultimate decision in Kinsey's favor. Between the notification of the seizure of the thirty-one photographs on May 11, 1951, and the final decision of *31 Photographs* on October 31, 1957, the cultural context around the case had changed dramatically. 1957 was the year that Grace Metalious' sensational best-seller novel, *Peyton Place*, dominated the silver screen with Lana Turner and the themes of rape, incest, adultery, pre-marital sex, and divorce aired in graphic detail. *A Summer Place* in 1959, *Psycho* in 1960, and *Homicidal* in 1961 extended the exploration, often in graphic terms, of disturbing sexual themes, including incest, illicit sex, transsexualism, transvestism, illegitimacy, abortion, and sexual slayings. The era of the 1957 decision in Kinsey's favor was also that of Britain's famous Wolfenden Report which decriminalized private adult sexual behavior including homosexuality and aspects of prostitution. Testing of the contraceptive pill was underway in Puerto Rico, soon to receive Federal

Drug Administration approval for release in the United States in May 1960.[12] Despite the visual coarseness of the thirty-one photographs, they become much less "raw" in light of contemporary world events and representations.

This study explores intriguing issues arising from the way the photographs were integrated into the institute's research program, their central position in the court case, and their historical meaning as cultural objects. To more fully comprehend the significance of the photographs, it is necessary to examine their contents and their roles in scientific, legal, and cultural contexts. The movement and function of the photographs across discourses suggest that the message presented by the images went beyond the surface, beyond evoking sexual arousal. It is important to investigate how the politics of representation coincided or collided with the politics and ideals of the era. Reviewing the actual and intended functions of visual material at the institute during the early years and the thirty-one photographs in the federal court case places this discussion in context.

THE ARTS AS SCIENTIFIC DATA

After receiving his doctorate from Harvard University, Alfred Charles Kinsey came to Indiana University (IU) in 1920 at the age of twenty-six to teach in the Department of Biology. Before beginning in sex research, Kinsey authored a number of books (including high-school textbooks) and was well respected as a researcher specializing in studies on the gall wasp.[13] Kinsey became involved in the emerging field of sex research in 1938 although he had been publicly advocating the need for sex education since 1935 (Jones, 1997, p. 305) and opposing censorship of student publications since 1927 (Gathorne-Hardy, 1998, p. 98). Kinsey began conducting his own research by interviewing students who were enrolled in the course on marriage that he was co-teaching.[14] His quest to accumulate data greatly expanded his efforts and his team.[15] Kinsey and his small staff ambitiously sought to collect 100,000 sexual histories. By the project's end, Kinsey and the members of the institute's research team had collected nearly 18,000 interviews. The Institute for Sex Research was incorporated as a not-for-profit Indiana corporation affiliated with Indiana University on April 8, 1947. Its purpose was to protect the confidentiality of the interview records and to clarify ownership of the data and the collections.

Alfred C. Kinsey, Wardell Pomeroy, and Clyde Martin published *Sexual Behavior in the Human Male* in 1948 and these authors, joined by Paul Gebhard, published *Sexual Behavior in the Human Female* in 1953. These two volumes, commonly referred to as "the Kinsey reports," made a huge impact on American society. The popularity of these volumes catapulted Kinsey's name into American culture in the form of song lyrics, cartoons, and polite conversation. So great was Kinsey's contribution that historian Paul Robinson has stated: "Kinsey has had probably a greater influence on modern sexual consciousness than any other thinker since Freud" (115). And, this "sexual consciousness" came not from obscenity trials, pornography, or popular culture, but from the "respectable domain of science" (D'Emilio and Freedman, 1988, pp. 284-85).

In addition to collecting sexual histories through interviews, Kinsey began to acquire a wide range of visual and literary materials relating to sexuality.[16] Supporters of the research encouraged Kinsey to collect, especially as the Second World War acquainted Americans with materials from countries like China, Japan, India, and Egypt. New York gynecologist Frances E. Shields was one such friend and advocate. She arranged for a friend who had become an expert on Japanese erotica during the war to act as Kinsey's agent in acquiring significant materials.[17] As Kinsey wrote her in 1947: "It becomes increasingly apparent that we must know this Japanese material."[18] This mid-1940s interest in cross-cultural comparison disposed Kinsey to include on his team Gebhard, an anthropologist, who also encouraged Kinsey to collect visual material systematically. The institute cultivated relationships with collectors of erotica, artists, and other individuals. The level of donations increased significantly when relationships with police departments, post offices, and prisons were established. These institutions sent confiscated material to Bloomington that would enhance Kinsey's scientific research program. The development of the visual collections was also augmented by the hiring of William Dellenback as staff photographer in 1949.[19] The building of the visual collection to enhance a scientific project reunited the arts and sciences in a fashion that echoed their close-knit relationship in the nineteenth century. However, the link Kinsey made did not rank art and science as equals.

Kinsey's vision is clearly outlined in the memorandum "Significance of Erotic Art and Literature in Scientific Studies," where the "arts" are put into the service of science.[20] In this two and a half page document, it is declared that "representations of sexual action . . . are indispensible [sic] sources of data for any scientific study of sex" because they provide information about the creators' and consumers' desires and sexual interests, attitudes about sexuality specific to social classes and entire cultures and also give insight into present-day attitudes and practices, sexual anatomy, and techniques of activity. Visual representations were also declared able to "elucidate a variety of other biologic, psychologic, medical, and social problems."[21] Yet, the actual historical implementation of images in scientific investigations by Kinsey or his colleagues, with reference to any specific image or group of images, remains uncertain.[22] Nonetheless, Kinsey clearly believed that visual materials, especially those that cut across "social levels" and cultures, provided further evidence of the "non-natural" features of prescribed patterns of traditional Judeo-Christian sexual behavior—particularly the missionary position. In the male volume, Kinsey identifies sex from the rear as the most "biologically natural" position in the animal kingdom and notes that the missionary position is a product of Anglo-American "human culture" (Kinsey, 1948, p. 373). The frank eroticism and diverse sexual positions he found, for instance, throughout Japanese materials had no American or European counterpart. Such materials, which he viewed as "data" rather than art, clarified beliefs and activities that were peculiar to American culture. Moreover, these materials identified a different significance for such representations in other cultures.

Although Kinsey's collecting priorities and methods attest to his belief in the cultural power of visual images to inform his scholarship, his aspirations became somehow reduced to parallel the alchemist's goal of completely transforming one property into another. Like alchemy, the scientific classification could not retain the complexity of the "original metal"; if the transformation was successful (and, of course, for alchemists it never was), it had to be complete. The photography collection received the most extensive treatment in this process of transmutation. Photographs were divided into four basic, though incongruous, categories: special photographic formats, special interests (like tattoo), sexual behaviors, and male and female figure photography. The majority of the photographs belong to the sexual behavior category and for these images, the sex act and the subjects' positions were given elaborate attention. At Kinsey's request, Gebhard painstakingly defined the categories and guidelines for "measuring" positions. Fellatio, the activity represented most often in the group of thirty-one photographs, is represented in the coding system as GO ⊠ (genital, oral, male). The description of this sexual behavior reads as follows: "Genital oral, male. Heterosexual, female mouth on male genitalia. For convenience, the position of the male is utilized [for subdivisions]." Then the images were further divided according to model position. Four of the nine images of fellatio are classified as GO ⊠ STND. The standing position is elaborately defined as "ventral and dorsal surface, lateral; torso axis, vertical Å 44%; leg, straight or not bent beyond 89% (angle between upper and lower leg); weight, chiefly on foot or feet; other, if body inclined forward and legs straight, position becomes prone when inclination exceeds 45%." This treatment moves the viewer to consider the photographs in a clinical manner. In fact, the classification of the activity in the images as heterosexual underscores the limitations of the scientists' interpretations of photographs.

The system of classification suggests that photographs were simply viewed as a transparent medium that provided "evidence" regarding the practice of an activity or, on a more sophisticated level, the popularity of its representation. In other words, photographs were read as accurate documents rather than as constructions designed for a consumer market does not embrace realities beyond the frame of the picture. For instance, the GO ⊠ classification excludes consideration of the subjects' sexual orientation beyond the heterosexual act portrayed in the photograph. By so classifying the images according to this system, institute staff effectively transformed the "visual data" into scientific data. The purpose of the system was to avoid collecting duplicates, one of Kinsey's pet peeves, and to assist the research by making images accessible according to specific behavioral interests.[23] But the result was far from golden, ultimately undercutting the potential for the visual images to contribute to scientific understanding of sexual practices shaped by specific cultures. Although the photographs do represent a wide range of human sexual behavior from a variety of geographical regions, the images were effectively divested of their original cultural context. In light of Allyn's analysis of Kinsey's focus on private sexual activity, it is worth noting that grounding the images in the sciences also removed them from the public and political spheres. During the test case, however, a number of erotic images resurfaced in a public, or more specifically, legal realm.

SEIZING THE OBSCENITY

During the 1950s, Kinsey challenged the U.S. censorship law prohibiting the importation of obscene materials. The Institute for Sex Research emerged from the battle in 1957 triumphant, based on the argument that erotic material was necessary to further Kinsey's scientific research into human sexual behavior. Thirty-one sexually explicit photographs, imported from Denmark in 1951, became the cornerstone of the case.[24] The defense of these photographs' value to research removed them from the realm of the senses, replanting them firmly in "cleaner," scientific soil.[25]

Before the legal battle began in 1950, Kinsey tried to avoid any difficulties that might arise from importing sexually explicit research materials. In 1947, Kinsey wrote to the Customs Bureau's legal advisor in Washington explaining his need to import erotica from abroad.

> In the attempt to understand the significance of sex in all aspects of human activity, it has been necessary to accumulate a considerable library of erotic publications and collections of erotic materials. These materials range from fine art to specifically pornographic books and objects. Scientifically, it is of considerable importance to understand the comparable material from cultures other than our own and, consequently, we need materials from various other parts of the world.[26]

Kinsey's concerns about foreign shipments reaching him in Bloomington were validated the next month when the first of many shipments was seized by Alden Baker, customs collector in Indianapolis, for being in violation of the tariff act of 1930. This law stated: "All persons are prohibited from importing into the United States from any foreign country . . . any obscene book, pamphlet, paper, writing, advertisement, circular, print, picture, drawing, or other representation, figure, or image . . . which is obscene or immoral."[27]

Although a *modus vivendi* (practical compromise) arranged by Indiana University law professor Leon Wallace made it possible for sexually explicit materials to pass through customs for the next three years, trouble erupted again in April 1950. Eugene Okon, the new assistant collector in Indianapolis, did not feel comfortable passing shipments to Kinsey without the government's sanction. Consequently, he requested guidance from Washington. The informal arrangement between the Indianapolis Customs Bureau and Kinsey collapsed as soon as David B. Strubinger, Assistant Commissioner of Customs, saw samples of the material Kinsey regularly received. Thereafter, many shipments to Kinsey were seized.[28] A great volume of imported material addressed to the Institute for Sex Research was detained over a number of years by customs officials in Indianapolis and New York who subsequently shipped it to Washington for evaluation. When Kinsey was asked to write a statement describing why the detained material was important to his study of human sexual behavior, he considered it the "equivalent of asking an explorer to tell how he is going to use the material he may find on a previously unexplored continent . . . before he knows what he is going to find."[29] Kinsey often complained bitterly about the disruption to his research that was caused by the detention of important material and the interruption caused by the legal test case itself.

After the first seizure by Okon in 1950, Kinsey sought advice from Morris Ernst, who had represented Random House in the *Ulysses* customs case of 1934 and was an authority on censorship. Harriet Pilpel, Ernst's junior partner at the New York law firm Greenbaum, Wolff & Ernst, became Kinsey's lead attorney. She tried to settle the matter out of court by arguing that "the exception for [legally importing] 'books of . . . established . . . scientific merit' under Section 1305 of the Tariff Act should be interpreted to mean books which are necessary for the *production* of works of 'established scientific merit.' "[30] However, in February 1956 the Customs Bureau in Washington refused to grant Kinsey an administrative exception to the law. After trying to resolve the matter out of court for over five years, "Kinsey reluctantly agreed to a court test. . . . [Kinsey's legal counselors'] proposed test case called for patently obscene materials to be sent to the institute through the New York customs office, where the deputy collector of customs agreed to seize the packages and the district attorney promised prompt federal proceedings" (Stevens, 1975, p. 302). From the beginning of the controversy, Kinsey felt confident that the court would reaffirm his right as a scholar to have access to the "*raw* material" that was necessary for his research—even if it was denied to the general public.

According to Kinsey, customs collectors passed even the most explicit erotic material if it was in another language or if the sexual content was otherwise obscure or understated.[31] Not everything that went through Indianapolis was being seized. As Kinsey noted: "Two small packages which came through yesterday had been opened for examination at Indianapolis Customs, and were passed because they did not contain such obviously erotic material."[32] Kinsey did not want *any* material to be restricted from him. For testing the matter legally, therefore, he needed to ensure that the sexually explicit content of the material coming through customs was obvious. This made it essential for Kinsey to import written works in English and, especially, visual images. From the materials detained by customs, Kinsey and his attorneys selected imported items for the test case that ranged "from sheer pornography in the form of French photographs . . . to well-known works of established scientific or literary merit."[33] This included the thirty-one photographs, eight books, forty-six prints and drawings, six paintings, nine three-dimensional objects, plus four cases of printed matter. This representative sample contained examples of heterosexual and homosexual activity as well as bestiality. The focus of the case became thirty-one black and white photographs.

These photographs were chosen to be the focal point because they were considered the most "openly erotic" works in the test case. As such, they ranked above Asian prints and paintings of explicit heterosexual intercourse, the written *Memoirs of Marquis de Sade*, and a portfolio of nine engravings (titled "Voyeurs") which visually depicted sexual activity between humans and animals. If Pilpel could convince the judge that Kinsey had a legitimate scientific use for these photographs, it would make any equally explicit and other more subtle forms of erotica permissible. So just what do the photographs depict? They show a variety of coital positions that deviate from the standard "missionary" position, cunnilingus, fellatio, "lesbian" activity, masturbation, exposed vaginas, and group sex. Not only were these photographs recognized as blatant obscenity by the customs collector who seized them, they were given the status of the most "openly erotic" material in a court of law in 1957. Was it the gritty quality of the poorly printed negatives that intensified the "dirtiness" of the photographs? Were they offensive because they threatened to corrupt viewers? Or was the real threat the "evidence" that such activity actually occurred?

The notion of obscenity did not enter the English and American court rooms until the nineteenth century. As the Kinsey Institute's photography collection readily attests, the activities represented visually do not move increasingly toward the "fringes" of sexual activity as time progresses. Activities, and representations of activities, were in existence long before legal interpretations deemed them obscene. A gamut of heterosexual, homosexual, sadomasochistic, and scatological activity is represented in the institute's earliest photographs dating from the 1880s to the 1920s. Sexual interests in behavior and in representation have not changed dramatically; what has changed is the technology that makes different poses, or visual products, possible.

Legal rulings on obscenity and debates on censorship have affected the suppression of American classics, such as the novels of Henry Miller, and foreign works alike. For instance, the film *In the Realm of the Senses* (1976) demonstrates how the current system accords a single individual the power to restrict a work that may later be recognized as a classic. This film, based on a historical event which occurred in 1936 in Japan, graphically depicts the obsessive sexual relationship between a servant, Sada, and the head of the household, Kichi. The sensation of sexual pleasure becomes the central motivation for their existence as the film title suggests. Their passion for one another is fraught with danger (of being caught) from the beginning and escalates with their sexual experimentation until Sada strangles her "master." The cinematic retelling of this "common man" tragedy may be read as a lesson for its viewers. However, the film's tenderness resists a satirical interpretation. Moreover, the censorship that shaped its production, editing, and screening carries a more ominous message.[34] The United States Customs office seized *In the Realm of the Senses* when it was shipped from Japan. No legal action followed the seizure, as the film was later released. However, the customs agents made clear their opinion that "pleasure in sexual gratification" as subject matter for a historically-based film was obscene.[35] Even its aesthetic merit could not exonerate the film from censorship. This temporary detention of *In the Realm of the Senses*, selected to debut at the New York Film Festival, effectively banned it from being viewed during the festival.

As attorney and founding director of the Arts Censorship Project of the American Civil Liberties Union Marjorie Heins points out, obscenity is a legal term, pornography is not (Heins, 1993, p. 16). Yet, what is or is not pornographic has become much contested ground in the cultural, academic, and political arenas.[36] And the contest will continue to be hotly debated as long any single government employee working for the U.S. Customs or postal office has the power to detain images and texts that they personally find objectionable. Apparently, few of the potential obscenity cases that arise from the thousands of seizures made annually by customs and postal authorities are actually prosecuted. Yet, as the example of the film *In the Realm of the Senses* poignantly shows, sometimes the temporary detention of an item considered offensive by one person can thwart the goals and aspirations of an entire group.

CULTURAL CURRENCY

The thirty-one photographs functioned as cultural objects prior to their insertion into the domains of science and law. In spite of the fact that the photographs were produced in Europe, probably during the 1940s, they need to be considered in the Cold War period of the United States—the context into which importation brought them. To better appreciate the cultural significance and power of these images, it is necessary to consider what they may have represented or meant to those who viewed them in the 1950s. The images were probably produced for a white, male heterosexual clientele, however, their audience went beyond that targeted group once they entered the legal domain. There, we know, that *at least one woman* (Harriet Pilpel) saw the photographs.

Perhaps, on the most immediate response level, the images were labeled "openly erotic" due to the photographic detail of bodies and genitals. Never mind that the poor quality of the photographs often results in dark areas that obscure the erotic action or areas of interest. The photographs may have been regarded as "evidence" by those who first glanced at them and found them offensive. As evidence, they "incriminated" the photographer and the subjects who participated in the action as well as the nebulous consumer for whom they were ultimately designed. Perhaps they

were viewed as a trace of reality with a photographer behind the camera
and the models in front of it. The activity did occur, *but it was staged for the
camera*. The realism of photography is often and easily mistaken for "truth"
without giving due consideration to the circumstances and motivation for
production. In all likelihood, this superficial perception was probably sufficient ground for some viewers to proclaim the images offensive. While this
sort of knee-jerk response to the photographs as documents may account for
the seizure of them by a customs officer, they have the capacity to impart
other meanings to other viewers which are worth considering.

Hovering just beneath the surface of post-war prosperity and consumerism was an atmosphere thick with panic over the nation's security and
"Un-American" or immoral activity. A wide-spread political investigation
originated to identify and punish non-conformists whether they were members of the communist party or the homosexual community. The fear of the
invisible social menace strongly recalls Francis Galton's mid-nineteenth-
century efforts to produce, through the use of composite photography, a
single, *optical* criminal type. Galton hoped to increase the safety of urban
dwellers by creating the visual appearance of the elusive (and as such dangerous) criminal type. Similarly, fear that pervaded the United States government during the Cold War rested on the invisibility of communists and
homosexuals, posing a particular threat because they could infiltrate the
government at any level (D'Emilio, 1989, p. 232). Historian John D'Emilio's
work on the "homosexual menace" shows the way in which homosexuals,
like communists, were targeted by government oppression: "An executive
order barred them from all federal jobs, and dismissals from government
service rose sharply. The military intensified its purges of gay men and lesbians. The Post Office tampered with their mail, the FBI initiated widespread surveillance of homosexual meeting places and activities, and urban
police forces stepped up their harassment" (D'Emilio, 1989, p. 229). This
degree of scrutiny devoted to investigating the private and public lives of
presumed homosexuals implies that all Americans, including heterosexuals,
were also subject to governmental surveillance, thus infringing on a precious
American freedom—the right to privacy. Police departments and post offices
did target images and texts containing homosexual content for confiscation.
Yet, the five photographs depicting two women were probably not the only
or even primary "threat" in the thirty-one photographs. In fact, it is more
likely that this "lesbian" scenario was staged by the photographer to satisfy
a male viewer's fantasy. Rather, the content and style of the photographs
were what sent a threatening message to some American viewers.

The traditional family unit emerged as a source and powerful symbol of
stability for Americans. Still, communist fears infiltrated this revered
familial domain by threatening the foundation of domesticity. Women who
may have wished to continue working outside of the home after the war
posed a threat to the patriarchal structure of the family. Propaganda and the
media that reinscribed the social and political position of women in the
home began to appear before the war ended.

[W]omen faced a barrage of propaganda informing them that their jobs really belonged to men and extolling the virtues of marriage and childrearing. In the media, pictures of sparkling, well-equipped kitchens occupied by young mothers with babies dangling from their arms replaced images of women in hardhats surrounded by heavy machinery. Popular psychology books and women's magazines equated femininity with marriage and motherhood. Where these methods failed, employers could simply fire women, since female workers lacked the support of either organized labor or federal antidiscrimination statutes. From 1944 to 1946 the number of women workers fell by four million. (D'Emilio, 1989, p. 236)

Although four million women left the workplace, it was not a simple or smooth transition. When one mother proposed in a 1947 edition of the *Atlantic Monthly* that the government fund nurseries to facilitate women's pursuits of careers outside of the home, a female reader responded harshly by stating that such a suggestion "invokes shades of Communism" (Tindall and Shi, 1992, p. 1272). If the desire to work outside the home could elicit such a hostile response, it is possible that sexual desire was even more contested terrain in this conflicted land. This was, after all, a decade of contradiction, as America struggled to recover institutional and cultural stability that had been disrupted by war.

Despite the fact that nineteenth-century marital boundaries of duty and sacrifice were being replaced by a growing understanding that marriage was based on emotional compatibility, white women were expected to find satisfaction and fulfillment in the home as wives and mothers. While historians John D'Emilio and Estelle B. Freedman contend that even in the context of companionate marriage, men and women often had different sets of expectations for their physical relationship—wives valued romance and displays of affection whereas husbands placed emphasis on intercourse and desired it at a greater frequency than their partners (D'Emilio and Freedman, 1988, p. 269). The friction between husbands' and wives' expectations is important considering the message conveyed by the visual images.

Most of the photographs present a heterosexual Caucasian couple involved in a wide range of sexual activity. Occasionally a woman is depicted alone or with another woman. Despite the specific activity or partner, the most striking feature in this group of images is that the *women* seem to be having *fun*. Fun is a light-hearted contrast to the "involuntary confession of bodily pleasure" (Williams, 1989, p. 50). The photographs portray women who smile widely and seem to be enjoying themselves. In the context of marriage, enjoying sexual relations is quite different from embracing the domestic responsibilities of cooking, cleaning, and caring for children. For a woman who may have experienced feelings of guilt for merely having sexual desires, even within marriage, the photographs offer an expression of guilt-free, good, clean fun.[37] For a man who wished to have sex more often than his spouse, these photographs offer images of an enthusiastic, receptive, fun-loving partner. This message was bolstered by new notions of "companionate" marriage that fostered an expectation for marital relationships to be egalitarian in the home, and in the bedroom.[38]

The customs bureau and the institute's director and legal counsel fully understood the potential offensiveness of the images' content. Yet, social history and Kinsey's own scientific studies reveal that "the younger generation of husbands and wives enjoyed greater variety in their lovemaking. Substantially more of them participated in oral sex, touched each other's genitals, and used a variety of coital positions" (D'Emilio and Freedman, 1988, p. 268). So, presumably many of these photographs seemed to fit within the socially accepted practices of sexual relations for a middle-class white heterosexual married, or perhaps engaged, couple. Yet the visual representation of these activities was prohibited from circulating among the general public. How can the majority of sexual activity in the thirty-one photographs be acceptable in reality and objectionable, or more accurately, obscene, in representation? First and foremost, acceptance of an activity and tolerance of its representation are not always equal. Kinsey's studies showed that participating in an activity and admitting to that participation were quite different (Halberstam, 1993, pp. 272). Similarly, engaging in a practice and visually representing that sexual activity are not at all the same. Second, the realism of the photographic medium enhances erotic fantasy in representation and perception (rather than acting merely as a visual document of a sexual behavior). Fantasies are not reality, but the more "real" a fantasy the more exciting it may be. One of the primary elements of fantasy is control (McElroy, 1995, pp. 137–38), and the ability to manipulate a more realistic scene is arguably more stimulating. Unfortunately, some radical pro-censorship feminists have recently blurred reality and sexual fantasy (Strossen, 1995, p. 170-74). The powerful reality of fantasy even in speech has recently become the target of legal investigations. The recent case of *United States* v. *Daniel Thomas DePew* involved an individual being prosecuted for verbalizing a violent, sexual fantasy (Kipnis, 1996, pp. 3–63).

Violence and the degradation of women became a focal point in discussions of sexually explicit images and films in the 1970s and 1980s. Prior to that time, the main fear of "pornography" seemed to be based on the image's potential ability to corrupt viewers. The thirty-one photographs, arriving on the scene prior to this focus of attention, do *not* depict violence. Conceivably, the thirty-one photographs were considered potentially corruptive due to their *recreational* element. This combined with the sparse setting, in which floral patterned wallpaper is the primary unifying visual component, may hint at a brief and "secret" rendezvous. Although sexual freedom had not been completely taboo during the war-time of the previous decade, the whisper of an illicit (pre- or extra-marital) interlude in the postwar era may have been perceived as a force capable of rocking the bastion of American stability, the family. The low quality of the photographs may have functioned to support the notion that the meeting was illicit. The lighting and poor print quality formally echo the "quick and dirty" content of the images. These visual elements may have appealed to potential male viewers, who supposedly had greater interest in engaging in extra-marital affairs than the women (D'Emilio and Freedman, 1988, p. 269).

Ultimately, the unprofessional quality of the images probably intensi-fied the potential threat of the images' contents. The lack of aesthetics or "niceness" in the pictures underscores the fact that the photographs were made by an amateur. The implications of this mode of production are two-fold: almost anyone could produce and virtually anyone could pose for such pictures. The makeshift studio was probably set up in either a bedroom or a hotel room, but more importantly, this bedroom could have been in any suburban household or respectable hotel. Unlike Hugh Hefner's monthly magazine, *Playboy* (launched in December 1953), which featured "ideal" female bodies, the women in the thirty-one photographs are not as glam-orous or young as Hefner's "bunnies." Hefner's first centerfold of Marilyn Monroe, nude and airbrushed to perfection, floating against a lush, red background, is clearly the product of a professional studio. By contrast, the thirty-one photographs offer a "peep" into anyone's bedroom. Kinsey, qui-etly advocating the freedom to engage in any form of private sexual inti-macy, may have conceptually included *viewing* sexually explicit imagery as a private act. These photographs suggest that producing and starring in such imagery could also be fairly private. Since Kinsey did not scrutinize public sexual behavior as it was, for example, depicted in the movies (Allyn, 1996, pp. 414–15), the amateur photographs embodied the goal of Kinsey's scien-tific project: to offer a glimpse into the sexual life of the "average" person.

Many scholars credit Kinsey's research for single-handedly bringing sex into public discourse. Undoubtedly, Kinsey's research did much to make such discussions acceptable and, of course, Kinsey's project was of profound importance. However, the male and female volumes were not the only cat-alysts responsible for putting sex into the public sphere. Legal attention to sexual practices and lifestyles, the sultry images on the silver screen, sexu-ally explicit adult magazines, and other scientific developments, for example, the invention of an effective form of oral contraception, also advanced the "arrival" of sex on the public scene in the 1950s. *31 Pho-tographs* was decided in the institute's favor not based on Kinsey's popular appeal (though this certainly must have made a contribution), but rather because of the team's solid and scholarly reputations as scientists.

CONCLUSION

The collections that once helped Kinsey and his staff in their efforts to better understand the range and expression of human sexuality have become of interest to scholars from a wide range of academic disciplines. Scholars are now engaged in questions regarding the production, presentation, and cir-culation of erotic images as well as formal analysis. This involves under-standing the complicated context in which the images were produced and viewed. Masters of studio art and scholars of art history, law, literature, folk-lore, philosophy, anthropology, history, psychology, sociology, journalism, gay studies, gender studies, and film studies are among the researchers now using the collection. Recent scholarship has underscored and explored the value and function of photography as a commodity. Of course, how an image functions depends largely upon its audiences' perspectives, varying according to gender, age, class, race, and economic background. Broader academic attention to the visual collections has also increased due to a heightened interdisciplinary interest in the power of the image as a mediator of culture, a theory which recognizes the image's ability to shape as well as reflect social practices and beliefs.[39] In essence, these are the two sides of the same coin: Kinsey and his staff saw the photographs as a reflection of and interest in actual practices and the government feared the ability of images to shape these practices.

The law which regulates access to the collections now seems too restrictive. However, the case set an important precedent for evaluating obscenity based on the audience. Judge Edmund L. Palmieri considered that it was necessary to assess the audience in order to apply the label of "obscene," casting aside the issue of immorality in his final decision. Today, it is the Miller test, a result of the 1973 *Miller* v. *California* case, that is usually referred to when assessing obscenity according to community standards (Heins, 23).[40] Although *31 Photographs* preceded the Miller test, recognition of the Institute's case has been minimal at best. It is important to remember that in 1957, before the Miller case, it was primarily the audience and their scholarly credentials that enabled the Institute to import and to house sexually explicit images. Not only did the federal ruling make it possible for the collections to be acquired, the court case also officially completed and sanctioned the transformation of visual images from the realm of the senses to the realm of the sciences. One challenge for contemporary scholars is to reclaim the original "soil," dirty as it may be, to understand this vast collection in a broader cultural context as well as appreciating the rationale for the original transfer to scientific turf.

The thirty-one photographs present a rare opportunity to investigate the intersection of fantasy and realism which emerges as document or evidence beyond the conflation, or rather unfortunately, at times, confusion, of these elements in the photographic medium. In *U.S.* v. *31 Photographs* fantasy and realism in visual representation became document in a legal realm. Photographs are regularly introduced as evidence in court nowadays. Art historian John Tagg names some of the multifaceted functions of photographic evidence in court rooms, which range from prosecutions of traffic offenses and crime scenes to forensic evidence and "proof" of adultery (Tagg, 1988, p. 77). In short, the legal currency of photographs is as physical evidence, often that of surveillance. Networks of surveillance that investigated private lives were certainly part of the Cold War era. However, in *31 Photographs,* the representations did not function as supporting or incriminating evidence. They became the direct target of an investigation through the legal analysis of obscenity. And the photographs "documented" not just sexual activity, but also sexual fantasy.

The Institute's treatment of the photography collection may not have matched Kinsey's vision for its potential use, but the photographs did stand up in a court of law, granting the scholarly use of sexually explicit materials legal protection. As scholars become increasingly involved in research that requires the use and perhaps importation of "obscene" materials, *31 Photographs* may become more significant for its legal precedent of supporting academic freedom. Kinsey's legacy is indeed great.[41] Not only did his pioneering research affect the social and scientific spheres, it attempted to integrate the arts and sciences in an intriguing way. Although he may not have achieved in practice his theory for using visual material, we, as scholars, are indebted to Alfred Kinsey's pursuit to obtain the legal right to amass the collection which remains well-preserved at the institute bearing his name. Kinsey's belief in academic freedom and understanding of the cultural importance of visual erotica not only a made an impressive mark in the law, but also left a great legacy of imagery in a fascinating bedrock of science.

NOTES

1. I am grateful for having had the opportunity to participate in the extraordinary interdisciplinary World Pornography Conference by presenting a shorter version of this paper. I would like to thank James Elias and Vern Bullough, the conference chairs, the other speakers on the "War Stories" panel, and the audience for making provocative conversations on the subject of pornography possible. I want to thank the director of the Kinsey Institute, John Bancroft, and associate director, Stephanie Sanders, for supporting my research on this subject in a number of ways. I am indebted to Judith Allen for her insight, generosity, and overwhelming support which contributed greatly to the shape of this project. I offer my sincerest thanks to Margaret Harter, Stephanie Sanders, and Liana Zhou, my wonderful colleagues at the institute, for their encouragement and constructive criticism. An examination of the thirty-one photographs would not have been possible without my friend and colleague Paul Burk who deserves special recognition for managing to find all thirty-one "needles" in a great, big "haystack." Finally, I would like to express my gratitude to Jon Yamashiro for his constant, caring support and critique of my work.

This paper will be expanded in my doctoral dissertation "Under the Microscope: The Kinsey Institute's Photography Collection." In my dissertation I will also examine the ideological structure which supported the collecting and classification of the photography collection and analyze the sexual fantasies that are represented in the photographs at the institute.

For an excellent summary of the court case see Kenneth R. Stevens, "*United States* v. *31 Photographs*: Dr. Alfred C. Kinsey and Obscenity Law," *Indiana Magazine of History* 71, no. 4 (1975): 229-318.

2. *United States* v. *31 Photographs*, United States District Court, Southern District of New York (1957). The final decision of the court case is in the Kinsey Institute (KI) Archives in Bloomington, Indiana.

3. *Roth* v. *United States*, 354 U.S. 476 (1957). A bookseller named Roth was convicted for sending the magazine *American Aphrodite*, which contained images of nudes and erotic stories, through the postal system. In 1957, the Supreme Court sustained the conviction while also recognizing that "sex and obscenity are not synonymous." In this case, the Court determined that obscenity appealed to a prurient interest.

4. Consistent with its *Articles of Incorporation*, the Institute makes its library, art/photography, and archival collections available to duly qualified students of sexuality, including university faculty, other scholars and professionals, and university students at least eighteen years old who have demonstrated research needs related to human sexuality, gender, and reproduction.

5. Walter Kendrick's investigation into the origins and subsequent development of pornography starts with archaeological excavations of ancient Roman cities during the nineteenth century. The sexually explicit images and objects unearthed at Pompeii were kept concealed, behind locked doors, at burgeoning national museums, thus creating "secret museums" within larger, publicly accessible collections. Only *gentlemen* who could afford to pay the custodian to unlock the chamber could gain admission to the so-called secret museums.

6. In 1996 Assistant Curator Paul Burk located the thirty-one photographs in the Documentary Photography Collection which contains approximately 50,000 photographs. The photographs were separated into almost twenty different subcategories of sexual behaviors.

7. The thirty-one photographs read most clearly as depictions of the activities outlined in the above text. However, according to the institute's classification scheme, one of the photographs that I have grouped with fellatio was originally classified as "group heterosexual" (KI-DC: 38294), in response to an "extra" hand in the picture frame. Since this reference to a third party is not the primary focus in the image, it reads most obviously as fellatio. Furthermore, two of the seven photographs featuring variations of coital *positions* were classified originally as variations of coital *activity* (KI-DC: 311 and KI-DC: 342). These two images were labeled as heterosexual anal intercourse, following the institute's definition which encompassed penetration as well as a situation where the penis is near the female anus. However, these photographs may also be interpreted as "sex from the rear" before entry.

8. Twenty or thirty years ago scholars attempted to reclaim sexually explicit imagery from the pornographic realm by rescuing them as erotica. Many scholars today have turned their attention to an array of more probing issues of representation in approaching sexually explicit imagery, such as the gaze (Abigail Solomon-Godeau), the issue of "framing" (Lynda Nead), pleasure (Linda Williams and Carole S. Vance), and female *and male* subjects (Melody Davis). However, some feminists, most notably Andrea Dworkin and Catherine MacKinnon, remain focused on identifying and defining pornographic representations that "degrade women."

9. Significance of Erotic Art and Literature in Scientific Studies, unpublished memorandum (KI Archives, Bloomington, IN).

10. Nadine Strossen points out that Andrea Dworkin and Catharine MacKinnon are two examples of feminists who remain focused on "rape and the rape myth (that women really want to be raped) as major symbols and instruments of women's oppression" (Strossen, 152). Strossen also discusses pro-censorship feminists' responses to representations of nude female bodies from ancient Greek sculpture to the Spanish painter Francisco de Goya (Strossen, 21-2). Dworkin and MacKinnon are staunch anti-pornography feminists whereas Strossen and Wendy McElroy are two scholars who champion the anti-censorship feminist position.

11. Judith Allen, George Chauncey, John D'Emilio, Estelle B Freedman, Andrea Friedman, and David Halberstam are among those who have made significant contributions to the revision of mid-twentieth-century American history.

12. For additional information please see Linda Grant's *Sexing the Millennium: Women and the Sexual Revolution* (New York: Grove Press, 1994).

13. According to Christenson's biography, Kinsey published forty-three books and articles during his lifetime. Philadelphia's J. B. Lippencott published many of Kinsey's early books: *An Introduction to Biology* (1926), *Field and Laboratory Manual in Biology* (1927), *New Introduction to Biology* (1933, revised and reprinted in 1938), and *Workbook in Biology* (1934, 1938), and *Methods in Biology* (1937). Indiana University Press published both of Kinsey's books on gall wasps: *The Gall Wasp Genus Cynips: A Study in the Origin of Species* (1930) and *The Origin of Higher Categories in Cynips* (1936). After Kinsey's death in 1957, his enormous collection of well over a million gall wasps was moved to the American Museum of Natural History in New York City (Christenson, 187). Kinsey's book written with M. L. Fernald, *Edible Wild Plants of Eastern North America*, was published in 1943 by Idlewilde Press in New York.

14. The Association of Women Students petitioned the university to offer a marriage course and Kinsey was asked to coordinate this course. He invited a number of IU professors to join the faculty for the course to discuss marriage from the social, political, economic, and biologic points of view. When the university later asked Kinsey to chose between teaching the class or conducting his research on human sexual behavior, Kinsey chose the research.

15. In 1939, Clyde Martin joined Kinsey in his endeavor, in 1943 Wardell Pomeroy came aboard, and in 1946 Paul Gebhard joined the research staff.

16. When the Institute was incorporated in 1947, Kinsey sold his entire collection of materials to the corporation for one dollar. Now one of the largest and richest repositories in the world, the Institute's extraordinary collections contain approximately 75,000 photographs; more than 7,000 original works of art; 86,000 books, journals, and scientific articles; about 6,500 reels of film and 5,000 videos; and 55 filing cabinets of original Kinsey Institute documents and correspondence.

17. Alfred C Kinsey to Frances E. Shields, March 12, 1947 (KI Archives, Bloomington, IN).

18. Alfred C Kinsey to Frances E. Shields, March 19, 1947 (KI Archives, Bloomington, IN).

19. Dellenback made many valuable contributions to Institute research projects by photographing objects from other collections and the Institute's own collections, making portraits of visiting scientists, and documenting sexual behavior in mammals, including chimpanzees, cattle, hogs, and, occasionally, humans.

20. "Significance of Erotic Art and Literature in Scientific Studies," unpublished memorandum (KI Archives, Bloomington, IN). The author of this memorandum is not identified, but it clearly maps out Kinsey's ideas for using visual images in his studies.

21. Ibid, 3.

22. Although no analysis of images has been found to date, an example of the scientific use of images is given in the "Significance of Erotic Art." In the seventh and final point, where it is stated that images and literature may provide insight into a variety of problems from the biologic, psychological, medical, and social perspectives, a single example is given. Their understanding of the difference between male and female response (to be included in *Sexual Behavior in the Human Female*) was derived from a number of anatomical studies and scientific laboratory investigations as well as looking at drawings done by well-known male and female artists, amateur artists, mental patients, and graffiti in public restrooms. This reference illuminates the range of material that might be considered, but it does not demonstrate more specifically what conclusions they drew from particular visual examples.

23. Such processing continued at least through the 1974-1975 fiscal year, with the exception of the fourth priority of female and male figure photography. In the

one-page document "Projects completed July 1, 1974 to June 30, 1975," (KI Archives, Bloomington, IN) it is reported that new acquisitions of photographic material was still being processed. However, a memo dated September 6, 1962 formalizes the decision made by Paul Gebhard, Wardell Pomeroy, and Blaine Johnson not to continue processing the female and male figure photographs. Because the material was so voluminous and figure photography was also represented in the library's collection, they decided to leave the figure photographs bundled, unmounted, and unfiled.

24. In a previous essay, "History of the Collections" in *The Art of Desire* exhibition catalog, I published that the photographs were French in origin and dated to 1939. Since that 1997 publication, I have uncovered material that confirms that the photographs were shipped from Denmark to the United States in 1951. At this time, I have not been able to locate any more concrete evidence about where they were produced. However, the customs case correspondence does seem to be a source for generating and perpetuating the rumor that the thirty-one photographs (indeed almost any photographs at the Kinsey Institute) were French in origin. In the correspondence, "French" and "sexually explicit" were used almost interchangeably as qualifiers.

25. All of the information about the visual images and objects included in the test case incorporated into this paper has come from the customs case correspondence files at the Kinsey Institute. Unfortunately, neither the Institute's archives nor the university archives has a copy of the actual transcript of the case which would illuminate the way in which images were viewed and discussed in court sessions.

26. Alfred C. Kinsey to Huntington Cairns, June 13, 1947 (KI Archives, Bloomington, IN).

27. This quotation was excerpted from Honorable Edmund L. Palmieri's note (on p. 2) in the final decision of *U.S.* v. *31 Photographs* regarding 46 Stat. 688 (1930), 19 U.S.C. Sec. 1305(a) (1952) to define the terms of the 1930 tariff act that conflicted with Kinsey's research needs (KI Archives, Bloomington, IN).

28. The customs case correspondence at the Kinsey Institute indicates that hundreds of shipments were seized and detained, although an exact number is not readily identifiable. This action by Customs began to occur regularly in 1950, and it is probably that it continued until 1957 when the issue was resolved in court.

29. Alfred C. Kinsey to Harriet Pilpel, June 3, 1952, (KI Archives, Bloomington, IN). Pilpel requested that Kinsey address the importance of the detained material, and the memo "Significance of Erotic Art" may have been written in response, though this is suggested by the contents of the memorandum alone.

30 Harriet Pilpel to Huntington Cairns, June 20, 1950 (KI Archives, Bloomington, IN). Emphasis is mine.

31. Kinsey to Philobiblon Bookseller (Copenhagen, Denmark), March 22, 1951 (KI Archives, Bloomington, IN).

32. Alfred C Kinsey to Harriet Pilpel, August 24, 1950 (KI Archives, Bloomington, IN).

33. Pilpel to Edgar Weber (Vice President of Tice & Lynch, a custom house broker and forwarding agent in New York), May 28, 1951 (KI Archives, Bloomington, IN).

34. Nagisa Oshima, the film's director, shot the film in Japan, but had to send it to France to be developed. "Originally the complete version of the film was only shown in countries without censorship. It ran for years in Paris, but had to be edited to various degrees before screening in other countries" (Buehrer, 224).

35. In Williams's summary of the Supreme Court decision of 1957 in *United States* v. *Roth,* she excerpts this phrase from Solicitor General Rankin's argument that

the existence of pleasure in sexual gratification is the central "idea" of hard core pornography. Put neatly into perspective by Williams: "To Rankin the 'social value' of such an idea was obviously nil" (88).

36. The public hearings and nearly two-thousand-page report of the Attorney General's Commission on Pornography (also referred to as the Meese Commission), which convened in 1985 and 1986, examined the power of visual images and attacked them for their ability to evoke sexual pleasure and desire. For an excellent review and analysis of this cultural and political phenomenon, see Carole S. Vance's essay in the book *The Critical Image*.

37. D'Emilio and Freedman tells us: "Wives exhibited guilt about premarital experience and the desire for sexual gratification within marriage" (265).

38. The term *companionate marriage* was coined as the title for a 1927 book by Ben Lindsey and Wainwright Evans.

39. Nead states: "Visual culture . . . does not simply absorb and transmit a pre-formed ideology; it is not a neutral vehicle which 'expresses' social meaning. Painting, for example, is a practice of representation and representation functions to transform and mediate the world through the specific codes it uses and the institutions of which it is a part" (8).

40. Heins provides an excellent summary and analysis of the Miller Test. She also presents this case in the context of other rulings on obscenity. According to Heins, the Miller case reversed the direction of recent rulings to eliminate obscenity laws and, instead, *Miller* v. *California* (1973) allowed obscenity laws to be expanded.

41. Kinsey died prematurely in 1956 at the age of sixty-two (b. 1894-d. 1956). Fortunately for scholars his Institute for Sex Research has survived. It was renamed The Kinsey Institute for Research in Sex, Gender, and Reproduction in 1982 in honor of its founder. Today, the Institute's mission to promote the interdisciplinary study of research on sex, gender, and reproduction is supported by a small staff of three scientists (the director, the associate director, and an assistant scientist), a departmental administrator, two librarians, a curator, a systems analyst/computer programmer, a research associate, an accounts manager, a receptionist, and several clerical staff members.

REFERENCES

Allyn, David. 1996. "Private Acts/Public Policy: Alfred Kinsey, the American Law Institute, and the Privatization of American Sexual Morality." *Journal of American Studies* 30: 405-28.

Billings, Dwight B., and Thomas Urban. 1996. "The Socio-Medical Construction of Transsexualism: An Interpretation and Critique." *Blending Genders: Social Aspects of Cross-Dressing and Sex Changes,* ed. Richard Edkins and Dave King. New York: Routledge, 99–117.

Buehrer, Beverley. 1990. *Japanese Films: A Filmography and Commentary.* Jefferson, NC: McFarland & Co.

Christenson, Cornelia V. 1971. *Kinsey: A Biography.* Bloomington, IN: Indiana University Press.

D'Emilio, John. 1989. "The Homosexual Menace: The Politics of Sexuality in Cold War America." *Passion and Power,* ed. Kathy Peiss and Christina Simmons. Phildelphia: Temple University Press, 226–40.

D'Emilio, John, and Estelle B. Freedman. 1988. *Intimate Matters: A History of Sexuality in America.* New York: Harper & Row.

Freedman, Estelle B. 1987. "Uncontrolled Desires: The Response to the Sexual Psychopath, 1920-1960." *Journal of American History* 74: 83–106.

Friedman, Andrea. 1996. "'The Habits of Sex-Crazed Perverts': Campaigns against Burlesque in Depression Era New York City." *Journal of the History of Sexuality* 7, no. 2: 203–38.

Gathorne-Hardy, Jonathan. 1998. *Alfred C. Kinsey: Sex the Measure of All Things: A Biography.* London: Chatto & Windus.

Grant, Linda. 1994. *Sexing the Millennium: Women and the Sexual Revolution.* New York: Grove Press.

Halberstam, David. 1993. *The Fifties.* New York: Ballantine Books.

Heins, Marjorie. 1993. *Sex, Sin, and Blasphemy: A Guide to America's Censorship Wars.* New York: The New Press.

Jones, James H. 1997. *Alfred C. Kinsey: A Public/Private Life.* New York: W. W. Norton & Co.

Kendrick, Walter. 1987. *The Secret Museum: Pornography in Modern Culture.* New York: Viking Press.

Kinsey, Alfred C., Wardell Pomeroy, and Clyde Martin. 1948. *Sexual Behavior in the Human Male.* Philadelphia: Saunders.

Kinsey, Alfred C., Wardell Pomeroy, Clyde Martin, and Paul Gebhard. 1953. *Sexual Behavior in the Human Female.* Philadelphia: Saunders.

The Kinsey Institute. 1997. *The Art of Desire: Erotic Treasures from the Kinsey Institute.* Bloomington, IN: The Kinsey Institute.

Kipnis, Laura. 1996. *Bound and Gagged: Pornography and the Politics of Fantasy in America.* New York: Grove.

McElroy, Wendy. 1995. *XXX: A Woman's Right to Pornography.* New York: St. Martin's Press.

Morantz, Regina Markell. 1977. "Scientist as Sex Crusader: Alfred C. Kinsey and American Culture." *American Quarterly* 29 (Winter): 563-89.

Nead, Lynda. 1988. *Myths of Sexuality: Representations of Women in Victorian Britain.* Oxford: Blackwell.

Pomeroy, Wardell. 1971. *Dr. Kinsey and the Institute for Sex Research.* New Haven: Yale University Press, 1971.

Robinson, Paul. 1977. *The Modernization of Sex.* New York: Harper & Row.

Stevens, Kenneth R. 1975. "*United States* v. *31 Photographs*: Dr. Alfred C. Kinsey and Obscenity Law." *Indiana Magazine of History* 71, no. 4: 229–318.

Strossen, Nadine. 1995. *Defending Pornography: Free Speech, Sex, and the Fight for Women's Rights.* New York: Scribner.

Tagg, John. 1988. *The Burden of Representation: Essays on Photographies and Histories.* Minneapolis: University of Minnesota Press.

Tindall, George Brown, and David E. Shi. 1992. *America: A Narrative History,* 3d ed. New York: W. W. Norton & Co.

Vance, Carole S. 1990. "The Pleasure of Looking: The Attorney General's Commission on Pornography versus Visual Images." *The Critical Image,* ed. Carol Squiers. Seattle: Bay Press.

Williams, Linda. 1989. *Hard Core: Power, Pleasure, and the "Frenzy of the Visible."* Berkeley: University of California Press.

2

How a Family-Planning Experiment Became a Sex-Products Business

Philip D. Harvey

I. THERE ARE LAWS AND THERE ARE LAWS

WHEN ADAM AND EVE FIRST GOT UNDERWAY SELLING CONDOMS BY MAIL in 1970, it was illegal to sell condoms by mail. A law dating back to 1872, called the Comstock Law in honor, if that's the correct term, of Anthony Comstock, who crusaded for decades to remove everything sexual from American life, classified birth control–the means for preventing conception, the means for terminating pregnancy, any information relating to these subjects–as "obscene" and therefore "unmailable" through the U.S. postal system.

In 1970 the U.S. federal government was investing increasing amounts of congressionally appropriated funds in family-planning programs for low-income Americans. That the federal government should be supporting, even paying for, "the means to prevent conception" with one hand and defining such materials and even information about them as "obscene" on the other hand illustrates three points:

1. Even the silliest and most stupid of laws can be very hard to change. Laws which attempt to regulate private morality are universally silly and stupid but they are very difficult to alter, as politicians are reluctant to stand up and be counted as opposing laws concerning obscenity, adultery, fornication, and sodomy, to name just a few.
2. Governments by their nature are hypocritical. The categorization of the means to family planning as important service to be appropriately provided by taxpayer funding is, of course, irreconcilable with the definition of contraceptives as obscene. But this is quite typical of government hypocrisy when government attempts to regulate private consensual behavior.

3. Stupid and silly laws–particularly stupid and silly laws that are meant to direct our private lives–are generally ignored and teach us all contempt for all laws. I should not overstate this. It is my belief that the vast majority of Americans can easily distinguish between laws which need to be obeyed for the conduct of a civilized and civil society, and laws which may be ignored, laws which, indeed *should* be ignored for the conduct of a civilized and civil society. There are some gray areas. There is a reasonable limit to which sexual messages, for example, may be "thrust upon unwilling recipients," to use the Supreme Court's phrase from *Miller* v. *California.* But generally, Americans understand that laws which attempts to govern private consensual behavior are bad and stupid laws, and laws that protect us from the depredations of our fellow citizens and even, to a very limited extent, laws which prescribe certain conduct in public, such as stopping at red lights, are necessary laws. I think most of us are able to distinguish between these two kinds of laws with reasonable ease. On the other hand, both kinds are enforced. And when the law-enforcement system goes berserk and doles out heavy punishment to people for their private consensual behavior, our contempt for all laws increases quickly. Further, just getting used to the routine violation of certain kinds of laws, like having oral sex with your spouse in North Carolina, is apt to vitiate our respect for our law makers and our law enforcers generally.

So, in 1970, my partner Tim Black and I were looking for ways to promote birth control through means other than clinics, which had been the traditional method of delivery of family-planning services up to that time. Both of us had come from working in developing countries, Tim from sub-Saharan Africa and I from India. We knew there could never be enough clinics in those parts of the world to meet the family-planning needs of the hundreds of millions of couples who clearly were interested in spacing and preventing births. We took a look at Europe and found that anywhere from 5 to 25 percent of all condoms in most European countries were delivered by mail. We took a look at the United States and found that virtually no condoms were being sent out through the mail because of the Comstock Law.

We consulted lawyers. Neither Tim nor I had consciously broken the law up to that time. Yet our contempt for this particular silly and stupid law was manifest, for reasons already noted. How much more silly and stupid can you be than to classify as "obscene" those very things which you are yourself making available to your fellow citizens at other taxpayers' expense? But the law could still be enforced. We consulted with the postal authorities and they were willing to go so far as to suggest that, with the federal government promoting family planning, the prosecution of mailers of FDA-approved non-prescription contraceptives would not be a very high priority for them. But they could not and would not assure us, even by clear inference, that they would not prosecute us in the event there was a complaint.

Planned Parenthood lawyers spoke darkly of long jail terms, which had Tim scratching his head because his wife and two young daughters did not relish the prospect of his serving time at that stage of their family's development. (Nor at any other stage for that matter!)

The lawyers we consulted did reassure us with some relatively recent court decisions upholding the right of physicians and other family-planning professionals to provide contraceptives "for a legal purpose." Nobody knew what "a legal purpose" was, but it clearly did not include the provision of contraceptives to unmarried minors, a group with which we were particularly concerned. Still, there was some reassurance in the fact that others had been found to be operating legally when they provided contraceptives, "obscene" though those items had been.

So we went ahead. We began selling condoms by mail.

Thanks to Mr. Comstock, we had no competition. The orders rolled in. We had simply stepped into an area of market demand that had been completely unserved because of this law, and in 1970 the embarrassment factor for purchasing condoms in drug stores where they were almost always kept behind or under the counter was substantial, thus greatly expanding the interest in mail-order purchasing. There were, of course, vending machines in the men's rooms of some gas stations, particularly in the South, and a few bars. But mostly, if you wanted condoms, you had to ask somebody behind the counter in a pharmacy. The mail-order condom sampler package was an attractive alternative to this transaction.

Neither Tim nor I knew anything about business. Tim was a physician, and I had come from an international assignment with CARE, feeding kids in India. Neither of us was even particularly interested in business. But we were just smart enough to know that when there was more money coming in than going out, we might have the makings of a business. On Fridays, I would ask Tim how much money we'd put in the bank that week, then I'd pay all our bills, look up cheerfully and say, "There seems to be some left over!"

Up to that point Adam & Eve had been part of a non-profit organization. Now we looked at each other and said "hey, maybe we've got the basis for a profitable company so let's start one."

The mail-order activity and the Adam & Eve name were transferred to a new corporation, and that, almost by accident, is how the Adam & Eve mail-order business got started.

By now I had read a few books about operating businesses and particularly about running mail-order companies. The management gurus, even then, stressed the importance of listening to the customer, of letting the customer lead the most important corporate decisions, of offering the customer what he or she wanted. We assumed, coming from our do-gooder backgrounds, that our condom buyers would be enormously interested in books about reproductive anatomy, birth control, and things like pregnancy testing. So we offered these kinds of books and products. Our pregnancy-testing service by mail was an interesting experiment. A woman provides a urine sample in a tightly capped–very tightly capped–container and sends it through the mail, and we deliver it to a lab and phone back with the results a few days later. But our customers' interest in services like this and in pure information books about reproductive physiology, human anatomy, and such was, to put it mildly, limited. At this stage of the game, it didn't even occur to us that we might enter the "sex business" because we had started on a platform of family planning and family planning, back in the 70's, was pretty unsexy. However, we also had learned the gurus' rules about listening to the customer. And every time we included in our brochures or flyers a book about reproduction that contained some erotic visuals, sales took off. We weren't so thickheaded as to ignore these obvious preferences, and, gradually, we added more and more items of erotica. We also worked very hard to promote non-erotic merchandise in our catalog offerings, everything from digital watches and clocks, to leisure wear, to jewelry, to shipbuilding kits. Nothing but yawns for most of those categories. We did see some early interest in lingerie, and in other sexually oriented merchandise that might or might not have visual erotic content. But it was this last, visual erotica, that our mail-order condom buyers most clearly wanted from us, and we could see no reason not to give it to them. I should repeat that this evolution was completely customer-driven. We came to analyze precisely the sales and profit-per-square inch, square inch by square inch in our catalog. We carefully calculated the most financially productive items, the amount of space that should be devoted to those items, etc. In other words, this evolution was done with great and scientific care in direct response to what our customers were telling us through their own purchases. I cannot imagine a clearer case of the American people making clearly known their interest in sexually oriented merchandise than this evolutionary process, particularly as, especially in the early days, we tended to resist the sexually oriented direction our customers were taking us.

Simple lesson: People like sex. People are interested in sex. People buy sexually oriented merchandise. We couldn't see anything wrong with that. We still don't.

I want to emphasize that this process was orderly, rational. Our catalog pages would be analyzed square inch by square inch. Customer preferences were expressed through their purchases.

As we move to the next stage, things became chaotic, irrational. All hell breaks loose, as the government enters the picture. (The government, of course, is supposed to make things orderly, controlled. But more often than not, as in our case, the government imposes chaos on order.)

The following remarks are from the affidavit of Shirley Sell, one of our employees:

I was working at Adams & Eve on the morning of Thursday, May 29, 1986. At approximately 9:00 A.M., while I was on the telephone with a customer, four or five men came into my work area with some sort of badges . . . and one of these men ordered me to hang up the telephone. When I told him

I was on the phone with a customer, he said he didn't care and that I should get off or he would hang the phone up, so I hung up on the customer. I did not know who men were, or what was going on. I felt very badly about hanging up on the customer.

An announcement was made over the public address system that all employees had to go to the warehouse. I asked the man who had made me get off the phone if there had been a bomb threat, and he said no, that I just had to go to the warehouse. I did not believe that I had any choice, so I went.

When I arrived, all of the other employees were there. We were told by one of the officers that they had a search warrant. One of the supervisors, Mr. Loy, came in and said that he was not permitted to talk to us, but that the agents did have a search warrant.

After we had all gotten into the warehouse, one of the agents told the supervisors and managers to form a separate group and stand away from the rest of the employees, which they did. The supervisors were subsequently escorted out of the warehouse area by some agents. The other employees and supervisors were told that we would be questioned, that after we were questioned we would be brought to the back door of the warehouse, and that we could not leave the building until we had a subpoena. There were armed guards at every door, and I was guarded when I went to the restroom. I was not permitted to bring my pocket-book into the stall of the restroom, and had to give it to the female agent who escorted me there.

This raid consisted of thirty-five armed Federal and state law enforcement agents who descended on our premises on Highway 54, seven miles west Carrboro, North Carolina. The group comprised sheriff's deputies from two countries, federal postal inspectors from the Eastern District of North Carolina and from the state of Utah, and state Bureau of Investigation agents from North Carolina. Our receptionist, Jodi Klomser, reported: "A man in a brown suit stuck his head inside the window between the lobby and my work space and told me to open the door. I said no, just one moment please, and continued to try to find a manager. The man in a brown suit said: 'You tell him if you do not open the door immediately, we will kick it in.' When Skip [the manager] arrived and opened the door, the men in suits swarmed into the building." Jodi went on: "I was taken to the lunch room and asked questions. I do not remember everything about the interview, because I was very frightened. I believed that I had to answer the questions before I could leave. The agent who interviewed me also gave me a grand jury subpoena.

After the interview, I was taken back to the warehouse, and one of the agents took my picture and then asked for my driver's license. I was told to leave through the back door, and had to show a sheriff's deputy guarding the exit my subpoena before I was allowed to leave."

A reporter for the Chapel Hill *Independent* summed up the day's major events in the March 27, 1991, issue: "By the end of the day, 118 employees had been 'processed', questioned, and photographed. Subpoenas were issued, pocketbooks searched, documents and computer ledgers confiscated.

Law-enforcement officers ordered employees to turn over their weapons and demanded to see the studio where sex videos were made. 'They acted like it was a drug raid, and I guess we were a real disappointment to them,' said Skip Loy, director of operations . . . 'The only weapons people had were their box cutter knives.' And I had to tell the officers, I said, 'there's no videos produced here. We just got things in boxes.'"

The raiders' abuse of our employees that day included "securing" all exits, segregating supervisory from non-supervisory staff, individually photographing and interrogating every employee before ordering them out of the building, and refusing our people access to an attorney even after one was available on the premises. Each of our 118 employees was issued a subpoena.

I was in New York when I got the call from North Carolina. The first thing I did was call a local attorney, Grainger Barrett, in Chapel Hill. Grainger treated the situation like the emergency it was. He hung up the phone with me at 10:10 and was at our offices, eight miles away, by 10:30. While he was doing that, I was in a taxi on the way to La Guardia Airport to hop the next flight to North Carolina.

Grainger reported, a few weeks later in an affidavit of June 23, 1986:

> After I arrived, one of the supervisors asked me if she could advise the employees that I was present and that they could speak to an attorney if they wished. I told her yes, and gave her some business cards to provide to employees. I felt it important to reassure them that an attorney for the company was in fact now on the premises and of my name. About two minutes later Inspector Charlton came up to me and told me he could not allow my cards to be handed out any further. I told Inspector Charlton that I wanted to let the employees know I was there and to let them know what their legal rights were if they wished this advice. I repeatedly assured him I would advise employees generally to be cooperative and that neither I nor the employees would interfere with or impede their search. Inspector Charlton told me something to the effect that the employees didn't have the right to consult with an attorney since they weren't under arrest, and I asked him if he was saying that persons not under arrest didn't have the right to talk to an attorney. Charlton then said that he didn't have to let me talk to the employees since I wasn't their attorney, but rather the company's attorney. At no time did Inspector Charlton ever permit me to provide legal advice to any of the employees being detained in the warehouse, despite my specific request to be allowed to do this. I heard one agent tell the employees in the warehouse that if they each talked to an attorney, they would be there all day and everyone would thus be greatly inconvenienced. During the three hours I was at PHE, Inc., from 10:30 A.M. until 1:30 P.M., none of the employees to my knowledge were allowed to leave the building without being interviewed, searched, photographed, and given a subpoena. All of the employees were restrained in a custodial atmosphere and the search was as intrusive and general a search as I have witnessed. It was clear to me that the majority of employees held there were intimidated, that (they) repeatedly asked whether they were under arrest, and they were extremely fearful and apprehensive about what was

happening to them. I hope never again to be called upon to provide legal counsel under such distressing circumstances and conduct by Government officials.

Adding to this, an employee reported that "the agents treated us like criminals and tried to scare us." The agents told employees that they were involved in disturbing obscenities "that influenced rapists and child abusers."

In addition to my anger and indignation, I learned something very important about people from this experience. Since virtually all of our employees had been subjected to this treatment, I assumed that we would lose many—perhaps half or more—of our staff and that we would be severely short-handed on the following day. But the next morning practically everyone turned up. They weren't scared, they were mad! It was, of course, patronizing of me to think that while my reaction was one of sputtering anger, other people would intimidated, and I was very glad to be wrong. Melinda Ruley recounted in the same *Independent* article, "Skip Loy, director of operations at the plant, is fond of telling how, the day after the raid, all but a handful of employees showed up for work as usual. Even a woman who had been filling out an application when the agents filed in came back, still hoping to be hired. 'It's a uniting experience,' Loy says of the legal trouble PHE and Phil Harvey have gone through. 'People have suffered through this thing together.' "

I will summarize very briefly the trial in Alamance County which followed ten months after this raid. The company and I were indicted in nearby Alamance in September of 1986, and the trial took place in March of 1987. In terms of trial tactics, I would like to emphasize particularly the point about jury selection. We had, I believe, nine days of trial and five of those days were spent in *voire dire* selecting the jury. This is a critical—an absolutely critical—part of any obscenity defense.

The jury took five minutes to find us not guilty on all nine counts of obscenity dissemination. They had watched five hours of tapes and reviewed several magazines. An interesting footnote is the fact that the jury, out of "respect for the prosecutor" remained in the jury deliberation room for about an hour after having made their decision. My own feeling is that the prosecutor in this case, Octavis White, did indeed do a responsible and professional job. I certainly have no regrets that the jury wanted to avoid embarrassing him.

What happened after the trial was particularly revealing of the zealousness of prosecutors who are obsessed with sexual issues. The U.S. Attorney for the Eastern District of North Carolina, Sam Currin, just days after our not guilty verdict in nearby Alamance, issued the following memo to his staff:

1. . . . We must regain momentum after the Adam & Eve verdict and come with as many indictments as possible. As I suggested to Paul by telephone last Friday, we need to do a complete analysis of what

went wrong in the Adam & Eve case and share this with the membership of the Pornography Task Force.

2. We need to keep working on our Adam & Eve case and be prepared to indict when Judge Boyle resumes jurisdiction over the case.

3. I want you to subpoena (Orange County District Attorney) Carl Fox to the federal grand jury as soon as possible. His role vis-a-vis Adam & Eve is going to continue to haunt every single prosecution of that company. Therefore, we need to bring him on in and question him about his entire role in this matter, including campaign contributions, etc. I don't want any delay on this. I personally believe he is in league with Phil Harvey on this matter and you might as well proceed with that assumption in mind. I want you to be tough as nails in questioning him in the grand jury.

4. We also need to locate some other District Attorneys who will prosecute Adam & Eve in their districts. Bob Thomas in Hickory is one who I believe will do so. Perhaps Peter Gilchrist will also prosecute. We need to get state indictments of Adam & Eve in some other districts.

5. Contact Utah and urge them to proceed with their indictments as soon as possible. Also discuss with [Washington NOEU head] Rob [Showers] whether he wants the Middle District to do a RICO on Adam & Eve. If so, he needs to work the RICO case out of Washington. I doubt anyone in the Middle District has the sense to do it. . . .

The idea that district attorney Carl Fox and I were "in league" is of course preposterous. I had made a $200 contribution to Fox's re-election campaign, hardly a conspiracy! Yet, here was Sam Currin, cooking up paranoid visions to support his determination to prosecute us, even in the face of an acquittal in a considerably more conservative jurisdiction in the same state. We are often told that prosecutors can be trusted to be reasonable. That they will not abuse the public when they are given wide latitude with laws like RICO, and civil asset forfeiture. Whenever I am inclined to give prosecutors the benefit of this doubt, I remind myself about Sam Currin and his persistent policy of abusing the power of his office in pursuit of his own personal agenda.

One very interesting aspect of the ensuing struggle—which went on for a total of eight years—was the assumption on the part of all the prosecutors that our employees must somehow be bad people. When our company had first been raided, several of those in the invading task force had remarked somewhat incredulously, "I've interviewed two grandmothers and a Sunday School teacher. What's going on here?" They just couldn't seem to believe, despite their own experience with our staff, that our employees were decent, hard-working, law-abiding citizens.

We hired a seasoned defense attorney, Fred Harwell, to represent those of our employees who were subpoenaed by Sam Currin's office to appear before the grand jury in Raleigh. Fred relates that the representatives of

Currin's office had considerable difficulty even believing the testimony given by our employees. He reports:

> I had to have a long conversation with the prosecutors and tell them that these PHE employees are ordinary, good people. They are not engaged in some huge international pornography conspiracy. They come to work in the morning, they do their job, they go home at night. They have high personal standards, a great deal of loyalty, but they understand that they need to tell the truth when they're asked to, and that's what they're trying to do. And you need to tell me, as their attorney, if you ever have any reason to believe that any of these of my clients has said anything to the grand jury that is not true, because I'll sit down and talk to them and take care of it right away. And I can tell you over this entire time for perhaps two or three years, not a single prosecutor or agent ever came to me and suggested that they had anything other than a *generalized* skepticism about my clients' testimony. They seemed to think that the testimony was just too good to be true, that the company could not be as well-managed as the employees were saying. And I said well, you're the ones that put the names on the subpoenas, I didn't pick them out!
>
> There was an acute disappointment on the part of prosecutors that people they wanted to make out to be devils were not. I believe that disappointment radiated right up the chain of command; there was an increasing sense of frustration on the part of the government that they couldn't really seem to break through to the reality that they thought existed. They kept bringing people in and bringing people in and just never could find anybody that fit the profile that I'm sure they had in their mind, the profile of people who worked at PHE who would be 'the key' to the inside. By then, of course, I knew that there was no key because I saw how the corporation was run. There wasn't a back door that you went through to a sweatshop operation.
>
> They sprinkled immunity agreements all over the landscape and got nothing in return except bad news for the prosecution.

Let me make just one main point and quickly summarize the battle between our company and the U.S. Justice Department over the next several years.

North Carolina never indicted. On the other hand, we were indicted under federal law in the District of Utah. Federal prosecutors in Kentucky conducted an active prosecution. Subsequently, federal prosecutors in Alabama conducted an active prosecution. Fairly early in this process, we sued the Department of Justice for having violated our constitutional rights by conducting a bad faith prosecution using threats of multiple indictments and multiple trials to muzzle us, as they had many others.

Along the way, we made some good law. In particular, our interlocutory appeal to the Tenth Circuit in Denver established that a company like ours has *a right not to be tried* when prosecuted in a bad faith context. This form of appeal and, most assuredly, this right, had never been established before. Here is a summary of the Tenth Circuit Appeals Court decision:

We conclude that appellants have already satisfied their burden of showing that the indictment is the tainted fruit of a prosecutorial attempt to curtail PHE's future First Amendment protected speech. . . . [T]he burden now shifts to the government to "justify its decision [to indict] with legitimate, articulable, objective, reasons." In considering whether such proper reasons exist, the polestar to guide the district court on remand will be the controlling precept it recognized in its previous opinion in this case:

> The inquiry is whether, "as a practical matter, there is a realistic or reasonable likelihood of prosecutorial conduct that would not have occurred *but for* the hostility or punitive animus towards the defendant because he exercised his specific legal rights."

As most of you know, we finally reached a settlement with the Feds in December of '93. We agreed to drop our civil suit, which was just about to go to trial, and agreed to plead guilty to a technical violation of a mailing regulation (the size of type in which the term "sexually oriented ad" had been printed on some of our mailing envelopes) in Alabama, in exchange for which the government agreed to drop all obscenity-related charges against us prior to the date of the settlement.

Now I'd like to examine briefly some of the whys behind all this. Why are we humans so upset about sex? Why are we so ashamed of the most creative human act?

I'd like to begin with three revealing quotations about women's sexuality and women's genitalia. I find these very revealing. The first is from Eve Ensler's "The Vagina Monologues":

> Down there? I haven't been down there since 1953. No, it had nothing to do with Eisenhower. No, no, it's a cellar down there. Its very damp, clammy. You don't want to go down there. Trust me. You'd get sick. Suffocating. Very nauseating. . . .
>
> There's rumbles down there sometimes. You can hear the pipes and things get caught there, animals and things and it gets wet and sometimes people have to plug up the leaks. Otherwise the door stays closed. It has to be there though cause every house needs a cellar otherwise the bedroom would be in the basement.[1]

The next quote is from Shakespeare's *King Lear*. See if you can recognize which of Shakespeare's characters characterizes women's sexuality in the following very graphic terminology:

> Behold yon simp'ring dame,
> Whose face between her forks presages snow,
> That minces virtue, and does shake the head
> To hear of pleasure's name,–
> The fitchew nor the soiled horse goes to't
> With a more riotous appetite.
> Down from the waist they are Centaurs,

Though women all above;
But to the girdle do the gods inherit,
Beneath is all the fiends';
There's hell, there's darkness, there's the sulphurous pit.
Burning, scalding, stench, consumption; fie, fie, fie!

Finally, Tertullian, an early and important Christian cleric, described woman as "a temple over a sewer."

It seems to me these remarks about the seat of women's sexuality, about the reproductive organs, about, perhaps most of all, men's fear of women's sexuality are very revealing.

Why this fear?

I believe it has something to do with control. Here are a few quotations on the subject of control and sex from other persons.

U.S. President Richard M. Nixon, denouncing the recommendations of the U.S. Commission on Pornography and Obscenity submitted to him in 1970, declared that we must "draw the line against pornography to protect freedom of expression[!] . . . If an attitude of permissiveness were to be adopted regarding pornography, this would contribute to an atmosphere condoning anarchy in every other field—and would increase the threat to our social order as well as to our moral principles."[2]

Here's Walter Kendrick's description of Anthony Comstock:

"Like his more sophisticated contemporaries in France and England, Comstock at bottom feared nothing so much as the universal distribution of information. The prospect called up nightmarish images of a world without structure, where all barriers had been breached and all differences leveled. It was appropriate that sex should become the focus of such nightmares, since long before the modern threat arose, sex already stood for loss of control and the scattering of substance. . . . On the surface pornography threatens nothing but the unleashing of sexuality; but that unleashing, as Nixon said, turns immediately into wantonness of every other kind, including the promiscuous redistribution of property."[3]

Lawrence Tribe notes that sexual imagery "threatens to explode our uneasy accommodation between sexual and social custom—to destroy the carefully spun social web holding sexuality in its place."[4]

Does anyone really believe that sexuality and pornography threaten property rights? Apparently so. Mary Klein adds this: "Authentic sexuality is ultimately revolutionary. It challenges gender roles by depicting women as lusty without being bad. It enfranchises us all as sexual beings—but for who we are, not for what we do. It returns to us the right and means to own and evaluate our own sexuality, rather than referring us to social definitions of what is "normal." It challenges the role of monogamy and the nuclear family as the exclusive source of emotional comfort. It undermines traditional religions by refusing to make procreation the primary purpose of sex. . . . It trusts people to take care of themselves during sexual encounters. Finally, it sees sex as a positive force we can use to explore and expand our human horizons, rather than as a negative force we must control and restrict to protect ourselves."[5]

In the same vein, political tyrants always do their best to suppress sexuality. "[M]ost tyrannies have a puritanical nature. The sexual restriction of Stalin's Soviet Union, Hitler's Germany, and Mao's China would have gladdened the hearts of those Americans who fear sexual images and literature. Their iron-fisted Puritanism wasn't motivated by a need to erase inequality. They wanted to smother the personal chaos that can accompany sexual freedom and subordinate it to the granite face of the state. Every tyrant knows that if he can control human sexuality, he can control life." (Hammill).[6]

This provides at least some insight into the issue of sexuality and the desire to control it. But why do we feel we must so vigorously control our sexuality? Why are we so embarrassed?

NOTES

1. In Judy Bloomfield et al., eds., *Too Darn Hot* (New York: Persea Books, 1998).
2. In Nadine Strasser, *Defending Pornography* (New York: Scribner, 1995), p. 177.
3. Ibid., p. 178.
4. *American Constitutional Law* (Westbury, N.Y.: The Foundation Press, 1988).
5. "Censorship and the Fear of Sexuality." *The Humanist,* July/August 1990.
6. Strasser, *Defending Pornography*, p. 219.

3

Art, Literature, and Obscenity in the United States Supreme Court

Stanley Fleishman

O N APRIL 22, 1957, I ENTERED THE GREAT MARBLE COURTHOUSE OF the United States Supreme Court to argue my first case before the High Court. My client, David S. Albert–a major distributor of sexy books and nude pictures–was convicted in California of distributing "obscene" books and pictures and was sentenced to sixty days in jail. Under California law, a work was "obscene" if it "has a substantial tendency to deprave or corrupt its readers or viewers by inciting lascivious thoughts or arousing lustful desires." Although federal and state obscenity statutes had been on the books for over a hundred years, the Supreme Court had not yet given serious consideration to the constitutional issues posed by these laws.

In my brief to the Supreme Court, I argued that "obscene" speech was merely "offensive" sexual speech and should be given the same First Amendment protection as offensive political or religious speech. Next, I argued that even if some obscene works might be outside the protection of the First Amendment, the test California used–exciting lascivious thoughts or arousing lustful desire–was too broad and encompassed works which enjoy First Amendment protection by any standard. Finally, I argued that "obscenity" was hopelessly vague and thus violated the Due Process Clause of the Fourteenth Amendment.

In 1957, America was a country with a tradition of blue-nosed puritanism. A book with the word "fuck" in it would be prosecuted and almost certainly found to be obscene. Similarly, a photograph showing the pubic area of a man or woman would be legally condemned. Oral sex was still considered an abominable and detestable crime against nature, punishable by a 15-year prison term. At the same time, the upheavals of the Second World War were being felt in virtually every area, and the sexual revolution of the 1960s was just around the corner.

Lawyers appearing before the Supreme Court give three arguments: the one they intend to give, the one they give, and the one they wish they had given. The argument I gave was mostly controlled by Associate Justice Felix Frankfurter, a former professor at Harvard Law School.

While I was rehearsing my argument, the sharp sound of the Marshal's gavel filled the courtroom. As everyone in the room quickly stood, the Court crier began to chant: "Oyez! Oyez! All persons having business before the Honorable Supreme Court of the United States are admonished to draw near and give their attention." Suddenly the red draperies parted and nine black-robed men appeared between the opening in the velvet, stepped forward, and took their places as the crier continued: "The court is now sitting. God save the United States and this Honorable Court."

In the center was Chief Justice Earl Warren. Warren was a man of great integrity. In his youth he had been a brakeman on freight trains in and out of Bakersfield, California. He had come up the hard way. He had served as Attorney General and Governor of California and was appointed Chief Justice by President Eisenhower in 1953. Warren had a passion for justice, for "constitutional law and order." But he had a blind spot on the obscenity issue. In his view, as I later came to learn, the Constitution gave no sanctuary to any indecencies. I did not know that then. Indeed, I was counting on Warren to be one of my supporters.

Sitting with the Chief Justice were Associate Justices Hugo L. Black, appointed in 1937, Felix Frankfurter, appointed in 1939, William O. Douglas, appointed in 1939, Harold H. Burton, appointed in 1945, Tom C. Clark, appointed in 1949, John Marshal Harlan, appointed in 1955, William J. Brennan, Jr., appointed in 1956, and Charles E. Whittaker, appointed in 1957. I knew that Black and Douglas believed that all utterances in publications were protected by the First Amendment, and assumed they would side with me. I also knew that Frankfurter disagreed with them, and that he would be against me. None of the other justices had plainly shown their hand, though I feared most of them would line up behind Frankfurter.

In a courteous tone, Chief Justice Warren announced: "Number 61, David S. Alberts, appellant, versus the State of California. Mr. Fleishman, attorney for the appellant, you may proceed."

I opened with the traditional:

Mr. Chief Justice may it please the Court.

I then explained that in California a book or picture was obscene if it had a substantial tendency to corrupt or deprave the reader by arousing lascivious thoughts and inciting lustful desires. Our first point, I argued, "is that because the statute applies only to thoughts and only to desires, and has nothing to do with conduct, it violates the First Amendment." Chief Justice Warren quickly broke in, and in an icy tone asked whether any of the books or pictures involved in the case were obscene. When I said "no," we had the following colloquy.

Chief Justice Warren: Well, I asked you if they were. You say they are not obscene.

Mr. Fleishman: That's right.

Chief Justice Warren: None of them are obscene?

Mr. Fleishman: None of them are obscene.

Chief Justice Warren: Well, I just wanted your viewpoint. That's all.

I knew then that I had lost the Chief. At that point Justice Frankfurter came after me.

Justice Frankfurter: Well, you say there is no such thing as obscenity controllable by law.

Mr. Fleishman: That is not what I say, Your Honor.

Justice Frankfurter: Well, what do you say?

Mr. Fleishman: I say that the standard California applies is a mental obscenity statute. I say that is no good. Now it may be that an obscenity statute which is narrowly drawn and which is related to conduct may reach some material which Your Honors think may be controllable.

Justice Frankfurter: What do you mean by related to conduct? That the book must say to whomsoever it's addressed to go out and do that, is that what you mean?

Mr. Fleishman: Yes, Your Honor.

Justice Frankfurter: That's what you mean?

Mr. Fleishman: That's what I mean. Yes. I believe that under our Constitution, the mere arousing of thoughts, any thoughts, bad political thoughts, bad religious thoughts, and bad sexual thoughts, may not be controlled by government.

Justice Harlan then asked: You are saying no matter how pornographic the subject matter of a particular book or a picture is, constitutionally you can't touch it.

Mr. Fleishman: I'm saying that we would have to have, Your Honor, a much narrower statute. I'm saying that our statute talks in terms merely of the effects it has on a person's mind. Now if, on the other hand, something that Your Honor may have in mind could be tied in with conduct, perhaps, and could be specifically defined, perhaps that would be reachable. I have in mind, for example, the views of Judge Curtis Bok and Judge Jerome Frank. That is their position also. Now, there is much in their opinions that may not satisfy all of us, but at least it shows the relevant factors. You have to have a narrow statute and you have to relate it to conduct. So far as it merely touches the mind, it's our position that we, as free Americans, have the right to choose.

Justice Harlan: Do any of the obscenity statutes meet that test? You say that unless the book or picture told an individual to go out and commit a crime, it can't be stopped.

Mr. Fleishman: I'm not prepared to draw up a statute that may meet the test Your Honor. My argument here is, merely, that our statute is so broad it includes what Your Honor has in mind when you say pornography as well as works of great value that all of us would admit have to be protected. If the State may control some part of this area, it must do so by narrower legislation than we have before us today.

Justice Frankfurter: Do you agree or disagree that there is such a thing as pornography? This isn't an academic question. You're asking us to strike down a statute that every state of the Union has, and when you say it isn't your business to draw a statute that would stand, it is, if I may say so, your business to enlighten me as to what the scope of–what the standard, what the tests are–which I'm to apply. And therefore it seems to me very relevant to ask you whether you concede there is such a thing as pornography in this world.

Mr. Fleishman: If Your Honor please, pornography means different things to me than it does to you. And I can't answer that question–because we're not talking in the same language.

Justice Frankfurter: May I say that you are here under a constitutional provision, the Due Process Clause, which may mean very different things to you from what it does to me and which is so vague that this Court constantly divides on it. The fact that the concept may have different content for different people doesn't mean it's unconstitutional.

Mr. Fleishman: Let me answer you this way, if I may, Your Honor. I believe that there is some material that is so highly erotic that perhaps most of us in this room and most people in America would say that this is so erotic as to offend most of us and therefore we personally don't like it. I will concede there is that much. But I do not concede that there is any way where you or anyone in this room can look at a book and say that book, that it's going to arouse lascivious thoughts, lustful desires and corrupt a person. I say that's impossible.

Justice Frankfurter: Well I think, if I may say so, you're raising two different questions. I understand you intellectually. I understand you when you answered a little while ago that mere arousing of thoughts or feeling, not incitation–now that's an ambiguous word–not telling me or somebody else to do something. That conduct must be carried not merely as a likelihood that conduct may come. You say unless a book says on its title page "this is calculated to have you go out and commit pederasty," or something like that. I understand you to say that it's necessary to have the additional fact of conduct. Now you say that maybe books so offend everybody–now offend is a personal feeling for a community of people. It has nothing to do with conduct.

Mr. Fleishman: That's right. And I think that is why the First Amendment forbids that, Your Honor.

Justice Frankfurter: Wait a minute, I understand you. Now if you stick to that I understand you. If you say that you take the position that no statute can outlaw or make it an offense or in an appropriate way prosecute books that have tendencies that may be deemed to offend the community, I understand you. But there must be the additional factor of making somebody go out and do something which the community may forbid. But you say that no matter how offensive it may be it must be protected, because if once you open the door, who is to judge what does and what doesn't offend?

Mr. Fleishman: If Your Honor please, perhaps I can clarify it this way.

Insofar as the material may offend, only offend, unrelated to conduct, the First Amendment absolutely prohibits criminalizing it.

Justice Frankfurter: By unrelated to conduct you mean that the author must indicate in a pretty unambiguous way that he wants the reader to do something. Is that what you mean?

Mr. Fleishman: Yes.

Justice Frankfurter: Alright, I understand.

Mr. Fleishman: The other point is that the statute violates Due Process. Nobody can tell in advance, neither the defendant nor the jury, or the judge, where the line is separating the constitutional work from the obscene. There is no line whatsoever.

Justice Frankfurter: You mean you can't determine it automatically. There is no formula.

Mr. Fleishman: You cannot determine it at all.

Justice Frankfurter: Professor Borchant wrote a book called "Convicting the Innocent." I am of the view that from time to time innocent people have been convicted of murder because of misjudgment. Does that mean that's so vague that juries send people to the electric chair unconstitutionally too?

Mr. Fleishman: In this case you can never prove that the jury's verdict was right or wrong. . . . I pose this to you Your Honor: If the State decided to bring a complaint against a bookseller for selling Kinsey's Report, might not a jury find under the standard used that the Kinsey Report might arouse lustful desires or lascivious thoughts and thereby corrupt and deprave a person? Now if it might, there would be no way of reversing this, because the jury makes the law as its decides the case. A jury says it's going to have this effect and then there is no way of disproving it.

Justice Frankfurter: But highest courts all over the place have said that a scientific book, as a matter of law, can't be brought within that rubric.

Mr. Fleishman: Justice Frankfurter, that's not the standard we use in California.

Justice Frankfurter: Well, you haven't told us what the standard is. You haven't told us a thing except your own elucidation for what you read the statute to mean, namely that a book in the office of any gynecologist is lewd, obscene and lascivious. That's all you've told us thus far.

Mr. Fleishman: If Your Honor please, in California a book is obscene if it has a substantial tendency to deprave or corrupt its readers by inciting lascivious thoughts or arousing lustful desire.

Now in the brief time left, I want to point out that the State of California has contended that the book *The Picture of Conjugal Love* is one of the most obscene books in the record. That book happens to be a classic. Any standard that will catch within its net this book must be an unconstitutional standard.

Justice Frankfurter: What is the book?

Mr. Fleishman: *The Picture of Conjugal Love* by Dr. Vinette. It was written in 1688. It was the first Kinsey report.

Justice Frankfurter: May I ask you what you would do with a case in which a careful abstract of the Kinsey report is mailed exclusively to boys in the famous prep schools of the United States? What would you say to that?

Mr. Fleishman: I think a narrowly drawn statute addressed to children would be a statute which would commend itself much more readily to me and to Your Honors.

Justice Frankfurter: Well, the fact that it's a classic doesn't answer all of the questions.

Mr. Fleishman: No, it doesn't.

Justice Frankfurter: And a classic may have illustrations. That may add an element to the classic text and make a difference.

Mr. Fleishman: If Your Honor please, this statute is not limited to children. It applies to the readers.

Justice Frankfurter: I'm just addressing myself to your suggestion that this book, which in my ignorance I have not heard of. Perhaps in my maturity I have not heard of, you call it a classic, therefore okay.

Mr. Fleishman: If your Honor please, this work illustrates to me one of the really difficult problems in this whole area. We all approach it, if Your Honor please, with a prejudice. I know it because when I handled my first case I was prejudiced also. But the fact of the matter is that in this area of sexual conduct the American people are undergoing great change.

Justice Frankfurter: Must I take that as a dogmatic proof, a scientific proof? These statements are made about what the American people think on sex. Are those all established tenets that come from Moses to Sinai via Kinsey?

Mr. Fleishman: I believe that it's at least as established as many of the things that are asserted as being the basis for obscenity laws.

Justice Frankfurter: That's where the function between the judiciary and the legislature comes in, because they are not susceptible of scientific proof. This Court doesn't sit here as a college of purity.

Mr. Fleishman: If Your Honor please, the legislature doesn't draw the standard of obscenity. The judge and the jury draw it. In each case the standard is made, the law is made for that case. That's not the function of courts.

Justice Frankfurter: So it is in negligence. So it is in the difference between manslaughter and murder. So it is in Sherman law cases.

Mr. Fleishman: Your Honor, in criminal law cases involving free speech, the standard has to be more specific.

Justice Frankfurter: Justice Holmes for this Court said what I supposed would put an end to these arguments, that simply because they run the risk of what a jury may have to decide doesn't mean the legislature has exceeded the constitutional speed limits. Although its been on the statute book of every state of this Union and of the United States–every state of the Union for 150 years–the statute in United States for almost 100 years, not quite, you've just discovered that there's no content to it because it's difficult to apply.

Mr. Fleishman: I say the California standard, and that's all we are attacking, which says that a defendant must know in advance that this book–*The Picture of Conjugal Love*–is going to so arouse people, incite such bad sexual thoughts in them, that they are going to be corrupted and depraved, I say that's unknowable by everyone in this courtroom.

The red light signalling my time was up went on and I backed away from the podium wondering what I could have said or should have said in answer to Justice Frankfurter's barrage of questions.

Two months later, on June 24, 1957, the Court announced its decision upholding Alberts' conviction by a vote of seven to two. Justice Brennan—who was to emerge in later years as one of the great defenders of the First Amendment—wrote the opinion for the Court.

Justice Brennan: The dispositive question is whether obscenity is utterance within the are of protected speech and press. Although this is the first time the question has been squarely presented to this Court, expressions found in numerous opinions indicate that this Court has always assumed that obscenity is not protected by the Freedom of Speech and Press. In light of our history, it is apparent that the unconditional phrasing of the First Amendment was not intended to protect every utterance. Implicit in the history of the First Amendment is the rejection of obscenity as utterly without redeeming social importance. This rejection for that reason is mirrored in the universal judgment that obscenity should be restrained. Accordingly, we hold that obscenity is not within the area of constitutionally protected speech or press.

It is strenuously urged that the obscenity statutes offend the constitutional guarantees because they punish incitation to impure sexual thoughts not shown to be related to any overt anti-social conduct which is or may be incited in the persons stimulated by such thoughts. It is insisted that the Constitutional guarantees are violated because convictions may be had without proof either that obscene material will perceptibly create a clear and present danger of anti-social conduct or will probably induce its recipients to such conduct. But in light of our holding that obscenity is not protected speech, it is unnecessary for us to consider the issues behind the phrase "clear and present danger."

It is argued that the obscenity statutes do not provide reasonably ascertainable standards of guilt and therefore violate the constitutional requirements of due process. Many decisions have recognized that the terms of obscenity statutes are not precise. This Court, however, has consistently held that lack of precision is not itself offensive to the requirements of due process. The Constitution does not require impossible standards: all that is required is that the language convey sufficiently definite warning as to the prescribed conduct when measured by common understanding and practices. The statutes give adequate warning of the conduct prescribed and mark boundaries sufficiently distinct for judges and juries fairly to administer the law.

Justice Douglas wrote a dissenting opinion, joined by Justice Black.

Justice Douglas: When we sustain this conviction, we make the legality of a publication turn on the purity of thought which a book or tract instills in the mind of the reader. I do not think we can approve that standard and be faithful to the command of the First Amendment.

The test by which the conviction was obtained requires only the arousing of sexual thoughts. Yet the arousal of sexual thoughts and desires happens every day in normal life in dozens of ways. The test of obscenity the Court endorses today gives the censor free range over a vast domain. To allow the State to step in and punish mere speech or publication that the judge or the jury thinks has an undesirable impact on thoughts but that is not shown to be a part of unlawful action is drastically to curtail the First Amendment.

Any test that turns on what is offensive to the community's standards is too loose, too capricious, too destructive of freedom of expression to be squared with the First Amendment. Under that test, juries can censor, suppress and punish what they don't like, provided the matter relates to "sexual impurity" or has a tendency "to excite lustful thoughts." This is community censorship in one of its worse forms. It creates a regime where in the battle between the literati and the Philistines, the Philistines are certain to win. If experience in this field teaches anything, it is that censorship of obscenity has almost always been both irrational and indiscriminate.

If the First Amendment guarantee of freedom of speech and press is to mean anything, it must allow protests, even against the moral code that the standard of the day sets for the community. In other words, literature should not be suppressed merely because it offends the moral code of the censor. The legality of a publication in this country should never be allowed to turn either on the purity of thought which it instills in the mind of the reader or on the degree to which it offends the community conscience. By either test, the role of the censor is exalted, and society's values in literary freedom are sacrificed.

Today the Court defines obscene material as that "which deals with sex in a manner appealing to prurient interest." But that standard, too, does not require any nexus between the literature which is prohibited and action which the legislature can regulate or prohibit. Under the First Amendment, that standard is no more valid than the standard used in the lower courts.

I do not think that the problem can be resolved by the Court's statement that obscenity is not expression protected by the First Amendment. I reject as well the implication that problems of freedom of speech and of the press are to be resolved by weighing against the values of free expression, the judgment of the court that a particular form of that expression has no redeeming social importance. The First Amendment, its prohibition in terms absolute, was designed to preclude courts as well as legislatures from weighing the values of speech against silence. The First Amendment puts free speech in the preferred position.

Freedom of expression can be repressed if, and to the extent that, it is so closely brigaded with illegal action as to be an inseparable part of it. As a people we cannot afford to relax that standard. For the test that suppresses a cheap tract today can suppress a literary gem tomorrow. All it need do is to incite a lascivious thought or arouse a lustful desire. A list of books that judges or juries can place in that category is endless.

I would give the broad the sweep of the First Amendment full support. I have the same confidence in the ability of our people to reject noxious literature as I have in their capacity to sort out the true from the false in theology, economics, politics or any other field.

Between 1957, when I argued the Alberts case, and 1995, I have been the attorney of record in some twenty-five Supreme Court cases involving the First Amendment. I represented Henry Miller in his fight against being extradited from Los Angeles to Brooklyn to be criminally tried for having written *Tropic of Cancer*, and Bradley Smith, the Los Angeles bookseller who was convicted by a Los Angeles jury for having sold *Tropic of Cancer*. I also took *Deep Throat* and a host of sexy books, magazines, videos and films to the Court. I sometimes felt that I was giving a basic sex education course to the Justices.

When I filed my petition to the Supreme Court for a writ of certiorari in the *Tropic of Cancer* case, I asked Henry Miller to write a letter addressed to me which I then attached to the petition. He wrote to me from Big Sur, California, on December 26, 1962.

Henry Miller: At your suggestion I am setting forth some of my views concerning the *Tropic of Cancer* case, which I understand is on its way to the Highest Court of the Land. I have often referred to this work as an ice-breaker. In writing it I found my own voice, liberation in short. This was due, undoubtedly, to the life I led, by which I mean not only the struggles and hardships of keeping alive in France but also as a result of a growing acquaintance with French literature, the French way of life, and the acceptance accorded me by French writers. Unwittingly, I found myself living that "bohemian" life which so many celebrated writers and artists before me had been obliged to live for one reason or another. My book might be regarded, I suppose, as a celebration of that splendidly miserable kind of life. In writing it, I ought to add, I had almost no hope of its ever being accepted by a publisher. It was something I had to do in order to preserve my integrity. It was a case of do or die. Certainly, the last thing I ever dreamed of was that it would one day be published in my own country.

Perhaps it is not a "pleasant" book. It has proved, however, to be an "instructive" one—for those who know how to read it. Of that I have had much interesting testimony during the years following its publication. In the files of the library at UCLA there are thousands of letters from readers of the book all over the world. The burden of most of these testimonials is that the book had a liberating affect, that it inspired hope and courage, and courage to live one's own life, come what may. It had this effect, I'm sure, because it is a naked vivid account of one man's struggles with almost insuperable odds, because it is a revelatory account of this man's life, sparing nothing. Many of the readers confess that it was the first time in all their reading experience that the whole man had been portrayed. They saluted the author as one who had restored a new kind of integrity to literature, to our literature at least.

The truth of these assertions I myself discovered later when I began to investigate the emasculative process which Anglo-Saxon literature has undergone these last few hundred years. With the tremendous upheavals which the Second World War brought about it became more than ever obvious to me, and others, that our literature was not rendering a true picture of the known behavior, sexual behavior particularly, of the citizens of the western world. Some measure of freedoms have been gained perhaps, though this is not always clear, but certainly no freedom of expression in literature.

Certainly, this book has provoked attention and discussion wherever it has been published. In every country there are those who believe that the author went too far, that certain things may be said but not written.

In my youth, my idols among American authors were such as Thoreau, Emerson, Walt Whitman; they still are, I should add. I regard them as revolutionary spirits. Men who were against the trend of the times. Perhaps I was drawn to such writers because I am myself a born rebel.

To come back to the free spirits . . . if they had been obliged to write down to the level of the "normal community standard" as the phrase runs, would we have today the works which make them famous. Why should any thinker in any field be required to make his thoughts palatable and acceptable to the ordinary citizen? As a member of a great community which boasts of the exceptional freedom its citizens are permitted to enjoy, it seems to me that this question is not out of place.

The question in my mind is not how far one should be permitted to go in expressing one's self freely, but how great is the gap, and how dangerous for the future of mankind, between the daring inspired by conviction and integrity and the conformity based upon inertia, stupidity, cowardice and hypocrisy? Are we here on earth to live like sheep, live in the heard, or to follow our own bent, our own conscience? Should we be fearful of revolutionary thinking or welcome it? Should we not as our fathers and forefathers be free and individually unique beings? And finally, is freedom itself to be interpreted and circumscribed by the few, the many, or by each man for himself?

Much has been said, during the course of the many trials which this book has provoked of the danger to society, particularly to the young which free circulation of the book involves. No one, to my knowledge, has yet pointed out a single instance where such has been the effect. And the book has had so far well over a million readers. We do not know, on the other hand, the disastrous effects upon adults, as well as young people, of drugs, tobacco, alcoholic beverages, weapons, even automobiles. Is it possible that we can adapt to certain hazards and not others? Are certain words and expressions, even those commonly used, to be employed in writing? Do they really constitute such a dangerous menace? Or is it not simply a matter of overcoming one more built in prejudice? We all know that when it comes to the classics, a liberal use of what is called obscenity may be found. On what presumption is the freedom to read the classics permitted? Is time the test? If so, what hope is there of obtaining new classics? I use the word classics deliberately. I regard *Tropic of Cancer* as such a classic. Despite all that has been said against it, despite all the efforts to suppress it, it continues to make its way, to find more and more readers. It is now almost 30 years since its first publication in Paris. It is still in its infancy.

I have been accused at times of having written expressly to make money, that is to say, of having purposely used objectionable language in order to make it appeal to certain readers and thus further its sale. Nothing, of course, can be further from the truth. I have never written anything expressly to make money.

I trust that it is apparent from the foregoing that I am not attempting to present myself as the author of a nice, clean, wholesome piece of work. I think of this work as a sincere, honest effort which, in liberating me as a person and a writer, has somehow done the same for many others. I make no attempt to evaluate it as literature, since that is the task of posterity, but I feel certain that it is a work which will live no matter what is said or done about it. I do not regard myself as a "monster," but as a sane and useful member of society. I have found life worth living even when unbearably difficult, and I think this view of life permeates not only the book in question but all of my work.

The Supreme Court ultimately ruled that *Tropic of Cancer* is not obscene. But it did so by the narrowest of margins—5 to 4—with Chief Justice Warren voting against the book.

From Alberts, argued in 1957, to *United States* v. *X-Citement Video*, argued in 1995, revolutionary legal changes transpired affording constitutionally protected status to sexually explicit materials, i.e., pornography. The material involved in the *X-Citement Video* case consisted of hard core videos depicting a minor (Traci Lords) performing sexual acrobatics. Neither the government nor the Supreme Court suggested that the fucking and sucking made the videos obscene. On the contrary, it was assumed by all that the tapes were constitutionally protected but presented a question because of Ms. Lords' minority.

The Supreme Court—acting as the Supreme Board of Censors—played a vital—if reluctant—role in liberating pornography. I had the good fortune of arguing on behalf of greater freedoms before 22 Supreme Court Justices, including 3 Chief Justices: Earl Warren, Warren Burger, and William Rehnquist. For better or worse, my footprints can be found in the cases in the United States Supreme Court Reports dealing with freedom for sexual expression. Notwithstanding the gains made, the "decency" war—part of the ongoing cultural war—is, of course, still very much alive. Today the battle rages over child pornography, internet porn, nude dancing, lap dancing, zoning laws, licensing, and the like. As I am writing this, a client is preparing an exhibit in her gallery depicting homosexuals engaged in explicit sexual activity and depicting the audience reaction to the conduct. The hope is that it will be seen on cable.

4

My Years Defending *Playboy*

Burton Joseph

OW SATISFYING IT HAS BEEN TO BE ON THE SIDE OF THE RIGHT, JUSTICE, and freedom. To be involved in the preservation and extension of the Bill of Rights, particularly the First Amendment. My life as an attorney has been highlighted by participation in numerous cases involving the protection of free expression and the preservation and extension of rights guaranteed by the First Amendment to the Constitution.

In the 1950s, and as a member of the Illinois Division of the American Civil Liberties Union, I had my first taste of the defense of freedom in a tangential way. This was during the trial of Lenny Bruce, who was charged with the offense of obscenity for a night club performance at which I was in the audience. Shock, dismay, provocation, indignation were some of the emotions that enveloped the audience while Lenny's monologue attacked puritanism, the Church, prudishness, and prevailing morality. Unsuspecting patrons stormed out of the Gate of Horn when they did not get the expected entertainment from what was billed as a "comedian." Lenny was that but far more. He taught a whole generation that freedom must tolerate dissenters and iconoclasts or there was no freedom at all.

Shortly thereafter, I assisted one of Chicago's finest attorneys in an action to restrain law enforcement officers from prohibiting the display and sale of Henry Miller's *Tropic of Cancer*. It was an exciting moment in my professional life. We were challenging the establishment in support of a book that only a short time before was allowed to be sold in the United States. Previously, only underground copies were available illegally brought into the country from Europe. Like Lenny Bruce, Henry Miller was almost universally believed to be without any redeeming social value—clearly obscene and of interest only to perverts and sex fiends, including bleeding-heart liberals and pseudo-intellectuals. Real Americans would not want this smut available in book stores, newsstands and certainly not in public libraries. In today's hardcore world it is difficult to imagine the universal judicial and legislative condemnation of what today are regarded as serious works of art and literature.

We obtained, in a very conservative jurisdiction from a very conservative judge, an injunction restraining the interference with the display and sale of Henry Miller's classic. Once having tasted success under the First Amendment I have since spent as much professional time as possible in protecting the First Amendment, not for money and not for glory but as a true-believer that the society that censors books, magazines and films is a society without faith in its citizen and the ideas of democracy.

After the 1968 Democratic National Convention in Chicago, described by one investigator as a "police riot," the stakes were raised for the right to free political and artistic expression.

At that time, I was asked by Hugh M. Hefner (who was a victim of "police riot" on the street near his home) to organize the Playboy Foundation to support civil rights and liberties, particularly rights guaranteed under the First Amendment. It was an exciting time. I was spending *Playboy*'s money as the Executive Director of its Foundation on issues in which I was involved. These include the fight against capital punishment, the pioneering effort toward abortion rights, prison reform, reform of juvenile law, decriminalization of the possession of recreational drugs, protection of women's rights and the rights of minorities and, particularly, the right of free expression.

I participated in the organization of a group later called the Media Coalition, a consortium of industry group that organized to oppose a censorship proposition that was to be before the voters in California. Through the dedication of this group, and with the good fortune of talking a movie cowboy named John Wayne into making a video on the evils of censorship, we were able to defeat this insidious proposition.

The Media Coalition thereafter became one of the most potent forces defending the right of free expression. Representatives of various mainstream organizations met on a regular basis to review proposed legislation that affected the right of free expression, to educate and advise state legislators and members of Congress, to urge their vetoes of restrictive legislation and to challenge the constitutionality of such restrictions through the courts.

As co-counsel in a case entitled *Playboy Enterprises, Inc.* v. *Boorstin,* I participated in an action in the U.S. District Court for the District of Columbia in a most unusual situation. Congress was considering the annual appropriation for the library of Congress as part of the general appropriation bill. A demagogic congressman discovered that the Library of Congress had a program called Books for the Blind that published books and magazines in a Braille edition. Each year among the top two or three magazines in popularity was a Braille edition of *Playboy*. (At this point I should point out it was text only, no pictures). In denouncing *Playboy* on the floor of the House, the Library of Congress was excoriate for using public funds to publish and disseminate "smut." The Librarian of Congress testified that the cost of publishing the annual Braille edition of *Playboy* magazine was $319,000. Congress, in an effort to protect us from sightless perverts, amended the appropriation bill to deduct from the Library of Congress budget $319,000–the amount allocated for the Braille *Playboy* edition. Not wanting to sidetrack the entire Nation's appropriation bill, the amendment passed and the bill was signed into law.

A unique challenge to government censorship followed with *Playboy* arguing that Congress need not appropriate any money for the Library of Congress, indeed need not appropriate any money for the Books for the Blind program, but once they elected to fund such program the First Amendment prohibited them from censoring lawful material based upon the content. The government argued the reduction in appropriation was not necessarily aimed at *Playboy* and was simply a reduction in the total budget of the Library of Congress. The argument was unpersuasive. The judge knew that this was a not-too-subtle directive to the Librarian of Congress to use the reduction to eliminate publication of the Braille edition of *Playboy*. The judge issued a mandatory injunction against the Librarian of Congress from using the reduction for the censorial purpose intended. A small victory, but one that incrementally enforced the idea that the government cannot decide what expression should be available as a result of general government support.

It was fashionable at a time among certain reactionary feminists, personified by Catharine MacKinnon and Andrea Dworkin, to argue that the subordinate place of women in our society was a result of the proliferation of explicit sexual material. Books, magazines and films that involve explicit sexual material were not expression, they argued, but rather were "action" unprotected by the First Amendment. This argument required a whole new category of "new-speak," where words were threats, images assaults. This led to a coalition of strange bedfellows, between Christian conservative and reactionary feminists united in attacking free expression. Each image was a "rape," they argued, and not expression so not protected by the First Amendment. The so-called MacKinnon-Dworkin Ordinance was proposed which provided that anyone allegedly harmed as a result of the actions of any persons who had been exposed to sexual material could bring an action for damages against the creator, distributor, publisher and retailer of any such book, film or magazine. Indeed, a cause of action was specifically granted for participants in explicit sexual films or pictures against the person employing them. The ordinance specifically stated that consent of the "victim" could not be considered a defense. This created a schism among feminists. Those such as Nadine Strossen of the ACLU argued that this paternalism was inimical to the interest of women. Like other laws designed to protect women, she argued, they only limited options and the freedom of women without any commensurate benefit. Women should be free to make a wide range of decisions, not only the ones that Ms. MacKinnon and Ms. Dworkin felt were appropriate. They argued that to equate words and images with action was not only irrational and an example of double-think but treated women as children–incapable of protecting their own interest.

On the other end of the spectrum were Catharine MacKinnon and Andrea Dworkin, who passionately argued that the principal cause of harm to women was the availability of obscene images. To tolerate such images was to condone the harm. They argued that no evidence was necessary to support the *nexus* between explicit words and imagery and harm to women. It was obvious, self-evident and required no empirical support, they argued.

The Indianapolis, Indiana, City Council passed the Ordinance, which was signed into law by then Mayor Hudnut. The Media Coalition filed a lawsuit to restrain enforcement of the Ordinance.

Michael Bamberger, representing the Media Coalition, other attorneys representing a consortium of plaintiffs, and I, representing *Playboy*, filed suit in the United States District Court in Indianapolis and promptly moved for a temporary restraining order against enforcement. The day before the ordinance was to become effective, in a most thoughtful opinion. Judge Sarah Evans Barker issued the restraining order and found the Ordinance unconstitutional under the First Amendment. Judge Barker was a conservative, appointed by a conservative President. Nevertheless, in her opinion, she found that the interest of women never justifies censorship, that words and images were just that, "words and images" and not action, and that the First Amendment prevented legislatures and City Councils from passing laws to abridge the right of free expression.

The City appealed the decision to the Seventh Circuit Court of Appeals. In a different analysis the three-judge Court sustained the lower court. Judge Easterbrook based his decision on the fact that the ordinance was viewpoint-based, that is that it favored once view of women over another, and therefore could not survive scrutiny because the government cannot by legislation favor one argument over another and must remain neutral under the law.

On appeal to the United States Supreme Court the decision of the Seventh Circuit was affirmed without argument and *American Booksellers Association* v. *Hudnut* became law of the land.

The original obscenity case from England, *Regina* v. *Hicklin* (1868), defined obscenity as that which tended to deprave and corrupt the most susceptible person into whose hands the material might fall. The determination need not consider the book as a whole but rather by any isolated passage. The Courts in England soon modified and repudiated the *Hicklin* test for obscenity long before the American courts analyzed it into oblivion. The courts here eventually held that obscenity could not be based on isolated passages but must consider "the work as a whole." Next the courts decided that obscenity cannot be judged upon its effect on the "most susceptible" person into whose hands it might fall but it must rather be based upon the reaction on a theoretical "reasonable person." Later, the Court wedded to the definition a requirement that the work must be "without redeeming social value" (a requirement later abandoned, and that the work must "appeal to the prurient interest in sex" and be "patently offensive" to the "average person," based upon "local community standards." Added to this obtuse analysis was a defense that precluded obscenity if it could be proven that the work had "serious literary, artistic, political, or scientific value."

Most recently a movement has arisen to "protect the children" that argues although some books, magazines and films might be appropriate for adults they should not be available or accessible to children who need protection from sexual words and images.

The courts long ago ruled that you could not justify the availability of sexually oriented material to adults by what might be suitable for children. This, the court ruled, was tantamount to "throwing out the baby with the bath water." The court did fashion a two-tier system of censorship, however, which permitted the availability of certain work to adults but denied its availability to children. This led to the passage of numerous laws that did not restrict the sale of sexually oriented material to adults but rather restricted the display where children might be present. In First Amendment terms this presented a problem. The clerk in the store could make a case-by-case judgment and refuse to sell a particular book, film or magazine to anyone he believed to be a minor. Since retailers know that what was appropriate for adults might be illegal in terms of minors, this decision protected both the stated public interest as well as the rights of the adult consumer. The problem was that these so-called "display laws" or "minor access laws" did in fact result in the diminution of material available to adults. It is axiomatic among retailers that display equates with sales. The schemes included in legislation–that material must be sold from under the counter and not in open display, racks had to be a minimum height if adult material was to be displayed, material could only be displayed with the title and in an opaque shrinkwrap and other variations–all substantially interfered with circulation because much of the purchases of this material was on impulse and if not immediately available was never seen and never sold.

A challenge was filed by the Media Coalition in which I participated on behalf of *Playboy* with Michael Bamberger in a case called *American Booksellers Association* v. *Virginia*. The court, in a defeat for the censors, said that although the display of some material might be restricted, it had to be determined to be "obscene as to minors." The standard was judged not on the basis of the youngest or the average minor but on the basis of the oldest, most sophisticated minor. The court designated this as "borderline adult obscenity." For all practical purposes this case severely restricts the use of display restrictions to prohibit the availability of lawful material to adults.

To prove that the appetite of the censor is insatiable one has to look at the insidious actions prompted by the report of the Attorney General's Commission on Obscenity and Pornography, commonly known as the Meese Commission (named for President Nixon's then Attorney General). Without conducting any research and without consulting scholars or experts on the subject, the Meese Commission sought to overrule the detailed findings of the prior President's Commission on Obscenity that concluded there should be no restriction on the availability of sexually explicit material except that involving child pornography and exploitation. President Nixon emphatically rejected these conclusions as immoral and sided with the few dissenters, principally Charles Keating. Pursuant to assumed authority, the Executive Director of the Meese Commission sent a letter to major retailers, including convenience store chains, specifically targeting *Playboy* and ominously advising the recipients that they may be in violation of the law for the sale of "pornography" by the sale and display of *Playboy* and similar magazines. *Playboy Enterprises, Inc.* v. *Meese* was immediately filed challenging the letter as an implicit threat to remove our magazine or suffer unnamed consequences. The letter, we argued, was in violation of the long standing prohibition against "prior restrain." The natural consequences of governmental threats is the removal books and magazines from circulation without a judicial determination of their legality. In response to our challenge the court strongly criticized the action taken by the Meese Commission in sending out the threatening letter and directed the Commission to communicate with the recipients of his original letter repudiating its import and advising that the sale of *Playboy* was not in violation of the law.

Whenever there has been a technological development that increased the potential audience for material though harmful by the State a surge of censorship resulted. From the invention of the printing press in the sixteenth century to paperback books, comic books, movies, broadcast television, cable television, and most recently the Internet, each development precipitated the same argument justifying censorship. The unrestrained, unrestricted, uncensored proliferation of words and images would cause the decline of society. That people could not be trusted was always the basis for censorship.

Recently Senator Diane Feinstein, without hearings and without any empirical support, proposed an amendment to the Telecommunications Decency Act by virtue of which the disseminators of "adult programming" on cable were required to insure that all nonsubscribers be protected against the phenomenon known as "signal bleed." There was no evidence that this occurred more than occasionally, or that children were exposed to these fleeting images and sounds, that there was any harm that would endue from such momentary "bleed," or that subscribers to cable television believed that a problem existed. Adult programmers were given an option to either assume the enormous, potentially bankrupting expense of installing electronic devices on all cable homes—whether requested, whether children resided there or whether any problem existed—or else to restrict programming between 10:00 P.M. and 6:00 A.M. of the broadcast day. A challenge to this law—Section 505 of the Telecommunications Decency Act—was filed in the United States District Court entitled *Playboy Entertainment Group, Inc.* v. *United States of America* challenging the constitutionality of the requirement. A three-judge court held that the provision was censorship based upon the content of the material and would be unconstitutional unless the statue attempted to address a compelling government interest by the "least restrictive means." Another section of the Act provided that upon request subscribers could obtain, without cost, a filter for undesired cable programming. The court held that even if a problem or "signal bleed" existed the availability of a filter upon request of the subscriber constituted a less restrictive means. The universal application of the statue was therefore in violation of the First Amendment. A scalpel, not a sledgehammer, was what was needed. The government has recently requested the trial court to amend or modify its judgement and simultaneously has filed a notice of appeal of the decision to the Supreme Court. In arguing our case we relied heavily upon the decision of the Supreme Court in *ACLU* v. *Reno, et al.* which struck down a congressional attempt to censor material on the Internet. That unanimous decision was a recognition that although the technology is new the Internet constituted a truly world-wide marketplace for ideas, speech and images contemplated by the First Amendment. Congressional attempt to restrict expression by any technology was both unwise and unconstitutional.

Since the appetite of the censor is insatiable I do not foresee any diminution of censorial efforts on the Internet, on television, cable, in libraries and of books, magazines and films. These efforts are an attempt to return to the *Hicklin* standard, where banning words and images is justified by the need to protect the "most susceptible" child who may hear or view the material. All we can do is to remain eternally vigilant. *Playboy* will continue to be at the forefront in this fight–not only for self-interest but as a matter of principle.

5

Freedom of Cyberspeech

Stephen F. Rohde

I N A HISTORIC DECISION IN JUNE, 1997, THE U.S. SUPREME COURT GUAR-
anteed cyberspace the fullest degree of First Amendment protection available under the Constitution. In *Reno* v. *American Civil Liberties Union, et al.*,
an opinion written by Justice John Paul Stevens, the High Court declared
that "[n]otwithstanding the legitimacy and importance of the congressional
goal of protecting children from harmful materials, we agree with the three-
judge District Court that the statute abridges 'the freedom of speech' protected by the First Amendment."

In *Reno*, a wide spectrum of organizations lead by the ACLU challenged
two provisions of the Communications Decency Act of 1996 ("CDA") which
had made it a crime to knowingly transmit "indecent" messages over the
Internet to anyone under eighteen years of age or to knowingly send or display to a person under eighteen any message that "in context" depicts or
describes, "sexual or excretory activities or organs" in terms "patently offensive as measured by contemporary community standards."

The Supreme Court found that the "Internet is 'a unique and wholly
new medium of worldwide human communication'" and that it is "no exaggeration to conclude that the content on the Internet is as diverse as human
thought." The Court agreed with District Judge Dalzell that the Internet is
"the most participatory form of mass speech yet developed" and is entitled
to "the highest protection from governmental intrusion."

THE INTERNET

The Supreme Court explained that the Internet has experienced extraordinary growth. The number of host computers–those that store information

and relay communications–increased from about three hundred in 1981 to approximately 9,400,000 by the time of the trial in 1996. Roughly 60 percent of these hosts are located in the United States. About forty million people used the Internet at the time of trial, a number that is expected to mushroom to two hundred million by 1999. The District Court had found that at any given time "tens of thousands of users are engaging in conversations on a huge range of subjects."

Sexually Explicit Material

Sexually explicit material on the Internet includes text, pictures, and chat and "extends from the modestly titillating to the hardest-core." "Once a provider posts its contents on the Internet, it cannot prevent that content from entering any community. Thus, for example, when the UCR/California Museum of Photography posts to its Web site nudes by Edward Weston and Robert Mapplethorpe to announce that its new exhibit will travel to Baltimore and New York City, those images are available not only in Los Angeles, Baltimore, and New York City, but also in Cincinnati, Mobile, or Beijing–wherever Internet users live. Similarly, the safer sex instructions that Critical Path posts to its Web site, written in street language so that teenage receivers can understand them, are available not just in Philadelphia, but also in Provo and Prague."

Age Verification

The District Court categorically determined that there "is no effective way to determine the identity or the age of a user who is accessing material through e-mail, mail exploders, news groups or chat room." The Government offered no evidence that there was a reliable way to screen recipients and participants in such for age. Moreover, even if it were technologically feasible to block minors' access to news groups and chat rooms containing discussions of art, politics or other subjects that potentially elicit "indecent" or "patently offensive" contributions, it would not be possible to block their access to that material and "still allow them access to the remaining content, even if the overwhelming majority of that content was not indecent."

In sum, the District Court found:

"Even if credit card verification or adult password verification were implemented, the Government presented no testimony as to how such systems could ensure that the user of the password or credit card is in fact over 18. The burdens imposed by credit card verification and adult password verification systems make them effectively unavailable to a substantial number of Internet content providers."

REJECTION OF PRECEDENTS RELIED ON BY THE GOVERNMENT

In arguing for reversal, the Government had contended that the CDA was constitutional under the three prior Supreme Court decisions: (1) *Ginsberg* v. *New York*, 390 U.S. 629 (1968); (2) *FCC* v. *Pacifica Foundation*, 438 U.S. 726 (1978); and (3) *Renton* v. *Playtime Theaters, Inc.*, 475 U.S. 41 (1986). But the Supreme Court found that a "close look at these cases however, raises–rather than relieves–doubts concerning the constitutionality of the CDA."

In *Ginsberg*, the Court upheld the constitutionality of a New York statute that prohibited selling to minors under seventeen years of age material that was considered obscene as to them even if not obscene as to adults. In four important respects, *Reno* found that the statute upheld in *Ginsberg* was narrower than the CDA. First, the Court noted that in *Ginsberg* that "the prohibition against sales to minors does not bar parents who so desire from purchasing the magazines for their children." Under the CDA, by contrast, neither the parents' consent–nor even their participation–in the communication would avoid the application of the statute. Second, the New York stature applied only to commercial transactions, whereas the CDA contains no such limitation. Third, the New York statute cabined its definition of material that is harmful to minors with the requirement that it be "utterly without redeeming social importance for minors." The CDA fails to provide any definition of the term "indecent" and importantly, omits any requirement that the "patently offensive" material lack serious literary, artistic, political, or scientific value. Fourth, the New York Statute defined a minor as a person under the age of seventeen, whereas the CDA applies to all those under eighteen years, and thereby includes an additional year of those nearest majority.

In *Pacifica*, the Court upheld a declaratory order of the Federal Communications Commission, holding that the broadcast of a recording of a 12-minute monologue entitled "Filthy Words" that had previously been delivered to a live audience could have been the subject of administrative sanctions. In *Reno*, the Court found that there are significant differences between the order upheld in *Pacifica* and the CDA. First, the order in *Pacifica*, issued by an agency that had been regulating radio stations for decades, targeted a specific broadcast that represented a rather dramatic departure from traditional program content in order to designate when–rather than whether–it would be permissible to air such a program in that particular medium. The CDA's broad categorical prohibitions are not limited to particular times and are not dependent on any evaluation by an agency familiar with the unique characteristics of the Internet. Second, unlike the CDA, the Commission's declaratory order was not punitive; the Court expressly refused to decide whether the indecent broadcast would justify a criminal prosecution. Finally, the Commission's order applied to a medium which as a matter of history had "received the most limited First Amendment protection," in large part because warning could not adequately protect the listener from unexpected program content. The Internet, however, has no comparable history. Moreover, the District Court found that the risk of encountering indecent material by accident on the Internet is remote because a series of affirmative steps is required to access specific material.

In *Renton*, the Court had upheld a zoning ordinance that kept adult movie theaters out of residential neighborhoods. The ordinance was aimed not at the content of the films shown in the theaters, but rather at the "secondary effects"–such as crime and deteriorating property values–that these theaters fostered "It is the secondary effect which these zoning ordinances attempted to avoid, not the dissemination of 'offensive' speech." According to the Government, the CDA was constitutional because it constitutes a sort of "cyberzoning" on the Internet. But in *Reno*, the Court found that the CDA applied "broadly to the entire universe of cyberspace." And the purpose of the CDA is to protect children from the primary effects of "indecent" and "patently offensive" speech, rather than any "secondary" effect of such speech.

THE INTERNET IS NOT
THE SAME AS BROADCASTING

In *Reno*, the Court declared that "[n]either before nor after the enactment of the CDA have the vast democratic fora of the Internet been subject to the type of government supervision and regulation that has attended the broadcast industry. Moreover, the Internet is not as 'invasive' as radio or television. The District Court specifically found that '[c]ommunications over the Internet do not "invade" an individual's home or appear on one's computer screen unbidden. Users seldom encounter content 'by accident.' " It also found that '[a]lmost all sexually explicit images are preceded by warnings as to the content,' and cited testimony that " 'odds are slim' that a user would come across a sexually explicit sight by accident.'"

Finally, unlike the conditions that prevailed when Congress first authorized regulation of the broadcast spectrum, the Court found that the Internet can hardly be considered a "scarce" expressive commodity. "It provides relatively unlimited, low-cost capacity for communication of all kinds. The government estimate that '[a]s many as 40 million people use the Internet today, and that figure is expected to grow to 200 million by 1999.' This dynamic, multifaceted category of communication includes not only traditional print and news services, but also audio, video, and still images, as well as interactive, real-time dialogue. Through the use of chat rooms, any person with a phone line can become a town crier with a voice that resonates farther than it could from any soapbox. Through the use of Web pages, mail exploders, and newsgroups, the same individual can become a pamphleteer. As the District Court found, 'the content on the Internet is as diverse as human thought.' We agree with its conclusion that our cases provide no basis for qualifying the level of First Amendment scrutiny that should be applied to this medium."

The CDA Is Hopelessly Vague

The Court found that "regardless of whether the CDA is so vague that it violates the Fifth Amendment, the many ambiguities concerning the scope of its coverage render it problematic for purposes of the First Amendment." For instance, each of the two parts of the CDA uses a different linguistic form. The first uses the word "indecent," while the second speaks of material that "in context, depicts or describes, in terms patently offensive as measured by contemporary community standards, sexual or excretory activities or organs." Given the absence of a definition of either term, the Court found that "this difference in language will provoke uncertainty among speakers about how the two standards relate to each other and just what they mean. Could a speaker confidently assume that a serious discussion about birth control practices, homosexuality, the First Amendment issues raised by the Appendix to our *Pacifica* opinion, or the consequences of prison rape would not violate the CDA? This uncertainty undermines the likelihood that the CDA has been carefully tailored to the congressional goal of protecting minors from potentially harmful material."

The vagueness of the CDA is a matter of special concern for two reasons. First, the CDA is a content-based regulation of speech. The vagueness of such regulation raises special First Amendment concerns because of its obvious chilling effect on free speech. Second, the CDA is a criminal statute. In addition to the opprobrium and stigma of a criminal conviction, the CDA threatens violators with penalties including up to two years in prison for each act of violation. The Court pointed out that the severity of criminal sanctions "may well cause speakers to remain silent rather than communicate even arguably unlawful words, ideas, and images." As a practical matter, this increased deterrent effect, coupled with the "risk of discriminatory enforcement" of vague regulations, poses greater First Amendment concerns.

The Court concluded that "[w]e are persuaded that the CDA lacks the precision that the First Amendment requires when a statute regulates the content of speech. In order to deny minors access to potentially harmful speech, the CDA effectively suppresses a large amount of speech that adults have a constitutional right to receive and to address to one another. That burden on adult speech is unacceptable if less restrictive alternatives would be at least as effective in achieving the legitimate purpose that the statute was enacted to serve."

In evaluating the free speech rights of adults, the Court has made it perfectly clear that "[s]exual expression which is indecent but not obscene is protected by the First Amendment. ('[W]here obscenity is not involved, we have consistently held that the fact that protected speech may be offensive to some does not justify its suppression')."

While the Court has repeatedly recognized the governmental interest in protecting children from harmful materials, that interest does not justify an unnecessarily broad suppression of speech addressed to adults. As the Court has explained, the Government may not "reduc[e] the adult population to only what is fit for children." And that "[r]egardless of the strength of the government's interest in protecting children, the level of discourse reaching a mailbox simply cannot be limited to that which would be suitable for a sandbox."

The CDA Is Unconstitutionally Overbroad

The breadth of the CDA's coverage is wholly unprecedented. The Court found that "[u]nlike the regulations upheld in *Ginsberg* and *Pacifica*, the scope of the CDA is not limited to commercial speech or commercial entities. Its open-ended prohibitions embrace all nonprofit entities and individuals posting indecent messages or displaying them on their own computers in the presence of minors. The general, undefined terms 'indecent' and 'patently offensive' cover large amounts of nonpornographic material with serious educational or other value. Moreover, the 'community standards' criterion as applied to the Internet means that any communication available to nation-wide audience will be judged by the standards of the community most likely to be offended by the message. The regulated subject matter includes any of the seven 'dirty words' used in the Pacifica monologue, the use of which the Government's expert acknowledged could constitute a felony. It may also extend to discussions about prison rape or safe sexual practices, artistic images that include nude subjects, and arguable the card catalogue of the Carnegie Library."

The Court gave two ominous examples of the reach of the CDA: "a parent allowing her 17-year-old to use the family computer to obtain information on the Internet that she, in her parental judgment, deems appropriate, could face a lengthy prison term. Similarly, a parent who sent his 17-year-old college freshman information on birth control via e-mail could be incarcerated even though neither he, his child, nor anyone in their home community, found the material 'indecent' or 'patently offensive,' if the college town's community thought otherwise."

The Court found that "[t]he breadth of this content-based restriction of speech imposes an especially heavy burden on the Government to explain why a less restrictive provision would not be as effective as the CDA. It has not done so. The arguments in this Court have referred to possible alternatives such as requiring that indecent material be 'tagged' in a way that facilitates parental control of material coming into their homes, making exception for messages with artistic or educational value, providing some tolerance for parental choice, and regulating some portions of the Internet— such as commercial web sites—differently than others, such as chat room. Particularly in the light of the absence of any detailed findings by Congress, or even hearings addressing the special problems of the CDA, we are persuaded that the CDA is not narrowly tailored if that requirement has any meaning at all."

The Government had essentially argued that a statute could ban *leaflets* on certain subjects as long as individuals are free to publish *books*. In invalidating a number of laws that banned leafleting on the streets regardless of their content the Court has explained that "one is not to have the exercise of his liberty of expression in appropriate places abridged on the plea that it may be exercised in some other place."

The CDA Fosters Censorship,
Not the Growth of the Internet

In the Supreme Court, though not in the District Court, the Government had asserted that—in addition to its interest in protecting children—its "[e]qually significant" interest in fostering the growth of the Internet provided an independent basis for upholding the constitutionality of the CDA. In *Reno* the Court noted that the Government apparently assumed that the unregulated availability of "indecent" and "patently offensive" material on the Internet is "driving countless citizens away from the medium because of the risk of exposing themselves or their children to harmful material."

The Court found this argument "singularly unpersuasive" and noted that the dramatic expansion of this new marketplace of ideas contradicts the factual basis of this contention. "The record demonstrates that the growth of the Internet has been and continues to be phenomenal. As a matter of constitutional tradition, in the absence of evidence to the contrary, we presume that governmental regulation of the content of speech is more likely to interfere with the free exchange of ideas than to encourage it. The interest in encouraging freedom of expression in a democratic society outweighs any theoretical but unproven benefit of censorship."

Is the CDA Dead?

Although civil liberties lawyers were calling the *Reno* decision an occasion for "dancing in the streets" and a "legal birth certificate for the Internet," unfortunately the celebration may be premature. Supporters of the CDA have already threatened to design new legislation to navigate around the defects the Supreme Court found in *Reno* to require Internet providers to implement cybertechnology to verify the age of the users or to "tag" material that is "indecent" or "patently offensive."

Any Supreme Court decision that bases constitutional protections on the state of *existing* technology (or the lack thereof) has within it the potential to eliminate those protections depending on the development of *future* technology. The *Reno* decision relied heavily on the elaborate findings of a special three-judge District Court which presided aver an extensive evidentiary hearing in Philadelphia last year. The key to the plaintiffs' success, engineered by a team of Internet-savvy ACLU lawyers and cyber experts, was twofold.

First, the District Judges (and by extension the Supreme Justices) were given a crash course in the Internet to convince them to resist their natural temptation to treat the *computer* screen the same as the *television* screen. Had the District Judges found that, for First Amendment purposes, the "*broadcasting model*" rather than the "*print* model" applied, the CDA might well have been upheld, since broadcasting holds a second-class status in the hierarchy of free-speech protection. For example, in 1978 using the "broadcasting model" the Supreme Court upheld the censorship of George Carlin's "Filthy Words" monologue in *FCC* v. *Pacifica Foundation*, but would not have done so had the monologue been published in a book or magazine, which are entitled to the highest level of First Amendment protection. Therefore, it was critically important in *Reno* for the judges and Justices to understand the differences between the operation and regulation of broadcasting versus the Internet.

The other key to the plaintiffs' success in the District Court was that the ACLU lawyers outfoxed the Justice Department on the issue of what may be called the current "technological vacuum." The constitutionality of the CDA raised two separate and conflicting technological questions:

(1) Did technology exist which Internet providers could use to "tag" indecent material or to verify the age of users seeking access to sexually explicit material? and

(2) Did technology exist to allow parents to block sexually explicit material they did not want their children to see?

If the courts answered the first question in the affirmative, then the CDA would pass the threshold constitutional hurdle, since the law would only require Internet providers to use available technology to block "indecent" material from children at the source. But if the courts answered the first question in the negative and the second question in the affirmative, then the CDA would be unconstitutional, because Internet providers would have to censor speech directed at adults in order to protect children but parents would have the tools to achieve that purpose at the point of reception.

The District Court (and the Supreme Court) found that the government had offered "no evidence" that there was a reliable way to screen recipients for age, but the plaintiffs had established that "a reasonably effective method by which parents can prevent their children from accessing sexually explicit and other material which parents may believe is inappropriate for their children will soon be available."

The Justice Department certainly was hobbled by the fact that there had been no Congressional hearing to establish the existence of effective tagging, age verification or any other technological aspects of the CDA. Justice Stevens pointedly observed that the CDA was but one Title out of seven comprising the Telecommunications Act of 1996 and that whereas the other six were the product of extensive committee hearings and reports, by contrast the CDA was added *after* the hearings on the floor during debate.

Thus, neither the legislators who wrote the CDA nor the government lawyers who defended it had done their homework. Congress had quickly enacted the CDA in response to frantic (and often exaggerated) reports of how children were getting access to "pornography" on the Internet. Likewise, the Justice Department, despite all of its resources, failed to effectively present reliable and persuasive evidence to show that the burden imposed by the CDA on "smut peddlers" to verify the age of their customers or to tag their "pornography" was constitutionally permissible, given the compelling interest in protecting children from "indecent" material.

But there is no rule which says that the government only gets one chance to censor the Internet. Indeed, the *Reno* decision itself may serve as a blueprint for a more sustainable "Son of CDA." Learning from their mistakes, supporters of a "CDA II" might try to do a better job next time by holding extensive hearings and writing elaborate reports to demonstrate that advances in technology have filled the vacuum found by the Courts. The *Reno* decision is particularly vulnerable on this count since it is so grounded in the *existing* state of technology. Indeed, Dan R. Olsen, a professor of human computer interaction at Carnegie Mellon University and a government witness in *Reno*, told the *Chronicle of Higher Education* that the Supreme Court only "took a snapshot in time of what the technology could do" and that while age-verification systems do not exist today they "are not far off."

The point has not been ignored by members of the Supreme Court, most prominently Justice Scalia. At the oral argument in *Reno* held March 19, 1997, he told Bruce Ennis, who argued the case for the plaintiffs, that "so much of your argument is based upon what is currently available. You know, I throw away my computer every five years. I think most people do. This is an area where change is enormously rapid. " Ominously, Justice Scalia, who joined in striking down the CDA, asked whether the law is "unconstitutional today" but "will be constitutional next week."

It remains to be seen whether a combination of repressive zeal and technological advances will lead to a new round of cybercensorship. Surely the Reno decision is a groundbreaking victory for the First Amendment. Just think of the consequences had the CDA been upheld. The Internet would be a vast wasteland of sanitized speech, cleansed of all but the safest of material dealing with the great mysteries of human sexuality, purged of anything provocative or controversial, stripped of words or images deemed offensive or shocking to those in power. To be true to our heritage of free expression, the CDA simply could not stand.

But James Madison warned us that the Bill of Rights was a mere "parchment" and that the cause of freedom lay in the hearts of our citizens. No single Supreme Court decision can permanently guarantee free speech anymore than the First Amendment itself can. Has the battle over censorship of the Internet been won? The battle, but not the war. So long as blue-nosed officials and self-appointed moralists claim the power and duty to dictate, on pain of fines and incarceration, what people can read and see, so long as the repressive spirit of Anthony Comstock lives on in the likes of Senators Helms and Exon, so long as parents abdicate their responsibilities to "Big Brother," the impulse to censor will survive and eternal vigilance will remain the price of liberty.

6

Reno v. *American Civil Liberties Union*: The 1996 Communications Decency Act

Marjorie Heins

THE BEGINNING

When Congress passed the 1996 Communications Decency Act, or "CDA," young computer hackers reveled in the irony that a bunch of middle-aged or older politicians who, unlike their children and grandchildren, had only the vaguest idea of how the Internet worked, had now enacted one of the most sweeping censorship laws in American history—in order, they said, to "protect" those same children and grandchildren from the devastating psychological harm that was supposedly caused by exposure to "patently offensive" or "indecent" online speech.

Of course, our esteemed legislators were not the only ones who lacked full understanding of cyberspace. Many of us at the ACLU were still struggling to master the most rudimentary computer operations in 1995 when Congress was considering what eventually became the CDA. Only the most electronically sophisticated among us were surfing the Internet, which was at that time more a participatory, communitarian network of newsgroups and chatrooms than the vast online shopping mall that it was soon to become. Most of us didn't have modems or e-mail. We all had to play catchup, including, as it turned out, the three federal judges in Philadelphia who first heard *ACLU* v. *Reno*, our challenge to the CDA.

What inspired the wildly overbroad, internally contradictory, sloppily drafted online censorship law that became the CDA? Sex, of course; and indeed, there was plenty of it on the Internet by 1995, although not so large a proportion as some of the law's promoters pretended. Within the original participatory online networks, newsgroups, chatrooms, and bulletin boards, there was plenty of sex talk, as well as an increasing number of pornographic sites and a brisk trade in sexual images. People *do* like to discuss sex, and initially a lot of this talk was not-for-profit. Then the World Wide Web's irresistible "hypertext markup language" and linking technology took over; commercial porn sites arrived, along with a variety of other, more mainstream consumer goods and services.

How could Congress control all this unbuttoned sexuality, available to anyone with a modem, software, and a teenager willing to show them how to use it? "Obscenity," of course, was already illegal, but even the vague and mushy *Miller v. California* three-part test for proving obscenity would be a difficult obstacle to the government in many Internet cases. After all, what jury these days was likely to rule the *Playboy* Website obscene? Yet surely the tender psyches of kids had to be protected from viewing it, along with lots of other pictures, writings, and conversations that were not nearly hard-core enough to be prosecuted under *Miller.* Whether genuine or simply politically convenient, concern for protecting minors became the vehicle for an online censorship law that went way beyond the hard-core pornography that might meet the *Miller* test for speech unprotected by the First Amendment.

The resulting CDA was a masterpiece of confusing and internally contradictory prose. One section criminalized any use of a "telecommunications device" to send "indecent" online communications to a person under eighteen. Another forbade use of an "interactive computer service" to send or "display in a manner available to" a person under eighteen any communication that, "in context, depicts or describes, in terms patently offensive as measured by contemporary community standards, sexual or excretory activities or organs." This language, of course, was lifted almost wholesale from the FCC's definition of "indecency" for purposes of regulating radio and television broadcasting, as approved by the Supreme Court in 1978 in *FCC v. Pacifica,* the famous George Carlin "seven dirty words" case. But Congress in the CDA did not bother to say whether it meant "indecency," as used in one part of the law, to be the same as "patently offensive as measured by contemporary community standards," as used in the other. Nor did it say exactly how, if at all, a "telecommunications device" might differ from an "interactive computer service."

More importantly, as you may recall, the *Pacifica* indecency standard did not require that the speech in question be "lascivious" or appeal to "prurient interests" in order to be regulated; it needed only be "patently offensive," according to "contemporary community standards," whatever those might be. Also, again unlike constitutionally unprotected obscenity, "indecent" speech as defined in *Pacifica* can have "serious literary, artistic, political, or scientific value." This meant that all manner of literary, artistic, and otherwise educational material was potentially criminal if displayed online. And this, of course, was precisely what Congress intended—a standard that went well beyond obscenity into the realms of protected and valuable speech—as long as the subject was sex, or, as in *Pacifica,* simply vulgar words.

In *Pacifica,* the Supreme Court's narrow five-justice majority justified banning "indecent" words from the airwaves—at least at times when children might be listening—on the rationale that broadcasting is uniquely invasive and accessible to children. Why was this such a bad thing? Justice Stevens's plurality opinion didn't really explain, but Justice Powell's concurrence, although differing with Stevens on the question whether dirty words "lie at the periphery of the First Amendment" (Stevens thought they did), straight-forwardly asserted that "shocking" and indecent speech "may have a deeper and more lasting negative effect on a child than on an adult."[1] Powell cited no authority for this proposition; he simply asserted that "the language involved in this case is as potentially degrading and harmful to children as representations of many erotic acts."[2] Powell's moralistic assumptions about what is "degrading and harmful" to children is still a powerful political sen-timent, and continues to drive the enactment of censorship laws.

One of the delightful ironies of *Reno* v. *ACLU* was that the entire, hilar-ious George Carlin monolog which precipitated the *Pacifica* case, had been reproduced as an appendix to the Supreme Court's *Pacifica* decision. Because the monolog had been officially judged indecent, and because the CDA used virtually the same indecency standard to criminalize online speech, any Internet sites containing the appendix to *Pacifica* (including, pre-sumably, lexis-nexis) could be guilty of violating the CDA.

This was true even though the CDA on its face only criminalized "patently offensive" or indecent speech that was "displayed in a manner available to" minors. Because minors traveling through cyberspace are gen-erally indistinguishable from adults, the CDA essentially banned such speech entirely. Under a line of cases starting with *Butler* v. *Michigan* in 1957, it was clear that the First Amendment forbids government from censoring speech in the interest of protecting minors if the result is to "reduce the adult population . . . to reading only what is fit for children." (The law struck down in *Butler* banned materials that "tend[ed] to incite minors to violent or depraved or immoral acts" and that "manifestly tend[ed] to the corruption of the morals of youth."[3])

Congress tried to address this *Butler* problem by writing defenses into the CDA for "good-faith" efforts to identify and screen out minors from indecent or patently offensive communications. But existing screening tech-nologies were both expensive and technologically limited; most individuals and nonprofit organizations had neither the financial nor technical ability to install them. Moreover, most of the organizations that joined as plaintiffs in *Reno wanted* to communicate on sexual subjects to young people, not screen them out. Among them was the ACLU itself (which hosted an online teen chat about masturbation after Joycelyn Elders was fired as Surgeon General for daring to mention the subject), Human Rights Watch (which offered fairly horrifying descriptions of torture and rape), Planned Parenthood, the Safer Sex Web Page, and the Critical Path AIDS Project (all of which pro-vided explicit discussions of contraception and safer sex), and the Wildcat Press (which published an online magazine for gay and lesbian teens).

II. PHILADELPHIA

Although most of us at the ACLU were still in cyberspace kindergarten as February 8, 1996 (the day President Clinton was to sign the CDA into law), approached, fortunately, we had a young lawyer, Ann Beeson, who was already an experienced Internet traveler. This was undoubtedly the first ACLU lawsuit in which most of our clients were recruited online, and Ann did most of the networking. Our lead attorney, Chris Hansen, is a superb, experienced ACLU litigator who was still fairly new to the intricacies of First Amendment doctrine but was a fast learner when the subject was speech about sex. (Chris would turn bright red if he knew I'd said this.) Having spent the previous five years heading the ACLU's Arts Censorship Project, I was the sex-and-free-speech guru on the litigation team.

We filed suit on February 8 in Philadelphia—an inspired choice, as it turned out, given the three judges who were assigned to the case. (The CDA provided for constitutional challenges before a three-judge court, and expedited review by the Supremes.) Dolores Sloviter is a Third Circuit judge with a good record of sensitivity to free-speech issues; during the trial, she expressed particular concern about the broad censorial effect that an "indecency" standard would have on art and literature. Federal district court judge Stewart Dalzell was the Internet whiz, enthused by the new technology. (He also was a tough case manager who forced the squabbling lawyers to get our respective acts together and come up with hundreds of detailed, technical stipulations in the short time between the filing of the case and the scheduled hearing on our preliminary injunction motion.) The third judge, Ronald Buckwalter, was quieter than Sloviter and Dalzell but had a commonsense appreciation of the astounding vagueness of the indecency standard.

The weeks after filing tested the endurance of lawyers on both sides. We were simultaneously engaging in a pretrial process that would ordinarily take a year or two, including sixteen depositions, briefing on a host of subsidiary legal issues, preparation of dozens of witness declarations, and selection of thousands of documents to introduce as exhibits, followed by five days of trial testimony spread through the spring of 1996. I found myself on more than one Saturday night in that spring of 1996 indexing, collating, and stapling exhibits, then searching the ACLU office desperately for tags and labels. The U.S. Courthouse ceremonial courtroom in Philadelphia was wired for computer access; *Reno* was the first case in history in which a cyberspace expert instructed federal judges on how to surf the Web.

A crucial part of the ACLU strategy in *Reno* was to introduce evidence of the valuable, nonharmful character of much online communication about sex, nudity, and even vulgar words that could be considered patently offensive and therefore illegal under the CDA. This strategy was designed to focus the courts, including, ultimately, the Supreme Court, on actually analyzing, perhaps even reconsidering, its past statements in *Pacifica* and later cases about the importance of protecting kids from "patently offensive" speech. Thus, we presented evidence describing explicit online sex and reproductive information; literature and art with sexual themes; and discussions about homosexuality, feminism, rape, and censorship. To our delight, the trial judges themselves chimed in with examples of their own. Two of my favorites came in questions to the government's expert witnesses. The first question was whether the famous *Vanity Fair* cover photograph of a naked, pregnant Demi Moore would be "patently offensive" and therefore indecent, according to the community standards of, say, rural Minnesota. The expert, a federal law enforcement officer who specialized in computer pornography, said that it could well be, since the photo was for "fun" rather than educational purposes. A different expert witness responded affirmatively when asked whether a vulgar comment such as "Fuck the CDA," in an online chatroom, would be indecent. The judges also wondered out loud whether *National Geographic* photos of erotic Hindu sculptures, news reports of female genital mutilation, and Henry Miller's *Tropic of Cancer* would be illegal under the CDA.

We also presented a psychological expert, Dr. William Stayton of the University of Pennsylvania, who testified that explicit sexual information, and even pornography, do not by themselves cause psychological harm to minors of any age, and that his views are in the mainstream among sex educators. I heard a few gasps of outrage from pro-CDA fundamentalists in the courtroom's spectator section as this testimony went in. Indeed, the alleged compelling government interest in protecting minors from crude or explicit sexual speech has for so long been a self-evident proposition in legal and policy circles that the Justice Department lawyers threw surprised looks at us when we argued that the government had the legal burden of proving not only that the sweeping criminal prohibitions of the CDA were necessary to accomplish the law's purpose in protecting minors, but that "indecent" speech harmed them in the first place.[4]

The government lawyers thus did not put on expert testimony to contradict Dr. Stayton. Instead, they conducted a brief Catharine MacKinnonesque cross-examination that focussed on whether pornographic images "depict a healthy view of women as sexual beings" or "socialize minors" to see women as sex objects. It didn't seem to phase the government attorneys that the First Amendment prohibits legislation targeted at ideas that the state disapproves or considers "unhealthy," whether about women as sexual beings or about sexual morality in general.

I have to admit that our strategy—both of presenting Dr. Stayton and of introducing sexually explicit evidence of online speech that we believed valuable, not harmful—was not arrived at without some contention. Several weeks after we filed *ACLU* v. *Reno*, a companion lawsuit with even more plaintiffs—twenty-seven to our twenty—was filed in the same Philadelphia court. Heading the list of plaintiffs in this second suit was the American Library Association, but the majority of plaintiffs were for-profit online corporations or trade associations, among them AOL, Compuserve, Prodigy,

Microsoft, Netcom., HotWired, and the American Booksellers and Publishers Associations. This second set of plaintiffs were ably represented by Jenner & Block, which assembled a formidable legal team headed by the redoubtable Bruce Ennis, once an ACLU legal director. Bruce Ennis and Chris Hansen both liked to recall that Bruce had initially hired Chris as an ACLU attorney more than twenty years before.

Although the industry plaintiffs opposed the broad and vague CDA for obvious reasons, many of them were wary of presenting politically controversial arguments that questioned the conventional wisdom that minors must be protected from sexually explicit speech. A less controversial strategy was simply to demonstrate that because the CDA's so-called good faith defenses were technologically and economically unfeasible for most online speakers, the law amounted to an unconstitutional ban on indecent speech for adults; and, moreover, that voluntary parental blocking software was available as a "less restrictive" and less constitutionally burdensome way of protecting minors.

It was probably inevitable that the availability of blocking software would be part of the legal strategy of both groups of plaintiffs, though it was a strategy with not-so-hidden dangers. Both the lower court and the Supreme Court eventually relied on this evidence in striking down the law, which naturally gave ammunition to the post-CDA proponents of Internet rating and blocking products, with all their attendant problems of subjectivity and overinclusiveness (see IV, below).

How did the Clinton Justice Department choose to defend the CDA? In line with its emphasis on the purported evils of pornography, the government's main trial strategy was to deluge the court with raunchy examples of online pornographic texts and images, meticulously downloaded and where possible printed in full color, and submitted as exhibits in a large looseleaf binder which the judges took to calling, affectionately, "Mr. Coppolino's book." (Tony Coppolino was DOJ's lead trial lawyer in the case.) My personal favorite in Mr. Coppolino's book was a long printout from an online site called "Bianca's Smut Shack," a sort of interactive version of the board game "Clue," in which participants could contribute their own fantasies as they traveled through various rooms in Ms. B's virtual "shack." The government's point here was to reinforce its position that the language of the CDA—"patently offensive as measured by contemporary community standards"—meant only, or at least *mostly*, "pornography," so that producers of safer sex Web pages or gay rights bulletin boards did not really have to worry; prosecutors would be prudent and sensible in their interpretation of the law. To this contention, Judge Sloviter responded in her separate opinion supporting the preliminary injunction (each judge wrote separately, after joining in fact findings and a brief legal conclusion), that she was dubious about "in effect, trust[ing] the Department of Justice to limit the CDA's application in a reasonable fashion"; this "would require a broad trust indeed from a generation of judges not far removed from the attacks on James Joyce's *Ulysses* as obscene."[5]

The Clinton Administration also argued to the three-judge court–as it later would to the Supremes–that cyberspace can be more heavily regulated than books, newspapers, films, music, or visual art (all of which, of course, are *found* online) because it invades the home, is pervasive, and is uniquely accessible to children. They relied, of course, upon the precedent of *Pacifica*, which had justified the FCC's regulation of radio and television on the theory that broadcasting invaded the home unannounced and uninvited, and was pervasive and particularly accessible to children. But of course many forms of communication are pervasive and accessible to children; and although the reasoning of *Pacifica* was troublesome, it had not been extended beyond broadcasting. (At the time of the three-judge trial, the Supreme Court had not yet decided the cable television indecency case, *Denver Area Educational Television Consortium* v. *FCC*, which extended the *Pacifica* rationale to cable.) The three Philadelphia judges rejected the argument for relaxed First Amendment scrutiny over laws regulating online speech. As Judge Dalzell wrote, "[a]s the most participatory form of mass speech yet developed, the Internet deserves the highest protection from government intrusion."[6]

III. EXPEDITED REVIEW

The government promptly appealed from our victory in *ACLU* v. *Reno*, and we probably had no hope of persuading the Supreme Court to dismiss the appeal for want of a substantial federal question. Nevertheless, we nobly made the attempt, arguing that the record was undisputed that because of technology and economics, the CDA's defenses were unfeasible, thus reducing the adult population of cyberspace to reading and speaking only what was fit for children, a result flatly unconstitutional under *Butler* v. *Michigan* and later cases. Such straightforward reaffirmation of longstanding constitutional law was not worthy of the Court's review.

If we suffered some palpitations after the Supreme Court accepted the appeal, though, the oral argument provided some comfort. Seth Waxman of the Solicitor General's office, gamely defending the law, made an unfortunate analogy to adults sitting around discussing sex; surely, he said, they would change the subject if a minor entered the room, so it was not problematic for Congress to expect adults to do the same in their online discourse.

This was a remarkable proposition. Adults may or may not censor their conversations in the presence of kids, depending on the age, maturity, and other characteristics of the particular youngsters involved, and the personal values of the grown-ups. But it was quite a leap for the government to suggest that adults should go to jail for two years if they choose not to censor themselves, and conduct an explicit sexual conversation in the presence of a child or teenager.

The justices were troubled by this and similar implications of the CDA. Justice Breyer asked Waxman whether a parent communicating via e-mail about sex or birth control with his seventeen-year-old college student son or daughter could be found criminally liable under the law. Waxman somewhat unenthusiastically admitted that there was no exemption for parents. Justice Breyer added another example: two teenagers communicating via e-mail regarding their sexual adventures or imagined adventures. This is known to happen in high school, Breyer remarked; Waxman conceded they could be prosecuted.

Like the three-judge federal court that initially struck down the CDA, however, the Supreme Court that affirmed the preliminary injunction a year later chose not to mention Dr. Stayton's testimony or to confront directly the longstanding assumption of harm to minors from sexual speech. Instead, Justice Stevens's opinion for seven members of the Court noted without elaboration: "we have repeatedly recognized the governmental interest in protecting children from harmful materials." Justice Stevens did not specify how such materials might be identified, but he did go on to explain that not all speech about sex fit within the "harmful" category; terms like "indecent" and "patently offensive" are so expansive as to threaten with criminal prosecution "serious discussion about birth control practices," homosexuality, prison rape or safer sex, in addition to "artistic images that include nude subjects," and "arguably the card catalogue of the Carnegie Library."[7] "Under the CDA," wrote Justice Stevens,

> a parent allowing her 17-year-old to use the family computer to obtain information on the Internet that she, in her parental judgment, deems appropriate, could face a lengthy prison term. . . . Similarly, a parent who sent his 17-year-old college freshman information on birth control via e-mail could be incarcerated even though neither he, his child, nor anyone in their home community, found the material "indecent" or "patently offensive," if the college town's community thought otherwise.[8]

This language was certainly a gratifying payoff for our strategy of confronting, not avoiding, the issue of minors and sexual speech. Reno is, I believe, the first case since Justice Brennan's peroration in Roth v. United States about sex being a "great and mysterious motive force in human life"[9] in which a Supreme Court majority has affirmatively acknowledged the educational, artistic and social value of sexually explicit speech, even for the young. I like to think that in writing Reno Justice Stevens was in some sense repenting the error of his ways in Pacifica. Certainly, it was a source of some pleasure to us that he specifically mentioned the George Carlin monolog, reprinted in the Pacifica decision appendix, as an example of the overbreadth of the CDA.

Reno v. ACLU also affirmed the Philadelphia judges' findings that the CDA's defenses were ineffective, thus rendering the law an unconstitutional infringement on the First Amendment rights of adults. In a section that was particularly heartening for those of us who had long been arguing the hopeless vagueness of the "indecency" standard, Justice Stevens's opinion explained why the standard was just that—too vague for anyone really to know what it meant, and to tailor her communications accordingly. Finally, the Court rejected the Justice Department's arguments that cyberspace should enjoy less First Amendment protection than books, magazines, or movies, and instead spoke in glowing terms of the tremendous potential of "this new marketplace of ideas"—the " 'most participatory form of mass speech yet developed,'" with content " 'as diverse as human thought.'"[10]

IV. THE FUTURE

Victories are always temporary in First Amendment litigation, and despite the stirring words of the Supreme Court in *Reno* v. *ACLU*, our euphoria had barely worn off when political players from the White House to the "Enough is Enough" anti-pornography campaign to industry giants like America Online began to float alternative proposals for controlling speech in cyberspace. Some were narrower versions of the CDA, imposing a "harmful to minors" (or "obscenity lite") rather than an "indecency" test, or regulating only commercial Web sites rather than all of the Internet. Other legislative initiatives focused on the wide variety of Internet rating and filtering programs that were by now flooding the market. A "harmful to minors" bill sponsored by Senator Dan Coats, as well as an Internet filtering requirement authored by Senator John McCain, were both passed by the Senate in July of 1998; the latter would have required any public school or library receiving federal aid for Internet connections to install software that rates and blocks purportedly "inappropriate" online sites.

Blocking software, however, is an extremely crude tool for controlling minors' access to cyberspace. It filters out large amounts of valuable, educational material. This is because the software must rely either on "keyword" identification, or on subjective human judgment about the relative offensiveness or controversiality of online speech. (Most products rely on both methods.) The keyword system cannot distinguish between the use of terms like "sex" or "breast" in pornography and in literature or medical information, thus blocking Internet sites that mention "Middlesex" County, "Anne Sexton," or "breast cancer." The subjective approach is equally problematic: it uses squads of individual screeners to make inevitably hasty, discretionary decisions about whether to label hundreds of thousands of Internet sites based on slippery, intangible categories of disapproved subject matter. Some software programs even block any online speech critical of their manufacturer. In a suit pending in 1998 against the Loudoun County, Virginia library board challenging its use of a program called "X-Stop," among the blocked websites were those of the American Association of University Women, Books for Gay and Lesbian Teens, Glide Memorial Methodist Church, the Society of Friends, the Heritage Foundation, Zero Population Growth, and the Yale Graduate Biology Program.

Blocking technologies are of course less coercive than criminal laws—at least as long as the government is not mandating their use. But they are still premised on the same or similar vague ideas about what is to be controlled–that is, primarily sexual speech–and the reasons why control is necessary: unexamined presumptions about psychological or moral harm to youth.

In this respect, the testimony of Dr. Stayton–and similar but more elaborate testimony by two experts in Burt Joseph's "Harry Met Sally" case (*Playboy* v. *U.S.*)[11]–will eventually become impossible for courts to ignore. For the fact is that there is no empirical evidence that exposure to erotica is psychologically harmful to minors. Indeed, the little social science and medical research that has been done suggests the opposite; a 1991 field study of juvenile sex offenders, for example, reported that although most of them had seen pornography, the primary causes of sexual offenses among these adolescent boys were their own histories of physical and sexual abuse.[12]

The courts will eventually have to acknowledge what has been, and remains, the true basis for the harm-to-minors presumption: notions of conventional morality; and fear that youths will be "corrupted" by knowledge about sex. A friend of the court brief filed with the Supreme Court in *Reno* by the "Enough is Enough" campaign and other groups brought this point home as it attempted to explain why the CDA was necessary. The brief asserted that pornography "is a powerful but deforming tool of sex education," and "encourages neither tenderness nor caring" in sexual relations.[13] I would like to think that one day–perhaps in my lifetime–politicians, opinion leaders, and judges will straightforwardly address the question whether it is really the job of government to encourage "tenderness and caring in sexual relations" by depriving minors of speech that a political majority believes may give them the opposite idea.

Litigating *Reno* v. *ACLU* was an unforgettable experience. The tremendous support we received in Websites, newsgroups, and chatrooms throughout cyberspace made this case very different from many First Amendment battles in which the ACLU is seen as a far-out extremist. Now, though, two years after the adrenalin rush has subsidized, I can only hope that the Supreme Court's encouraging words about the value of sexual speech will be read and pondered.

NOTES

1. *FCC* v. *Pacifica Foundation*, 438 U.S. 726, 757-58 (1978) (Powell, J., concurring).

2. Ibid., p. 758 (Powell, J., concurring).

3. *Butler* v. *Michigan*, 352 U.S. 380, 382-83 (1957).

4. For background on the legal development of the harm-to-minors concept, see Marjorie Heins, *INDECENCY: The Ongoing American Debate Over Sex, Children, Free Speech, and Dirty Words*, Andy Warhol Foundation for the Visual Arts Paper Series on the Arts, Culture, and Society, no. 7 (1997).

5. *American Civil Liberties Union* v. *Reno*, 929 F.Supp. 824, 857 (E.D.Pa. 1996).

6. Ibid., p. 883.

7. *Reno* v. *ACLU,* 117 S.Ct. 2329, 2344–48 (1997).

8. Ibid., p. 2348.

9. 354 U.S. 476, 485 (1957).

10. *Reno* v. *ACLU,* 117 S.Ct. at 2351, 2344, 2340 (1997) (quoting in part the findings and opinions of the three lower court judges: *ACLU* v. *Reno,* 929 F.Supp. at 883 (Dalzell, J.); ibid., p. 842).

11. See 30 F. Supp. 2d 702 (O. Del. 1998). The case involved a challenge to sections of the CDA requiring cable operators to block "signal bleed" (i.e., the sounds of sex) from adult cable channels.

12. Judith Becker and Robert M. Stein, "Is Sexual Erotica Associated with Sexual Deviance in Adolescent Males?" *International Journal of Law & Psychiatry* 14, 85 (1991); see also sources discussed in Heins, INDECENCY.

13. Brief *Amici Curiae* of Enough is Enough et al. in *Reno* v. *American Civil Liberties Union,* no. 96–511 (Jan. 21, 1997), pp. 11, 10.

SECTION 2
EXPERT WITNESSES

E XPERT WITNESSES ARE USED IN SOME TRIALS BUT NOT IN OTHERS, AND the decision is dependent upon the judge and the attorneys involved. Sometimes the role of the expert witness is crucial. For example, one of the editors of this volume (Bullough) acted as an expert witness in one of the Meese-originated trials on pornography. Many of these were carefully staged, and jurisdictions were selected because of cooperative district attorneys and because it was assumed that juries in certain areas would be more likely to convict. Cities such as Salt Lake City; Little Rock, Arkansas; and Buffalo, New York, were favored, and one of the major trials on gay porn took place in Buffalo. Since the defense attorney wanted to get a local expert witness if possible, I was selected. The judge threw out much of the material which had been collected by the attorney general's office to demonstrate pornography, since most were available for sale and consumption in Buffalo book and video stores and had long been tolerated by the community. The trial ended up with a handful of video tapes and magazines, and both the jury and I sat through screenings of the videos and read the magazines in question or least skimmed them.

After this had been done, the prosecuting attorney began an almost scene-by-scene questioning of me as to whether there was any serious "literary, artistic, political, or scientific value" in the materials. One of the first scenes he questioned me about was one in which two men were engaged in oral-genital contact while in the corner of the room another man was self-masturbating with his penis in his mouth. I answered that the film had been educational to me because although I had known that some people were contortionists enough to put their penis in their mouth, I had never seen such action before, and was interested in seeing how it was done. The court room erupted in laughter, especially the jury, and the judge eventually gaveled us to silence, but in effect the prosecuting attorney abandoned any more scene-by-scene activity. When the jury eventually came in with a decision, they had voted for acquittal on all but one charge, and on that one there had been a hung jury. The lawyers felt my response had tipped the balance in favor of the defendant.

This only emphasizes, however, the potential dangers of using expert witnesses, since a chance remark can complicate the issues at trial. Richard Green, a lawyer and a physician as well as a leading sexologist, is often in demand, and he summarizes two of his cases and gives some words of caution about the use of expert witnesses. William Simon, a sociologist, has often appeared as an expert witness, and he summarizes his experiences and indicates the complexity of the issue. The third contributor to this section, Marilyn Fithian, is in many ways made a much more desirable expert witness than others who might have had better academic credentials. She was a mother, a grandmother, a woman active in scouting, PTA, and other community groups which involve so many parents. She in a sense was a typical American housewife, but she also was a sex therapist who felt the need to produce her own sex films in order to fill the therapeutic needs of her own clients.

7

Pornography: The Expert Witness

Richard Green

I N THE U.S. THE ROLE OF EXPERT WITNESSES IN OBSCENITY TRIALS HAS BEEN tortuous. Early cases argued whether the prosecution had to offer expert evidence to prove material obscene and whether the defense must be allowed to offer expert evidence to rebut. The Supreme Court held in 1959 that it is a defendant's right to enlighten the judge or jury. "Community standards or the psychological . . . consequences of questioned literature can as a matter of fact hardly be established except through experts. Interpretation[s] ought not to depend solely on the necessarily limited, hit-or-miss, subjective view of what they are believed to be by the individual juror or judge." *Smith* v. *California* (1959), 361 U.S. 147, 164-166 [Frankfurter, J., concurring]. However, the prosecution need not introduce expert testimony. It need not offer expert evidence that the materials are obscene when the materials are placed in evidence. "The films are the best evidence of what they represent." *Paris Adult Theatre I* v. *Slaton* (1973), 413 U.S. 49,56.

Some federal courts have given experts short shrift. "No amount of testimony by anthropologists, sociologists, psychologists, or psychiatrists could add much to the ability of the jury to apply [the] tests of obscenity." *Kahm* v. *United States* (1962), 300 F. 2d 78, 84, n.3, and another court: "To hold, in effect, that we must turn the application of the obscenity statutes over to a collection of randomly chosen PhD's as expert witness . . . is to require abdication of the judicial function of the judge or jury as triers of fact." *U.S.* v. *Groner* (1973), 479 F.2d 577, 587.

In *Paris Adult Theatre I*, The Supreme Court scornfully observed "the expert witness practices employed in these cases have often made a mockery out of the otherwise sound concept of expert testimony."

In an obscenity prosecution, to secure a conviction, the pornographic material must be shown, when taken as a whole, to appeal to the prurient interest of the average person, to be patently offensive to community values and to lack serious literary, artistic, political or scientific merit. *Miller* v. *California* (1973), 413 U.S. 15.

Expert witnesses have difficulty in addressing these three *Miller* criteria. First, consider "prurient" interest. Psychiatrists and other doctors met "pruritis" in dermatology training where it meant itching. Thus, in the area of sexuality, prurient might mean a stimulus that demands relief. However, as defined by the Supreme Court, prurience is a "shameful, morbid (unhealthy) interest in nudity, sex or excretion." This definition evokes the provocative question, "What is a *healthy* interest in nudity, sex or excretion?"

More complicated still than determining prurient interest is in whom to find it. The jury must decide whether the "average person" would find that specific material appeals to a prurient interest. Is a juror with a *healthy* sexual interest to determine which small group of persons with an *unhealthy* sexual interest would find the material appealing? No. Appeal to the weak link of society was no longer the test after *Roth* rejected the earlier English-derived *Hicklin* test. *Roth* v. *U.S.* (1957), 354 U.S. 476. Under *Hicklin*, courts were concerned with "a tendency of the material to deprave or corrupt those whose minds were open to such immoral influences." *Queen* v. *Hicklin*. L.R. 3QB (1868).

Thus, prurient appeal should be found in the average person. This is an "original sin" view of human sexuality. Everyone has the capacity for a morbid, shameful, unhealthy interest in sexuality.

Some defendants in obscenity prosecutions have attempted to harness the prurient appeal prong of the *Miller* test by turning it on its head. In a case involving bestiality the defendant argued that the film was so repulsive it could not be erotic to the average person and so could not be found obscene. The Court agreed with the defendant's characterization of the film as "absolutely disgusting," but found it would "have an appeal to the prurient interest of an otherwise sexually normal person." *U.S.* v. *Gugliemi* (1987), 819 F.2d 451.

The next obstacle for experts is determining "patent offensiveness." Can a random sampling of persons be shown examples of currently available erotic material? Not easily. Further, is the availability of comparable material in the community an indication that it lacks patent offensiveness? Not necessarily. The other material might be prosecutable. Does availability reflect community tolerance? Some Courts have rejected that equation, e.g., *Commonwealth* v. *Trainor* (1978), 374 N.E. 2nd 1216. The court barred polling a community sample because of "the absence of any indication that the willingness, the lack of willingness, or the indifference of a group to the sale of sexually explicit magazines or the showing of sexual explicit films has any relevance ... (to the question of) whether the particular sexual conduct involved ... was depicted or described in a patently offensive way."

In an Illinois case the trial court refused to admit a public opinion poll on community standards. It ruled that the survey and interpretation of results invaded the province of the jury. However, the trial court was reversed because the Illinois criminal code permits evidence showing "the degree of public acceptance of the material." The appellate court held that the survey was relevant to whether the explicit sexual depictions were "patently offensive" and appealed to the "prurient interest." *People* v. *Nelson* (1980), 410 N.E. 2d 476.

A third obstacle for experts is determining whether the material has "serious literary, artist, political or scientific value." What is serious scientific value? Is depiction of the genitals scientific? Is it seriously scientific? If education is science how formal must the process be for it to be "serious?" If similar material is used by medical schools to educate students to a range of sexuality for patient care in counselling or taking a sexual health history, is that sufficient? If so, can this be extended to the general public that desires sexual education? Is sex therapy science? If similar material is used by therapists with their patients, is that sufficient? If so, what of the public that may want comparable therapeutic advantage but views the material without a therapist?

UNITED KINGDOM

The Obscenity Test

At the core of the U.K. test for obscenity is the *Hicklin* test. Justices in Wolverhampton, England issued a warrant under an 1857 Act to seize copies of a pamphlet "The Confessional Unmasked: Showing the Depravity of the Roman Priesthood, the Inequity of the Confessional, the Questions put to Females in Confession."

At a trial before the Justices, one of whom was Benjamin Hicklin, the materials were found to be obscene and ordered destroyed. The defendant appealed and initially succeeded where it was found that the material was not kept for publication for gain, or to corrupt good morals.

The Queens Bench reversed, holding that the publisher's innocent motive or object was *not* relevant. Chief Justice Cockburn set out the meaning of obscenity. It is "whether the tendency of the matter charged as obscenity is to deprave and corrupt those whose minds are open to such immoral influences and into whose hands the publication of this sort may fall." *R.* v. *Hicklin* (1968) L.R. 3 QB 360 at 371. The emphasis in the test is on the effect of the work. With the phrase "whose minds are open to such immoral influences," the Court regards "deprave and corrupt" as signifying "to make morally bad." Lord Cockburn remarked further "now with regard to this work it is quite certain that it would suggest to the mind to the younger of either sex or even to persons of more advanced years thoughts of a more impure and libidinous character." The Court regarded effect on thoughts as a sufficiently immoral influence. A mere tendency to that effect is sufficient for conviction. Obscenity is a matter for the jury which is to decide three questions: the identity of the audience, the influence the material has on the audience and whether that influence is immoral.

The later Obscene Publications Act 1959 evolved in the same directions as the American Supreme Court decision in *Roth* where "patent offensiveness" was introduced as an element of obscenity. In the US there had been the shift of emphasis from *effect* to the *nature* of the material. This began to be considered in English law as well. Thus, serious literary work would be protected.

The Court felt some obligation to help the jury with the meaning of "deprave" and "corrupt" in the *Lady Chatterley's Lover* case. It provided the jury with the *Oxford English Dictionary* definition of the two words. Deprave is to make morally bad, to pervert, to debase or corrupt morally. Corrupt is to render unsound or rotten, to destroy the moral purity or chastity, to pervert or ruin a good quality, to debase or defile.

An article is not necessarily obscene because it is repulsive, filthy, loathsome or lewd. It is open to an accused to shown than an article is so unpleasant or disgusting that it would not corrupt and deprive, but instead would cause persons to revolt from the activity. *R. v. Calder and Boyers Ltd.* (1965). (Prosecution of *Last Exit to Brooklyn*, by Hubert Selby Jr).

The Obscene Publications Act 1959 and 1964 is not merely concerned with the corruption of the innocent but protects equally the less innocent from further corruption. The test of obscenity depends on the article itself and not upon there being an intention to corrupt. The article must tend to deprave a significant portion of those likely to read it.

An article is deemed to be obscene "if its effect, or where the article comprises two or more distinct items, the effect of any *one* of its items, if taken as a whole, tends to deprive and corrupt persons who are likely . . . to read, see or hear it." The issue of obscenity is usually entirely one for the jury and expert evidence on the issue is not admissible. An exception was expert evidence in a trial on the effect of publications on children. Also, expert evidence is admissible if not aimed at establishing the tendency to deprave and corrupt, but is scientific evidence essential to ensure that the jury has necessary information. The opinion of experts is further admissible in relation to the defense of public good, that the material is in the interests of science, literature, arts or learning (similar to one prong of the *Miller* test in the U.S.).

CASE EXAMPLES

I will close with two cases in which I testified. They are a quarter of a century apart.

A 1973 case was the first in which I testified—*People* v. *Parker* (33 Cal. App. 3rd 842). The producer was being prosecuted for producing an obscene film and for directing an act of oral copulation, fellatio, an act which was a felony in California at that time.

Normative Behavior

[At the time of the trial the books *The Sensuous Man, The Sensuous Woman,* and *Everything You Always Wanted to Know about Sex (but Were Afraid to Ask)* were on the best-seller list.]

Attorney: With respect to each of these books, are there passages running on at some length which describe various oral-genital sexual techniques?

Green: In both *The Sensuous Man,* and particularly in *The Sensuous Woman,* there are passages running several pages describing a variety of procedures with respect to oral-genital sexual contact. *The Sensuous Woman* instructs the woman on the oral techniques which are described as the most exciting to the male. *Everything You Always Wanted to Know about Sex* is not so much a book on technique, but is designed to dispel people's preconceived notions or prejudices against participating in oral sexuality. Essentially it is instruction in trying to desensitize or disinhibit such people against this behavior, but does not in fact offer a course of instruction as do the other two best-selling books.

Attorney: Does the fact that these books have become best-sellers have any particular meaning to you as a psychiatrist?

Green: It does. These are behaviors which have been widely practiced, if we can believe the data from the Kinsey books, but not publicly acknowledged, and carry with them a certain amount of guilt because of the secrecy clouding such behavior in the past. It is behavior which is not only being practiced, but more openly discussed. I would submit that as an accompaniment of more open acknowledgement and discussion of such behavior the majority of persons who practice such behavior would benefit psychologically because of assuagement of guilt and conflict over what they are practicing.

Effects of Proscription

Attorney: Have you, Doctor, had the opportunity to read California Penal Code Section 228(a) which purports to prohibit any kind of oral-genital sexual contact?

Green: Yes, I did.

Attorney: Is the prohibition itself, Penal Code Section 288(a), in your opinion, psychologically harmful?

Green: I would have to say Yes. From the time of the classic writings of Freud, there has been an emphasis on conflict over sexuality. Traditionally this has been seen as one of the cornerstones out of which springs a variety of psychologic conflicts. Based on my experience with patients, when one is confronted with a pattern of behavior which is practiced by most, if not all of us, and one is then told either by a religious authority that it is immoral or sinful, or by a penal authority that it is illegal, and one is essentially responding to a biological drive, a normal part of sexuality, then conflict is generated in the person. It can only lead to inner conflict, it can only lead to guilt, it can only lead to anxiety. These are psychological phenomena which are harmful.

Effects of Viewing the Film

[Testimony was given that sexually explicit films showing oral-genital sexuality are shown to medical students.]

Attorney: Referring to the films you have seen which you have made reference to, those shown in the medical school setting depicting oral-genital sexuality, if those films were to be shown in a metropolitan theatre, do you have an opinion as a psychiatrist whether or not the film would have social value?

Green: Based on clinical interviews of patients who have seen so-called adult films, by and large I would say that these people report, first of all, not being offended by them, and secondly, report that they have been able then to introduce more communication with their spouses regarding their own sexual relationship. In some cases they have been able to introduce new varieties of sexual technique into their marriage. In one of the studies reported in the [Pornography] Commission report, in which some 250 people were interviewed after leaving adult film houses in San Francisco or Los Angeles, a majority of people reported to the interviewers that their sexual relationship was more enjoyable and that there was more communication about sexuality following their having seen these films. These were married people who had been frequenters of adult film houses. Only 1 percent of all the subjects reported a negative effect on sexual adjustment after seeing the films.

Attorney: Is there anything about the fact that a given type film, namely the type that you have seen and that you are now discussing, is taken outside of a medical classroom and shown in a metropolitan theatre that in any way detracts from the kind of social value and utility that you are discussing? For example, the absence perhaps of a medical lecture by a psychiatrist or physician to accompany the film, would that detract from it, in your professional judgement?

Green: No. The films which are being shown this year [in the university human sexuality course] will not be accompanied by lectures during those hours. They will merely be the film presentations. That would be comparable to a public viewing in which there would not be an accompanying medical or scientific lecture.

The film was found by the jury not to be obscene, but its producer was convicted of conspiracy to commit oral copulation. His conviction was upheld on appeal.

The second case is: *Playboy Entertainment* v. *United States of America* (1998), Civil Action 96-94/107.

The case involved the Playboy channel, a soft core pornography television channel, available on subscription to viewers who can receive the film broadcasts unscrambled. Non-subscribers see a scrambled picture but may received unscrambled sound.

The court is concerned with effects of the *scrambled images* with unscrambled sound on minors.

General Effects

Attorney: Briefly, what is your opinion (of the effects on teenagers and children)?

Green: Very briefly, there are no adverse effects.

Attorney: Well, is it possible for you to prove a negative?

Green: In scientific or logical terms, one can never prove the general negative, no.

Attorney: So if that's the case, what is the basis for your conclusion?

Green: The basis of my conclusion rests on several considerations. Firstly, there is no body of empirical data or empirical research demonstrating an adverse effect on children or adolescents of viewing explicit sexual materials.

Attorney: Well, if there isn't empirical research, is there clinical data?

Green: I think most tellingly that, in addition to the absence of empirical research or empirical data, there's no credible body of clinical data or clinical experience demonstrating it either. This is especially important when one considers the extent, the volume of such material that is available.

Attorney: Where we cannot conduct direct empirical research, what do you think might be the best evidence that we can look to to determine whether or not there are negative effects?

Green: We look to a variety of sources.

Erotic Non-Violent Material

[Evidence from studies of persons viewing erotic, non-violent materials was presented.]

Green: Essentially what these studies show is that just viewing, nonvi-
              olent erotic materials doesn't have much, if any, effect on the
              viewers in terms of aggressive acts in these laboratory settings
              or on attitudinal shifts. But when one introduces into the sexu-
              alized medium, violence, then one may well see, at least on
              paper and pencil measures, some immediate or short-term
              changes in attitudes towards women. So, it's the violence ele-
              ment that seems to be of concern, not the sexual element.

Primal Scene Viewing

Attorney: What is the primal scene?
Green: The primal scene is children witnessing their parents having
              sexual intercourse. The primal scene holds a central position
              for early psychosexual development in traditional Freudian
              psychoanalytic theory. It essentially occurs during the time of
              the so-called family romance, Oedipal conflict, a time when
              little children are being burdened by castration fear and penis
              envy. By theory it should be sexually frightening and dam-
              aging.
Attorney: Have there been studies of this phenomenon?
Green: There are two published reports of persons who are reported as
              having witnessed the primal scene when they were young chil-
              dren.
Attorney: And could you describe the results of those studies?
Green: In a very abbreviated form, the results of these two studies do
              not find these dire consequences on these individuals' general
              personality development or on their sexual development that
              would have been predicted from the traditional Freudian
              model.
Attorney: Dr. Green, do those research findings surprise you?
Green: They don't surprise me. Firstly, I think that the notion of the
              primal scene consequences derive to a large extent from a later
              Victorian, European and early twentieth-century concept of
              sexuality and modesty about just what people do sexually. In
              the context of history, that's a relatively recent role. For cen-
              turies, many, if not most families, lived in single-room
              dwellings, where inevitably there must have been opportunity,
              continued opportunity, for exposure of parental intercourse
              and parental sex acts for children.
Attorney: Now, that's when you are seeing live sex.
Green: Yes.
Attorney: Would you expect the potential psychological effect to be
              greater on a child or similar when you're talking about wit-
              nessing video images of sexualized behavior?
Green: Seeing his or her own parents engage in sexuality should have

a more profound impact on the child, compared to seeing some anonymous stranger in a two-dimensional video screen. Firstly, the parents are far more salient or significant figures to the child than some anonymous television actor or actress. And, importantly, too, children, all of us growing up, probably shared the myth that our parents don't have sex. It's hard for most children, when they grow up as adults, to actually imagine their parents engaged in lustful sexual activity.

TV Violence

Attorney: As another analogous area, you mentioned studies on the possible effects of televised violence. Don't these studies prove the existence of adverse effects?

Green: In reading and rereading these materials, first, let me say—there's less uniformity or less consensus in this area than is popularly believed. There is a substantial body of researchers who are convinced that the laboratory studies and some of the field studies show a–at least a correlation, maybe even a casual relation, between children and adolescents viewing aggressive or violent media and increased aggressive or violent behavior amongst these viewers. But, there's also a body of credible scientists who do not believe that causation in any way has been proven. There is some concern about these data in extending them from those laboratory studies, when one finds that people who have witnessed or viewed more of these aggressive materials are, in fact, more aggressive. There is a cart and horse problem, whether the children who have an interest in aggressive behaviors are those who preferentially seek out aggressive media as opposed to children who would have been neutral coming into the system and then, because of seeing aggressive media, become aggressive themselves.

Attorney: Do the researchers know whether or not their findings are replicated outside the laboratory?

Green: There's a lack of consensus in that area.

Attorney: And even when the studies find some kind of effect, isn't it true that those studies don't have any findings of a long-term effect?

Green: They are essentially short-term, laboratory-induced changes. My understanding is that there's no consistency over time between studies in attempting to document a prospective or longitudinal impact.

Attorney: Well, to whatever extent studies of televised violence might find some effect, short-term or not, can you apply those findings to imagery of sex–sexually orientated imagery?

Green: I don't think so. They're really not relevant to children watching explicitly sexual behaviors in media. A principal reason is the term salience or relevance or significance to the child. Certainly, at least in pre-teen years, the salience of aggressive themes is–its far more powerful, far more salient, than sexual themes. Children are preoccupied with aggressive themes beginning in very early years. They watch cartoons. Cartoons are funny, but they're funny because there's a lot of aggression in them. There's a lot of chasing and animals being splashed to smithereens. The principal theme in cartoons is violence, is aggressive.

Additionally, beyond that, whether it's science fiction films or adventure films, whatever it is, aggression holds, captivates children's interest. By contrast many clinicians ascribe to the Freudian notion of the latency period, in which Freud said after the Oedipal period of age 3-5 years and the family romance issues are resolved then, prior to puberty, there was this latency period, where children had very little interest in sexuality. Whether you ascribe to that theory or not, there's just little interest in sexualized content, sexualized materials in children during this age, much less so than in aggressive themes or violent themes.

So in order to postulate that the materials would have substantial impact on the viewer, you have to look to the extent to which the material is relevant to the viewer's interest. If it's not at all relevant or has much diminished interest or salience to the child, you would not posit anything resembling the TV violence effect.

Availability of Erotica and Sex Crimes

Attorney: You mentioned that the general availability of sexually orientated materials in society might be one place to look for effects. What has research found in that area?

Green: Research has been conducted in the U.S. as well as in Europe. The general finding is that there's no positive relationship between the availability of explicit sexual materials in a community, and the rates of sex crimes.

There's some evidence from some of the European countries, that there's an inverse rate. With the higher availability of explicit sexual materials, certain sex crimes, especially notably sex offenses against children, have dropped. The posited explanation for that finding is what's called the catharsis model. The availability of sexual materials provides a vicarious outlet, sexual outlet, for persons who might otherwise commit a sexual offense.

Notwithstanding whether that interpretation has merit, the fact is that in some Western nations, especially in particular research by Berl Kutchinsky in Denmark, there's a lower rate of sex offenses, particularly sex offenses against children, with the increased availability of erotic materials.

In this country, a number of studies have looked at, either state-wide or community-based, or metropolitan-area based, availability of sexual materials and commission of sex offenses. The correlations with sex offenses seem to be related, not to the availability of erotic materials, but to other, third factors.

For example, rates of divorce in the community, urbanization, some measures of poverty. And interestingly, circulation rates of nonsexual magazines, certain macho magazines.

Attorney: What of exposure of erotica to convicted sex offenders? Could you generally tells us what the findings have been in that area?

Green: Generally, sex offenders, persons convicted of sex offenses, have either lower rates of exposure to a wide range of pornographic materials during adolescence or have later exposure to such materials.

This is of substantial interest in that one would—one might well expect persons who are convicted of sex offenses to report higher rates of exposure in what's described as the scapegoat phenomenon. If a person, a sex offender, can point to some variable, some influence, that promoted their aggressive sexual behavior, then this might in some way dilute their responsibility for those acts.

Attorney: The devil made you do it?

Green: The devil made me do it.

General Effects

Attorney: Then, finally based on your experiences as a psychiatrist, including your clinical experience, do you believe that there are negative effects from the exposure of children to sexual materials in and of themselves?

Green: I don't believe so. I have been a clinical psychiatrist for about twenty-five years. I've seen children and adolescents and adults who do and don't have sexual problems. And as psychiatrists, we take histories.

We try to determine from what people tell us what the sources of concern may be, what they think and what we might conclude have contributed to problem areas in their lives, be it sexual or otherwise.

And I can tell you that one just doesn't hear this, one doesn't have a parade of witnesses, a parade of clinical witnesses, patients, who come forward and say that because of this kind of influence, because I've seen erotic materials, because I've seen pornography, this has caused me to have general psychological problems or specific sexual problems. Clinically, you just don't see this.

These materials that are available for children or adolescents have been available over a substantial period of time. If there were adverse effects, certainly by now one would have available a substantial body of clinical data, peer reviewed in publications, presentations at scholarly meetings, reporting or documenting in some clinical way these adverse effects.

If one takes seriously the position of some professionals in this field, that there's essentially—for every child, almost universally, some adverse impact or some consequent emotional disturbance on the child or adolescent from viewing such materials, one would have expected by now some credible body of clinical data published, presented at meetings, demonstrating this.

But the fact is there isn't any.

The three-judge federal court struck down the statute challenged by *Playboy.*

8

Importance of Knowledge as an Expert Witness

Marilyn A. Fithian

I N THE PAST, PORNOGRAPHY BEGAN AS SEX EDUCATION FOR THE LOWER class. The rich, powerful, well-educated, and affluent have always been able to obtain or purchase sexual material, sometimes having it privately printed. The first laws against pornography were passed during 1853 in England. There were strong feelings against pornography prior to this since some saw pornography as the influence of the devil. Comstock, an early condemner of pornography, was eloquent in this regard.

Three articles appeared in the *International Journal of Sexology* one in 1951 and two in 1952 and two important issues were discussed. Material that was deemed pornographic and prosecuted in England, Denmark and Belgium was material that had been readily available to people of the upper class. One article pointed out that the material from the publication discussed came from forty-four well-accepted writers whose books, although expensive, were considered acceptable and available to the wealthy. These books were only considered pornographic after the contents were put into language for the less-sophisticated reader and sold at an inexpensive price. The material was no longer printed in Latin but in the language of the street. This caused a great deal of controversy at the time, and pornography was seen as that of the illiterate with the crude language of the "lower classes." This was true in art as well as literature. Any sexual material not meeting the ideals of the upper class was condemned.

When pornography laws were initially passed, many in the population could barely read or write. Often their depiction of sexual material, both written and visual, were seen as crude. Therefore, early pornography tended to reflect the social position of those involved with it.

* * *

In the early 1950s, pornographic laws, in Belgium, were influenced by politics and the strong political position of the Catholic Church. Attempts to control and suppress pornographic material in the United States is currently often lead by church groups some of whom have attained strong political power.

Equally important in those three early articles were the fact that material deemed to be pornographic ten years before, was now considered acceptable. This has also been true in the United States. For instance, a song I liked as a teenager was not played on the radio because it was considered pornographic. It was a featured song thirty years later in a Mormon road show and the content of the song had not changed.

Another example was a picture that looked identical to the one I testified about in the early 1970s appeared in a Mormon magazine last December and was called the Blessing of the Prodigal son. Just because the man is kneeling in front of a man with a robe and his head is penis height does not mean he is having oral sex. The picture in question was depicted in an underground newspaper. There was no nudity or any display of genitalia. One would have to imagine that oral sex was going on since there was no actual evidence of such behavior. I pointed this out in court. When asked by the prosecuting attorney if I did see anything in the newspaper as pornographic, I said yes, and he became very excited. The judge asked me for the paper and I handed it to him. He laughed. It contained a picture of a war scene with a small nude child running down the middle of the street. It was the war scene I was referring to, not the child. It is a well-known picture, and probably many of you are familiar with it. That picture appeared on the front page of most of the newspapers in this country. Could this picture be published today with some states restrictions on pictures of nude children? Since child pornography is not covered in the Supreme Court's decision, child pornography it is still a murky area.

It appears that it is not only the depiction of the pornography but where it is published that are key factors as to whether something is labeled obscene or not. It is all right to show pictures of children being chopped up, but you can not show them nude or in any type of sexual behavior.

There are currently two publishing houses being prosecuted for pornography in books with photographs of children that have appeared in exhibits in museums around the country.

Is the reluctance of studios in releasing the new *Lolita* film due to fears of prosecution?

The National Foundation of the Arts may again be funding projects but due to the assault for funding works by artists whose work was considered either obscene or sacrilegious it is unlikely future grants will be based on artistic merit but on content of material presented.

WHAT IS PORNOGRAPHY?

What is pornographic and what is not. Understanding and identifying it is complicated by the fact that there is not a clear cut definition of what is pornographic. This poses a problem for people attempting research in pornography and doing comparative studies. Researchers say that they used pornography for a study but they do not state what that "pornography" was in terms of content and why it was considered pornographic by the researchers. Were they sexually aroused when they saw it? Did someone tell them it was pornographic, so they used it? Did they themselves consider it pornographic? Did they buy it as pornography? Or was it pornographic in the eye of the beholder.?

The first laws regarding pornography in England were passed in 1853. The first significant law on pornography in the United States was passed 20 years later in 1873. It was called the Comstock law after its strongest advocate, Anthony Comstock. This made it a felony to deposit in the United States mail any obscene, lewd, or lascivious book, pamphlet, picture, writing, paper or other publication if it was indecent. This was enforced by the inspector of the Postal Service:

In 1956, the Supreme Court, for the second time in three years, ruled that Nudist magazines Sunshine and Health and Sun were not obscene.

New definitions of pornography were made in 1957 with the *Roth* v. *The United States* that stated:

- The dominant theme of the work as a whole must appeal to a pertinent interest in sex;
- The work must be patently offensive by contemporary community standards, and
- The work must be devoid of serious, literary, artistic, political or scientific value.

In 1969, it was ruled that private possession of obscene material was not a crime. In 1970, the President's Commission funded a research projects for experts in the field to study the effects of pornography. It was determined that soft and hard core pornography did not lead to anti-social behavior. It was recommended that the obscenity laws be abolished except for those concerning minors.

In 1973, in *Miller* v. *U.S.* it ruled that defenders of an obscene work prove that this was a "serious literary, artistic, or scientific work."

The Meese commission in 1986 took a different approach. They asked anyone to step forward and state their position. Hence, those who had strong negative feelings about pornographic material came forward and expounded on the evils of pornography. From this, the commission concluded that there was a causal relationship between pornographic material and crimes sexual in nature.

In 1987 the Supreme Court attempted to reshape the Roth/Miller decision by making it "a reasonable person" not an ordinary person.

I testified in court cases for Stanley Fleishman and others in the late 60s and early 1970s, regarding both written and visual material under the Roth decision that was laid down by the Supreme Court in 1957.

Deep Throat was probably the best known film I testified about although, there were others I liked better. At this time, there was a shift in pornography from those that contained straight sex scenes to those that contained a story line. These were popular for a while and included some classic films such as *Behind the Green Door* and *Alice in Wonderland*, to name two.

I based my testimony on my belief that there was merit in such films since, I saw them as educational. They could be educational to anyone who had an normal interest in sexual behavior and function. A person didn't have to possess prurient interest in the material to find them helpful.

COMMUNITY STANDARDS

There have been a number of studies on community standards. It has been assumed that community standards are defined by a geographical area containing a common unit of government. A town or city would be the smallest unit. Where there are no studies of the nation as a whole, I think that if we look at the distribution and national income from such material we will have some idea about how the nation as a unit stands on pornography.

There were 600 million adult videos purchased and rented in 1997.

Playboy has long been considered to be pornographic and at one time or another was banned from the mail. It has a circulation of 4,250,324 copies, which exceeds both *Time* and *Newsweek*.

Several people besides myself have viewed romance novels with their graphic depictions of sex as soft core pornography. I base my opinion on having read pornographic material, both hard and soft, since 1935, and over two hundred romance novels in the last few years. Research subjects and clients both told me that they gained their sex information from them, so I felt I should read them and see what they said.

In 1998, romance novels were a billion-dollar business. They were up from 855 million in 1997. Fifty-three percent of the mass market in paperback sales in the United States are from romance novels. An estimated forty-five million women in North America and an unknown number of men are readers of such books. Harlequin Enterprises say that some of their readers read fourteen of these books a month. Other sources speaking of all such publications said the number average five a week for many readers. I know people who read that many.

From this information, it would seem that there is a great deal of exposure to both hard- and soft-core sexual material.

Lest we believe that an interest in pornographic material is new, around the late 1880s, Comstock wrote a letter to the Young Men's Christian Association and sent a copy to Kellogg stating that Comstock, as Post Master General, had destroyed "Obscene photographs, stereoscopic and other pictures, more than one hundred eighty two thousand; obscene books and pamphlets, more than five tons; obscene letter-press sheets, more than two tons; sheets of impure songs, catalogues, hand bills, etc., more than twenty-one thousand; obscene microscopic watch and knife charms, and finger rings, more than five thousand; obscene negative plates for printing photographs and stereoscopic views, about six hundred and twenty five."

In looking at the more local or regional areas where studies on community standards have been conducted, most of which have been done by direct random dialing, we see that the range of approval rate for pornographic material runs from 60 percent for the lowest to 79 percent at its height. Even in Utah, which has a large conservative Mormon population, 67 percent said sexual material shown on cable TV was acceptable.

Even when the ratings are the lowest, it was not clear if it was the content of the film seen or pornography itself. What pornography are we talking about?

The only major area of concern in the studies I have read is child pornography. It is not clear if it is the depiction of nude children, children in some sex act, children seeing the material, or all three.

In testifying I had no problem with community standards since I knew them very well from my forty-year background of living and working in the community, graduating from the local grammar school, high school, and the area college, working in industry, teaching in high school and college, raising four children (three boys and a girl), being active in PTA, being a member and attending a local church, active in Boy Scout for seven years as a den mother, secretary to the district scout masters, assistant scout master to a handicapped troop, den mother coordinator for the district and the Los Angeles County Coordinator. I received several recognitions, including district, community, and college awards as well as the prestigious Scouter's Award. Thus, I had community, city, and L.A. County experience with people from all walks of life.

I knew the people and their values in the community well. The person testifying for the prosecution in the first case I testified for was someone I knew, and I would have expected him to take the negative position that he did. His community background was limited. He came from a strong religious background from a conservative church. The church encompassed his social life. Even the troop of Boy Scouts he was in charge of was church sponsored. He was a postal inspector.

It has been suggested that even though research data on community standards in an area accepts pornography, people who testify or sit on a jury are more likely to go along with their personal beliefs rather than research findings.

THERAPY

Many problems we encountered in sex therapy were related to the lack of knowledge. At that time, there were no films strictly used for sex education. We, therefore, had been viewing pornography in nearby theaters. When we found something that seemed appropriate for clients we sent them there to see the film.

There were three major problems with this. The location of theaters were typically in a bad neighborhood. Second, the audience was often predominately male. Women felt somewhat uncomfortable with both of these. The last problem we encountered was that there was often something else on the bill that was not particularly appropriate for the clients. We concluded that we would develop our own films for use with clients. Most of our clients had middle-class values, and it turned out that tattoos and dirty feet that often appeared in these films bothered them. They said, however, that they learned a great deal from the films and felt they were worth seeing.

We made a concerted effort to try and make films that were not just another porn film, however. Some showed nudity, masturbation, sexual positions and intercourse. We attempted to avoid the porn label by talking through the films and telling the viewer what we wished them to see, or be aware of, to make them as non-pornographic as possible. We showed them to people including a lawyer from the D.A.'s office that prosecuted pornography cases. We asked if he saw them as pornographic. Everyone said no. We used people in the films from helping professions, such as therapists, social workers and others. None of them were professional actors. Many professional people considered us pornographers in the early years of our work.

We had not intended to make films for use aside from their use in our therapy practice. We started training other therapists by using films. They said they were trained with something that was not available. This encouraged us to make films that were available to them. To make this financially feasible, we had to make them available to other professionals, colleges, universities and medical schools. There are currently many people who make better quality films suitable for this use.

Others have seen pornography as a way that people could learn about sex. There are people in society who oppose pornography because they believe it is a powerful motivation not only to try different modes of sexual behavior, but more of it. This, to me, is a positive factor in its continued use.

AROUSAL

Much of the research done studying pornography has measured arousal. In 1968, we measured response patterns on a group of male and female subjects. We found that both males and females responded, but at different scenes. Females reacted more to the robber peeking in on the woman undressing, preparing for bed, whereas men responded more to the sex act itself. However, men experienced their highest arousal when the actor put his hand into the woman's vagina up to his wrist watch. All but one man responded. That was a complete turn-off for him. It not only showed on the recorder, but he said so as well. The instrumentation was not where he could see it or hear it. The man was a gynecologist.

Men and women may be aroused by different things, and some people will not respond in the same way as other people to the same event. One of the films produced no arousal at all for either sex, although it contained nudity of both sexes and intercourse. It was a comedy and was reacted to with laughter rather than arousal. It was the final film watched which may have also been a factor in the lack of response. This would suggest content of the film is important, as well as the background of the research subjects.

Other researchers have found that both males and females respond to films. They found that reported arousal was less for women than for men but when measurements were used they found that women's self-report of arousal was significantly less than what the instrument indicated.

This is not unusual in our experience. Working with clients, women are often unaware of any arousal that is occurring to them during lovemaking situations with their partner. However, in talking to them it is clear arousal is occurring they just don't identify what is happening as such. A sample of twenty-one women were monitored in the laboratory. All reported they were not orgasmic. The instrumentation showed that three-fourths of them were indeed having orgasm. After identifying it for them, all but one was able to identify it the second time they were monitored. This would indicate that there are probably a lot of women who do not recognize orgasm or arousal when it is occurring to them. Males can see an erection, but women do not have the same easily identifiable response.

In research on pornography, arousal should be expected, since that is supposed to be what pornography does. Arousal is one of the complaints made by those opposing pornography. They may assume that arousal automatically means someone has to do something about it. This of course is not true.

Studies have shown that films are more arousing than slides with the same content. Colored films are more aesthetically pleasing to subjects. They physiologically responded equally to black and white films and colored films as well. Homosexual males did not respond to films with females but did respond to same-sex films. They also did not respond to lesbian films as the heterosexual males did. Lesbians responded to lesbian films but not to homosexual films.

There seems to be a difference in arousal patterns between social classes. The better educated, less religious and more sexually experienced are more likely to report being aroused than those who are less educated, more religious with less sexual experience.

There was no indication that frequency of exposure to sexual material increased arousal or changed the subjects forms of sexual behavior. There was no change in the frequency of orgasm. Their behavior outside of the laboratory showed no change.

Where a study has not been done, it has been suggested that male interest in pornography has to do with brain wave differences between the sexes.

When a study is done to "prove" something I always question the results. This study attempted to show that erotic video tapes interfere with sexual arousal and response. Shock and negative feedback were effective strategies for interfering substantially with sexual arousal.

DEVIANT BEHAVIOR

Some have taken an uncritical view of *The Meese Report* where they concluded there was a causal relationship between pornography and sex crimes. This has resulted in a number of people believing there is a relationship between all kinds of sex crimes, deviant behavior, and pornography. They tend to belong to the ultra-conservative religious group.

Michael Goldstein at UCLA found that sex offenders and rapists, in particular, had much less exposure to pornographic material of all sorts than the non-rapists, non-sex offender population which were the controls. Kathleen Barry disputes this data claiming sex offenders were exposed to pornography as youngsters. I have taken sexual histories of men who never had such exposure, but that was rare. I wonder if the amount of exposure is a factor since I suspect most males have had some exposure to pornography.

Whenever a sex crime is committed the police always search the home of the suspect. If there is any pornographic material found this is always mentioned, although, they may not mention anything else. The police never state the kind and amount of material found. It could be copies of *Playboy* or any other items that may be commonly be found in a household. Since the definition of pornography is unclear it is hard to speculate what was found.

SEX CRIMES

Rapists, according to the Goldstein study, came from homes that were sexually repressive. Others have found similar things. When the ban on pornography was lifted in Denmark, sex crimes went down 31 percent.

VIOLENCE

There are some women who vehemently condemn pornography. There seems to be a strong reaction to pornography from the militant woman's liberation movement. They see pornography as full of violence. I have seen well over five hundred pornographic films over the last thirty years. My initial reaction to that was that I don't remember seeing violence against women in any of them. The nearest to that was one made for women by women.

In researching the material for this paper I viewed over one hundred films looking specifically for behavior I would consider violent. I did a content analysis of all of the films I saw. Three men who were in different sequences in one film with different partners slapped the buttocks of their partner so that you could see the hand print, and one woman slapped a man on a film. This was the most violence I saw outside of the s&m film *Sick* where the man drives a nail through his own penis. This certainly was not against women. In fact, the woman was doing things to him.

I didn't like the film but it is one I think anyone working in the sexual area should see. It is a film that makes you think. It is informative. I do not recommend men driving a nail through their penis.

Some stimulation of both male and female genitalia was rough, but not unusual having observed well over a thousand people in masturbation and intercourse I can say I have seen much rougher behavior in laboratory observations than what I saw in pornographic films. Research subjects were asked to do what they would do at home in the privacy of their own room. After observations, they were asked how close it was to what would occur there. Even slapping the buttocks was not unusual since spanking does produce arousal in some people and they often use it in their lovemaking activity.

The films I viewed came from a number of sources. Some I had, some I borrowed from several other people, some that had been given to us, some were purchased. I would say that the amount of violence was negligible at the most three percent. A man who studied violence found less than 10 percent of the films he saw contained violence.

Either these women who view pornography as violent have viewed unusual pornographic films and/or have only seen a very few that happened to have violent content. One woman who has complained about the violence of pornography had seen only three films.

Kathleen Barry believes women in pornography are "murdered in an orgy of sexual pleasure" for the gratification of men. I would like to know what it was she saw so I could judge for myself.

Eisler claims that pornographic films show "women (sometimes little girls as merely male sex objects), we find women in chains, women being humiliated, degrade, beaten tortured, and even killed." She claims that Marquis de Sade, Caligula et al. are examples of man's insatiable sexual cruelty and violence. That is like saying that Charlie Manson is the typical male in our society.

In all the pornography I have seen, I have never seen any of the things she claims typify pornography. I have tried to find such films and have been unable to locate them. When there were first rumors of snuff films I made a concerted effort to locate that material without success. The police have never been able to locate that kind of material either. If anyone knows where to find it I would be interested.

That does not mean that sick people do not do sick things and in fact some photograph their violent behavior with women but these are not pornographic films found in the market place and should not be confused with them.

The material written by de Sade is interesting only because it is not usual behavior. It is like the breasts of the women in *Playboy*. It's not the common thing. That is why such material sells. It has been sixty years since I have read his material. I found it beneficial. If you know that kind of behavior exists and you don't want to be involved, be careful who you date. Or check out their sexual proclivities before you have sex with them. If that kind of behavior interest you, then what is the problem?

There may be some films out there that have violent content but no one I have talked to has said they have seen any of them. They certainly appear not to be the norm. If they were popular, there would be more of them.

The more radical feminists believe women are harmed by pornography and the sex industry. They not only view pornography, but working in the area, as demeaning and an example of the victimization of women. I have talked to some women who work in the pornographic industry and they like their work and for them it is a choice. Would these same women tell another woman she should not be a police woman?

I was at a professional meeting of sex therapists where two women got up and walked out when a pornographer was lecturing. I personally felt his talk was informative and interesting. I don't have to watch pornography if I don't want to and I usually don't. It was a real chore looking at over one hundred films. Luckily, many of them were only five or six minutes long, although, a number of them on tape were over an hour.

PERSONALITY AND EARLY CONDITIONING

How adults tend to respond to pornographic material tends to be related to how they were reared as children. Those in childhood who have been conditioned to react negatively to sexual cues are the ones who react the most negatively to erotic material. They are the ones who are the most likely to see pornographic materials as offensive and dangerous. Those who are reared in a home where sexual topics and material were a part of their normal family life tend to be much more comfortable with it. One does not need to like it to be tolerant of it. Those with an authoritarian personality tend to feel the strongest against such material. They not only wish not to be exposed to it but also don't want others to be exposed to it either.

Those who are better educated, less religious, and reared to be more tolerant are more likely to be the least negative about it.

LEARNING

It was pointed out that pornography was originally sex education for the lower classes. It now has become sex education for the masses. The way we learned about sex is slowly dissipating. In the past, people all slept in one bed or lived in one room where sexual behavior could be learned by close contact. Today, except for the very poor, people live in houses with multiple bedrooms with little chance to learn about sex.

I found that in therapy many couples with young children under a year would not have sex with their infant in their bedroom with them.

Childhood sex play, once a fairly common means of learning, has been increasingly restricted by laws making such behavior subject to legal punishment. I have worked with children whose parents were seen as unfit for not keeping closer watch on their children's behavior because one four year old and neighboring five year old boy had been exploring each other's genitalia in the playroom of the little girl's home. Sex education courses in colleges, universities, and medical schools have decreased in the last few years although there seems to be continued student interest.

I was a substitute teacher in a local high school and many of the children were barely or not able to read. When asked what they were interested in learning about, they almost all said sex. I had thought that I might be able to bring books to class in areas of their interest since they were not interested in reading *This Is a Dinosaur*, which was the text one class of seniors were supposed to be reading.

Being aware of community standards, I did not take sex books into them. However, I did not take sex books away from them if they brought them in to read.

In teaching at California State University of Long Beach, the Marriage and Family class always had at least a hundred students in it. It is no longer taught. Where sex was not a major part of the class it was certainly discussed. A later Human Sexuality class was also popular. At one time seven different departments had a class in human sexuality. Most departments no longer have a class and where they do it is limited in size and not offered all the time. This cut back has occurred in other schools of higher learning with some no longer having these classes at all. Medical schools have drastically cut back on human sexuality classes even though doctors are the ones that most people ask about sexual problems. Their research has shown to be the most conservative and they tend to know the least about sex.

When we decided to open The Center for Marital and Sexual Studies, in 1965, we started preparing ourselves for practicing therapy and research. Wardell Pomeroy told us we should start observing sexual behavior which we did. Where do you go to observe sexual behavior? We went to theaters and looked at pornography. A five-year study of social nudism had introduced us to couples who were into swinging behavior. We ask them if we could observe them. Their first reaction was no. Since they were intelligent people, one in a masters program at a local university, they changed their minds, saying that it was important that someone do it and they were willing to help.

As a couple, they were never observed but they opened their house to us and were able to convince many of their friends that this work was important. Observations of sexual behavior was important, and in the thirty some years of our work, we observed well over a thousand people in various kinds of sexual behavior.

This included many non-swingers. People over the years who felt our work was important volunteered or said yes when we asked if they would be a research subject. When we could afford the costs, we filmed people in intercourse for study. This allowed us to look at films repeatedly. Most of those film are now in the library in Northridge for scientific use. Those research subjects I have talked to about their disposition have felt positive about this. Where do serious researchers see how non-professional people function? From these films we selected those including intercourse using a modified Bales chart to show our clients in therapy.

Sex therapy is primarily sex education. Even male clients who saw themselves as sexually sophisticated told us at the completion of therapy that they couldn't believe how much they didn't know. A lot of what they learned were things that they saw on films.

Lack of knowledge still plagues us today. A publisher pirated one of our books, and we know when he prints more copies since it brings a deluge of letters from people seeking sex information. A writer will call asking for fifteen minutes of my time and three hours later is still asking me questions.

As limited as it is I still see pornography as an important purveyor of sex information. In my reading a number of writers spoke of the learning aspect of pornography even for themselves. It provided new and different positions they had not thought of before. Things they were reluctant to try became acceptable after seeing it. In therapy, seeing films gave women an opportunity to engage in some behavior that they were aware of and wished to try without their partner wanting to know how they knew about it.

SOME OBSERVATIONS

Opposition to pornography in the beginning seemed to be the crude content of the material and a desire to keep sexual knowledge from the masses. This became acceptable when there was something else to attack. Pornography was not initially focused on arousal, violence, sex crimes or the degradation of women. As some new reason arose to condemn pornography, research would show that the fear was irrational since it did not contribute to the behavior that those who opposed it expressed. The violent content of pornography has been inconsequential when you look at the total body of the material. The degradation of women has, and is, an issue, but when there is content analysis of films that may not hold up. In my viewing of pornographic material my impression was that the women often took the role of the aggressor. Perhaps that is what women's lib objects to. They may talk about equality but want something else. Until they clearly define what they are talking about that will apply to most of the pornography films or at least a substantial number, the question of violence towards women and demeaning of them is not substantiated by the material when looked at in quantity and randomly. As these two areas begin to have less support, the focus tends now to be on childhood sexuality and its depiction. I am not at all clear what it is that people object to. Is it childhood nudity, sex acts performed by children, adults and children, children viewing pornographic material, or all of the above? When is someone old enough to view such material? There are those who would say never.

Until there is a clear definition of what pornography is, it remains in the eye of the beholder, making scientific research difficult and laws meaningless.

AN EFFECTIVE EXPERT WITNESS

Once you know the etiology of the subject and are aware of the research that has been done and the findings of such research, it is important to see what has occurred over time. What has been the effect in areas where restrictions have been lifted and/or laws have changed?

It is important to look at community standards even though there may not have been any research done in an area where a case is being tried. Collateral research may be important to point out the findings in areas that may have similar or like values.

What is going on in the general media? Is it much different than what has been termed pornography? Or is it a class difference in how sexual material is presented, and is it a clash between social values?

What is going on in other areas of the country in regard to pornography? What is now the popular focus of the field? How is it now different or newer than it was in the past?

What do the current laws say? Are they reasonable and clear, do they discriminate, or are they subject to interpretation?

The more prepared we are with knowledge of what has gone on in the past, what is going on currently and what is likely to go on in the future, the more likely we will be effective and successful expert witnesses. To have greater overall knowledge of the field than the prosecutor is helpful in the defense of a case.

BIBLIOGRAPHY

Journal Articles

Amoroso, Donald, and Marvin Brown. "Problems in Studying Effects of Erotic Material." *Journal of Sex Research* 9, no. 3 (August 1973): 187–95.

Berger, Alan S., William Simon, and John Gagnon. "Youth and Pornography in Social Context." *Archives of Sexual Behavior* 2, no. 4 (December 1973): 279–308.

Brown, Coke, Joan Anderson, Linda Burgess and Neal Thompson. "Community Standards, Conservation and Judgments of Pornography." *Journal of Sex Research* 14, no. 2 (May 1978): 81–95.

Craig, Alec. "Recent Developments in England in the Law of Obscene Libel in England." *International Journal of Sexology* 5, no. 4 (May 1952): 185–97.

Crepault, Claude. "Sexual Fantasies and Visualization of Pornographic Scenes." *Journal of Sex Research* 8, no. 2 (May 1972).

Diamond, Milton, and James E. Dannemiller. "Pornography and Community Standards of Hawaii: Comparison with Other States." *Archives of Sexual Behavior* 18, no. 6 (December 1989): 475–95.

Farrell, Warren. "Pornography by Any Other Name." *Sexual Harassment and Sexual Consent, Sexuality and Culture* (New Brunswick, N.J.: Transaction Publications, 1998), pp. 213–18.

Gebbard, Paul H. "Sex Differences in Sexual 'Response' " *Archives of Sexual Behavior* 2, no. 3 (June 1973): 201–203.

Goldstein, Michael, et al. "Experience with Pornography; Rapists, Pedophiles, Homosexuals, Transsexuals, and Controls." *Archives of Sexual Behavior* 1, no. 1 (1971): 1–15.

Hale, Valerie, and Donald Strassberg. "The Role of Anxiety on Sexual Arousal." *Archives of Sexual Behavior* 19, no. 6 (December 1990): 569–81.

Hatfield, Elaine, Sue Sprecher, and Jan Traupmann. "Men's and Women's Reaction to Sexually Explicit Films: A Serendipitous Finding." *Archives of Sexual Behavior* 7, no. 6 (November 1978): 583–92.

Henrichsen, Steen. "In Defense of Pornography." *International Journal of Sexology* 4, no. 4 (May 1951): 230–32.

High, R. W., H. B. Rubin, and Donald Henson. "Color as a Variable an Erotic Film More Arousing," *Archives of Sexual Behavior* 8, no. 3 (May 1979): 263–67.

Julien, Elise, and Roy Over. "Male Sexual Arousal with Repeat Exposure to Erotic Stimuli." *Archives of Sexual Behavior* 13, no. 3 (June 1984): 211–22.

Kelly, Kathryn. "Sex, Sex Guilt, and Authoritarianism; Differences in Response to Explicit Heterosexual and Masturbatory Slides." *Journal of Sex Research* 21, no. 1, (February 1985): 68–85.

Laan, Ellen, and Walter Everaerd. "Habituation of Female Sexual Arousal to Slides and Film." *Archives of Sexual Behavior* 24, no. 5 (October 1995): 517–41.

Laan, Ellen, Walter Everaerd, Gerdy van Bellen, and Gerrit Hanewald. "Women's Sexual and Emotional Responses to Male- and Female-Produced Erotica." *Archives of Sexual Behavior* 23, no. 2 (April 1994): 153–69.

Lanval, Marc. "Obscene Books and the Law in Belgium." *International Journal of Sexology* 1, no. 1 (August 1952): 33–35.

Luria, Zella. "Sexual Fantasy and Pornography: Two Cases of Girls Brought up with Pornography." *Archives of Sexual Behavior* 11, no. 3 (October 1982): 395–404.

Marshall, W. L. "The Use of Sexually Explicit Stimuli by Repeat, Child Molesters and Nonoffenders." *Journal of Sex Research* 25, no. 2 (May 1988): 267–88.

Meyer, Timothy P. "The Effect of Sexually Arousing and Violent Films on Aggressive Behavior." *Journal of Sex Research* 8, no. 4 (November 1972): 324–31.

Norris, Jeanette. "Social Influences Effects on Responses to Sexually Explicit Material Containing Violence." *Journal of Sex Research* 28, no. 1 (February 1991): 67–76.

Palmer, C. Eddie. "Pornographic Comics: A Content Analysis." *Journal of Sex Research* 15, no. 4 (November 1979): 285–98.

Quackenbush, Debra M., Donald S. Strassberg, and Charles W. Turner. "Gender Effects of Romantic Theme in Erotica." *Archives of Sexual Behavior* 24, no. 1 (February 1995): 21–35.

Rubinsky, Hillel, David Eckerman, Elizabeth W. Rubinsky, and Chip R. Hoover. "Early Phase Physiological Response Patterns to Psychosexual Stimuli: Comparison of Male and Female Patterns." *Archives of Sexual Behavior* 16, no. 1 (February 1987): 45–56.

Sandford, Donald. "Patterns of Sexual Arousal in Heterosexual Males." *Journal of Sex Research* 10, no. 2 (May 1974): 150–55.

Scott, Joseph E., and Steven J. Cuvelier. "Violence in *Playboy* Magazine." *Archives of Sexual Behavior* 16, no. 4 (August 1987): 279–88.

Scott, Joseph, and Jack L. Franklin. "Sex References in the Mass Media." *Journal of Sex Research* 9, no. 3 (August 1973): 196–209.

Schmidt, Gunter, and Volkmar Siguch, trans. Fred Klein Switzerland. "Sex Differences in Responses to Psychosexual Films and Slides." *Journal of Sex Research* 6, no. 4 (November 1970): 268–89.

Smith, David, and Ray Over. "Correlates of Fantasy-Induced and Film-Induced Male Sexual Arousal." *Archives of Sexual Behavior* 16, no. 5 (1987): 395–409.

Wallace, H. Douglas, and Gerald Wehmer. "Pornography and Attitude Change." *Journal of Sex Research* 7, no. 2 (May 1971): 116–25.

———. "Evaluation of Visual Erotica by Sexual Liberals and Conservatives." *Journal of Sex Research* 8, no. 2 (May 1972): 147–53.

Waring, E. M., and J. J. Jeffries. "The Conscience of a Pornographer." *Journal of Sex Research* 10, no. 1 (February 1974): 40–46.

Weneck, Charles, and John T. Evans. "The Relationship Between Nonenforcement of State Pornography Laws and Rates of Sex Crime Arrests." *Archives of Sexual Behavior* 25, no. 5 (October 1996): 439–53.

Wineze, John P., and C. Brandon Qualls. "A Comparison of Sexual Arousal in Male and Female Homosexuals." *Archives of Sexual Behavior* 13, no. 4 (1984): 361–70.

Books

Allgeir, Albert Richard, and Elizabeth Rice Allgeir. *Sexual Interactions.* Lexington, Mass.: D.C. Heath, 1988.

Baker, Robert, and Frederick Frederick Elliston, ed. *Philosophy of Sex.* Amherst, N.Y.: Prometheus Books, 1984.

Bancroft, John, Clive M. Davis, and Deborah Weinstein. *Annual Review of Sex Research.* Society for the Scientific Study of Sex, 1990.

Barbach, Lonnie. *For Each Other.* New York: Anchor Press, Doubleday, 1982.

Berger, Fred R. "Pornography, Feminism, and Censorship," *Philosophy of Sex,* ed. Robert Baker and Frederick Elliston, 2d ed. (Amherst, N.Y.: Prometheus Books, 1984), pp. 327–51.

Braun, Saul, "Underground Comix." *Catalog of Sexual Consciousness.* New York: Grove Press, 1975.

Brusendorff, Ove, and Paul Henningsen. *The Complete History of Eroticism.* Castle, New Jersey, no date in U.S.

Bullough, Vern, and Bonnie Bullough. *Human Sexuality: An Encyclopedia.* Library of Social Science 685. New York: Garland, 1994.

Byrne, Donna, and Lisa Schulte. "Personality Dispositions as Mediators of Sexual Responses," pp. 93–117. *Annual Review of Sex Research,* ed. John Bancroft, M.D.; associate ed. Clive M. Davis, Ph.D., Deborah Weinstein, MSW. Society for the Scientific Study of Sex, 1990.

Cornog, Martha. "Language and Sex," pp. 341–17. *Human Sexuality: An Encyclopedia. Library of Social Science,* vol. 685, ed. Vern L. Bullough and Bonnie Bullough. New York: Garland Publishing Co., 1994.

De Lora, Joann S., Carol A. B. Warren, and Carol Rinkleib Ellison. *Understanding Human Sexuality*. Boston: Houghton, Mifflin and Co., 1980.

Eisler, Raine. *Sexual Pleasures*. San Francisco: Harpers, 1995.

Ellis, Albert, and Albert Abarbanel, ed. *The Encyclopedia of Sexual Behavior*, vol. 2. Hawthorn Books, 1980.

Francoeur, Robert. "Pornography and Erotica," pp. 201–205. *Sexuality in America*, ed. Patricia Barthalow Koch and David I. Weis. New York: Continuum, 1998.

Gary, Ann. "Pornography and Respect for Women," in *Philosophy of Sex*, ed. Robert Baker and Frederick Elliston. Amherst, N.Y.: Prometheus Books, 1984.

Hartman, William E., and Marilyn A. Fithian. *Any Man Can*. New York: St. Martin's Press, 1984.

———. *Treatment of Sexual Dysfunction*. New York: Jason Aronson, 1972.

Hartman, William E., Marilyn A. Fithian, and Donald Johnson. *Nudist Society*. New York: Crown Publishers, 1970.

Hyde, Janet Shibley. *Understanding Human Sexuality*. New York: McGraw Hill, 1979.

Jones, James. *Kinsey*. New York: W. W. Norton, 1997.

Katchadourian, Heraant A., and Donald T. Lunde. *Fundamentals of Human Sexuality*. New York: Holt, Rinehart and Winston, 1975.

Kellog, J. H. *Plain Facts for Old and Young.*, Burlington, Iowa: I. F. Segner and Co., 1889.

Kimmel, Michael S., ed. *Men Confront Pornography*. New York: Meridian, Penguin Books, 1990.

Kinsey, Alfred C., Wardell B. Pomeroy, and Clyde E. Martin. *Sexual Behavior in the Human Male*. Philadelphia: W. B. Saunders Co., 1948.

Klatt, Heing, and Joachim Klatt. "Sexual Harassment Policies as All-Purpose Tools to Settle Conflicts." *Sexuality and Culture*, vol. 1, ed. Barry M. Dank and Roberto Refinetti. New Brunswick (U.S.A.): Transactions Publisher, 1998.

Kronhausen, Eberhard, and Phyllis Kronhause. "Pornography, The Psychology of." *The Encyclopedia of Sexual Behavior*, vol. 2, ed. Albert Ellis and Albert Abarbanel. Hawthorn Books, Inc., 1961.

Kronhausen, Eberhard, and Phyllis Kronhause. "The Psychology of Pornography," in *Sexuality in America*, ed. Robert T. Francoeur, Patricia Barthalow Koch, and David L. Weis. New York: Continuum Press, 1998.

———. "The Psychology of Pornography," *The Encyclopedia of Sexual Behavior*, vol. 2, ed. Albert Ellis and Albert Abarbanel, Hawthorn Books, 1961.

Lambert, James. *Porn in America*. Lafayette, La.: Hunington House, 1997.

Love, Linda. *Encyclopedia of Unusual Sex Practices*. Fort Lee, N.J.: Baracuda Books, 1992, pp. 215–17.

McCormick, Naomi. "Feminism and Sexology," in *Human Sexuality*, Reference Library of the Social Science 685, pp. 208–12, ed. Vern I. Bullough and Bonnie Bullough. New York: Garland Press, 1994.

McCumber, David. *The Mitchell Brothers, A True Story of Sex, Money, and Death*. New York: Simon & Schuster, 1992.

Mosher, Donald L. "Pornography," in *Human Sexuality: An Encyclopedia*, Reference Library of Social Science 685, pp. 474–77, ed. Vern L. Bullough and Bonnie Bullough. New York: Garland Publishing, 1994.

Paglia, Camille. *Sexual Personae*. New York: Vintage Books, 1990.

Queen, Carol. *Live Nude Girl*. Pittsburgh: Cleis Press, 1997.

Rembar, Charles. *The End of Obscenity*. New York: Bantam Books, 1969.

Rosario, Verrnon. *The Erotic Imagination*. New York: Oxford University Press, 1997.

Strossen, Nadine. *Defending Pornography.* New York: Scribners, 1995.
Walker, Brooks R. *The New Immorality.* New York: Doubleday, 1968.
Weis, David. "American Demographics and a Sketch of Diversity, Change and Social Conflict," in *Sexuality in America,* ed. Robert T. Francoeur, Ph.D., Patricia Barthalow Koch, Ph.D., and David I. Weis, Ph.D. New York: Continuum Press, 1998, pp. 1–9.

Films and Video

Bold and the Beautiful, June 25, 1998, depicted a main character with pelvic nudity emphasizing pubic hair by having it framed by a corset that forced focus on area. Few seconds.

Erotica from the Past, 12 films, 1899 to 1929, Passion Video: Total time 1 hour 2 minutes 20 seconds.

Sexographies

Untitled 5 minutes 41 seconds
Untitled 4 minutes 21 seconds
Untitled 5 minutes 52 seconds
Untitled 5 minutes 34 seconds
Untitled 11 minutes 27 seconds
Untitled time not kept for these two films
Untitled
Untitled 5 minutes 18 seconds
Untitled 5 minutes 25 seconds
Untitled 4 minutes 39 seconds
Untitled 4 minutes 42 seconds
Untitled 5 minutes 10 seconds

Antique Erotica no. 1, Elite Visuals, 1 hour 13 minutes 19 seconds
Untitled 11 minutes 8 seconds
Keyhole Portraits, 13 minutes 2 seconds
Wonders of the Unseen World, 11 minutes 4 seconds
Untitled, 13 minutes 16 seconds
Untitled, 10 minutes 10 seconds
The Price of Love, 11 minutes 19 seconds

Antique Erotica no. 2, Jerico Films 1930–1950, 1 hour 14 minutes 30 seconds.
Untitled, 10 minutes 34 seconds
The Good Life, 11 minutes 14 seconds
Dear John, 11 minutes 33 seconds
Rome, 12 minutes 8 seconds
Candid Camera, 13 minutes 50 seconds
Butcher Boy, 14 minutes 36 seconds
Antique Erotica no. 3, Jerico Films, Elite Visuals, 17 separate films, total time 1 hour 13 minutes
Untitled 4 minutes 26 seconds
Untitled 5 minutes 31 seconds
Untitled 2 minutes 54 seconds
Untitled 1 minute 30 seconds
Untitled 5 minutes 12 seconds
Untitled 4 minutes 33 seconds
Untitled 3 minutes 4 seconds

Untitled 3 minutes 27 seconds
Untitled 4 minutes 42 seconds
Untitled 5 minutes 21 seconds
Untitled 5 minutes 12 seconds
Untitled 5 minutes 1 second
Untitled 4 minutes 30 seconds
Untitled 5 minutes 26 seconds
Untitled 5 minutes 5 seconds
Untitled 3 minutes 10 seconds
Untitled 3 minutes 17 seconds

Classics No. 2, Erotica from the Past 5 films total time 1 hour 15 minute 2 seconds
  The Smart Alec, 10 minutes 5 seconds
  The Payoff, 9 minutes 13 seconds
  Bachelor Dream, 9 minutes 33 seconds
  Goodyear, 10 minutes 39 seconds
  Wet Dreams, 10 minutes
  Untitled 10 minutes 52 seconds
  Untitled 2 minutes 40 seconds
  Untitled 10 minutes 1 second

Classic Erotica # 3, Old Time Erotica, 1 hour 10 minutes 17 seconds
  Hotel Romance, 12 minutes 30 seconds
  My Wife, 14 minutes 13 seconds
  The Village Girl #4 9 minutes 10 seconds
  Groovy, 11 minutes 21 seconds
  Hungry Pussy, 9 minutes 38 seconds
  Bridge Game, 8 minutes 58 seconds

Wild Night, Jerico Video, 14 minutes 21 seconds
The Dick Diddlers, Jerico Video, 15 minutes 20 seconds
Three Way Lust, Jerico Video, 13 minutes 38 seconds
Any one Can Play, Jerico Video, 12 minutes 51 seconds
Bed Party, Jerico Video, 23 minutes 23 seconds
Honey Buns, Western Visuals, 63 minutes
Long Dong Silver, 12 minutes 23 seconds
Poof, Western Visuals, 24 min. 16 seconds
Sick, the Life and Death of Bob Flanagan. Produced by Kirby Dick. One hour and thirty
  minutes.
Sluts and Goddesses. Produced and directed by Maria Beaty and Annie Sprinkel, 1992.
  Fifty-two minutes.
Sunset Blvd., Western Visuals, 2 min. 55 seconds.
World Sex Tour, Vol. 1., Anabolic Video, 5 separate pictures not identified by name.
  Shortest 6½ minutes to 39 minutes 58 seconds. Entire film runs about 1½ hrs.
Gay Erotica from the Past #2, Jerico Video
    The Snow Boy, 5 minutes 25 seconds
    No Rest for the Wicked, Zenith Pictures, 6 minutes 18 seconds
    The Magic Pool on the Isle of Desire, 4 minutes 31 seconds
    Marble Illusion, 6 minutes 45 seconds
    Closed on Vacation–Wanted Model, 6 minutes 26 seconds
    Call Me Stud, 6 minutes 55 seconds.
    Strangers at Play, 7 minutes 8 seconds
    Wrestling Match, 2 minutes 45 seconds

Tim and Jim, 7 minutes 16 seconds
Three Is a Crowd, 13 minutes 15 seconds
The Golden Age of Erotic Video No. 1, Jerico Video, Clothing and hair looked like late
thirties. Time 1 hour 6 minutes 10 seconds
    Games You Have to Play, 13 minutes 6 seconds
    The Crowded Bed # 3, 12 minutes 44 seconds
    Crazy Kat, 12 minutes 23 seconds
    Mary Poppens, 14 minutes 37 seconds
    Candid Camera, 14 minutes 10 seconds
The Golden Age of Erotica #2 Jerico Video, Time 1 hour 23 minutes 58 seconds
    The Radio Repairman, 13 minutes 26 seconds
    Wife's Revenge, 13 minutes 28 seconds
    Swinging Debs, 20 minutes 34 seconds
    The Lady in Blue, 12 minutes 33 seconds
    Miss Lonely, 13 minutes 6 seconds
    I Love You, 11 minutes 51 seconds
Old Time Erotica No. 2., Jerico Video 3, featuring Marilyn Monroe 1930-late 1950.
Total time 1 hour 43 minutes and 41 seconds
    The Apple, the Knocker and the Coke, 8 minutes 3 seconds
    The Toni Twins, 12 minutes 16 seconds
    Torchy the Red Hot Red Head, 13 minutes 5 seconds
    The Bachelor and the Maid, 10 minutes 49 seconds
    The Cat Burglar, 15 minutes 8 seconds
    Bed Party 1, 11 minutes 34 seconds
Beach Bum Adventures Vol. 29, sometime in 1990. Total time 3 hours 47 minutes
    advertisement two lesbians 42 seconds
    Untitled 26 minutes 51 seconds
    Untitled 21 minutes 51 seconds
    M and C, 36 minutes 14 seconds

Book Reviews
Newspaper Articles

Crutchfield, John. "The Fractured Life of Jeremy Strohmeyer," *Los Angeles Times*,
July, 19, 1998, pp. A1, A18–20.
Eller, Claudia. "In Hollywood, Almost Anything Goes–Except for Lolita," *Los
Angeles Times*, 1998, pp. D1, D5.
"Grand Jury Indicts Barnes & Noble for Books Depicting Nude Children," *Los
Angeles Times*, February, 19, 1998, p. A10.
Lacy, Mark. "House, in Shift, Backs Funding for Arts Agency," *Los Angeles Times*, pp.
A1 and A15, July 22, 1998.
Lowenstein, Daniel. "Should Law Be Politics Savvy?' " *Los Angeles Times*, March 22,
1998, pp. M1 and M6.
McLellan, Dennis. "Embracing the Romance Novel," *Los Angeles Times*, July 31,
1998, pp. A3, A34, A35.
"The Modern Library's Choice," *Los Angeles Times*, July 22, 1998, p. E6.
Moehringer, J. R. "Child Porn Fight Focuses on Two Photographers' Books," *Los
Angeles Times*, Sunday, March 8, 1998, pp. A1 and A22.
"*Ulysses* Tops List of Best Novels," *Los Angeles Times*, July 21, 1998, p. A9.

Personal Conversations

Jay Mann, Ph.D.
Henry Miller
Person from President's Commission, 1969
Person from Meese Commission, 1986
Man from *Hustler*
Stanley Fleishman, JD

9

The Social Scientist as Expert Witness

William Simon

INTRODUCTION

To ENTER THE COURTROOM AS AN "EXPERT WITNESS" IN TRIALS DEAL-
ing with explicit representations of sexual behavior or near sexual
behavior is to enter a field describable as confused and conflicted as the discourses of sexuality. Moreover, at the same time, it is to enter the domain of
social science research that is equally confusing and conflicted. And perhaps
no less than the confusions and conflict within the legal domain itself.

Over the past twenty-five years, I've come to recognize that a major
aspect of my role as an "expert witness" in trials that involved the display or
distribution of explicit representations of the sexual, was not merely the protection of freedom of expression. This is an issue that is admittedly of considerable importance to me. Equally important, however, is a desire to
respond to the effects of such research in sustaining a discourse of sexuality
that I believe is not only erroneous, but is as injurious as it is empty of significant theoretical content.

Recent litigation provided me with an opportunity to survey a substantial part of what is offered as "scientific evidence" supporting the inference
that exposure to sexually explicit representations of sexual activity has a
harmful effect upon children and adolescents. I stress "inferential" because
there is to my knowledge no body of work that offers conclusive or even
substantial evidence of such direct effects. As part of the same effort, I also
reviewed the literatures on possible negative effects of such exposures on
adults, coming to the same conclusion: that there is no creditable evidence
of a significant effect beyond the anecdotal or clinical literatures.

Concerns for the effects of exposure to sexually explicit materials upon
children are based upon no direct research whatsoever. One most typically

encounters arguments resembling the classic "When did you stop beating your wife?" approach. With seeming candor, those defending the efforts at restricting distribution of such material will often admit that there is no direct evidence of a direct effect because it would be unethical, under most protection of human subject provisions, to expose minor children to the potentially toxic effects of such exposure. This is a strategy that assumes as fact what has yet to be demonstrated. This, in turn, provides the rationale for either relying on highly questionable inferences derived from what are themselves drawn from highly questionable theories of psychosexual development, and anecdotal reports from law enforcement officers and clinicians.

The traditions of anti-pornography research have come to resemble nothing so much as a self-reproducing process going absolutely nowhere. While replication is a significant aspect of the process of scientific inquiry, it becomes a cynical caricature of scientific inquiry when research is characterized by either of the following: (a) when the research rests upon the identical (and largely unexamined or articulated) assumptions regarding the nature and sources of human sexuality, or (b) questionable application of otherwise conventional research strategies. Unfortunately, most of the articles and essays that I reviewed were guilty of both of these pitfalls.

META-THEORETICAL ASSUMPTIONS REGARDING HUMAN SEXUALITY

The need to shelter children, if not adults, from representations of sexual interaction tends to rest on rarely examined assumptions. The first of these, following Freud and neo-Darwinians, assumes that the sexual is a high intensity, primary drive that is inherently threatening to social life unless it is carefully regulated and monitored. In other words, the sexual need not be explained, but rather is a given. This is a view of the sexual that clearly permeates the current prevailing themes of "folk psychology"; a view that lust and shame are inherent in our capacity to be sexual and that, as a result, can directly touch all individuals, down to the very youngest. A second common assumption involves the conflation of sex and violence—a legacy of both the moral ideologies and science of the Victorian era. It is assumed that the capacity for sexual expression and violence are inherent in human affairs because they are part and parcel of our "animal" natures. Such universal human propensities are assumed to represent the evolved capacity emergent out of the brutality of a natural order that at its roots knows no conscience beyond the blind practices that ensure survival of the species.

While the record of the human species is replete with episodes of extreme sexual preoccupation and "acting out," there is little reason to assume that such behavior is the manifestation of raw nature making its appearance because of some lapse in mechanisms of social control. Indeed, the surviving legacy of the disordering effects of sexual desire may reasonably be seen as the derivative of cultural discourses, as Foucault among other have suggested, that are the source of the meanings and emotions we've come to associate with the sexual. The very conception of the inherent toxicity of unregulated sexual expression is part of the justification of such efforts to regulate the sexual, as well as endow the sexual with the capacity to generate powerful emotions. In other words, it may be more fruitful to think about the sexual, in virtually all its appearances, as coming through the experience of sociocultural life than as a pressure upon socio-cultural life. From such a perspective the sexual can neither be seen as a permanent threat to collective well-being nor a force, once fully liberated, that will point us to some ultimate, joy-filled utopia.

QUESTIONABLE USE OF OTHERWISE CONVENTIONAL RESEARCH STRATEGIES

Data regarding the effects of exposure to sexually explicit materials generally derive from three distinct channels, each with their own claims for validity, each with its own methodological limitations and embarrassments. The first—and historically the earliest of these—is clinical or case studies. Among the most accessible and dramatic of these sources of insight, it is also the most suspect methodologically. Among the major fault-lines characterizing this research strategy is a double question of sampling and mis-sampling. For the very same reasons that the clinical or case study approach offers attention focusing images, more often than not, they represent the extreme expressions of a specific form of behavior or desire. As a result an entire category of sexual interest will be defined by what may in fact be only a small sub-set of a larger population, a small sub-set typically over-represented in both public and scientific discourses. As a result, there rarely is any consideration of alternative uses of exposure to sexually explicit material; most of which may fail to contribute to any behavior manifestly sexual or to the performance of behaviors that fall fully within the realm of the conventional.

An additional bias derives from the social locations from which observations are made and the mandates implicit in such locations often conflate this bias of case selection. Most typically, these locations are within mental health or law enforcement contexts, often a combination of the two. One consequence of this bias of location is to *assume* that the presence of sexually explicit materials is causal rather than being, at best, symptomatic. This "over-reading" of the significance of the presence of exposure to sexually explicit materials in part derives from pressures to provide definitive explanations for unexpected or undesirable developmental outcomes which, in fact, may follow from no one source. Moreover, given the bias in case selection, there almost never is any attempt at understanding what role the identical "symptom" might play in the lives of those for whom there is no reason to attract the attention of agents of either mental health or law enforcement establishments.

A second research strategy avoids many of the pitfalls of the clinical or case-study approach by seeking to obtain information from large groups of individuals, most commonly referred to as "survey research." This was an approach used by many of the projects sponsored by the Commission on Pornography of the 1970s. It was precisely the attempt to place exposure to or use of sexually explicit in a broad context that persistently led to findings of no measurable, direct toxic effect of exposure. However, the absence of an effect is the most difficult of all outcomes to establish. Legitimate questions of about sampling, question wording, as well as a prevailing skepticism in the general population regarding the willingness of respondents to provide honest answers to questions involving socially undesirable behavior tends to be out weighed by the commonly held, if questionable, concepts of the inherent dangers of the sexual and the vivid imagery of clinical and law-enforcement reports.

The third strategy is offered as the environment of the *controlled* experiment. The possibility of "before and after" testing of the effects of various specific kinds of measured exposures, and sophisticated statistical techniques for "testing" outcomes for very small groups of experimental subjects, provided an illusion of newly achieved scientific precision. It is the findings of such research efforts that have largely dominated recent discussions. Here despite a persistent unevenness of findings as well as significant methodological concerns, a general image that the toxic effects of exposure to sexually explicit material—especially when associated with violence—has been accepted by a large segment of the social sciences, as well as in the public media. In part this acceptance of the "fact" of a relationship between exposure and some negative effects has been furthered by its consistency with the traditional "wisdom" regarding the toxicity of the sexual, as well as the exploitative reporting of sensational case material in the public media.

Despite self-advertising as controlled experiments, virtually all such research might be viewed with caution given persistent methodological concerns. First and foremost, there is the persistent unevenness of research findings. A few report substantial or hearty effects, most report largely marginal, though "statistically significant" effects, and a few no effects. The large number of research reports of this middle group can be accounted for in several ways. A major factor has to do with an implicit bias in favor of reporting positive findings, in professions where academic publication is a critical determinant of reputation. This tends to generate replications with minor variations. A second, even more disturbing contributor, is the dilution of the concept of peer review as, with the proliferation of academic journals, many of a proprietary nature, peer review frequently involves review by peers who share the same essential methodological practices. The latter, a sharing of methodological practices leads to an incestuous toleration of methods that others find questionable.

While adorned with the formal images of the "hard" sciences, the environment of "controlled" experiments is almost invariably referred to as a laboratory. This costuming of research, in its unreality, creates a bias of its own. The subjects, most typically undergraduate students earning credit for some introductory psychology course, may either be cynically indifferent to the "experiment" or anxious to please the researcher by providing responses they think the research desires ("the sponsor effect"). In any event, neither the reader nor the researcher knows. And in many cases, given pressure upon academics to publish, I suspect that many do not care to know.

This last point suggests a bias of location, though one markedly different from that of the clinical or law enforcement bias. The pressure to publish just mentioned is one. This is a bias that to a considerable degree encourages utilization of the "laboratory" control model of doing research in that it is a relatively inexpensive way of generating publishable data, inexpensive in terms of both time and money. A more fundamental bias derives from the over-specialization that describes contemporary social science practice, where researchers increasingly can be described as "knowing more and more about less and less." For many of the contributors to this literature, the effects of explicit representations of sexual behavior or violence, as the case might be, is the only area where they have done work. One effect of this "anomic division of labor" is that researchers frequently lack the breadth of knowledge to be able to effectively interpret their own results except in the most formal statistical terms or, worse yet, the assumption that their particular set of attributes are the singly most significant in determining behavior.

This brings us to what is for me one of the major short-comings of the work undertaken in this tradition—letting statistics do the thinking or the tendency to treat "*statistical* significance" as if it were synonymous with "*substantive* significance." The former is the product of the application of abstract statistical theories; the latter is a judgement based upon a presumed appreciation of the full complexity of the phenomena. For example, the measurements of a before and after experiment finds that the measures taken after the exposure of an experimental group to a specific intervention (i.e., viewing films of a sexual nature) produce a statistically significant difference from the initial observation. All this means, however, is that this observed difference is unlikely to have happened by chance. However, it must fall to the observer to assess the *substantive* significance of the observed difference. Though often shrouded in the formal language of hypothesis testing, in virtually all of the research I reviewed the differences were *substantively insignificant* in that it was only the responses of a minority of the research subjects that produce the observed difference.

Another lacunae, one shared by many areas of research, is a general neglect of the researchers to fully commit to the priority of the "null hypothesis," i.e., the application of thoroughgoing skepticism regarding all findings. More concretely, this means that even when statistically significant findings occur, the research has a moral obligation to fully examine the possibility that significant finding is really artifactual of some other unrecognized or unmeasured factors. Beyond a minimal regard for bias in the selection of subjects, little of this effort is detectable in this literature.

There are other fundamental criticisms of "laboratory" research, which by far represents the larger source of recent publication on this issue might be described. These would include the predominance of focusing upon atti-tudes with little concern for behavior and inarticulate measurement of phys-iological reactions. However, the larger point that published research on this topic out of the controlled experiment, for the most part, does not even having the distinction of being wrong, the vast majority of it being either profoundly inconclusive or irrelevant.

CONCLUSION

As of the present moment, as I said at the outset, I believe there is to my knowledge no body of work that offers conclusive or even substantial evi-dence of direct injurious effects of exposure to explicit representations of sexual behavior. My role as "expert" witness is to affirm this seemingly neg-ative finding and to affirm the significance of negative findings, while knowing that this language is far less impressive to many juries than the manifestly more dramatic accounts provided by law enforcement agents or clinicians. Moreover, it is typically very difficult to enter testimony to the effect that a major aspect of the "redeeming social merit" of such material is to be found in the idea that the very attempt to suppress such material is far more injurious than any exposure that it might occasion. As I noted above, it may well be the perpetuation of the image and ideologies of the sexual as the beast within that contributes most to occasions where the sexual appears beastly. What is needed, and rarely tolerated, is the full contextualization of this issue within sensible concepts of human sexuality, as is currently being done with increasing effectiveness with regard to such issues as homosexu-ality or transgendering.

SECTION 3

SEX, CENSORSHIP, AND THE BATTLE OVER MORALITY

T HIS SECTION, SEX, CENSORSHIP, AND THE BATTLE OVER MORALITY, provides a full range of articles from a psycho-sexual discussion about the fear of sexuality to Australian censorship, religion, and body ornamentation.

Marty Klein moves from the legal perspective to that of a clinician who focuses on the fact that many would censor what they fear as a resolution of their personal conflict about sexuality. Dr. Klein sees fear of one's own sexual being projected onto others with myths created to rationalize that fear. He goes on to examine the elimination of sexual secrecy by the public-izing of sex through sex education, thus bringing sexuality into the public arena, which threatens sex-negative people. Marty Klein sees censorship as a special case of sex-negativity. Dr. Klein looks at the issue of childhood sexual exploitation and discusses the association between pornography and other forms of sexual dialogue and the fear that this will cause sexual exploitation. He provides us with a series of suggestions about how to deal with this fear of sexuality and the resulting censorship.

Yolanda Corduff, an Australian journalist, provides a personal perspective on the issue of censorship by the Office for Film and Literature Classification. She cites the "guidelines so ambiguous you could drive a truck through them, yet so restrictive you can never be sure what will pass and what won't." The process has led to self-censorship by journalists and publishers prior to submitting their material to the OFLC. Ms. Corduff provides a series of situations in which either censorship or self-censorship is evident.

As president of the Eros Foundation, Fiona Patten spends much of her time dealing with the politics and politicians in Australia, which has recently adopted a new category for sexually explicit films and videos–NVE, Non-Violent Erotica. Ms. Patten traces the history of attitudes toward sex and pornography in Australia with its roots in "mother" England. She defines the issues before the Australian Parliament and how the sex industry combined to lobby the governmental officials for the establishment of the new code of Non-Violent Erotica.

Miss Charlie Latour provides personal insight into her world of strong religious convictions and sexual permissiveness. She traces religious thought on sexuality as filtered, first of all, through the philosophy of the Stoics, who rejected pleasure, sex, and marriage. The second movement was that of Gnosticism which "preached abstinence from marriage, meat, and wine." Latour attributes the repression of sexuality largely to these two movements. She follows the works of Augustine and Thomas Aquinas, Luther and the Protestant Reformation. Miss Latour discusses the Puritan movement with the Gnostic influences leading to sexual pessimism. As she continues her discussion, Miss Latour concludes that, "From Sodom to Corinth to the San Fernando Valley the history of sexual pessimism can be traced not to God but to man."

Maureen Mercury's article, "America Unchained: Tattoos, Piercings, and Porn," sees the society from a different perspective. She views the body as "soulscape" with a connectedness to the sensate. Ritual plays a significant role. Tattooing is examined in terms of an initiatory "rite of passage." The stages of initiation as practiced by indigenous people can be applied to the tattooing, with the various stages of the initiation mimicked in the process of obtaining a tattoo. She sees the trend of piercing as another form of initiation, except that it has an emphasis on sensate response. Mercury discusses the common piercings and the more uncommon body modification of pockets. Scarification is another form of bodily modification. She focuses on why this is desirable and finds her answers in sexual pleasure and reaching a state of feeling unattainable by other means. Ms. Mercury takes a Jungian approach to viewing sexuality and describes what she sees as a neurotic culture caught in an "erotic conflict." Pornography is a means of resolving the erotic conflict, although in the tattoos, piercings, and porn are defenses against the psychological fear of death.

10

Censorship and the Fear of Sexuality

Marty Klein

CENSORSHIP IS FREQUENTLY DISCUSSED AS A CIVIL LIBERTIES ISSUE. As the title of this talk suggests, I want to discuss it in another way, on a more psycho-social level.

Most Americans do not want to discuss sexual issues rationally. Their sexuality poisoned by the culture, they just want their emotional pain taken away. To people afraid of sexuality, censorship looks attractive. It appears to be a solution to the pain. This pain, this fear of sexuality, leads people to support censorship.

Talk of censorship typically leads to thoughts of "pornography." But that's only one aspect of sexual censorship. Other targets include sex education, contraceptive advertising, fiction, sex surveys, and public nudity. *The Color Purple, Our Bodies Ourselves*, and *Ms*. magazine, for example, have all been banned from various high school libraries in supposedly liberal California. I think it's important to talk about the availability and restriction of all these aspects of sexuality, not just of pornography. This will help us understand censorship on a deeper level.

I think of "censorship" as a strategy people use to eliminate certain kinds of sexuality-related displays or opportunities from their lives. The forms of sexuality typically censored include one or more of the following:

1) Sex not bounded by love. In our culture, love is supposed to make sex sane and wholesome and controlled. That's "good" sex. In contrast, "bad" sex gives people "too many" choices–inappropriate partners, hedonistic activities, etc.

2) Sex strictly for pleasure. American culture mistrusts pleasure as a motivation for sex; in fact, many people consider it to be dangerous.

3) Sex that isn't bounded by arbitrary social rules. The values of honesty, responsibility, and consent are the foundation of democratic,

civilized society, and are deemed sufficient criteria for most activities. Many people, however, feel that sex requires additional rules.
4) Sex that honors losing control (within a secure environment). Lust,
passion, ego loss, timelessness—while these are qualities some people
associate with good sex, they also describe the loss of control during
sex that censorship attempts to eliminate.

These factors are missing or underplayed in forms of eroticism that are
not typically censored, such as romance novels, slasher films, and football
cheerleaders. We'll return to this point later.

At one time or another, many people in this room have said something
like, "If you don't like porn films, strip clubs, or sex surveys, don't participate in them. But don't prevent the rest of us from doing so!" Let's now
examine the emotional context that makes censorship look absolutely essential to many people.

Instead of addressing their personal fears about sexuality directly, many
Americans displace them. Sexuality and sexual material itself is seen as the
source of problems out in the world; thus, restricting or eliminating sexuality and sexual materials out in the world is seen as the solution to those
problems, a solution that will supposedly eliminate the personal fears.

We need to look at the emotional pain people are in about sex, and
examine why and how such displacements of this pain occur. Doing so will
help explain why censorship is popular, why it feels so good, and how we
can address it more effectively.

A. FEAR OF OUR OWN SEXUALITY, PROJECTED ONTO OTHERS

We all know the many ways kids learn that sex is bad. This is harmful
enough. But what reason are kids given for sex being bad? None: "It just is."
The lack of a reason is crucial, because the belief can't be refuted or tested.
It's like a religion. Sex is bad: "It just is."

Children know they're sexual, so most conclude that they are bad.
Unconsciously, kids fear being abandoned or destroyed because of their
sexuality. This is not a metaphorical fear—for young children, 100 percent
dependent on the caretaking and good will of their parents, it is a literal fear.
In terror, kids learn to hide, deny, repress, and distort their sexuality. Using
a familiar process we call internalization or introjection, children soon take
over the life-and-death job of scrutinizing their sexuality from their parents.

Freud observed this, but interpreted it incorrectly. He mistakenly
believed that during a "latency period" from roughly six to eleven years old,
kids lost their sexual interest. But this isn't so; kids just learn to hide their
sexuality. And sadly, many continue doing so after they grow up.

As a result, many adults feel that trusting their own sexuality is dangerous. Unconsciously, they fear being punished or abandoned for their

sexual fantasies, desires, and feelings. Like other therapists, I have heard heart-rending "confessions" about sexuality that patients are sure must never be shared with anyone who loves them. But once you reject your own sexuality, it becomes impossible to imagine others accepting your sexuality. The research for my first book, *Your Sexual Secrets,* revealed how much people were afraid that their partners would reject them if they told the truth about their sexuality. People felt they could handle their partner's sexual secrets, but feared their partners couldn't handle theirs.

Developmentally, the dynamic typically goes further: "if my sexuality is so dangerous, yours must be too." And so people start fearing others' sexuality. Jimmy Swaggart is a perfect example. He spent an entire career railing against people doing "perverted" things—and then we found out he was doing them too! Why was he criticizing others' sexuality—in fact, warning everyone about their dangerous impulses? Because he was afraid of his own. His call to disarm others' sexuality was a call, in code, about wanting to disarm his own. Progressive people, of course, don't think Swaggart's sexual desires were sick. But imagine how terrified he must have been of them.

Rather than talk about these fears on a personal level, our society has developed myths to justify them. These myths include, for example:

- Homosexuals want to seduce straight adults and children into homosexual activity;
- Sex education stimulates sexual interest in adolescents;
- People can become "addicted" to sex, pornography, prostitution, and masturbation;
- STDs ruin people's lives;
- Sexual experimentation leads to compulsive fetishes and uncontrollable sexual acting out;
- There is a vast underground industry that kidnaps children for sexual purposes.

Supported by social myths, then, people talk about the fear of their own sexuality primarily in metaphor.

To illustrate, this is one reason the concept of sex addiction has become so popular, and why these people so frequently want to restrict everyone's sexual options. Feeling victimized by their own sexuality, they want to protect others from being victimized by their sexuality. These twelve-steppers want to keep the tools of self-destruction out of people's hands, like the temperance marchers of eighty years ago did.

Normality anxiety is another part of Americans' sexual development. Sheltered from accurate information, prevented from asking meaningful questions, told that our sexuality is bad—without being given criteria we could use to refute the judgement—we learn to worry that our sexuality is not "normal," and that being sexually normal is very important. Many of my patients have fantasies or desires they believe are unusual. Unaware of anyone else having similar ones, they typically assume they must be abnormal.

This anxiety is reinforced in people by social institutions such as the government, the media, organized religion, and the advertising industry. Having created the anxiety, these institutions then offer to soothe it. The church creates sin, then offers salvation. Advertising creates sexual insecurity, then offers products to make people feel adequate. The government criminalizes victimless behaviors, then offers people the chance to be law-abiding citizens.

Most people walk around oppressed by normality anxiety. It reminds me of what physician Harvey Caplan said during my very first sexuality training twenty years ago. "People don't come to us wanting two-hour orgasms or help in finding orgies," he said. "They mostly want their emotional pain taken away."

And most people will do anything to have the anxiety taken away. For many, twelve-step programs serve this purpose. For others it's organized religion. I have a patient who recently quit being a stripper after ten years. She's now heavily involved in Catholicism, which she loves—says she likes the structure and rules, says it makes her feel normal. Says she's learned masturbation is a sin. She'd rather keep doing it, but she feels that giving it up is a small price to pay for the peace of mind she gets. For the first time in ten years, she isn't afraid that she's a pervert.

Pornography and other kinds of publicly acknowledged sexuality (such as condom advertising) increase such people's anxiety about what's normal. Declaring pornography, sex education, and homosexuality "bad" is soothing for them. By defining "good sexuality" and "bad sexuality," they psychologically split, unconsciously putting their bad sexuality "out there" where it can be disowned.

Given that so many people are afraid of their own sexuality, here are some aspects of pornography that will seem scary to them:

- Pornography shows people experimenting as sex objects. For people who fear they aren't sexually adequate, this is scary. The social myth covering this personal fear is that consumers of pornography will begin to see all men or women that way. This naive, inaccurate assumption also denies the healthy dynamic of lovers agreeing to objectify each other during their sexual interactions.
- Pornography also shows people experimenting via sex. This is a scary concept for those who fear that their experimenting can lead to trouble. In truth, when experimentation is consensual, physically safe, and non-self-destructive, it's almost impossible for people to do something wrong. The vast majority of American pornography shows legal, fairly vanilla sex. But in depicting people unafraid to experiment, it looks dangerous to those afraid to experiment. By censoring pornography, such people feel they are keeping others out of danger.
- Pornography invites viewers to get in touch with their fantasies, which are, of course, irrational. Fantasies are used specifically to get aroused—i.e., uncontrolled. They depict sex where people relinquish

control, and where they enjoy sex without the context or boundaries of romantic love. The primitive fear is that getting "too excited" will destroy the ability to defer gratification and to reason in other areas; this is why the concept of "morality" often comes down to controlling sex. Eroticism is a metaphor for being out of control, for compromised decision-making.

So in a culture where people learn to fear their own sexuality, sex appears to require censorship if it is sex for pleasure, healing, or self-expression, and not bounded by love; and if it doesn't require an institution, ritual, or sanctioned person to approve it. When people have been taught to fear the lack of rigid boundaries in their own sexuality, they fear what appears to be the lack of them in others.

B. THE ELIMINATION OF SEXUAL SECRECY, OF THE PUBLIC-IZING (VS. PRIVAT-IZING) OF SEX

Who controls our common cultural space with regard to sexuality? This is a political question very much like the question of who controls the public airwaves. Sexologist David Steinberg points out that most of us limit how much we fondle our partners in public, out of "respect" for those uncomfortable with others' sexuality. But, he asks, why does society agree that we have to accommodate the least erotically comfortable people? This trivializes the discomfort of more erotically comfortable people who are forced to repress themselves in public. Instead, why not have "fondlers" set the standards, and expect others to deal with their discomfort? Our culture assumes that repressed people's exposure to erotic activity is more painful (and therefore needs more protection) than non-repressed people's being prevented from expressing themselves erotically. Why?

Because we live in a sex-negative culture, many people want eroticism kept private throughout society. This is their social policy response to their individual discomfort, similar to institutionalizing personal racism via the social policy of apartheid.

By their very nature, some acknowledgements of sexuality are public— let's call these public-ized sexuality. These include, for example, sex education, contraceptive advertising, gay bars, nude beaches, and the rental availability of X-rated videos. When these exist, they are part of a community's public consciousness. Such activities declare that aspects of sex such as pleasure, self-expression, and high states of arousal are legitimate, are not shameworthy, and are an integral part of emotional life for one's fellow citizens.

When sexuality is brought into the public arena in this way, therefore, it threatens sex-negative people. It undermines their illusion of a cultural community's consensus in which they can feel safe. The very existence of this public-ized sexuality challenges the cherished belief that the community is not a sexual community, a pretense that sex-negative people need. By asserting that "everyone in this community is a sexual being, and that's OK," public-ized sex confronts and acknowledges everyone's desire, not just the desire of the consumers of a particular sexual activity.

For people who unconsciously feel, therefore, that their desire is illicit, public-ized sex makes them outlaws–even though they have not actually participated in the activities. For such people, the existence of public-ized sex by definition means they participate–without their consent. Their psychological defenses pierced, they now feel dirty and unsafe, and want to hide. This shame is a profound existential loss for them.

What is indecent about "indecent material" is that it transforms sex from private to public. When people say that sex education should be done only in the home, they mean it should be done without necessarily accepting sexuality, and, more importantly, without participating in any ongoing community acceptance of sex. When people oppose contraceptive advertising on TV–even on stations they don't watch, like MTV–they say, in effect, they don't want to live in a place in which people feel comfortable with such images on TV. They don't want little Jennifer asking questions. So in an erotophobic culture, it's indecent to provide a vehicle for people–and thus, the community–to accept and honor sexuality.

Some people claim a right to not be discomfited with regard to sex, a right that they don't claim in other arenas. They justify this on the grounds that since sex "should" be private and intimate, they shouldn't be forced to deal with the psychological impact of it being in the public sphere. But this is a phony reason. For example, society accepts an ongoing public display/dialogue about money, even though we all say that money is a private matter and that many people are uncomfortable with it.

We get an interesting insight when we see people making the same moral judgments about the depiction or discussion of an activity as they do about the activity itself. Some people equate, for example,

- pictures of sex=actual sex;
- a nude beach with sensual bodies=a beach with sexual bodies;
- ads for contraception=encouragement for non-reproductive sex, i.e., pleasure;
- enjoying a fantasy of taboo sex=desiring or doing taboo sex.

In fact, many people make worse moral judgments about depictions of sex, because the depiction implies an acceptance of the sexuality that the activity doesn't necessarily imply. That is, "it's bad enough that you're sexual–at least feel guilty about it, and therefore keep it private. Public-ized depictions of sex, on the other hand, mean you feel so good about it that you think it's OK to acknowledge it in public."

Censorship is a special case of sex-negativity. While sex-negativity is a judgment primarily applied to the individual's own life, censorship is an action-oriented, activist stance taking that judgment to a broader plane.

It says that the censor's sexuality requires a certain kind of cooperation in order to maintain itself in the less-threatening way s/he desires; or, to put it another way, that if others don't cooperate in creating a certain kind of psycho-socio-sexual environment, the censor will, inevitably, suffer from erotic self-consciousness and self-criticism. The censor fears having to deal with disturbing fantasies, the fear of losing control, sexual shame, and other frightening internal experiences. The censor may express this fear as concern for individual others ("we must help people who risk their health for casual sex") or for the community ("we must protect our adolescents from sex perverts"); the truth is, these are socially-acceptable motivations for what is really self-protection.

In the debate over whether a community, local or national, can allow sex to go public, most sexologists and progressives say that sex should be treated like all other classes of activity in a democracy—i.e., restricted only when there is a clear and present danger to some because of the behavior or options of others. It's hard to find this clear and present danger in, say, a nude beach or a Playboy channel, particularly if people who don't want to patronize such things have the option of staying away.

Would-be censors reply that there's something special about sexuality that requires special rules. But they only say this about certain kinds of eroticism—eroticism that accepts itself on its own terms, without the need to be bounded or redeemed.

Romance novels, for example—women's pornography, for sale in every supermarket in America—don't get censored even when sexually explicit. That's because 1) they make sex mysterious and illicit; 2) they uphold conventional morality by requiring that sex be redeemed by love, and 3) everyone pretends that readers are not having sexual fantasies. To the extent that the romance novel is a category of eroticism, it has the courtesy to not be too self-accepting about the sex.

Despite the huge number of readers, romance novels are actually "private-ized" rather than "public-ized" sex because they don't demand that the community redefine conventional sexuality, and they therefore do not require the community to "participate" in their use. The definition of "participate" is the key issue, because progressive say, "You don't like nude beaches, don't go to a nude beach." Censors say, "Having one in my town forces my psychological participation"—because its very existence challenges everyone's definitions of acceptable sexuality.

Censorship is aimed at material that is believed to be unspeakable, too private to be public. This betrays an erotic self-hatred which is not about real practical danger but about felt emotional danger. And that's why First Amendment or other logical arguments inevitably fail in disputing the appropriateness of censorship. In terms of the private-ized/public-ized dichotomy, sex-negative people are right—without institutionalized restrictions, they are forced to psychologically participate in kinds of sexuality that they don't like. The real question is, whose problem is that, and what should be considered acceptable solutions to it.

C. THE RESTIMULATION OF CHILDHOOD SEXUAL EXPLOITATION

We know that many children who are forced into sexual contact with adults suffer psychological and sexual problems. It's important that our society is finally looking at this reality.

One aspect of childhood sexual exploitation getting too little attention, however, is the residue of fear and anger being displaced onto a demonized sexuality. This internal psychological process is gaining increasing support as a public policy. Too many survivors and professionals are saying that sex is the problem. The enthusiastic support of the anti-sex Right is well-documented.

Many survivors fear pornography and other forms of sexual dialogue will somehow cause other children and adults to be exploited. The scientific data doesn't support that fear; as Dr. Mickey Diamond told us in yesterday's plenary, high-pornography-availability societies like Germany, Holland, Sweden, and Japan have much lower molest and rape rates than more restrictive societies like the U.S. and Ireland. Even the Meese Commission Report, on pages 951 and 975, said it could establish no causal link between pornography and anti-social behavior.

But I don't think truth is the important issue, because there's more going on here than reasoned judgments about what's dangerous. Many survivors of sexual exploitation are still in pain about past experiences that are restimulated in the present. And a crucial part of that experience is powerlessness. The residue of feeling is so powerful, and so close to the surface, that many survivors can be catapulted right back into the past simply by being exposed to something that reminds them of sexual powerlessness. I believe that the desire to avoid this experience motivates a great deal of censorship, consciously or unconsciously. Again, this is a public policy response to a private psychological need.

Once we understand the deep desire of survivors to avoid having their pain restimulated, we can see many reasons they would want to censor "unbounded" forms of sexual expression like pornography. Let's examine a few.

- The fantasy depictions of "limitless" sex—i.e., sex without constraints such as love or properness—can restimulate the true powerlessness of being coerced. Pornography actors are shown unprotected from lust, passion, and the urgent drive for satisfaction. To someone who has actually been victimized by irrationality in the past, this can be a painful reminder, even if exploitation is not being depicted.
- Pornography sometimes shows voluntary dominance and submission, depictions that can restimulate memories of true powerlessness in survivors of coercion. Would-be censors talk about "sex and violence" as a single category, wanting to eliminate such depictions. (Susie Bright sarcastically says the expression "sex and violence" makes her want to kill people who won't let her talk about sex.)

Additionally, many people who have been victimized simply can't imagine voluntarily submitting to domination, so they assume that any depictions of it are real, not fantasy.

- Many survivors still feel shame about having somehow invited the exploitation; seeing pornography actors inviting sex restimulates that shame. In restimulated pain, survivors forget that inviting sexuality can be an act of authentic sexual power and adulthood.

Actors are in control of their decision-making when they invite sex on-screen. Survivors have trouble grasping that, because they did not have such control at the time, and because what's being invited on-screen seems so much like what has caused so much pain in the past. Many survivors (and others) tend to over-identify with porn actors as human beings; there isn't enough suspension of disbelief. In contrast, no one talks about actors being exploited in *Rambo* or slasher films; in *Silence of the Lambs*, was Jodie Foster exploited because she had to deal with really terrifying stuff as part of making the film?

In talking about how these actors are allegedly exploited, survivors (and others) forget that they're on screen voluntarily, getting paid. Yes, porn actors are objects—they are choosing to be objects. The victim of childhood exploitation did not consent to being an object at the time. Survivors attempt to rid themselves of their shame by ridding actors of it.

We should be very sympathetic about the pain of those sexually exploited as children. Their pain renders living in a sexualized society, in a sexual body, a great challenge. But while we need to support these people in healing themselves, we should not do it by crippling or restricting society and other individuals. Helping people to protect themselves from danger that no longer exists isn't right, and it isn't helpful.

I also want to note the large number of professionals who do not help their survivor patients see that sex or lust is not the problem. This keeps the patients stuck as victims forever. Some professionals do this as an unconscious way of acting out their own sexual distress. Others do it as a cheap way of emphasizing that survivors are not to blame for what happened. I have a big quarrel with therapists who say that sexual trauma is the central, defining feature of a person's life. This does not do any patient a favor. Instead, we need to empower people by reminding each one: "you are bigger than your wound."

D. A FEW THOUGHTS ON AUTHENTIC SEXUALITY

Depictions of real eroticism kick up other feelings too, which some people simply don't want to deal with. Some depictions of lust represent sexuality that has the capacity to be revolutionary—that is, to challenge the personal, social, and political status quo. In this sense, it is rational for some people to fear it, and, therefore, to want to censor it. Thus, expressions of sexuality that are subject to censorship are those which:

- challenge traditional gender roles
- challenge the concept that sex is primarily for procreation
- empower people
- undermine authorities who define sexual normality
- challenge advertising based on creating sexual insecurity
- see sex as a positive force to expand our horizons

Contrast this to forms of sexual expression that are not subject to censorship, because they support society's status quo:

- romance novels
- Ken and Barbie dolls
- girls' heartthrob teen idol magazines
- titillating yet moralistic TV shows like *Dallas* and *Baywatch*
- slasher films
- the Miss America Pageant
- Sears underwear ads–because they're about being comfortable, not about being sexy

E. WHAT WE SHOULD DO

Let me end by suggesting what we should do about the psychological dynamics that drive the desire to censor or otherwise restrict sexual material.

- When discussing censorship, we need to talk about the fear of sexuality, not only about civil liberties or facts. We need to empower people to identify and deal with their fear of sexuality, and remind them of their inner resources. We should invite pro-censorship people to talk about their personal discomfort with sex. It can be uncomfortable to listen to–upsetting, sad, boring. But the more we can help these people acknowledge their personal pain, the easier it will be for them to listen, and to see that their comfort lies in personal solutions rather than public policy ones.

  Remember, most people are less interested in facts than in having their pain taken away. In his books *The Politics of Meaning* and *Surplus Powerlessness,* Michael Lerner has shown how talking about powerlessness can attract the support of people from a wide range of backgrounds and ideas. We can then talk about how fear should not be the basis of public policy.
- Demand that those exploited as children, as well as counselors and prosecutors, work through their anger. Confront their subtle or blatant concept that sexuality is the problem.

We should talk about the real sources of childhood exploitation: sexual repression, family power dynamics, alcoholism, poor anger management. As educator Sol Gordon says, "I've never heard of a molester with a healthy attitude toward masturbation." We must fight the idea that sex crimes result from sexual liberalism.

- Identify and discuss the difference between being the victim of someone's sexual acting out, vs. the healthy, voluntary relinquishing of control during sex. Talk about the consensual nature of erotic power play. Underline that temporarily relinquishing control during sex can be an act of power. It isn't something that a marginalized group of weirdos do—it's a mainstream sexual activity enjoyed by millions.
- Talk about the connection between censorship and opposition to sexuality-enhancing institutions like school sex education and legal contraception.
- Talk about how fantasy is not the same as desire. Sources as diverse as Robin Morgan and Bernie Zilbergeld remind us that all fantasy, even a rape fantasy, can be an act of power because we direct the scene, we create ourselves as an object of desire, and we control the access others have to us.
- Know the statistics on the large numbers of Americans who participate in sexuality-enhancing activities. For example,
  - ~ Every Gallup Poll since 1980 says that at least three-fourths of Americans approve of school sex education.
  - ~ 500 million X-rated videos were rented last year, one-half by couples or women.
  - ~ The majority of American Catholics (and all other American groups) use "artificial" contraception, and favor its availability.
- See sexual repression as a form of child abuse: teaching that masturbation is wrong, for example, or refusing to tell kids about menstruation or wet dreams, is as irresponsible as not teaching kids how to take care of their teeth.
- See full female sexuality, including lust, as a key part of the women's movement. Social scientist Leonore Tiefer notes that social restrictions on sexuality are typically aimed at the most culturally deviant expressions, which now include women's experimentation. Tiefer says censorship will ultimately allow only the most traditional types of sexuality, which will hurt women.

Sexual repression also hurts women by strengthening the Right. As Richard Enrico, the founder of Citizens Against Pornography, told me many years ago, "First we eliminate trash like *Playboy*, tomorrow filth like sex education, and eventually, abominations like homosexuality and birth control."

Those of us who trust sexuality must not allow ourselves to be controlled by those who fear it.

11

Censorship by Any Other Name

Yolanda Corduff

THE BIG "C" OF THE PUBLISHING WORLD MAY NOT BE A REFERENCE TO cancer but what it does refer to is just as insidious and just as deadly. Censorship or, as it's now defined in Australia, classification, has made a big come back in recent years, leading many people to question the value of our new classification system.

Some consider Australia a world leader when it comes to the classification of film and literature and it's easy to see why. Public interest, politicians and political correctness have culminated in new legislation, new standards and the formation of the OFLC–the Office for Film and Literature Classification.

Now in its tenth year of operation after replacing the Film Censorship Board of the 1980s, the OFLC is there to ensure film and literature is classified in a consistent manner that balances the rights of adults to "read, hear and see what they want" while protecting minors from "material likely to harm of disturb them." There are other considerations too like protecting everyone "from exposure to unsolicited material . . . they find offensive" and heeding community concerns about depictions condoning or inciting "violence, particulary sexual violence" and "portrayals of people in a demeaning manner."

These sound like reasonable objectives but how does it all work in practice? And what could we have forfeited in the process?

As a freelance journalist working in Australia, I have come to understand what classification really means to the publishing world. It's just another name for censorship, in particular self-censorship as practiced by Australian journalists and editors in an effort to avoid official censorship by the OFLC.

You may think that the OFLC is not responsible for decisions made by others to self-censor but think again. Self-censorship is a symptom of a much bigger problem that no one's talking about. The existence of the OFLC is reducing everyone's access to information as editors seek to comply with guidelines so ambiguous you could drive a truck through them, yet so restrictive you can never be sure what will pass and what won't. Yes, the new legislation has teeth and does bite so no one's keen to take on the OFLC and that's led to self-censorship.

How does self-censorship work?

First you ring an editor with a story idea. He or she mulls it over for a few moments then says something like, "The idea is good but we might have problems with censorship. A few years ago, a story like that was fine but you never know these days. Tell you what, write it up and we'll run it past our lawyers and see what happens. Now don't censor yourself, mind you, we'll do that for you once we see the piece."

Call me old-fashioned, but when I'm told something like that, I find it hard not to censor myself. I don't do it on purpose, it's just that the idea I should be "careful" stays with me. As I write, I'm thinking, will this be okay or should I cut it out. As I re-read and edit my work, I find myself looking for controversy to remove therefore ensuring I get the sale. After all, editors do and are rejecting articles of public interest every day based on fear of censorship.

My efforts to remain unaffected by thoughts of impending censorship are draining and futile. At the end of the day, I want the sale, I need the money, so I end up doing what it takes, we all do. That's the danger of self-censorship in a commercial environment, after all, no one wants to write great articles that are never published.

It's not just the written word that is being self-censored either. Photos and graphics are also being judged unsuitable for publication. Images that two years ago wouldn't be classed "offensive," are now.

For example, photos of female genitalia in over-the counter girlie magazines are now commonly doctored to changed their appearance with all detail carefully air-brushed away to avoid offense. The resulting image is unrealistic and deformed yet passed off as a photo many will interpret as "realistic." Women's magazines like *Cosmopolitan* and *Australian Women's Forum* prefer to avoid the issue altogether by not publishing "explicit" photos at all, even with articles that rely on them for educational purposes.

Take the recent case of the Australian women's magazine *Cleo* doing a feature on female genitalia. The article, provided in a sealed section within the magazine, discussed the confusion and distress many women experienced from lack of knowledge about how they should look.

"We'll show you what you're supposed to look like," the magazine promised but didn't deliver. While the article did provide some photos of the female anatomy, none were explicit enough or provided enough variety to truly give the readers the information they required. Any woman hoping to gain self esteem and confidence about her body from reading the article would have been sadly disappointed.

The tragedy of this case is that it's not even unusual. Australia's new classification system has led many publications to reconsider items that might not even be refused classification in a growing trend towards conservatism.

The OFLC would have us believe that when an article is not approved for general consumption, it may find a market in restricted publications, such as those sold in plastic covers (Restricted Category 1) and those sold in adult book shops or by mail order (Restricted Category 2).

Perhaps in an ideal world this would be true, but this is far from an ideal world.

Penthouse, Playboy and *Hustler* are all magazines that publish three different versions in Australia, one for each of the three classification categories. Aspiring journalists covering controversial issues often turn to these kinds of publications as an outlet for their work.

Unfortunately, the publishers of these magazines won't buy printed material specifically for the restricted versions of their magazines so articles that do not meet the standard of a general publication aren't published anywhere.

What all this means is that in practise, most Australian journalism is now targeted towards the lowest common denominator. In other words, if it's not likely to harm or disturb minors, it will be published while material of public interest that's only suitable for an adult audience is not.

So, in examining whether the OFLC has ensured their primary goal, that of allowing adults to read, hear and see what they want, I would have to argue they have fallen painfully short. Without specifically setting out to censor Australia's publishing industry, the OFLC has certainly achieved that gain.

Perhaps this is not such a great burden if the other goals of the OFLC have been met. So have they?

Are minors really being protected from material likely to harm or disturb them? Only if they live in a vacuum where they don't watch television, surf the Internet or see TV advertising. I say this because all of the above are not covered by the OFLC's classification guidelines and would certainly not meet their standards, should they be applied. Nevertheless, all are highly visible, common-place and likely to be seen by minors in greater numbers and greater frequency than film or literature that is classified.

For example, *Kia Mentor* is a new brand and model of car being advertised on Australian television at present. Their ad is certainly eye catching as we watch a leather and fishnet clad mistress dominating her subservient, leather-bound male partner, declaring they like to "stand out." The *Kia Mentor* therefore being a car that allows you to stand out. This advertisement is played regularly, at all time slots, and, while not offensive in nature, certainly exploits the ideas of kinky fetishes, demeaning others and sex and violence.

By comparison, an informative and well-researched article on B&D professionals, without pictures or graphics, was recently turned down by "gun-shy" *Penthouse*.

"The lawyers say we'll never get it past the OFLC," says the disappointed editor, self-censorship rearing its ugly head again.

Why the double standard?

Television advertising in Australia is governed by a comprehensive code of practise endorsed by the ABA, that's the Australian Broadcasting Authority, and tested by advertisers intent on pushing the limits further. Ads like the *Kia Mentor* are only pulled from air if enough written complaints are made to the

TV stations and the ABA. I call this the re-active approach to censorship, that which actually offends is removed as a consequence of public complaints.

The OFLC, on the other hand, takes a pro-active approach. That is to say, publishers and film makers must first submit their work for "classification" and, in the process, censorship or "RC–refused classification" if their material is deemed unsuitable for Australians to view or access.

So while the OFLC doesn't aim to censor, it clearly does since the same topics, images and information that can be viewed on television, on the internet and in advertising can't be seen in print or in films. This indicates the OFLC's guidelines are not representative of the "standards of morality, decency and propriety generally accepted by reasonable adults" since controversial subject matter is regularly viewed without complaints on other mediums.

The OFLC is also responsible for protecting everyone "from exposure to unsolicited material that they find offensive," an almost impossible task from the way it's worded. How can any organisation or person hope to determine what "everyone" will find offensive?

For example, I consider doctoring photo's of the human body and passing them off as real most offensive. The OFLC has not only failed to protect me from this kind of material, it's encouraged the existence of such material. With the variety of tastes, cultures, sexualities and taboos in existence in the cultural melting pot that is Australia, very little material is universally acceptable or offensive.

Finally, does the OFLC take into account community concerns about "depictions that condone or incite violence, particularly sexual violence; and the portrayal of persons in a demeaning manner"? It certainly tries to but again, this is so open to interpretation that mostly it's used to censor otherwise acceptable material. After all, there's no specific community mandate on such issues so the OFLC must draw its conclusion from the personal experiences of their staff and other representatives' and the assumptions they make about the rest of us.

Unfortunately, a proactive censorship process can never be representative of the general community. To be proactive by definition means to presume what will offend rather than find out what actually does.

In the end, the OFLC's decisions are only a reflection of their staff's personal viewpoints, and then only those they were comfortable expressing publicly.

These are not decisions that will protect everyone from unsolicited offensive material. Nor are they decisions guaranteed to protect our children from material likely to harm or disturb them.

They are, however, decisions that will ensure censorship and self-censorship continue to thrive in Australia for years to come.

12

Sex Fights Back:
How to Succeed in Politics
Without Being Elected

Fiona Patten

INTRODUCTION

I N AUSTRALIA THE "P" WORD MEANS TWO THINGS. PORN AND POLITICS.
For the purposes of this discussion I define pornography as sexually explicit material designed to titillate rather than educate and containing no violent actions or language.

When Australians read the word "pornography" in their daily newspaper these days, it is invariably followed by a political commentary of one kind or another. In many ways this has been the outstanding success of Australia's sex industry association—the Eros Foundation.

Within a decade, Eros has managed to force the issue of explicit sex into the corridors of Parliament House and the offices of the senior Ministers of the day.

For many Australian politicians, dealing with the sex industry's association is now no different from dealing with the Motor Trades Association.

Calls to the Federal Attorney General's office are returned within forty-eight hours by his Senior Advisor, bimonthly meetings with the Prime Minister's Senior Advisor were a feature of our 1997 diary and monthly lunches with our state Premier have been a permanent fixture for over two years.

And against all odds, Australia's sex industry recently caused the most conservative Prime Minister in years to direct his Cabinet to create a new category for sexually explicit films and videos—Non Violent Erotica (NVE).

With once-progressive countries like Sweden now turning back the clock and banning commercial sex and old stalwarts like China still executing pornographers, there is an urgent need for sex industry associations and free speech groups around the world to develop better political strategies. Global communications means world markets are within the reach of all traders in adult erotica. You think that European markets are important to annual profit and loss sheets? Try thinking about China, Indonesia and India.

The challenge of the next ten years is to borrow and adapt the political strategies of those countries where the sex industry has been successful in lobbying governments and adapt them to those countries who are still having problems.

EARLY ATTITUDES TO SEX

Australia's attitudes to sex are largely imported from "mother" England. Along with the Westminster style of government, Australia's early politicians learned how to instinctively react to questions of sexual politics with what has been described by one popular writer as "visceral clutch"–an instinctive form of self-denial born of guilt and ignorance and involving genital grasping, breath retention and wild gesticulation!

These early attitudes were modified by waves of European immigration in the 1950s, which romanticized and freed up the traditional English attitudes to sex. Australia's warm climate, its open spaces and proximity to beaches have also had a strong influence on morality.

When you combine this with a fairly laconic attitude to social issues in general, it's no wonder that a dozen national opinion polls taken over the last decade in Australia have revealed a strong 75 percent support for sexually explicit media.

Some say this is also the result of Australia being colonized by convicts, as opposed to the Puritans who colonized the U.S. and the barbarians who colonized the U.K.

OPPOSITION TO PORNOGRAPHY

But this has still not stopped a very small but well-organized minority from spoiling everyone else's fun. In 1984, the British moral's campaigner, Mary Whitehouse, joined the Reverend Fred Nile in successfully banning X-rated videos in all states of Australia bar two. In the late 1980s a U.S. fundamentalist Christian and ex-McDonald's manager, Jack Sonneman, immigrated to Australia and gave us our first taste of Southern Baptist politics. He quickly toured another U.S. anti-porn campaigner, Judith Reisman, as a lead up to a major assault on X-rated videos in 1988.

The Dworkin/McKinnon school of feminist fundamentalism has major enclaves in two Australian universities. Although impotent in the lobbying process, they nonetheless provide some feminist politicians with timely arguments and the moral courage to enter the pornography debate from time to time.

The most interesting opposition to pornography in Australia of recent times though, has come from the gun lobby. There have been three major shooting massacres in Australia over the past decade and after each one, the Shooters Party and other gun lobbyists have immediately blamed the tragedies on X-rated videos. This response has been a calculated one by shooters and has back-fired on them with far-reaching gun controls being enacted by the Federal Government, almost at the same time as the government agreed to more liberal pornography laws.

CURRENT LAWS ON
SELLING PORNOGRAPHY

Australia's laws on "pornography" are basically contained within one Federal Act of Parliament known as the Classification Act.

It describes a number of different 'categories' of films, videos, publications and computer games, which basically represent degrees of sexual explicitness – although they are also affected by levels of violence and profane language. (Outlines of the system are available for conference participants to study.) It does not include free to air or pay television, nor does include material published on line.

This is not a voluntary system nor is it regulated by the entertainment industry that it serves. The federal government provides a number of trained censors (pornographers by another name) who look at a video master or magazine mock-up before it is sold and give it an official rating. The current cost of this service to industry is approximately U.S. $400 per X-rated video and approximately U.S. $75 per magazine. If you don't sell your product according to the regulations covering that particular category or if you sell it without getting it classified to begin with, the state's police force can bust you with jail sentences of up to two years and fines of U.S. $26,000 per offense.

Each of Australia's eight States and Territories have different laws regarding which parts of the Federal Classification scheme they adopt. This system has meant that the retail sale of X-rated videos is only legal in two states and in only one of these can you actually duplicate large numbers of X-rated videos. Each state also has differing rules for publications though not as varied as here in the U.S.

However, Australia's Constitution is such that it permits the sale of a product that is legal in one state, to be legally mailed into any other state. This Constitutional protection has led to the establishment of a national mail order system in X-rated product from the Australian Capital Territory—the home of the Eros Foundation.

SEX INDUSTRY SPIN DOCTORS

Through the 1980s Australia's X-rated video industry ran political and media campaigns to stop numerous attempts to ban its products at a federal level under the banner of the Adult Video Industry Association, AVIA. It won battle after battle. But by the early 1990s the industry knew that unless it structured a new and long term industry association, it could kiss a lot of sexually explicit media goodbye.

Our first task was to try unite all the different ends of the Australian sex industry under one banner. This was seen to make the best use of all possible resources. It meant that pornographers had to get into bed with sex workers, as well as table top dancers, magazine publishers, condom manufacturers, phone sex services and many others.

At this point I was running a sex worker outreach program and joined up with AVIA's lobbyist Robbie Swan to help form the new super sexual Coalition to be known as the Eros Foundation, so named after the Greek God of love and lust.

As it turned out, I not only grabbed the Presidency of this new group but I grabbed the lobbyist as well and we have been in our own little association alongside the bigger political one, for as many years now.

Seriously, this was an important step in putting a united front to governments and politicians. They clearly wanted to talk to a group that represented the whole of the sex industry and not just one segment of it.

From a distance, it would appear that in the U.S. and in some European countries there is a reluctance for the different ends of the sex industry to unite. From our experience, politicians see this as "division" and a sign of weakness and we would advise all industry lobby groups to look more favorably on this sort of amalgamation.

With new technologies our industry cannot be so easily defined into individual streams. Phone sex services are now providing intimate online conversations with pictures. Brothels are setting up on line services so that sex workers can chat with clients and show them pictures and videos of themselves. At this point are they sex workers or porn stars? The only real answer is, of course, "It doesn't matter."

On line magazines often have moving pictures. Are they publications or films? Traditional geographical borders are also blurred. State lines and even national borders mean nothing in cyberspace and our politicians are increasingly ignorant in this area.

Most politicians in western style democracies are middle-aged men who are not confident with their computer abilities and feel very much out of their depth when debating regulation of the new sex industry. They have enough trouble speaking about sex in their own lives, let alone sex and new technologies. This technological revolution is bringing all aspects of the global sex industry to a much more common ground and it is logical that the industry itself should present to government as a united front.

ARMING OURSELVES FOR BATTLE

Over the last decade the Australian sex industry has commissioned a dozen national community opinion polls using the same pollsters that the major political parties used at election times. Although expensive to conduct, these polls have consistently shown legislators that there is a strong but silent 75 percent support for non-violent erotica or pornography.

Because Eros has cultivated a good and personal relationship with many journalists in the Australian Press Gallery (equivalent to the White House Press Corps) these polls generally get page 3 coverage in the quality newspapers.

The effect of this is hard to quantify but we believe that it has been very successful in letting members of the public know that they are not alone out there in suburbia in buying X-rated videos or hardcore Category 2 Restricted magazines. This, in turn, gives people the confidence to write letters to the editor, to call radio stations, to tackle politicians, and so forth.

Paid advertising, as a means of lobbying or getting a message across appears to be a total waste of money for us in Australia and has even been damaging. Most Australians assume that the sex industry is incredibly wealthy and paid large advertisements just confirm the "throw money at it" approach favored by wealthy corporate "thieves."

The most successful and far reaching lobbying tool that Eros has developed has been the irrefutable demonstration of the large numbers of people who buy via mail order sexually explicit material and the threat that the sex industry is prepared to use such a large mailing list against particular politicians and political parties at election times.

In the run up to the last federal election Eros decided that there was little point in trying to change the mind of conservative opposition leader John Howard about his thirteen-year pledge to ban X-rated videos, if he ever became prime minister.

Instead, we began a campaign to have the conservatives adopt a more restricted video category called Non Violent Erotica which would contain only "vanilla" sexual depictions.

We then hatched a plan, that I will describe in my workshop session, to create a map of X-rated video watchers in Australia that would show up to 14 percent of some federal electorates as regular buyers of X-rated videos.

We took this map to the political party bosses and told them that if they would not agree to the new adult video category, we would mail the entire list, urging people to vote against them. We had done this in the past with startling results.

With a little more arm-twisting, they agreed and eighteen months later and in government for the first time in thirteen years, they stayed true to their word and adopted the NVE category.

OTHER POLITICAL STRATEGIES

Eros has its offices strategically located within a mile of Parliament House. We ensure that at least one of our team has an unrestricted access pass into Parliament House.

We make sure that we have at least one lunch or dinner date per month with a member of Parliament.

We regularly send quality X-rated videos into the State and Federal Parliaments whenever the opportunity arises–they rarely say no or send them back.

A few years ago when a threatened ban on X-rated videos loomed, we sat down and matched up Government Ministers and their portfolios with popular X-rated videos and sent them off.

The Treasurer got the 1980s classic *Liquid Assets*, the Foreign Affairs Minister got *Lust on the Orient Express* and the Leader of the redneck farmer's party received a copy of *An Unnatural Act.*

The story was front page on every major newspaper the next day and politicians laughed and joked about "pornography" on the six o'clock news that night. We won that battle, with the Senate voting down the ban on X videos the next day and the value of humour indelibly edged into our campaign agenda thereafter.

The fall of morals campaigners and the rising numbers of pedophile priests have given us a focus for letter-writing to the major daily newspapers and we are now starting to see large numbers of the general public pick up this line of argument whenever the church or religious groups attack us in the media. This has taken a couple of years of persistent letter-writing but in the end it has paid off.

We have also pushed the idea of the emergence of a new psychological disease in Western countries known as the Swaggart Syndrome, in honor of your wonderful campaigner Jimmy Swaggart.

We have promoted the fact that when public figures get up and take an unusually hard line on sexual or moral issues, that in all likelihood they are trying to assuage their own guilt in some sexual matter. We even wrote a formal letter to the peak government health authority in Australia, the National Health and Medical Research Council, asking them to formally investigate this new "disease" in public figures.

It is the persistence in making claims like these, that eventually wins public support.

Whether a prostitute is stoned to death in Iran or an X-rated video producer jailed in Mississippi, the discrimination, the bias and the blatantly political attitudes of those who condemn both of them are the real enemies of the sex industry.

We urgently need a United Nations of Sex, an Amnesty International for the release of pleasure-prisoners, and a World Bank of Love to help struggling sexual economies in the third world.

The future of the sex industry is to that half of the world's population who are currently forbidden to see it.

13

Sex, Pornography, and Religion: From Sodom to Corinth to the San Fernando Valley

Miss Charlie Latour

I WAS BLESSED TO BE THE DAUGHTER OF A PROFOUNDLY INTELLIGENT MAN, a man who dedicated his life to Jesus Christ and the most disadvantaged in our society. He, like his denominational founder, Martin Luther, had great concerns for the outside influence on the interpretations of Scriptures. My father was a scholar, who studied ancient Greek so he could better understand the words of the original texts and what they meant. He influenced me in a manner that has allowed me to pursue my beliefs in sexual freedom while maintaining my strong Christian faith. Understanding why some deeply religious people, Christians, Jews, Moslems and secular, anti-sex feminists project a sexual pessimism can help us better protect our sexuality and individual freedoms, while respecting their cultural and philosophical beliefs. I will state now that I am not a religious scholar. I do not come before you offering anything which is startling or new. What I offer is my view from both worlds. I have lived in the world of sexual permissiveness, where licentious behavior is the norm and at the same time I have maintained and actively participated in my religious beliefs, as well as, my secular pro-sex, pro-female ideals. The purpose of my presentation is to draw a line from Antiquity and the Old Testament, through the New Testament and tying it to the sexual pessimism we face today. From Sodom to Corinth to the San Fernando Valley, people have faced a humanly induced sexual pessimism and unless we understand the historical basis or rationale behind the pessimism we will continue to be repressed by it.

What, might you ask, does this have to do with the current rage against sex in general and pornography is particular? Simply, it is my firm belief that if you understand the history and reason for an action you can better understand those promoting and defending those actions. In logical form if you understand the actions of those who oppose you there is a greater likelihood that you can effectively counter their influence. While religious zealots gain the vast majority of media exposure in our current society for their puritanical anti-sex philosophy the secularists, who have been influenced by Stoicism and Gnosticism, are in many cases far more dangerous in a society founded on the separation of church and state. Ours is such a society and we are being seriously challenged in our basic right of freedom of person.

Why our society is so pessimistic about sexuality and why certain elements in our society go to great lengths to hide or eliminate sexuality are questions that need historically accurate and complete explanations. In this case, we have to look at the most distant dates and work methodically up to our current situation. Sexual pessimism, the philosophical and religious thought which so permeates our society predates the birth and growth of Christianity. The first record of sexual pessimism goes as far back as the sixth century before Christ when Pythagoras expounded on the negative health consequences associated with sex. Plato, Aristotle, and Hippocrates all believed that the sexual act was dangerous, draining the man of his energy. Of course, in typical fashion, sex never affected women. After all, to these men, women provided nothing but a receptacle for their pleasure. Therefore, the societal trend against sex and the concomitant pessimism predates modern events, including the dreaded Meese Commission Report.

There are two very important, intersecting philosophical and religious schools of thought which guide our sexual identity into the twenty-first century. The first is the hideous and thoroughly degrading philosophical analysis of sex as developed and promoted by the Stoa, by far the most influential school of ancient philosophy. This school of thought was at its zenith from 300 B.C. to A.D. 250. It is from this body of thought that we get the word "Stoic" which means passionless behavior. The Stoics rejected pleasure, sex and marriage.

Their philosophy elevated celibacy to a higher plane than marriage. The historically significant Stoic philosopher, Seneca, professed that we should "do nothing for the sake of pleasure" and said that "nothing is more depraved than to love one's spouse as if she were an adulteress." Notice the trend of meeting reproductive needs but vilifying the woman as a dangerous pleasure object. This will crop up again and again. The second was a modifying religious movement that came from the East, probably Persia, called Gnosticism. This movement attempts to undermine the idea of the existence of good by claiming to have recognized the worthlessness of life. Gnosticism was the counter-culture movement of the early Christian church. It drew upon religious symbols from Persia, Babylon, as well as the Greek, Jewish and Christian beliefs. This religious philosophy preached abstinence from marriage, meat and wine. Gnosticism had a major influence on Christianity during the early stages of the church, but it found a way to effect Judaism, which had, until this stage, rejected most ascetic lifestyles. We are just now finding out the full impact of Gnosticism since the discovery in 1946 of an entire library of Gnostic literature near Nag Hammadi in upper Egypt. These two movements combined to repress sexuality more than any other single event in the history of man.

The sexual pessimism of today manifests itself in a myriad of ways. In each and every way the roots extend back to either the philosophy of Stoa or to the Gnostic religious movement of the second century. Much of the interpretation of religious Scriptures is influenced by these schools of thought. Prior to Christianity the dominant Greek and Jewish cultures interfaced with varying degrees of cross culture influence. The development of Stoicism in Greece had a profound influence on the lifestyle of the inhabitants and their negative sexual interactions with women. Judaism's cultural traditions of subordination of women when interfaced with the Greek Stoicism compounded sexual thought. A singular good and kind God was the basis of Judaism. Stoicism, a philosophy not a religion, allowed the Jewish people to maintain their belief in a singular good and kind God, while enhancing cultural traditions. It was Philo of Alexandria who had the greatest influence in this cross cultural exchange. He was a Jewish-Greek philosopher who lived at the time of Christ. After the crucifixion of Christ and up until the fourth century this blend of Jewish tradition and Greek Stoic philosophy began to parallel the early Christian philosophy. Since people of good will always try to seek areas of agreement these non-conflicting philosophies of the Stoic/Jewish group and the Gnostic/Christian group were the genesis for the growth in the pessimistic anti-sex atmosphere, particularly as we see it in the dominant Judeo-Christian American culture.

In the Old Testament, women held a much lower status than men. A prime example is the prohibition on adultery, as stated in the Old Testament. "Thou Shall Not Commit Adultery" had a different meaning for men. It was common belief that adultery for a man was sex with another man's wife. To a woman, it was sex with anyone besides her husband. It all has to do with possessions. A woman was a man's possession, therefore, defiling her was devaluing his possession. In other words, a married man could have sex with any unmarried woman without being accused of adultery. More evidence can easily be found in the Old Testament that open the gates to the sexual pessimism projected by the Stoics and Gnostics. The Harlot at Tim'nath and Sodom are some of the most vivid. In all of my studies, the story that brings the pessimism so vividly to life is the story of the Rape of the Levite's Concubine (Judges 19:1-30). In fact, before and at the time of Christ, except for the Qumran sect, polygamy was rampant in Jewish society. Jesus' teachings challenged the patriarchal system. The followers of Christ you read about were predominately men. Noting their cultural traditions with women you can better understand the disagreements they must have had over this, a cultural right handed down from generation to generation. Jesus, in the embodiment of man, was a Jew, so he understood the cultural traditions. I believe this is why He was so effective in his teachings.

I had mentioned earlier the Jewish sect at Qumran, known since Antiquity, as Essenes. This sect was geographically headquartered near the area where Jesus taught. During the second century, Gnostic influence altered this powerful Jewish group which had already been influenced significantly by Stoic philosophy. They emphasized the rejection of sex, marriage and pleasure, donned a self doubting and pessimistic religious viewpoint which allowed them to easily intermingled with the growing early Christian church. The great Jewish historian, Josephus wrote about the Jews of Essenes in The Jewish Wars II, . . . "they are . . . convinced that no woman is true to her husband." Here it can be noted a blending of the cultural Jewish tradition of a lower status for women with the sexual pessimism as projected both by the Stoics, which had already influenced this important Jewish community, and the Gnostics, which followed in the second century. This historical significant evidence provides a roadmap for understanding how the integration of the Stoic philosophy into basic Jewish culture was accomplished, why the overlapping of Gnostic influence in the Qumran sect was a natural and significant occurrence and how these events ultimately influenced the growth of anti-sexual Christian thought and theology.

Equality of partners was one of the most difficult parts of Jesus' teachings for the local population to understand. The Jewish tradition of a lower status for women and the shamefulness and unhealthfulness of sexuality, as projected by the Stoics was countered by Jesus. First, Jesus treated women with dignity and respect. There are many accounts of Jesus speaking with women when in traditional Jewish culture this was considered shameful and punishable. Jesus, upon his resurrection first appeared to a woman, who thereupon went to the men and told them of his rise from the dead. In all of my studies of Jesus, I can not find one shred of evidence, other than that which has been interpreted by sexually negatively influenced individuals for the purposes of philosophical reasons, where He projects a sexual pessimism. On the contrary, His positive relationship with women and his direct teachings (those directly and indisputably attributed to Him) give no hint at pessimism. But it was not long after his crucifixion that the sexual pessimism was instituted by the leaders of the Christian movement. The Gnostic influences of the second century are profound and long lasting. Changes occurred in text, not only the New Testament but the Old Testament, as well. Jerome, who in the late third and fourth century translated the Bible into Latin (the Vulgate) actually altered the language to elevate the concept of virginity to a religious symbol. He changed the meaning of some of the Old Testament by deleting statements which were not consistent with his Gnostic views. Celibacy, a state thought of long before Christianity, was not a belief of Jesus. He never spoke of celibacy. What he did speak about was the need for kindness and respect and what an ideal marriage was. He was misquoted and re-interpreted by celibate clergy, thereby justifying their Gnostic and hypocritical views and place in heaven.

To continue a reasonable line of logical thought you need to accurately follow the actions and words of those who followed Jesus and continued to interpret his teachings. The most visible and controversial was Saul of Tarsus, the persecutor, who became Paul the apostle to the Gentiles. This educated man studied Jewish law with the great rabbi Gamaliel in Jerusalem. The influence of his Jewish heritage and that of the Stoics is unmistakable. When confronted with difficult theological problems I

believe Paul would fall back on this background because he drew comfort
from it. To avoid the difficulty in addressing all of Paul's work, which I feel
others are more competent to do, I want to maintain my focus on the reasons why we have so much sexual pessimism today. To do this we need to
focus on I Corinthians, written in A.D. 55, which came at the end of Paul's
three-year ministry in Ephesus. When you evaluate the writings of other
church scholars who followed Paul you find that they use this letter most frequently when discussing sexual issues. Corinth was an important city, with
major implications in the area of commerce and trade. There were two
patron deities, Poseidon, god of the sea, which was obvious because of the
seafaring nature of the city, and Aphrodite, goddess of sexual love. The
temple of Aphrodite was central to her worship and boasted one thousand
female prostitutes available to citizens of the city and all visitors. This made
Corinth a very popular place to visit and live. The growth of the Christian
church in this city was beset with problems, not the least of which was the
inability or unwillingness of the local church leadership to deal with issues
of morality. Since Paul had started the church in Corinth he maintained
close ties to it. The reports and rumors he was hearing about Corinth presented him with problems so he took the opportunity to answers questions
put to him by the Corinthians and also to address issues of concern to him.
The point where I have parted with many theologians is in the meaning of
his writings. There is no doubt that the letter was a letter of pastoral theology
not doctrinal theology. There is a big difference. In a pastoral letter the
pastor, in this case Paul, attempts to interpret for the situation, rather than
just state what Jesus has said. In this manner you begin to see Paul's background begin to seep into his work. A very close analysis of the sections on
morality and sexuality indicate a Stoic influence, not unlike the later Gnostic
influence that would invade the writings of Augustine and Thomas Aquinas.
Brilliantly he chose the issue of incest which was particularly disliked by
Jews, Christians, Greek Stoics and most pagans. By using incest to make his
point he chose a topic that would offend the fewest people and gain the
broadest support. In this decision he was right. But he begins to broaden his
attack on sexuality in areas which have little, if any relevance, to Jesus'
teaching. His writings on sexuality in and outside of marriage show his
strong ties to his Jewish background and the influence the Stoics had on
him. Many Gnostic leaders in the second century say they draw their philosophy from Paul. To this day some theologians believe that Paul was the
founder of the Gnostic movement. But in reality Paul was faced with a difficult task. On one hand he had a fledgling church that was composed of the
broadest possible spectrum of people, each bringing some previous teaching
with them. To some of them the interest in Aphrodite was purely sexual and
they did not want to give up their sexuality. To combat the pleasure seeking
nature of Aphrodite, Paul felt compelled to offer his pastoral thoughts, not
doctrinal teachings. This is critical to any logical line of thought about how
we have gotten from there to here. It was the writings in I Corinthians that
activated the Gnostic beliefs in those who followed Paul. The evolving

sexual pessimism draws support from this one letter. There is little doubt that Paul, called by some as the greatest apostle of all, had more influence in the development of the Christian church than any one person. These are Paul's pastoral interpretation not Christ's teachings. Unlike his other letters, such as Galatians and Romans, which were doctrinal in context, I Corinthians was truly a pastoral letter.

The man most responsible for the dislike of sex within the Christian community was Augustine during the fourth century. But he did something that forever changed the willingness of most Christians to pursue their sexuality. A basic tenet of Christianity is redemption. We, as Christians, can been redeemed and therefore enter the Kingdom of Heaven. Therefore, most Christian spend their entire lives seeking redemption. Take that away and a Christian has no hope, no eternal life, no salvation. Augustine knew this so he tied his personal hatred for sexuality to original sin, that sin that may forever place you in a position of outcast. The process was now started to have the church proclaim that sexuality was the road to hell, not because God the Father or Jesus spoke of such, but because hypocritical men choose for God the way to separate the loyal from the disloyal. He blended the one good God with the sexual pessimism of Gnostics, not unlike the Jewish sect at Qumran. This explains why today, religious zealots will tell you of God's forgiveness while telling you that you are evil if you like sex. To Augustine, marriage was more of a duty than a partnership, in stark contrast to Jesus' teachings. Having children, or procreation was noble, yet sexual pleasure was evil. This dichotomy has led to a form of sexual schizophrenia. To have children you need to have sex, but you should not enjoy what you are doing. This was very similar to the Stoic philosophy of previous centuries. At the same time as Augustine there was a Catholic bishop by the name of Julian. He was a married priest from Pelagian. He had a very positive attitude towards sexuality. He looked upon sexuality as a positive part of life given by the grace of God. He lost his battle with Augustine and was eventually excommunicated and considered by some to be a heretic. Julian's sixth sense of sexual desire would be lost forever and the "sin" of sexuality institutionalized within the church body. Augustine elevated the pleasure of sex to a sin so evil that even God could not redeem you.

This trend continued through the Early Scholasticism period of the twelth and thirteenth century. Thomas Aquinas was a shining example of this period, but he took the anti-sexuality theme even further. He wrote that any sexual position, other than the missionary position, was an unnatural act and sinful, worse than having sex with your mother, incest, rape and adultery. Included in these unnatural acts were masturbation, homosexuality, anal and oral sex. Remember Paul's letter to the Corinthians where he used incest as a coalescing point, Aquinas took the next step. The Gnostic religious elite were now in the business of determining the level of evil with different sex acts. Jesus never spoke of oral sex, why should he! Not until Martin Luther was there any ray of hope for sexuality. This is not to say that Luther was a libertine, but his doctrine of justification did loosen the noose on sexuality. To Luther you attained redemption through "faith alone" and, therefore, you were not always committing sins. But as with all movements the Protestant reformation developed offshoots which again brought the Gnostic philosophy front and center. The Puritan movement was extremely Gnostic in the Augustinian way. As the Puritans found themselves under attack in England and on the European continent they moved to the new world. With them they brought the Gnostic sexual pessimism with them. In fact, it became a form of blood sport to find the person who did not meet their artificial standards. America became the focus of immigrants bringing with them their own form of philosophical and religious beliefs. The three religious groups who have had the most impact on American sexual behavior have been the Gnostic Puritanized Protestants, the Gnostic Celibate Catholics and the Stoic Jews. By following the line from Antiquity to modern day America you can readily see why we face a growing number of problems associated with sexual pessimism. To the pessimists the adult industry is a foretelling of the end times, the end of man brought about by a God, who neither legislated sexuality, nor banished it. A God who created man in His image, including His sexual being.

Now what do we do? Hopefully we better understand why the religious zealots and the secular anti-sex feminists are such pessimists. But this still does not solve the problem. What are we missing? Like many other forms of study, theology can be subject to intensive and overbearing scrutiny. By studying something too much scholars have a habit of discovering what does not exist. The Gnostic tendency or the Stoic influence will manifest itself in the area of study because it adds a new avenue. What I have attempted to do is to avoid the buffet approach to the Bible and other sacred texts. People will tend to pick and choose what they like and what the don't like. I believe those who re-interpreted the Bible did exactly that all throughout history. They chose to eliminate certain statements or add certain statements so that their point of view could be made. What God did not speak of in the Old Testament, or what Jesus did not preach about in the New Testament was added by those who felt compelled to do so. From my study and my own analysis the sexual pessimism that is pervasive in our society today is a direct result, not of God's intention, or of Jesus' preaching, but of the influences of the Greek Stoics and the Gnostic philosophy. But how do you overcome this effect. We are talking about thousands of years of changes and billions of people who are believers in one form or another.

The first step to be unashamed of what you believe. Whether you are Jewish, Christian or Moslem you can read your own texts and evaluate their meaning based on the knowledge of the historical events that took place at that time. I know I am an unashamed Christian. I understand my lineage because I believe in the Creation. I am a believer in salvation through faith alone and nowhere can I find that my sexuality or gender will render me sinful or unworthy of redemption. From Sodom to Corinth to the San Fernando Valley the history of sexual pessimism can be traced not to God but to man. Yes, there is right and wrong, yes, there is a proper way to do things.

Yes, you must at all time respect a person and their beliefs (or lack thereof). But none of these common and logical conditions of life limit what God has given to me. I truly believe that I have been made in the image of the Lord. I have come to believe that my sexuality has set me free to understand the kind, gentle and rewarding preaching of Jesus Christ. Sexual pessimism is like a jail that imprisons your spirit. Staying away from sexual pessimism is staying free. Much like the Negro spiritual, made so famous by the wonderful speech by Dr. Martin Luther King Jr.: "Free, Free at Last, Thank God Almighty, I'm Free at Last."

14

America Unchained:
Tattoos, Piercings, and Porn

Maureen Mercury

THE BODY AS SOULSCAPE

A DISCUSSION OF BODY AS LANDSCAPE OF EXPERIENCE MUST BE PRE-ceded by an exploration of the ensouled flesh. This is our canvas. I believe soul is grounded in the body as the body is grounded in soul. Hillman (1972), beautifully captures the essence of the word soul saying:

> Not a diamond but a sponge, not a private flame but a flowing participa-tion, a knotted complexity of strands whose entanglements are also "yours" and "theirs." The collective nature of the soul's depths means simply that no man is an island. (24)

This collectivity is the soul of the culture. Loss of soul, loss of connectedness to sensate body, is a collective loss. The individual is the "identified patient" of a culture in conflict.

How does the pathology of this "patient" manifest in the world? It appears as literalizing and concretizing attempts at soul-making. Hillman (Ibid.) explains, "We act out not only by running away into concrete life; we act out equally in the flight upward into the abstractions of metaphysics, higher philosophies, theologies, even mysticism. The soul loses its psycho-logical vision in the abstract literalisms of the spirit as well as in the concrete literalisms of the body" (137). What we are seeing in the burgeoning cultural trends of tattooing, piercing and consumption of pornographic materials, is humankind's quite human attempt to connect to individual and world soul through core sensations. Sadly, what has happened, in most cases, is that in this unconscious frenzy for connectedness, through the literalizing of the body, a lesser coniunctio experience is attained. Thus, after one has fallen

174

into mortificatio and putrefactio realms, one attempts, through the same means of acting in or acting out, to reach a greater coniuctio. A feedback loop of failure is assured each time.

The possibility of changing this pattern lies in ritual. Engagement in the "ritual" of initiation, loving, performance, prayer, require concrete actions: these ritualized actions holding much more than they literally seem to be. Hillman (Ibid.) continues, "Ritual offers a primary mode of psychologizing, of deliteralizing events and seeing through them as we 'perform' them. As we go into a ritual, the soul of our actions 'comes out'; or to ritualize a literal action, we 'put soul into it'. . . . Ritual brings together action and idea into an enactment" (p. 137).

This enactment then moves the initiate into sacred space and offers, at the least, the possibility of the pre-conditions of separation, and at the most, the chance for transformative experience.

Ritual brings the flesh body into soul, and soul into flesh. This body, the body that is tattooed, the body that is pierced, and the body that fornicates or is voyeur to fornication, through ritualization may become "subtle body." Hillman (Ibid) explains:

> . . . the moment we realize body also as a subtle body—a fantasy system of complexes, symptoms, tastes, influences and relations, zones of delight, pathologized images, trapped insights—then body and soul lose their borders, neither more literal or metaphorical than the other. Remember: the enemy is the literal, and the literal is not a concrete flesh but negligence of the vision that concrete flesh is a magnificent citadel of metaphors. (p. 174)

The tattooed, the pierced and those with a predilection for graphic sexual imagery are attempting to plumb the depths of those metaphors. Through examination of each body modification, this will become clear.

CONTEMPORARY TATTOOING

Inkslinging as Initiation and
Actualization of Archetypal Imagery

The society of the twentieth century Western world suffers the lack of rituals to aid its members in crossing the thresholds of developmental stages of life. Community and familial support does not exist to celebrate or note this crossing. Hence, citizens of the West are left to devise their own rites of passage, and to mark the threshold experience (often literally) during their initiation process, alone. Choosing an image and placing it on skin through tattooing is becoming an important means of such an initiation.

Tattooing contains all of the elements of initiatory rituals as chronicled by van Gennep (1960) in his work "The Rites of Passage." The stages of initiation, as practiced by indigenous people, of 1) separation, 2) marginality or liminality, and 3) reaggregation, are aptly mimicked through tattooing.

The separation of the tattooee from his social structure (or family unit) is evidenced by two facts: first, according to law, one must be eighteen in order to get a tattoo, and second, most first tattoos are gotten by the underaged without parental permission, and illegally. So one must separate out, perhaps break the law, in order to actualize an image on skin. In this separation, one moves into the sacred space of the tattoo studio.

Turner (1995) discusses liminality as a dynamic process rather than a static state of the psyche. In this process the initiate enters into ritual time and space between ordered categories of existence. Here is the space where the soul connects to psychoid numinosum.

Even if the tattooee is completely unconscious of the reasons for getting a tattoo (as most are), this occurs. It occurs because of the biophysical responses of the body to needle stimulation. That is, when an area of the body is stimulated (injured or pleasured) the release of dopamine and/or endorphins from brain neurons not only masks or heightens the sensation (depending on whether it is perceived as painful or pleasurable), but presents a "high" feeling. Thus, the initiate benefits, albeit temporarily, and does achieve an altered state of consciousness. Remember, the consciousness with which one enters the process ultimately determines the quality of the experience and the capacity for the experience to be of value for transformation.

During this liminal time, in the tattoo studio, the sacra (myths and mysteries of the tribe) are communicated. The initiate receives the image from an adept, one who has gone before, and is mythically linked to the marked ancestors that have preceded him. The natural world is taken apart as the body part that has been chosen for marking receives the tattoo. This phase of liminality, called ludic recombination, closes with the marking becoming complete and the initiate receiving aftercare instructions for tending the wound.

Lastly, in the rites of passage ritual, is the reaggregation phase. The initiate is returned to the everyday world a changed man. In linear space and time he wears the badge of the initiation with pride. The tending of the wound enhances all of the processes. The slow healing lengthens the memory of the initiation ritual.

Imagery

The images chosen for marking are as important as the process of inscription. The source of these marking is the vast reservoir of images of the objective psyche. Hillman (1983) defines these images that actualize to consciousness as psyche itself in its imaginative visibility. They do not "stand for anything" they exist in their own right. Image is primary datum. By examining one's skinscape, we gather a soul history.

Images of meaning carry the experiences of the soul. Experiences of the outer world owe their existence to the natural symbol-forming nature of the psyche (Hillman, 1964). Integration of the images of the psyche comes through recognizing and experiencing them as "pictures of meaning," as symbols (Whitmont, 1969).

Differentiated and primitive, conscious and unconscious we are united in symbol, as well as all other psychic opposites. Whenever such a symbol comes spontaneously to light from the unconscious, it is a content that dominates the whole personality, "forcing the energy of the opposites into a common channel," so that "life can flow on . . . towards new goals." Jung called that unknown activity of the unconscious which produces the real, life-giving symbols the *transcendent function*, because this process facilitates a transition from one attitude to another. (Von Franz, 1980, p. 83)

Hence, every image for marking, whether it be designed by the initiate or chosen from a flash (tattoo design) board in the studio, is an image of value. The fact of soulular resonance of an image denotes its charge.

Charged images have archetypal importance. In carrying a charge, ". . . they develop *numinous* effects that manifest themselves as affects" (von Franz, ibid., p. 85). By actualizing these archetypal images of the unconscious to consciousness, a psychic healing may occur, in that the initiate gains a primary experience of his own psyche.

PIERCINGS

Soft Tissue Body Modification

The exploding cultural trend of piercing as a body modification can be likened to an initiatory rite of passage (with the psychic processes similar to the tattooing experience) with the exception of its emphasis on sensate response. The use of the word "pain" will be avoided because of its subjectivity. An extreme sensate response is sought as a path of connection to numinosum, and this is where piercing deviates from tattooing. In discussing piercings, we will examine both forms of adornment and ritual practices of the contemporary body modification community.

What is currently happening today bears some semblance to practices indigenous to tribal people, but with modern twists. The jewelry for adornment is far more "user friendly" with the advent of surgical steel and titanium (which is not as prone to infect as wood, bone leather and shells). The piercing needles are also autoclaved and the piercers wear surgical gloves. However the actual piercings mimic tribal placements.

There is no place on the body that is not being explored by those engaged in body modification. Common piercings include: tongue, eyebrow, nose, navel, lips (upper and librette), ear (all parts of outer and inner cartilage), male genitalia (penis formations of guiche, Prince Albert, hafada, apadravya, ampallang, dydoe, foreskin and frenum) and female genitalia (labia, clitora, clitoral hood) (Juno, 1989).

More uncommon body modifications are: pockets (in which a titanium rod is pushed through skin to "pocket" at both ends and just show in the middle of the rod), implants (in head with spikes protruding and changeable colored balls fixed on the spikes), branding and scarification on all parts of the body (with hot metal or more recently laser, the purpose of which is to keloid scar tissue in patterns), sewing of lips (closed, i.e., Christlike) and of necklaces on collar line, stretching genitalia with suspension weights, and cutting genitalia.

There are historical precedents for most of these modifications. Subincision, the splitting of the penis down the shaft, is discussed by Eliade (1958) as an initiatory practice among the Pitta-Pitta and the Boubia tribes of northwestern central Queensland in Australia. He explains that the novice, once subincised, is then called "one with a vulva" (p. 26). The notion of a male being incomplete without his feminine side derives from the origin myths of the tribe. The novice is subincised to invoke *divine totality*, the coming together of male and female in one body. "The androgyne is considered superior to the two sexes just because it incarnates totality and hence perfection. For this reason we are justified in interpreting the ritual transformation of novices into women—whether by assuming women's dress or by subincision—as the desire to recover a primordial situation of totality and perfection" (Ibid.).

Many body modifications found in America today are still being practiced around the globe. Scarification of elaborate keloiding patterns is still practiced among the Nuba in Sudan. Wealthy women in Malaysian Borneo have jewels and gold implanted in their teeth, as well as very extended earlobes laden with heavy hoops. Men in the upper Sepik River area of New Guinea wear bone or ivory tusks through their nasal septums. The Kayaw women of Burma wear heavy metal rings below their knees that reshape their calves (Camphausen, 1997).

As for female labial adornment, Camphausen (Ibid.) states:

> . . . female labia minora—the small, inner genital labia—have been adorned and/or enlarged in some cultures. Among the Hottentot people, a woman was judged beautiful and powerful if she had large inner labia extending far beyond the outer ones. They were purposely elongated with weights and by daily manipulation and have been reported to be very large indeed. Early ethnologists called this modification the Hottentot apron. Other African tribes, such as the Basuto, Dahomey, Tonga, Urua and Venda people, have followed the same practice, as have contemporary women in the East and West. (p. 74)

One of the most interesting ritual piercings that is proliferating today is that of Kavandi. Several Web sites on body modification show modern men of the West practicing this Indian and Malaysian ritual. Kavandi is an Indian word derived, in part, from the word *kavaca* (a metal corselet and/or coat of arms), and in part from *kavadi* (a vow to make a pilgrimage). These rituals are performed in the East by men in their annual religious processions. One day a year, these men undergo the outrageous torture of walking in the procession bearing heavy weights on their shoulders and flesh-hooks with weights attached. Campenhauser (Ibid.) says that these men are not professional yogis, but instead, ordinary people who are making an appeal to the deities for attention to their problems. He adds, "Trance-consciousness is so powerful that once the procession is over and the deities, in the form of the priest, have accepted the offering, the wounds of the practitioners heal in a day and become simply invisible"(p. 86).

In contemporary culture, there is no procession, even though the goal of the ritual is the same. A trance state through which one touches the divine, is the desire of the participants. This is an admirable goal. However, without adequate spiritual preparation, correct separatio, once again it could all too easily become a lesser coniunctio experience: temporarily satiating the participant, but leaving him to move into more extreme sensate responses and impossible tortures in his quest for the stone.

Having interviewed many "committed" piercers and also casual piercers, a primary question on my list is why body modification is desirable. Overwhelmingly, the same responses are echoed: the adornment factor is important, many piercings enhance sexual pleasure, and the experience of overcoming pain and reaching a state of "twilight of feeling," quite unattainable through any other means, is sought. I have no doubt that in the moment of transcendence of sensation, where pleasure and pain are indistinguishable, one touches the psychoid archetypes of the objective psyche and experiences the numinous. I can't help but ponder, however, if there isn't another way to get there that doesn't exclude the body, but that doesn't abuse it. Some people find an answer to that question in sex.

PORN

The dynamic energy field of the personal unconscious is the first arena in which a clue to the attraction to non-affective sex is found. This is the realm in which thoughts and behaviors unacceptable to ego are relegated, to form shadow elements of the personality. The drives and urges which are in opposition to persona values cannot be integrated into ego's image of itself, hence they become repressed. "It is most important to note that those qualities which at this point are repressed as incommensurable with persona ideals and general cultural values may be quite basic to our fundamental personality structures, but owing to the fact of their repression they will remain quite primitive and therefore negative" (Whitmont, 1969, p. 163).

These primitive shadow elements do not go away. They are always lurking just below the surface of consciousness. When shadow elements push to actualize we are engulfed by their energy. Jung (1959) states:

> The unconscious no sooner touches us then we *are* it—we become unconscious of ourselves. That is the age-old danger, instinctively known and feared by primitive man, who himself stands so very close to this pleroma. His consciousness is still uncertain, wobbling on its feet. It is still childish, having just emerged from primal waters. A wave of the unconscious may

easily roll over it, and then he forgets who he was and does things that are
strange to him. (p. 318)

In America today the consciousness of sexuality is very primitive, and
"wobbling on its feet." Indeed, the way in which the issues of sexual education, abortion, birth control and sexually transmitted disease are treated on
a national level, can be described as split-off. What we are witnessing in the
proliferation of sexually explicit materials is, at one level a grandiose acting-
out as a defense against the affect constellated by emerging archetypal energies of instinctual urges-turned-shadow material of a culture.

According to Lionel Corbett in his work, "The Religious Function of the
Psyche"(1996), there is a therapeutic benefit to conscious recognition of
actualizing shadow. He asserts:

> The usual goal is increased consciousness and mastery of the personal
> shadow, which reduce the autonomy of split-off sectors of the personality
> from holding sway. We are then able to suffer the shadow without inflicting
> it or projecting it onto others. But an important caveat is that such con-
> tainment is only possible if the self structures are strong enough to with-
> stand the intense affects, such as terror, envy, rage, shame and guilt, which
> are involved. These should not be underestimated; it is to avoid them that
> much acting out occurs. . . . Consciousness of the personal shadow allows
> humility and understanding for others to develop; increasing awareness of
> the personal shadow actually undermines the ego's existing categories,
> allowing them to expand or alter to include material that was previously
> unassimilable. (p. 201)

Jung (1953) discusses the legions of laymen who understand nothing
about themselves, and patients who are" . . . utterly unaware of their actual
conflicts" (p. 257. par. 426). The conflict in the psyche, generated by overi-
dentification with pornographic imagery can be labeled as "erotic conflict."
Man is the symptom of his neurotic culture, and his conflict is shared with
the culture in which he lives. Jung continues on this subject saying:

> . . . man possesses in the unconscious a fine flair for the spirit of his time;
> he divines his possibilities and feels in his heart the instability of present-
> day morality, no longer supported by living religious conviction. Here is
> the source of our [erotic] conflicts. The urge to freedom beats upon the
> weakening barriers of morality; we are in a state of temptation, we want
> and we do not want. And because we want and yet cannot think out what
> it is we really want, the [erotic] conflict is largely unconscious, and thence
> becomes neurosis. (Ibid., p. 261, par. 430)

This analysis of the cultural neurosis of Jung's day can be easily applied to
contemporary American politics today. The nation's intense preoccupation with
the President's sexuality, indeed the President's alleged extra-marital affairs, all
present as the symptoms of a neurotic culture caught in "erotic conflict."

Part of the appeal of pornographic material is the voyeuristic position one is able to take vis-à-vis the fantasy subject, thus temporarily suspending consciousness of the "erotic conflict" generated by the material. Another aspect of the appeal is the important component that is lacking in adult entertainment today, the exhibition of any form of affect in heterosexual contact (this changes somewhat in gay and lesbian interactions). The adult industry produces approximately 150 new films a week, with minimal affective content normally present in intimate sexual relations. In fact, they place a disclaimer at the beginning of most films (as suggested by the Free Speech Coalition) that indicates that these films portray neither healthy intimacy nor safe sex. Heterosexual film interaction involves mostly lubricating the vagina or female anus with either saliva or lotions, positioning the body for penetration, penetrating in various ways and positions and shooting sperm in women's mouths. What is the appeal of this?

I contend that if we listen, if we attune our senses, we are hearing screams of soul loss or "depersonalization" of humankind. Hillman (1975) defines "depersonalization" as ". . . a condition in which the 'personal coefficient' standing behind the ego and its relation with self and the world is suddenly absent" (p. 44). This soul-less sex, devoid of signs of affect (kissing, fondling, laughing, crying) is appealing precisely because of its lack of affect.

It is interesting that man is simultaneously drawn to exaggerated depictions of anima figures (with large implanted breasts and suctioned fat) while in deep terror of the charge of his own archetypal anima energy. Thus his attraction to bogus anima representation. For us to experience the reality of the self and the world, the "personal coefficient" must be a functioning psychic component (Ibid., p. 45). Jung (1959) speaks of the anima saying:

> The anima is not the soul in the dogmatic sense, not an *anima rationalis*, which is a philosophical conception, but a natural archetype that satisfactorily sums up all the statements of the unconscious, of the primitive mind, of the history of language and religion. It is a "factor" in the proper sense of the word. Man cannot make it; on the contrary it is always the *a priori* element in his moods, reactions, impulses, and whatever else is spontaneous in psychic life. It is something that lives of itself, that makes us live; it is the life behind consciousness that cannot be integrated with it, but from which, on the contrary, consciousness arises. For, in the last analysis, psychic life is for the greater part the unconscious life that surrounds consciousness on all sides—a notion that is sufficiently obvious when one considers how much unconscious preparation is needed, for instance, to register a sense-impression. (p. 27, par. 57)

For Western men in search of their anima aspects, who are terrorized by the face of those aspects, pornography exacerbates the conflict. With the push to integrate anima and the pull of soul-less bogus intimacy, he remains forever caught, with not even a chance at lesser coniunctio experience. Without living, breathing interaction, without the tension that comes from real relationship, without love, he remains on a hamster wheel.

In conclusion I assert that my only objection to the proliferation of sexually explicit materials, termed pornography, is that it is non-relational. That is has exploded in consumption is evidence of the cultural trend towards staving off feelings and fears emerging from the unconscious, personal and collective, about death.

The three fleshworks we've reviewed at the deepest level are humankind's defense against death. We have the impending death of the century, and we are experiencing the deaths of traditional religious archetypes and cultural morals. At the risk of "throwing in the kitchen sink" I will add that it is not coincidental that the development and widespread prescription of narcoleptic drug therapy (Prozac, Paxil, etc.) coincides with the rise in fleshwork activity. There is a frenzied attempt by humankind to reconcile the anxieties and fears that accompany death, and to chose the body as the locus for healing.

In examining these fleshworks, my goal is to generate discussion, make people angry, make people think. If a dialogue can begin in communities throughout America about these skinscapes, then maybe something will change. In relationship we see ourselves reflected as we reflect others. We become more than ourselves, we become part of the whole.

REFERENCES

Camphausen, R. (1997). *Return of the tribal.* Rochester, Vermont: Park Street Press.
Corbett, L. (1996). *The religious function of the psyche.* New York: Routledge.
Eliade, M. (1958). *Rites and symbols of initiation.* Dallas, Tex.: Spring Publications.
Hillman, J. (1964). *Suicide and the soul.* Dallas, Tex.: Spring Publications.
———. (1972). *The myth of analysis.* New York: HarperPerenial.
———. (1975). *Re-visioning psychology.* New York: HarperPerenial.
———. (1983). *Archetypal psychology.* Dallas, Tex.: Spring Publications.
Juno, A. (1989). *Re-search: Modern primitives.* San Francisco: Re-Search Publishing.
Jung, C. G. (1959). *The archetypes of the collective unconscious* (R. F. C. Hull, trans.). New York: Princeton University Press.
Turner, V. (1995). *The ritual process: Structure and anti-structure.* New York: Aldine de Gruyter Publishing.
Van Gennep, A. (1960). *The rites of passage.* Chicago, Ill.: University of Chicago Press.
Von Franz, M. L. (1980). *Projection and re-collection in Jungian psychology* (W. Kennedy, trans.). London: Open Court.
Whitmont, E. (1969). *The symbolic quest.* Princeton, N.J.: Princeton University Press.

SECTION 4

WOMEN, FEMINISM, SEXUALITY, AND CENSORSHIP

FOR A TIME IT WAS POLITICALLY INCORRECT FOR ANYONE WHO CLAIMED to be a feminist to speak favorably of pornography. The pornography issue was so dominated by anti-porn feminists that even those women who eventually came to the defense of porn did so not in the name of pornography but of Feminists Against Censorship. Some possible explanation for this is given by Molly Merryman, who, in a brief overview of modern feminism, finds that the tide has changed, and that women against pornography are very much in a minority. Unfortunately none of the prominent members of the anti-porn groups were willing to appear at the World Conference on Pornography without requiring fees of thousands of dollars, and even when this was being discussed they refused to come unless they could control the agenda.

Merryman argues that feminists against porn were not radicals, but conservative reactionaries, defending the traditional image of women as above any interest in sexuality. She believes that to accept women fully as sexual beings is a revolutionary thought which many, if not most Americans, are not yet prepared to accept. Jo Weldon picks up on some of the issues raised by Merryman, and holds that women against porn simply are not facing reality with their arguments. One example she uses is the presence of a Dominatrix in a significant portion of male porn, a symbol, she believes, of female power. She is especially concerned about the unity of images set forth by women against pornography in which all males are portrayed in the same way and so are females. Pornography, she argues, is not a homogenous entity, and neither is male or female sexual identity.

Emphasizing the variety of female responses is Nina Hartley, a feminist, an actress in X-rated movies, and a nurse, who feels that women have to acknowledge their sexual desires before they know what they need or want sexually. She believes the deliberate, therapeutic use of sexually explicit imagery is an aid to help people unlearn negative conditioning about sex. Similarly, Veronica Monet, who among other things, calls herself a whore, and who is well known as an actress, believes that there is a real need for feminist porn, that is a porn which empowers women not only on the screen but off camera as well. Sex, in her words, becomes degrading only when the person, male or female, loses the power to choose.

15

Removing Sex from Sex: Mainstream Feminism's Incomplete Dialogue

Molly Merryman

T HIS PRESENTATION ADDRESSES THE CULTURALLY CONSTRUCTED CLI-
mate the current feminist pornography debate resides within, and
seeks to answer these questions: Why is the anti-porn/pro-censorship view
believed by most people (and pushed by the media) as the sole articulation
of feminists? Why has this critique of sexual expression continued to manifest itself for more than a decade with no advancement of its treatises and in
light of the real damages its legal enactments have caused feminists and
sexual minorities? Why have the majority voices of feminists opposed to
anti-porn measures (either on the principle of anti-censorship or from a pro-
sex/pro-porn perspective) not been recognized in the public dialogue? And
why is it that academic women's studies is seemingly influenced by anti-
porn feminist philosophy?

The feminist discourse on pornography, particularly the academic feminist pornography stance, is widely believed to be the anti-pornography
arguments put forth by Catharine MacKinnon, Andrea Dworkin and their
followers. This is the common knowledge of the populace, a knowledge bolstered by the media, which commonly refers to this faction as "the" feminist
view of pornography. Yet a survey of the literature available in university
libraries under the combined key words feminism and pornography reveal
that only 18 percent of the feminist works on pornography widely disseminated within the academy reflect the anti-pornography viewpoint.[1] Twenty-
eight percent are comprised of or debate both viewpoints, while 53 percent
are of either the pro-porn/pro-pleasure or the anti-censorship approach. Yet,
the stereotype of feminists, particularly academic feminists, as hysterical,
sex-hating censors continues unabated.

I want to provide some condensed theories about why this is, from the
perspective of one who is a feminist academic and cultural historian. Be-

185

cause the feminist porn debate is well documented in other venues, this presentation is limited to the hegemonic construction of this debate and the implications it has on women living in contemporary American culture.

To begin, I need to put forth the definition of pornography from which I work. Mine is quite simple: pornography is the media representation of sexual expression. This is a basic definition that isn't value-laden, thus it simply sets aside material categorically more than it reveals what turns me on and off. I define media as the mass production of images and ideas, and the category includes books, magazines, audio tapes, video tapes, CD-ROMs, Internet sites, comics, etc.

What lies at the heart of the contemporary feminist pornography debate and the positioning of that debate within a larger culture is not even pornography. What is being contested are not the images or the manufactured ideas, but what they represent: sexual expression and more significantly, the control of sexual discourse and sexuality, and ultimately the very assumption of natural difference between genders. It is the very notion of sexuality and its expression that has removed feminists from the public discourse on pornography, for sexuality is not accepted by dominant culture to be the domain of women. Advocates of feminist anti-porn theory and referendums thus fall into a larger cultural construction that essentializes women and female sexuality, and positions that women are of the emotional sphere and men of the physical, thereby constructing the realm of genital sex, sexual pleasure and sexual representation as the domain of men, a domain that is exclusive and thus poses a threat to all women.

I would now like to offer an exceedingly brief historical overview of American feminism and its relationship with topics dealing with sexuality in order to further contextualize this notion of cultural construction as it pertains to the domain of sexuality and gender. The feminist movement for all practical purposes began in 1848, with the Declaration of Sentiments at Seneca Falls. Many of the goals put forth at this time have continued to be relevant: the rights of women to have political control, economic control, and bodily control. These ideas were expressed with demands for fundamental access: the right to vote, the right to have legal control over money, and in the arena of sexuality, access to birth control and abortion to confront the tremendous fatalities caused by child birth, and laws to make violence against women in the forms of spousal abuse and rape illegal. Yet at the same time the Document of Sentiments was becoming known in this country, the free-love movement was also spawning important feminist speakers and writers, most notably Victoria Claflin Woodhull, incidentally the first woman in the United States to run for President. While also advocating for reliable contraception and abortion and denouncing physical abuse of women, Woodhull added a discourse of female sexual pleasure that resulted in her being branded by the public at large, disregarded as a cultural critic and excluded from the first wave of American feminists.

In the first decades of the twentieth century, the next significant movement of American feminism arose, although it is categorized as an extension of the 1840s movement because its focus was on obtaining the vote, a goal which had not yet been obtained. Other issues raised at Seneca Falls were also being contested, and Margaret Sanger, a nurse who dealt with the tragic results of women not having access to birth control or basic knowledge of their reproductive organs, began a crusade to educate and provide for the reproductive health of women. Around this same time, an anarchist, Emma Goldman, was also writing for the sexual emancipation of women, and included in her assertions was the idea that women had a basic right to sexual pleasure, a right that could not be realized within state-controlled heterosexual marriage.

The next formal wave of feminism arose in the 1960s and grew throughout the 1970s. Known as the Second Wave of American feminism, this movement was broadly defined, with followers demanding unilateral equality between women and men. Among the expressed goals of this movement that were swept away in the conservative 1980s was the demand for sexual pleasure. This wave of feminism was closely linked with the sexual revolution, and technological advances in birth control combined with the legalization of abortion in 1973 allowed for the feminist discourse of sexuality to move for the first time beyond critical needs. Feminist discourse on sexual expression arose from two factions: a heterosexual contingency that explored the idea of sexual pleasure removed from marriage and monogamy, and a lesbian faction that argued that in an unequal society, sexual pleasure could best be achieved between those of the same gender. Both factions soon found themselves on the outs from the self-proclaimed feminist mainstream, with academic feminists arguing that feminist adaptations of tenets from the sexual revolution espousing non-monogamous sex and the autonomy of pleasure, as put forth by Helen Gurley Brown of *Cosmo* and sexy feminist cover girl Germaine Greer, were a co-optation of feminism by men, who really only wanted non-committal sex; while at the same time Betty Friedan spoke against the "Lesbian Menace" to feminism, and NOW and other major feminist organizations removed lesbian issues from organized efforts and removed vocal lesbian theorists, such as Jill Johnson, from the front.

What is important to notice in this thumbnail sketch on the history of feminism is that there occur consistent elimination of any discourse regarding the sexuality of women from the public positioning of feminism. Attempts by feminists to define sexuality through pleasure or autonomy and identity are attacked, and women are only permitted to talk publicly about sex through the manifestations of the problems it creates in women's lives, such as pregnancy and child birth, domestic violence and rape–although it should be noted that the introduction of these issues into cultural discourse also did not come easily. Over this timeline occurs the continual rejection of feminists who advocate for sexual pleasure from the mainstream. While this rejection does manifest itself in part through mainstream feminists leaders, this only followed public attacks against feminist sexual expression when the mainstream feminists themselves were implicated in the outcry of opposition to those who dared further ideas of women's sexual drives that ran counter to cultural constructions of womanhood. In the examples I gave from Victoria Woodhull to Jill Johnson—feminists who came forward espousing a platform of sexual freedom and sexual pleasure for women received the greatest attacks from the public at large, and were singled out for personal attacks, being called, among other things, godless and unnatural.

In this attack on the feminist ownership of sexual discourse, many patterns arise, two of which I will point out because of their bearing on the contemporary issues of a public construction of anti-porn feminists as being the only discourse in town. First, we see that feminist leaders who are fighting for more tangibles than sexual authority back away from pro-sex feminism because the virulence of public attacks are so strong as to undermine the implementation of such tangible goals; and within this formulation we see that these tangibles—the end to violence against women, economic injustice, poor health care, etc.—are positioned not as feminist issues or rights for women, but of larger societal values. In other words, feminist goals have only been achieved when feminist activists could convince the larger culture that these goals were for the good of all and that they reflected the values of a society that imagined itself fair and equitable. And in what has consistently been a Puritanical culture (with 1970s sexual revolution as the only significant countering of that), feminists have not been successful at getting their culture to rally forth in defense of the rights of women to control and achieve their own sexual pleasure. For, in fact, this culture barely allows sexual expression for its privileged men.

The second pattern that arises within this discourse is that any positioning of sexual autonomy for women is met with attacks so virulent that simple Puritanism cannot be the explanation. Continually, we see women who espoused sexual freedom, sexual pleasure and lesbian sexuality silenced and named unnatural and godless. The ferocity of these attacks bears witness that this silencing is not about societal morality, but is much deeper. In fact, the very notion of the sexual autonomy of women disrupts culturally accepted notions of sexual difference. Constructions of the differences between the sexuality of men and women are so deeply entrenched in defining who comprises the categories of women and men that eroding the notions of essentialized sexuality (whether from feminist authority or queer sensibilities) erodes the very premise of rigid biological differences between the sexes. Accept that women have a sexual identity based on pleasure rather than reproduction (or that women are aggressive or competitive), then the idea that women and men are not categorically formulated but are culturally constructed must also be accepted. This is why the arena of women's sexuality is as contested as that of women in the military: these are the key areas through which sexual difference have been defined, explained and substantiated. There is a continued cultural insistence that men are sexual beings and women are emotional beings. Accepting the discourse of pro-sex feminists means the deconstruction of the basic belief systems that legitimize sexual oppression, by destabilizing cultural expectations about masculinity (i.e., male sexual prowess) and revealing the fraud of any purportedly natural progression of men and women into separate spheres.

So let us return now to the current feminist pornography debates. If we accept that sexuality represents one of the most vulnerable domains of cultural constructionism, then we would expect that any idea deflecting the threat would be embraced and espoused within this culture. Therefore, the contentions by the MacDworkinites that all women perceive sexual expression (i.e., pornography) as a real threat because all women have sexual drives that differ from men's, and that all women are sexual victims needing protection are readily accepted by our culture because they contest no ground and in fact substantiate essentialized constructions of gender difference because they rise purportedly from a feminist critique of that very same culture.

The feminist timeline also reveals that we are embroiled in an ideological battle where the very notions of gender and sexuality are heavily contested. Ground won by Second Wave feminism has been lost, and basic feminist tenets, having been erased over and over again, are being reintroduced into a culture hostile to change. There emerges a climate ripe for the likes of Catharine MacKinnon and Andrea Dworkin, for what they represent more than feminist autonomy and power are patriarchal and culturally constructed values about women and their sexuality. Despite the self-labeling of this feminist branch as radical, there is nothing radical about the notions of sexuality put forth, which is why dominant culture allows this faction to control the discourse on feminist views of pornography and consequently of sexuality. This positioning serves dominant culture in several ways: it deflects the truly fearful notion that women can be in control of their sexuality and even sexually dominant; it brands all feminists as women who hate and fear sex and thus men; it erases all notions of queer sexuality that would confound ideas not only of who consumes pornography, but also ideas of there even existing a proper or natural sexuality; and it distances women who might otherwise follow feminism, because they don't want to be labeled men-haters or they don't identify with this anti-pleasure construction of feminist thought.

By viewing the rise of anti-porn feminist sentiment within this cultural climate, we also see why some feminists hold onto an ideology that has clearly conspired with right wing fundamentalism and which in practice has been revealed to oppress the sexual expressions of feminists and sexual minorities. In a culture of sustained and damaging backlash against women, in a state where the last feminist gains were the implementation of Title IX in 1972 and the passage of *Roe* v. *Wade* in 1973 (both of which continue to undergo pervasive and sustained attack), in this culture and climate, the acceptance of MacKinnon's anti-pornography measures and sexual harassment standards are the only substantive gains put forth by self-described feminists in twenty-five years. For feminists continually beleaguered in defending the same torn ground, it is not surprising that some would set aside the real threats and ideological boundaries of this stance to be on the winning and "righteous" side.

It is also not surprising that MacDworkinite philosophy seems to be most consistently embraced within academic women's studies programs and among feminist faculty, for this represents the most beleaguered of the feminist institutions.[2] Despite the rhetoric that women's studies is a controlling entity within universities and despite the popular assertion that universities are sites of cultural contestation, the realities of the academy are that women's studies remains disenfranchised and underfunded, women faculty still constitute the minority and do not hold controlling positions, and universities as a whole are struggling to survive under corporate interests and governmental regulations that increasingly restrict free speech, threaten academic integrity and undermine any semblance of student activism that existed thirty years ago.

In this climate some academic feminists embrace the one platform of feminist thought that does not render them under siege only because it reflects dominant hegemonic values. It is this same mechanism that places an undue focus in women's studies texts on other acceptable notions such as equal employment opportunity, ending violence against women, and providing health care. These same tantamount issues as put forth in Seneca Falls in 1848 are what still are being debated in women's studies classes across this country because of backlashes so successful that most college students believe that ERA passed, and that women and minorities have obtained disproportionate power.

As a result of the dominant silencing of sex positive theorists and gender flux critics, their space in the public discourse is occupied by feminist anti-porn/pro-censorship theorists, status quo assumptions about women's sexuality and gender construction stand, and feminists are publicly regarded as hysterical and fearful women who are quite willing to erode the civil liberties of society to further their cause. As a result, we have spent two decades going over the same ground and contesting opposing sides within feminism, rather than confronting dominant cultural values and reaping positive change.

To change this, there needs to occur a positive, synergistic relationship between free speech advocates and pornography industry leaders with academics, particularly those most under siege for teaching sexual materials, such as women's studies, gender studies and queer studies faculty. Just as exists the need for feminists within the porn industry to transform the product to reflect feminist values and women's perspectives, and for feminists to support their sisters within the industry, there also exists the need for free speech advocates and pornography industry leaders and workers to support feminist academic discourse and work to create an environment where students can be taught about gender, sexuality and its representational form, pornography.

NOTES

1. I chose this approach over reviewing published texts because of the assumption that the university (and the feminist scholars who order such books for their libraries) decidedly follow anti-porn ideology. These numbers were culled from Ohio Link, July 1998.

2. I say "seems" because I have not done an empirical study, and because there exists considerable diversity among and within academic programs and faculty. I base this assumption on recognized textbooks that rarely include readings on sexual pleasure and frequently include MacDworkinite essays, National Women's Studies Association conferences, at which I have participated and chaired national caucuses for several years, reviews of academic feminist journals and magazines that rarely include the pro-porn/anti-censorship stance, and my experience involved with women's studies programs featuring a range of feminist interpretations on pornography at five universities over twelve years.

16

Topping from Below: Does Female Dominant Pornography Endorse the Rape of Women?

Jo Weldon

BECAUSE MOST OF YOU ARE UNFAMILIAR WITH MY WORK, AND FRAMING lends a great deal to the interpretation of ideas, I will tell you from the start that I am an anti-censorship feminist. While I find the views of supporters of censorship of pornography dangerously paternalistic, I also find dangerously irresponsible the views of those who believe that no consensually achieved orgasm should be subject to critique.[1] However, I am not in the middle of the road; I am firmly on the anticensorship side.[2]

The works of both the Marquis de Sade and Leopold von Sacher-Masoch portray a great deal of sadism and domination deployed by women upon men. Both are also social commentaries on the ways in which inequality between genders and power structure among classes create environments in which domination, sadism, masochism, and submission thrive. Both writers were actively engaged in the sexual and social practices of *sadism* and *masochism*; and both criticized the conditions which they believed created their tastes because the original paper included information on the etymology of the terms *sadism* and *masochism*, as well as more explication. However, that is not necessary to this paper in this context.

The definition of pornography as harm continues to be used as the basis for legislation in the United States and other countries. (One may wish this subject would go away, or may consider the debate outdated, but the recurrence of proposed legislation based on these principles raises the stakes, so that the debate must continue.) The legal definition is almost always based on the definition provided in the Minneapolis and Indianapolis pornography ordinances,[3] written by Catharine A. MacKinnon and Andrea Dworkin. Those who favor this definition will hereafter be referred to as "MacDworkinites" for purposes of convenience.[4] The three harms of pornography constituted by MacDworkinites are: 1) harm to the women who perform in it, who, whether or not they appear to consent to participate in it, are being exploited and economically or physically coerced to do so; 2) harm to the women who do not participate in it but are denied their own, supposedly non-pornographic, sexuality, because they are encouraged to perform the unpleasant acts depicted in it by men who are enculturated by it; and 3) harm in the sense that the depicted acts are the equivalent of shouting "fire" in a crowded building, leading directly to conditions of endangerment (particularly of being raped) for all women.

Regarding the first harm, such coercion is already illegal. Regarding the second harm, annoying attempts to persuade are certainly not prosecutable under any law, except when they occur within the context of sexual harassment, which is also already illegal. Regarding the third harm, rape is already illegal, and so is incitement to rape. This paper will consider whether endorsements of rape, if not incitements, occur in female dominant pornography.[5]

The views of antipornography feminists, and those whose theories preceded and followed them, frequently apply to all pornographic media a concept which corresponds to Laura Mulvey's theory of the cinematic male gaze, the idea that media (particularly film, but also photographs and text) are constructed to suit a sadistic male eye.[6] This gaze is assumed to be sadistic whenever it is set upon a woman though not to be submissive when set upon a man.

This male-identified voyeurism is assumed to constitute an invasion of the woman's identity and an abuse of her body, by using both as objects upon which to project sadistic male fantasy. Through this gaze a portrayal of female sexual pleasure is perceived as subordination by assuming that her pleasure is feigned or is the result of brainwashing,[7] a portrayal of a man receiving sexual pleasure from giving another man sexual pleasure is further female subordination (by assuming that the man giving pleasure is in the female position),[8] and a portrayal of a woman committing violence against a man is yet further female subordination (by assuming that the woman is in the masculine position and the man is in the feminine position).[9] Applied to female dominant pornography, it constructs the dominatrix as a male figure to which the male submissive relates, rather than relating to his submissive role.[10] If this is true, then female dominant pornography endorses rape of women by endorsing violence against women as portrayed by that which the male submissive is subject to.

It is my contention that the concept of the male gaze is generally applicable only to items of media which conspicuously portray violence against women. In other words, if the dominant figure is defined as male by the position of dominance (and so it is in this concept, to the point that the female survivor in a horror film can be said to be perceived as male when she kills the monster[11]), then the argument is tautological. The argument seems to be that wherever there is an imbalance of power, dominance is the definition of male, and male is the definition of dominance. If there is no definition of a dominant female, then the argument begs the question every time by stating that the second the female becomes dominant, she becomes a male figure.

Let us turn the MacDworkinite version of the male gaze upon pornography which features a dominatrix playing the role of the character in power and a submissive male playing the role of the character who must submit to this power. In such pornography, the dominatrix explores her power over the male by forcing him to submit to outrageous whims: she may expect him to tolerate physical torture which is not the result of infraction of rules, but is administered for her amusement; she may expect his face to serve as an inanimate footrest under her table while she eats; she may expect him to clean her toilet with his tongue. In doing all this she is assumed to be exerting not physical domination but "the strength of her superior will is over the helplessness of the male in the face of her goddess-like presence."[12] That the male finds her commands incomprehensible is proof of his inferiority, and he may not object. His pleasure is to serve her, not to analyze her. According to the MacDworkinite gaze, the dominatrix is degraded by participating in this fantasy, in which the actual male, by playing the female role, identifies with and is empowered by the portrayal of the dominatrix.[13]

In this we can see that MacDworkinites would have us believe that the effect of the male gaze is absolute. Accurately perceiving the bulk of pornography to be produced for male consumers, their perception is followed by these assumptions: all porn represents women as objects to be consumed, all men consume it, and no women have the sexuality portrayed in it. The tautology of MacDworkinite-defined male sexuality,[14] when applied to gay male porn, is pushed to its absolute limits, but manages to locate the subordination of women therein nonetheless.[15] If this is a possibility, it is easy to believe that the image of a man licking a woman's boots really represents the ability of the man to force her to lick his own.[16] As Edward de Bono says, "A myth is a fixed way of looking at the world which cannot be destroyed because, looked at through the myth, all evidence supports that myth."[17] If the male gaze serves here as the MacDworkinite myth of demonized male sexuality, the implication is clear.

In fact, the idea that the person playing the part of the submissive in an S/M scene may actually be the one in charge is acknowledged by most practitioners of consensual S/M. They have a term for it: "topping from below." This is a term many sado-masochists use to describe the situation when a person calls himself (or herself) a submissive, but will not play unless the supposed dominant follows a strict script for the scene. In such a case the submissive is actually controlling the scene, although he or she may be being thoroughly beaten and humiliated. This is generally not considered to constitute abuse of the dominant, whether the dominant is male or female. It is merely considered bad form.

The term "topping from below" can also indicate the recognition by the S/M community that a responsible dominant is constantly aware of the desires and limits of his or her submissive subjects. In this sense, the topping from below is indicative of the consensuality of the scene, rather than of the subject's pretension to true submission: it is an acceptance of the fact that knowing a submissive's limits concerning tolerance of pain and humiliation is part of competent dominance.[18] This is part of the skilled dominatrix's job, and does of course verify the theory that the true power balance may not tip in her favor.

The dominatrix is a complex sexual subject, as well as a complex sexual object—too complex to be thoroughly analyzed in a paper such as this. In brief, I will say that, to some observers, she is the ultimate symbol of female supremacy, a patently erotic woman who tortures the men who find her sexy and gratifies her sexuality in a mysterious elsewhere populated only by her mutually respectful equals. To others, she is the ultimate symbol of female subordination, her very role a mockery of her true position in society, socioeconomically enslaved to the perversions of her male clients.[19]

For each dominatrix, the sense of which of these views corresponds correctly to her experience is on a point anywhere along the line between the two extremes. However, this paper is not about the sense of self imbued in the role-playing activity of the dominatrix. It's about the dominatrix portrayed as a character in the pornographic imagination, and how one's degree of belief in the concept of the male gaze determines one's perception of her cultural affect.[20] This is about the dominatrix as object. The imagery is pornography in the dictionary sense that its primary purpose is to sexually arouse. It is also pornography in the MacDworkinite sense, because women are shown in positions of display (usually of their feet) therein, and the women may be shown in servile positions (usually serving the man a bowl of dog food).[21] Since the man is aroused, of course, a woman is being subordinated; to arouse a man is practically the definition of subordination, according to the MacDworkinite gaze.

However, through a more objective gaze, the submissive male might be perceived as one who is not acting out the fantasies of standard heterosexual porn. Certainly all masochistic or fetishistic males are not submissive, and even if they were, they would not all be heterosexual. However, assuming the submissive role before a woman may offer a heterosexual male an outlet for his frustration with the role society forces upon him: to turn over, at least symbolically, not only the responsibility but also the undeserved status.

I suggest that the theories which create the basis for the MacDworkinite gaze are ineffective. They offer no believable explanation for how the male submissive, in the act of reinforcing gender stereotypes, experiences the knowledge that he can be at the bottom. If, in this power scenario, he shows the ability to be weak, to do unmentionable things, he has done much more than merely reinforce gender stereotypes.[22] He has truly transgressed. This is nothing like a war story which can be told over beers in a strip joint. He cannot share these experiences with his dominant male friends, engaging in male bonding.

Louise Kaplan claims that the acting out of perverse scenarios, such as the dominant female/submissive male scenario, merely reinforce gender stereotypes and may block the possibility of delving deeper into one's psyche.[23] In this there appears to be some support for the theory of the male gaze. She neglects to say, however, that therapy also generally fails to cure the perverted.[24] If the only purpose of the therapy is to cure the perversion, and the therapy generally fails, perhaps the perversion is an adequate coping mechanism.[25]

Those critical of alternative sexualities never adequately describe the healthy sexuality from which the perverts deviate. Certainly, it would not be indecent or pornographic to do so, particularly after the nature of the perversions they so lingeringly describe. In the case of (Dines co-author) Robert Jensen, he alludes to his struggles with heterosexual porn and the unacceptable acts he may have committed upon women under its influence, but in the end he reveals that he now identifies himself as homosexual.[26] Of course his sexual preference has no bearing on his critical faculties, including those applied to pornography, but it does leave one wondering—why does he not tell us how the self-aware, non-female-subordinating male may have intercourse with a woman?[27] Does he dare? Can there can be a lens prescription to reform the male gaze when no 20/20 standard is offered to alter it to?

What many anti-porn feminists seem to be advocating is a sexuality which is innocent of both personal and cultural history. They indicate, by their associations of sexual abuse and rape with alternative sexualities (such as sex work and S/M), that these sexualities involving domination and submission are all illnesses which must be cured. They indicate by their associations of these illnesses with crimes (such as rape and sexual abuse) that the price of deviation is too great for society to bear. In reality they are doing nothing but trying to homogenize sexuality, to create a standard similar to monogamous marriage which they claim to deplore, and relying on the acceptability of this oppressive and decidedly misogynist standard for the validation of their arguments. This is not to say that monogamy is, in and of itself, an oppressive state, but only to say that enforced monogamy, which is to say monogamy as the only acceptable standard, whether it is sanctioned by society or by law, has always historically been used to inhibit not only the social liberties of women, but particularly the sexuality of women.

Pornography must be critiqued like other genres of media, on a case by case basis. To group every item of pornography together as if pornography were a homogenous entity is to deny the reality of pornography. To assume that male sexual identity is homogenous, whether due to nature or nurture, is sexist. The presumption that all males perceive erotic pleasure only in fantasies or realities of imposing sex upon women through physical, economic, or emotional coercion may be an interesting theory to espouse in a discussion panel on human sexuality, but it is no fit basis for legislation.

Consider that in the decades during which the works of the Marquis de Sade were censored in the United States, women's rights were not particularly enhanced. It would seem that the ability to have access to works by Betty Friedan and Gloria Steinem coincides with the ability to have free access to pornographic works. One may argue that the spread of sexist pornography is a backlash, but it is, in fact, the nature of the free flow of speech that examples of contradictory ideals will be issued simultaneously. Further, the use of hardcore pornography continues to carry the stigma of a lower-class form of entertainment, indicating that it does not participate in the violation of women's socio-economic rights. Pornography is not offered as a solution to male poverty.

Not only does the notion that all men are culturally inclined to rape or insult women, but it places women in a position which denies them their own agency by indicating a need for coerced protection.[28] It can put women in the category of children, who have no judgement, no civil rights, and no agency, and must be restricted from certain actions for their own good. Pornography does not create the conditions conducive to the kinds of violent crimes to which women are particularly vulnerable; poverty does,[29] just as it does for the violent crimes to which men are particularly vulnerable.

Pornography must be critiqued, but with each item observed on an individual basis, rather than as a homogenized mass of which every element has a common epistemological basis. Items of pornography vary too greatly from each other, not only in content but also in availability to the public, for the whole of all of them to be considered part of a contiguous media influence on society. Even examples of male-dominant S/M pornography vary from each other. Many of the anti-pornography critiques of particular items of pornography are correct, but they are not applicable to pornography as a whole.

To blame rape, which is present in all the history preceding mass media and in those countries in which pornography is absent, on such sexist but non-violent images as the classic pinup[30] makes feminism more difficult to take seriously. And the concentration on pornography as the root of rape, discrimination, and violence against women is a distraction from the endeavor to find real causal relationships, real solutions, and real liberation from the controls society maintains against the free movement of women through our systems of achievement and validity. And these are conditions that both the Marquis de Sade and Leopold von Sacher-Masoch found so reprehensible in the first place.

While pornography may be constructed for a male consumer, and while this is in fact a society, like all other societies, dominated by males, it is not true that all pornography suggests and encourages sexual abuse of women.[31] The dominatrix may in fact be in a service industry that provides a place for the acting out of the male fantasy to be submissive. However, rather than representing yet another way in which men get women to do things to gratify a misogynist male sexuality, she may represent the need of the male to transgress the boundaries of that prescribed, which is to say male-dominant, sexuality. The existence of female dominant pornography shows that the influences of society can be responded to in different ways.

Whether or not a taste for images of dominant women constitutes an improvement in perceptions of women over the attitude which creates a taste for images portraying women as Dworkin's "masochistic sluts,"[32] it does not show endorsement of the rape of women. And the images do, however inadequately, show a male dissatisfaction with the image of women as masochistic sluts. This dissatisfaction implies that pornography which shows women as such is not an absolute enculturating force for every male, as MacDworkinites would have one believe. While female dominant pornography, or, if one wishes to call it so, male submissive pornography, does not empower women in any significant way, it does deny the theory that all men who objectify women also desire to rape them. As the dominatrix so often finds, some males respond to depictions of the rape of women with the desire to be in the places of the women in the pictures, and not in those of the men. Whether or not this is good news,[33] it is proof that the male gaze is not always what the anti-pornography gaze perceives it to be.[34]

PARTIAL BIBLIOGRAPHY

Assiter, Allison, and Avedon Carol, eds. *Bad Girls and Dirty Pictures: The Challenge to Reclaim Feminism.* Boulder, Colo.: Pluto Press, 1993.

Brame, Gloria G., William D. Brame, and Jon Jacobs. *Different Loving: The World of Sexual Dominance and Submission.* New York: Villard Books, 1993.

Brownmiller, Susan. *Against Our Will: Men, Women, and Rape.* New York: Bantam Books, 1976.

Butler, Judith. *Excitable Speech: A Politics of the Performative.* New York and London: Routledge, 1997.

———. *Gender Trouble: Feminism and the Subversion of Identity.* New York: Routledge, 1990.

Califia, Pat. *Public Sex: The Culture of Radical Sex.* Pittsburgh and San Francisco: Cleis Press, 1994.

Carter, Angela. *The Sadeian Woman and the Ideology of Pornography.* New York: Pantheon Books, 1979.

Chapkis, Wendy. *Live Sex Acts: Women Performing Erotic Labor.* New York: Routledge, 1997.

Clover, Carol. *Men, Women, and Chainsaws: Gender in the Modern Horror Film.* Princeton, N.J.: Princeton University Press, 1992.

DeGrazia, Edward. *Girls Lean Back Everywhere: The Law of Obscenity and the Assault on Genius.* New York: Random House, 1992.

Dijkstra, Bram. *Idols of Perversity: Fantasies of Feminine Evil in Fin-de-siecle Culture.* New York: Oxford University Press, 1986.

Duggan, Lisa, and Nan D. Hunter. *Sex Wars: Sexual Dissent and Political Culture.* New York and London: Routledge, 1995.

Dworkin, Andrea. *Pornography: Men Possessing Women.* New York: Dutton, 1989.

Ehrenreich, Barbara, and Deirdre English. *For Her Own Good: 159 Years of the Experts' Advice to Women.* Garden City, N.Y.: Anchor Books, 1979.

Gabor, Mark. *The Pin-up: A Modest History.* New York: Universe Books, 1972.

Goldberg, Steven. *Why Men Rule: A Theory of Male Dominance.* Chicago and LaSalle, Ill.: Open Court, 1993.

Goodwin, Jan. "Where Women Are Stoned to Death for Adultery." *Marie Claire,* August 1998, pp. 50–58.

Grosiz, Elizabeth and Elspeth Probyn, eds. *Sexy Bodies: The Strange Carnalities of Feminism.* London and New York: Routledge, 1995.

Hagan, Margaret A. *Whores of the Court: The Fraud of Psychiatric Testimony and the Rape of American Justice.* New York: Regan Books, 1997.

Henkin, William A., and Sybil Holiday. *Consensual Sado-masochism: How to Talk about It and How to Do It Safely.* San Francisco: Daedalus Publishing Co., 1996.

Hentoff, Nat. *Free Speech for Me–But Not for Thee: How the American Left and Right Relentlessly Censor Each Other.* New York: Harper Perennial, 1992.

Hunt, Lynn. *The Invention of Pornography: Obscenity and the Origins of Modernity, 1500-1800.* New York: Zone Books, 1996.

Itzin, Catherine, ed. *Pornography: Women, Violence, and Civil Liberties.* New York: Oxford University Press, 1992.

Jackson, Stevi, and Sue Scott, eds. *Feminism and Sexuality: A Reader.* New York: Columbia University Press, 1996.

Janus, Sam, Barbara Bess, and Carol Saltus. *A Sexual Profile of Men in Power.* Englewood Cliffs, N.J.: Prentice-Hall, 1977.

Juno, Andrea, and V. Vale, eds. *Angry Women.* San Francisco: Re/Search Publications, 1991.

Kaplan, Louise J. *Female Perversions: The Temptations of Emma Bovary.* New York: Doubleday, 1991.

Kimmel, Michael S., ed. *Men Confront Pornography.* New York: Meridian, 1990.

Kipnis, Laura. *Bound and Gagged: Pornography and the Politics of Fantasy in America.* New York: Grove Press, 1996.

Lorelei. *The Mistress Manual: The Good Girl's Guide to Female Dominance.* Springfield, Pa.: Berkana Press, 1994.

MacKinnon, Catharine A. *Feminism Unmodified: Discourses on Life and Law.* Cambridge, Massachusetts, and London, England: Harvard University Press, 1987; paperback edition 1994.

McClintock, Anne. *Imperial Leather: Race, Gender, and Sexuality in the Colonial Contest.* New York: Routledge, 1995.

——, ed. *Social Text: Sex Workers and Sex Work.* Durham, N.C.: Duke University Press, 1993.

McElroy, Wendy. *XXX: A Woman's Right to Pornography.* New York: St. Martin's Press, 1995.

McNair, Brian. *Mediated Sex: Pornography and Postmodern Culture.* New York: St. Martin's Press, 1996.

McWilliams, Peter. *Ain't Nobody's Business if You Do: The Absurdity of Consensual Crimes in a Free Society.* Los Angeles: Prelude Press, 1993.

Meyers, Marian. *News Coverage of Violence Against Women: Engendering Blame.* Thousand Oaks, Calif.: Sage Publications, 1997.

Mill, John Stuart. *The Subjection of Women.* Cambridge, Mass., and London: MIT Press, 1981 (first published 1869).

Miller, William Ian. *The Anatomy of Disgust.* The President and Fellows of Harvard College, 1997.

Mort, Frank. *Dangerous Sexualities: Medico-Moral Politics in England Since 1830.* London and New York: Routledge and Kegan Paul, 1987.

Nagle, Jill, ed. *Whores and Other Feminists.* New York: Routledge, 1997.

Parenti, Michael. *Inventing Reality: The Politics of News Media.* New York: St. Martin's Press, 1993 (2nd ed.).

Plachy, Sylvia, and James Ridgeway. *Red Light: Inside the Sex Industry.* New York: Powerhouse Books, 1996.

Queen, Carol. *Real Live Nude Girl: Chronicles of a Sex-Positive Culture.* Pittsburgh and San Francisco: Cleis Press, 1997.

Rose, June. *Marie Stopes and the Sexual Revolution.* London: Faber and Faber, 1993.

Shellogg, Susan. *Unnatural Acts: A Dominatrix Talks.* New York: Barricade Books, 1994.

Shrage, Laurie. *Moral Dilemmas of Feminism: Prostitution, Adultery, and Abortion.* New York: Routledge, 1994.

Solanas, Valerie. *The SCUM Manifesto.* San Francisco: AK Press, 1996. First self-published in New York, 1967; first Olympia Press Edition, 1968.

Strossen, Nadine. *Defending Pornography: Free Speech, Sex, and the Fight for Women's Rights.* New York: Scribner, 1995.

Tisdale, Sally. *Talk Dirty to Me: An Intimate Philosophy of Sex.* New York: Doubleday, 1994.

Von Sacher-Masoch, Leopold. *Venus in Furs, and Selected Letters.* New York: Masquerade Books, 1989 (originally published 1860?).

Wallace, Jonathan, and Mark Mangan. *Sex, Laws, and Cyberspace: Freedom and Censorship on the Frontiers of the Online Revolution.* New York: Owl Books, 1997.

Warren, John. *The Loving Dominant.* New York: Masquerade Books, 1994.

Weinburg, Thomas S., ed. *S&M: Studies in Dominance and Submission.* Amherst, N.Y.: Prometheus Books, 1995.

Williams, Linda. *Hard Core: Power, Pleasure, and the Frenzy of the Visible.* Los Angeles and Berkeley: University of California Press, 1989.

Wray, Matt, and Annalee Newitz, eds. *White Trash: Race and Class in America.* New York: Routledge, 1997.

NOTES

1. Amber Hollibaugh in Jackson and Scott examines the problem of restricting pleasure for political reasons, and also of forsaking politics in the pursuit of pleasure. Jackson and Scott, pp. 224–29.

2. Author's note: I wrote this introduction at a time when I beleived that antipornography feminists would be attending the World Pornography Conference. However, they did not attend.

3. Author's note: These ordinances have been determined to be unconstitutional. For detailed objections to the ordinances, see the amicus brief filed by the Feminist Anti-Censorship Taskforce (FACT) in the U.S. Court of Appeals in 1985. The brief is available in Duggan, pp. 205–47.

4. See Strossen, p. 13, footnote 6 (p. 281), regarding the origin of this term.

5. "Exposure to some of the pornography in our definition . . . makes normal men more closely resemble convicted rapists attitudinally, although as a group they don't look all that different to start with." MacKinnon, p. 187. (Author's note: Does the observation that the difference is so small indicate that pornography is not the cause?)

6. "The theory that constructs the female either as anatomical 'lack' or, with respect to the phallus, as lacking 'lack' in comparison to the masculine subject's more complete entrance into the symbolic begins, in its reliance on so exclusively masculine an assumption of masculinity, to block the difficult, though not foreclosed, discovery of power and pleasure for the female subject and spectator." Williams, p. 286.

7. MacKinnon claims that the real pleasure of pornography is in seeing women abused, then reminds us that Linda Marchiano said, "What people remember is the smile on my face." MacKinnon also says (when asked why women claim to enjoy sex when, if the conditions she describes are true, they surely do not), "Many people want to believe that they already have [sexual connection undominated by dominance] more than they want to have it," p. 217, *Feminism Unmodified.*

8. John Stoltenberg in Itzin, p. 156. Also Sheila Jeffreys in Jackson and Scott, pp. 238–47.

9. Clover, p. 47.

10. "Freud's original assumption [was] that masochism is simply the flip side of sadism—a deflection onto the self of a 'death instinct' that in sadism is directed outward toward others." Williams, p. 211. (Author's note: Williams does not concur.)

11. As in footnote 7. Clover, p. 47.

12. Author's note: In practice, this is not the only kind of client who wishes to employ a dominatrix. It is, however, the basis for most pornography portraying dominant females. Thus the fantasy life of the male consumer of such pornography may be assumed to be at least partially constituted of such scenarios.

13. "So whether the participant assumes the bottom role of helpless child or the top role of parent-caregiver-lawgiver, he or she is identifying with both roles . . ." Kaplan, p. 448. "Perversions are an instance of the erotic passions frantically trying to restrain impulses toward destruction and death. And fortunately, most of the time, the controlled ritual of a sadomasochistic scenario is successful in achieving this aim." Ibid., p. 27. (Author's note: Kaplan does not consider this harmless.)

14. MacKinnon and Dworkin say that they define pornography by "look[ing] at the existing universe of the pornography industry and simply decrib[ing] what is there..." In Itzin, p. 437.

15. John Stoltenberg in Itzin, p. 156.

16. ". . . [U]sually her humiliation is the secondary outcome of being forced to degrade and humiliate the fetishist." Kaplan, p. 22.

17. Quoted in McWilliams, footnote, p. 202.

18. Author's note: S/M is primarily a role-playing activity. The submissive is playing the role of one who will tolerate any punishment the dominant wishes to dish out; the dominant is playing the role of the merciless disciplinarian and torturer. In fact, the submissive usually has what is called a "safe word," which is a word (other than the word "no," which is never used as a safe word because of the erotic possibilities inherent in being overwhelmed against one's objections) the submissive can use to stop the dominant partner whenever his or her limits have been or are about to be exceeded. This is not considered a way of topping from below but a way of letting the dominant know what's going on down there, since the dominant cannot, in fact, feel the submissive's pain.

19. Kaplan, p. 35 and p. 258.

20. In *Crumb*, Terry Zwigoff's 1994 film documentary about the life of misogynist (by his own admission) comic artist Robert Crumb, Deirdre English comments that women need not recoil in fear from misogynist sexual images, saying that the strength of the fantasy comes not from the fantasizer's ability to exert power over women, but from his *inability* to do so. I mention this to point out, not that all misogynists are harmless, but that there is more than one valid interpretation of the implications of sadistic male fantasy. Therefore, there is likely more than one valid interpretation of submissive male fantasy.

21. "The term 'subordination' refers to materials that, in one way or another, are active in placing women in an unequal position." MacKinnon, p. 201. (Author's note: If you study her carefully, you will see that she is misrepresenting herself here.)

22. "If you want to know who is being hurt in this society, go see what is being done and to whom in pornography and then go look for them in other places in the world. You will find them being hurt in just that way." MacKinnon, p. 188. (Author's

note: It is this essentialism which the supporter of the MacDworkin ordinances must consider, since it forms the basis of the legislation.)

23. "Perversions are psychological strategies that enlist social gender stereotypes as a way of forgoing the search for the sources of our shared human miseries and insights." Kaplan, p. 518.

24. Hagen, p. 141–49.

25. Author's note: If it is assumed that the coping mechanism does not involve behavior including bodily harm (pain is not necessarily injury), child molestation, etc.

26. Jensen in Dines, p. 145.

27. Author's note: Valerie Solanas advocated asexuality, unable to conceive of pleasure or good purpose in either heterosexual or homosexual sex. "Sex is the refuge of the mindless." Solanas, p. 26.

28. Author's note: In many societies in which pornography is verboten, women are frequently denied their rights. They may be forced to wear veils and to marry without choice. In this it can be seen that pornography cannot be the primary cause of inhibition of, discrimination against, nor of violence against, women. See particularly the religious laws of the Taliban which force women to wear veils, not only to protect women from the lustful and dangerous gazes of men, but to protect men from the lust-inciting and dangerous faces of women.

29. Author's note: I do not mean to imply that only impoverished women are vulnerable to rape and domestic violence, only that they are the most likely victims. I suggest that impoverished women are also less likely to take the time and spend the money to prosecute perpetrators of violent crimes against them. Also, although men with greater socio-economic privilege may commit crimes of violence against women of their own class, they are in fact less likely to do so, having been more enculturated to fear prosecution. I am perfectly aware that no one of any gender or class is invulnerable to violence.

30. "Reflected in the pin-up is the masculine view of woman as passive—an object to be pinned up—existing for men's pleasure in whatever form it might take." Joan Nicholson in the introduction to Gabor's *The Pin-up: A Modest History*, p. 15.

31. One S/M pornographer comments that "90% of my stuff (video product) is female dominant because it's a much bigger market (than male dominant)." Plachy, p. 48.

32. "In a certain sense, the SM parlor provides a safer and more socialized nursery than the domestic nurseries where real fathers and mothers abuse children." Kaplan, p. 449. (Author's note: not wishing to misrepresent Kaplan, I must add that she does not consider this healthy.)

33. Author's note: I'm willing to pull the rank of personal experience to comment on this. My frequent contacts with such men have led me to believe that to consider the client's desire to be in the raped woman's position as a further proof that men believe that women enjoy being raped would be to oversimplify human sexual response and social interaction. It seems more likely to me that such men share many women's ambivalence about the consequences of their longings to be penetrated and translate it into rape fantasies in which they cannot be held accountable for their desires. I suggest that men suffer from sexual stigmas, if not to the same degree that women do. The fag stigma can be as dangerous as the whore stigma, even when the man is not homosexual and the woman is not providing sexual services for money.

34. "When all you have is a hammer, everything looks like a nail." Original source of this quote unknown; quoted to me by Judith Bradford.

17

Using Porn to Bridge
the Mind-Body Gap

Nina Hartley

W HAT FOLLOWS IS AN OVERVIEW OF MY PRESENTATION AT THE WORLD Pornography Conference in Los Angeles in August 1998. I spoke out of my own experience, as an actress with fifteen years and 460+ movies to her credit; as a lifelong feminist; as a health professional (RN) and as a formerly shy person with an insecure self-image. The points that I made came directly out of my personal experience and observations.

It is well-documented that large numbers of people are alienated from their bodies. They feel disconnected, unable to achieve intimacy, incapable of experiencing real pleasure and joy. Many people feel unworthy, that pleasure is for others, that they'll never be "good" enough to really feel at home in their skins. Some people have had their connection with their bodies stolen by an abuser. Others don't feel "beautiful" enough to be worthy of sexual connection, be it with themselves or with others. The reasons why individuals feel so are as varied as the individuals themselves yet each person must find their own way back to their center to feel truly comfortable in their skins.

How can we know what we need or want sexually if we can't even acknowledge our desires? How can we live our sexual lives to the fullest if we fear and despise our own flesh? How can we learn to look at ourselves with compassion and awareness, to understand our negative conditioning and how it causes suffering, so that we may move beyond our pain and truly experience intimacy?

Of the many tools currently in use to assist people who have embarked on the long journey toward wholeness, one that has been largely overlooked is the deliberate, therapeutic use of sexually explicit imagery (i.e., "porn") to help people recognize (so as to unlearn) negative conditioning. Sexual matters are commonly shrouded in shame, secrecy, guilt and denial. There are few, if any, socially sanctioned venues where a curious person can just LOOK at the naked human body let alone watch others engaged in sex, whether it's to satisfy curiosity, aid understanding or develop self-confidence.

A person can go to school to learn any skill except sexual ones; this forced ignorance fosters avoidance behavior, and a vicious cycle is begun. People can get so trapped in their pain, their need, their desire, that they can't bear to look at what is really going on. As long as they can't look, they can't begin to even think about changing their beliefs and subsequently, their behavior and experiences.

Since sex is so highly charged, looking at photos or videos of sexual activity often precipitates a strong emotional response by the viewer. "Gut wrenching" is not too strong a term to use when describing what people can (and do) experience when they are confronted with images of their greatest fantasy, deepest fear or most painful/joyful experience(s). These reactions can, with the compassionate guidance of a sex-positive therapist, lead a person toward a deeper understanding of themselves and their beliefs, and how these beliefs, in turn, influence their sexuality.

My use of porn was self-guided, but it helped (and continues to help) me find my way toward the fullest expression of my sexual self. Each person's use of porn will take them to a different place depending on what they seek. Porn can play a part in bringing behavior, desire and self-awareness into a healthy balance.

The first step, for me, was reading porn and the self-help books of the early mid 1970s. I also devoured the underground comics of that day as well as art books (erotic and otherwise) and took note of what turned me on, what turned me off and what confused me. My background in feminist theory told me that I had a right to sexual satisfaction, that I had an obligation to explore it safely and that the golden rule of sex was "consent." With consent, there could be no "sin." My first porn movie was a revelation. I was finally SEEING what had fascinated me for years: genitalia in action. It was powerful and beautiful and changed my life forever. By the time I started experimenting with partnersex about a year later, I had had a lot of "book learning" about sex but was without any practical experience. Putting into practice what I knew intellectually proved comically problematic.

My early forays into the land of partnersex were frequently cases of "the blind leading the blind," my first bedmates being as inexperienced as I was myself. When I met my husband a whole new world opened up for me; his unabashed, enthusiastic enjoyment of my physical body, combined with his skill as a passionate lover invigorated me and gave me confidence. He was excited, not threatened, by my interest in stripping, porn and multi-partner sex.

Soon after we moved in together, I suggested we put a mirror next to our bed and he agreed. It was the single best thing I ever did for myself. Instantly, I became both subjective participant as well as objective observer of my own private "porno movie." I learned to see myself as attractive, sexy, strong and capable. The voyeur in me loved watching the action as we played naked in bed; the exhibitionist in me loved having him watch us work as a team. Eventually, I was able to see myself as others saw me. I was finally able to move beyond the culturally sanctioned narcissism that so epitomized Berkeley in the 1970s and take my first real steps toward adult consciousness, and with them, adult responsibility for my own feelings and actions.

Through learning to love looking at myself having sex, I recognized the fatal flaw in the lesbian-feminist anti-objectification rhetoric of that time: it was based on hate, not just of men's but of women's sexuality as well. Their loudly voiced opposition to depictions of sex, characterizing them as "degrading" and "violence against women" was, I realized, their own pain and anger projected onto neutral images. As I saw it, their analysis of porn said more about themselves and their state of mind than it ever did about the images they abhorred. It spoke volumes about their internalized fear and mistrust of sexuality, especially their own. Being unable to experience sex as a positive force in their lives rendered them unwilling to believe that it could be (and was) so for others, even when told so directly. "Sisterhood is powerful" did not extend to women who made different sexual choices than they would have made for themselves.

My personal philosophy encouraged me to examine that which made me most fearful, angry, insecure or pained. Looking at images in books or movies helped me to understand what my beliefs actually were as opposed to what the culture said they "should" be. Seeing myself from the outside in as sexy, attractive and powerful permitted me to grow out of my idea of myself as clumsy, uncool and inept. Once my sexuality served to center me instead of keeping me off-balance, I felt whole and well on my way to being healed. It enabled me to tap into a wellspring of compassion, deepened my understanding of the world and gave me confidence that I could overcome any obstacles that life throws my way.

In 1994 I started putting out explicit material that took advantage of my nursing degree as well as my practical experience as a sex professional. My sex education tapes were designed to counter our culture-wide "sexual illiteracy" through a blend of factual biological, anatomical, physiological, historical and cultural information coupled with explicit demonstration and a touch of titillation. I wanted to pass on what I had learned.

As the teacher/participant in each of the eight tapes completed so far, I explain what is happening sexually as it is happening. This demystification, coupled with factual knowledge, in turn enables the viewer to relax and work through any fears or discomfort they may have that inhibit them from having positive sexual encounters.

In my fifteen years as an advocate for a sex-positive lifestyle, I have gotten a lot of feedback from my fans. While there have always been couples who enjoy my movies, the increase in women and couples as a subset of porn consumers has grown exponentially in recent years. Both through the mail and in person, I hear from people who are eternally grateful for my movies. Women tell me how watching me has been instrumental in their achieving greater confidence and satisfaction, in life as well as in bed.

Countless men have thanked me for helping their partners throw off child-hood conditioning to become enthusiastic sexual participants and for what they, themselves, have learned about women's sexuality.

I know from firsthand experience the transforming effects of porn in my own life. I hear the same from others who know how much it has helped them find their way to a positive integration of sexuality into their lives. Porn can help us to accept our physical selves and our sexuality; it can aid in healing the disconnection between our minds and our bodies that affects every aspect of our life and culture.

My educational tapes may be ordered from Adam and Eve at 1-800-765-ADAM.

18

What Is Feminist Porn?

Veronica Monet

L AST WEEK, I APPEARED ON THE TELEVISION SHOW *POLITICALLY INCORRECT* with Charo, John Schneider, and Howie Mandell. Since I am a sex worker and we were taping from Las Vegas, Nevada (the only state in the union where prostitution takes place legally), the subject of the show was the legalization or decriminalization of prostitution. Naturally, I was in the hot seat since among other things, I am a whore. John Schneider (the tall blonde in the tight jeans from the show *Dukes of Hazard* for those of you old enough to remember) has after his stint of selling sexual images on television become an ardent conservative. He lampooned me repeatedly with his very physical interpretation of the sexual positions he supposes I sell to my clients, getting up from his chair several times to bend over and show his ass or spreading his legs in an exaggerated fashion while still seated. He claimed to be illus-trating his point that prostitution is not glamorous, nor is it a valid career option because when reduced to the sex acts performed it is degrading. I am being quite generous to John Schneider at this point since I am providing the dialogue that seemed to fail him while the cameras were rolling.

My first impulse was to feel some embarrassment. This despite the fact that I not only have sold sex for years, but I have also performed sex on camera in several X-rated videos. There comes a time in a sex worker's career when one supposes, little can embarrass. Of course, that isn't always true. When I feel embarrassment, I tease it to its origins. I am not content to shrink from the uncomfortable feeling. I want to discover why it exists.

The presumption at the root of my embarrassment turns out to be that sexual positions usually assumed by females in heterosexual sex are inher-ently degrading. Bending over to receive a penis or some other object for penetration of the vagina or rectum, and spreading one's legs for penetra-tion of the vagina or rectum seem to be the main offenders. Performing a blow job is a close second, but giving a hand job seems more embarrassing to its recipient. This is in stark contrast to the laughs and applause a male can receive for imitating the thrusting and gyrating of performing sexual intercourse on many comedy shows. Our cultural stance seems to be that the person who moves and/or penetrates is powerful and the person who holds still and/or is penetrated is degraded. How convenient for the male power structure.

It is not the natural way to perceive sex nor is it the only way. In times past, the vulva was worshiped and considered the holy source of life. Not something dirty or disgusting or embarrassing. The vagina swallowed and devoured and conquered. It produced life. It was active and alive. Not some dark dead hole, like our culture seems bent upon relegating female genitalia to now. One could see the person penetrating the vulva as being in service to the vulva. Certainly a lot of my male clients feel a great deal of pressure to perform up to the expectations of their female partners. A few of them experience anxiety of such great degree that it interferes with their sexual function and pleasure altogether.

This brings me to my answer to the question: What Is Feminist Porn? I do not believe that we should put limitations or proscriptions on feminist porn of the variety that find certain positions, camera angles, etc. degrading to women. As long as we believe that women are degraded by close-ups and impersonal sex, we are buying into the patriarchal definition of power. True feminism refuses to play by the current power structure's rules. True feminism makes its own rules and defines its own reality. Sexual intercourse is not degrading. Vaginas are not embarrassing. Sex for the sake of sex instead of love, relationships, procreation or any other ideal is not degrading to women.

Women are degraded whenever their free will choice is removed however blatantly or subtlety. Degradation takes place in a marriage, on the job, while filming a porn film, or in conversation, ad infinitum. Degradation is not contingent upon the players, the situation, the context or action. Degradation results only because of intent. The intention of the people involved defines degradation. It is not that you marry, but why you marry that can lead to an uplifting or demoralizing marriage. Likewise, the intention of the female actress in a porn production is what makes us as women either feel OK or angry. Other factors determine whether the film/video is our cup of tea personally. It may or may not turn us on or entertain us. But as women we know instinctively when we have been assaulted and/or insulted. We feel it in our guts and it is visceral and palpable. We make the mistake of assuming that we feel this way because of a protracted close-up of the woman's vagina. The real reason we respond so vehemently is because we have been assaulted and insulted once again with the intention of the male players/producers/directors/etc. to express power over another in however subtle a manner and in the intention of the female actress to acquiesce to that male power. Instead of dancing with roles and sexual interaction, the person who wants to obtain power through sex is intent on maintaining control. It is not the sex act per se but the male's insistence on orchestrating and instructing and manipulating and thereby controlling the entire sexual inter-action, that is degrading.

For example, the scene may involve the male taking a supposedly sub-missive role where he is being dominated and "degraded" by the female, but he literally tells her how to do it to him. He is still in power while feigning helplessness. Another really tired scenario is the one where the guy tells the two girls how to make love to each other. In all these situations and so many more like them, the woman/women are not in power. I have also been insulted and felt assaulted when the female actresses were taking very forceful roles in front of the camera but it was only too obvious that they were being told what to do by the director/producer behind the cameras. In other words, the intention of the actress is to follow very specific orders, instead of being empowered to employ her skills as an actress. You could say this is merely bad acting but it feels like so much more. Perhaps the insult is when men repackage and reinterpret female sexuality in a way that coopts it for their personal pleasure and puts it under their control. For instance, most girl/girl porn videos have zero to do with real lesbian or bisexual sex between women. It is as if the reality of women having sex with women is too threatening to men so they try to redefine it into a male fan-tasy that they have control over.

In my search for a definition of feminist porn, I was only able to find a definition of feminist fiction which nonetheless I find very helpful. Aliz Kates Shulman, author of *Memoirs of an Ex-Prom Queen* which sold over a million copies, became required reading in universities and was hailed as the first important novel to emerge from the women's liberation movement (1972) supplied the following answer to the question "What Exactly is Fem-inist Fiction?"

"The feminist and scientist Naomi Weisstein says that feminist fiction is fiction that does not admire patriarchy or accept its ideology. It does not portray its male characters as naturally more exciting, more important, or more valuable than its female characters. Female characters are presented in their full humanity, whether they are villains or heroes, and sympathetic female characters are not necessarily nice or beautiful. Fiction that contains these elements challenges the patriarchal belief in the fixed and eternal nature of men and women. I like Weisstein's description because it closely resembles the vision that inspired me to become both a feminist and a nov-elist in the first place. So I do call my novels 'feminist fiction.' "

Likewise, I apply the same standards to porn when deciding what is feminist porn. I am not concerned with whether the subject matter interests or offends me (to be offended or sexually turned off is quite different from being insulted or assaulted as a woman). I am not interested in whether romance or pussy shots are employed. I could care less if it is called erotica or pornography. Feminist pornography does not admire or accept patri-archy's ideology. Consequently, feminist pornography must not only empower women on screen, but off camera as well. Female performers must be dealt with in a manner which is respectful and acknowledges them as whole human beings and empowers them as employees. Feminist pornography should challenge patriarchal assumptions about what sexually arouses women, how women feel and what women think. Feminist porn must not accept patriarchal assumptions about the relationship between men and women or even the assumptions regarding gender in general.

So in answer to John Schneider's attempts to remind the viewing public that sex work can never be fulfilling, rewarding or glamorous work because it involves the degradation of the female through sex acts which require spreading one's legs or bending over, I respond that as a feminist sex worker I can only reject the premise that I am degraded as a woman simply by my biology and anatomy. The very idea that bending over or spreading my legs (acts which are required in one form or another to have heterosexual intercourse if you are female) is degrading, pays homage to the oppressive idea that to be female is to be inferior, that the female position is degraded, that degradation and submission are dictated by biology and anatomy. As a feminist prostitute and porn actress and sometimes producer of porn, I soundly reject these patriarchal ideals and embrace my anatomy, biology, sexuality, and individuality. I will not believe the lie. Sex becomes degrading when any person, male or female, loses the power to choose. This can happen when someone perceives a loss of choice as with an authority figure. But the lie that sex can degrade women in a way that it cannot degrade men is simply a lie and it is the true degradation of all of us.

19

Women Who Make Porn: The Influence of Gender on the Content and Approach of Porn Videos

Patti Britton

OVERVIEW

D ESPITE THE PLETHORA OF ADULT VIDEOS (HEREAFTER REFERRED TO AS porn) released into the marketplace since the advent of the home-based VCR, few are produced/directed/written by women. This article is based on an in-depth study conducted in 1991 to assess the content and approach, from a sexological perspective, of female-directed porn videos compared with male-directed porn videos released during 1980-1990.

In 1991 adult industry data indicated that 65 percent of porn purchasers and 40-50 percent of porn renters were women or heterosexual couples. Interestingly, those figures declined by 1998. In 1998, 71 percent of renters were men alone, according to data from Adult Video News Entertainment Guide, the industry standard. In 1991 almost two thousand porn titles were released, as compared to 1998 in which over nine thousand titles hit the marketplace for purchase. Additionally, in 1998 adult revenues reached $4.1 million versus $1.2 billion in 1991, and rentals escalated from 410 million in 1991 to over 686 million in 1998. With the infusion of Internet sites that offer private access to porn purchasing and/or the viewing of adult materials, it is not surprising to note the significant increases in porn rentals and purchases.

LITERATURE REVIEW

Previous literature reviews revealed interesting trends. Most research on porn relies on viewer effects and presents a rather sex-negative bias. It relies heavily on the perceived incidence of violence and the degradation of women as its focus. Previous studies relative to this study include the works of: Hain and Linton (1969), Palmer (1979), Malamuth & Spinner (1989), Winick (1985), Fiedler (1988) and Pickett); only five studies on films/videos were in the literature at the time of the research, by Palys (1986), Pfaus et al. (1986), Cowan et al. (1988), Garcia & Milano (1990), and Fiedler (1988). Further, the filmographies and anthologies that lent insight into the research included Rimmer's *X-Rated Videotape Guide(s)*, Holliday's *Only the Best*, and Faust's *Sex and Pornography: A Controversial and Unique Study.*

THE STUDY

In this eleven-year retrospective study of the content and approach of forty-four titles, 50 percent directed by women and the remaining award-winning titles directed by men, the following elements were investigated: Elements of plot, such as noticeable themes; composition of plot, including length, mix and frequency of sex acts; the roles and images of women, such as if lead females/males were named, if lead females/males had identifiable career roles; the number of female-initiated sex acts; the number of female/female sex acts; descriptive use of "female-positive" or "female-negative" language; and a detailed analysis within each porn title of forty-nine specific sexual behaviors and their frequency.

The initial phase of this study involved personal contacts with notable experts and documentarians in the fields of sexology and adult entertainment. These included IASHS faculty, Laird Sutton, Ph.D., luminary pioneer of sexual pattern films, Jim Holliday, Sam Stetson, Bill Margold, Candida Royalle, Susie Bright, and Juliet Anderson, among others. The thrust of much of the interviews was to verify the identity of each female director and to qualify their actual involvement with the porn they directed. Only those females who could be validated as being the actual director/writer/producer and as having a significant influence over the content and approach of their film or video were selected for research inclusion.

The following titles were selected as the forty-four titles for this study:

From the Female Directors:

Year	Title	Director
1980	*Ball Game*	Anne Perry
1980	*Screwples*	Clair Dia
1981	*Desire for Men*	Carol Connors
1981	*Bad Girls*	Svetlana
1982	*The Playgirl*	Roberta Findlay
1983	*Little Girls Blue II*	JoAnna Williams
1983	*Smoker*	Veronica Rocket
1984	*Educating Nina*	Juliet Anderson

1984	*Stud Hunters*	Suze Randall
	Adventures of Rick Quick, Private Dick	Kristin Leavenworth
1985	*How Do You Like It?*	Marga Aulbach
1986	*Behind the Green Door II*	Sharon McKnight
1986	*Three Daughters*	Lauren Neimy/Candida Royalle
1987	*Miami Spice II*	Svetlana
1987	*Hotel California*	Patti Rhodes
1987	*Taste of Ambrosia*	Candida Royalle/Veronica Hart
1987	*Rites of Passion*	Veronica Hart/Annie Sprinkle
1988	*Sensual Escape*	Gloria Leonard/Candida Royalle & Per Sjostedt
1989	*Retail Slut*	Sharon Mitchell
1989	*Rainwoman*	Patti Rhodes
1989	*Queen of Hearts*	Britt Morgan
1990	*Mistaken Identity*	Tina Marie

From the Male Directors:

Year	Title	Director
1980	*Insatiable*	Godfrey Daniels
	Talk Dirty to Me	Anthony Spinelli
1981	*Nothing to Hide*	Anthony Spinelli
1981	*Outlaw Ladies*	Henri Pachard
1982	*Roommates*	Chuck Vincent
1983	*Devil in Miss Jones II*	Henri Pachard
1983	*Suzie Superstar*	Robert McCallum
1984	*Throat 12 Years After*	Gerard Damiano
	Every Woman Has a Fantasy	Edwin Brown
	New Wave Hookers	Gregory Dark
1985	*Desperate Women*	Ned Morehead
1986	*Flesh and Fantasy*	Gerard Damiano
1986	*If My Mother Only Knew*	Paul Vatelli
1987	*Deep Throat II*	L. Vincent
1987	*Careful, He May be Watching You*	Richard Pacheco
1987	*1001 Erotic Nights II*	Edwin Durell
1987	*Firestorm II*	Cecil Howard
1988	*Jamie Loves Jeff*	Paul Thomas
1989	*Second Skin*	Louie T. Beagle/John Leslie
1989	*Bratgirl*	Paul Thomas
1989	*Taboo VII*	Kirdy Stevens
1990	*Night Trips II*	Andrew Blake

METHODOLOGY/INSTRUMENTS

The Britton Content Analysis Assessment Tool (BCATT) was utilized containing sixty-seven variables for the assessment of each of the forty-four titles for content and approach, with special emphasis on the forty-nine selected sexual behaviors. These forty-nine behaviors, which may have occurred solo, in groups, with a same-sex partner or opposite gender partner, include the following acts: caresses body with hands; deep tongue kissing; licks, sucks female breasts/nipples; licks, sucks male breasts/nipples; fingers female vulva/vagina/clitoris; licks, sucks female vulva/vagina/clitoris; analingus; female hand on and around, rubbing penis; licks, sucks penis and/or scrotum/testicles (with or without condom); dildo used in female vulva/vagina/anal penetration; male penile penetration of female vulva/vagina in varied positions; penis in between female breasts; male ejaculatory response (location); male sexual response during ejaculation (such as camera speed, angles, facial expressions); female orgasmic response (such as observable patterns of vaginal lubrication, pelvic thrusting, heavy breathing, facial expression, vagina/anal contractions, shaking thighs, erect nipples); post-coital afterplay (such as kiss, caress). After coding each of the forty-four titles, an individual profile was generated about each title, noting variables. Some of these variables included lead actors, distributors, designated plot type (such as fantasy or crime story or romantic love story), total minutes of real running time, total minutes to first sex act, number of perceived pseudo-violent or coercive sex scenes, a detailed narrative describing the content of the individual film/video and comments about the work itself, such as interesting sexual objects used in the filming, directorial style or signature techniques, unusual behaviors, ambiance, distinguishing features of the director or the work itself.

RESEARCH RESULTS

No statistically significant differences were found in these categories: (1) number of minutes before the first sex act with a mean/average of five minutes per film/video; (2) number of sex acts, with a mean/average of seven acts per film/video; (3) number of pseudo-violent or coercive acts with a mean of .55 in the females (directors) and a mean of .73 in the males (directors) and a range of 0-4 for both females and males; (4) female/male leads with names; (5) career roles; (6) female-initiated sex acts, with a mean/average of 3.5 in females and 3.4 in males; (7) incidence of female/female sex acts.

However, within the forty-nine selected sexual behaviors results showed only four statistically significant findings and two trends. The four statistically significant findings are: (1) Among the Female Directors it was more common to find incidences of females placing their hands on and around, and/or stroking or rubbing the male's penis, especially during female-to-male oral sexual activities (fellatio); (2) among the Female Directors it was more common to find incidences of females, while experiencing penile penetration of female vulva/vagina (coitus), sitting on top of the male, facing his face, in the female-superior position; (3) among the Female Directors it was more common to find incidences of females audibly and/or visibly breathing hard during sexual stimulation, including male penetration of female vulva/vagina (coitus) or male-to-female oral sexual activities (cunnilingus); (4) among Male Directors it was more common to find incidences of erect nipples on females during sexual stimulation, including male penile penetration of female vulva/vagina (coitus), male-to-female oral sexual activities (cunnilingus). Finally, the one trend was noted among the Male Directors, in which it was more common to find incidences of male ejaculating on the female partner's face.

CONCLUSIONS

In summary, the one noted exception to the patterns observed in the Female Directors was from the groundbreaking director Candida Royalle, Femme Productions. Her work is deliberately constructed from a female perspective, known as women-friendly erotica, created by and for women alone and/or with their heterosexual partners as a couple. In her works assessed during this eleven-year period, women are depicted as "in charge" of their own erotic destiny. In the works from Femme there are no "cum" or "money" shots, no open female genitalia, exclusive use of safer sex and a sensual more than a sexual tone throughout the works.

The remainder of the female-directed works showed no significant overall differences from their male counterparts. This author concludes that porn films/videos are industry- and formula-driven products of their commercial venue. Despite the intention for a female presence in this industry, during the years of the 1980s no such influence on content and approach, other than from Femme Productions, is discernible overall. The need is keen for more women, such as Royalle, Shames and others, to develop and disseminate new materials. Furthermore, it is essential that more studies be conducted on the market impact of porn videos on both men and women in the current milieu of the Internet-affected world. There is a crying urgency for more refreshing formulas for porn videos today and a healthy challenge for adult entertainment providers to broaden the scope of explicit sexual imagery to reflect equally the wide range of male and female fantasies.

BIBLIOGRAPHY

Adult Video News Entertainment Guide. (1999). Van Nuys, Calif.: Adult Video News.
——. (1992). Upper Darby, Pa.: Adult Video News.

Cowan, G., et al. "Dominance and Inequality in X-rated Videocassettes." *Psychology of Women Quarterly* 12 (1988): 299–311.

Faust, B. (1980). *Women, Sex, and Pornography: A Controversial and Unique Study.* New York: Macmillan.

Fiedler, H. (1988). "Diversity in Adult Autoerotic Behaviors: A Survey and Comparison Study of Pictorial Representatives." Doctoral dissertation. San Francisco: The Institute for Advanced Study of Human Sexuality.

Garcia, L. T., and L. A. Milano. "A Content Analysis of Erotic Videos." *Journal of Psychology and Human Sexuality* 3, no. 2 (1990): 95–103.

Hain, J. D., and P. H. Linton. "Psychological Response to Visual Sexual Stimuli." *Journal of Sex Research* 5 (1969): 292–302.

Holliday, J. (1986). *Only the Best: Jim Holliday's Adult Video Almanac and Trivia Treasury.* Van Nuys, Calif.: Cal Vista Direct Ltd.

Malamuth, N. M., and B. A. Spinner. "A Longitudinal Analysis of Sexual Violence in the Best-Selling Erotic Magazines." *Journal of Sex Research* 16, no. 3 (1980): 226–37.

Palmer, C. E. "Pornographic Comics: A Content Analysis." *Journal of Sex Research* 15, no. 4 (1979): 285–98.

Palys, T. S. "Testing the Common Wisdom: The Social Content of Video Pornography." *Canadian Psychologist* 27 (1980): 22–25.

Pickett, P. F. (1991). "Sexually Explicit Advertisements in Women's Magazines: Characteristics of Erotic Content." Doctoral dissertation. San Francisco: The Institute for Advanced Study of Human Sexuality.

Winick, C. A. "Content Analysis of Sexually Explicit Magazines Sold in an Adult Bookstore." *Journal of Sex Research* 21, no. 2 (1985):

SECTION 5

THE RESEARCH ON, EXPERIENCE OF, AND EFFECTS OF PORNOGRAPHY

MUCH OF THE EXPRESSED FEAR ABOUT PORNOGRAPHY IS OVER ITS effect on the viewer but such fears are based more on emotion and belief than on research. Ray Anderson summarizes the nature of the discussion very effectively. Probably the most massive attempt to survey and present the research was the Presidential Commission on Obscenity and Pornography which issued its multi-volume report, published by the U.S. Government Printing Office, in 1970.

Interestingly, President Nixon refused to accept the report, mainly because the assembled experts and their studies found that pornography in itself is not harmful. President Nixon was not alone in refusing to accept the findings and the opponents, like the ostrich, buried their heads in the sands rather than closely examine the data. So antagonistic were some of the anti-porn crusaders that Edwin Meese, the attorney general under President Reagan, appointed his own commission to re-examine the issue. This time, however, no research reports were allowed, and instead relied upon emotional testimony of anti-porn individuals and organized groups.

Ray Anderson in the lead article in this section recounts his experience in trying to explain to an audience what research had shown about pornography. The audience and the press for that matter were not interested; instead the anecdotal evidence of the porn haters was accepted as demonstrating that porn was harmful. Anderson, who deals with sex offenders in his practice, holds that pornography is not a factor in sex abuse, rather the issues are the lack of social skills and of self concept. Pornography, however, sticks in the public mind and makes headlines.

One of the most comprehensive of recent studies is that of Milton Diamond. He presents data reviewing on a world-wide scale the effects of pornography and its relation to sex crime with special emphasis on Japan, the United States, and Shanghai, China. He found that with an increase in pornography, there is a dramatic decrease in sexual crimes. He argues that rather than removing pornography from society, we should strive to make better pornography so that preferred role models are portrayed and more segments of society can come to appreciate or at least understand and tolerate its value. At the same time we should turn our research away from the false issue of pornography to serious studies designed to eliminate or reduce the social ills of rape and other sex crimes.

Similar findings are reported by Esau Tovar, James Elias, and Joy Chang in their review of current literature. Study after study suggests that pornography is not the issue in sexual violence; rather violence itself may in fact cause sexual offending. Pornography, in fact, can have a helpful effect in preserving marriage and family life since both males and females respond to it by being aroused. William Griffit argues that by studying the responses in a serious way, we can help married couples recover some of the vitality and elan present when they were first married. He believes, as do some of the other presenters, that what is needed is not to ban pornography but to make it better.

Laurence O'Toole, who examines the experiences associated with pornography, found on his informal survey that most people had their first conscious exposure to pornography in their early teens. Often the experience was described as disconcerting since they were both aroused and repulsed by it. Others however, found it only exciting. He emphasizes that there is no such thing as an average porn user and the only thing porn users have in common is that they all like porn, although they do not all like the same thing. For many it simply is a kind of escape literature. For others it is educational. Still others can identify with individuals or situations being depicted or enacted. In short, porn and its users and viewers and participants is not a subject for which there are easy answers.

20

The Pornography Question:
Main Event or Sideshow?

Ray Anderson

A T LEAST SINCE THE 1960S AND PROBABLY BEFORE, THE IDEA THAT exposure to pornography generates sexual offending has been popular in some circles. Professional discussions regarding the issue, focus groups devoted to the "problem" and published treatises regarding the dynamics seem never to diminish in their popularity. By comparison, few clinicians who specialize in the assessment and treatment of sexual offenders are impressed with the impact of pornography on their patients based on anything that comes up in actual treatment or assessment. I have specialized in the treatment and assessment of sexual offenders for over thirty years and have been impressed by how infrequently the issue of pornography spontaneously arises in the treatment or assessment sessions of these patients compared with the emphasis placed on the issue elsewhere.

If one takes the view that most research should stem from issues raised in treatment or assessment, then one might question why this issue has such a robust life. Had I been asked to submit a list of the ten most urgent areas for research in this area based on my clinical experience, the exposure to pornography as an etiological factor would not have made the list at any point in my career in this field.

In the late 1960s, a presidential commission sponsored a number of research projects relating to this issue. The projects were carried out both in this country and abroad (The Commission on Obscenity and Pornography, 1970). To the surprise of no one who has followed current developments in this research, the results of the various studies commissioned at that time were negative as to any important relationship between the generation of the various disorders leading to sexual offense and the possession or use of pornography. In fact, some felt that an inverse relationship between the

219

availability of pornography and the incidence of sexual offense was uncovered by some of the research.

Shortly after these results were reported, I was asked to give a talk as part of a panel convened to discuss the issue. My experience during this panel presentation suggested to me that the issue was driven mainly by persons who cared little about discovering causal connections in sexual offending. The most ardent proponents of this type of thinking seemed to be, at that time, persons who were interested in banning pornography for reasons having nothing to do with the scientific investigation of sexual disorder.

At first, I complained to those who were organizing the panel that the issue was so clearly understood by the research just completed that, perhaps, a panel would not be the proper format to present the results. I was assured that my participation would be most appreciated and that the panel would be the best format. When I arrived on the site, to my surprise, I was to be the only presenter taking the position that there was little, if any, evidence of such a causal link. Three of the four presenters would enthusiastically take the opposite position. I began to feel like the victim of an ambush.

All the other presenters were very sensitive to indirect or even anecdotal "evidence" tending to imply this causal relationship. One of the presenters, a psychologist who was an excellent and dynamic public speaker, gave a series of indirect and anecdotal reasons why pornography should be considered a major factor in sexual offending.

This presenter was so well accepted that the proceedings were suspended temporarily while the print and visual media pressed in on this eloquent presenter to gain more details regarding his point of view. A brief statement was recorded for the evening television news telecast. My data-oriented talk was politely ignored both by the press and by the audience. I later learned that the audience was somewhat self-selected for attitudes opposed to pornography in general.

Another presenter actually suggested that the causal relationship was so clear that the First Amendment to the Constitution should be repealed or at least amended so that appropriate steps could be taken to protect society. As part of the proof, this presenter distributed a fairly large number of pornographic pictures to the audience.

The audience was then asked to view the pornography and then decide for themselves whether it would cause sex offending or not. I was annoyed at such an unscientific approach. What I personally felt was a rather comic moment ensued, however, because some members of the audience kept a large portion of the pornography for themselves. Even though I could see no outward evidence of laughter in what I later learned was this rather monolithic audience, I was privately amused at this presenter's angry demand that the pornography be returned.

To me, the above events are somewhat paradigmatic of an emotional, polemic, and even political approach to what should be a balanced and scientific examination of these data and experiences. This is not to diminish the importance of emotional or even political motives in social change. The readiness to exaggerate the practical importance of this issue to our specialized practice, however, is not welcome and probably detracts from clarification in other areas of our practice.

My impression is that exposure to pornography, if it is relevant to the genesis of sexual offending at all, is a somewhat peripheral issue at best. The relative scientific importance of the issue is clearly a more important consideration than whether there is any relationship at all between the possession or use of pornography and the development of a subsequent sexual disorder. After all, we want to clarify relationships that will lead to practical improvements in the treatment of these offenders. I am aware of the findings of the Meese Commission, but there are a number of methodological problems with this research, and it appears to be out of the mainstream of research and clinical experience in this area (Meese, A. G., 1986).

It would appear that, whatever causal relationship exists, the strength and importance to public policy of such a relationship is probably exaggerated by the degree of emphasis on this topic. To illustrate this point, my research for this paper regarding the influence of pornography in sexual offense yielded ninety-three "hits" from the clinic's internal sex offender data base when the keyword "Pornography" was used.

By contrast, using "Social Skills" as a keyword hits were limited to thirty-seven using the same data base. Hits using "Self Concept" were reduced to a mere nineteen in spite of the acknowledged and unchallenged importance of this topic in the treatment and assessment of sexual offenders. I believe most of us who specialize in this area of practice would agree that both of these latter topics are far more important issues in sex offending than exposure to pornography.

In actually treating sexual offenders, one gains the impression that few sex offender patients possess pornography and, for those who do, the pornography is not an important part of their disorder. For many, it seems to be something of an after-thought. Sometimes, pornography appears to be a significant side issue but many of this rather small number of patients actually appear less likely to offend when some form of pornography is available.

The child sexual abuser, specifically, who is interested in collecting pictures, is more likely to collect pornography depicting normal heterosexual contacts. Those who do collect pictures of children are more likely to collect clothed pictures or even pictures from commercial clothing catalogues rather than examples of child pornography. Again, we appear to be discussing a rather tiny proportion of the overall child sexual abuser population. For most, the collection or use of picture or written pornography is not an issue.

Much of this clinical data is obtained from passive listening. That is, the patient produces the information spontaneously; not in response to specific questioning. This form of date gathering is arguably more likely to be objective than posing specific questions (especially when the form of the question implies the desired answer).

My impression is that the research literature largely supports the above clinical impression (Kant, 1971; Goldstein, 1973). Examples of studies supporting an important link between exposure to pornography and the genesis of sexual offending tend not to be based on studies of offenders but may be based instead on other types of indirect research, interpretations of general data or mere conceptual reasoning (Russell, 1988; Nemes, 1992; Sharp, 1986). However this may be, the burden of proof would appear to be on proponents of this type of reasoning (Murrin & Laws, 1990).

Again, it is useful to contrast this area of interest with "Self Concept," a known important area that includes most offenders, not just a few. There is little controversy that this is an important issue with this treatment population (Segal & Marshall, 1985). Often, statistical probability levels in this type of research are so clearly significant that little doubt remains as to what an important area this is for the sex offender patient.

REFERENCES

Commission on Obscenity and Pornography, The. (1970). *The report of the commission of obscenity and pornography.* Washington, D.C.: U.S. Government Printing Office.

Goldstein, M. J. Exposure to erotic stimuli and sexual deviance. *Journal of Social Issues* 29, no. 3 (1973): 197–219.

Kant, H. S. Exposure to pornography and sexual behavior in deviant normal groups. *Corrective Psychiatry and Journal of Social Therapy* 17, no. 2 (1971): 5–17.

Meese, A. G. (1986). *Attorney General (Edwin Meese) Commission Report.* Washington, D.C.: U.S. Government Printing Office.

Murrin, M. R., & D. R. Laws (1990). The influence of pornography on sexual crimes. In William L. Marshall & D. R. Laws, eds., *Handbook of sexual assault: Issues, theories, and treatment of the offender* (pp. 73–91). New York: Plenum Press.

Nemes, I. The relationship between pornography and sex crimes. *Journal of Psychiatry and Law* 20, no. 4 (1992): 459–81.

Russell, D. E. Pornography and rape—A causal model. *Political-Psychology* 9, no. 1 (1988): 41–73.

Segal, Z. V., & W. L. Marshall (1985). Self-reported and behavioral assertion in two groups of sexual offenders. *Journal of Behavior Therapy and Experimental Psychiatry* 16 (3): 223–229.

Sharp, I. Pornography and sex-related crime—A sociological perspective. *Bulletin of the Hong Kong Psychological Society* 16–17 (1986): 73–81.

21

The Effects of Pornography: An International Perspective

Milton Diamond

F OR THOSE WHO WISH TO STUDY THE EFFECTS OF PORNOGRAPHY, REAL-
world studies seem rare. Depending upon the field of the experimenter and his/her expertise, different research methods are employed.

Teaching psychologists usually use random samples of people but most
often employ students, either volunteers or not, as subjects. These subject
are then presented with a sequence of exposures to different media, usually
video or film clips for varying periods of time. Then some paper and pencil
test or artificial situation is fabricated to measure what the experimenter
thinks is a reflection of the subject's experience. The experimenter can ask
of the subject's subsequent masturbation, or coital frequency, attitudes
toward hypothetical situations or even place the subject into an artificially
manipulated situation in which he or she is supposedly reacting in a way
molded by the exposure experience. This is often contrived with the use of
a confederate to goad the subject to react. Examples of such studies are
those of Zillmann and Bryant (Zillmann, 1984; Zillmann & Bryant, 1982;
1984; Zillmann & Weaver, 1989), Malamuth & Donnerstein (Donnerstein,
1984; Donnerstein, Donnerstein, & Evans, 1975; Donnerstein, Linz, &
Penrod, 1987; Malamuth & Donnerstein, 1984).

Another research technique, somewhat closer to the real world, is often
used by clinicians. These investigators interview persons who have committed some sort of sex offense and compare their experiences with pornography with those who have not committed sex crimes. Here come to mind
the work of Abel (Abel, Barlow, Blanchard, & Guild, 1977; Abel & Becker,
1985; Abel, Mittelman, & Becker, 1985), Becker (Becker & Stein, 1991;
1991) and Kant and Goldstein (1970) (Goldstein, Kant, Judd, Rice, & Green,
1971; Goldstein & Kant, 1973).

Comparably, one can research either the victim of sex crimes or interview police investigators and record how pornography might or might not have figured in any criminal incident. Unfortunately, there is usually no official police record kept of the more common occasions when *no* pornography is involved while it is common to record when it *is* found to be involved. These studies consist mostly of anecdotal or hearsay materials with little or no control on recall, bias, or selection of spokespersons interviewed. Crusaders for either side of the issue on pornography are fond of this anecdotal "research" technique. Most noted for using such stories on the anti-porn side, those *for* censorship, are the sex-negative feminists Andrea Dworkin (Dworkin, 1981; 1985; Dworkin & MacKinnon, 1988) and Catharine MacKinnon (MacKinnon, 1989; 1993) the members of "Women Against Rape" (WAR) and members of "Women Against Pornography" (WAP). Also notable here is Susan Brownmiller (1975) and her well-known work *Against Our Will: Men, Women and Rape.*

Those *against* censorship also use this technique, although much less frequently. They include authors such as Beatrice Faust (1980) with her book *Women, Sex and Pornography.* Usually, those against censorship show how it is devastating to art, education and social order. That approach is exemplified by such groups as "Women Against Censorship," the Feminist Anti-Censorship Task Force (FACT) and the "National Coalition against Censorship (NCAC)."[1]

An excellent research technique, only occasionally used due to its cost, is to interview a cross-section of "normal" randomly chosen individuals and compare the experiences of those who have voluntarily consumed pornography with those who have not. Large selected populations too can be canvassed. Investigators who use this technique search to see if more of those exposed to sexually explicit materials (SEM) were involved with sex crimes or other anti-social activities than those who have not been similarly exposed. It may be difficult to get honest answers to actual illegal or anti-social behaviors such as rape, child or spouse abuse, however. Nevertheless, polls and surveys, if done well, often approach this technique. Gebhard, Gagnon, Pomeroy, & Christenson (1965), Smith (Smith & Hand, 1987), Diamond and Dannemiller (1989), Lauman, Gagnon, Michael and Stuart (1994) and others have used this method. Major national opinion polls typically use such techniques.

Lastly, one can compare how pornography has effected total societies when the material has gone from being illegal and relatively scarce to being legal and plentiful. Or vice versa; one can investigate what happens when a community goes from having relatively large amounts of sexually explicit materials (SEM) to relatively small amounts. Researchers using this technique question: "What happens over the years to sex crimes and other anti-social activities?" Within a single society these comparisons can also be made, where different geographical areas–individual states or provinces for instance–contain relatively large amounts of pornography in contrast with those that have little or none. Perhaps the best known of these societal studies are the works of Berl Kutchinsky of Denmark, who studied different countries [see, e.g., Kutchinsky, 1978; 1985a; 1990; 1991].

This paper focuses on these last types of studies. It will attempt to show how the prevalence of pornography in a locale has or has not had an influence on sex crimes, particularly rape. The focus on rape reflects the opinion of those most opposed to available pornography. They claim the more sexually explicit material present in a community, the more rape. Or, as it has been alleged: "Pornography is the theory and rape is the practice" (Morgan, 1980). Findings around the world are reviewed with initial attention to the countries of Denmark, Sweden, and Germany. Then, I focus on Japan, a country quite different from those in the West. In regard to pornography in Japan, the swing from prudish and restrictive to relatively permissive and nonrestrictive was dramatic. Some limited data from Shanghai and new data from the United States follow. Several conclusions are then offered. These real-world types of findings most accurately reflect the broad crime-related effects pornography has on modern societies.

Pornography is a term in popular use but can also be a legal term. For the purposes of simplicity in the present discussion, *pornography* is broadly defined as any sexually explicit material primarily developed or produced to arouse sexual interest or provide erotic pleasure. It can be so-called soft-core or hard-core and it can extend from pin-ups which might be offensive to XXX fetish or materials involving children (so-called child-porn). The term is often, in itself, seen as pejorative. I view it as neutral. It can be in any media and it might be legal or illegal. Pornography, to be illegal, generally has to further be found *obscene.* Here too *obscenity* is a legal term and each jurisdiction, e.g., country, province or state, defines such material differently.

SOME BACKGROUND

In the 1960s the U.S. Supreme Court issued rulings that dramatically changed how our country was to, thereafter, deal with censorship. These were rulings regarding the imported books: *Lady Chatterley's Lover, Tropic of Cancer,* and *Fanny Hill* (Rembar, 1968). Before 1966 these books could not legally be published in America; afterwards writings that had literary merit were no longer to be considered obscene even if they contained material considered sexually explicit. These books and others like them not only became available but widely popular, and are still considered as classics. (Suffice it to say that, in their time and later, proven literature such as Aristophanes, Balzac, Boccaccio, Chaucer, Galileo, Maimonides, Ovid, Shakespeare, Socrates, Spinoza and Swift have all suffered from the censor's prejudice.)

The response to the Supreme Court decision regarding these now-recognized literary treasures, from the conservative, moralistic populace (a possible majority at the time), was outrage and fear that obscenity would flood the country. The *New York Daily News* fueled some of this with a headline that read "BLAME COURTS FOR FLOOD OF PRINTED FILTH." Significantly, two years later, *The Wall Street Journal* published an article on the *Daily News* detailing how the *News* attained their readership, the second largest in the nation, by exploiting–you guessed it–sex in its photos and stories (Rembar, 1968). But the stage was set: There was a clamor against pornography and an attempt to identify what was obscene. In response to this clamor, President Lyndon B. Johnson appointed a commission to study the problem.

This presidential Commission reported (Pornography, 1970), no such relationship of pornography leading to rape or sexual assault could be demonstrated as applicable for adults or juveniles. This Commission, chaired by William B. Lockhart, past President of the Association of American Law Schools, sponsored various surveys and research studies and concluded: "In sum, empirical research designed to clarify the question has found no evidence to date that exposure to explicit sexual materials plays a significant role in the causation of delinquent or criminal behavior among youth or adults. The Commission cannot conclude that exposure to erotic materials is a factor in the causation of sex crime or sex delinquency (pp. 27)."[2] Indeed, the Commission concluded that pornography has a sex education effect that can be beneficial.

When President Ronald Reagan entered the White House, to placate his conservative constituency, he rejected the findings of the President Johnson Commission and, in 1984, appointed a commission to be headed by his Attorney General.[3] In 1986 the findings of this United States' Attorney General's Commission were released (Meese, 1986). This commission found, in contrast with the previous Presidential Commission, that: "substantial exposure to sexually violent materials . . . bears a *causal relationship* to antisocial acts of sexual violence and, for some subgroups, possibly to unlawful acts of sexual violence (pp. 326) [emphasis mine]." In distinction to the Presidential Commission, however, this Attorney General's Commission was politically, not scientifically, constituted.[4]

This "Meese" Commission was primarily composed of nonscientists who did no research of their own and commissioned none. It solicited testimony mainly from specific parties and organizations which it anticipated would be sympathetic to its goals while ignoring testimony from those it suspected would be disagreeable. Many critics took this Meese Commission to task for the bias of their work; e.g., Lab (1987), Lynn (1986) and Nobile & Nadler (1986).

The Meese Commission's own minority report, by two of the only three women on the panel (Judith V. Becker, & Ellen Levine)–one of whom had a great deal of experience in sex research with sex criminals (JVB)–dissented from the majority report in saying the findings were not in keeping with the amassed social science data (Meese, 1986). The statistical methods as well as research methods were also significantly found wanting (Smith, 1987). Parenthetically, nation-wide studies in the United States, done essentially at the same time as the Meese Commission's work, also seemed to find no strong evidence that rape rates were associated with porn as measured by circulation rates of pornographic magazines or the presence of adult theaters in a community (Baron & Strauss, 1987; Scott & Schwalm, 1988a, b).[5]

In Britain, the privately constituted Longford Committee (Amis, Anderson, Beasley-Murray, & al., 1972) reviewed the pornography situation in that nation and concluded that such material was detrimental to public morals. It too dismissed the scientific evidence in favor of protecting the "public good" against forces that might "denigrat(e) and devalu(e) human persons." The officially constituted British (Williams) Committee on Obscenity and Film Censorship, however, in 1979 analyzed the situation and reported (Home Office, 1979): "From everything we know of social attitudes, and have learnt in the course of our enquires, our belief can only be that the role of pornography in influencing the state of society is a minor one. To think anything else . . . is to get the problem of pornography out of proportion" (p. 95).

A 1984 Canadian study found similarly. A review by McKay and Dolff for the Department of Justice of Canada reported "There is no systematic research evidence available which suggests a causal relationship between pornography and the morality of Canadian society . . . [and none] which suggests that increases in specific forms of deviant behavior, reflected in crime trend statistics (e.g., rape) are causally related to pornography" (McKay & Dolff, 1985). The Canadian Fraser Committee, in 1985, after a review of the topic, concluded the evidence so poorly organized that no consistent body of evidence could be found to condemn pornography (Canada, 1985).

Among those European/Scandinavian societies investigated for any relation between the availability of pornography and rape or sexual assault, again no such correlation could be demonstrated (Kutchinsky, 1985a; 1991). For the countries of Denmark, Sweden and West Germany,[6] the three nations for which ample data were available at the time, Kutchinsky analyzed in depth the crime statistics and pornography availability for the years from approximately 1964 to 1984. Kutchinsky showed that as the amount of pornography increasingly became available, the rate of rapes in these countries either *decreased* or remained relatively level. These countries legalized or decriminalized pornography in 1969, 1970 and 1973 respectfully. In all three countries the rates of nonsexual violent crimes and nonviolent sex crimes (e.g., peeping, flashing) essentially decreased also.

According to Kutchinsky, only in the United States did it appear that, in the 1970s and early 1980s as the amount of available pornography increased, did some increase in rape occur (Kutchinsky, 1985a; 1991). But Kutchinsky also noted a change in how rape was recorded which could account for the apparent increase in the American sex crime rate.

Following Kutchinsky's work no other large scale study has been reported. Considering the volume and intensity of debate still current in Europe and the United States and elsewhere surrounding the possible link between pornography and sex crimes it is valuable to see how another nation, one quite different from those in the West, compares in the availability of SEM and the occurrence of rape and other sex related crimes. Japan, an Asian culture with its ancient tradition of male prerogative and female subservience and thirteen year post-World War II period of legal prostitution provided a sufficient cultural contrast to that of the United States and the other Western countries investigated (see Diamond & Uchiyama, 1999).

Presently in Japan, sexually explicit materials which cater to all sorts of erotic interests and fetishes are readily available. These include video tapes, books, and magazines as well as sexually obvious comic books (*manga*) without age restrictions as to availability. Public phone booths in commercial areas and city newspapers contain advertisements for sexual liaisons of every sort. However, this widespread availability of modern pornography is relatively new. Essentially since the end of World War II with the imposition of American military rules, which lasted until 1951, there was prohibition of any sexually explicit material. In Japan almost all sexually explicit visual material was seen as legally obscene. This continued under the Japanese government into the late 1980s; until then, images or depictions of frontal nudity were banned as were pictures of pubic hair or genitals. No sex act could be depicted graphically.

There are many indications that document an increase in the number and availability of sexually explicit materials in Japan over the years 1972–1995. Under the auspices of "Juvenile Protective Ordinances" formulated within and for each prefecture (except Nagano prefecture), data had been collected of items that might be "considered harmful for juveniles." Once items are so designated they are forbidden to be sold or distributed to minors under eighteen years of age. Collected by local authorities, these are statistics on items such as sexually explicit films, books, magazines and video tapes. It also included explicitly violent materials. These data are forwarded yearly to the Youth Authority in Somicho (Government Management and Coordination Agency). Items so listed increased almost four-fold from some 20,000 items in 1970 to roughly 76,000 in 1996, the last year for which such data are available. Since 1989 the greatest increase in such materials were accounted for by sexually explicit video tapes. Despite any such categorization, these materials remain readily available to persons of any age.

The main concern, however, was not against videos but against sexually explicit comic books available to children. Conservative groups and the media began to call for government action to stem the rising tide of pornography they saw occurring. For instance the citizens of Wakayama prefecture loudly called for the control of sexually explicit *manga* directed at children (Mainichi-shinbun, 1990).[7]

For reasons that are unclear, these calls were not effectively heeded. Indeed, while the laws themselves were not modified, interpretation of them changed. Judges during this period became increasingly liberal allowing more pornography of wider scope to be considered "not obscene." Concomitantly with this, as might be reflected by the widely reported uproar regarding a case of rape by American servicemen of a young Okinawa girl in 1995, this crime is taken quite seriously in Japan (Desmond, 1995).

In 1991, twenty-one prefecture governments designated forty-six specific sexually-oriented publications as being "harmful to juveniles" and complained of them to the publishers (Burrill, 1991). The companies involved accepted the criticism and its industry's "Publishing Ethics Council" voted for self regulation and advised its member firms to place an "Adult Comics" mark on sex oriented *manga* (Anonymous, 1991a). The Council further advised their distributors to maintain these comics in the "adult corner" of their stores. This advice was not always followed. Sales of such sex-filled comics totaled more than ¥ 180 billion in 1990, a figure up 13 percent from the year before (Burrill, 1991).

Production of the classic Japanese love film *Ai no corrida* ("In the Realm of the Senses") was banned from Japan due to its nudity and erotic content. This film by Nagisa Oshima was produced in France in 1976 and quickly became a sensation at film festivals in New York and Cannes. When first shown in Japan, however, in October of 1976, the film was seized by authorities. Based on a true story well known in Japan, its content—involving the vivid depiction of asphixiophilia—was, nevertheless, considered too obscene for public viewing in Japan. The producer and script writer were taken to court and charged with obscenity but found not guilty (Okudaira, 1979; Oshima, 1979; Uchida, 1979). An expurgated version of the film was subsequently released. Frontal nudity was permitted to appear on film for the first time at the 1986 Tokyo film festival (Downs, 1990).

The American college sex text book *Sexual Decisions* (Diamond & Karlen, 1980) was republished in a Japanese edition in 1985 (Diamond & Karlen, 1985). Depictions of sexual positions and other images were allowed only after the book was edited to reduce the number of illustrations with pubic hair or exposed genitalia. It was the first college level sex text in that country. The first art photo book with full frontal nudity of women was also published in 1985 (Downs, 1990). As with the text, *Sexwatching*, a trade book for general readership illustrated with some three hundred images, first published in England and the United States in 1984 (Diamond, 1984) was published in Japanese in 1986 (Diamond, 1986). Again, several of the original illustrations, considered middle-of-the-road in the United Kingdom and the United States, had to be replaced with images considered less sexually explicit.

Change in Japan from the conservative posture of the 1960s, 1970s and early 1980s began to most markedly shift toward permissive in the late 1980s and early 1990s. Magazines such as *Playboy* and *Penthouse*, due to their display of pubic hair, were banned totally in Japan until 1975. They were then allowed to be imported into Japan if the offending images of genitalia were "sand-papered" or otherwise rendered opaque.

This original ban against the display of pubic hair was applied so routinely that objective commentators noted that obscenity standards occasionally blocked distribution of serious art works but were ineffective in slowing the increasing availability of sexually explicit materials (Anonymous, 1992). In June 1991 the *Japan Times* described the influx of pornographic comics into the market as showing a rampant growth that "depict sexual perversions and violence, including the utter debasement of women, in graphically appalling detail even if pubic hair is not shown." (quoted in

Woodruff, 1991). Almost simultaneously, the *Asahi Shinbun* newspaper reported that police would no longer prosecute "pubic hair" pictures for obscenity since the social trend has moved to accept photos of this type and concluded "the decision not to prosecute indicates that pubic hair is no longer a uniform standard for obscenity" (Woodruff, 1991).

In the early 1980s, European and American pornographic video tapes were the most prevalent form of contraband seized by Japanese custom agents from travelers returning from aboard (Abramson & Hayashi, 1984). These materials were routinely confiscated. Now such tapes are locally produced and available. They often contain minors as actresses. There is a "Child Welfare Law" in Japan which prohibits child prostitution. However, there are no specific child pornography laws in Japan and SEM depicting minors (particularly uniformed school girls) is readily available and widely consumed. Most charges of obscenity presently are related to portrayal of group or violent rape or realistic and graphic film or video descriptions of sexual behaviors considered deviant and dangerous (as in *Ai no corrida*).

In 1989 a survey of *manga* in book shops and magazine stalls by a voluntary citizen's group, the "Tokyo Bureau of Citizens and Cultural Affairs," found that more than half of the stories depicted sex acts. They reported: "in many cases, female characters were treated simply as sex objects for the satisfaction of men" (Anonymous, 1991a).

Again in 1989, a report by the Japanese "Publishing Science Research Institute" presented statistics for the legal production of Japanese publications. *Playboy* and *Penthouse* were among the best selling adult men's magazines. Semi-annual sales figures for *Playboy* averaged some 900,000 monthly for each issue in 1977. The monthly value of magazines with sexual content increased from ¥ 3,264 million in 1984 to ¥ 3,665 million in 1988 (Shupan Nenkan, 1988, 1997).

In February 1991, the Liberal Democratic Party asked its members to introduce legislation to regulate sexually explicit *manga* (Anonymous, 1991a). The motion failed but again served notice that the increase in pornography available to children was of widening social concern. In that year a "Survey on Comics among Youth" by the "Japanese Association for Sex Education" (J.A.S.E., 1991) found that among Middle School students 21.6 percent of males and 7.6 percent of females regularly read "porno-comics." In 1993 a survey by the Youth Authority of *Somucho* (Government Management and Coordination Agency) (Somucho, 1993) found that approximately 50 percent of the male and 20 percent of the female Middle and Upper High School students were found to regularly read "porno-comics."[8]

Another index of sex related materials available in Japan might be reflected in the number of sex related industries (*fuuzoku kanren eigyou*) registered with and monitored by the police. These industries include strip theaters, so-called love hotels (rooms available by the hour), "adult" sex shops (for the purchase of pornography or paraphernalia associated with sexual activities), and "soap lands" ("massage" or "shampoo" parlors known to offer sexual services). The authorities use such statistics in monitoring potential influences on minors. According to statistics from *Roposensho*, the Japanese National Police Agency (JNPA), an organization akin to the American Federal Bureau of Investigation (FBI), these numbered approximately 7,500 establishments in 1972 and more than 12,600 in 1995. The largest segment increase was seen in the number of so-called fashion massage parlors in operation which offered sexual services. A newer type of "body shampoo parlor" is also now available (Roposensho, 1995).

Telephone sex lines have become increasingly common. In the first 18 month period since they started operation, a commercial business information service, "Dial Q2", which at first provided sports results, advertisements and medical guidance, in 1991 switched more than one-fourth of its lines to telephone sex services (Anonymous, 1991b). This remains a popular form of sexual commerce even though, unlike here in the United States where anyone can call such services, individual households must initiate a special request to even participate. "Telephone clubs" have also proliferated. In such clubs men wait for calls from girls and women. The phone numbers to call are widely advertised as free for the female caller; "excitement" and "romance" are promised. This is often an outlet for prostitution contacts (Stroh, 1996). It is also of general social concern since informal surveys by the police have found that some one-fourth of high school girls have made contact via a telephone club.

While, in 1992, authorities occasionally continued to cite magazines and newspapers for public indecency if they showed nude pictures, or if genitals or any pubic hair were visible, police confiscation became uncommon and prosecutions inconsistent. Peculiarly these legal challenges might have occurred even when these images were clearly artistic works (Anonymous, 1992). By 1993 that type of prosecution became rare.

In 1993 the *Shukan Post* became Japan's top-selling magazine. This appeared due to photos containing glimpses of pubic hair and feature photos of nude girls and articles on sex. Circulation jumped from about 850,000 in the first six months of 1993 to about 867,000 for the first six months of 1996. This popularity spawned two additional magazines which were even more sexually explicit: *Shukan Bunshum* and *Shukan Shincho*. In 1995 these magazines had average weekly sales of more than 600,000 copies (Shupan Nenkan, 1988, 1997).

The changing public attitude toward pornography might be considered reflected by the number of police cases where the arresting charge was "distribution of obscene materials." Despite the rise in available SEM, arrests and convictions for the distribution of obscene materials significantly declined in Japan from 3,298 in 1972 to 702 in 1995 (Roposensho, 1995). [Table 1].

Currently, not only are visuals with pubic hair and exposed genitalia present, but cartoon images of hard-core sexual encounters in *manga* as well as in adult reading materials are available. These can be pictures and stories involving bestiality, sadomasochism, necrophilia and incest; the characters involved may be adults, children or both. Essentially, anything goes.

Two additional measures of erotica available in Japan are noteworthy. The first is that reported by Greenfeld (1994) that approximately 14,000 "adult" videos were being made yearly in Japan compared with some 2500 in the U.S. And the average Japanese watched nearly an hour more of TV a day than did Americans. The second measure is a recent report by Keiji Goto, a senior official at the Japanese National Police Agency. *Roposensho* estimates that about 1200 commercial child pornographic internet sites exist in Japan. And there are no anti-child porn laws in Japan (Anonymous, 1998a). And while a bill to outlaw child-porn, on and off the Internet, was introduced into the Diet early in 1998, the bill did not make it onto its agenda and was not likely to come up for consideration (Anonymous, 1998a).

EFFECTS OF PORNOGRAPHY

While all these changes were occurring we investigated how the occurrence of sex crimes in general and rape in particular correlated with the increasing availability of pornography. For comparison and as "control" measures the incidence of *Murder* and nonsexual *Violent crimes* for the same period was looked at. We particularly attended to any influence the introduction of widely available pornography might have had on juveniles (Diamond & Uchiyama, 1999).

The period chosen for investigation includes the twenty-three years from 1972 to 1995. These are years for which official data from Japan are available. Prior to 1972 the data collection methods and associated definitions used in Japan were significantly different from those presently in use and are not suitable for comparison. These years, 1972–1995, cover a time period during which Japan transitioned from a nation whose laws, or their interpretation, relating to pornography changed from sexually prudish to a country whose sex censorship laws can now be classified as permissive.

In application, when Japan was in its prudish phase, not only might pornography include so-called hard core erotica, but until the 1970s and into the 1980s this included material that graphically presented genitals, pubic hair, or frontal nudity. Depictions of any sexual act in educational material or work of art might fall under this definition. Public and official attitudes toward such materials, appeared to gradually relax from the 1970s on. Particularly in the years 1990 and 1991, major shifts became apparent in how this law was interpreted; fewer materials were being charged as obscene and even fewer convictions obtained. The reasons for this shift are not obvious.

The jury system is not used in Japan. Final determination of which materials or acts meet any criteria of criminality are typically decided by a panel of three judges to whom the material or incident is presented. In Japan, the laws are applied nationally but often interpreted regionally; judges in the cities are often more lenient regarding pornography than are those in rural areas. To promote uniformity across the country, approximately every three years the judges are rotated to a different prefecture. As in other countries, initial determination of criminality is first made at a lower level, e.g., the local policeman or custom agent. Alleged obscene material is confiscated with a determination of actual obscenity to be made later.

PORNOGRAPHY & SEX CRIME DATA

JAPAN

Data on the actual number of reported sex crimes in Japan are from the files of *Roposensho*. The JNPA has been maintaining crime statistics for Japan since 1948. Basically yearly reports from all forty-seven Japanese prefectures including Okinawa are collated. These official crime records are based on independent police investigations. During the period under review there has been no known change in the method of collecting and recording of data.

Data regarding sex crimes, consistently and regularly recorded in police records, are clearly more available and definitive than those for quantitative or qualitative measures of pornography. It is readily obvious from the data that the incidence of rape and other sex crimes had steadily and dramatically decreased over the period under review. [Table 1]

The incidence of rape has progressively declined from 4677 reported cases with 5,464 offenders in 1972 to the 1995 incidence of 1,500 cases with 1,160 offenders; a dramatic reduction in incidence of some two-thirds. The character of the rape also changed markedly. Early in our period of observation many of the rapes were gang rapes (more than a single attacker) thus accounting for the number of offenders exceeding the number of rapes reported. This has now become increasingly rare. In 1972, 12.3 percent of the rapes by juveniles were conducted by two or more offenders. Over the years, the percentage decreased so that in 1995 only 5.7 percent of the rapes were of this category.

The number of rapes committed by juveniles has also markedly decreased. Juveniles committed 33 percent of the rapes in 1972 but only 18 percent of the rapes perpetrated in 1995. The number of juvenile offenders dramatically dropped every period reviewed from 1,803 perpetrators in 1972 to a low of 264 in 1995; a drop of some 85 percent. [Table 1]

For this same period the incidence of sex assault had also decreased from a 1972 incidence of 3,139 cases to fewer than 3,000 cases for the years 1975 to 1990. In 1995, however, the incidence of reported sexual assaults rebounded to 3,644 cases. Since all figures in these tables represent actual cases rather than rates, it can be seen that even the proportion of sex assault cases did not increase. During these intervening years the population of Japan had increased more than 20 percent, from approximately 107 million in 1970 to more than 125 million persons in 1995 (Nihon, 1996). Thus, the actual rate decreased slightly from .0292 to .0290 per thousand persons. It is also noteworthy that during this period, according to JNPA records, the rate of convictions for rape increased markedly from 85 percent in 1972 to more than 90 percent in the 1980s and more than 95 percent in the 1990s. This might be because, increasingly, in these latter years the rapist was less likely to be known to the victim; proving lack of consent became easier.

The data regarding public indecency (e.g., flashing) was more in keeping with those for rape than assault. The incidence of reported public indecencies decreased about one third over the period. Considering the concomitant increase in population this corresponds to a rate decrease of some 50 percent. [Table 1]

Police statistics use the victim age categories: 0-5, 6-12, 13-19, 20-24, 25-29, 30-39, 40-49, etc. The first three age categories reflect ages associated with "preschool," "elementary and beginning middle school," and "later middle school and high school" years. It also reflects the Japanese consideration of twenty being the age at which one reaches legal majority.

The most dramatic decrease in sex crimes was seen when attention was focused on the number and age of rapists and victims among younger groups. [Table 2] We hypothesized that the increase in pornography, without age restriction and in comics, if it had any detrimental effect, would most negatively influence younger individuals. Just the opposite occurred. The number of victims decreased particularly among the females younger than thirteen. In 1972, 8.3 percent of the victims were younger than thirteen. In 1995 the percentage of victims younger than thirteen years of age dropped to 4.0 percent; a reduction of greater than 50 percent.

In 1972, 33.3 percent of the offenders were between fourteen–nineteen years of age; by 1995 that percentage had decreased to 9.6 percent. Thus, over the period in question, there was a major shift in the proportion of victims and offenders away from the younger categories to older categories.

Lastly, in Japan, while the total number of rapes decreased, the percentage of rapes by a stranger increased steadily from 61.6 percent of the rapes reported in 1979 to 79.5 percent of the rapes in 1995. Thus, date rape and familial rape decreased significantly.

As a statistical control measure of sorts we analyzed the cases of murder and non sexual violent physical assaults reported during the years 1972 to 1995. [Table 1] Here also dramatic decreases occurred over the period reviewed. Murders dropped by some 40 percent and non-sexual physical assaults decreased by about 60 percent. In these last two categories of crime, however, there was no comparable shift in the age groups involved in these activities either as victim or offender.

COMMENTS ON JAPANESE DATA: Comparisons

Within Japan itself, the dramatic increase in available pornography and sexually explicit materials is apparent to even a casual observer. This is concomitant with a general liberalization of restrictions on other sexual outlets as well. Also readily apparent from the information presented is that, over this period of change, sex crimes in every category, from *rape* to *public inde-*

cency, sexual offenses from both ends of the criminal spectrum, significantly decreased in incidence. Most significantly, despite the wide increase in availability of pornography to children, not only was there a decrease in sex crimes with juveniles as victims but the number of juvenile offenders also decreased significantly.

These findings are similar to, but are even more striking than, those reported with the rise of sexually explicit materials in Denmark, Sweden and West Germany. The findings from Europe were, in turn, more dramatic than those reported for the United States. Kutchinsky (1991) studied the situation in Denmark, Sweden, West Germany and the U.S.A. following the legalization or liberalization of the appropriate pornography laws in those countries. The first three countries mentioned, decriminalized the production and distribution of sexually explicit materials in 1969, 1970, and 1973 respectively. In the U.S.A. there was no widespread decriminalization or legalization but, as in Japan, interpretations of the laws seemed to change and prosecution against SEM decreased markedly. Concomitantly, the availability of pornography increased commensurably. Kutchinsky studied the course of sex crimes for the twenty-year period 1964 to 1984. Thus his period of study overlaps with the first half of ours.

Kutchinsky (1991) found that in Denmark and Sweden adult rapes, for the years studied, increased only modestly and in West Germany not at all. Indeed, by 1989 (the last date for which data were available to Kutchinsky and the year in which East and West Germany were reunited) in West Germany the rape rate continued to decline since 1983 to a historic low ever reported; 8.0 cases per 100,000 (Kutchinsky, 1994, p. 6); a 27 percent decrease in the last six years. In all three countries, nonviolent sex crimes decreased. The slight increase in Denmark and Sweden, was thought by some most probably due to increased reporting as a result of greater and increasing awareness among women and police of the rape problem (Kutchinsky, 1985a, p. 323). In Japan too, over the two decades reviewed in the present study, there was also most probably an increasing likelihood of reporting which makes the decrease in sex crimes seen in Japan even more impressive.

Similar to our findings in Japan, in Denmark and West Germany the most dramatic categories of sex crime to show a significant decrease were rapes and other sex crimes against and by juveniles. Consider: 1) Between 1972 and 1980 the total number of sex crimes known to the police in the Federal Republic of Germany decreased by 11 percent; during the same period the total number of *all* crimes reported *increased* by 50 percent; 2) Sex offenses against minors (those under fourteen years of age) had a similarly slight decrease of about 10 percent during this period. For those victims under six years of age, however, the numbers decreased dramatically more than 50 percent (Kutchinsky, 1985a).

Other researchers have similar findings. In Denmark homosexual child molestation decreased more than 50 percent from 1966 to 1969 (Ben-Veniste, 1971). These decreases in sex crimes involving children are particularly noteworthy since in Japan, as in Denmark, for the time under review, there were no laws, and still are no laws, against the personal non-commercial possession or use of pictures of children involved in sexual activities; so-called child-porn (Kutchinsky, 1985b, p. 5; Anonymous, 1998a). Considering the seriousness in how sex crimes against children are viewed in both cultures, this drop in cases reported represents a real reduction in the number of offenses committed rather than a reduced readiness to report such offenses.

The decrease in gang rapes in Japan had been similarly reported to occur elsewhere. In West Germany, from 1971 to 1987, group rape rates decreased 59 percent. In contrast with findings in Germany where rape by strangers decreased 33 percent (Kutchinsky, 1991, p. 57), in Japan the number of rapes committed by individuals known to the victim, decreased and rape by strangers increased. Since rapes by strangers or groups are more likely to be reported than date or marital rapes, again there is little doubt these findings in Japan represent real differences. It is also noted that the Japanese police focused more heavily on the control of rape by strangers than on date rape or rape by a known assailant.

Some might, e.g., Court (1977) attribute the overall decrease in the number of sex crimes recorded in Japan as reflecting a public attitude change concomitant with the increasing availability of pornography. This is doubtful. While it might be true for relatively minor offenses as those of public indecency, rape has always been taken seriously. Indeed, one can argue that the inhibitions to reporting have decreased. The case can be made that the increased prevalence of SEM makes it easier for children or women or likely victims to be less inhibited in talking with their parents, partners or authorities about sexual matters; particularly about any sex offense.

Another factor to encourage reporting is that special police rape investigation units sensitive to women's issues were established in September, 1983 and women no longer are treated as if they are the offenders. This was often so in the 1970s. Also significant is that Japan, in the 1990s, established a women-run rape crisis center in Tokyo and women's centers in major cities throughout the country. In 1996 the police also started public awareness campaigns which encouraged the victims of sex crimes to report. Sex educators too deserve credit. Sex education, K-12, is standard in Japanese schools and has been so since the 1970s. Sex educators have increasingly become schooled in rape theory, prevention, and reporting, and added such materials to their classroom presentations.[9]

It is accepted that the application of the appropriate laws or the social forces at play might not have been consistent over time. Any short term glitch in how the data were volunteered, solicited or recorded, however, should not effect the overall trends. Regardless, it is safe to say that over this prolonged period, interpretations of the definitions of obscenity have been getting less rigid with more material passing as acceptable and entering public awareness while the prosecution of laws relating to rape and sexual assault have been getting tougher. Currently less sexual "license" for sex crimes is accepted by the general Japanese population or by victims than was true twenty-five years ago. And surely one can not attribute the decrease in murder and nonsexual violent assault to a reluctance to report concomitant with an increase in SEM.[10]

It has been said that "pornography historically has been an integral part of Japanese culture" (Abramson & Hayashi, 1984). It is more true to say that erotic and fertility themes have been a traditional part of Japanese culture. Indeed religious shrines, ribald stories and both suggestive and explicit art have incorporated sexual icons and representations without shame and without the sin aspect associated with sex in the West. Traditionally these views of sex were in keeping with cultural or Confucian themes seen as enhancing family solidarity through child bearing and as a form of sex education (Abramson & Hayashi, 1984) and a way to enjoy the "good life."

This attitude essentially remained with the people even with the modernization of Japan ushered in with the 1868 Meiji Restoration. However, the government of the Meiji era, to enhance respect from the West, began to modify Japan's attitudes toward sex by adopting some of the West's comparatively restrictive and conservative mores. For example, the then common practices of nudity and mixed bathing, were newly forbidden in public bath houses (Dore, 1958). This ordinance was actually randomly enforced and basically only in the major cities. But this was a small part of the Meiji government's plan which came to be called *wakon-yoosai* (Japanese spirit and Western technology); a plan to develop and strengthen the nation by melding Western knowledge and technology with the Japanese spirit and culture (Hijirida & Yoshikawa, 1987).

During World War II many sexual restrictions were relaxed in Japan as they were in the West. Following the war, the United States' forces occupying Japan imposed Western ideas of morality and law. The Japanese slowly came to adopt some of these ideas and practices. The *wakon-yoosai* attitude reemerged (Hijirida & Yoshikawa, 1987). Negative ideas of pornography, foreign to Japanese culture, were accepted and particularly applied to visual images since they were the ones most likely recognized and thereby criticized by Westerners. Little attention was given to written SEM since foreigners would be unlikely to read Japanese and thus would not notice and criticize these (Abramson & Hayashi, 1984). Other visible sex related matters were bent to Western ways. Prostitution, for instance, previously legal and accepted, was declared illegal in 1958.[11] In the late 1950s and early 1960s separate-gender toilets and public baths began to replace the ubiquitous uni-sex facilities. Interestingly, while visual depictions of erotic themes were increasingly restricted, written pornography was slowly becoming more prevalent, more risqué and more fetishistic in tone. This was seen by some as a liberating reaction to the restraints of both Confucian feudalism and Western morality (Kuro, 1954). These were the laws and situation that basically existed in Japan during the early years of our study.

In the ensuing years, sexually explicit materials, first gradually and then in the late 1980s and into the 1990s rapidly increased in prevalence. The years 1990 and 1991 seemed a watershed. Major shifts developed in how much pornography was produced and how the obscenity laws were interpreted. Fewer materials were being charged as obscene and even fewer convictions recorded. Once more this was similar to findings elsewhere.

In Denmark the repeal of the ban on pornographic literature in 1967 was a consequence of provocative publishers producing and distributing to a waiting market and increasingly permissive court rulings (Kutchinsky, 1973b). In Japan the production and relaxation of control seemed to occur simultaneously; not one obviously causing the other.

The types of pornography available in Japan is also of interest relative to sex crime. The SEM produced caters to every taste and fetish and is typically much more aggressive and violent than that seen in the United States. And there are rarely enforced age restrictions in the purchase of or posing for these materials. This too was essentially similar to the situation in Denmark (Kutchinsky, 1978). Kutchinsky further found that while the available SEM increasingly became fetish oriented and aggressive, such materials were not necessarily more often used. It appeared to remain a small portion of the pornography available. In Denmark, Kutchinsky (1978) estimated hard core sadomasochistic materials and the like comprised no more than approximately 2 percent of all obtainable. Winick (1985) found about the same among U.S. materials. Giglio (1985) argued that Kutchinsky's data may not be applicable elsewhere considering a climate where violent pornography may be more prevalent. While we did not analyze in detail the pornographic materials in Japan for sadomasochistic or violent content it appears from inspection that such content is certainly much higher in Japan than in Denmark, the U.S.A. or elsewhere (Abramson & Hayashi, 1984; Yamada, 1989).

Kutchinsky (1973a), in his studies, found that the least serious sex crimes decreased the most and rape the least. We on the other hand found the opposite. In Japan, rapes decreased 79 percent while public indecency decreased 33 percent. The reason for the difference is not clear. We believe the compulsivity generally associated with the crimes considered under the public indecency law are less easily modified than is rape. Also, the incidence of peeping and flashing might already have been at a low incidence close to a base line. Public shame and interpersonal relativism is an extremely strong social force in Japan (Lebra, 1976) and can be a major factor in controlling public indecency.

Our findings regarding sex crimes, murder and assault are in keeping with what is also known about general crime rates in Japan regarding burglary, theft and such. Japan has the lowest number of reported rape cases and the highest percentage of arrests and convictions in reported cases of any developed nation. Indeed Japan is known as one of the safest developed democratic countries for women in the world. This not withstanding, Japanese social critics and feminists think things can be better still (Radin, 1996). Many women's advocates think the police authorities can be more responsive to women's concerns and women themselves less reluctant to complain. This comment can probably be applied everywhere. But, in essence, Japan can be rightly proud of these findings of diminished sex crimes in all categories and its non-censorship of sexually explicit materials.

SHANGHAI, CHINA

Parenthetically, some data from Shanghai, China are of comparative interest. The era of Classical China, particularly of the Ming (1368-1644) and Ching (1644–1911) dynasties still have a rich history of erotic art (Humana & Wu, 1984) and literature (Ruan, 1991). Nevertheless, government censorship against erotic (and politically sensitive) materials developed particularly in the thirteenth to fifteenth century but decreased from the sixteenth to the twentieth. For the modern period, the censorship policy of the Republic of China (1911–1949) was inconsistent; at times restrictive, at times permissive. During the Republic period prior to World War II authorities were often even critical of anatomy or physiology texts considered too explicit. Distribution of such texts was often restricted (Dikötter, 1995).

Contemporary China, however, is considered much more conservative in regard to sexual matters. After the founding of the People's Republic of China in 1949 the government imposed a complete nationwide ban on erotic fiction and SEM of any kind (China, 1949; Ruan, 1991). During the Cultural Revolution (1965–1968) the Red Guards were particularly destructive not only of Western images and pornography but even classical Chinese art was subject to their ravages. The destruction and confiscation was so effective that from the 1950s to the mid 1970s "almost no erotic material was to be found" (Ruan, 1991). What remains to the present from pre-Cultural Revolution days had been buried or hidden. Presently even consensual non-marital sex among adults is considered a serious crime. Nevertheless, and not surprisingly, sexual artifacts and writings continue to be of interest. In 1997 a museum of classical Chinese erotic art open to the public has been permitted in Shanghai under the directorship of Professor Dalin Liu. (Liu is considered the Alfred Kinsey of the P.R.C.)

Despite the ban, a rapid increase in available pornography was ushered in with the influx of increased tourism and lowering of trade restrictions following Nixon's visit to Beijing in 1972 and the United States' official recognition of the P.R.C. in 1979. These products were introduced mainly through Hong Kong. The government strongly reacted to this influx. A new anti-pornography law was instituted in 1985 with much harsher punishments than indicated in the 1949 law (China, 1985). Then, in 1987, the government began to enact most draconian policies. To be sure these repressive tactics were also used as political measures since the definition of *pornography* used was vague (Ruan, 1991). Nevertheless, the suppression of SEM was extensive and could have been more political than sexual. From 1985 to 1987, 217 publishers were arrested and 42 publishing houses were forced to close (Ruan, 1991).

One example of the extreme government prudishness is illustrative of the extremes to which the government moved. A high ranking government official, author and former deputy minister of the Cultural Ministry of the State council, Zhou Erfu, was removed from his vice-president's post of the Association for Foreign Friendship and expelled from the Chinese Com-

munist Party for having visited an "adult sex" shop and patronizing a prostitute while on a visit to Japan (People's Daily, 1986).

The move against pornography reached a low point in 1988 when the
Standing Committee of the 6th National People's Congress declared that
major porn dealers shall be sentenced to life imprisonment and Deng
Xiaoping, China's head, declared that some publishers of erotica even
deserved the death penalty (*Centre Daily News*, cited in Ruan, (1991, p. 103).

For the period 1965 to 1990, data on the cases of rape in Shanghai were
collected; so too were the number of pornographic items confiscated by the
government. These data are usually handled confidentially as government
secrets in China but were made available for research purposes. During the
five year interval 1986–1990 there was a twenty-five fold increase in the
number of pornographic items seized by the Shanghai police. Nevertheless,
as seen elsewhere in the world, there was no change in the incidence of rape
which has remained relatively constant over the twenty-five year period
reviewed. This is particularly noteworthy considering the in-migration to
the city population rise over the same period (Table 3).

UNITED STATES

Data from the United States are equally persuasive. By whatever methods
of documentation, it can be stated that the amount of pornography available
now in the United States is considerably greater than thirty or even twenty
years ago. One can consider alone the increase in home video rental and
sales; more than one in ten women and two in ten men bought or rented an
XXX-rated film or tape in the year 1993 (Laumann, 1994) and estimates are
that 600 million adult videos were rented or bought in the U.S. in 1997–
more than two for every person in the United States (Phillips, 1998). Hotel
guests in 1996 spent some $175 million to receive porn in their rooms and
those at home spent some $150 million to receive pay-per-view in their
homes (Schlosser, 1997). And considering the volume and number of
Internet/web porn sites, over the last decade–with a market value of some
$750 million to $1 billion in 1998 alone (Leland, 1998; p. 65)–a dramatic
increase in the availability of pornography, even of the XXX type, cannot
be denied. Such sexually explicit materials is available to satisfy almost
every paraphilia including a minority of illegal child pornography (e.g.,
Thornton, 1986, U.S. Customs, 1994).

Since the times of the Presidential and Attorney's General commissions
the standards for obscenity have been changing. Presently the basic decision
of whether something is obscene depends upon proving three prongs (the
so-called *Miller* v. *California*, 1973, test): (1) the average person, applying
contemporary community standards would conclude that the work taken as
a whole, appeals to prurient interest–a demanding drive to sexual fulfillment; (2) it depicts sexually explicit conduct, specifically defined by law, in
a patently offensive manner; and (3) it lacks serious literary, artistic, political

or scientific value. These are increasingly difficult tests to meet especially since no major community in the U.S. has decided that anything other than child-porn was outside its standard (Diamond & Dannemiller, 1989).[12] [13]

Despite this availability of SEM, according to FBI Department of Justice statistics we can see that the incidence of rape declined markedly over these last twenty years from 1975 to 1995. This was particularly seen in the age categories 20–24 and 25–34 [Table 4]. In the other categories, the rate of rape essentially did not change. During the years 1980 to 1989 the contrast is great between the rates of rape, declining or remaining steady, while the rates of non-sexual violent crimes continued to increase (Flanagan & Maguire, 1990 pp. 365). The decreases in criminal victimization to sex crimes are particularly dramatic when attention is focused on the latter years, 1993–1996 [Table 5] for which data are available. This is especially so for the last years for which full data are at hand. In those years there has been a decrease by some 60 percent in the incidence of rape, but all categories of crime associated with rape also declined. Indeed, in the latest FBI announcement, they report that murder in 1997 dropped 8.1 percent to its lowest rate in 30 years and that rape declined in number and rate in every region of the country (Anonymous, 1998b). Attorney General Janet Reno reported that in 1997 rape, in number and rate, has declined in every region of the country (Anonymous, 1998b).

A further consideration is that, while teen drug use continued to rise, a study by the Centers for Disease Control and Prevention reported "a steady decline" in the proportion of high school students who have ever had sex, a trend that began in 1991. Boys accounted for nearly all of the decline (Leland, 1998; p. 64). Part of this may be accounted for by increased sex education classes in the U.S. and a concomitant or independent increased awareness of AIDS.

GENERAL DISCUSSION

With these data from a wide variety of countries and cultures, we can better evaluate the thesis that an abundance of sexual explicit material invariably leads to an increase of illegal sexual activity and eventually rape (e.g., Liebert, Neale, & Davison, 1973; MacKinnon, 1989; Morgan, 1980). Similarly we can now better reconsider the conclusion of the Meese Commission that there exists "a causal relationship to antisocial acts of sexual violence and . . . unlawful acts of sexual violence" (Meese, 1986; p. 326). Indeed, the data we report and review suggests that the thesis is myth and, if anything, there is an *inverse* causal relationship between an increase in pornography and sex crimes.

Christensen (1990) argues that to prove that available pornography leads to sex crimes one must at least find a positive temporal correlation between the two. It appears from these new data from Japan, the United States, and Shanghai, as it was evident to Kutchinsky (1994) from research in Europe and Scandinavia, that *a large increase in available sexually explicit materials, over many years, either has no effect on the incidence of sex crimes or is correlated with their decrease.*

Objectivity now requires that an additional question be asked: "Does pornography use and availability prevent or *reduce* sex crime?" This hypotheses seems to have been tested and substantiated, over prolonged periods, in Denmark, Sweden, West Germany and now in Japan and the USA and somewhat in Shanghai, China.

The first question/concept we discussed, that of sex crime *cause*, is quite different from that of sex crime *prevention*. And the two concepts are not even mutually dependent although they seem to be so intuitively. Accepting or rejecting one thesis is independent from accepting or rejecting the other. Kutchinsky (1994) considering the political implications of these questions has written:

> Criminalizing or legalizing pornography should depend on whether it can be shown to be seriously *harmful or not*; not whether it is found to be *harmful or beneficial*. If pornography cannot be shown to be seriously harmful, it should be legalized. (emphasis in original)

In a similar vein additional evidence is available which should be considered. The countries of Singapore and Union of South Africa as well as the Australian State of Queensland, during the same period investigated by Kutchinsky (1964-1974), were firmly against any pornography. Their anti-obscenity laws were quite broad. In Singapore rape rates *increased* by 69 percent, in South Africa the rape rate *increased* by 28 percent and in Queensland the *increase* was 23 percent (Court, 1984).[14]

There are reasons to believe increases in available SEM can lead to legal sexual expressions but no measure was taken of such activities. Couples might have increased their love-making frequency, artists might have created newly inspired works of art,[15] multitudes might have used the pornography as vehicles for sex education and not a few have probably used the material for reading or viewing pleasure and masturbation. All of these are positive, legal and constructive, or at least nondestructive, social outlets. In Japan, as elsewhere, publishers and others maintain that erotic stories, even in comics, serve as a means of relaxation for adults who feel suffocated in Japan's' "controlled society" (Burrill, 1991). This probably holds similarly for all societies.

Many individuals, in polls and surveys around the USA and Japan have indicated that pornography has been useful in their own love-making and relaxation and not a few, even among senior citizens, have indicated it has also often been instructive and pleasurable (Brecher & Editors, 1984). Further, in general, no American state-wide community ever polled has voted to ban pornography; even Maine (1986) and Utah (Fahy, 1984; Seldin, 1984), typically considered conservative American states, have refused to do so (Diamond & Dannemiller, 1989).[16]

While no population study has demonstrated a link between pornography and sex crimes, there are, however, occasional research reports of a linkage. One, for example, stated:

> Retrospective recall provided the basis for estimating the use of sexually explicit materials by sex offenders (voluntary outpatients) and non offenders during pubescence, as well as currently . . . Rapists and child molesters reported frequent use of these materials . . . Current use was significantly related to the chronicity of their sexual offending . . . (Marshall, 1988, p. 267)

The actual evidence in this report, however, seems at closer scrutiny, to indicate that pornography used by adult sex offenders is viewed immediately prior to their offense. Unstated, but contained within the Marshall study, is evidence that pornography was usually absent from the offenders' experiences during formative years.

This lack of exposure to pornography seems to be a crucial consideration. Most frequently, as it was found in the 1960s before the influx of sexually explicit materials in the United States, those who committed sex crimes typically had *less* exposure to SEM in their background than others and the offenders generally were individuals usually deeply religious and socially and politically conservative (Gebhard, Gagnon, Pomeroy, & Christenson, 1965). Since then, most researchers have found similarly (e.g., Ward & Kruttschnitt, 1983). The upbringing of sex offenders was usually sexually repressive, often they had an overtly religious background and held rigid conservative attitudes toward sexuality (Conyers & Harvey, 1996; Dougher, 1988); their upbringing had usually been ritualistically moralistic and conservative rather than permissive. During adolescence and adulthood, sex offenders were generally found *not* to have used erotic or pornographic materials any more than any other groups of individuals *or even less so* (Goldstein & Kant, 1973; Propper, 1972). Among sex offenders, violent rapists had seen no more pornography than had sex "peepers" or "flashers" (Abel, Becker, Murphy & Flanagan, 1980). Walker (1970) reported that sex criminals were several years older than non-criminals before they first saw pictures of intercourse. Thirty-nine percent of convicts surveyed by Walker agreed that pornography "provides a safety valve for antisocial impulses."

Increased exposure to pornography is also, I believe, a major reason we are seeing a downturn particularly in sex crimes with juveniles, either as perpetrators or victims. Youngsters, particularly in the past but still somewhat at present, have fewer outlets for their sexual curiosity or desires than do adults. Available pornography and other SEM allows an outlet for developing sexuality that was heretofore unavailable; the sexual drives and needs of minors can now be somewhat satisfied by fantasy made real by pornography.

Many who deal with rapists feel rape is a sexual act for a nonsexual problem, e.g., a defeat or frustration at work might motivate rape (Groth, 1979). Others see rape as an expression of power (Groth, Burgess, & Holstrom, 1977). Goldstein and Kant concluded that "few if any" of the sex offenders they interviewed had been appreciably influenced by pornography. They concluded: "Far more potent sexual stimuli" are real persons in the environment for the sex criminal (Goldstein & Kant, 1973). Danish experts, including feminist criminologists who have studied rape in Denmark, also agree that there is no relationship between pornography and rape (Kutchinsky, 1985b).

Nicholas Groth, a specialist in the treatment of sex offenders, has written:

> Rape is sometimes attributed to the increasing availability of pornography and sexual explicitness in the public media. Although a rapist, like anyone else, might find some pornography stimulating, it is not sexual arousal but the arousal of anger or fear that leads to rape. Pornography does not cause rape; banning it will not stop rape. (Groth, 1979, p. 9)

Wilson (1978) found that "Males who develop deviant patterns of sexual behavior in adulthood have suffered relative deprivation of experience with pornography in adolescence." He suggests that pornography not only can, but does, help to prevent criminal sex problems (p. 176). Wilson claims exposure to sexually explicit materials can have therapeutic advantages and, among couples, help by promoting greater communication and openness to discuss sexual matters, and provide sex education. It can also help by providing an anxiety and inhibition-relieving function.

Several other explanations have been offered to account for the decreasing and low incidence of sex crimes in Japan. Abramson and Hayashi (1984) attribute the low incidence of rape in Japan to internal restraint which is part of the Japanese national character instilled by the tight society. While that might be so, it is difficult to imagine that restraint stronger in the 1990s than it might have been in the more conservative environment of the 1970s.

Kutchinsky (1973b) credits the reduction in sex crimes associated with the high availability of SEM in Europe and Scandinavia to "most of the population became familiar with pornographic literature: but very quickly the point of saturation was reached, mainly because the interest was based on curiosity rather than a genuine need." Some credit the overall decrease in crime in the USA to a decrease in drug use and availability (*U.S. News & World Report*, 1998).[v]

Other factors associated with the decrease in rape and sex crimes are probably involved. For instance, over the period under review, 1972 to 1995, concomitant with the decrease in male sex crimes there has been an increase in female consensual sexual availability. In addition to females available as sexual partners via prostitution and other commercial sex outlets, the "girls next door" are now more ready to accept and even solicit nonmarital consensual sexual activities than was common two and three decades ago (Kinsey, Pomeroy, Martin, & Gebhard, 1953; Laumann, Gagnon, Michael, & Stuart, 1994; Liu, Ng, & Chou, 1992; Tavris & Sadd, 1977; Uchiyama, 1996).

Many laboratory experiments are alleged to prove a negative societal influence from exposure to pornography. Results from different experiments supposedly demonstrated that exposure to pornography, particularly that which includes violence, leads to the degradation of women, the trivialization of rape and increased likelihood of aggression or acceptance of violence against women (for overview of this area see, e.g., Malamuth & Donnerstein, 1984; Zillmann & Bryant, 1989; Zillmann & Weaver, 1989).

The laboratory-school experiments or brief exposure experiments (less than a week or less than a semester) are hardly comparable to situations in the real world and may not be relevant at all. The typical laboratory experiment exposed college students to different types of pornography for various durations and attempted to measure their subsequent attitudes and behaviors. Further, and considered crucial, the situation was often manipulated so that the students were placed into situations that confounded the experimental design interpretations (e.g., Donnerstein, 1984; Donnerstein & Barrett, 1978; Zillmann, 1984; Zillmann & Bryant, 1984; 1989; Zillmann & Weaver, 1989). Often the findings themselves are inconsistent. For instance Zillmann and Bryant (Zillmann, 1984; Zillmann & Bryant, 1984; 1988a; 1988b) reported that their results indicated, on the one hand, that large amounts of exposure to pornography reduced the willingness of student subjects to aggress against another after erotic stimulation [inferred positive effect] but led to "a general trivialization of rape," decreased satisfaction with the present partner and supposed lessening of "family values" [inferred negative effect]. These laboratory studies have been seriously critiqued e.g., by Becker & Stein (1991), Brannigan (1991), Brannigan & Goldenberg (1986; 1987a,b), Christensen, (1990), Reiss (1986) and Rosen & Beck (1988), for being methodologically flawed and inappropriate for practical consideration. And even experimenters in this area of *class*–room research have significantly criticized how the data have been extrapolated for the *court*–room (e.g., Linz, Penrod, & Donnerstein, 1987).

Lab experiments typically do not take into account context and other crucial social and situational factors in considering the audience or the material. The real-world results we find for Japan, Shanghai and the USA, and those Kutchinsky reports for West Germany, Denmark, and Sweden, and Court has found for Singapore and elsewhere, are from huge diverse populations that have had years of exposure to sexually explicit materials. These materials could be chosen or not, used or not and modified or not to taste. No person was obligated to expose him or herself to experiences found distasteful while, on the other hand, anyone could exploit any available material or opportunity available. Individuals in real life could use the material alone in private or with partners. In real life, individuals can elect to experience some pornography for minutes or hours, at a single session, or over years. In real life, individuals are free to satisfy different sexual urges in ways unavailable to students in classroom situations.

Kutchinsky (1983, 1987, 1992, 1994), has discussed the relative merits of lab studies compared to events outside the laboratory. Basically Kutchinsky believes that pornography, in the real world, offers a substitution for the sexual and nonsexual frustrations that might, in other circumstances, lead to sexual offenses (Kutchinsky, 1973a). He wrote:

> If availability of pornography can reduce sex crimes, it is because the use of certain forms of pornography to certain potential offenders is functionally equivalent to the commission of certain types of sex offences: both satisfy the need for psychosexual stimulants leading to sexual enjoyment and orgasm through masturbation. If these potential offenders have the option, they prefer to use pornography because it is more convenient, unharmful and undangerous. (Kutchinsky, 1994, pp. 21)

This too we believe is only a partial answer. There is also the likelihood that repeated exposure to SEM can lead to a response of habituation, boredom or fatigue.

What other societal factors, aside from an increase in pornography, might have led to the decrease in crimes in Japan or the USA? If pornography doesn't lead to rape and sex crimes, what does? Obviously these are complicated multifaceted questions. In response, we agree with many (e.g., Brannigan, 1987b; Fisher & Barak, 1991; Gottfredson & Hirschi, 1995) that crimes in general are not simply a matter of "monkey see-monkey do." It is not as Byrne (1977, p. 346) suggests evident that "In this way, the erotic images prevalent in a culture become transferred to private erotic images which are later translated to overt behavior." Most sex crimes are usually opportunistic, given little forethought and typically committed by individuals with poor self or social control. And such individuals are often identifiable before they would be exposed to any substantial SEM. More than half of adult sex offenders were often known to be adolescent sex offenders (Abel et al., 1985; Knopp, 1984). As Gottfredson and Hirschi (1990) state:

> . . . the origins of criminality of low self control are to be found in the first six or eight years of life, during which time the child remains under the control and supervision of the family or a familial institution . . . *policies directed towards enhancement of the ability of familial institutions to socialize children are the only realistic long-term state policies with potential for substantial crime reduction.* (pp. 272–73) [emphasis mine]

I believe this conclusion has great merit. Consider that in Japan the competitive nature of the educational and employment situation over the last two decades has pressured more time being devoted to school achievement starting in preschool and continuing through college; hours of homework and extra tutoring after school (*juckyu*) are common (Effron, 1997). And Japanese mothers usually remain at home to supervise their children through the middle school if not the high school years. We believe this in itself reduces the opportunity for anti-social or criminal activity and helps socialize the child to avoid unlawful behaviors as an adult.

Ellis (1989) attributes sex crimes to innate motives toward sexual expression and a drive to possess and control. The increased early age times under family jurisdiction can help modify these drives. So too can standard K-12 sex education programs take some credit. Sex education programs are routine school offerings in Japan, Denmark, Sweden and Germany (but not in China). Thus, socially positive proactive forces, in themselves, may account for much of the reduction in the crimes seen. Other forces responsible for the reduction of sex crimes rates have yet to be determined. [17, 18]

A companion question also arises: "Might there be negative effects of the increase in pornography availability other than measured by our inspection of documented sex crimes?" Feminists, religious conservatives and other moralists consider pornography a problem even if it can not be proven that it leads to an increase in sex crimes (see e.g., Cline, 1974; Court, 1984; Dworkin, 1987, 1988; MacKinnon, 1984, 1993; Osanka & Johann, 1989).

Some see it as violence against women *per se*. Andrea Dworkin, for instance claims: "The question is not: does pornography cause violence against women? Pornography is violence against women, violence which pervades and distorts every aspect of our culture (Dworkin, 1981)." And Gloria Steinem (Steinem, 1983) has written: "pornography is about power and sex-as-weapon—in the same way we have come to understand that rape is about violence, and not really about sexuality at all" (p. 38). Catharine MacKinnon (1993) considers even written pornography degrading and harmful to women by its mere existence.[19]

It must be simultaneously recognized that many feminists consider pornography to be liberating for women. They see SEM as expanding their social and sexual options; offering them choices of fantasies, behaviors and artistic expression. On the other hand, they see the stereotypic views of femininity and female roles in the popular so-called women's magazines, to be stultifying and restrictive; keeping women in "their place." Such feminists include Wendy McElroy (1995) with her book "XXX: A Women's Right to Pornography" as well as Marjorie Heins (1993), Nadine Strossen (1995)– head of the American Civil Liberties Union–and Leonore Tiefer (1995). As with so many other aspects of pornography, much is in the eye of the beholder and neither all feminists nor all religious conservatives can be painted with the same brush.[20]

There are certainly anecdotal reports of negative consequences, aside from sex crimes, attributed to pornography. These range from domestic violence, e.g., Sommers & Check (1987), to child abuse, e.g., Burgess & Hartman (1987). There is, however, no evidence that pornography is in anyway causal or even related to such terrible and regrettable crimes (Howitt & Cumberbatch, 1990). These anti-social and criminal acts are, as mentioned above, more likely due to the poorly parented and inadequately schooled individuals with long lasting poor self or social control.

Another potential ill effect of pornography is reviewed by Howitt and Cumberbatch (1990); the possible negative effects of pornography on men. These authors review reports (e.g., Moye, 1985; Fracher & Kimmel, 1987; Tiefer, 1986) of men reduced to impotence by "performance anxiety" and not being able to match the ever-potent, hugely endowed, skilled "studs" in pornography. Howitt and Cumberbatch, despite an apparent selective anti-pornography bias in the data they consider, conclude that the factors actually responsible for impotence and performance anxiety eventually probably have nothing to do with pornography and have also yet to be determined. It is most probably that porn turns some people "on" while it turns other people "off." Actually, pornography is often the poor man's Viagra®. There is little doubt, however, that it provides many with positive returns and pleasurable and legal outlets for sexual urges.

A last thought: I believe it part of nature's evolutionary heritage that reproductively relevant scenes be part of any individual's development. Since until recent times, privacy has been a luxury afforded only to the very few and then to the very rich. Only in modern times are children expected to develop without witnessing their parents or others, and certainly animals, in sexual activities. As such, a basic feature of evolution, reproduction, would not be left completely to chance. Attraction of so many to pornography and other sexual themes is most likely our biological and social heritage from this fundamental aspect of life. It is only culture and politics which make it seem unusual or negative.

CONCLUSIONS

The concern that countries allowing pornography and liberal anti-obscenity laws would show increased sex crime rates due to modeling or that children or adolescents in particular would be negatively vulnerable to and receptive to such models or that society would be otherwise adversely effected is not supported by evidence. It is certainly clear from the data reviewed, and the new data and analysis presented, that a massive increase in available pornography in Japan, the United States and elsewhere has been correlated with a dramatic *decrease* in sexual crimes and most so among youngsters as perpetrators or victims. Even in this area of concern no "clear and present danger" exists for the suppression of SEM. There is no evidence that pornography is intended or likely to produce "imminent lawless action" (see *Brandenberg* v. *Ohio*, 1969). It is reasonable that the U.S. Supreme Court has consistently rejected the principal that speech or expression can be punished because it offends some people's sensibilities or beliefs. Compared with "hate speech" or "commercial speech" there seems even less justification for banning "sex speech."[21, 22]

Sex abuse of any kind is deplorable and should be eliminated. Rape and sex crimes, like any criminal activities, are blights on society which should be expunged. The question remains "How best to do this?" Most assuredly, focusing energy in the wrong direction, or taking actions just to placate victims, politicians or irate citizens will not solve the problem nor help. Nor will spreading myths or misinformation. Removing pornography from our midst will, according to the evidence, only hurt rather than help society.

I think it is better to expend our energies in two directions: 1) Make better pornography so that preferred role models are portrayed and more segments of society can come to appreciate or at least understand and tolerate its value[23]; and 2) turn our research to other directions to eliminate or reduce the social ills of rape and other sex crimes. The best place to look is probably in the home during the first decade of life. But it is only by research that we can continue to understand how to most effectively meet this social challenge. Governments as well as the pornography industry itself would do well to finance and encourage such research.

REFERENCES

Abel, G. G., Barlow, D. H., Blanchard, E. B., & Guild, D. (1977). The components of rapists' sexual arousal. *Archives of General Psychiatry* 34, 895–903.

Abel, G. G., & Becker, J. V. (1985). *Use of pornography and erotica by sex offenders.* Paper presented at the International Academy for Sex Research, Seattle, Washington.

Abel, G. G., Becker, J. V., Murphy, W. D., & Flanagan, B. (1980). Identifying dangerous child molesters. In R. B. Stuart (Ed.), *Violent behavior: Social learning approaches to prediction, management and treatment.* (pp. 116–37). New York: Brunner/Mazel.

Abel, G. G., Mittelman, M. S., & Becker, J. V. (1985). Sexual Offenders: Results of assessment and recommendations for treatment. In M. H. Ben-Aron, S. J. Huckle, & C. D. Webster (Eds.), *Clinical criminology: The assessment and treatment of criminal behavior* (pp. 191–205). Toronto: M & M Graphic.

Abramson, P. R., & Hayashi, H. (1984). Pornography in Japan: Cross cultural and theoretical considerations. In M. N. Malamuth & E. Donnerstein (Eds.), *Pornography and sexual aggression* (pp. 173–183). New York: Academic Press.

Amis, K., Anderson, J. N. D., Beasley-Murray, G. R., et al. (1972). *Pornography: the Longford Report.* London: Coronet Books: Hodder Paperbacks, Ltd.

Anonymous. (1991a). Racy comics a labeled lot now in Japan. *Honolulu Star-Bulletin and Advertiser.* 31 March.

Anonymous. (1991b). Tokyo telephone sex. *Honolulu Advertiser,* 5 February.

Anonymous. (1992). Police warn magazines over nudes. *The Japan Times,* 2 October, p. 2.

Anonymous. (1998a). Lax law leaves child porn on Net almost untouchable in Japan. *Honolulu Star-Bulletin,* 26 November, p. A-18.

Anonymous. (1998b). Serious crimes down for sixth straight year, latest FBI report says. *Honolulu Star-Bulletin,* 23 November, p. A-3.

Baron, L., & Strauss, M. A. (1987). *Four theories of rape in American society: A state-level analysis.* New Haven: Yale University Press.

Becker, J., & Stein, R. M. (1991). Is sexual erotica associated with sexual deviance in adolescent males? *International Journal of Law and Psychiatry* 14: 85–95.

Ben-Veniste, R. (1971). Pornography and sex crime: The Danish experience. *Technical Report of the Commission on Obscenity and Pornography* (pp. 245–261). Washington, D.C.: U. S. Government Printing Office.

Berger, R. J., Searles, P., & Cottle, C. E. (1991). *Feminism and pornography.* New York: Praeger.

Brandenberg v. *Ohio.* (1969). re: Ku Klux Klan free speech decision 395 U.S. 444.

Brannigan, A. (1987a). Mystification of the innocents: Crime comics and delinquency in Canada. *Criminal Justice History* 8: 111–44.

——. (1987b). Sex and aggression in the lab: Implications for public policy? A review essay. *Canadian Journal of Law and Society* 2: 177–85.

——. (1991). Obscenity and social harm: A contested terrain. *International Journal of Law and Psychiatry* 14: 1–12.

Brannigan, A., & Goldenberg, S. (1986). Social science versus jurisprudence in Wagner: The study of pornography, harm, and the law of obscenity in Canada. *Canadian Journal of Sociology* 11(4): 419–31.

——. (1987a). Pornography studies: The second wave, a review essay. *Law in Context* 5: 56–72.

——. (1987b). The politics of pornography research. *Contemporary Psychology* 32, no. 8: 761.

Brannigan, A., & Kapardis, A. (1986). The controversy over pornography and sex crimes: The criminological evidence and beyond. *Australian and New Zealand Journal of Criminology* 19 (4): 259–84.

Brecher, E., & Editors. (1984). *Love, sex and aging: A Consumers' Union report.* Mount Vernon, N.Y.: Consumers Union.

Brownmiller, S. (1975). *Against our will: Men, women and rape.* New York: Simon & Schuster.

Burgess, A. W., & Hartman, C. R. (1987). Child abuse aspects of pornography. *Psychiatric Annals* 17 (4): 248–53.

Burrill, J. (1991). Lowering the boom on sex comics. *Limousine City Guide*, 33.

Byrne, D. (1977). The imagery of sex. In J. Money & H. Musaph (eds.), *Handbook of sexology* (pp. 327–50). Amsterdam: Excerpta Medica.

Canada. (1985). *Report of the special select committee on pornography and prostitution.* (Report): Ottawa; Supply and Services.

China, People's Republic of. (1949). Rules for the Control of and Punishments Concerning Public Security of the People's Republic of China (pp. Article 5, para 7).

——. (1985). The State Council's Regulations on Severely Banning Pornography .

Christensen, F. M. (1990). *Pornography: The other side.* New York: Praeger.

Cline, V. (Ed.). (1974). *Where do we draw the line? An exploration into media violence, pornography and censorship.* Provo, Utah: Brigham Young University Press.

Conyers, L., & Harvey, P. D. (1996). Religion and crime: Do they go together? *Free Inquiry* 16, no. 3 (Summer): 46–48.

Court, J. H. (1977). Pornography and sex crimes: A reevaluation in light of recent trends around the world. *International Journal of Criminology and Penology* 5: 129–57.

——. (1984). Sex and violence: A ripple effect. In N. M. Malamuth & E. Donnerstein (Eds.), *Pornography and sexual aggression* (pp. 143–72). New York: Academic Press.

DeBenedictis, D. J. (1992). Keating's legal woes mount; convicted S & L chief faces another prosecution, myriad civil suits. *ABA Journal* 78 (February), 30 (1) (SIC code : 6035).

Desmond, E. W. (1995). Rape of an innocent, dishonor in the ranks. *Time*, 146, October 2.

Diamond, E. (1990). Breaking a covenant? *New York Post* 23 (1): January 8, p. 16.

Diamond, M. (1984). *Sexwatching: The world of sexual behavior.* London: Macdonald.

——. (1986). *Sexwatching* (Japanese edition). Tokyo: Shogakukan.

Diamond, M., & Dannemiller, J. E. (1989). Pornography and community standards in Hawaii: Comparison with other states. *Archives of Sexual Behavior* 18 (6): 475–95.

Diamond, M., & Karlen, A. (1980). *Sexual decisions.* Boston: Little, Brown.

——. (1985). *Sexual decisions* (Japanese edition). Tokyo: Shogakukan.

Diamond, M., & Uchiyama, A. (1999). Pornography, rape and other sex crimes in Japan. *International Journal of Law and Psychiatry* 22, no. 1: 1–22.

Dikötter, F. (1995). *Sex, culture and modernity in China.* Honolulu: University of Hawaii Press.

Donnerstein, E. (1984). Pornography: Its effect on violence against women. In N. M. Malamuth & E. Donnerstein (Eds.), *Pornography and sexual aggression* (pp. 53–81). New York: Academic Press.

Donnerstein, E., & Barrett, G. (1978). The effects of erotic stimuli on male aggression toward women. *Journal of Personality and Social Psychology* 36: 180–88.

Donnerstein, E., Donnerstein, M., & Evans, R. (1975). Erotic stimuli and aggression: Facilitation or inhibition. *Journal of Personality and Social Psychology* 32: 237–44.

Donnerstein, E., Linz, D., & Penrod, S. (1987). *The question of pornography: Research findings and policy implications.* New York: Free Press.

Dore, R. P. (1958). *City life in Japan.* Los Angeles: University of California Press.

Dougher, M. J. (1988). Assessment of sex offenders. In B. K. Schwartz & H. R. Cellini (Eds.), *A practitioner's guide to treating the incarcerated male sex offender* (pp. 72–88). Washington, D.C.: U.S. Department of Justice, National Institute of Corrections.

Douglas, J. J. (1998). Special Supplement: Testimony of J. J. Douglas, Executive Director, Free Speech Coalition. Before the Subcommittee on Telecommunications, Trade and Consumer Protection, United States House of Representatives. Sept. 11.

Downs, J. F. (1990). Nudity in Japanese visual media: A cross-cultural observation. *Archives of Sexual Behavior* 19 (6): 583–94.

Dworkin, A. (1981). *Pornography: Men possessing women.* (Book Cover) New York: Putnam.

———. (1985). Against the male flood: Censorship, pornography, and equality. *Harvard Women's Law Journal* 8: 1–29.

Dworkin, A., & MacKinnon, C. (1988). Pornography and civil rights: A new day for women's equality. *Minneapolis: Organizing Against Pornography* (pp. 138–42). Minneapolis.

Effron, S. (1997). In Japan, even toddlers now attend cram schools. *The Honolulu Advertiser,* February 16, p. A-6.

Ellis, L. (1989). *Theories of rape: Inquires into the causes of sexual aggression.* New York: Hemisphere Publishing.

Fahy, K. (1984). Defeat of cable TV act fails to shake resolve of regulation proponents. *Deseret News,* November 7.

Faust, B. (1980). *Women, sex, and pornography: A controversial and unique study.* New York: MacMillan.

Fisher, W. A., & Barak, A. (1991). Pornography, erotica, and behavior: More questions than answers. *International Journal of Law and Psychiatry* 14: 65–83.

Flanagan, T. J., & Maguire, K. (Eds.). (1990). *Sourcebook of criminal justice statistics-1989.* Washington, D.C.: U.S.G.P.O.

Friedan, B. (1985). How to get the women's movement moving again. *New York Times Magazine,* November 3, p. 26.

Gagnon, J. H., & Simon, W. (1973). *Sexual conduct: The social origins of human sexuality.* Chicago: Aldine.

Gebhard, P. H., Gagnon, J. H., Pomeroy, W. B., & Christenson, C. V. (1965). *Sex Offenders.* New York: Harper & Row.

Giglio, D. (1985). Pornography in Denmark: A public policy for the United States? *Comparative Social Research* 8: 281–300.

Goldstein, M. J., & Kant, H. S. (1973). *Pornography and sexual deviance: A report of the Legal and Behavioral Institute.* Berkeley: University of California Press.

Goldstein, M., Kant, H., Judd, L., Rice, C., & Green, R. (1971). Experience with pornography: Rapists, pedophiles, homosexuals, transsexuals, and controls. *Archives of Sexual Behavior* 1: 1–15.

Gottfredson, M. R., & Hirschi, T. (1990). *A general theory of crime.* Stanford, California: Stanford University Press.

——. (1995). National crime control policies. *Society* 32: 20–36.

Greenfeld, K. T. (1994). *Speed tribes.* New York: Harper Collins.

Groth, N. A. (1979). *Men who rape: The psychology of the offender.* New York: Plenum.

Groth, N. A., Burgess, A. W., & Holstrom, L. L. (1977). Rape, power and sexuality. *American Journal of Psychiatry* 134: 1239–43.

Heins, M. (1993). *Sex, sin and blasphemy: A guide to America's censorship wars.* New York: The New Press.

Hijirida, K., & Yoshikawa, M. (1987). *Japanese language and culture for business and travel.* Honolulu: University of Hawaii Press.

Home Office. (1979). Committee on obscenity and film censorship. London: Her Majesty's Stationary Office.

Howitt, D., & Cumberbatch, G. (1990). *Pornography: Impacts and influences. A review of available research evidence on the effects of pornography.* Commissioned by the British Home Office Research and Planning Unit.

Humana, C., & Wu, W. (1984). *Chinese sex secrets: A look behind the screen.* New York: Gallery Books.

J.A.S.E. (1991). *Survey on comics among youth* (Survey Report). Tokyo: Japanese Association for Sex Education.

Kant, H. S., & Goldstein, M. J. (1970). Pornography. *Psychology Today* (December): 59-76.

Kinsey, A. C., Pomeroy, W. B., Martin, C. E., & Gebhard, P. H. (1953). *Sexual behavior in the human female.* Philadelphia: W. B. Saunders Company.

Knopp, F. H. (1984). *Retraining adult sex offenders: Methods and models.* Orwell, VT: Safer Society.

Kuro, H. (1954). *Nikutai bungaku no seiri.* (Vol. 4). Tokyo: Shisoo no Kagaku.

Kutchinsky, B. (1973a). The effect of easy availability of pornography on the incidence of sex crimes: The Danish experience. *Journal of Social Issues* 29: 163–81.

——. (1973b). Eroticism without censorship. *International Journal of Criminology and Penology* 1: 217–25.

——. (1978). Pornography in Denmark–a general survey. In R. Dhavan & C. Davies (Eds.), *Censorship and obscenity: Behavioral aspects* (pp. 111–126). London: Martin Robertson.

——. (1983). Obscenity and pornography: Behavioral aspects. In S. H. Kadish (Ed.), *Encyclopedia of crime and justice* (Vol. 3, pp. 1077–86). New York: Free Press.

——. (1985a). Pornography and its effects in Denmark and the United States: A rejoinder and beyond. *Comparative Social Research* 8: 301–30.

——. (1985b). *Experiences with pornography and prostitution in Denmark* (Revision of Chap. 5 in J. Kiedrowski and J. M. van Dikj: *Pornography and prostitution in Denmark, France, West Germany, the Netherlands and Sweden.* Stencilserie Nr. (30): Kriminalistisk Instituts Stencilserie.

——. (1987). Deception and propaganda. *Transaction, Social Science and Modern Society* 24 (5): 21–24.

——. (1991). Pornography and rape: Theory and practice? Evidence from crime data in four countries where pornography is easily available. *International Journal of Law and Psychiatry* 14: 47–64.

——. (1992). The politics of pornography research. *Law & Society Review* 26 (2): 447–55.

———. (1994). Pornography: Impacts and influences: Critique of a review of research evidence. [*Preprint sent to me before Kutchinsky's death*], 1–30.

Lab, S. (1987). Pornography and aggression: A response to the U.S. Attorney General's Commission. *Criminal Justice Abstracts* 19: 301–21.

Laumann, E. O., Gagnon, J. H., Michael, R. T., & Stuart, M. (1994). *The social organization of sexuality: Sexual practices in the United States*. Chicago: The University of Chicago Press.

Lebra, T. S. (1976). *Japanese patterns of behavior*. Honolulu: University of Hawaii Press.

Leland, J. (1998). Let's talk about sex. *Newsweek*, Dec. 28–Jan. 4, pp. 62–65.

Liebert, R. M., Neale, J. M., & Davison, E. S. (1973). *The early window*. New York: Pergamon Press.

Linz, D., Penrod, S. D., & Donnerstein, E. (1987). The Attorney General's Commission: The gaps between findings and facts. *American Bar Foundation Research Journal* 4: 713–36.

Liu, D. L., Ng, M. L., & Chou, L. P. (Eds.). (1992). *Sexual behaviour in modern China: A report on the nation-wide "sex civilisation" survey on 20,000 subjects in China*. Shanghai: San Lian Bookstore.

Lynn, B. W. (1986). *Polluting the censorship debate: A summary and critique of the final report of the Attorney General's Commission on Pornography*. Washington, D.C.: American Civil Liberties Union.

MacKinnon, C. A. (1989). Sexuality, pornography, and method: "Pleasure and patriarchy." *Ethics* 99: 314–346.

———. (1993). *Only Words*. Cambridge, Mass.: Harvard University Press.

Maine. (1986). Attorney General's Office Re: Obscene materials referendum of June 10. *Personal communication*.

Mainichi-shinbun. (1990). Wakayama Prefecture calls for control of manga. *Mainichi-shinbun*. November 23.

Malamuth, N. M., & Donnerstein, E. (Eds.). (1984). *Pornography and sexual aggression*. New York: Academic Press.

Marshall, W. L. (1988). The use of sexually explicit stimuli by rapists, child molesters, and nonoffenders. *Journal of Sex Research* 25 (2): 267–88.

McElroy, W. (1995). *XXX: A woman's right to pornography*. New York: St. Martin's Press.

McKay, H. B., & Dolff, D. J. (1985). T*he impact of pornography: A decade of literature*. Working Papers on Pornography and Prostitution 13: Canadian (Ottawa) Department of Justice.

Meese, E. (1986). *Attorney General Commission Report*. U.S. Government, U.S.G.P.O.

Miller v. *California*. (1973). [*Re: community standard evaluation in determination of obscenity*] (413 U.S. 15).

Morgan, R. (1980). Theory and practice: Pornography and rape. In L. Lederer (Ed.), *Take back the night: Women on pornography* (pp. 134–40). New York: William Morrow.

Nihon No Tokei (Japan's Statistics). (1996). Tokyo: Somucho Tokei Kyoku (Statistics Bureau).

Nobile, P., & Nadler, E. (1986). *United States of America vs. sex: How the Meese Commission lied about pornography*. New York: Minotaur Press.

Okudaira, Y. (1979). Indecency and social culture or custom. *Hogaku-Seminar*, 1979 (December): 2–9.

Osanka, F. M., & Johann, S. L. (1989). *Sourcebook on pornography*. Lexington, Mass: Lexington Books.

Oshima, T. (1979). What's wrong in indecency? *Hogaku-Seminar* (December): 10–15.

People's Daily. (1986). Re: Dismissal of official for visiting porno shop & prostitute. *People's Daily, Overseas Edition.* March 4.

Phillips, K. (1998). Under Clinton, stocks and porn rise together. *International Herald Tribune*, p. 8. March 26.

Pornography. (1970). *Report of the U.S. Commission on Obscenity and Pornography* (Technical Report): U.S. Commission on Obscenity and Pornography. Washington, D.C.: U.S.G.P.O.

Propper, M. M. (1972). *Exposure to sexually oriented materials among young male prisoners.* Technical Report of the Commission on Obscenity and Pornography, vol. 8.

Radin, C. (1996). Rape in Japan: The crime that has no name. *Boston Globe*, p. A-1. March 8.

Reiss, I. L. (1986). *Journey into sexuality: An exploratory voyage.* Englewood Cliffs, N.J.: Prentice Hall.

Rembar, C. (1968). *The end of obscenity.* New York: Random House. Bantam Books.

Roposensho, J. N. P. A. (1995). *Annual report of Japanese crime statistics.* Tokyo: Japanese National Police Agency.

Rosen, R. C., & Beck, J. G. (1988). *Patterns of sexual arousal: Psychophysiological processes & clinical applications.* New York: The Guilford Press.

Ruan, F. F. (1991). *Sex in China: Studies in sexology in Chinese culture.* New York: Plenum.

Schlosser, E. (1997). Most of the outside profits being generated by pornography today are being earned by businesses not traditionally associated with the sex industry. *U. S. News & World Report*, February 10, pp. 43–50.

Scott, J. E., and Schwalm, L. A. (1988a) Pornography and rape: An examination of adult theater rates and rape rates by state. In Scott, J. E. and Schwalm, L. (Ed.), *Controversial issues in crime and justice.* Beverly Hills: Sage.

——. (1988b). Rape rates and the circulation rates of adult magazines. *Journal of Sex Research* 24: 241–50.

Seldin, C. (1984). Vote rejecting cable measure by a 3–2 ratio. *Salt Lake Tribune*, November 7.

Shupan Nenkan. (1988, 1997). *Annual report for publishers.* Shupan Nenkan.

Smith, M. D., & Hand, K. (1987). The pornography-aggression linkage results from a field study. *Deviant Behavior* 8 (4): 389–99.

Smith, T. W. (1987). The polls–A review: The use of public opinion data by the Attorney General's Commission on Pornography. *Public Opinion Quarterly* 51: 249–67.

Sommers, E. K., & Check, J. (1987). An empirical investigation of the role of pornography in the verbal and physical abuse of women. *Violence and Victims* 2 (3): 189–209.

Somucho. (1993). *Survey of youth reading manga.* Tokyo: Management and Coordinating Agency [of the Japanese] Youth Authority.

Steinem, G. (1983). *Outrageous acts and everyday rebellions.* New York: Holt, Reinhart and Winston.

Stroh, M. (1996). Girls who offer sex upset Japan. *Los Angeles Times*, p. 1. September 30.

Strossen, N. (1995). *Defending pornography: Free speech, sex, and the fight for women's rights.* New York: Scribner.

Tavris, C., & Sadd, S. (1977). *The Redbook Report on female sexuality.* New York: Dell.

Thornton, M. (1986). U.S. Customs: Crusaders in the child-pornography War. *The Washington Post National Weekly Edition*, September 8, p. 34.

Tiefer, L. (1986). In pursuit of the perfect penis. *American Behavioral Scientist* 29 (5): 579–99.

———. (1995). *Sex is not a natural act & other essays.* Boulder: Westview Press.

Tjaden, P. J. (1988). Pornography and sex education. *Journal of Sex Research* 24: 208–12.

Uchida, T. (1979). Diary of a lawyer in charge. *Hogaku-Seminar* (December): 16-31.

Uchiyama, A. (1996). A study on the attitude of girls toward the commercialization of sex. Research on Prevention of Criminal Delinquency (Reports of the National Institute of Police Science): 1–3.

U.S. Customs. (1994). *Combating child pornography: U.S. Customs Service arrests 65 in first half of FY-98* (Press Release): U.S. Customs Service. September 8, p. 34.

Witkin, G., et al. (1998). The crime bust. *U.S. News & World Report.* 124 (20): 28–40.

Walker, C. E. (1970). *Erotic stimuli and the aggressive sexual offender.* Technical report volume 7 (pp. 91-147): U.S. Commission on Obscenity and Pornography.

Ward, D., & Kruttschnitt, C. (1983-1984). *Comparison study of imprisoned sex offenders, non sex offenders and others* (for City Council hearing): University of Minnesota. Reported in Reiss, Ira L. "Journey into sexuality: An exploratory voyage" (1986), pp. 181.

Wilson, W. C. (1978). Can pornography contribute to the prevention of sexual problems? In C. B. Qualls, J. P. Wincze, & D. H. Barlow (Eds.), *The prevention of sexual disorders: Issues and approaches* (pp. 159–79). New York: Plenum Press.

Winick, C. (1985). A content analysis of sexually explicit magazines sold in an adult bookstore. *Journal of Sex Research* 21: 206–10.

Woodruff, J. (1991). Japan's police finding it difficult to enforce informal ban on nudity. *Sunday Honolulu Star Bulletin & Advertiser,* July 7, p. A-26.

Yamada, T. (1989) Personal communication. Kinjo Gakuin University, Nagoya, Japan.

Yoakum, R. (1977). The great *Hustler* debate. *Columbia Journalism Review,* May/June 53-58.

Zillmann, D. (1984). *Connections between sex and aggression.* Hillsdale, N. J.: Erlbaum.

Zillmann, D., & Bryant, J. (1982). Pornography, sexual callousness and the trivialization of rape. *Journal of Communication* 32: 10–21.

———. (1984). Effects of massive exposure to pornography. In N. M. Malamuth & E. Donnerstein (Eds.), *Pornography and sexual aggression* (pp. 115–38). New York: Academic Press.

———. (1988a). Effects of prolonged consumption of pornography on family values. *Journal of Family Issues* 9 (4): 518–44.

———. (1988b). Pornography's impact on sexual satisfaction. *Journal of Applied Social Psychology* 18 (5): 438–53.

———. (1989). *Pornography: Research advances and policy considerations.* Hillsdale, N.J.: Lawrence Erlbaum.

Zillmann, D., & Weaver, J. B. (1989). Pornography and men's sexual callousness toward women. In D. Zillmann & J. Bryant (Eds.), *Pornography: Research advances and policy considerations* (pp. 95–125). Hillside, N.J.: Lawrence Erlbaum.

NOTES

1. The persons involved "for" or "against" pornography do not identify, nor necessarily see themselves comparably. Those "against" pornography and for censorship

are usually direct. They are against pornography and all it applies to them. They may also be in favor of censoring other things as well; such as materials they consider anti-religious or pro-abortion. Often times those against pornography are an unusual alliance of sex-negative femanists and religious fundamentalists. Those "for" are not necessarily in favor of pornography but more usually announce themselves as against censorship and for choice in private adult matters such as abortion and religious beliefs. In other regards they may be for "choice" in regard to abortion. This latter group may, indeed be in favor of pornography and whatever it might imply to them. In this case it would be a different spectrum of feminists that support this cause.

2. One of those dissenting in the vote was Charles H. Keating Jr. He felt the need to defend our country's "sinking morality." Appointed by President Nixon to the commission he was founder and president of the anti-pornography group "Citizens for Decency through Law" (Yoakum, 1977). He was later convicted as one of the major offenders in the Bank and Savings & Loan scandals of the 1980s (DeBenedictis, 1992).

3. I have an impression that another of the driving forces to look at porn again was the increasing prevalence of the "pocket book" (first appearing in 1935) and the increasing availability of VCRs and porn movies in the 1980s. In the past, pornography was mostly available to the rich and privileged. Now, as more and more pornography was inexpensively getting to the masses, the concern was something akin to: "While rich, educated and conservative people can deal with it, the masses can not." Anti-pornography censorship is a form of elitism where the "antis" are convinced that they can restrain themselves from the demoralizing power of SEM but others can not.

4. For instance, it included James Dobson, head of Focus on the Family, a noted Right Wing conservative organization It also included Reverend Bruce Ritter, who would later be indicted for child sex abuse (Diamond, 1990).

5. Only the states of Alaska and Nevada and the District of Columbia were an exception. In these two states there was a positive correlation between the distribution of sexual magazines and rape (Scott & Schwalm, 1988b).

6. Kutchinsky's study was completed prior to the reunification of East and West Germany in 1989.

7. In the 1930s to the 1950s, with the advent and popularity of crime comics in the West, from the United States, and Canada to Britain and Australia, and elsewhere there was a similar outcry against their alleged damaging influence on children. They were believed to be "criminogenic." Many obscenity laws were rewritten to include them. As shown by Brannigan (1987), however, the actual evidence was against their having any substantial influence on juvenile or adult offenses.

8. Tjaden (1988) surveyed the impact of pornography as a source of adolescent sexual information for American youth. He found that both male and female adolescents listed porn as their least important source of sexual information.

9. I myself have given many sex education workshops to Japanese sex education teachers since 1972. In almost all of them I have included sessions on rape prevention, reporting and related matters.

10. Many murders and violent assaults in Japan were, on inspection, found to be the actions of *boryokudan* and *yakuza* (protection and extortion) criminal gangs. Enhanced police efforts specifically directed against these criminal elements are believed at least partially responsible for the decreased incidence of murder and violent assault.

11. Although prostitution presently is illegal and streetwalkers are uncommon, suffice it to say there is no shortage of available prostitutes.

12. The U.S. government, aware of the community standard requirement, endeavors to try its antipornography cases in communities it thinks most conservative in religious, political and sexual matters rather than in the community in which the alledged violation occured (Yoakum, 1977).

13. Among the earliest definitions of obscenity, used in the U.S. for more than one hundred years, was the so-called English *Hicklin* definition. It held that "the test of obscenity is this, whether the tendency of the matter charged as obscenity is to deprave and corrupt those whose minds are open to such immoral influences, and into whose hands a publication of this sort may fall." Justices Black, Bok, Hand and others have, over the years, essentially concluded the term is basically undefinable in relation to sexual materials and the Court itself has confused the term rather than defined it. From a legal point of view it is long established in American jurisprudence that any crime must be known as such before its commission; the government cannot, *post hoc*, establish something as illegal.

14. Court's work (1984), particularly his analysis with its anti-pornography bias and selective use of evidence, has been severely criticized (Brannigan & Kapardis, 1986; Kutchinsky, 1994). Peculiarly he presents these data on Singapore and elsewhere as if they *support* his anti-porn bias by considering that matters could be much worse if porn laws were liberalized in those communities.

15. Leo Tolstoy, the great Russian novelist, has written: ". . . from the very commencement of my activity, that horrible Censor question has tormented me! I wanted to write what I felt; but at the same time it occurred to me that what I would write would not be permitted, and involuntarily I had to abandon the work. I abandoned and went on abandoning, and meanwhile the years passed away."

16. This doesn't mean that zealous federal and state attorneys have not brought charges of obscenity and won cases in those states. In so doing, for the cases in question, however, community standards were not surveyed or, if surveyed, not allowed into evidence. In other instances where the charges were made, the individual charged pled guilty to save legal fees, and other costs.

17. In the USA lately some are attributing the drop in crime as due to decreased drug use (*U.S. News & World Report*, 1998). Drugs were and are not a major factor in any of the other countries we mentioned. If anything, we would have to say that drug use was, during the time in question, on the *increase* in those societies rather than vice versa.

18. Some would likely credit an increased punishment associated with sex crimes leading to a decease in their frequency. Other than in China, however, there is no evidence that such punishments have increased over the years in the locales studied.

19. A study by Ira Reiss (1986; pp 183-184) of national samples of women who go or do not go to see pornographic films found that those who went were more, not less, gender equal than those who chose not to go. They did not see such films as encouraging the subordination of women. Those women who chose not to go typically had stereotypically conservative ideas of the roles proper for women, e.g., only 72 percent of those who chose not to attend X-rated films were more likely to approve of the statement: "Do you approve or disapprove of a married woman earning money in business or industry if she has a husband capable of supporting her?" Of those women who voluntarily view X-rated films, 81 percent approved. The difference is statistically significant.

20. Founder of the National Organization for Women Betty Friedan (1965) argues against women riling against pornography. She writes:

Get off the pornography kick and face the real obscenity of poverty. No matter how repulsive we may find pornography, laws banning books or movies for sexually explicit content could be far more dangerous to women. The pornography issue is dividing the women's movement and giving the impression on college campuses that to be a feminist is to be against sex . . .

21. On June 26, 1997, President Clinton signed the Communications Decency Act forwarded to him by Congress. It was their attempt to control and limit SEM on the internet. The U.S. Supreme Court, however, ruled the Act was an "unconstitutional intrusion on adults' free speech." Justice John Paul Stevens wrote for the court majority: "Notwithstanding the legitimacy and importance of the congressional goal of protecting children from harmful materials, we agree with [the lower-court ruling] that the statute abridges "freedom of speech" protected by the First Amendment.

22. The right to free speech and free press does not include the right to subject unwilling individuals to sexual utterences, materials or displays they find obscene. Such unwilling persons, however, cannot deprive access to others who welcome such.

23. The Free Speech Coalition, an adult film industry support group, has advocated, and adult film makers have adopted, a condom-only policy for their productions. In other ways also they work to improve the products being offered to the public (Douglas, 1998). Erotic films can also promote contraceptive use and recipracative consensual adult relationships.

TABLE 1
SEX CRIME STATISTICS IN JAPAN
(Actual Cases)

Crime	1972	1975	1980	1985	1990	1995
Rape victims (total)	4,677	3,692	2,610	1,802	1,548	1,500
Rape offenders (total)	5,464	4,052	2,667	1,809	1,289	1,160
Rape offenders (juvenile)	1,803	1,319	958	658	346	264
Sex assaults (events)	3,139	2,841	2,825	2,645	2,730	3,644
Sex assault offenders (total)	1,915	1,570	1,420	1,334	1,143	1,464
Sex assault offenders (juvenile)	641	439	440	497	341	321
Public indecency	1,651	1,706	1,335	1,182	947	1,108
Obscenity convictions	3,298	1,824	894	2,093	736	702
Violent crimes (events)	89,235	73,198	52,307	48,495	37,899	35,860
Murder (events)	2,060	2,098	1,684	1,780	1,238	1,281

Public indecency = flashing, frottage, etc.

Violent crimes = as grouped by the JNPA; includes those in which assault or injury occurs.

TABLE 2
RAPE IN JAPAN
Percentage of Victims in Each Age Range
for Each Year Examined

Age of Victim	1972	1975	1980	1985	1990	1995
0-5	0.7	0.5	0.5	0.2	0.1	0.1
6-12	7.6	9.5	8.9	12.5	5.4	3.9
13-19	35.4	36.3	33.4	34.7	39.8	36.4
20-24	29.6	22.0	23.0	22.7	24.5	33.0
25-29	9.0	11.5	11.6	8.8	11.4	12.2
30-39	10.6	11.2	12.5	10.8	8.6	7.1
40-49	4.7	5.5	5.5	5.2	5.5	4.3
50-59	1.6	2.3	3.1	3.3	2.3	1.9
60-69	0.7	1.2	1.0	1.2	1.3	0.6
70-79	0.0	0.0	0.5	0.6	1.0	0.5

TABLE 3
SHANGHAI PORN & RAPE

Year	Rapes	Pornography Items Confiscated
1972	456	•
1973	573	•
1974	398	•
1975	411	•
1976	359	•
1977	390	•
1978	310	•
1979	205	•
1980	258	•
1981	348	•
1982	447	•
1983	774	•
1984	439	•
1985	442	14,182
1986	410	•
1987	426	170,739
1988	360	265,951
1989	336	367,030
1990	456	•

• = no data available

TABLE 4
FEMALE RAPE: VICTIMIZATION RATES (/1000) IN USA
(Bureau of Justice Statistics)

Age of Victim	1975	1980	1985	1990	1995
12–15	1.6	1.3	1.0	3.4	2.2
16–19	4.7	5.0	4.3	2.5	5.7
20–24	4.7	3.9	3.4	3.5	3.0
25–34	2.3	2.2	2.0	.9	2.0
35–49	.4	.8	.6	.5	1.4
50–64	.4	0	0	.1	.1
65 >	.1	.2	.1	.1	0

Table 5
RATES OF CRIMINAL VICTIMIZATION
AND PERCENT CHANGE, 1993-1996, IN USA
(Bureau of Justice Statistics)
Victimization rate (per 1000 persons >12 y.o.)

Crime	1993	1994	1995	1996	% Change
Rape/Sexual Assault	2.5	2.1	1.7	1.4	−44.0
Rape/Attempted Rape	1.6	1.4	1.2	.9	−43.8
Rape	1.0	.7	.7	.4	−60.0
Attempted Rape	.7	.7	.5	.5	−28.6
Sexual Assault	.8	.6	.5	.5	−37.5
Completed Violence	15.0	15.4	13.8	12.4	−17.3
Attempt or Threat Violence	34.9	36.4	32.8	29.6	−15.2

22

Effects of Pornography
on Sexual Offending

Esau Tovar, James E. Elias,
and Joy Chang

THE DEBATES OVER WHO COMPRISES A SEX OFFENDER VARIES WIDELY and rather than attempt to provide a variety of definitions, one provides the comprehensiveness necessary for this review of the literature. The Kinsey Institute for the Study of Sex, Gender and Reproduction in an earlier book, *Sex Offenders* by Gebhard, Gagnon, Pomeroy, and Christenson (1964) defines sex offenders as "individuals who are ultimately convicted for committing overt acts for their immediate sexual gratification that are contrary to the prevailing sexual mores of their society and thus are legally punishable." It should be noted that this definition of sex offender differs from those individuals who are deviant, but are never arrested and from those classified in the *Diagnostic and Statistical Manual of Mental Disorders IV* (1994) as paraphilias. The differing views of the legal and psychiatric professionals have generally been in conflict and there is no reason to expect convergence or agreement on what comprises either the offender or the offense. We therefore wish to focus our review on data based studies which provide evidence to test the research question *Does exposure to pornographic materials lead to antisocial behavior in the form of sex offenses?*

Before beginning the review of the literature, note must be taken of the questions raised by Bauserman (1996) with respect to research on pornography and offenses. According to Bauserman, two questions arise in the study of pornography and its relation to sexual offending, "whether or not exposure to pornography plays a role in the *development* of offending behavior and whether use of pornography plays a role in the *commission* of actual offenses" [emphasis added]. This paper will focus on the second of these questions, as the literature provides much clearer data with respect to the commission of the offense as opposed to the development of a pattern of behavior which is subject to the interpretation of the researcher from extensive background materials.

Theories of Sex Offenders

There are numerous theories of sex offenders, which need to be presented before one can focus on the variable of pornography. These explanatory perspectives of sex offenders usually fall into categories which are crafted by different researchers. The theories can be classified as (1) Individual, (2) Psychological, (3) Social, or (4) Cultural explanations of the offending behavior with the level of explanation usually being reflected by the discipline and training of the researcher. Others, such as Siegel and Senna (1994) take a different approach dividing the explanations for deviant or criminal behavior into groups: (a) Individual, which is composed of choice and trait theories; (b) Social Structure Theories, which are made up of social disorganization, social strain, and cultural deviance; (c) Social Progress Theories, made up of labeling and conflict types. Another addition to this group is that of Feminist Theory. Looking at the work of Barbara Schwartz (1995b) in her paper on "Theories of Sex Offenses" we see a list of no less than twenty different theories used to explain the behavior of sex offenders including Ego, Neurosis, Jungian, Psychoanalytic, Cognitive-Behavioral, and an Integrated Theory of Rape. In looking at the characteristics and typologies of sex offenders, Schwartz (1995a) indicates a number of characteristics associated with the sex offenders, however, pornography was not one of them. Typologies which can classify groupings of sex offenders into categories providing insight into their patterns, behavior and possible motivations make a significant contribution to the field. These have been developed mainly for two types of sex offenders—pedophiles and rapists. It is worthwhile noting, however, that "research into the characteristics of sex offenders can become a meaningless list of traits. Typologies may be reduced to labels that do more harm than good" (Schwartz, 1995b).

Upon reviewing the literature, the position serious researchers have taken with respect to pornography is one in which the antisocial or deviant behavior is preexisting and that the role of pornography is that of providing justification and rationalizations for their behavior in addition to being a source of sexual arousal.

One of the variables that is often cited in association with pornography is that of aggression. It is this link that provides much of the fodder for emotional appeals based on experiential evidence. The research most often cited is that of Malamuth and Donnerstein reported in the book *Pornography and Aggression* (1984). Their research has often been misinterpreted and misstated for political purposes. In their research, Donnerstein and Linz (1986) conclude that "There is no evidence for harm-related effects from sexually explicit materials. But research may support potential harmful effects from aggressive materials. Aggressive images are the issue, not sexual images."

The Debate Over the Effects of Pornography

The debate over the effects of pornography can be seen in three positions: (1) those supporting the relationship between pornography and sex offenses, (2) those whose results are mixed or conflicting, and (3) those studies which show no relationship between pornography and sex offenders. A brief discussion of the two polar positions may provide a clearer picture of the debate as there is a movement to present opinion as data and mix the politics of pornography with what pretends to be scientific research. However, it is very important to look at the source of the data and conclusions drawn by the different positions.

The position that sees pornography as directly related to sex offenses is most strongly held in a wing of the feminist perspective, namely following the work of Andrea Dworkin (1981) and Catharine MacKinnon (1993). The basis in Feminist Theory is explained on the grounds of a patriarchal, oppressive society. Dworkin and MacKinnon

> believe that pornography is at the root of every form of exploitation and discrimination of women. Dworkin, MacKinnon, and numerous other feminists also believe that violence against women is not merely reflected in some pornography, it is caused by all pornography. (Turley, 1986)

To support this position, the work of Donnerstein and Malamuth (1984) is frequently cited along with the support of the profeminist men's group NOMAS (National Organization of Men Against Sexism) strongly supported by M.S. Kimmel (1992).

Leading the fight against the Dworkin-MacKinnon position have been the female sex workers who are the focus of the "exploitation." These women form the foundation for a strong pro-porn or pro-erotic position with respect to women and sexuality. The position of the academic women who support them, such as Linda Williams, Camille Paglia and others do not find pornography as oppressive of women. In fact, their position supports the thesis that pornographic material releases women to express their sexuality. This is further reinforced by sex workers like Annie Sprinkle and filmmakers such as Candida Royalle.

When strong personalities make strong political arguments, the data may very well become lost in the rhetoric. This paper will try, as much as possible to eliminate the politics of pornography and focus instead on data derived from research. The research should stand on its own and the interpretation should be based on the conclusions derived from data and not from the political positions of conflicting groups. It is with that intention that this review of the data was undertaken.

STUDIES REFUTING THE
PORNOGRAPHY-SEX OFFENSE LINK

Pornography, Rape, and Sexual Arousal

Asked about why sex offenses may occur, individuals in the general population believe that reading and viewing pornographic materials "lead people to commit rape" (Abelson et al., 1970). This is also contended by many law enforcement officials. Dworkin (1981, 1985) and MacKinnon (1989) maintain that pornography constitutes hate literature against women, that it facilitates aggression, and that it encourages men to see women as sex objects. Misleading statements such as "Pornography is the theory and rape is the practice" (Morgan, 1980; Bowen, 1987) further carry on this belief. However, as suggested by analyses of crime data on sexual offending in the United States and abroad do not support this causal connection between the availability/circulation of pornography and the commission of sex crimes among juveniles or adult sex offenders. In fact, it has been shown that although the availability of pornographic materials has sharply increased over time, arrests for sex offenses have remained relatively stable or decreased compared to other violent crimes.

Examining Uniform Crime Reports compiled by the Federal Bureau of Investigation from 1960 to 1969 Kuperstein and Wilson (1970) found an overall decrease on sex offenses, with the exception of forcible rape, prostitution, and commercialized vice. However, these accounted for less than 2 percent of arrests from 1960 to 1969. Compared to the forcible rape, arrests for criminal homicide, robbery, grand larceny, and auto thefts increased to a greater extent. Juvenile sex offenses decrease by 4 percent during the same period.

Comparative studies conducted in the United States and European countries have found no causal relation with the availability of pornography and the commission of sex offenses. A Danish study revealed that the number of arrests for sex offenses dramatically decreased from 1958 to 1969, despite an extensive increase in the circulation of pornographic material (Ben-Veniste, 1970). A more recent study conducted by Kutchinsky (1991) found similar results.

Studying the role of pornography on rape rates in Denmark, Sweden, West Germany, and the United States from 1964 to 1984, Kutchinsky reports that the availability of both hard-core pornography (combining sex with aggression and or explicit dominance) and non-aggressive pornography experienced rapid growth during this period in all four countries. Rape rates, however, differed among them. That is, rape rates in West Germany remained relatively steady; Denmark and Sweden experienced moderate increases; and the United States experienced a higher increase. Kutchinsky suggests that "it is likely that at least some of the increase is due to increased reporting and registration of rape, as a result of growing awareness of the rape problem among women as well as the police" (Kutchinsky, 1991).

Despite the increase of reported rapes, these did not differ from non-sexual violent crimes such as aggravated assault from 1964 to 1984. The rates for rape and aggravated assault in the United States experienced similar growth; assault increased at a faster pace than rape rates in Denmark, Sweden, and West Germany. Kutchinsky suggests that "the two developments [rape and aggravated assault] are related and should be explained in the same terms." This is consistent with the view that rape is an act of aggression, not a sexual act (Russell, 1980) and "refute[s] the belief that explicit sexual material is somehow related to rape" (Scott & Cuvelier, 1993).

Yet another study conducted in the United States examining arrest data in Maine, North Carolina, Pennsylvania, and Washington during the periods of time when these states' pornography statutes were inoperative, found an upsurge in explicit pornographic media, a decrease in murder and robbery arrest, and an increase in rape and aggravated assault. Despite these increases, however, arrest rates for sex crimes were well below the national average (per 100,000 arrests in those states: ME=5.77; NC=11.32; PA=13.36; WA=12.56; ALL=14.46) over the fourteen-year period studied. Compared to the pre-suspension periods, no significant changes occurred in observed rates of arrest for rape, prostitution, and sex offenses. Winick & Evans (1996) offer various interpretations for their findings. They postulate the possibility that there may not exist a relationship between the use of pornography and the commission of sex offenses, or that the availability of pornography may alternately increase rates of sexual offenses for one group, decrease it for others, or have no impact on the majority of individuals.

Challenging the belief that increased availability and circulation of pornography in effect leads to an increase in rates for rapes, Kimmel and Linders (1996) found just the opposite, mainly, that rape rates along with aggravated assault increased while pornography consumption decreased. Thus, it is evident that "a steady decline in consumption of printed pornography and a steady rise in rape rate" (Kimmel & Linders, 1996) was in effect. It was also found that among the cities studied (Cincinnati, Cleveland, Indianapolis, Dallas, Jacksonville, and Louisville) "the proportion of rapes reported for the core cities had decreased from 1979 to 1989 in Cincinnati, Indianapolis, and Louisville, remained fairly stable in Cleveland and Jacksonville, and [slightly] increased in Dallas." Additionally, a negative correlation (r= .79) between circulation rates and rape rates between 1979 and 1989 was found nationwide. Even after removing *Penthouse* and *Playboy*, which account for the majority of the circulating material as included in the study, this negative correlation remained substantially high (r=-.54). Similar correlations were found at the state level, Kentucky (r=-.75), Ohio (r=-.82), and Texas (r=-.61). Positive correlations were found in Florida (r=.30) and Indiana (r=.04). The authors conclude that "just as legalizing pornography has not, and . . . will not lead to an increase in rape rates, banning pornography [as was done in Cincinnati and Jacksonville] will not lead to a reduction in rape rates," contrary to beliefs held by Dworkin (1981, 1985), MacKinnon (1989, 1993), and Brownmiller (1975).

Allegations have also been made in reference to increased violence depicted in sexually explicit materials, including sadomasochistic and bondage representations (Smith, 1976; Winick, 1977; Attorney General's Commission on Pornography, 1986; Zillman & Bryant, 1986; Marshall & Barbaree, 1984). However, as reported by Kutchinsky (1983) sadomasochistic representations accounted for less than 2 percent in the available material in Denmark. Winick (1985) also reports that among 430 magazines found in a representative adult bookstore, sadomasochistic material accounted for only 1.2 percent of the total available pornographic material, while that of bondage was slightly higher (4.9 percent). Yet another bookstore study analyzing three hundred magazines found that only 7 percent of the women and 9 percent of the men portrayed in these magazines were seen in sadomasochistic or bondage submissive positions (Soble, 1986).

Furthermore, a content analysis of all cartoons and pictorials included in *Hustler* magazine from 1974 to 1987 was conducted by Scott & Cuvelier (1993). The study focused on any depictions of violent and nonviolent portrayals in such pictorials. Sexually violent depictions included references to rape, sadomasochism, and exploitative/coercive sexual relations. Contrary to popular belief, researchers found no evidence to the assumption that violent pornography was increasing. In fact, the average number of sexually violent depictions per year was 5.77, or .48 per issue. According to the authors "there has not been a monotonic increase in either violent or sexually violent cartoons or pictorials in *Hustler* magazine from 1974 to 1987." Authors also note these findings were unexpected given that the number of cartoons and pictorials substantially increased from one issue to another. In fact, without controlling for the number of pages or the number of pictorials and cartoons included in each issue of the magazine, a decrease in violent depictions is observed.

In addition to refuting the so-called increase in sexually violent portrayals, Scott & Cuvelier (1993) state that "these data [also] question the alleged link between increased sexual violence in adult magazines and rape rates" by citing relevant literature. They argue that given the increase in X-rated video rentals in the U.S., one would expect that rape rates would have increased if the assumption that pornography causes individuals to rape held true, but this has not occurred.

Additional research has been conducted to assess the effects of pornography, violent and nonviolent. Citing Malamuth and his colleagues' work, Donnerstein & Linz (1986) state that a non-rapist population will show increased sexual arousal after having been exposed to "media-presented images of rape," especially when the female victim demonstrates signs of pleasure and arousal. This exposure may also lead to a lessened sensitivity toward rape, acceptance of rape myths, increased self-reported likelihood of raping and self-generated rape fantasies. According to Donnerstein & Linz, exposure to nonaggressive pornography may have one of two effects: either (1) individuals predisposed to aggress who are later exposed to nonaggressive pornography increase their experiencing aggressive behavior; or (2) exposure to nonaggressive pornography may have the opposite effect, it may reduce subsequent aggressive behavior. They go on to state that no evidence exists "for any 'harm'-related effects from sexually explicit materials. But research may support potential harm effects from aggressive materials. *Aggressive* images are the issue, not sexual images" (Donnerstein & Linz, 1986).

Jaffee & Straus (1987) report that sex magazines circulation rates, poverty, urbanization, and divorce rates of males are statistically associated with the incidence of reported rape as measured by the FBI's Uniform Crime Reports. Having reviewed their findings the authors conjectured a theoretical model explaining how rape might occur. They state, "it is the joint dependence of sex magazine readership and rape on hypermasculinity, rather than the influence of exposure to sexually explicit materials per se, that produces the correlation between sex magazine readership and rape."

Studies assessing the impact of pornography on men's fantasies, attitudes, and aggressiveness toward women have also been conducted. Such was the purpose of Fisher & Grenier's study (1994), where a group of men was assigned to one of three experimental conditions or one control condition where they were told they would view a video (edited to fit three scenarios) depicting a man and a woman who had met at a dance and either (1) the man forced the woman into the bedroom and raped her but the woman ultimately enjoyed the experience (positive outcome); (2) the man forced the woman into the bedroom and raped her, and after the incident she fell into a deep depression (negative outcome); (3) the couple were quite attracted to one another and wanted to express their feelings; and (4) the neutral (control) group was explained the rules of a television game show. Pre-exposure arousal of subjects (as measured by the Sexual Arousal Self-Report Grid) revealed equivalent arousal levels across all conditions. Post-exposure measures indicated that in all, but the neutral condition, arousal levels had increased significantly. It was found that exposure to the neutral, erotic, and pornographic stimuli had no effect on subjects' fantasies or attitudes toward women. No man produced sexually aggressive fantasies; men had positive attitudes toward women, rejected interpersonal violence toward them and contrary to other studies, rejected rape myths. Fisher & Grenier concluded that "These observations are consistent with the conclusion that exposure to violent pornography, as often studied in this research area, is not a reliable cause of antiwoman fantasies or antiwoman attitudes."

Conducting a second experiment on the "effects of exposure of pornography on men's aggressive behavior toward women," Fisher & Grenier (1994) found that twelve of fourteen men assigned to the exposure to violent pornography, positive outcome condition did not experience antiwoman aggression following a negative evaluation by a female confederate by means of electric shock and exposure to violent, positive outcome pornography–confirming the researcher's hypothesis. The two other men had from the onset of the experiment expressed an interest in using the shock machine to provide feedback to the female confederate on a poorly performed memorization task. Because no significant effects were found in this experimental condition, the remaining conditions were not carried out. These results go on to suggest that:

> The current research findings do tell us–together with the empirical, methodological, and conceptual problems identified in the literature–that the reliability of effects of violent pornography on men's fantasies, attitudes, and behavior toward women remains to be demonstrated within the experimental procedures that have often been used to study such effects. (Fisher & Grenier, 1994)

Sexual and Physical Abuse and
Family Violence among Sex Offenders

Although allegations continue to be made that sex offenders consume comparatively substantially more pornography than the general population, research does not support this premise, rather it seems other variables may instead affect sexual offending more aversively. Howitt (1995) conducted extensive interviews with eleven pedophiles undergoing treatment. The interviews probed a variety of areas as they related to sex offenses. Howitt characterized these offenders as fixated, that is, their offenses did not extend to adult women, for example. During the interview, sex offenders were asked about their experience with pornography, fantasy, and sexual history pertaining to childhood sexual abuse. Exposure to heterosexually oriented softcore pornography was typical of the men, however, "commercial pornography was rarely a significant aspect of their use of erotica." Although exposure to child pornography was not significant among offenders, some generated their own erotic materials from such items as catalogs and newspaper advertisements. No reports were made by the offenders regarding exposure to sexually explicit materials prior to their first sexual abuse offense or prior to their own victimization. Howitt concludes "there is no evidence that early exposure to pornography was a cause of later offending."

To the extent that pornography did not play a significant role in their offending, a strong association with childhood sexual abuse was readily evident. Ten of the eleven pedophiles had been sexually victimized as children. The eleventh man witnessed a pedophilic assault of another child. Howitt argues that early sexualization of these men as children might help explain why masturbatory experience occurred at a relatively young age.

Becker & Stein (1991) conducted a study investigating (1) the number of adolescent sex offenders using sexual erotica, (2) the type of sexually explicit material used, and (3) the relationship between use of erotica, alcohol/drugs, history of victimization, and number of victims. One hundred and sixty adolescent males charged with or convicted of a sex crime participated. Results indicated that 35 percent of the offenders used magazines and 26 percent viewed pornographic videotapes most often than other media. Eleven percent reported not viewing sexually explicit materials at all.

Asked about the effect of pornography on their sexual arousal, the majority (67 percent) reported an increase in sexual arousal. No differences were found in terms of number of victims for type of material used. However, a significant relationship was found on the use of alcohol and number of victims. In general, those subjects who believed alcohol increased their sexual arousal had a mean of 3.1 victims, compared to 2.1 for those believing it decreased their arousal, 2.0 for those believing alcohol had no effect on their arousal, and 1.7 for those not using alcohol.

Subjects who were sexually abused had a greater number of victims (M=2.8) than those with no sexual abuse history (M=1.7). Those with no prior history of sexual abuse, were more likely to have had female victims (73 percent), while those reporting no sexual abuse had approximately the same number of male and female victims. Physical abuse history was also significant. Specifically, physically abused offenders had a greater number of victims (M=2.4) than those with no physical abuse history (M=1.7). Arriving at similar conclusions as did Howitt (1995), Becker & Stein (1991) suggest that:

> Sexual victimization can provide a powerful basis for the development of sexual deviance. A young victim of sexual abuse may fantasize about his own victimization or about committing similar abuse while masturbating. This pairing of masturbation and the experience of abuse only serve to strengthen deviant sexual interest. Therefore appropriate sexual interest may not have the opportunity to develop.

Thus, pornography may not significantly contribute to sexual offending. Of twenty offenders selected for further inquiry, Becker & Stein found fourteen sex offenders believed pornography had no effect on their offending. Only one reported having seen a video which perhaps "may have unconsciously given me the idea."

Studying characteristics that might be predictive of sexual offending among juvenile sex offenders (rapists and child molesters), violent nonsex offenders, and status offenders, Ford & Linney (1995) found that child molesters differed from status offenders in observing and being victims of parental violence; reported more intrafamilial violence than status offenders and rapists; and were sexually victimized more frequently than other offenders. The study revealed juveniles in all groups were exposed to soft-core and hard-core (bondage, violent sexual acts, paraphilia) pornography. While 42 percent of the sex offenders were exposed to hard-core pornography only 29 percent of violent and status offenders were exposed to the same types. Results also indicated sex offenders were exposed to sexually explicit materials at a younger age (five–eight). Of the two sex offender groups, child molesters were more frequently exposed. No difference was found in exposure to X-rated movies or sexually explicit television programs among offenders. However, violent offenders reported earlier exposure to explicit movies and television programs that showed violence associated with sexual intercourse. "The salience of these early memories suggests that exposure to violence during early childhood, either within the home or elsewhere, may be a significant antecedent risk factor for violent and sexual offending" (Ford & Linney, 1995).

Finally, a review of the literature on pornography and its relation to sexual aggression concludes that "pornography in its purely erotic form" has failed to demonstrate "any significant detrimental effect on human behaviour," especially its effects on psychological development (Fukui & Westmore, 1994). It is further noted that no causative link has been demonstrated between sex offenders' deviant behavior and pornographic material. Fukui & Westmore go on to state that:

> The psychological problems are traced back to childhood [38] and involve issues of intimacy and loneliness [39] inability to control feelings of anger and hatred, and disturbances of identification [40]. The functional disturbances demonstrated by sexual offenders are often extensive, particularly in those who commit rape or sadistic sexual assault. However, pornographic stimulation acting either as a "trigger" for the offending behaviour or indeed as a "kindling" phenomenon has not been identified [their brackets].

Degree of Exposure to Sexually Explicit Materials Among Sex Offenders

One of the most extensive studies conducted to-date (Gebhard, Gagnon, Pomeroy, & Christenson, 1965) analyzed sexual offenses among 1,356 white male sex offenders, 888 male nonsex offenders, and a control group of 477 volunteer males from the general population. The study found that exposure to sexual materials was common among all three groups, and sex offenders did not differ statistically from the nonoffender group and the control group in the degree of exposure to sexual material. Additionally, sex offenders reported less arousal from using pornography.

A study conducted by Condron & Nutter (1988) on sixty-two men (thirteen reporting a paraphilia (exhibitionism, cross-dressing, infantilism, voyeurism, fetishism, bestiality, klimaphilia, sadism, masochism, bondage, or discipline), a control group of eighteen men from a service club, a control group of fifteen men being treated for a sexual dysfunction, and a nonincarcerated sex offender group of sixteen men (offenses included rape, incest, child molestation, exhibitionism, voyeurism, and telephonicophilia). Although age differences in pornography exposure did not differ statistically, results indicated sex offenders were generally exposed to pornography at a later age than were non-offenders (sex offenders: M=14.90; paraphiles: M=13.40; sexual dysfunction group: 13.33; service group: 12.80). Thus dispelling the common belief that sex offenders are exposed to pornography at earlier ages and somehow causing them to offend. In all four groups studied, first masturbation experience occurred prior to exposure to pornography. Specifically, 63 percent of the sex offenders; 91 percent of paraphiles; 47 percent of sexual dysfunction patients; and 41 percent of men in a men's service group had masturbated prior to exposure to pornographic materials. As Lipton (1976) suggests, "In general, sex offenders report sexually repressive backgrounds and immature and inadequate sexual histories" (Condron & Nutter, 1988).

Becker and Stein (1991) also reported that nearly 90 percent of 160 adolescent sex offenders had been exposed to sexually explicit materials, two-thirds of which reported having been aroused by it. However, no relation was found between the number of victims and the type of materials used. Of twenty individuals questioned in more detail, only two felt that sexual materials may have contributed to the commission of their sexual offense.

Several studies reported by the U.S. Commission on Obscenity and Pornography (1970) suggest that sex offenders are not exposed to pornography or to more unusual types of it during childhood or adolescence to a greater extent than non-offenders. For example, Cook and Fosem (1970) compared imprisoned sex offenders and non-sex offenders in the degree of exposure to soft-core and hard-core pornography. Compared to non-sex offenders, sex offenders were exposed to significantly lower levels of soft-core and hard-core pornography during pre-adolescence and early adolescence periods. Although both groups experienced increased sexual activity after exposure, sex offenders resorted to masturbation, whereas, non-sex offenders resorted to interpersonal sexual activity.

Also writing for the Commission, Johnson, Kupperstein, and Peters (1970) conducted a study on erotica and sex offenders. Compared to a national sample of 652 adult males, forty-seven probationary sex offenders, including rapists, pedophiles, homosexuals (deemed deviant at the time of the study), and exhibitionists answered a questionnaire identical to that of a national sample. It was observed that sex offenders came into contact with sexual materials including hard-core pornography (whips, belts, spankings) at later ages than the national sample. Their reported arousal level to such materials was similar, however (7 percent and 6 percent, respectively). Questioned about whether pornography had led them to commit their sexual offense, only one pedophile claimed that pornography had led him to commit rape. Walker (1970) too, assessed the effects of erotic stimuli among sixty imprisoned aggressive sex offenders, sixty matched incarcerated non-sex offenders, and ninety non-matched non-offenders controls from colleges and men's service clubs. Results indicated controls were exposed more frequently and at an earlier age to erotic materials than were the sex offenders. However, an unspecified "small but significant minority" of sex offenders believed pornography contributed to their sexual offense.

Goldstein and Kant (1970) found no differences in exposure to pornography among rapists, pedophiles and controls (Black and white non-offenders) during adolescence and rapists were exposed to hard-core pornography at similar rates of exposure as were the low-income blacks, whereas, whites were exposed to such materials less frequently. Exposure to pornographic materials during the past year was not significantly different among sex offenders and controls.

Together, these findings suggest there is no readily identifiable causal connection between sex offenses and exposure to pornographic materials. The rare instances in which individual offenders reported their belief that pornography caused them to commit their sex crimes, must not be taken at face value given the possibility that offenders may in fact be rationalizing their deviant behaviors.

STUDIES SUPPORTING THE PORNOGRAPHY-SEX OFFENSE LINK

Few data based studies have been conducted to-date on the effects of exposure to pornographic materials and its relation to sexual offending. It is here that much of the politicization of pornography occurs. Allegations are made by numerous individuals who often interpret findings in an effort to advance their own agendas. Nonetheless, there exist a few studies supporting the pornography-sex offense link. Typical studies in this area involve the utilization of undergraduate psychology students in experimental research where they are exposed to varying degrees or forms of pornography. They are then given a series of questionnaires or tasks designed to reveal the extent to which pornography may have a deleterious effect on those participating, and their interactions with female confederates. One such study was conducted by Zillman & Bryant (1986) which explored the relation of pornography on beliefs about sexuality and on dispositions toward women. Eighty male and eighty female undergraduate students participated in the study which took place over the course of six weeks. Subjects were assigned to one of three experimental conditions (massive, intermediate, or no exposure to pornography) or a control group. While the experimental groups were assessed at different times during the six weeks, the control group, with no prior exposure to pornography was introduced to the study during the third week. Subjects in the experimental groups were exposed to six eight-minute films and were asked to evaluate them for aesthetic aspects. Those assigned to the massive exposure group watched a total of thirty-six films, approximating four hours and forty-eight minutes; those in the intermediate exposure condition watched eighteen erotic films and eighteen non-erotic films constituting two hours and twenty-four minutes of erotic material; finally, those assigned to the no exposure condition watched thirty-four non-erotic films. All of the erotic films depicted heterosexual content (fellatio, cunnilingus, coition, anal intercourse). Films did not depict coercion or deliberate infliction of pain. During the third week, participants were asked to estimate the percentage of adults performing a given sexual activity. They were also introduced to a rape case by reading a newspaper article describing a case where a female victim had picked up a hitchhiker who later raped her. Subjects were asked to recommend a prison sentence for the offender. The authors postulated the length of prison sentences would indicate the degree to which individuals would exhibit callousness toward women, especially reflected in lower prison terms. Subjects also asked to report their support for the women's liberation movement. Subsequently, they were exposed to a sexually explicit novel and were asked to rate their affective reactions, and their objections regarding the distribution of pornographic material. Finally, only all male participants filled out a questionnaire assessing sexual callousness toward women.

For the purpose of this paper only those aspects regarding pornography and rape and men's sexual callousness toward women will be discussed. According to the authors, the disposition to rape—as measured by prison sentences—was readily evident in the assigned prison terms of the offender. Specifically, those exposed to the massive pornography condition (men and women alike) assigned significantly shorter prison terms. Additionally, the men exposed to the same condition were more likely to express an increased sexual callousness toward women. The authors conclude that "massive exposure to standard pornographic materials devoid of coercion and aggression seemed to promote such callousness (in particular, the trivialization of rape), the findings are suggestive of further anti-social consequences" (Zillman & Bryant, 1982).

Moving beyond the study of length of exposure to pornographic material, Emerick & Dutton (1993) assessed observed differences in reported sex offenses of adolescent offenders. Seventy-six adolescent males reported for, charged with, or adjudicated of a sexual crime including voyeurism, exhibitionism, bestiality, sexual abuse, rape, child molestation, fetishism, and obscene phone calling were included in the study. No specific numbers for each type of sexual offense were noted. Data regarding assault history disclosure was gathered by means of collateral documents (legal and clinical documents), clinical interview, and polygraph examination. Pornography was classified as depicting (1) "commercial objectification of women," (2) "commercial exploitation of women," and (3) consisting of hard-core pornography. Seventy percent of subjects reported having been exposed to pornographic materials: 27.2 percent to #1, 17.1 to #2, and 55.7 percent to #3. Nearly 79 percent reported viewing pornography while masturbating. Additionally, those using hard-core pornography while masturbating had a higher number of female child victims (M=2.75) than those not using it or viewing commercial pornography (M=1.69). Additionally, they too had a greater number of female adult and child victims combined (M=3.29 vs 2.04). Finally, when put together, those using hard-core pornography had a higher number of victims of both genders (M=4.33 vs 3.00). Emerick & Dutton also found a strong association with the sexual victimization of the offenders themselves, specifically, 63.5 percent had been sexually abused.

Employing yet another research technique to study the effects of pornography, Marshall (1988) conducted a retrospective study in which fifteen incest offenders, eighteen homosexual child molesters, thirty-three heterosexual child molesters, and twenty-three men accused of rape or attempted rape participated. An additional twenty-four men with no prior history of sex offending were matched to child molesters on socioeconomic class, intelligence, and age. Each of the offenders was interviewed twice to

assess their sexual preferences, and a third time to inquire about their exposure to and use of sexually explicit materials. Subjects were asked to focus
on only hard-core materials defined as "those available only in specialized
stores (or from illegal sources) and depicting explicit sexual acts with
nothing left to the imagination." Results indicated that child molesters did
not have significantly more access to "kiddie porn" than the other groups.
Additionally, rapists did not differ from child molesters and non-offenders
in their use of material concerning forced sex.

Although the type of sexually explicit material used by sex offenders
did not differ from non-offenders, significant differences were found in the
use of pornography during pubescence and current use. Specifically, 33 percent of heterosexual child molesters, 39 percent of homosexual child molesters, 33 percent of rapists, and 21 percent of non-offenders reported using
pornography during pubescence. Although rates for current use of pornography did not differ significantly among sex offenders, these rates were
much higher than those reported during pubescence (67 percent for both
heterosexual and homosexual child molesters, 100 percent for incest
offenders, 83 percent for rapists). Non-offenders reported less current exposure than any of the other groups (29 percent). Additionally, 53 percent of
the child molesters and 33 percent of the rapists reported pornography
served as an instigator to their offenses. That is, they intentionally viewed
these materials in preparation to commit their offense.

Marshall also found that compared to non-offenders and incest
offenders, child molesters and rapists masturbated more frequently
(one–two per week vs greater than one time per day). They were also more
likely to report deviant fantasies during masturbation and non-masturbatory
daydreams. Heterosexual and homosexual child molesters with three or
more victims were more likely to have used sexual stimuli in preparation to
commit their offense. Frequent masturbators (greater than one time per day
or three–six times per week) who were current users of pornography were
more likely to use it in preparation to commit their offense.

Marshall states that "The demonstration of relationships between the
use of sexual stimuli as instigators to offend, the strength of deviant sexual
interest (as measured by deviant quotients), and the rates of masturbatory
activities, strengthens the conviction that child molesters (in particular) are
preoccupied with deviant thoughts that unfortunately appear to mediate a
high rate of sexual offending." Marshall goes on to say

> It is possible that the use of these stimuli by sex offenders reflects the gen-
> erally deviant sexual appetites of these men. According to this view, rather
> than exposure to sexual materials contributing to their deviance, the fact
> that these offenders seek it out is simply another manifestation of their
> basic deviant interests. (Marshall, 1988)

Indirect findings on the effects of pornography have been reported in
the literature. Silbert & Pines (1984) carried out a field study analyzing

sexual abuse experienced by street prostitutes prior to and following entrance into prostitution. Although the intent was not to directly look at pornography, it became clear during the course of the study that many prostitutes reported incidents in which their clients behaved in a manner which is portrayed in many pornographic movies. That is, many of the clients engaged in violent sexual acts as viewed in the movies. Authors caution against any firm conclusions about these findings given that victims, not perpetrators, contributed the information on violent pornography. Nonetheless, they go on to state that their "results lend considerable support to the 'imitation model' of pornography. Many of the references to pornography noted by the subjects indicated that their abusers were imitating the abusing males in pornographic materials, and believed that, as the victims in pornography, their victims [too] must enjoy the abuse" (Silbert & Pines, 1984).

DISCUSSION

Studying the purported link that pornography may have on antisocial behavior, particularly in the form of sexual offending has proved a difficult task. Numerous methodological and logistical problems have been reported in the literature, including the lack of inclusion of control groups when gathering data from sex offenders. In conducting retrospective studies it is not uncommon to find that offenders attempt to provide an explanation on why they offend and cite the use of pornography as the instigator of their offending. However, this may instead prove to be no more than a rationalization for their deviant behavior. Laboratory experiments too suffer from a number of limitations, namely, whether findings from a laboratory setting be generalized to the general population.

As with many other areas of sexuality, pornography is frequently cited by the feminist wing as being harmful and degrading to women, and how men consuming it become callous and violent toward them. Many findings—often with low correlation values between pornography and sex offenses—are exaggerated and exploited through the media in an effort to advance an agenda supportive of one's point of view. There is also a trend to portray opinion as data, thus politicizing the study of pornography. The Effects Panel of the United States Commission on Obscenity and Pornography (1970) acknowledged that in conducting their studies, "social forces" impeded and limited carrying out given studies. The Attorney General's Commission (1986) was even more political than scientific. Most of its reported findings were based from opinion and not data.

To briefly summarize the findings of this literature review, consistent with many of the findings of the U.S. presidential commission on pornography, no causal links can be established between the use of pornography and sexual offending. Study after study suggests that pornography is not the issue in sexual violence, rather violence itself may in fact cause sexual offending. Juvenile and adult offenders report similar use of pornographic material as nonoffenders. Age of exposure to such materials varies widely, however, sex offenders become exposed to it at later ages than nonoffenders. The review of several studies reported in this paper suggest that sexual abuse, physical abuse, and drug/alcohol use may better serve as predictors in sexual offending. Researchers have hypothesized that individuals who are sexually abused may fantasize about their own abuse while masturbating, which in turn may lead them to believe that offending may not be an inappropriate behavior. Sexually repressive backgrounds are also reported extensively in the study of sex offenders where pornographic materials are not readily available. Notwithstanding these findings, the view that pornography may serve as an instigator for sex offending cannot be ignored in its entirety. It is possible as Marshall (1988) found that pornography may be used by some offenders in preparation to commit their offenses. However, the opposite can be true.

REFERENCES

Abelson, H., Cohen, R., Heaton, E., & Slider, C. (1970). Public attitudes toward and experience with erotic materials. *Technical Reports of the Commission on Obscenity and Pornography*, vol. 6. Washington, D.C.: U.S. Government Printing Office.

American Psychiatric Association. (1994). *Diagnostic and statistical manual of mental disorders*. 4th ed. Washington, D.C.: Author.

Attorney General's Commission on Pornography. (1986). *Final Report*. Washington, D.C.: U.S. Department of Justice.

Bauserman, R. (1996). Sexual aggression and pornography: A review of correlational research. *Basic and Applied Social Psychology* 18: 405–27.

Becker, J., & Stein, R. M. (1991). Is sexual erotica associated with sexual deviance in adolescent males? *International Journal of Law and Psychiatry* 14: 85–95.

Ben-Veniste, R. (1970). Pornography and sex crime: The Danish experience. *Technical Reports of the Commission on Obscenity and Pornography*, vol. 9. Washington, D.C.: U.S. Government Printing Office.

Bowen, N. H. (1987). Pornography: Research review and implications for counseling. *Journal of Counseling and Development* 65: 345–50.

Brownmiller, S. (1975). *Against our will: Men, women, and rape*. New York: Simon & Schuster.

Commission on Obscenity and Pornography. (1970). *The Report of the Commission on Obscenity and Pornography*. Washington, D.C.: United States Government Printing Office.

Condron, M. K., & Nutter, D. E. (1988). A preliminary examination of the pornography experience of sex offenders, paraphiliacs, sexual dysfunction patients, and controls based on Meese Commission recommendations. *Journal of Sex & Marital Therapy* 14: 285–98.

Cook, R. F., & Fosen, R. H. (1970). Pornography and the sex offender: Patterns of exposure and immediate arousal effects of pornographic stimuli. *Technical Reports of the Commission on Pornography*, vol. 7. Washington, D.C.: United States Government Printing Office.

Donnerstein, E., & Linz, D. (1986). Mass media sexual violence and male viewers: Current theory and research. *American Behavioral Scientist* 29: 601–18.

Dworkin, A. (1981). *Pornography: Men possessing women.* New York: Perigee Books.

——. (1985). Against the male flood: Censorship, pornography, and equality. *Harvard Women's Law Journal* 8.

Emerick, R., & Dutton, W. A. (1993). The effects on polygraphy on the self-report of adolescent sex offenders: Implications for risk assessment. *Annals of Sex Research* 6: 83–103.

Fisher, W. A., & Grenier, G. (1994). Violent pornography, antiwoman thoughts, and antiwoman acts: In search of reliable effects. *Journal of Sex Research* 31: 23–38.

Ford, M. E., & Linney, J. A. (1995). Comparative analysis of juvenile sexual offenders, violent nonsexual offenders, and status offenders. *Journal of Interpersonal Violence* 10: 56–70.

Fukui, A., & Westmore, B. (1994). To see or not to see: The debate over pornography and its relationship to sexual aggression. *Australian and New Zealand Journal of Psychiatry* 28: 600–606.

Gebhard, P. H., Gagnon, J. H., Pomeroy, W. B., & Christenson, C. V. (1965). *Sex offenders: An analysis of types.* New York: Harper & Row.

Goldstein, M. J., Kant, H. S., Judd, L. L., Rice, C. J., & Green, R. (1970). Exposure to pornography and sexual behavior in deviant and normal groups. *Technical Reports of the Commission on Obscenity and Pornography,* vol. 7. Washington, D.C.: U.S. Government Printing Office.

Howitt, D. (1995). Pornography and the paedophile: Is it criminogenic? *British Journal of Medical Psychology* 68: 15–27.

Jaffe, D., & Strauss, M. A. (1987). Sexual climate and reported rape: A state-level analysis. *Archives of Sexual Behavior* 16: 107–23.

Johnson, W. T., Kupperstein, L., & Peters, J. (1970). Sex offenders' experiences with erotica. *Technical Reports of the Commission on Obscenity and Pornography,* vol. 7. Washington, D.C.: U.S. Government Printing Office.

Kimmel, M. S., & Linders, A. (1996). Does censorship make a difference: An aggregate empirical analysis of pornography and rape. *Journal of Psychology and Human Sexuality* 8 (3): 1–20.

Kimmel, M. S., & Messner, M. A. (Eds.). (1994). *Men's lives* (3rd ed.). Needham Heights, Mass.: Allyn & Bacon.

Kupperstein, L., & Wilson, W. C. (1970). Erotica and anti-social behavior: An analysis of social indicator statistics. *Technical Reports of the Commission on Obscenity and Pornography,* vol. 7. Washington, D.C.: U.S. Government Printing Office.

Kutchinsky, B. (1983). Obscenity and pornography: Behavioral aspects. In S. H. Kadish (ed.), *Encyclopedia of crime and justice,* vol. 3 (pp. 1077–86). New York: Free Press.

——. (1991). Pornography and rape: Theory and practice? *International Journal of Law and Psychiatry* 14: 47–67.

Lederer, L. (Ed.). (1980). *Take back the night.* New York: William Morrow.

Lipton, M. A. (1976). Pornography. In B. J. Sadock, H. I. Kaplan, & A. M. Freedman (Eds.), *The sexual experience,* pp. 584–93. Baltimore, MD: Williams & Wilkins.

MacKinnon, C. A. (1985). Pornography, civil rights, and speech. *Harvard Civil Rights-Civil Liberty Law Review* 20 (1): 1–17.

——. (1989). Sexuality, pornography, and method: Pleasure under psychiatry. *Ethics* 99: 314–46.

——. (1993). *Only words.* Cambridge, MA: Harvard University Press.

Malamuth, N., & Donnerstein, E. (Eds.). (1984). *Pornography and sexual aggression.* New York: Academic Press.

Marshall, W. L. (1988). The use of sexually explicit stimuli by rapists, child molesters and nonoffenders. *Journal of Sex Research* 25: 267–88.

Marshall, W. L., & Barbaree, H. E. (1984). A behavioral view of rape. *International Journal of Law and Psychiatry* 7: 51–57.

Morgan, R. (1980). Theory and practice: Pornography and rape. In L. Lederer (Ed.), *Take back the night: Women on pornography* (pp. 134–40). New York: William Morrow.

Russell, D. (1975). *The politics of rape.* New York: Stein & Day.

———. (1980). Pornography and violence: What does the new research say? In L. Lederer (Ed.), *Take back the night.* New York: William Morrow.

Schwartz, B. (1995a). Characteristics and typologies of sex offenders. In B. K. Schwartz & H. R. Cellini (Eds.), *The Sex Offender: Corrections, treatment, and legal practice.* Kingston, N.J.: Civic Research Institute.

———. (1995b). Theories of sex offenses. In B. K. Schwartz & H. R. Cellini (Eds.), *The Sex Offender: Corrections, treatment, and legal practice.* Kingston, N.J.: Civic Research Institute.

Scott, J. E., & Cuvelier, S. J. (1993). Violence and sexual violence in pornography: Is it really increasing? *Archives of Sexual Behavior* 22: 357–71.

Silbert, M. H., & Pines, M. A. (1984). Pornography and sexual abuse of women. *Sex Roles* 10: 857–68.

Smith, D. D. (1976). The social content of pornography. *Journal of Sex Research* 16: 16–24.

Soble, A. (1986). *Pornography, Marxism, and the future of sexuality.* New Haven, CT: Yale University Press.

Thornton, N. (1986). The politics of pornography: A critique of liberalism and radical feminism. *Australian and New Zealand Journal of Sociology* 22: 25–45.

Turley, D. (1986). The feminist debate on pornography: An unorthodox interpretation. *Socialist Review* 16 (3–4): 81–96.

Walker, C. E. (1970). Erotic stimuli and the aggressive sexual offender. *Technical Reports of the Commission on Obscenity and Pornography*, vol. 7. Washington, D.C.: United States Government Printing Office.

Winick, C. (1977). From deviant to normative: Changes in social acceptability of sexually explicit material. In E. Sagarin (Ed.), *Deviance and social change.* Beverly Hills, CA: Sage.

———. (1985). A content analysis of sexually explicit magazines sold in adult bookstores. *Journal of Sex Research* 21: 206–10.

Winick, C., & Evans, J. T. (1996). The relationship between nonenforcement of state pornography laws and rates of sex crime arrests. *Archives of Sexual Behavior* 25: 439–53.

Zillman, D., & Bryant, J. (1982). Pornography, sexual callousness, and the trivialization of rape. *Journal of Communication* 10–21.

———. (1986). Shifting preferences in pornography consumption. *Communication Research* 13: 560–78.

23

Pornography as a Research Tool: Exploring Fundamental Issues in Human Sexuality

William Griffitt

M ATERIALS THAT ARE REFERRED TO UNDER THE POORLY DEFINED rubric "pornography" are most often discussed in terms of controversies involving "free speech," decency, artistic value, depiction of gender relations, and in a number of other emotionally laden contexts. Beyond these concerns, however, pornography has, and will continue to do so, served as a valuable tool in the investigation of fundamental issues in human sexuality. There have been two predominant approaches to studying these issues, each of which involves its own advantages and disadvantages. Survey research has the advantage of involving a large number of respondents but the disadvantage of relying on retrospective reports that may be distorted by under or over reporting or faulty memory. Experimental laboratory research has the advantage of directly exposing respondents to the materials of interest but the disadvantages of relatively small numbers of respondents and the possible lack of generalizability of findings to the larger population. Frequently these methodological differences produce different findings. The purpose of this presentation is to, rather superficially, highlight major issues that have been investigated by both methods. Other presentations have focused in detail on some of these issues, but I want to address the overall value of the use of "pornography" address the overall value of the use of "pornography" as a research tool in investigating important questions regarding human sexuality.

INDIVIDUAL DIFFERENCES IN SEXUAL
AND EMOTIONAL RESPONSES

Sexual Responses

No historical review is necessary to document long-standing beliefs that there are major differences between the genders in interest in sex and responsiveness to sexual stimuli. The assumption, of course, is that male responsiveness exceeds that of females. Early Kinsey survey research addressed this issue using retrospective reports of responses to various categories of materials with sexual content. The results indicated that more males than females reported sexual responses to "explicit" materials but that the responses of females equalled or exceeded those of males to materials with implied sexual activity accompanied by themes of romance or affection. Subsequent survey research sponsored by the President's Commission on Obscenity and Pornography in 1970 supported the early Kinsey findings regarding gender differences in response to "explicit" materials. The Commission work basically opened the door to laboratory research in which respondents are actually exposed to the materials of interest and sexual responses are assessed following exposure through the use of self-reports of subjective arousal, of experienced physiological arousal, or sexual arousal through the measurement of sexually related physiological responses. Using such methodologies, the picture radically changed with males and females displaying remarkably similar responsiveness to sexual materials. Thus, from our own and others' work it appears that male and female responsiveness to sexual stimuli is more similar than previously thought to be.

Kinsey's conclusion that the presence of romance and affection in sexual stimuli (or situations) is crucial in female sexual responsiveness has proven to be very difficult to examine experimentally. The available research in which this variable has been investigated, however, does not support this assumption. The question remains unanswered.

A number of "personality" and social history variables have been investigated with regard to differential arousability but few have proven to be "good" predictors. For example Don Mosher's concept of sex-guilt sometimes emerges as a correlate with those high on this variable reporting less arousal to sexual stimuli than those who are lower in guilt. The same is sometimes found with Introversion-Extroversion with extroverts manifesting more arousability.

A number of studies have reported that high sexual experience is positively related to arousability in general and, from our own studies, to arousal to depictions of specific acts with which respondents have substantial experience. There are some findings that relate arousability to particular characteristics of the viewer. Not surprisingly gay men and lesbians are more responsive to depictions of same-sex activities than opposite-sex activities. In addition, the work of Abel indicate that rapists are more responsive to depictions of coercive sex and the work of Freud and that pedophiles are more responsive to depictions of children than to those of adults.

Emotional and Affective Responses

Sexual stimuli, and of equal importance, sexual situations and sexual matters in general, elicit sometimes strong emotional and affective responses in people. These can, in turn, enhance or detract from the pleasure of one's own sexual life. Pornography and "erotica" research has contributed substantially to our understanding of the nature of these responses and individual differences in these responses and their potential effects on sexuality. First, from the work of Donn Byrne and that from our own research, it has become clear that reactions to sexual stimuli and sexuality in general involve a mixed bag of both positive and negative emotional responses.

Many personal and social variables have been shown to be predictive of emotional and affective responses to pornography and erotica and sexuality in general. For example, it has been repeatedly reported that female affective responses to explicit depictions of sexual action are more negative than are those of males even though their sexual responses appear to be similar.

A number of personality and attitudinal variables have been shown to be related to affective responses to erotic stimuli and issues. A sampling of these variables (though not comprehensive) will be mentioned here.

The concept of *sex-guilt* was first introduced by Don Mosher within the framework of Social Learning Theory in the 1960s and has proven to be a valuable variable for prediction of a number of aspects of sexuality. It has been repeatedly shown in the research of a number of investigators that those scoring high on this variable are more negative emotionally regarding many sex-related variables including responses to pornographic materials. The related concept of *erotophobia-erotophilia* of Donn Byrne is also predictive of affective responses to pornography and sexually-related behaviors. In addition, our own work and that of others indicates that *Authoritarianism* is related to affective responses with high authoritarians reacting more negatively than low authoritarians. Other research suggests that Byrne's concept of *Repression-Sensitization* is related to acknowledged affective responses to sexual stimuli with sensitizers reporting more negative responses than repressors but that repressors' responses may be of the same intensity but their defensive style leads them to under-report emotional reactions.

These findings, are, of course, just representative but are exemplary of the use of pornographic materials as symbolizations of sexuality to investigate the myriad of differences among people in their emotional and affective feelings regarding sexual matters.

SATIATION AND RENEWAL OF
SEXUAL RESPONSES

A problem often reported by long-time sexual partners is that their sexual routine has become ritualized and that one or both of the partners becomes less and less sexually stimulated and responsive to the other. In other words, they become satiated (or, perhaps, bored) in a sexual sense to their partner. Support for this observation comes from animal studies of rodent males and from anecdotal observations of human sexual behavior. For example, the rodent studies show that a male animal may copulate multiple times with a single female and then appear to lose interest. His interest is revived, however, when a new estral female is introduced and his copulatory behavior is actively renewed with the new partner. Similar observations have been noted in separated, divorced, and widowed males when they become involved with a "novel" sexual partner and in females who become involved in "swingers" groups with new sexual partners.

Pornography offers an excellent tool for the investigation of this issue. In research published to date it does, in fact, appear that, at least among males, repeated exposure to pornographic materials results first in strong sexual reactions and preferences for viewing the materials followed by a rapid decline in arousal and interest as the stimuli are repeatedly presented.

When, however, novel (new) stimuli are introduced responsiveness and interest are renewed only to decline with repeated presentations of the same stimuli. Though a complete explanation of these findings is not available, they seem to follow what we know about satiation, boredom, and novelty in general. Findings among females are less consistent.

BEHAVIORAL AND OTHER EFFECTS
OF EXPOSURE TO PORNOGRAPHY

Sexual Behaviors

One of the major missions of the President's Commission in the late 1960s was to determine what, if any, effects exposure to pornography would have on common sexual practices. In a number of studies, respondents were first assessed regarding their frequencies of various sexual practices including heterosexual intercourse, masturbation, and conversations about sexual matters. They were then exposed under varying circumstances to pornographic materials and assessed following exposure regarding their behavior. In the vast number of studies no significant changes were reported. Some studies, however, reported minor and short-lived increases in behaviors in which the respondents normally engaged. No evidence was found that "new" behaviors resulted.

Antisocial Behaviors

Another charge to the President's Commission was to determine relationships, if any, between exposure to pornography and various forms of antisocial behavior. Using survey, experimental, quasi-experimental, and historical data the Commission concluded that that there was little relationship between the availability of and "use" of pornography and the probability of the commission of sex crimes, non-sexual crimes, and juvenile delinquency.

During the interval between the 1970 President's Commission and the subsequent Attorney General's Commission on Pornography (the Meese Commission) in 1986, research continued in many quarters. From the research of Ed Donnerstein, Neil Malamuth, Bob Baron, and others it seems clear that negative behavioral effects from pornography exposure are dependent on the juxtaposition of violence with sexually arousing materials. Non-violent materials tend not to produce similar effects even though Dolf Zillmann and a few others do not agree.

Pro-social Effects

Rarely recognized and cited are various pro-social effects of exposure to sexually arousing materials that depict consensual sexual behaviors. In our own work we have found that such materials may increase positive feelings and sexual attraction toward members of the opposite sex in terms of ratings of attraction and visual attentiveness. Other research indicates heightened feelings of love of a "loved one" following exposure to consensual erotica and enhanced perceptions of the attractiveness of opposite-sex people. This appears to be the result of enhanced attentiveness to the positively evaluated characteristics of physically attractive others and to the negatively evaluated characteristics of physically unattractive people since they are seen as less sexually desirable

CONCLUSION

Pornography or erotica can serve as a "stand in" for the actual observation of actual behavior. Those of us using such materials, however, face a number of challenges in our efforts. First, there is virtually no standardization in the stimulus materials that are available to the the investigator. Standardization is, of course, one of the cornerstones of programmatic research. Second, most of us in the academic community face problems that block our own production of standardized materials that allow us to vary and control various aspects of the content of research material. These include legal, technical, financial and other obstacles. It might be argued that "those in the industry" might be able to assist in helping us in sexual science to overcome some of these obstacles further enabling us to clarify some of the issues and controversies surrounding the many issues that need to be addressed.

24

The Experience of Pornography

Laurence O'Toole

I WOULD LIKE TO OFFER JUST A FEW BASIC IDEAS AND STARTER OBSERVATIONS on the experience of pornography.

How does it feel watching porn? There's a silence concerning those who put porn to use. It is porn's greyest area. Studies are meager, and too preoccupied with attaching gizmos to gonads, with measuring tumescence and blood flows, rather than subjective experiences. There are few porn surveys. In part this is because it has never occurred to anyone to ask porn users what's going on. Or maybe folks think they already know all there is to know about porn users: they look at dirty images, they become aroused, they're sad. "To talk about pornography," writes Sallie Tisdale, "means having to talk about the millions of people who like to watch it, read it, think about it. If we talk about pornography with disdain, we have to talk about these millions of people with the same disdain."

Such contempt makes for difficulties in researching the subject. In the mainstream media, with a few exceptions, porn users remain virtually silent. TV and radio shows complain of difficulties persuading people to come on and talk positively about porn. Considering the negative cultural stereotypes of dirty, raincoated tossers, of hairy-palmed no-mates, of wastrels, lotharios, sexist dogs, misogynists (and that's just male porn users), it's really little surprise that people would rather not discuss it.

There's a need to make people think differently about porn and porn use. One way of thinking differently is not to look on porn as inherently problematic—a predicament and not a pleasure. There is also a general cultural difficulty with something that appeals to the love muscle rather than the thought center. Porn has a very basic function. Though it can be educational and entertaining, the hard and soft-core truth is that arousal is porn's main event.

In the autumn of 1994, *The New Yorker* reported on a major sex survey,

"Sex in America," which had discovered that the most notable thing about most (American) people's sex lives, is how unremarkable they are, and that "36 percent of men aged eighteen to twenty-four had no sex with a partner in the past year or had sex just a few times." In the same year, *Playboy* magazine gathered up a few quotes that catch a mood of carnal temperance in the nineties: "Abstinence makes the heart grow fonder," runs a virginity ad campaign. ("You can go farther when you don't go all the way.") Bill Lancaster, a producer for the TV show *Geraldo* declares, "These days, there's nothing bold or innovative about saying you sleep around. What takes a lot of guts is to say you're a virgin. Virginity has become the new sexuality." So it would seem that people in the U.S.A. are having less sex, or waiting till wedlock before they start doing it. Meanwhile, in the U.K., in the autumn of 1996, the TV health show *Pulse* and *Top Sante* health magazine reported that a "major new survey" of British sexual habits which found increased monogamy an emerging trend.

Apart from the fact that such reports of sexual restraint might suggest a deeper moral corruption—that is, a tendency for people to lie when asked about bedroom matters—there was little doubt that masturbation is on the rise. It was to America's self-loving generation that *Sky* magazine paid a visit in the summer of 1995, and found droves of young people watching piped-in cable soft core and calling it "Wet TV." The dull college campus life, the date-rape minefield, safe sex, the virginity push, cathode addiction and slackeritis were all cited as reasons for the boom. A "panic" on the American nightclub scene was alleged as a consequence of a generation of youngsters lost to the porn demon. With twenty million American homes with access to pay-to-view porn channels like Spice and Playboy at $5 an hour, who needs sweaty clubs, warm beer, bad drugs? *Sky* met a college student knocking back five hours of cable porn a day, costing him a fortune, and culminating in a regular late evening rendezvous with his love-tool: "I like to wait toward the end of the day before I actually put hand to penis."

Typically, having used a porn story to pepper the editorial content, the magazine then seized the moral high ground, speaking of bleak addictions, dysfunction, an alienation from real life: Wet TV is "great for sad men who'd rather sit at home and watch the boob tube than go out and pull a real woman." To *Sky*'s predominantly late adolescent readership the word is that solo sex is for deficient types. A magazine that month-on-month assiduously courts the young male reader by featuring near-raunch glamour shots of leading female celebrities—Liv Tyler, Alicia Silverstone, the Spice Girls—proffers a righteous disapproval of a kind that would not have been out of place in the late Victorian era.

Sky magazine is not alone in the continued slighting of masturbation. Celebrating the tenth birthday of *Arena* magazine, apparently the first magazine in Britain "that looked at the world with a man's eye," Tony Parsons praises the magazine for having contributed to a cultural shift over a decade that has seen men becoming not only more familiar with the pleasures of Italian tailoring and Japanese beer, but also more in touch with their "inner lives." Before

Arena, "we could never really open up our hearts," and men were unable to be "unashamedly male." One thing *Arena* "knew," and still knows, Parsons assures us, is that most men are not "stroke merchants." In the same issue, *Arena* pays tribute to ten great British sex symbols of our times, fashion models, singers and actresses–Louise, Elizabeth Hurley, Anna Friel, Kate Moss–and features all of them doing cheesecake poses, lips pouting, legs parted, maybe tugging at their hipster-trouser waistbands, revealing bare midriffs and heading lower with the enticing promise of some elusive celebrity privates. These pictures may be more "tasteful" and "arty" than gynecological, but they are nonetheless images to contribute to a masturbator's visual repertoire, fantasy gear made for "stroke merchants." Clearly men getting in touch with their inner lives means never admitting to masturbation.

The denial of masturbation, its roping off as a queasy state of incompleteness, and the rumored revival of virginity and monogamy, all persist in awkward conjunction with the continuing sexualization of mainstream culture. So many magazines, so much television, every other billboard poster campaign sells you sex, or features sex as the hook for selling other products, from holidays to motor cars, pensions and alcohol. Nevertheless, masturbation is required to maintain its shadowy existence. "Fetching come," "flapping yourself," "jilling," "bashing the bishop," "going solo," "spanking the monkey," "paddling your own canoe" shall not be discussed. As the science-fiction writer Brian Aldiss observes, "people pretend to be so enlightened about sex these days, they talk happily about copulations and such subjects, about adultery and homosexuality and lesbianism and abortions. Never about masturbation though. And yet masturbation is the commonest form of sex, the cheapest and most harmless pleasure."

This is not to say it should be headline news each time a person delivers the goods single-handedly. It is more about turning thoughts of isolation to a recognition that you're not alone, of switching from images of desperation to horns of plenty, from the image of the "hideously atrophied male genitalia" that the writer Andy Darlington found in medical text books during his adolescent years, to images of better blood circulation, mental comfort, stress therapy and idle recreational abandon. "Masturbation is not some kind of lonely, pathetic thing that happens when you're not getting laid," writes Lisa Palac. "Everybody masturbates," declares Audrey, "but it's only the British and some buttoned-down yanks who deny it."

Steve Perry urges a re-evaluation: "Wanking's cool. You don't have to have anyone else there, you don't have to spend any money, you don't have to worry about driving home pissed. You can have fantasies about all these gorgeous women that you're never going to meet. That is why porn is such a wonderful commodity."

Another feature of porn consumption seldom examined is the strange and complicated business of looking. Take for instance excerpts from the story of Kate, a feminist porner. Her confessions commence in her childhood. Before she was five, Kate started having s/m fantasies. Growing up in the English countryside she couldn't wait to go horse-riding and be intimate with a leather saddle. From around the age of ten, Kate started making use of porn, masturbating to British top-shelf, soft-core magazines. She does not remember the very first time she saw porn, although she remembers that her parents left such materials about the home, rather than stashed away in some out-of-reach cubbyhole.

The first view of porn can be pivotal for some, and barely memorable for others. Most of those who spoke to the author about porn had their first porn moment in early teens with a glimpse of something mainstream. "I discovered *Penthouse* magazine at about age 10." Or, "I remember finding a collection of *H&E* in my stepfather's wardrobe while looking for something else. I was about eleven or twelve at the time."

"Well, my first experience with pornography was when my cousin showed me a *Penthouse* he had stolen from one of my uncles," an anonymous contributor recalls. "I was nine or ten at the time and I remember liking the pictures of naked women, but what really impressed me were the sexual cartoons. I spent a couple hours flipping through his collection, and I may not have looked at every photo, but I read all the cartoons. I still get equally aroused at a painting or drawing as I do at a photograph." A gay man describes his initial view. "My first exposure was at six years old. Even then the men interested me more than the women."

The first time is not always recalled as the best time. Writing in the porn 'zine *Batteries Not Included,* Rachel James outlines an uptight Catholic upbringing, where sex education was virtually non-existent except for a guide book called *A Doctor Talks to Twelve Year Olds,* which described copulation as so: "When a man and a woman love each other, they hold each other close in a special embrace." James found her dad's *Playboy*s stowed away in the basement at home between *Popular Mechanics* and *Popular Science* and realized there was something about being adult and intimate that she wasn't aware of yet. Later on, still eager to find out all she could, James let her boyfriend take her to see a porn film. She was into the porn house and out again in near record time. On sitting down, first thing she saw on-screen was a woman on her knees just finishing a blow job, who then turned to face the camera, "and let all the cum pour out of her mouth." James recalls feeling horrified: "I could feel my mouth drop open and I just sat there transfixed for a few minutes." Before getting out of there fast: "I simply was not ready to see all THAT on a wide SCREEN."

Which might have been it. But, because she liked her boyfriend, and really wanted to find out, she went again, and again. And then, one day, all the right things happened on screen for her. The right stuff came along in the shape of the actor John Leslie, like it seems to have done for several female porn converts: "But John Leslie . . . WOW!" Brandy Alexandre similarly fell in love with the on-screen Leslie. Alexandre also found watching porn films as her most vital lead-in experience to real-life sex: "After seeing a few adult movies in the Pussycat Theater," she writes at her home page on the world wide web, "I decided I was old enough to put the knowledge I gathered into practice. WOW! Why did I wait so long? I did it three times that night."

Others remember their first time with porn as similarly positive. "I found some porno mags when I was about eleven years old," writes Kerri Sharp. "I thought they were funny but wasn't upset by them. It made me realize that there was a whole subterranean psyche to grown-ups (they didn't just think about jobs and money) and it made me want to grow up fast so I could start having sex." For one contributor, a childhood European vacation brought an unexpected revelation. "My family was visiting Denmark and we got our car stolen. My parents were forced to stay at the hotel so they sent my brother and I (I was ten at the time) out to see the town of Copenhagen. We went into a bookstore and I saw photographs of fellatio. I was thunderstruck and delighted. My brother (nine) was disgusted. The world of sex opened up for me." When Tuppy Owens saw her first Danish porn magazine she thought it was "wonderful, so exciting," and was annoyed she hadn't seen it earlier. She decided to make her own, taking pictures of herself in a boat on the local river at five o'clock in the morning, "with a doll stuck up my pussy." Owens feels her life might have taken a different course if it hadn't been for her discovering porn, "I'm really lucky that porn came into my life when it did."

Into her teens, and Kate's interest in horse-riding declined, while her interest in porn grew. Her family were quite strict in many respects, she says, but not concerning sex. She thinks it likely her parents knew about her hobby, and chose to say nothing about it to her. When friends were going to London, Kate would give them money to buy porn magazines for her. She collected them all. Kate has never identified her sexuality as lesbian. She is an example of a straight woman who has regularly turned for arousal to top-shelf material made for men, predominantly featuring photo sets of naked women, and without a male member, or even a male, in sight. Julia shares similar tastes, finding the general explicitness of the photography to be the source of masturbatory excitement. Tuppy Owens says she gets turned on by the women in *Penthouse*, finding porn made for men more to her liking than the porn specifically angled at her own sex: "The magazines made in the U.K. for women are utterly dull. They are not like my sexuality at all. They're not funny enough and they're not dirty enough."

In Kate's experience, she feels she lusted over pictures of naked women because she found the imagery erotic in the broadest sense. Many porn users speak of being stirred just by the general "sexiness" of simply watching other people aroused, rather than the exact bearing of the representation. In the porn 'zine *Batteries Not Included*, a lesbian reviewer observes, "I'm finding more and more women who love to get off on other people getting off without imagining themselves in one or the other positions. After all we are a nation of watchers." "Writing as a gay man who likes porn," the critic John Lyttle admits, "the porn that truly revs my motor these days is mean dyke porn."

It is also true that many straight men confess to queer occurrences watching porn. Sure-thing heterosexuals, they thought, who've seen an erection on-screen and found themselves getting aroused by this, and wondering what that was all about. Hardly what you'd expect from the last bastion of absolutely het maleness. Inevitably the hetero male's hard-core experience involves looking at other men's penises, getting an eyeful of pumping erections. For most men it's the only place they see such things. Likewise watching men orgasm. Many find this fascinating; they want to compare it to how it works for them. Some men tell of how if they ejaculate simultaneously with the man on screen it makes the experience more complete. (Other men, however, say that they don't care about the porn stud on-screen, or his appendage.) It could be that a form of homosexual desire is going on with some men watching hetero hard core. After all, it is staring us in the face—the penis. Consider that, for the ten or fifteen years prior to video, millions of American and European males went to cinemas to sit in front of large screens and watch the male member, blown up to the size of a big log, and coming towards them. So, is the whole hetero porn thing the longest homoerotic alibi in history? Are straight men coming out to themselves as bi-men, masturbating over the sight of other hard-ons? Could be, but probably not. Meanwhile porn directors guide the situation carefully, making sure in any three-way number involving two men that the two penises shall not touch. Nevertheless, the penis is still there, taking care of business, and any analysis of the curious business of porn-watching better not forget it.

In *Sex Exposed* the feminist academic Anne McClintock speaks about her early days with hard core. As an "innocent" in early adulthood she ventured into an adult book store, looking for the "hot stuff" magazines that catered for women, only to be told there weren't any. McClintock was not so easily brushed off, however, and her porn search continued. From a state of exclusion, over time she found a way inside by tapping into feature-length hard-core movies. In sex films supposedly made for hetero men, she found a space for herself to watch, recognizing that there's possibly more than one thing going on with porn. *Devil in Miss Jones* was a key moment. Watching Georgina Spelvin perform a girl–girl number, it seemed to McClintock that the presence on screen of the man and his penis was there as a fig leaf maintaining a pretense of heterosexuality. Understanding Spelvin to be "out" as a lesbian in real life at this time, and seeing the actress and her female co-star really "doing" it, made the critic aware of how the "uninvited" viewer might possibly take something from this "men-only" porn.

Plainly the porn viewing experience is more involved than first meets the eye; where the actual imagery is sometimes less significant than the feelings, thoughts and associations going on inside the viewer's head. Though the soft-core magazines Kate used didn't directly address her sexuality, neither did they thwart or contain her own particular longings. Instead they served as a base camp building to other, more personal fantasies concerning a very different transgressive scene. The simple fact that it was porn, and explicit, and socially "reprehensible," meant the commonplace soft core functioned as a "deviant" stand-in.

These complex ways of seeing illustrate the potential for mobility in the user's point of view. An intersubjectivity that, for example, goes far beyond the usual reckoning which declares that all men who watch porn see themselves having sex with the woman. This is not necessarily so. "I generally do not place myself into a porn fantasy that I am watching or reading," says a porn fan who goes by the alias of "Burkman." "My interests are usually more voyeuristic." Geoff is equally clear about this. "No, I do not," he says, "and I don't tend to do this when I read regular fiction, either." Then again, for others, a simple transference is indeed the way of things: "One or more smiling beautiful girls looking straight at me while working a cock," writes "Demaret," from Sweden. "By preference I like it when the girl(s) lick. I can then admire beautiful eyes and smiles close up and fantasize that the smile is an invitation for me to be there with her/them. In fact I often fantasize that I am there." An anonymous female admits, "I always project myself into the action, sometimes 'feeling' the enjoyment of both the male and the female."

The obvious conclusion to be drawn is that there's no such thing as an average porn user, or "only in the sense that there's an average height of human beings," suggests Nicholas White. "It's a meaningless conflation which tells us nothing about the individual subtleties and variations . . . the only thing that porn users have in common is that they all like porn." To know the way porn works is to recognize the variety of responses a single porn work may engender. The porn viewing experience can be a distinctly personal and complex happening, involving not just the fantasy scenario on screen, but the viewer's own fantasy extracts, projections and flashbacks from their personal erotic memories. These particular brain images may leak and mix with events on-screen, or on the page, cutting and cross-cutting like a series of fast edits. A type of cross-subjectivity may occur watching porn, where viewpoints switch and change. Writes Anne McClintock: "Identification in porn can be multiple and shifting, bisexual and transsexual, alternately or simultaneously." A long-term porner recalls, "While wanking over the pictures . . . the meeting of my unrestrained lust and the explicit images of girls often produced an almost trance-like state in which I felt as if I were experiencing sex from the female side as well as the male." And yet, he says, "This wasn't a latent homosexual desire to be penetrated, but a kind of ecstatic identification with aroused femininity."

Desiring the porn figure so dearly, many men may also want to temporarily become that figure, because being so dearly desired is enviable. To say, therefore, that all hetero men have the same porn emotions, which is, to reiterate, that they all want to be having sex with the porn woman, misses the complexity of desire. This fits with a tendency in recent times to characterize male heterosexuality as an unshakably single-minded business. This reduction often occurs in combination with mass-communication theories that fail to take into account what audiences make of media signals within their own specific context of personal experiences, values, preferences, psychology, or simply whatever mood they happen to be in at the time. "The variability of interpretation is the constant law of mass communications," writes Umberto Eco; and what matters is "not where the communication originates, but where it arrives."

In America, during 1983–84, a colossal 180 million telephone sex calls were made. In New York in the same financial year, during a twenty-four hour period, a certain pre-recorded erotic message was called up 800,000 times. In her book *The War of Desire and Technology*, the cultural anthropologist Sandy Stone writes of the time she spent with a small community of women in the San Francisco Bay area who operated a telephone sex line. Stone was curious about phone sex and the process of parceling up and sending erotic arousal downline: "The more I observed phone sex," she writes, "the more I realized I was observing very practical applications of data compression." The phone-sex women were collecting the five senses, the full sensual range, and compressing them into an auditory package. In order to convey so much in such small packages, the words used by phone sex operators, the sighs, pauses, delays, giggles, amount to a highly sophisticated code, a compendium of erotic communication for the dialer to receive and decompress by adding themselves, their own detailed experiences, fantasies and predilections to the mix. "The sex workers took an extremely complex, highly detailed set of behaviors, translated them into a single sense." And then, "At the other end of the line the recipient . . . reconstituted . . . a fully detailed set of images and interactions in multiple sensory mode." From this combination emerges a very elaborate, individual erotic occurrence.

Information compression is not exclusive to phone lines. I was once talking with someone about the problem of never being able to remember more than a couple of details about books that you nonetheless proclaim to love. From a five hundred-page biography of the writer Vladimir Nabokov, my only strong recollection concerns the image of the author as an old man taking great sensual pleasure from bath-times, and how he'd submerge his bath sponge, let it fill with water, lift it over his head and slowly squeeze out the water, letting it trickle over his head and shoulders and down his back. That's all that comes to mind when I think of this long, detailed book. This was the book's "punctum" for me, it was suggested: a very condensed and personalized summary. In *Camera Lucida*, Roland Barthes speaks of two kinds of apprehension when looking at the photographic image. There is the studium, the trained, commonplace effect of a photographic composition, and then there may also be what he calls the punctum, the quirk within the aesthetic play that for some reason captures the viewer's eye and begins almost to stand for the whole photographic experience: "this element which rises from the scene, shoots out of it like an arrow, and pierces me."

It's true. What appeared as a pleasant but slight detail actually contains in notation the feeling taken from the book. The impression of Nabokov as a sensualist contains also in shorthand the sensuality of experience and rapture particular to reading one of his novels. The single image of the author's bath-time was satisfactorily carrying a freight-load of meanings, memories, feelings. And so decompression isn't just something computers and modems do, or auditory erotic tokens passed down a telephone line. Like phone sex, people bring so much to porn. Porn is its own compressed delivery system. The ostensibly limited imagery contains in précis a whole range of information, erotic ideas and gestures. To it we bring our selves, and the two interrelate: like a man plunging from a plane with a small tightly packed square attached to his back, which, once the string is pulled, bursts forth into this capacious parachute, many times the size of its original container. The parachute, the punctum, the image decompressor, the pornography—so simple, and yet so densely packed.

Despite all of this mental input and output, porn continues to be seen in the main as repetitive dick fodder for dullards. Where porn and men are concerned, Catharine MacKinnon is sure that the brains and genitals aren't speaking to each other. In her demonology of the male, the mind–body split is fundamental. Referring to the Yiddish maxim, "a stiff prick turns the mind to shit" (her rough translation), she is very clear about this: "The common point is that having sex is antithetical to thinking." And because it does not aim for the mind, merely the lap region, porn cannot be speech, in any legally defensible sense. We are immediately aware when we look at porn that we are being communicated with, and yet some anti-porners say otherwise, that in fact we are merely being triggered like Pavlov's dog. As Drucilla Cornell observes, MacKinnon's behaviorist, mechanical version of man amounts to just another spin on the Freudian notion of anatomy as destiny: "A man becomes his penis. He cannot help it . . . He is reduced to a prick." Cornell doubts the use of such a crude model in seeking to explain how the body, consciousness, fantasy and desire interrelate: "I think that men can think and have an erection at the same time."

The notion that porn use doesn't mean using your head is clearly ill-considered. "I think that using porno is cerebral," observes the writer Dennis Cooper. "It's like a study. It's like a text." In fact, if it weren't so much about the body being moved and aroused, you'd be excused for thinking that porn is really a head thing. "I started reading porno when I was really young," says Cooper, "and like a lot of people I read a lot of porno before I had sex. By the time I was having sex, I expected it to be like porno. When it wasn't, I invented porno to go with my sex, because while you're doing your limited little things with your body, there's all this stuff going on in your head about what could be happening."

An online porn fan provides a small, light-hearted example of the porner's non-vegetative reach, interrupting and reconfiguring the media flow with what he describes as his *Porn Star/Celebrity Equivalencies Handy Reference List!* Whenever he tires of formula porn, he imagines the same scenarios but featuring substitute celebrities who are porn star lookalikes: "Nina Hartley = Goldie Hawn; Amber Lynn = Melanie Griffith; Annette Haven = Jane Seymour; Tori Welles = Raquel Welch after a big meal; Ginger Lynn = Meg Ryan; Buttman = a less-talk-more-action Seinfeld; Tom Byron = a Klingon having a bad hair day." The porn fan as art-worker recommends additional gain through switching between porn tape and a film on television featuring one of the celebrity doubles: back and forth, back and forth, "until the two begin to become indistinguishable in your mind!" You might even forgo sound, it is suggested, and improvise your own narrative from the joined-together mainstream and porno movie. "Yes boys," our fan declares, aware that he's starting to sound a little cranky, "your Good Doctor has been snowed in a little too long!"

The perfectly "useless" nature of such activity is as interesting as the signs of mental activity. Discussing entertainment applications for new technologies, science-fiction novelist Pat Cadigan says, "Let's face it . . . it's not so terribly inaccurate to say that we've done some of our best work for the sake of relieving our boredom, ennui, or Weltschmerz." In this way might the alleged passivity of the porner be better grasped as a kind of socially unacceptable, non-utilitarian activity. Porners are perhaps misrepresented as slothful, idiot perverts when in fact they are flaneurs in a late twentieth-century setting of consoles, cathodes and couches, wastrels who feel that time spent with a close friend is time well spent indeed. So, which is it to be, porn a waste of valuable time, or porn a valuable waste of time?

The counter-accusation laid against the sex industry, of course, is that it contributes to a culture that sees sex not as idle pleasure but as hard work, requiring constant effort if it's to be any good. Where "doing it, having it, getting it, wanting it is our duty, our task, our vocation. Boast of your idleness in other areas of your life," writes Suzanne Moore, "but not in this one." It's true that porn shows great athleticism and prodigious energy expenditure. Yet critics who represent this as a version of Marxist alienation from the "natural" pleasures of the flesh are missing the most crucial point: that it's not the viewer who's doing the work, it is the well-paid porn performer. Do porn fans really absorb the porn work ethic, or do they just watch it in action? The viewer can watch, get horny, orgasm, then fall asleep.

The criticism of porn for creating a compulsiveness in viewers emerges from similar ideological terrain. Hard core's failure to wholly render the "truth" of physical female sexual pleasure, it is suggested, means that it lacks for something, that it cannot fully deliver on its promises, and so porn viewers compulsively keep going back to try to get it all, to finally find out. These fugitive pleasures—forever out of reach—make porn the ultimate Marxian commodity. Because we keep on coming back for more, porn becomes a money pit, offering easy earnings for the pornocrats. Porn, however, tends to plateau in terms of sales. Also, the approach that sees porn as compulsive is offered by critics who like to keep their distance. Unable or unwilling to get inside to the sensualities of porn, they're therefore almost bound to view repeated porn use as unsatisfactory. These observations are determined by a particular view of experience. Notions of the "elusive" circle back to a Freudian version of wants and desires, which has desire being fueled by the person's need to find resolution, to be completed. Alternative versions might figure human longing as not a thing of lack but more concerned with replicating pleasure, of repeating loops. With desire made of such "moreness," notions of deficiency, of longing gone wrong, become less tenable. For what if porn isn't a problem after all? Beyond the arguments, perhaps it is really straightforward. You watch it, you get off, watch it again and get off; again, get off. What if, after all the bickering, it's as simple as that?

But of course, it is never as simple as that. But, that's another story . . .

SECTION 6

PORNOGRAPHY, CENSORSHIP, AND THE CLASSROOM

COLLEGES, UNIVERSITIES, AND "THE CLASSROOM" HAVE BECOME A target of abuse through their use or exhibition of pornography. In the first article in this section, David Austin discusses the use of sexually explicit material in the classroom without leading to sexual harassment, and Bill Paul's experience with an exhibition of his work which became the subject of a major attack by the Christian Coalition of Florida.

Virginia Elwood, a librarian, documents a case on campus in which men's magazines were to be removed from the California State University, Northridge, Bookstore. The initial response by a female journalism student was taken up by the Women's Study Program which formally requested that the offending material be removed from the bookstore. Although the executive committee of the Faculty Senate agreed with Women's Studies, the body of the Faculty Senate overturned the vote of the executive committee in favor of First Amendment rights. Thus, the Foundation Executive Committee that ran the bookstore reversed their position and replaced the magazines. To help mend the rift that had taken place on campus a symposium of experts debated the issue. While this has proved helpful, the same issue has resurfaced time and time again.

"(Sexual) Quotation without (Sexual) Harassment? Education Use of Pornography in the University Classroom" by David F. Austin shows what he considers to be the right discussion of sexuality which can help prevent harassment as opposed to the wrong sort which actually can be harassment. Professor Austin describes three legitimate uses of sexually explicit material in the university classroom: (1) legal studies, (2) studies of sexuality and its representations, and (3) social scientific and medical investigations. He offers five uses of sexual quotation which are not considered sexual harassment and provides a guideline for a syllabus in sexuality which has pornography as its focus. He also provides an extensive set of referents for his work and class.

In contrast, Professor Bill Paul's paper is a narrative which describes his background and the outcry of the Christian Coalition over an exhibition of his work in Florida. His role as an artist and professor of art places Paul in a unique position to assess the impact of censorship on art. He expresses his personal feeling about this attack on his work and indicates how it has changed him and brought to the surface his concerns over personal freedoms and responsibilities.

25

Porn Wars on Campus

Virginia Elwood-Akers

U NIVERSITIES ARE SUPPOSED TO BE DEDICATED TO LEARNING; TO THE free exchange of ideas; to intellectual freedom. Unfortunately, even on a University campus, censors lurk. Censors aren't always piggy-eyed rednecks or blue-haired ladies from Boston. Sometimes they are well-meaning academics; people who would describe themselves as liberal; even, dare I suggest it, as feminists.

At California State University, Northridge, in the Fall of 1984, a student named Jill Schultz–a feminist–decided that the sale of adult magazines in the Campus Bookstore was an affront to her feminism, and began to circulate a petition demanding that the Bookstore no longer stock such magazines. The depressing fact was that Schultz was a Journalism major, and presumably had heard of the First Amendment. She was quick to point out, however, that what she proposed was certainly not censorship, because she was not advocating that adult magazines not be published, but simply that they not be sold. The magazines named in the petition were *Playboy*, *Penthouse*, *Gallery*, and *Oui*.

Schultz began her campaign with the Steering Committee of the Women Studies Program, which responded by sending a letter to the Bookstore manager, Lew Herbst, asking that the store reconsider the sale of these four magazines, and also the sale of "particularly tasteless calendars featuring peepshow type photographs of women's breasts and buttocks."[1]

On October 20, 1984, reacting to the petitions which Schultz was circulating on campus, the Associated Students Senate approved a resolution opposing the sale of "commercial publications . . . that depict sexually and/or violently exploited people."[2]

Lew Herbst decided to pass the responsibility on to the CSUN Foundation Board of Trustees, which set Bookstore policy, but he was quoted in the school newspaper, the *Daily Sundial,* as saying, "It is not my job to censor material that is sold in the bookstore."[3] In this same article the members of the Women Studies Program Committee were quoted as insisting that their action was not censorship, but students interviewed for the article weren't buying that argument. "I am completely outraged," said one. "I object to someone telling me what I can and can't read on campus."[4] Another student pointed out that no one was forcing anyone on campus to read the magazines. Clearly the issue was not as straightforward as had been hoped by Schultz and the members of the Women Studies Program Committee.

The campus divided into two camps as opinions for and against the ban on the sale of the magazines appeared in the *Daily Sundial,* and demonstrations were held by both factions. On November 6, the Executive Committee of the Faculty Senate entered the foray by voting unanimously to recommend that the Faculty Senate support the Associated Students' resolution calling for the ban. Ten days later the entire Faculty Senate met to debate the issue. Despite the unanimous vote of their Executive Committee, after heated debate the Faculty Senate decided to support the First Amendment and voted to reverse the Executive Committee's recommendation.

By this time the *Los Angeles Times* had picked up the story. As one of two female faculty senators who had spoken in opposition to the ban of sales of the magazines, I was interviewed in a November 16 *Times* article on the Faculty Senate vote and was quoted as saying that censorship in the name of feminism is a horrible idea. "Anti-feminists can come in next week and take away feminist literature," I said.[5] Remember that quote; it will be important later.

On November 28, despite the Faculty Senate vote, the Foundation Board of Trustees voted to develop a policy which would ban the sale of sexually explicit magazines on campus, and the issue would have seemed to be ended. But the students and faculty would not accept the policy. The University Student Union, a separate entity from the Associated Students, voted to continue sales of such magazines in its tiny store. The campus Republican Club joined forces with the CSUN Young Democrats (surely a first!) to oppose the Foundation's ban. Individual faculty members called for a boycott of the Campus Bookstore. Letters and opinion columns filled the pages of the *Daily Sundial,* the *Los Angeles Times,* and the *Los Angeles Daily News.* All of the newspapers firmly supported the First Amendment, and called for an end to censorship on campus.

Faced with a barrage of bad publicity, on December 10th the Executive Committee of the Foundation suddenly reversed itself and voted to recommend that the ban be rescinded. The following day the Associated Students Senate followed suit, voting twenty to one to rescind *its* original October 30th resolution. With the tide of public opinion clearly turned against banning sales of the magazines, and the University being held up to ridicule by the city's newspapers, the Foundation Trustees Board as a whole voted unanimously on December 20th to reverse the ban, stating rather disingenuously that its earlier action had been "widely viewed as improper censorship."[6]

So the issue ended, but it didn't really end, since both proponents and foes of the ban were still firm in their opinions. In an attempt to mend the rift, the Center for Sex Research sponsored a symposium on April 10, 1985, to which speakers on both sides of the issue were invited. It was hoped that the symposium would educate the campus community about the complexities of the issue of pornography and censorship, and that some understanding and agreement might be reached.

Speakers at the symposium included Neil Malamuth, a psychologist who had done research on whether pornography caused violent behavior, anti-pornography activist lawyer Catharine MacKinnon, Betty Brooks of the Feminist Anti-Censorship Taskforce, First Amendment lawyer Robert Smith, and William Simon, who had been a researcher for the Kinsey Institute for Sex Research. Simon's scholarly analysis and Malamuth's statement that evidence of any connection between pornography and violence was inconclusive, were politely listened to by the audience of about two hundred, but things livened up when Catharine MacKinnon argued that men used the First Amendment as an excuse to continue their exploitation of women, calling anyone who supported the sale of *Playboy* a "misogynist sexist." When Smith took the floor he pointed out that MacKinnon's ideas on pornography were learned from Linda Lovelace, star of the pornographic film *Deep Throat*, who had testified at hearings held on MacKinnon's proposed anti-pornography law in Minnesota. When MacKinnon insisted that Lovelace had been coerced into acting in the film, Smith produced testimony to the contrary. Smith and MacKinnon's debate disintegrated into an argument which ended with her calling him a "pimp" for defending publishers of pornography. The most reasoned arguments at the symposium came from Betty Brooks of the Feminist Anti-Censorship Taskforce. As a feminist who had herself been the victim of a censorship campaign when she was fired for discussions of Lesbianism in a Women Studies course, Brooks implored those who oppose sexism to concentrate on *real* issues instead of pornography.

Understanding and agreement were probably not reached at the symposium, but the issue seemed to have ended at CSUN. Ten years later, however, a mini-version of the same controversy occurred when a zealous Bookstore employee decided on his own that *Playboy*, *Penthouse*, and *Playgirl* should not be sold in the Campus Bookstore. This time the removals seemed to be due to a lack of communication and the magazines quietly reappeared after Dr. Veronica Elias from the Center for Sex Research and I paid a visit to the Bookstore manager.

Do you remember my quote about feminism and censorship? In November 1997 the Women Studies Department of the State University of New York at New Paltz sponsored a one-day conference called "Revolting Behavior: The Challenges of Women's Sexual Freedom." Among the issues discussed at the conference were masturbation and lesbianism. Alas for the Women Studies Department, the conference was attended by a trustee of the University named Candace de Russy, who ran screaming from the conference calling for the resignation of New Paltz President Roger Bowen, declaring that the conference was a "travesty of academic standards and process."[7] De Russy was supported at first by New York Governor Pataki, who declared that the issue had "nothing to do with freedom of speech and everything to do with the proper expenditure of tax money."[8]

Bowen refused to give in to pressure, and was ultimately vindicated in a report from a committee set up to investigate the conference. The report chastised Pataki by stating that "taxpayer support cannot depend on the wishes of individual taxpayers or the disagreement of specific taxpayers with particular activities."[9] Although Bowen held his ground, and later received a commendation from the American Association of University Professors for his refusal to give in to censorship, de Russy is still muttering in the background and the issue is not yet dead. In a June 18, 1998 editorial, the *Indianapolis Star* took AAUP to task for the giving Bowen the commendation, reporting in shocked tones that "we can only fear for our children when a college president is lifted up by his colleagues for promoting sexual deviancy on campus."[10]

So the porn wars on campus continue; only the names of the players change. Shortly before the World Pornography Conference I went into the CSUN Campus Bookstore to check on the availability of *Playboy*, and what do you suppose? That's right . . . it was gone again! When I inquired of bookstore employees I was told that the magazine was no longer sold because "there had been a complaint." After the conference I was told that there had been a mistake and the magazine was back. In November 1998 a reporter for the *Daily Sundial,* following up on the story, asked for *Playboy* in the Campus Bookstore and was told "We don't sell that kind of thing." Here we go again!

NOTES

1. Letter from Women Studies Program Committee to Matador Bookstore manager Lew Herbst, dated October 12, 1984. CSUN University Archives.

2. CSUN Associated Students Resolution SB #5, urging public policy regarding Matador Bookstore merchandising. Approved October 30, 1984. CSUN University Archives.

3. CSUN *Daily Sundial,* November 5, 1974.

4. Ibid.

5. *Los Angeles Times,* November 16, 1984., F8.

6. *Los Angeles Times,* December 21, 1984., F8.

7. *New York Times,* November 7, 1997., B5.

8. Ibid.

9. *New York Times,* December 23, 1997,. B5.

10. *Indianapolis Star,* June 19, 1998., A16.

26

(Sexual) Quotation Without (Sexual) Harassment? Educational Use of Pornography in the University Classroom[1]

David F. Austin

I N A PAPER ABOUT QUOTATION, IT SEEMS APPROPRIATE TO BEGIN WITH SOME quotations. They'll help to introduce the questions on which I want to focus.

> The universities . . . were now [during the 1980s] seeing . . . verbal assaults so degrading and vicious I found I could not report some of them, *even for educational purposes.* . . .[2]

Others strike a different note:

> To understand how pornography works, one must know what is there.[3]
>   One of the problems you have with pornography is that in some cases you cannot adequately describe it. You have to . . . confront the art.[4]
>   I have come to dislike talking about the effects of pornography with people who have not seen it for themselves, . . . discussions on this controversial topic frequently descend into verbal combat totally removed from the reality. . . .
>   Many people are more convinced of the harmful effects of pornography after seeing visual examples of this material than by reading about the now considerable scientific evidence of harm. Many women find the visual evidence particularly convincing–*if* they look at it. But few women *do.* Others find the combination of theory and visuals particularly effective. I therefore decided to include in this book a summary of some of the scientific research on the impact of pornography together with examples of visual pornography.[5]

The right sort of classroom discussion of sexuality can help prevent harassment; the wrong sort can *be* harassment. How can we distinguish these two sorts? I want to urge careful attention to context in characterizing "hostile learning environments," and I'll do this by looking at real and hypothetical cases where sexually explicit material is used in educating those who are legally adult.[6] My purpose, therefore, is to raise a question about some hard cases in the hope that we can work on finding an answer. I don't now know what the answer is. Throughout this discussion, I'll use the phrase, "hostile learning environment" as a shorthand for "learning environment that unreasonably interferes with an individual's education or is intimidating or hostile," modeled on the U. S. EEOC guidelines on sexual harassment [(29 C.F.R. §1604.11(a)(3)].

Although my focus will be *sexual* harassment in the *classroom,* current law provides characterizations of at least six other sorts of harassment–corresponding to the broader categories of discrimination based on race, color, national or ethnic origin, religion, age or disability–and it is important even for my limited purposes to keep this in mind. It is at least arguable that many of the same kinds of principles that apply to one sort will apply to the others as well, and this can provide an important constraint on such principles. I'll return to this point later.

Are the sorts of cases I'm concerned about unusual? Some hope so. But the hope is bound to be disappointed: any course that counts among its topics any one of the seven sorts of discrimination (and how to move beyond them) is likely to have an educational need to "quote hate speech," to make use of potentially objectionable representations. Courses in many areas–e.g., anthropology, art, biology, communication, economics, film, gender studies, history, law, literature, medicine, music, philosophy, political science, psychology, religious studies, sociology, theater and performance art–will often be affected.

I suspect that there's so little written about these hard cases because they're hard, not because they're uncommon. But even if these sorts of cases were unusual, it would still be worth figuring out how to address them. In doing so, we will gain a far deeper understanding of our more general ideas about harassment, and such understanding will have great practical utility. Hard cases don't always make bad law. After all, there's nothing more practical than a good theory, and there's no better test of a theory than a hard case.

To the best of my knowledge, there are only two published discussions that attempt to address this issue directly in anything approaching the relevant detail, and even these are far too brief to deal adequately with the relevant subtleties and complexities: Catharine MacKinnon gives a few paragraphs to the issue, Mari Matsuda, a few pages.[7] To highlight those subtleties and complexities, I'll conclude with a brief discussion of some changes in MacKinnon's own pedagogical practices.[8]

I'll begin by describing three apparently legitimate uses of sexually explicit material in the university classroom, each involving "sexual quotation" sexually explicit material is presented in class to make feasible fully informed discussion. These uses fall into three categories, pertaining to legal studies, study of sexuality and its representation, and social scientific investigations.[9] I'll then present five increasingly refined principles that say how to avoid sexually harassing students while quoting sexually explicit representations; recognizing the principles' flaws will give us a deeper understanding of our question.

Not everyone who sees a need for "sex quotes" conceives the issue in quite the same way as do the Reverend Wildmon and Professor Russell[10]:

> As a teacher of a university course on pornography, I can sympathize with Russell's opening statement: "I have come to dislike talking about the effects of pornography with people who have not seen it for themselves. . . ." If there's one thing I dislike even more, however, it's talking about pornography with people whose only exposure to porn has been a narrow band within the broad spectrum of pornographic materials, carefully pre-selected by the anti-porn feminists.[11]

These remarks, together with those already quoted, suggest that there may well be a place for pornography in the classroom. To bring the matter even closer to the focus of this conference, and to begin my presentation of examples, consider the following case.

SEXUALLY EXPLICIT MATERIAL IN LEGAL STUDIES

"Gender and the Law" is a required, team-taught course in the prelaw and law school curricula. A female, feminist legal theorist, co-teaching the "sexual harassment law" portion of the course seeks to make the issues as vivid as possible by bringing to class samples of the "pin-ups" that saturated Lois Robinson's work environment at Jacksonville Shipyards, Inc., some of which involve "full frontal nudity" of women.[12] Suppose (contrary to fact) that a porn video, *Hell Bent*, had been left by coworkers in Robinson's locker; its central character is an over-sixty-five, hemophiliac, Afro-American nun with AIDS, who wants to make up for lost time in her sex-life. (This character is therefore relevant to seven categories of discrimination in the law.) After Robinson discarded the video without comment, someone retrieved it from the trash can and arranged for it to be playing the Ku Klux Klan rape scene on the cafeteria TV monitor when Robinson arrived for lunch the next day.[13] The instructor wants to show her students just how powerfully one such incident contributes to making a work environment hostile. So she proposes to show some of the most explicit segments in class. (To help her male students gain a keener appreciation of the issues, she wants also to show a gay video, paralleling the one displayed to Robinson.[14]) Her co-instructor, a self-described "First Amendment hawk," agrees that it's worth showing those segments, mainly because she believes that they are not legally actionable—the tape is "protected speech."

A co-instructor for the First Amendment portion of "Gender and the Law" argues strongly in favor of civil-rights based regulation of pornography, and shows his class videos that would meet the law's definition, as well as sexually explicit videos ("erotica") that would, he believes, be exempt. Another co-instructor might have doubts about or even reject this approach, perhaps because she endorses Lars Ullerstam's view[15] (i.e., tolerance for allegedly harmless, victimless practices of most perversions) and argues for the essentially fluid performativity of socially constructed gender identity, which she highlights with a wide range of videos.[16] Of course, obscenity law already regulates some pornography, and (otherwise?) obscene material might need to be shown for informed classroom discussion.

STUDY OF SEXUALITY AND ITS REPRESENTATIONS

A faculty film theorist offers a course focusing on Linda Williams's long, intricate argument, beginning in her 1989 book *Hard Core*, that pornography constitutes an evolving film genre worthy of academic study.[17] (Possibly, this evolution indicates changes in what's wrong with contemporary attitudes towards sexuality.) Williams cites particular pornographic films as key to the genre's definition, including *Deep Throat, Behind the Green Door* and *Insatiable*. (Williams cites more than fifty films.[18]) Williams continued her argument in a 1992 paper[19] in which she argued that pornography depicting "perversions" (e.g., butch/femme lesbian sex, BD and SM, and bisexuality) should not be censored since viewing it may help to raise important and useful questions about the characterization of sexual normality and the standard categories of sexual practice that are used to discuss these questions. Some of these sexual practices (esp. lesbian sadomasochism[20]) and their depictions have been at the center of debate over MacKinnon-Dworkin anti-pornography ordinances. Williams cited an additional eleven videos in her paper.[21] A representative sample of the movies must be viewed to assess her argument fairly and thoroughly—say, two per week for fourteen weeks. [Suppose (contrary to fact) that one of them is a poorly shot amateur video of lesbian sadomasochism depicting anal and vaginal fisting and excretory functions.][22] The course might also include study of sexually explicit feminist anti-pornography films,[23] as well as study of any attempts by feminist anti-pornography activists to meet repeated challenges to present a clear and positive vision of human sexualities: erotica that makes a contribution towards the creation of "the uncompromised women's visual vocabulary."[24]

Who better to give a course on these topics than Professor Williams herself? Because she had the following sorts of reservations, she was nevertheless not the first to offer such a course:

> . . . I was genuinely not convinced that undergraduates, even the highly motivated, upper-division ones I would want to gear such a course towards, could or should be asked to handle the anxiety produced by materials whose aim is to put you in the throes of sexual arousal. After all, if I taught a course on comedy it would be imperative to talk about what made us laugh; if I taught a course on horror it would be imperative to talk about what made us cringe in terror; if I taught a course on pornography would we not need to talk about what turned us on—or off? Could we, should we, talk about that[?]

Despite these and other reservations, Williams decided to go ahead with the course:

> In 1993, Catherine MacKinnon reignited the "porn wars" in feminism with two highly inflammatory publications which made me recognize that these [wars] still needed fighting and that a pedagogy of pornography might be an effective way to counter the kind of scapegoating of pornography that MacKinnon promulgates.
>
> . . . [MacKinnon's] are the kinds of arguments that can . . . fly [only] if you don't know much about visual pornography, its history, its conventions, and its various uses among very different kinds of viewers. . . . [T]he study of moving image pornography is the best antidote to the widespread belief among anti-pornography feminists that pornography is pure misogynist violence against women. Among other things, such a study can point out that a good proportion of visual pornography produced since the early seventies hasn't had anything to do with women at all.
>
> This, at least, was my reasoning in putting together a [n upper division, undergraduate Women's Studies and Film] course. . . .
>
> The course was designed to survey the history of moving-image pornography from the early, underground stag films for all-male audiences to the quasi-legitimate "couples" films of the seventies to the proliferating varieties of gay male, lesbian, bisexual, straight, sadomasochistic, fetishist pornographies that are available now that low-budget video shooting and home VCR viewing predominate.
>
> We saw a group of hard-core stag films the very first day and we continued to see at least one work of hard-core, feature-length pornography each week and sometimes twice a week.[25]

SOCIAL SCIENTIFIC AND MEDICAL STUDIES

Faculty in anthropology, philosophy, psychiatry, psychology, sociology and statistics offer a course on methodological issues, concerning links among viewing, attitudes and action, that arise in doing studies of the effects of viewing sexually explicit material. The therapists among them are especially concerned with treatment of sexual disorders and dysfunctions (including the paraphilias, as well as what's colloquially known as "porn addiction").[26] Altogether, the published studies specify, say, fifty sexually explicit movies that have been used in various experiments. The studies come to significantly different conclusions (e.g., "It's not the sex, it's the violence," "It *is* the sex," "It's the *combination* of sex and violence," "There *is* a reliable distinction between erotica and pornography," "There's *no* reliable distinction between erotica and pornography" . . .). These differences might very well be caused in part by the studies' varied uses of different types of films, and verbal descriptions of the films do not provide sufficient relevant detail, so some of them must be viewed in class.[27] Two co-instructors who are experienced therapists and researchers on psychological trauma report that although viewing some sexually explicit material may be harmful to some people, the harm is on a par with the effects of viewing Holocaust films, the powerful pro-life film *Silent Scream*, and videos of the Vietnam War, material that they regularly show in their courses on trauma; they report further that no student has found such material inappropriate for the courses.[28] The course is offered, but not without encountering some objections from other faculty; in an interview with a local newspaper reporter, one objector protests:

> It's irresponsible to test a chemical on people who are more likely than not to suffer bad side effects (some of them quite serious). It's just the same for porn: in our sexist society, we're primed for the worst effects of viewing hardcore. You just can't inoculate against the effects through this sort of "education." What are we going to say to the women who are raped by "participants" in this course (the "excess rapes" [!])? "Don't blame us—we were engaged in the scholarly pursuit of knowledge. Be glad that you've helped us to understand how attitude affects action." Nazi social science is no better than Nazi medicine! And informed consent is either impossible or useless here: either you tell the subjects so little that the consent can't be informed, or you tell them so much that you bias the selection of subjects in irremediable ways.

Finally, we might imagine *The Ultimate Meta-Course, Contemporary Controversies in Sexuality and the Law*, where controversies arising from the aforementioned situations (and others) are thoroughly investigated and debated anew.

What do all of these apparently legitimate uses of sex quotes have in common? One shared feature is the obvious direct relevance of the material to the courses' topics. This suggests:

(P1) Sexual quotation in the classroom is not sexual harassment if and only if a purpose of the course is to study the quoted material.

Had (P1) not actually been proposed at some universities (e.g., University of Texas, Dallas), it would not even be worth refuting. This principle is far too undiscriminating—it yields neither necessary nor sufficient conditions. It ignores the way in which material is presented, and so it ignores any effects specific to the quotational mode of presentation.[29]

Let's try (P2): Sexual quotation in the classroom is not sexual harassment if and only if it is reasonable to believe that the quoting causes no offense.

Reasonable according to whom? "the" reasonable person? man? woman? victim? student? instructor? This is a very large question that will affect every proposal. Because it has been so widely discussed and debated, I'll focus on other issues or approach this one obliquely, but this issue never goes away, and my formulations will continue to reflect this.[30]

(P2) is far too restrictive in disallowing any offense whatever. As many feminist instructors have emphasized, sexists may need to have their sexist attitudes challenged, and the instructors' classroom practices reflect this. Some religious conservatives might be offended by depictions of women working outside the home,[31] but, if they're enrolled in the course, that's not by itself a good reason to exempt them or to exclude the material.[32]

At some point, however, the level of offensiveness may become so great as to inflict harm on those exposed to the material.[33] (Defenders of obscenity law often raise this point.) So the effects that we should be concerned about are the harmful ones:

(P3) Sexual quotation in the classroom is not sexual harassment if and only if it is reasonable to believe that the quoting causes no *harm*.

Despite its welcome shift in focus, (P3) is still too restrictive; it ignores the fact that education is often risky and can be painful. Over a decade's experience teaching the creationism controversy to more than five thousand Bible Belt engineering students helps me to remember that education is often quite risky and can be very painful for students who have previously regarded as fully settled, or even off-limits, questions nevertheless worth raising; trauma specialists tell me that studying trauma is often risky or painful, but still worthwhile for their students (even, or especially, for some of the trauma survivors). Our purpose is not to cause pain, we do what we can to help (where "we" sometimes includes therapists and counselors), we encourage our students to speak (see the sample syllabus), and we listen to them carefully (including, in many cases, their thanks). Three additions to (P3) suggest themselves:

(P4) Sexual quotation in the classroom is not sexual harassment if and only if it is reasonable to believe that the quoting causes no *unnecessary* harm; *informed consent* is obtained; and *substitute work or no-penalty withdrawal* are permissible to prevent unnecessary harm.

With each of the three additions comes important questions: (a) What is informed consent? How is it to be secured? (and how well informed can the consent be when the main purpose of sexual quotation is to go beyond mere description,[34] with effects that are difficult to predict?); (b) How in general are necessary and unnecessary harms to be distinguished? (and how should we weigh risks to the more vulnerable?) (c) Since actual psychological damage need not occur for (a legal finding of) sexual harassment (to be made),[35] is (P4) strong enough? I'll comment on each of these questions in turn.

On (a): Securing informed consent from students[36] and permitting students to substitute assignments for those that would be too harmful are both important measures, but I wouldn't want to (be legally forced to) exempt from most assignments or courses the student whose deeply held, possibly religiously inspired, beliefs entail racism, sexism, homophobia, creationism, advocacy of genital mutilation and/or opposition to all non-natural termination of pregnancy. Here we need to remember that "religion" is one of the categories in the relevant body of law; any restriction that is imposed here to avoid a gender-hostile environment must also have its parallel for avoiding religious (and other designated sorts of) harassment. There is so much that is deeply offensive to some religious (etc.) group or other that exempting every potentially offended student would leave us with a badly undereducated student population.

Informed consent, understood in part as willingness to tolerate a specified risk of incurring a specified harm, is, I'd guess, as difficult to secure in sexual as in surgical matters, where the pain of embarrassment (more gen-

erally: social disadvantage) as well as the pain of trauma are notoriously difficult to anticipate.[37] Just as a patient can sue for malpractice discovered well
after receiving substandard treatment, informed consent should also not
foreclose the possibility of a student's discovering later that s/he was
harassed and has a course of legal action.[38]

On (b): Apart from the clear case where a student's pain is so great that
it overwhelms any possibility of learning, thus qualifying the student for a
substitute assignment or even for no-penalty withdrawal from the course,
I'm not sure exactly how to distinguish in a general, principled way between
necessary and unnecessary harm. The first question we should ask is, For
which educational purpose is the harm necessary? Presumably, pursuit of
some purposes, but not all, is worth a given risk. Which are the worthwhile
ones? Implicit in any assessment of harm is some notion of (bounds on)
normal function, where the latter is a normative, as opposed to merely statistical, notion, and is surely very complex, relational and context–and subject–dependent; it's no less difficult to get a handle on this notion than on
human nature itself.[39] In the correlative sense of "harm," it is recognized that
sometimes harm must be done now to bring about later normal function ("It
took a long time to heal after my surgery, but it was worth the suffering.").
Since in education, the psychological functioning is far more complex than
the physical functioning at issue for most kinds of surgery, the "pedagogical
malpractice" cases are typically much more difficult than the already difficult medical ones; with sex in the picture, things get even tougher.[40]

Faculty sometimes complain that they cannot reasonably be expected
to warn students about any topics that *might* be disturbing since, as noted
above, so many topics might disturb some student at some time; one can't
make all higher education risk-free. While the latter is true, there is, however, a simple strategy that can provide some very useful information. Faculty can survey their students at the course's beginning to discover student
attitudes and ignorance on topics that the course covers;[41] responses can be
anonymous, and a statistical analysis can be a topic for class discussion.[42]
Quite apart from issues of harassment, this practice would be a good idea;
the bravest faculty will repeat the survey at the course's end, to see if they
have had any effect at all on their students' attitudes.[43]

On (c): Can we get help from social psychologist Susan T. Fiske, who
testified in both *Price Waterhouse* v. *Hopkins* and *Robinson* v. *Jacksonville Shipyards, Inc.*?[44] In her expert testimony, she argued that a workplace environment that promotes sex-role stereotyping is more likely to be hostile, where
four factors contribute to stereotyping: extreme minority status,[45] priming,[46]
hierarchical power structure and tolerance for unprofessional conduct.[47] So
let us augment (P4) accordingly:

**(P5) Sexual quotation in the classroom is not sexual harassment
if and only if it is reasonable to believe that the quoting causes no
unnecessary harm and *promotes no significant misuse of sex-role stereotyping*; informed consent is obtained; and substitute work or no-
penalty withdrawal are permissible to prevent unnecessary harm.**

Applying this to the classroom is even trickier than applying it to the workplace. Since not all (sex-role) stereotyping is in itself bad, and, as common sense and cognitive psychology tell us, some benign stereotyping is inevitable for the sake of cognitive efficiency, we need to distinguish uses from misuses—no small task. Extreme minority status is often avoidable by enrolling a sufficient number of women (etc.) in a course. There might be justification for having some all-women (and some all-men) courses, but having mixed classes would be educationally valuable, too; and we might have male and female students view and discuss material in separate groups or individually as well as together.[48] Some priming is inevitable in classes where material is presented to illustrate stereotypes. But how much priming occurs will depend heavily on mode and context of presentation, and it may be feasible to overcome the effect by careful construction of the mode and context. And that, of course, is where we came in: with concerns about how to construct the educational context! Hierarchical power structure is a feature of academic contexts, but not in the same ways as in the workplace; including female instructors and feminist methods of pedagogy can help.[49] Tolerance for unprofessional conduct is intolerable, and there are plenty of clear cases of such conduct, but we need some principled way of sorting out the inevitable controversial cases. It might be inappropriate for an instructor to exclaim during a video, "Wow, look at those!" as a remark about a performer's physical attributes, but would an expression of amazement (e.g., "Gee, I didn't know that was possible!") *always* be objectionable? Fiske's own work suggests that it is the disinclination of the powerful to pay attention to the powerless that is a major factor in the misuse of stereotypes by the powerful.[50] Here, educational contexts often enjoy a major advantage over the typical workplace environment. In each of the examples I've considered, the roles of stereotypes[51] being presented, as well as their (mis)uses, are also being studied; because such educational uses of pornography are so very likely to be reflective and self-conscious, the likelihood that habitual misuse of those stereotypes will be reinforced is correspondingly diminished, though not, of course, eliminated.[52]

I conclude that (P5) doesn't so much resolve as highlight and focus the relevant questions.

Consequently, appealing to the legal precedent of *Robinson v. Jacksonville Shipyards, Inc.* is not particularly useful when it's learning environments that are concerned. This means, however, that there are no particularly useful legal precedents to guide us here.

In closing, I consider some remarks by Catharine MacKinnon, who seeks to raise serious doubts about the legitimacy of any course-required sexual quotation. Where I am cautiously optimistic, she is profoundly pessimistic. In her most recent, and perhaps only, published comment directly on the educational use of pornography, MacKinnon writes:

Teachers who wish to teach such materials should be prepared to explain what they are doing to avoid creating a hostile learning environment and to provide all students the equal benefit of an education. . . .

Pornography, under current conditions, *is* largely its own context. Many believe that in settings that encourage critical distance, its showing does not damage women as much as it sensitizes viewers to the damage it does to women. My experience, as well as all the information available, make me think that it is naive to believe that anything other than words can do is as powerful as what pornography itself does [*sic*]. At the very least, pornography should never be imposed on a viewer who does not choose—then and there, without any pressure of any kind–to be exposed to it. Tom Emerson said a long time ago that imposing what he called "erotic material" on individuals against their will is a form of action that "has all the characteristics of a physical assault." Equality on campuses, in workplaces, everywhere, would be promoted if such assaults were actionable. (*Only Words*, 108–9, italics in original)

This passage seems to recommend extremely stringent requirements for informed consent. The phrase "then and there" suggests frequent checks on students' mental and other states. How frequent should they be (and of what sort, done by whom)? The phrase "without any pressure of any kind" could even be interpreted to mean: *never*–since, as MacKinnon's own writings have emphasized, the pressure of sexism is omnipresent, and the power differentials in the classroom can increase it ("Fiske in the limit"). So, what I've called a "major advantage" for educational contexts, MacKinnon sees as far less significant, at most.

It's safe to assume that no one's given more thought to these issues than MacKinnon has. It is a sign of their difficulty that MacKinnon herself has not always behaved in accord with the most stringent restrictions. In the fall of 1983, ten years before giving the lectures from which this quotation is taken, she and Andrea Dworkin taught a course at the University of Minnesota-Minneapolis covering pornography and its harms. Then, they did require their students to view pornography and to attend at least one live-sex show; a list of bars in Minneapolis where the shows could be viewed was provided with the syllabus.[53] The penalty for either not viewing or not attending was a failing grade in the course. A more recent episode reflects MacKinnon's apparently changed practice.

A controversy arose during Fall 1993 over the planning of a University of Michigan Law School conference on prostitution. The law students initially invited Detroit artist Carol Jacobsen to assemble a videotape on prostitutes' experiences. The students, many of whom had studied with MacKinnon, later asked Jacobsen to withdraw the tape because they feared that at least part of it was pornographic. Here are four remarks attributed to MacKinnon by Liza Mundy in "The New Critics."[54] These remarks bear on MacKinnon's views about the permissibility of research and teaching about pornography.

(1) "Have you [Liza Mundy] seen the tape?" MacKinnon asks me on the phone. [Mundy says that she has not yet seen it.] "Depending on your own history of sexual abuse," she comments offhandedly, "you might want to be prepared for what it might do to you" (28, col 1).

(2) When a speaker at the conference called her about the video, she says, she phoned the students and advised them to take a look at it. Later, she spoke with them again and warned them of the dangers of showing pornography, even in an academic context: She had felt compelled to stop teaching a class she and Dworkin gave on the subject, she told them, after "several students had mental breakdowns as a result of remembering things that happened to them as children." Then she urged the students again to look at the tape: "I said, 'I haven't seen this stuff, I don't know if it is pornography, but, if it is, people need to think about its impact in an academic setting–and not assume that an academic setting is stronger than the pornography" (29, col 3).

(3) Female artists, she says, haven't begun to escape the miserable self-image foisted upon them by dastardly pornographers. Luckily, though, she has: "What you need is people who see through literature like Andrea Dworkin, who see through the law, like me, to see through art and create the uncompromised women's visual vocabulary" (30, cols 1–2).

(4) The compromise that will allow Carol Jacobsen's work to be shown has also failed to reconcile the pro- and anti-porn feminists on the University of Michigan campus. Indeed, Catharine MacKinnon and her supporters are sure Jacobsen's video will only strengthen their claim that porn cannot be transformed by context. Asked whether the video, as porn that at least aspires to be art, is still porn, MacKinnon replies, "It's not even a close call. This is sexually explicit material; women are being hurt, used, violated, stripped" (33, cols 1–2).[55]

So, if these quotes are accurately reported, it appears that MacKinnon has changed her mind on an important matter.[56] Perhaps MacKinnon's current attitude can be expressed by varying a Kantian slogan:[57] "I have therefore found it necessary to deny *knowledge*, in order to make room for *equality*."[58] I find no clear indication in her published work of exactly how MacKinnon proposes to balance these values in educating for a better future.[59]

I would tentatively recommend a more moderate course of action, as illustrated by the draft syllabus in Appendix I, below: Students are given "fair notice" in the syllabus, in individual pre-enrollment discussions (before the first class meeting), and during the first class meeting; the team of three instructors, one male and two female, is alert to issues of both pleasure and danger,[60] assisted in part by analysis of the initial survey of students' attitudes; and provisions are made for substitute work or withdrawal in cases where students are so pained that their learning cannot continue.

Because, however, I have not resolved most of the questions that I have raised, I end pretty much where I began, without precise instructions on how to use sex quotes without sexually harassing students. But I hope that you'll agree that it's worth seeking better answers than any we've now got, and that (P5) is a good place to *begin* looking. More generally, I would urge *all* sides of the debates about sexuality to address these sorts of hard cases in sufficient detail to make it clear exactly how they propose to balance the values[61] that they take to be implicated.[62]

Since I began with some pertinent quotations, I'll end with a quotation that nicely encapsulates our present difficulty.

What is most disconcerting about Dworkin and MacKinnon, finally, is that they do not parody pornography or the gothic; instead they madly identify with these genres. . . . [S]eeing the harm that pornography causes necessarily involves the very splitting and dissociation, the appropriation, that in turn problematizes the critique. With MacKinnon and Dworkin, it is no secret that theory produces what it also describes. Their mad identifications remind us that *the space within quotation marks is no sanctuary.*[63] (italics mine)

David F. Austin, Department of Philosophy and Religion, NCSU[64]

APPENDIX I: GUIDELINES FOR SAMPLE SYLLABUS

PHI 498/588 Sexuality: Regulation and Choice
We investigate the notions of norm and choice as they arise in sexuality by examining a variety of controversies about sex work and its representation, especially in pornography.

Prerequisites: Two courses in relevant topic areas (e.g., in philosophy, psychology, film or cultural studies, sociology) at the junior-level or above, and instructors' permission; enrollment limited to 15 students.

Course Format: One seminar meeting each week, and one viewing session each week.

How to Get a Grade: (i) Seven 750–1000 word papers on obscenity and the empirical evidence of harm; the civil rights approach and criticisms of it; porn in the classroom; anti-porn stars; porn stars and other sex workers; children and sexuality; porn puzzles; due by dates specified in schedule; specific questions set by instructors (40 percent of grade); (ii) 1250 word paper (10 percent of grade) on lessons learned from 'mock jury' determinations on selected material: for each item studied (or a specified subset, depending on time constraints), all fifteen seminar members (twelve jurors, and three alternates) will apply (a) the US Supreme Court *Miller* standard; (b) NC state obscenity law; and (c) the MacKinnon/Dworkin model ordinance to determine if the material is obscene [(a), (b)], pornographic [(c)] or erotica [neither obscene nor pornographic]. A worksheet specific to each standard will be supplied. Time permitting, some items may be viewed and evaluated a second time at the course's end. If feasible, a mock trial will be held for some material, if cooperating attorneys can be found. (iii) Final project–3000+ words (40 percent of grade). This may be a further development of one of the short papers in (i). Additional topics will be suggested by the instructors. An abstract and annotated bibliography for the paper is due three weeks before the end of the semester. Collaborative efforts may be undertaken only with the instructors' permission; everyone in the group will receive the same grade. {? (iv) journal on videos viewed and related discussion; will be read and graded by instructors; 10 percent of grade?} The work of graduate students taking the course as PHI 588 will be evaluated with criteria appropriate to their more advanced academic standing. All students will also be expected to complete class surveys on topics pertinent to the course. A summary of the results will provide material for class discussion, but individual responses will be kept confidential. The surveys may be repeated at the course's end to help gauge any changes in student views.

How to Get an Even Better Grade: If your course grade is on a borderline, you may boost it into the higher range by providing well-written, well-argued 250–500 word reviews of any three of the movies viewed in the course.

On-Line Resources and Participation: (i) One or two listserves will be set up to allow discussion with anti-pornography activists and with sex workers; all students are expected to at least monitor the discussion {and write about it in their journals}. (ii) The course will have a web page with readings and links to other web resources. Students are expected to make use of this page in preparing for discussion and in writing their papers. {At least ten links must be discussed in the journal, with their specific bearing on a course topic made clear.}

[Consider holding a symposium in your geographical area on the more general topic of "Dangerous Knowledge" to run concurrently with the seminar or shortly afterwards.]

Guidelines for Students Enrolled in This Course:[65] The sort of material that we will be viewing can elicit strong responses; among common responses are amusement, anger, anxiety, arousal, boredom, disgust, embarrassment, sadness—any of which may be accompanied by characteristic physical reactions. (Some instructors' experiences suggest that arousal is far less common than might be expected, perhaps because of the group setting for viewing and the analytical approach taken towards the material. There have also been reports that viewing this sort of material can cause memories to surface, including memories of abuse.) These responses and reactions can serve as data for class investigations. It is therefore important for us to work to make this classroom a safe place for students to share experiences, feelings, and ideas. Here are some rules to help us. Students may propose new rules or amendments to these rules if they wish.

•There will be no interruption of any student by another. The instructors will moderate all discussion and invite the next comment when the current speaker is finished.

•There will be no personal criticism of any kind directed by any member of the class to any other member of the class. You are entitled to comment on the intellectual content of another student's words, to contribute your own feelings and thoughts to the discussion, and to pose questions to other students, but you are not entitled to tell your peers that they are "crazy," "perverted," "stupid," "sexist," or anything else of this nature. Treat peers with respect, civility and kindness. This includes treating any silences with respect, as well. Of course, none of this precludes exercising one's sense of humor, but it should be done with appropriate care.

•Some students may choose to give accounts in class of their personal experiences, though no one will ever be required to do so. These accounts are welcome in this class if and only if they relate directly to the discussion. Since they are true accounts, students in this class should respect others' privacy and observe the rules of confidentiality—if you tell someone else's stories outside of class, please omit the student's name and any other identifying features. No one may tape any session of the course for any purpose (except as necessary to assist any disabled students).

•This class is not a therapy session, and the instructors cannot serve as any student's therapist. Feelings and personal experience may be introduced into discussions if and only if they contribute to the class's understanding of the particular topic under discussion. Students who wish to explore the option of therapy may speak with the instructors privately for a list of on- and off-campus resources.

•Some students may find it necessary to take an occasional "breather" during class; they should feel free to stand up and walk out of class if they find themselves in need of a short break. It's OK to ask a classmate to accompany you during such a break. (Joking about this is alright only if it's friendly; see above.)

The ideal for discussion will be defined by Richard Feldman's *Reason and Argument.* Although the ideal may not always be attained, we will always aim for it.

Participation in Studies: Aside from the in-class surveys, you may be invited to participate in one or more academic studies on the effects that taking this course has on your attitudes. Any such study would have been reviewed and approved by the University Committee on the Use of Human Subjects. *Participation would in any case be strictly voluntary and is not a course requirement.* If you did choose to participate, any study could be discussed in one of your shorter required course papers [see (i), in How to Get a Grade, above].

Disability-Related Student Needs: It is University policy to provide, on a flexible and individualized basis, accommodations to students who have disabilities that may affect their ability to participate in course activities or to meet course requirements. We strongly encourage any students with disabilities to contact us as soon as possible to discuss their individual needs for accommodations so that those needs can be met in a timely manner. Course material can be made available in alternative formats upon request.

Texts and Materials on Reserve:
Topics: [Specify videos to be viewed under each topic]
I. Dangerous Knowledge—Preventing Harm
 The Harm of Offensiveness: Background on Current U.S. Obscenity Law
 Evidence of Harm Caused by Pornography:
 Pornography Regulation: A Civil Rights Approach
 Criticisms of the Civil Rights Approach
 Sexual Harassment, Speech Codes and a Hostile Academic Environment
 Pedagogy of Pornography
 Dangers of Inquiry
II. Making Choices and Giving Consent

Could a Free Woman Choose Porn?
Anti-Porn Stars, Left and Right
Porn Performers and Other Sex Workers
Developing Choices—Children and Sexuality
III. Abnormal or Just Unusual? Genders and Sub-genres—Puzzles Raised by Porn
[At least the first four topics in class, with others for student papers
and/or presentations.]
Gay Porn
Lesbian (vs. girl/girl) Porn
Painful Pleasures—Bondage, Domination and Sadomasochism (BDSM)
Bi Porn and Transgender Porn—How many genders? How many sexes?
Why ask why?
Slash (Kirk/Spock) Porn: Gay (?) Porn by Women, for Women
Other SciFi (Robo- and Alien) Porn
Black and other (Inter)racial Porn
White Trash Porn
Fat Porn
Medical Porn
Disabled in Porn
"Period" and "Puke" Porn: Beyond Disgust
Norms Abroad: International Porn
Long time pornful: Japan and The Netherlands (or Denmark) Societies
in Transition: Ireland and Russia

APPENDIX II: OBSCENITY LAW: DOES EDUCATIONAL VALUE MATTER?

Obscenity law must also be taken into account in decisions about classroom use of potentially obscene material. The answer to the question, Does educational value matter?, is that educational use clearly can sometimes confer some serious scientific and/or political value on otherwise obscene material, but the situation remains less clear than is desirable because there is so little directly relevant case law. Another paper should be written about these issues, but here, I'll simply pass along some practical suggestions from a variety of attorneys with whom I've discussed the matter informally.

Does your locality's obscenity law offer explicit protection for material that has serious educational value? If not: (i) Request that your institution's attorney seek a declaratory judgment to immunize against prosecution. (Because of the expense involved, many institutions will refuse, but it's still worth asking.) (ii) Take reasonable measures to insure that no legal minors participate in the course. (iii) To minimize the risk of illegal dissemination of the sexually explicit materials, limit use of the materials to students in the course and any faculty with a legitimate research interest in the materials; implement a system, either through the library or department(s), to verify that material is checked out only to those authorized individuals (e.g., have IDs checked against a list). (iv) Direct a large proportion of class lecture and discussion and student study to non-obscene materials. (v) Inform students that if they disseminate any of the sexually explicit materials, then they, too, are at risk of prosecution. (vi) At the end of the class, collect any sexually explicit material distributed to students. (vii) Close to the time when the course is to be offered, let your institution's attorney review materials to be distributed to students so that their risk can be minimized and so the administration will not be surprised if a student's parent calls to inquire about the course.

To further reduce the risk of prosecution: (viii) Keep the video material to just a few items. Generally, videos are riskier than still photographs, which are riskier than non-pictorial print material, though even use of the latter is not without risk. (ix) Use materials that are readily available in the community, which speaks to the issue of "community standards," a key provision of the *Miller* test for obscenity. (x) Rely on university funding sources (e.g., library or department budgets) in acquiring materials (for purchase or rental)– although this also leaves a public institution open to attack for "misuse of public funds." (xi) Have students write a paper about a particular item. (xii) Have students participate in social scientific research on the effects of any material viewed to help make the case for material's in-context serious scientific value. (xii) Include discussion of feminist and/or conservative religious perspectives on regulation of pornography to help make the case for the in-context serious political value of the material viewed.

I'd add two other pieces of advice: First, it helps to be protected by tenure before attempting such a course. Second, it's not unlikely that some prominent First Amendment attorney(s) would offer to defend you pro bono if the local district attorney decided to prosecute, but there would be other expenses, and the experience might not be a lot of fun even if the charges are eventually dismissed or you're found not guilty.[66]

Most important: Obscenity law is always local and political, so you should seek the advice of an attorney who is experienced with local obscenity law and who is therefore familiar with the local political climate.

NOTES

1. I'm not an attorney, and I'm not offering legal advice. Nor is my primary focus the law, though I do look to the law for advice about what we ought to do in the classroom. This is part of a larger project on hate speech and informed consent, which is in turn part of an even more ambitious project on unity in philosophy of mind and language and moral theory.

2. Mari Matsuda, *Words That Wound: Critical Race Theory, Assaultive Speech, and the First Amendment* (Westview Press, 1993), quoted in Introduction, 13 (italics added) Matsuda repeats and elaborates on the point in another essay:

At every single university at which I spoke–north, south, east, and west–I learned of serious incidents of racist, homophobic, or anti-Semitic hate. University administrators reported that they had never seen anything like it. A pattern emerged in the 1980s of the new integration colliding with the new racism—or the new old racism. The universities, long the home of institutional and euphemistic racism, were now seeing something different: the worst forms of gutter racism. Asian-American students spat on; Nazi literature appearing on Jewish holy days; and cross burnings, racist slurs, and homophobic insults so degrading and assaultive that I found I could not in good conscience reprint them, even for educational purposes, in the book I wrote on the topic. (105)

Mari Matsuda, "Assaultive Speech and Academic Freedom," reprinted in: *Where Is Your Body? and Other Essays on Race, Gender and the Law* (Boston: Beacon Press, 1997), 103–117. The book Matsuda refers to is: Mari Matsuda and Charles Lawrence, *We Won't Go Back: Making the Case for Affirmative Action* (Houghton Mifflin, 1997).

3. Catharine A. MacKinnon. "Pornography as Defamation and Discrimination," *Boston University Law Review* 71 (November 1991): 793 (text attached to n11). MacKinnon continues with a characteristically graphic description:

In the hundreds and hundreds of magazines, pictures, films, videocassettes, and so-called books now available across America in outlets from adult stores to corner groceries, women's legs are splayed in postures of sexual submission, display, and access. We are named after men's insults to parts of our bodies and mated with animals. We are hung like meat. Children are presented as adult women; adult women are presented as children, fusing the vulnerability of a child with the sluttish eagerness to be fucked said to be natural to the female of every age. Racial hatred is sexualized; racial stereotypes are made into sexual fetishes. Asian women are presented as so passive they cannot be said to be alive, bound so they are not recognizably human, hanging from trees and light fixtures and clothes hooks in closets. Black women are presented as animalistic bitches, bruised and bleeding, struggling against their bonds. Jewish women orgasm in reenactments of actual death camp tortures. In so-called lesbian pornography, women do what men imagine women do when men are not around, so men can watch. Pregnant women, nursing mothers, amputees, other disabled or ill women, and retarded girls, their conditions fetishized, are used for sexual excitement. In the pornography of sadism and masochism, better termed assault and battery, women are bound, burned, whipped, pierced, flayed, and tortured. In some pornography called "snuff," women or children are tortured to death, murdered to make a sex film. The material features incest, forced sex, sexual mutilation, humiliation, beatings, bondage, and sexual torture, in which the dominance and exploitation are directed primarily against women.

Would a reading of this description suffice to yield the required kind of knowledge? Why?

4. Reverend Donald Wildmon, in his testimony at the Wojnarowicz defamation trial, 6/25/90, US. District Court, NY; quoted in C. Carr, "Trying Times," *On Edge: Performance at the End of the Twentieth Century* (Wesleyan University Press, 1993), 262. Wildmon was defending himself against the charge that he had defamed artist David Wojnarowicz by excising fourteen images from the latter's allegedly pornographic work and mailing them to media and congressional leaders.

5. Diana E. H. Russell, *Against Pornography: The Evidence of Harm* (Russell Books,

1993), vii. Russell has also said that she is considering writing a similar book on child pornography, which would include pictorial examples of the latter. Other pertinent remarks, the first "con" and the rest "pro":

> . . . they don't want other visions laid out . . . as equally valid alternatives. The word *heresy* is rooted in *haeresis,* meaning "choice." . . . "mere exposure" . . . *does* affect students' values.

Stephen Bates, *Battleground: One Mother's Crusade, the Religious Right, and the Struggle for Control of Our Classrooms* (Poseidon Press/Simon and Schuster, 1993), Chapter 11: "Beyond Providence," 309. [Members of minorities are typically quite sensitive to the fact that there's often nothing "mere" about "mere exposure." In this case, the minority is a subgroup of Christian Fundamentalists, (or, as some prefer to say instead, finding the latter term offensive, "Orthodox Christians") but the lesson is general.]

> Diana Russell has given us the ultimate proof of the impact and reality of pornography . . . used properly, it could save women's lives.–Gloria Steinem, back cover, *Against Pornography: the Evidence of Harm*
> As they say, "A picture is worth a thousand words." . . . . No academic has ever dared to reproduce the pornographic images themselves and then comment on them. The effect is profoundly enlightening, sobering and challenging. *Brava,* Diana, for your determination and originality.–Phyllis Chesler, back cover, *Against Pornography*
> . . . Now when we speak about pornography, we all will know precisely what we are talking about. Bravo and thank you Diana Russell for your brilliant analysis, your courage and commitment.–Jane Caputi, back cover, *Against Pornography*
> . . . for the first time in a feminist book about pornography, she shows us the images which, she says, teach men to rape women, so the reader can see for herself what the pornography debate is all about. *Judge for yourself!*–Melissa Farley, inside front cover, *Against Pornography*
> . . . after attending Diana's feminist anti-pornography slide presentation . . . I was moved to tear up several hundred *Hustler* magazines in convenience stores . . . –Nikki Craft, inside front cover, *Against Pornography*
> This book takes a risk in using illustrations from contemporary pornography. Women may find it distressing to see the sexually explicit violence and subordination of women this multi-million dollar industry is selling. Men–and women too–may find it sexually arousing: that's what it is intended to do. But information is power. Men need to know what pornography means and does to women. The text that accompanies the picture provides this information. And women can be empowered by knowing what is being done to them in the name of sex, even if that knowledge is painful or frightening. The pornography industry thrives on ignorance, secrecy, shame and silence. Exposing it is a risk worth taking.–Catherine Itzin, facing title page, *Against Pornography*

6. Although I am concerned primarily with hostile environment harassment, and not the generally less controversial targeted harassment, there does seem to be good reason to connect the two, See my "A Note on Universal Targeting and Hostile Environment Harassment" (unpub. ms.) for an argument worth considering.

7. Matsuda, in the "Hard Cases" section of her, "Public Response to Racist Speech: Considering the Victim's Story," (repr *Words That Wound,* 37–44); and MacKinnon in *Only Words,* 107–9.

8. For an excellent review of prevailing First Amendment concerns about hate speech codes, see Rodney A Smolla, "Academic Freedom, Hate Speech, and the Idea of a University," in William W. Van Alstyne (Ed.), *Freedom and Tenure in the Academy* (Duke University Press, 1993), 195–225. See also William W. Van Alstyne, "The University in the Manner of Tiananmen Square," *Hastings Constitutional Law Quarterly* 21, 1 (1993), about how the road to hell can be paved with the best intentions. Also helpful are: Patricia Meyer Spacks (Ed.), *Advocacy in the Classroom: Problems and Possibilities* (St. Martin's Press, 1996) and Louis Menand (Ed.), *The Future of Academic Freedom* (University of Chicago Press, 1996). The best defense of hate speech codes, sensitive to a wide range of concerns, is Joshua Cohen, "Freedom of Expression," *Philosophy and Public Affairs* 22, n. 3 (1993): 207–64. The best brief critique of MacKinnon's work from a Rawlsian (or any other) perspective is Joshua Cohen, "Freedom, Equality, Pornography," in Austin Sarat and Thomas R. Kearns (Eds.), *Justice and Injustice in Law and Legal Theory* (University of Michigan Press, 1996), 99–137.

9. These categories are not meant to be either exhaustive or exclusive. For the most part, my examples will involve the subclass of 'sex quotes' that might be called "video porn quotes," because these are among the most controversial. There are, of course, many uses of the term "porn" (and its cognates), and it is crucial to be clear on which use is being made. Here, I'll let the examples indicate the kind of use. One good working definition of "pornography" has been offered by my colleague Donald VanDeVeer:

> Pornography is the sexually explicit depiction of persons, in words or images, created with the primary, proximate aim, and reasonable hope, of eliciting significant sexual arousal on the part of the consumer of such materials (987). [This characterization is population-relative:] Important in deciding whether material is likely to evoke significant sexual arousal [an admittedly somewhat vague term] is its probable effect on an average person in a certain population. . . . The reactions of particular individuals are inconclusive. (988)

Encyclopedia of Ethics (Garland, 1990), 986–89. If the population has just one member, this yields a person-relative definition. Additional context-dependency would make the definition much more useful and complex.

10. Of course, their reasons for fighting pornography are different–the same might be said for Catharine MacKinnon and Beulah Coughenour, who fought together to pass an anti-pornography ordinance in Indianapolis in 1983–though Wildmon and Russell agree that a necessary part of the fight is confronting pictorial material that they would both take to be pornographic.

11. Jen Durbin, "When a Scientist Stacks the Deck: A Review of Diana E. H. Russell's *Against Pornography: The Evidence of Harm,*" *Spectator Magazine* 33, n. 2, issue 835 (Sept 30–Oct 6, 1994): 4.

12. *Robinson v Jacksonville Shipyards, Inc.* 760 S. Supp. 1486 (M.D.Fla. 1991).

13. On a relevant subgenre, see Gloria Cowan and Robin R Campbell, "Racism and Sexism in Interracial Pornography: A Content Analysis," *Psychology of Women Quarterly* 18 (1994): 323–38.

14. It is, I think, an interesting question just how close the parallel can be; I leave this matter for another occasion.

15. In his *Erotic Minorities* (New York: Grove Press, 1966). The work of Judith Butler on performativity and gender is relevant here. See her *Gender Trouble* (Routledge, 1990), *Bodies That Matter* (Routledge, 1993), and, for a more direct connection to issues raised in this paper, *Excitable Speech: A Politics of the Performative* (Routledge,

1997). Butler use of "citation" in "citationality" is fairly close to my somewhat extended use of "quotation."

16. One can readily imagine a series of parallel examples with other sorts of hate speech regulations at issue.

17. Three other film theorists who have done important work on the genre are Constance Penley [e.g., "Feminism, Psychoanalysis, and the Study of Popular Culture," in Lawrence Grossberg, Cary Nelson and Paula A. Treichler (Eds.), *Cultural Studies* (Routledge, 1992), 479–500; "Brownian Motion: Women, Tactics and Technology," in Constance Penley and Andrew Ross (Eds.), *Technoculture* (University of Minnesota Press, 1991), 135–61]; Mandy Merck [e.g., "More of a Man," *Perversions* (Virago Press, 1993), 217–35]; and Tania Modleski [*Feminism without Women: Culture and Criticism in a "Postfeminist" Age* (Routledge, 1991)].

18. Other uncited films may also be important for assessing her argument, e.g., amateur videos, the most rapidly growing portion of this video market; the most popular non-amateur tapes produced in the last six years, since Williams's book was finished, to indicate changing themes; meta-porn, e.g., *Making of a Porn Movie, Porn Screen Tests, Tori Welles Goes Behind the Scenes*, or, for the purposes of supposed contrast, the *Better Sex Video* series, sexually explicit videos (widely advertised in "mainstream" periodicals, e.g., the *New York Times*) produced by sex educators and therapists to teach approaches for adult heterosexual activity.

19. "Pornographies on/scene, or diff'rent strokes for diff'rent folks," in Lynn Segal and Mary McIntosh, eds, *Sex Exposed: Sexuality and the Pornography Debate* (London: Virago Press, 1992), 233-265. See also: Linda Williams, "Second Thoughts on Hard Core: American Obscenity Law and the Scapegoating of Deviance," in Pamela Church Gibson and Roma Gibson (Eds.), *Dirty Looks: Women, Pornography and Power* (London: BFI Publishing, 1993), 46–61; and "A Provoking Agent: The Pornography and Performance Art of Annie Sprinkle," in the same collection, 176–91. And see: Arthur and Marilouise Kroker (Eds.), *The Last Sex: Feminism and Outlaw Bodies* (St. Martin's Press, 1993), as well as Laura Kipnis, *Bound and Gagged: Pornography and the Politics of Fantasy in America* (Grove Press, 1996).

20. See, for example: Elizabeth A. Meese, *(Sem)erotics: theorizing lesbian: writing* (NYU Press, 1992), *and* references cited therein. Mandy Merck, "The Feminist Ethics of Lesbian S/M," *Perversions* (Virago Press, 1993), 236–66. Patrick D. Hopkins, "Rethinking Sadomasochism: Feminism, Interpretation, and Simulation," *Hypatia* 9, n. 1 (Winter 1994): 116–42. Claudia Card, *Lesbian Choices* (Columbia University Press, 1995).

21. *Punishment of Anne* (1979), *Every Woman Has a Fantasy* (1984), *Suburban Dykes* (1990), *Bi-Coastal* (1985), *Bisexual Fantasies* (1986), *Bi-Night* (1985), *Bi-Dacious* (1985), *Bi-Mistake* (1985), *Karen's Bi-Line* (1989), *Bi-and Beyond: The Ultimate Union* (1986), *Bi-and Beyond III: The Hermaphrodite* (1991).

22. An issue worth considering is: where should the funding for material purchase or rental come from? This issue also arises in connection with obscenity law's application to the classroom; see Appendix II, below.

23. E.g., *Not a Love Story*. For criticism of NALS, see B. Ruby Rich, "Anti-Porn Soft Issue, Hard World," in Patricia Erens (Ed.), *Issues in Feminist Film Criticism* (Indiana University Press, 1990), 405–17; and I. C. Jarvie, *Thinking about Society: Theory and Practice* (D. Reidel, 1986). A similar example can be constructed concerning the practice, common in some cultures, of female genital mutilation, which is the focus of the documentary, *Warrior Marks: Female Genital Mutilation and the Sexual Binding of Women* (Pratibha Parmar, producer; accompanying book from Harcourt Brace, 1996), inspired by Alice Walker's novel, *Possessing the Secret of Joy* (Harcourt Brace, 1992).

24. The quoted phrase has been attributed to MacKinnon; see remark (3) reported by Liza Mundy, below. MacKinnon appears to allow for the possibility of erotica, in Gloria Steinem's sense of the term, "premised on equality." See "Francis Biddle's Sister," repr. in *Feminism Unmodified* (Harvard University Press, 1987), 176. See also James Lindgren, "Defining Pornography," *University of Pennsylvania Law Review* 141, n. 4 (April 1993): 1153–1275. Lindgren gives examples of works that, MacKinnon reportedly said (during a phone interview with him) are erotica: specified passages in Andrea Dworkin, *Ice and Fire*; Marilyn French, *The Women's Room*; and Deanne Stillman and Anne Beatts (Eds.), *Titters: The First Collection of Humor by Women.* Examples of pornography cited are: specified passages in Georges Bataille, *Story of the Eye*; Pauline Reage, *Story of O*; and pictorial material from much so-called lesbian erotica (non-sadomasochistic and produced by lesbians for lesbians), as well as *Hustler, Penthouse* and *Playboy.*

25. Linda Williams, "The Pedagogy of Porn: Censorship, Self-Censorship and the Undergraduate Curriculum," 2, 4–8, UC 'Censorship + Silencing' Series, UCSB, 11/4/94 Similar courses have been given at University of California/Santa Barbara (UCSB), University of California/Berkeley (even before Professor Williams moved there), and, I believe, at NYU, Duke and other universities. [See "Teaching Sexual Images," Special Section of *Jump Cut* n. 40 (March, 1996).] Professor Constance Penley taught a similar course during Winter quarter, 1993, at UCSB, and will soon teach it again; she describes her experience in, "Porn Pedagogy: Teaching Pornography as a Popular Film Genre," also delivered at the 'Censorship + Silencing' Series. Her class enrolled about seventy students, about evenly divided between men and women. Penley reports several surprises in teaching the course:

. . . when I got in front of the class and looked up, what I saw were 70 terrified faces. That is when I realized that they thought they were going to be seeing slasher films with sex, that is, films in which the most misogynistic violence and sex were one and the same. Their terror was not the terror of their own embarrassment about watching sex writ large on the silver screen in a room full of other people; embarrassment turned out not to be such a big deal. . . . Rather, it was that they believed, often without having read any of the feminist anti-porn books, but through having absorbed those prevailing ideas through the media's presentation of them, that porn was nothing but the violent subjugation and degradation of women by men. (4)

Yet another surprise for me was that, in contrast to every other class I have ever taught, here or at other universities, it was the women in the class who took the lead in class discussions. . . . What I realized is that there is no available public discourse for men to speak about pornography in anything but a denunciatory way, given the way pornography has been typified as male violence against women. Even when male students come to understand that this typification is wildly skewed and have begun to think about the interests behind such a campaign of disinformation, they still cannot speak as freely as the women can about what they have learned. (5–6)

. . . [W]ould you rather the professor put the materials on reserve for you to check out to take home or would you prefer watching them in the classroom with other students and the professor? Unanimously, they said they wanted to watch them together, in class. . . . They wanted the sanction of the classroom, of the academic, scholarly setting. . . .(7)

I said that every class is a kind of community for the duration of the class and this one would be no different, but that they should try to be sensitive to their own and other's possible embarrassment and ambivalence given the fact that people do not usually see these materials in such a setting. Within two weeks the class . . . had become a workable community. . . . I have never had a more well-behaved, disciplined, harder working group of students. (8)

There is another reason, directly linked to the genre, why watching these films turned out not to be so embarrassing, which is the high level of humor found in them, or rather the high level of low humor. (8)

Penley ends her description with these remarks:

Any talk about knowledge inevitably brings us to a discussion of fear. Pedagogy is about the joy of teaching and learning but it is also about learning to negotiate one's own fear of learning and all the horrible obstacles set up on the outside to block learning. Toward the end of the class the students, now with a working knowledge of what pornographic film is, and what it is not, began asking, "In whose interest was it to have us be so afraid, so very afraid? Who and what interests does it serve to have sexually explicit films be such a bogeyman?" . . . Nothing could have made me happier as a teacher that a course that had begun in fear was able to end with a thoughtful discussion of the socially coercive uses of fear. (14–15)

26. See the *Diagnostic and Statistical Manual of Mental Disorders IV* (DSM IV) (American Psychiatric Association, 1994), 493–538, as well as 417-423, 621.

27. Supreme Court decisions highlight the protected status, under the First Amendment, of some medical educational uses of otherwise obscene material [eg., *Miller* v. *California* 413 U.S. 15 (1973) and even *New York* v. *Ferber* 458 U.S. 747 (1982)]. But, as Rosalind A. Coleman and James Rolleston, "Anatomy Lessons: The Destiny of a Textbook, 1971–72," *South Atlantic Quarterly* 90, n. 1 (Winter 1991): 153–73, shows, a medical context is no guarantee of 'purity in representation'. The anatomy text discussed used out-takes from *Playboy* centerfold photo sessions to illustrate female anatomy; male anatomy was not similarly favored with *Playgirl* photos.

28. On powerful material: here are (close paraphrases of) remarks on student experience with classes that have included viewing of pornography:

Women's Studies classes are the *one* place where it would be safe to discuss this material. *Please* try to find a way to include it in your classes. There is a lot of confusion and anger around the issue of pornography, sex, etc., and if we can't discuss it in Women's Studies, where will we be able to deal with it?

Several students reported being very disturbed by *Dreamworlds* [a video on sexist images in MTV Rock]–more than one to the point of actually vomiting after leaving class. But [even] the students who were physically ill thought we should continue to use the video in the future.

Several students felt they had to leave the room, but none of them suggested that this video [*Not a Love Story*] be dropped from this course.

Do not be afraid to broach subjects that may cause a student to remember his/her trauma.

I think we forget how strong people are.

I saw *The Silent Scream* [a powerful anti-abortion film] in a Women's Studies class as an undergrad, and it was pretty horrible to watch, but it never occurred to me that it wasn't appropriate for the class. [Why shouldn't the same be true of porn?]

29. Although it might be pedagogically unwise to introduce a unit on porn in, say, an endocrinology or a thermodynamics course, doing so won't be harassment unless it's done "in the wrong way" ("This'll get you really hot!"), and we're trying to figure out what that way is. To give an example of an arguably legitimate departure from a course-description: suppose that Greene College has been embroiled in debate over a recent showing, in a Women's Studies class, of *Deep Throat*, often cited by Andrea Dworkin and Catharine MacKinnon as a document of the abuse of its female lead, Linda Marchiano (aka "Linda Lovelace"). The instructor for Thermodynamics sees that students are distracted from their studies in physics by the heated debate, and so decides, with the students' agreement, to spend one or two classes helping students to organize their thoughts on the matter, with the reasonable hope that this will help them focus on physics in subsequent classes. This might well be an effective measure under the circumstances, and even if other means would be better, it's not clear that we should rule out this measure in advance. (P1) also places no constraints on the range of courses and purposes; see the discussion of (P5), below.

30. See Nancy Tuana, "Sexual Harassment in Academe: Issues of Power and Coercion," *College Teaching* 33, n. 2 (1985): 53–57, 61–63; repr. in Edmund Wall, *Sexual Harassment: Confrontations and Decisions* (Prometheus Books, 1992) 49–60. One of Tuana's main conclusions is this: "Sexual harassment can occur even in situations in which the instructor has no intention of threatening the student. Given an instructor's obligations to the students, if it was reasonable for a student to perceive a threat, then the instructor is morally responsible for the sexual harassment even though he or she did not intend it." (59) See also, Robert Nozick, "Intention and Coercion," *Journal of Applied Philosophy* 5, n. 1 (1988): 75–85. A *very* interesting case for considering the question, Should s/he have known better?, is Professor Jane Gallop's; see: Margaret Talbot, "A most dangerous method: The disturbing case against Jane Gallop, feminist provocateur," *Lingua franca* 4, n. 2 (Jan 1994): 24ff; Jane Gallop, "Sex and Sexism: Feminism and Harassment Policy," *Academe* (September–October 1994): 16–23; Jane Gallop, *Feminist Accused of Sexual Harassment* (Duke University Press, 1997).

31. Or, in a geophysics course, by discussion of radiometric dating and the challenge it presents to some versions of creationism; see the discussion of (P3), below.

32. In Christianity and its art, disturbingly realistic descriptions and depictions of Christ's crucifixion, Biblical rapes and the deaths of martyrs are common and play a significant role in religious education and indoctrination—even when children are involved. Thorough–going opposition to use of potentially offensive images therefore seems unwise for those who believe these depictions should be allowed. It will not be easy to craft a principle that allows such imagery while prohibiting the educational use of such work as Andres Serrano's "Piss Christ," intended by its maker as pro-Christian, and made famous by Senator Jesse Helms. (For a brief review of Serrano's art that places his most well-known work in a larger context, see Celia McGee, "A Personal Vision of the Sacred and Profane," *New York Times*, 1/22/95, Section 2, 35.) Of course, Christianity is far from unusual among religions in its educational use of powerful and potentially offensive imagery. This range of examples also pertains to (P4) and (P5), below, which contain the distinction between necessary and unnecessary harm. See also: Cheryl Smith Blum, "The Place of Art in Catharine MacKinnon's Legal Theory," *Journal of Contemporary Law* 19, n. 2 (1993): 445–82.

33. In the physician's oft-repeated adage, "First, do no harm," the term "harm" is typically taken to mean: unnecessary pain or damage I am not here building "unnecessary" into the meaning of "harm," for reasons that will become clear presently.

34. It is often remarked (see above) that "one picture is worth a thousand (or ten thousand) words" Since quotation is a kind of demonstration, and demonstratives' meanings are not expressed by any descriptions, the remark understates the difference. (See also the discussion of "shock value," in notes below, where the difference between demonstrating and describing hate speech is at issue.)

35. *Harris* v *Forklift Systems, Inc.* 976 F.2d 733 (6th Cir 1992), 113 S.Ct. 1382 (1993). Justice O'Connor wrote for a unanimous court:

> Certainly Title VII bars conduct that would seriously affect a reasonable person's psychological well-being, but the statute is not limited to such conduct. So long as the environment would reasonably be perceived, and is perceived, as hostile or abusive, . . . , there is no need for it also to be psychologically injurious.

Justice Ginsburg concurring:

> The critical issue . . . is whether members of one sex are exposed to disadvantageous terms or conditions of employment to which members of the other sex are not exposed. . . . [T]he adjudicator's inquiry should center, dominantly, on whether the discriminatory conduct has unreasonably interfered with the plaintiff's work performance. To show such interference, the plaintiff need not prove that his or her tangible productivity has declined as a result of the harassment. . . . It suffices to prove that a reasonable person subjected to the discriminatory conduct would find, as the plaintiff did, that the harassment so altered working conditions as to ma[k]e it more difficult to do the job.

36. At the question and answer session after I gave a brief version of this paper, Professor Penley expressed this concern: actively seeking informed consent could well be taken as an unwarranted concession that sexually explicit material is especially dangerous in the classroom, and remarked that her own administration has not required any notice to students beyond a typically informative syllabus and has been otherwise supportive of her pedagogical efforts in this are. I'm glad that some instructors work in such supportive environments, but since law, as well as all politics, is local, it should not be assumed that all are similarly favored. The degree of caution exercised in securing informed consent should probably depend in part on local considerations, and having students sign a form may be, all relevant factors considered, the wisest precaution in some locales.

37. The MacKinnon/Dworkin ordinance expresses profound skepticism about the efficacy of the usual means for securing informed consent. Here is the text of the relevant section:

> Coercion into pornographic performances. Any person, including transsexual, who is coerced, intimidated, or fraudulently induced (hereafter, "coerced") into performing for pornography shall have a cause of action against the maker(s), seller(s), exhibitor(s) or distributor(s) of said pornography for damages and for the elimination of the products of the performance(s) from the public view. (1) Limitation of action. This claim shall not expire before five years have elapsed from the date of the coerced performance(s) or from the last appearance or sale of any product of the performance(s); whichever date is later; (2) Proof of one or more of the following facts or conditions shall not, without more, negate a finding of coercion: (a)

that the person is a woman; or (b) that the person is or has been a prostitute; or (c) that the person has attained the age of majority; or (d) that the person is connected by blood or marriage to anyone involved in or related to the making of the pornography; or (e) that the person has previously had, or been thought to have had, sexual relations with anyone including anyone involved in or related to the making of the pornography; or (f) that the person has previously posed for sexually explicit pictures for or with anyone, including anyone involved in or related to the making of the pornography at issue; or (g) that anyone else, including a spouse or other relative, has given permission on the person's behalf; or (h) that the person actually consented to a use of the performance that is changed into pornography; or (i) that the person knew that the purpose of the acts or events in question was to make pornography; or (j) that the person showed no resistance or appeared to cooperate actively in the photographic sessions or in the sexual events that produced the pornography; or (k) that the person signed a contract, or made statements affirming a willingness to cooperate; or (l) that no physical force, threats or weapons were used in the making of the pornography; or (m) that the person was paid or otherwise compensated.

It seems that (l) is to be read as including nonphysical threats to the individual in question; (2) would then cover a case in which all the other conditions [(a) - (k) and (m)] were met, and where the woman's child was being held hostage by her estranged husband. The one sort of case that is said to be common and would meet all of the conditions in (2) is one of severe economic coercion: a woman is desperate for money, and so performs in pornography. This might be thought of as a "hostile economic environment," seen as depriving the performer of a capacity freely to consent. Similarly, a woman who derives a significant measure of her self-esteem from pornographic exhibitionism would be seen as confined in a "hostile social, psychological and political environment," unable fully to appreciate the nature of the alternatives from which to choose, and so unable to give truly informed consent. Economic, social, psychological and political pressures all operate to some degree in the classroom, and there is thus an argument to be made along these lines for extreme caution in securing informed consent from students who are being asked to view pornography. Until the argument is fully specified by advocates of this approach to informed consent, it will be difficult to determine how they believe one should prepare for discussions of pornography.

38. This might be different from a situation in which no informed consent is given and the person realizes this well after the event; in this instance, informed consent is given but is not sufficient to protect the surgeon from future legal action (Suppose the surgeon, whose patient is a surgeon in the very same subspecialty, encounters extremely unlikely circumstances that were not reasonably foreseeable and deals with them substandardly.) One could stipulate that the latter was not really *informed* consent (part of the information was that the surgeon agrees to deal with unlikely circumstances in a way that meets standards, and the standards say what's reasonable in those unlikely circumstances), but it might be better to acknowledge that in very complex matters, there are limits on how well informed the person can or should be and that pedagogical or surgical malpractice is consistent with consent that's as fully informed as could reasonably be expected. For a useful general discussion, see David Archard, *Sexual Consent* (Westview, 1998).

39. For many of the same reasons, characterizing reasonableness is difficult: in this

sense, a reasonable person is one whose capacity for reason is functioning and being applied normally While many have written at length about these more general issues, MacKinnon among them, no one has presented a sufficiently clear and detailed picture to yield immediate answers to the questions about quotation discussed here. For helpful discussion of the related notion of agency, see Kathryn Abrams, "Sex Wars Redux: Agency and Coercion in Feminist Legal Theory," *Columbia Law Review* 95 (March, 1995): 304. Susan Etta Keller, "Viewing and Doing: Complicating Pornography's Meaning," *Georgetown Law Journal* (July, 1993): 2195, (also cited by Abrams) makes room for classroom use of pornographic material without, however, resolving many questions about what sorts of uses should be allowed.

40. Matsuda offers advice based on her classroom experience:

I have seen too many students confused by the claim that unless we let hate mongers into the room, critical inquiry will not take place. In fact, as a teacher, I have found that exactly the opposite is true. One of the hardest things to do in the classroom is to have honest, mutually critical discussions about racism, anti-Semitism, homophobia, and misogyny. We do not have enough of these discussions. We do not have models of how to have them, and a screaming match is the worst possible model. Hard-and-fast rules against name-calling and requiring listening before attacking are ways I have managed to get these discussions started in my classroom. *I have also had to ask more than one student to remain in the room when they wanted to run out in tears. These are hard conversations,* and pornography, anti-Semitic, racist, and homophobic epithets do not further critical, probing dialogue. (142) (italics mine)

It is the value of speech I hope to promote by suggesting that we many need to limit some speech. This is indeed a paradox—no easy walk to freedom, no easy civil liberties. (143)

Both passages from "Progressive Civil Liberties," reprinted in: Mari Matsuda, *Where is Your Body? and Other Essays on Race Gender and the Law* (Beacon Press, 1997): 131–45.

41. Asking questions carries some risk, since they, too, can be disturbing, but in this case, the risk does seem a reasonable one to take. (Though this, too, requires some argument.)

42. This suggestion presupposes that a course's topics are pretty much settled in advance. But don't we want to allow for spontaneity, tailoring of focus to student interest, and mid-course corrections? We do, and it would still be prudent and good pedagogical practice to check with those enrolled to see if newly proposed topics or materials hit any "hot spots." If they do, then use of substitute assignments or withdrawals may be offered. (An example may help: Suppose that the members of a Metaphysics seminar find that it would suit their collective interests and purposes to include a discussion of abortion. One of the participants speaks to the instructor privately, explaining that she's just had an abortion and is still too upset to engage such material with any educational benefit. Is there any serious question about what's reasonable in such a case?)

While this is a reasonable way to deal with mid-course corrections, it does not address the issues raised by the pedagogical utility of shock value. Here is an example, based directly on an actual case, that will help to explain what I mean: A white, male professor of First Amendment law is teaching a law school class at a large state university. He has a well-deserved reputation on campus of being a stalwart "friend of minority interests." He seeks to illustrate the power of speech with vivid examples, and, thinking that "Fuck the Draft" is too familiar to jolt anyone, instead writes, "Fuck all niggers" on the blackboard. The African-American students in the class complain to the administration, and the professor apologises to them. It was clear to everyone involved that the professor's intent was to illustrate the power of hate speech, not to endorse the message it carried. In a recent discussion of this case, there was sharp and deep disagreement among experienced legal academics, all of whom had previously shown considerable sensitivity to hate-speech issues, about the acceptability of the professor's example. Is shock value no value at all? How shocking is too shocking? Are some sorts of shock "off limits," regardless of their intensity?

43. With current computer and networking technology, it would be feasible to do surveying on a departmental or university scale. It would be helpful to study the dynamics of students' views during their educations. At a time when higher education is being asked to pay more attention to assessing effectiveness in teaching, the data provided by such surveys could be genuinely (as opposed to merely-'PR') useful.

44. *Price Waterhouse* v *Hopkins* 490 U.S. 228, 104 L.Ed. 2d 268, 104 S.Ct. 1775. See also Susan T. Fiske et al., "Social Science Research on Trial: Use of Sex Stereotyping Research in *Price Waterhouse* v. *Hopkins,*" *American Psychologist* 46, n. 10 (October 1991): 1049–60. More recently, she has summarized research that helps to further explain the role of stereotyping: "Controlling Other People: The Impact of Power on Stereotyping," *American Psychologist* 48, n. 6 (June 1993): 621–28; this article also discusses *Robinson* v. *Jacksonville Shipyards, Inc.* 760 S. Supp. 1486 (M.D.Fla. 1991). An approach similar to the one endorsed by Robinson has been taken more recently in *Jenson* v. *Eveleth Taconite Co.* 824 F.Supp. 847 (D.Minn. 1993); see esp. 879–83, on Dr. Eugene Borgida's expert testimony. For an earlier proposal sensitive to this range of issues, see: Helen E. Longino, "Pornography, Oppression, and Freedom: A Closer Look," in Laura Lederer (Ed.), *Take Back the Night: Women on Pornography* (William Morrow, 1980).

45. Or, rarity: "solo or near solo status, which exists when the individual's group comprises 15–20% or less of the environment's population."

46. Or, category accessibility, is a "process in which specific stimuli in the . . . environment prime certain categories for the application of stereotypical thinking, e.g., availability of photographs of nude or partially nude women, sexual joking and sexual slurs."

47. E.g., "tolerance of profanity and sexual joking."

48. See Fred von Lohmann, "Single-Sex Courses, Title IX and Equal Protection: The Case for Self-Defense for Women," *Stanford Law Review* (1996) on the legal permissibility of gender (etc.) separated classes, courses and programs.

49. Some helpful references: Frances A. Maher and Mary Kay Thompson Tetreault, *The Feminist Classroom,* (Basic Books, 1994); Amanda Konradi, "Teaching About Sexual Assault: Problematic Silences and Solutions," *Teaching Sociology* 21 (Jan 1993): 13-25; Susan Swartzlander, Diana Pace and Virginia Lee Stamler, "The Ethics of Requiring Students to Write about Their Personal Lives," *The Chronicle of Higher Education,* February 17, 1993, B1–2. Some of the best of these methods were used by Socrates.

50. She advocates ". . . a theory of the mutually reinforcing interaction between power and stereotyping, mediated by attention. The powerless attend to the powerful who control their outcomes, in an effort to enhance prediction and control, so forming complex, potentially nonstereotypic impressions. The powerful pay less attention, so are more vulnerable to stereotyping. The powerful (a) need not attend to the other to control their outcomes, (b) cannot attend because they tend to be

attentionally overloaded, and (c) if they have high need for dominance, may not want to attend. Stereotyping and power are mutually reinforcing because stereotyping itself exerts control, maintaining and justifying the status quo." (Abstract for "Controlling Other People," 621.) Although Fiske is only one of many social psychologists who have done relevant research, I focus on her work because of her prominent role in two high-visibility court cases. For a helpful review of the psychological literature, see: D. L. Hamilton and J. W. Sherman, "Stereotypes," in R. S. Wyer Jr. and T. K. Srull (Eds.), *Handbook of Social Cognition* 2nd ed. Vol. 2: Applications (Lawrence Erlbaum Associates, 1994): 1–68 (esp. 47–56, Stereotype Change). This review notes that it has been found to be very difficult to change or dislodge stereotypes. While this is discouraging, it also suggests that students will not be significantly more sexist after the hypothesized exposure to pornography. For a more nuanced perspective on the (limited) explanatory power of *stereotype*-based hypotheses and policies, see Elisabeth Young-Bruehl, *The Anatomy of Prejudices* (Harvard University Press, 1996).

51. As the example using Linda Williams's work reminds us, courses with sex quotes can hardly help dealing with many different sexual stereotypes, including gay, lesbian, African-American, etc, and many sub- and cross-types.

52. Of course, there's more that needs to be said about what kind of reflectiveness is helpful. Psychologists Krafka, Donnerstein, Linz and Penrod present evidence for the hypothesis that exposure to "hard-core" and violent pornography need not reinforce sex-role stereotyping and that follow-up debriefing can successfully counteract any of the negative effects that they found. See Daniel Linz and Neil Malamuth, *Communication Concepts 5: Pornography* (Sage Publications, 1993), for relevant summaries and citations. But see also: C. Neil Macrae, Galen V. Bodenhausen, Alan B. Milne and Jolanda Jetten, "Out of mind but back in sight: stereotypes on the rebound," *Journal of Personality and Social Psychology* 67, n. 5 (Nov. 1994): 808–18; Macrae et al. suggest that an active attempt to inhibit stereotypical thinking can have an unwanted rebound effect, and this needs to be kept in mind in designing any debriefings.

53. As MacKinnon has explained, the MacKinnon/Dworkin model antipornography ordinance is intended to allow some porn quotes: "The definition [of pornography in the ordinance] does not include all sexually explicit depictions *of* subordination of women. That is not what it says. It says, this which *does* that: the sexually explicit that subordinates women." "Francis Biddle's Sister," 176. The ordinance also contains an exemption for library archiving of pornography: "City, State, and federally funded public libraries or private and public university libraries in which pornography is available for study, including on open shelves shall not be construed to be trafficking in pornography but special display presentations of pornography in said places is sex discrimination." And it makes actionable forcing of pornography on a person: "Any woman, man, child, or transsexual who has pornography forced on them in any place of employment, in education, in a home, or in any public place has a cause of action against the perpetrator and/or institution." Classroom showing might be relevantly similar to a special display presentation in a library; forcing might be avoided by securing informed consent, though other parts of the ordinance (on defenses against a charge of coercing someone into performing in pornography) make it clear that securing consent is not a straightforward matter. Neither the language of the ordinance nor the surrounding commentary by its authors suffice to answer the questions about quotation discussed here.

54. *Lingua Franca*, vol 3, no. 6 (Sept/Oct 1993): 26–33. I have not verified the accuracy of any of these attributions.

55. In her *Sense and Censorship: The Vanity of Bonfires* [an early version of her *Sex and Sensibility: The Vanity of Bonfires* (Ecco Press, 1994)], Marcia Pally reports that Dworkin has claimed to be willing to give up her current legal right to publish books like *Mercy* if that will help the cause of women's rights The preceding suggests that MacKinnon might agree to something similar for research and teaching about pornography. But MacKinnon has reportedly indicated that Nabokov's *Lolita* may be misread as an endorsement of teenage sexuality, instead of an indictment of child sexual abuse—but that that is no reason to ban the book. [Reported by Katie Roiphe, *The Morning After: Sex, Fear, and Feminism on Campus* (Little, Brown, 1993), 143–44. MacKinnon's remarks were made in answer to Roiphe's question after one of Mac-Kinnon's Gauss seminars on criticism at Princeton in 1992. These lectures are the basis for MacKinnon's *Only Words* (Harvard University Press, 1993).] It is not clear to me exactly how one would allow for the 'misreading defense' of a work while at the same time limiting research and teaching uses of pornography. I have not verified the accuracy of either Pally's or Roiphe's reports.

56. The point here is not character assassination, but the difficulty of the issues involved. Changing one's mind is not the same as being hypocritical or inconsistent at a time. Some of MacKinnon's critics need to remember this.

57. "I have therefore found it necessary to deny *knowledge*, in order to make room for *faith*" Immanuel Kant, *Critique of Pure Reason* (Kemp Smith trans.), B xxx.

58. Matsuda's "hard cases" focus on racist hate speech. In her discussion of The Case of the Dead-Wrong Social Scientist (*Words that Wound*, 41–42), "who makes a case for racial inferiority in an academic setting based on what is presented as scientific evidence," she comments, ". . . outlawing this type of speech *might* be inappropriate. Assuming the dead-wrong social science theory of inferiority is *free of any message of hatred and persecution*, the ordinary, private solution is sufficient: Attack such theories with open public debate and with a denial of a forum if the work is unsound in its documentation." (italics added) But without being told more about what constitutes freedom from "any message of hatred and persecution," it is not clear how to apply this here, especially given Matsuda's emphasis on the "special vulnerabilities" and "captive" status of students (The Special Case of Universities, 44–45). Perhaps the latter could be used to support MacKinnon's current position. Did MacKinnon change her mind because she came to see requiring pornography-viewing as too much like *quid pro quo* sexual harassment? This would assimilate "Fuck or fail" and "Eat porn or fail," an assimilation which seems required by Mac-Kinnon's views. The puzzle would then be to explain her earlier pedagogical practice. But explaining her present practice along these lines would allow her to reject the Kantian slogan, since, on this line, there's either no knowledge, or no knowledge with any net worth, denied.

59. Two of the most interesting kinds of criticisms of MacKinnon's work are developed by Robin West and by Drucilla Cornell. West, who writes with unusual clarity, argues that MacKinnon is insufficiently attentive to the complexities of the psychological data about women's sexuality yielded by the technique of consciousness raising. Cornell faults MacKinnon for failure to develop a positive vision of human sexuality, and so for failure to explain how to get from awful 'here' to better 'there'. (I see West's and Cornell's points as two aspects of one deeper criticism.) See: Robin West, "The Difference in Women's Hedonic Lives: A Phenomenological Critique of Feminist Legal Theory," *Wisconsin Women's Law Journal* 3:81, 1987, 81–145; Robin West, "The Feminist-Conservative Anti-Pornography Alliance and the 1986 Attorney General's Commission on Pornography Report," *American Bar Foundation Research Journal* no. 4

(1987): 681–711; and "Pornography as a Legal Text: Comments from a Legal Perspective," in Susan Gubar and Joan Hoff (Eds.), *For Adult Users Only: The Dilemma of Violent Pornography* (Indiana University Press, 1989), 108–30; and Drucilla Cornell, *The Imaginary Domain: Abortion, Pornography and Sexual Harassment* (Routledge, 1995).

Since MacKinnon herself claims to have seen far more pornography than almost any male in her audiences, and remains nevertheless a *very* "high-functioning" individual, her own goals would seem to require explication of those features of, for example, her and Dworkin's personalities and circumstances that allowed their apparent transcendence of the worst negative effects. Is anti-pornography activism somehow protective against these effects? If so, how exactly? Perhaps closely studying such people will help us to discover how to make the transition from a pornographic society to an erotically healthy one; if pornography is rape-like, then the literature on survivors of sexual abuse should yield pertinent information about what makes it feasible for the abused to grow beyond their abuse. For insightful remarks about which speech acts MacKinnon believes herself to be performing, see Stanley Fish, *Doing What Comes Naturally* (Duke University Press, 1989), 16–23, 25. In "Performance and Paradox: How MacKinnon Shows What Cannot Be Said," (unpub. ms.), I suggest that MacKinnon's written work might best be interpreted under the hypothesis that she is a political performance artist who has (deliberately?) trapped herself in the role of Most Radical Feminist, with the consequence that the strongest affirmation she can now make of her gender identity is, as she is quoted as saying, "not not a woman." [Dinitia Smith, "Love is Strange," *New York* (March 22, 1993) 36-43.]

60. The Guidelines in the syllabus (see Appendix I, below) will be crucial in helping to ensure that, in Justice Ginsburg's words, "members of one sex are [not] exposed to disadvantageous terms or conditions of [education] to which members of the other sex are not exposed"

61. In her review of Richard A Posner, *Sex and Reason*, and Edward de Grazia, *Girls Lean Back Everywhere: The Law of Obscenity and the Assault on Genius* ("Pornography Left and Right," *Harvard Law Review*, Winter 1995), MacKinnon objects:

The two authors converge in complaining that the civil rights approach to pornography does not take the "value" of the materials into account, as obscenity law does. Because obscenity law criminalizes sexual materials defined as morally bad, it makes sense to allow their value—moral good— to outweigh it. The civil rights law, by contrast, defines pornography in terms of the sex discrimination—the real harm—it does. It makes pornography civilly actionable when coercion, force, assault, defamation, or trafficking in sex-based subordination can be proven. . . .

There is something monstrous in balancing "value" against harm, things against people, this on which left and right speak as one. It is not only balancing the value of human rights against the value of products that violate them. It is not only balancing rape, murder, sale, molestation, and use against pleasure and profits, or even aesthetics and politics. It is not only writing off the lives and dignity of human beings as if that were a respectable argument in a legal and academic debate. It is not even that this position that elevates the rights of pimps and predators over their victims and targets is part of current law. It is prior: when injury to women and children can be balanced against the "value" of pornography, women and children do not have human status—even though, pace de Grazia, women stand up everywhere.

I hope that it is clear that the balancing I speak of here is not of the monstrous sort.

62. Here is a homework assignment to encourage consideration of educational uses of sex quotes *outside* the classroom: Suppose that I had illustrated this paper with visual porn quotes and given it as a talk. Would I thereby have sexually harassed any members of the audience? What if the speaker had instead been well-known to the audience as a female anti-pornography activist (e.g., Diana E. H. Russell, or Catharine MacKinnon in 1983)? Consider also a wide range of possible prior warnings, illustrative material, display conditions and kinds of audience members. For discussion of an actual case, see the discussion of Professor Gail Dines's lectures in Eithne Johnson, "Porn-education Road Shows," *Jump Cut* n. 41 (May 1997). Reports are due by semester's end. No incompletes! Submission via e-mail encouraged: david_austin@ncsu.edu.

63. Naomi Morgenstern, "'There is Nothing Else Like This': Sex and Citation in Pornogothic Feminism," in Thomas Foster, Carol Siegel, and Ellen E. Berry (Eds.), *Sex Positives? The Cultural Politics of Dissident Sexualities* (NYU Press, 1997), 60.

64. For helpful discussion or correspondence, thanks to Priscilla Alexander, Randy Carter, Ailan Chubb, Drucilla Cornell, Jill Dahlmann, Gail Dines, David Drooz, Judith Ferster, Cynthia Freeland, Ruth Ginzburg, Thomas Grey, Charlotte Gross, Catherine Itzin, Robert Jensen, Susan Keller, Carol Leigh, Barbara Levenbook, Naomi McCormick, George Panichas, Jennifer Parchesky, Constance Penley, Robert Peters, Maria Pramaggiore, Ann Rives, Alix Schwartz, Barbara Herrnstein Smith, Wendy Stock, John Stoltenberg, Nancy Tuana, William Van Alstyne, Eugene Volokh, Lee Wentz, and Linda Williams. Apologies to those I've inadvertently omitted, and to those who wish they had been omitted.

65. Adapted from rules developed by Dr. Kali Tal, a female instructor (George Mason University, Yale) and therapist, who has taught a number of courses on sensitive subjects and worked extensively with groups of Vietnam veterans, Holocaust survivors and rape/incest survivors.

66. Here's a real case involving obscenity law: Professor Thomas Tedford, Professor of Communications at UNC/Greensboro and author of a nationally known textbook, *Freedom of Speech in the United States*, presented his undergraduate class COM 532 "Freedom of Speech and Censorship" with a half-hour slide show to illustrate the sorts of sexually explicit material that were the focus of controversy. At the urging of some local ministers, several students signed up for the course in order to be present at the slide show so that they could file an obscenity complaint with the DA under the extremely strict NC obscenity statutes (as amended in 1985), which define "disseminating obscenity" very broadly and which make the offense a felony punishable by a fine and imprisonment for up to three years. A key way in which the NC law was made stricter in 1985 was through the removal of a prior exemption for material that has educational value. Tedford's attorney (an ACLU member) and the General Counsel for the UNC-General Administration both told Professor Tedford to withdraw the visual aids. Since he did not have the resources to finance a protracted legal battle, Tedford decided to spend his time updating his textbook and advises other researchers who consult him about their research and teaching, "If you are serious about your research . . . find a school in another state where the state obscenity law protects academic teaching and research." This case alerts us to the additional problems that may be caused by obscenity law. See Appendix II for some advice.

27

Intention versus Interpretation: Personal Experiences with the Radical Right (Pornography Didn't Make Me Do It . . . the Christian Coalition Did)

Bill Paul

I GREW UP IN AN AREA OF GEORGIA WHICH WAS MADE FAMOUS BY ERSKINE Caldwell's *Tobacco Road* and *God's Little Acre,* by Walker Evans's photographs, and to some extent, by the photographs of Margaret Bourke-White and Dorothea Lange. At that time, there was a feeling of righteous indignation and a counterpoint of overblown confidence in the air as some folks reacted to what many writers had to say about the South in general and what Caldwell had to say about Central Georgia in particular. They believed that writers and artists in the late twenties and thirties had turned private matters into public issues of regional embarrassment when they portrayed poverty and ignorance in the South. Critics in the South rejected the southern stereotype on the one hand, but reinforced that stereotype by their behavior on the other. They didn't hesitate to say, "If you don't like it here, you can always leave."

Albert Key was my high school English teacher. He correctly surmised that most of my peers, twenty-four seniors at Wadley (Georgia) High School, would not go to college. Instead of spending a lot of time with traditional poetry, novels, and short stories, Mr. Key developed a curriculum which focused on important twentieth-century literature. We were assigned books and stories by some of the great writers of the current century: Somerset Maugham, William Faulkner, Pearl Buck, Theodore Dreiser, John Steinbeck, Willa Cather, Henrik Ibsen, and others.

In contrast to the wisdom of Mr. Key, one of the ministers in my hometown (he held a Ph.D. in philosophy and religion, by the way) objected to the material presented to the class. He maintained that high school students shouldn't be exposed to "unsavory" issues such as pollution, venereal disease, and out-of-wedlock sex. The minister's successful complaint ironically overlooked the rise in the divorce rate, unwanted pregnancies, and other matters that have reshaped American demographics during and after World War II. Partly because of this minister's interference, Mr. Key accepted a teaching assignment in another state. This was my first direct contact with censorship in the arts—and with censorship led by a man of the cloth. Other samples of repression existed at that time, but these situations were presented, without judgment, as simply the way things were.

One of the ladies in our community, learning of my intention to study art, warned me of the basic moral corruption that would result from a study of drawings, paintings, and sculptures of nude figures. She had no idea that a large variety of Tijuana Bibles (adult comic books) were readily available in Wadley, Georgia. Alas, not only did I study paintings of "naked" people during my first year in college, I actually drew and painted from nude models—male and female. Before the beginning of my sophomore year, I had already witnessed amazing things in Amsterdam and Paris, including wonderful reconstructions of some of those beautiful Baroque and Rococo masterpieces from art history at the *Folies Bergeres*, famous at the time for its spectacular *tableaux vivants*. I never told Mrs. Heath about those European experiences, or any others for that matter, and I'm sure she was a happier person without this knowledge.

There was quiet, and sometimes not so quiet, social turbulence in those years. After church, folks gossiped and wondered in whispers about early television images, the emerging power of the NAACP, about Elvis Presley, the Beatles, and that notorious kiss on the beach. Everybody innocently loved "Leave It to Beaver" and "The $64,000 Question." Needless to say, only a small number of TV watchers caught the coded double entendres and changing mores that were being introduced by this new medium at that time. Few had visions of what future technologies might bring. The public, still filled with images of prohibition and women's suffrage, appeared to be stunned and shocked by the national scope of the quiz show cheating scandal.

Most of us at the art school were painting very nice portraits, landscapes, and still life images. To spice up the scene, however, someone would occasionally tell about a trip to the House of Mysteries at Pompeii, or a packet of photographs of artists' models from Al Urban's studio would surface, and school buddies tried to ignore but ended up watching DeeDee tweeze out her boyfriend's chest hairs one by one. Waxing wasn't available at that time.

It took a while for the impact of the civil rights movement, the challenges of the 1968 Chicago Democratic Convention, the rise of abstract expressionism and other vanguard movements in art, and the growth of a mobile, media-based, Nielsen-rated society to emerge into the pluralistic era of Post Modernism and Deconstructionism, an era of cultural homogenization and reduced regional cultural differences. Clearly the social reforms that were being thought about in the 1960s, 1970s, and 1980s are now being implemented. As a result, the ethical and moral questions at the end of the twentieth century make certain images in art—traditional landscapes, portraits and still life paintings—seem at best retrograde and irrelevant. Outsider art, on the other hand, has gained value because of its idiosyncratic origins and eccentric forms, and because its sources seem to reaffirm the integrity of personal vision. The complexity of shifting customs suggests that traditional values, including the notion of personal accountability, may need to be reaffirmed. Basic social principles have been seriously altered by the speed of communication systems, by the predictability of "poll-tested language," and by the sound-bite superficiality of information conveyed through advanced technology. In my view, our basic cultural values have not been eroded by blasphemy or pornography or Christianity bashing as some would have us believe. Rather, we are adjusting to technologies and knowledge which are changing all aspects of our behavior patterns.

The sharp contrast between complex research in science and the public comprehension of this research has caused confusion and cultural paranoia. Personal differences and uniqueness have been diminished by the changes necessary to embrace the new information landscapes of global communication. Economic and political mutations of the past fifty years have also contributed to our cultural anxiety. The cultural and moral impact of technological evolution is vigorously debated today, but many of the solutions offered for problems which have arisen pose serious threats to our social and political structure. The debate surrounding the culture, image, and information wars has been fractious, acrimonious, and painful.

A major problem has emerged because those who would impose absolute order in the culture have mounted revisionist campaigns to suppress information especially about personal matters such as sex education, abortion, and the spread of sexually transmitted diseases. Sometimes called the thought police, their campaigns, programs, and draconian measures discriminate against large segments of society by limiting education, information, and economics. These authoritarians support repression that threatens to erode basic rights and privileges guaranteed by the Constitution. This tendency to regulate all transmission of information is profoundly dangerous to all of the freedoms of our society. The homogeneity and societal dilution that have resulted from corporate-based consumerism may be even more dangerous.

Groups which desire stricter limitations on society abhor pluralism, cultural diversity, and difference. They want to restore or impose elitist, parochial systems on an era already marked by awesome social, cultural, and scientific achievements which make such restrictions archaic and antiquated. Within the context of this retrograde pressure, it is easy—but nevertheless appalling—to realize that the U.S. Surgeon General could be fired because she dared to acknowledge that masturbation was safe sex and that the subject should be included in sex education curricula. The gag order that limited abortion information provided by federally funded health clinics was discriminatory, ridiculous, and frightening. That both Republican and Democratic administrations in Washington have succumbed to such hypocritical pressure is shocking.

Revisionists have established powerful agendas to implement their belief that stabilization of the society through authoritarian order is desirable at almost any cost to the democratic process. Radical moralists, seemingly with no other vision, are especially concerned with policing gender boundaries. Clearly, they say, we need to close the zippers and tighten the Bible belts. They concentrate on the singular notion that much if not all of civil and personal violence as well as other cultural disorders in society begin with uncontrolled exposure to the human body, especially those parts below the waist. They feel that solutions must come from strategies and paradigms of narrowly focused commitment to actions which they believe to be of traditional value.

On the other hand, those who want open, continuing, and progressive discussions of wedge issues are denigrated or politically discredited by the right wing. Attempts at discussion of hot button issues are met with charges of blasphemy, pornography, sickness, and sin. Gender identity, women's issues, almost any kind of sexual matter, abortion, reproduction rights, racial bias, and certain imagery in art have become taboo subjects. Pat Robertson continues to rant about what he identifies as "garbage, homosexuality, pornography, kiddie porn, and other offensive, blasphemous material against God, against Jesus, against the Pope . . . terrible stuff that doesn't need to be." He and others completely ignored the fact that Andres Serrano is a deeply religious person when they attacked "Piss Christ," which is his commentary on religious hierarchies and church politics. The evangelicals and others on the right turn a deaf ear to opinions other than their own and simply refuse to participate in the dialogue—as in the case of this conference.

As I've said, revisionists' arguments about the so-called wasting of society almost always migrate to the crotch, and the extremists' solution for social order clearly advocates intellectual and emotional chastity belts. They encourage suppression of any knowledge or action that would interfere with their concepts of social stabilization. They have established taboo subjects and lobby for limitations of support for all art forms, especially in literature, music, and the visual arts when "taboo subjects" are essential to the content of the art. It is unfortunate that people in the creative community—artists such as Jock Sturges and Sally Mann and those who publish their work—have been vilified and exploited by the right wing at great expense to both the artists and their advocates.

In the conservative program, community standards are frequently cited as guidelines for "decency" and as benchmarks for accountability. Even a recent Supreme Court decision endorses consideration of community standards of decency in determining grant support from the National Endowment for the Arts. The sole dissent to this decision was written by Justice Souter who held that "the 'decency' clause violates the First Amendment" and "fails to respect . . . diverse beliefs and values . . . of Americans." What are these community standards in the global society? What constitutional rights will be jeopardized by this decision when combined with similar actions in Congress? Will these judgments encourage even greater repression of free speech and of freely voiced opinions? I have heard speaker after speaker at this conference discuss the extent and influence of community standards that limit their work because of this legal restriction.

Advocates of repressive reforms have openly complained about the Bill of Rights as a nuisance. Some of these folks maintain an attitude of moral supremacy; at the same time, they exploit migrant workers and other low-income groups; and they appear to give tacit approval to unauthorized surveillance of our private lives.

As amazing as it seems, the American public has already acquiesced slowly—and perhaps innocently—to many of the systems which invade and erode our personal and private integrity. Some liberal programs to protect the individual have been corrupted and misused. Although the practice is against the law, we readily use Social Security numbers for identification, and, the concept of issuing identification numbers for health care, if implemented, will greatly increase the possibility of further invasion of personal and private freedoms. How many surveillance systems record our lives and transactions every day? How many metal detectors have we walked through this week? How much and what kind of personal information about our lives is immediately available at mail order switchboards as soon as our calls are answered? Nevertheless, the American people have become enamored of corporate structure and corporate wealth; we have embraced consumerism, corporate paternalism, and convenience. We have accepted corporate replacements for personal initiative and responsibility, and as I have suggested, this makes censorship possible on a grand scale . . . the most onerous, of course, being self-censorship by artists, curators, collectors, producers, or directors.

In 1990, an exhibition of my work was the subject of a major attack by the Christian Coalition of Florida. I was drawn into a process that I didn't understand when the artwork became a flashpoint in a significant fund-raising drive. The intention of my exhibition was twisted and distorted beyond belief. This attack included letter-writing campaigns with messages and copies of surreptitiously obtained (and out of context) photographs from my installations to all members of the Florida legislature, press releases to major wire services and nationally circulated newspapers, and a profile on *The 700 Club* that I learned about only after it had been broadcast.

Members of the Christian Coalition mailed an estimated 287,000 letters opposing my exhibition and asking for money to support their efforts to challenge work which they described as pornographic, blasphemous, Christianity-bashing, and unpatriotic. This campaign was reinforced by evangelical radio and television programs where charges against my work were restated over and over with inflammatory rhetoric. I was overwhelmed by the distortion of my ideas, and I felt helpless to defend the integrity of my work and my exhibition.

The symbols used in my work come from many cultures and civilizations, but today some groups, such as the Christian Coalition and the American Family Association, have tried to assume proprietary control over how some of these symbols may be used. Radical conservatives reject the idea that symbols can represent anything other than the meanings they proscribe.

In public lectures, when I was explaining the origins of the symbols and images in my installations, I was challenged by conservative representatives in the audience. The entire matter took on a life of its own and ran its course with little concern for the truth about my intentions and motivations. Wedge issues were imposed on the work, but my larger themes were ignored or denied. As an individual and unaffiliated artist, I had no elaborate public relations network to employ in my defense. It's ironic and frustrating that the themes of my exhibitions—the need to develop compassion and understanding for all groups in the society and man's inhumanity to mankind—would generate the distortions and hostility that they did.

An O. Henry closure to part of this conflict with the Florida Christian Coalition came last year when one of the three preachers who led the attack on my work, a loud and persistent man of the cloth, was convicted of hiring a hit man to kill his girlfriend's lover.

The conflict about my work in Orlando was one of several to erupt during the past eight years, but the challenges have accomplished several important things. Without that debate in 1990, I am certain that I wouldn't be at this conference today; without that debate, I am certain that I would not have thought so much about the value of personal freedoms and responsibilities as I have over recent years. Without that debate, I am certain that the content of my work would not be as explicit as it is today. Since that incident in 1990, I have come to understand that our differences are what make us wonderful. Since that time in 1990, I have come to profoundly understand that we are a very lucky people—we are free to challenge the status quo. We are free to challenge those who want to suppress our ideas, and, in fact, we have an obligation to do so. We are free to love the writings on the list prepared by my high school teacher Albert Key; and we can also enjoy the writings of Marquis de Sade, Jean Genet, Georges Bataille, Michele Foucault, William Boroughs, Marlon Riggs, Dennis Cooper, or Mike Kelly, if we wish. We are free to defend, support, and even celebrate the lives and works of Tom of Finland, Robert Mapplethorpe, Andres Serrano, Robert Flanagan, Tim Miller, Annie Sprinkle, or Karen Finley. And, if we choose, we can champion the careers and art of John Holmes, Al Parker, or Jeff Stryker and their colleagues. On the other hand, we are free to ignore or despise all of these things, but under no circumstances should we have the power to force others to accept what we like or to expect others to forfeit their ideas about what we might hold in disdain.

We are free to acknowledge and accept the systems, idioms, and images usually assigned to pornography as part of mainstream society, its culture, and its art. This assimilation happened in Europe long ago. In spite of threats from the political right and the moral extremists, segments of the public in this country are beginning to understand and accept these visual and verbal experiences as positive and life affirming. However, artists concerned with cutting edge genres are losing their performance and exhibition venues because of conservative influences on the arts during the past decade; exhibition space for certain art forms and content is virtually non-existent. Trustees and administrative directors of arts institutions fear the possible loss of financial support from sponsors and benefactors if their programs include controversial material. They are concerned about having to spend excessive time and energy and money to respond to charges from the right wing that ideas and concepts in exhibitions or performances are "offensive." We must, however, have the courage to resist these politics of guilt, intimidation, fear, and self-loathing. These politics cannot, they must not, prevail in a free society.

We must also understand that without sensuality and eroticism the entire society will lose its reason for being. Sensuality and eroticism must be celebrated as essential components of a rich and dynamic democratic form of life. We must be careful, however, not to allow expression of sensuality and eroticism to become predictable and mechanistic.

Without sensuality and eroticism there would be no art, no literature, no drama, no music, no architecture, no religion, even no family values, and no freedom of any significance. The presence of sensuality and eroticism has been an essential characteristic of all great cultures in the past. It's essential today, too.

We live in the most saturated image-based society of all time; given that fact, it is absolutely amazing that paintings, sculptures, photographs, architecture, literature, theatre, and other art forms still have the power to move the individual and the public to action—but that is possible only if these art forms can be discussed or seen or heard or lived with.

SECTION 7

A VIEW OF
FILM AND VIDEO
AS A GENRE

SEXUALLY THEMED PHOTOS BEGAN ALMOST WITH THE FIRST DEVELOPment of photography and similarly loops of erotic film appeared with the first projection machines. Now, the study of such films has become an academic specialty on some campuses. One of the major experts is Linda Williams, who is the author of *Hard Core: Power, Pleasure and the Frenzy of the Visible* (Berkeley: University of California Press, 1999). Her essay in this book, a reprint of the epilogue to that book, examines the elusive issue of what constitutes "Hard Core" pornography. Interestingly different stages of the development of moving-image pornography have produced different degrees and kind of "carnal" responses in the viewers. It might well be that pornography itself involves a process by which spectators themselves lean to vicarious experiences and then to enjoy different varieties of visual and visceral pleasures. This implies that pornography might not necessarily represent the original sexual predilection of the viewers.

One of the big shifts in pornography took place with the development and popularity of the VCR, which ultimately led to the demise of the pornographic movie houses. Jim Holliday, looking back at the films which were produced between the end of World War II and the 1980s, feels that the VCR also changed the nature of what was being produced. Three major areas–New York City, San Francisco, and Los Angeles–produced most of the films and each of these, he claims, had a different style and effect. He summarizes the New York productions as having more plot and grittier sex and what he rather sexistly calls "ugly chicks." San Francisco emphasized kinky sex, adequate story, and hippie looking women. Los Angeles for its part had "cuter" female actresses, playful and fluffier sex, and minimal plots. He lists and analyzes many of the films.

Another radical change taking place in the late 1980s was on which Jay

Kent Lorenz calls "gonzo" films. These were films featuring a male narrator-host who doubled as the videographer and was often involved in the video's sexual activity. Tracing its ancestry to documentary film, the narrative is often rudimentary dependent upon what the camera is able to capture on film. Often the camera is handheld. Several individuals, such as John Stagliano and Ed Powers, were important in the development of such films and Lorenz summarizes theirs and others contribution to the field. Peter Lehman goes further in examining in some detail the work of Powers. He feels Powers' brand of video porn (and gonzo porn in general) is somehow seen by its viewers as "real" making it different from the movies that preceded it, and in a sense harkening back to the audience response in the early days of film making.

28

A History of Modern Pornographic Film and Video

Jim Holliday

SINCE THE LATER HALF OF THE 1970S THE VCR HAS ENABLED MILLIONS of normal adults and closet perverts to enjoy "fuck films" in the privacy of their own homes. Slowly but surely pornography has become chic and/or hip once again. No longer must men and women depend on the virtually defunct adult theaters or the still surviving video peep show grind houses/combo strip joints to enjoy the brilliance and dreck found in cinematic intimacy. Somewhere in the United States, if you know where and how to look, you can find anything you want, legal or not.

Regard the following as a cocktail party bluffer's guide to porn history, to demonstrate that you can hang with anyone when it comes to understanding the times, the key trends, the major players (directors and stars), and the superior and significant movies of the first twenty-five years of explicit cinema. If other movies, facts or names that are alien to you slip into the conversation, dismiss them as not worthy of true greatness and smugly raise your nose to dismiss them and show your contempt in the haughtiest manner you can muster.

This chapter deals with "explicit films," my area of expertise. "Shot on video" features, or shit on video as many have termed them, is a whole different breed. Not better or worse in my opinion, just different. Any movie indicated with an asterisk (*) was included in the thirty landmark films presented at my film presentations at the World Pornography Conference. A small disclaimer is in order. At least three hundred worthy films have been omitted for reasons of space, and all movies discussed should be considered far superior to the run of the mill features of each era. You can read elsewhere about social significance and societal impact. I'm only concerned with historical accuracy.

GETTING THERE IS HALF THE FUN

David F. Friedman, former carnival dude and chairman of the Adult Film Association of America (and a guy I dubbed "the first citizen of the adult industry"), used to remark that five minutes after the motion picture camera was perfected there was probably a naked woman posing in front of same. Explicit loops, known as stag films, can be traced to the early 1900s and were still being produced as 8mm gems even into the 1970s. The birth of exploitation movies came in the 1930s and 1940s, playing in obscure theaters, usually ending with some guy who did the "square up"–the double talk explanation of legitimate content significance to satisfy the local law. The most famous exploitation film of all time was Kroeger Babb's *Mom and Dad.*

Post WWII, the 1950s waded into nudist colony territory and by the end of the decade "nudie cuties" were emerging from the underground into art houses. 1957 saw *Garden of Eden,* the first key nudist colony film, followed by Bambi Allen in *Daughter of the Sun* in 1959.

1959 was also the year of the big three soft core landmark features–Russ Meyer's *Immoral Mr. Teas,* Dave Friedman's *The Adventures of Lucky Pierre* and *Not Tonight, Henry* from Ted Paramore, the guy who would later become explicit producer Harold Lime.

Hard core had existed in the form of classic stags like *The Smart Aleck* with stripper Candy Barr, *The Nun* and the ancient *Grass Sandwich,* but in the late 1960s, film exhibitors grew bold enough to release features. The movies that first tested the new waters were the pseudo-documentaries, quasi-documentaries or in rare cases the real deal. Alex deRenzy's *Censorship in Denmark,* released in San Francisco paved the way for John Lamb's *Sexual Freedom in Denmark* in Los Angeles and Gerard Damiano's *Sex U.S.A.* and *(This Film Is) All About* in New York. SF, LA and NY quickly became the three major production centers for porno.

DeRenzy released *A History of the Blue Movie* and Bill Osco (of the Drug chain family) produced *Hollywood Blue,* both collections of classic stags. Matt Cimber, best known for being Mr. Jayne Mansfield, made *Man and Wife,* the first nationally distributed 35mm hard core feature. *Electro Sex '75,* made by 'Motorcycle' Mike Henderson, was the first advertised feature in the major New York papers over Labor Day of 1970.

THE EARLY DAYS OF
PUSHING THE ENVELOPE

In 1970 Bill Osco and Howard Ziehm collaborated on a feature called *Mona (The Virgin Nymph)*–* and history was made. This film had a full blown plot centering on Freida "Fifi" Watson's fixation on oral sex. There were no external "cum" shots because such things had not been invented by producers or the audiences. The reason for heavy doses of oral sex, and later anal sex, is simple. The filmmakers gave the audience what they couldn't get at home. The early pornographers had a great theatrical tag line: "For those who never knew . . . and those who can only remember."

I will cop to the fact that female porn viewers are growing in numbers but not to the extent some claim. And I will stick to the death to this original sound bite: "Porn is, was and always will be primarily the province of the lonely guy." Although I consider myself far removed from the raincoat crowd, I firmly believe the purpose of explicit cinema is to get the viewer off.

The President's Commission on Obscenity and Pornography concluded that pornography was not harmful to society in 1970. The group was appointed by L.B.J. and reached its conclusion when Tricky Dick was in the White House. Funny what would happen a mere fifteen years later.

Much of the early days were spent determining the new boundaries and pushing the envelope to see when problems would arise.

An Act of Confession (made in 1972 by Anthony Spinelli under the name Sybil Kidd) featured a Christlike character getting head. Self censorship by theater owners and distributors came into play. Movies like *The Taking of Christina* featured violent rapes and murders.

(Angela) The Fireworks Woman had just about everything, including a nun's rape, a fish used as a dildo, urination, fisting, a nude six-year-old kid walking the beach, etc. It played theatrically at the time, but has been cut to shreds ever since. The legitimate adult industry has *never* dealt with children or animals, although the pinheads in the mainstream media want to believe otherwise.

In 1971, *School Girl* was a San Francisco hit and having actresses of legal age play Lolita-types soon became another element for industry self censorship. *Hot Circuit*, same year, same city, was the first movie to introduce the La Ronde concept to porn.

Fist fucking scenes were the rage through the 1970s until distributors deleted them from the tapes to avoid prosecution. Some of the classic fister movies included *Love Bus, Story of Eloise, Anyone But My Husband, Candy Stripers (2), Little Orphan Dusty (2), Ms. Magnificent, Taxi Girls, Heavenly Desire, Her Name Was Lisa,* Damiano's *Fantasy, Tropic of Desire, 800 Fantasy Lane, Tigresses,* and the Marilyn Chambers short *Never a Tender Moment.* All were from the 1970s. In the 1980s, *Desire for Men, Platinum Paradise, Neon Nights, Peepholes,* and *Satisfiers of Alpha Blue* contained fisters that were cut after the "Mi-Porn" investigations of 1980.

Like 1959 was for soft core, so was 1972 for explicit cinema. Three landmark movies emerged.

Deep Throat–*, made by Gerard Damiano on a shoestring, starred Harry Reems, loop star Dolly Sharp and the infamous Linda Lovelace, whose subsequent accounts differ from all others involved with her porn appearances. The movie became the "porno chic" darling of mainstream New York pinhead critics who obviously went ga-ga over a routine, one-joke film. The one positive was in public acceptance of the new explicit visuals being presented on screen.

Worthy of far more praise was Damiano's *Devil in Miss Jones–**, made at the end of the year and released in early 1973. It still ranks as one of the first and the best serious film of its time.

Georgina Spelvin's performance as a spinster suicide is classic, and the film introduced the "one of every type" sex scene approach to the audience. Realistic story and hot sex.

The west coast entry was The Mitchell Brothers *Behind the Green Door*–*, based on the legendary short story, shot in San Francisco and starring former Ivory Snow model Marilyn Chambers. Her amazing sexual appetite and enthusiasm made the film one of the top sellers ever and the first to reach many sales levels. Former boxer Johnny Keyes demonstrated that pornwatchers must prepare themselves for interracial sexual encounters at this early developmental stage. *Teenage Fantasies* and *Teenage Sex Kitten*, both starring former soft core princess Rene Bond were the 1972 Los Angeles contributions.

Over the years, viewers have pretty much summed up the differences of the three locations.

New York–ugly chicks, gritty sex, more plot . . . San Francisco–decent looking hippie chicks who love to fuck, kinky sex, adequate story . . . Los Angeles–cute tan blondes, fun and fluff sex, minimal plot if any. Generalizations and stereotypes are always dangerous, and there are tons of exceptions from each locale, but damned if the fans didn't seem to get it early on.

In 1973 *Wet Rainbow* and *Resurrection of Eve* were produced, both very realistic dramatic stories with solid sex, but more and more pure sex grinders were appearing on the market to exploit the new found audience. Perhaps the first consciousness level raising comedy was made in 1974 by soft core genius Radley Metzger, under the name Henry Paris. *The Private Afternoons of Pamela Mann*–* was a breed apart–in script, in style, in editing, in overall enjoyment. Barbara Bourbon (rape victim in A DIRTY WESTERN a year later) and Marc Stevens provided the true "deep throat" scene the fans were waiting for and the "can you top this" fever was born. Every step, every trend spawns imitators till someone reached the point of overkill. Sweden's *Young Butterflies* with Maria Forsa and *High School Fantasies* were the other landmark efforts and, amidst the continued envelope pushing, a new level had been reached.

THE GOLDEN AGE

In the late 1980s, a publisher asked me to determine the so-called Golden Age of Adult Cinema. At that time my assessment was 1976 to 1981. Since then, with over a decade to reflect, I have now expanded the period to include 1975 through 1983. During this nine year period over 70 percent of the best films ever made were produced. The average high end budget for that era was seventy five to one hundred thousand dollars and a couple of dozen features actually reached the quarter of a million dollar mark. Shooting schedules were from six days to three weeks. In today's marketplace, budgets and shooting schedules would be considered absurd by virtually all video porn producers.

In 1975, Howard Ziehm pieced together some of his hottest loops with newly shot wrap around footage set at a fictitious magazine to create *Honey-pie–*, the hottest loop-carrier ever made.

In addition to proven starlets Serena and Sharon Thorpe, the film introduced cult legend Jennifer Welles and featured both a double penetration and a sandwich scene with Terri Hall, one of the legendary early east coast stars.

That same year on the west coast, Robert McCallum made his explicit film debut with *3AM–*. Starring Georgina Spelvin and Clair Dia, this one ranks as one of the most carefully crafted realistic porn films of all time. It could easily be a television show about a family in turmoil that happened to contain explicit sex. Rarely are characters developed as fully as those in *3AM.*

Radley Metzger's contribution to excellence in 1975 was *Naked Came the Stranger*, the funniest of his handful of classics. Also released that year was *The Punishment of Anne* (also known as *The Image* or *L'Image*), a film shot in France that barely qualifies, since it contains only three actual hard core oral scenes. The movie did introduce Rebecca Brooke (Mary Mendum to *Playboy* readers), one of the true beauties to grace the porn screen. *Passions of Carol* was the Charles Dickens "A Christmas Carol" take-off that still holds up to this day. Lasse Braun, pseudonym of Italian director Alberto Ferro, released the French classic *Sensations*, which I have always ranked as one of the five best foreign films ever made. It starred American Bridgette Maier and proved that when it comes to the trouser mouse factor, Braun was the Alex deRenzy of Europe. Gerard Damiano's *Story of Joanna* rates as a must own item for fans of kinky sex from the world of S&M and B&D. Jamie Gillis provides one of the ten greatest acting performances of all time and Terri Hall gained status as an actress as well as superb sexual artist.

The Opening of Misty Beethoven– was released in 1976 and is arguably the finest all around fuck flick ever made. Every other year, I screen this just to make sure that it stands up, both sexually and cinematically. Radley Metzger's masterpiece, made under the Paris pseudonym, stars Jamie Gillis and Gloria Leonard. They are great, but one shot wonder Jaqueline Beudant and Constance Money (film debut for the girl you know as Susan Jensen in *Playboy*) steal the show. There are movies to top it in certain areas, but none as totally polished and sophisticated.

The other three great films of that year are difficult to impossible to track down. Alex deRenzy's masterpiece *Femmes de Sade* has been off the market for several years due to content (rape, violence, a simulated shit scene, heavy B&D, etc.). Many consumers fail to realize that video manufacturers are not going to risk lawyer's fees, fines and possible jail time just so that they can get their jollies. *Felicia* and *Kinky Ladies of Bourbon Street* are both French films and extremely difficult to find, since the distributor now has the masters in a vault in New York city. The former featured Mary Mendum doing explicit sex and the latter found American expatriate Dawn Cummings and three gorgeous French stars in a hot sex/bummer ending winner.

Cry for Cindy was made by the folks at *Hustler* magazine and starred their centerfold Amber Hunt. Anthony Spinelli made the movie under a female pseudonym. More proof that hot sex, plot and production values can be found in an era when some say it never existed.

Not to be outmagazined, *Playboy* centerfold Kristine DeBell starred as the title character in *Alice in Wonderland*, a Bill Osco, Bud Townsend collaboration. This is the porn version of the Lewis Carroll classic and while not as scorchingly hot as the typical grinders of the day, it will more than pass muster with male audiences. Hollywood character actors can be found sprinkled among the non sex performers.

Autobiography of a Flea was the Mitchell Brothers entry for 1976, with John Holmes and Jean Jennings starring in another of the early films made by a woman—in this case Sharon McKnight. Ann Perry, Sandra Winters and Roberta Findlay may have predated Ms. McKnight, but this was the first female directed box office blockbuster.

1977 provided five great films, starting with the Harold Lime/Ramsey Karson production, *Desires within Young Girls*—*, one of the first of the multiple babes classics. This one featured Annette Haven, Clair Dia, Joan Devlon, Bonnie Holiday and Stacy Evans as the cupcakes and Georgina Spelvin as the grand dame. Annette Haven also starred in Radley Metzger's *Barbara Broadcast*—*, the slickest and best shot of his films, one of the first pornos to take place in a restaurant.

Eruption—* took 3 weeks to shoot in Hawaii and was the porn version of 1944's *Double Indemnity*, with John Holmes and Lesllie (*sic*) Bovee as Fred and Barbara. That would be MacMurray and Stanwyck, not their character names. If you question Ms. Bovee's induction to the adult hall of fame or her ranking as one of the Top 50 Adult Stars of all time, just check this puppy out.

Baby Face—* is currently off the market due to content, a condition that shows how daring Alex deRenzy was when it came to pushing the envelope. Underage female characters may be acceptable for Hollywood and *Lolita*, but not for fuck films at present. *Mary! Mary!* starred Constance Money and John Leslie and many of the classic unsung San Francisco female sirens of the era, and it rates among the slickest of the decade. *Inside Jennifer Welles* was the first major porno to profile a major female, relying on her star power to draw fans to the box office. Later, Evart Productions and Eric Andersson would perfect the formula.

Virtually anyone worth half a shit would rank 1978 as the premier year for classic American porn film release. More great movies and great selling movies (meaning that the porn public loved them) came out in 1978 than any other. For starters there was Bob Chinn's *Candy Stripers*—*, the definitive nurse/patient/hospital flick. The current version on the market deletes the two classic fist fuck scenes, one with Amber Hunt and the other being a double fister into cute little Nancy Hoffman. Throw in cult stars like Cris Cassidy, Sharon Thorpe, Eileen Wells, Phaedra Grant, Mimi Morgan and

Lauren Black for starters, and you get a glimpse as to why I consider Bob Chinn my movie making mentor. Give the predominantly male audience the really hot ladies they want to see, not just the big stars who lay there like potato sacks, even if the fans don't know their names.

Anna Obsessed was the first and only explicit on screen lesbian pairing of Annette Haven and Constance Money. Add John Leslie and a rape/psychological thriller plot and a couple of newcomers movie boys made themselves a cult classic. *Easy-** was an Anthony Spinelli triumph that introduced Jesie St. James to the screen in a sexual performance that could easily be called the hottest single female deal ever. Far from a classic beauty, Jesie was just plain erotic, as evidenced by the lesbian scene with Georgina Spelvin. For those who appreciate the so-called "couples" films, this is one of the first and best. Susannah French rivaled Jesie's heat as the title character in Sam Norvell's *The Other Side of Julie-**. The scene with John Leslie and one shot wonder Jackie O'Neill ranks among the three steamiest, stickiest all timers.

Anthony Spinelli also directed *Sex World-**, regarded by many as his masterpiece. A huge all star cast combining for one superbly erotic scene after another places this futuristic flick into most expert's Top 20. Alex deRenzy introduced dizzy Desiree Cousteau, she of the gravity defying tits, in *Pretty Peaches*, another classic now off the market. Her character thinks every sexual encounter is a rape. Even though a moron could get the comedy, law enforcement types apparently don't.

Little Girls Blue is an interesting study. Typical school girls in outfits fluff, but now under prohibitive video release. This film and *Expensive Tastes*, a film about raping for kicks, are among the current no-nos and among the most controversial ever made, yet both were made by Joanna Williams, a woman who currently directs mainstream episodic television shows. Points out the hypocrisy about porn's ability to use the first amendment. Feminist sob sister porn bashers have to live with the fact that a woman made two of their all time "worst violation" movies.

Take Off-*, made by Armand Weston of Hollywood movies, is arguably the second best adult film ever made. Slicker than owl shit and more sophisticated than all but a few, the only flaw is lack of relentlessly sustaining eroticism. It's still hot enough, just not raunchy enough for many. *V-The Hot One* has Annette Haven as the lead in a Robert McCallum movie that delivers plenty of plot with the spicy sex he shot during the late 1970s and early 1980s.

1978 was the year of a national porn phenomenon, Jim Clark's *Debbie Does Dallas- **starring Bambi Woods. The film is not all that bad, but it is far from superior, yet no film other than *Deep Throat* is better known for never having been watched. The title has become mainstream synonymous as porn reference Americana. The Cowboy Cheerleader box cover made it one of the top five sellers and most people are still unaware that the girls never got within 2000 miles of Dallas.

In addition to all the landmark entries, 1978 also produced such classics as *Gail Palmer's Erotic Adventures of Candy*, a Terry Southern rip starring cult queen Carol Connors and John Holmes; *Fiona on Fire*, the Gene Tierney

Laura of porn; Wesley Emerson's *The Health Spa* with Abigail Clayton; Gerard Damiano's *Skin Flicks*; Ramsey Karson's loop masterpiece *Untamed*; Bob Chinn's *China Cat* (one of the best Johnny Wadd movies); Radley Metzger's kinky *Maraschino Cherry* and the film voted by the industry as best of the year was *Legend of Lady Blue*, made by A. Fabritzi. In real life he was the late Jesse Pearson, the guy who played Conrad Birdie in the Hollywood film *Bye Bye Birdie*. Throw in another three dozen movies and clearly no single year in porno history offered as much creativity or diversity as 1978.

The Ecstasy Girls– was the first major collaboration between producer Harold Lime and director Robert McCallum and this 1979 film still ranks among the all time top ten. Pure fun and fluff, with an all star female cast, a wacky comedy plot and the steamy sex necessary to qualify as a step beyond superior.

On the east coast, Richard Mahler delivered the first of his dark side epics, *Her Name Was Lisa*. Please regard this, along with Mahler's *Midnight Heat* (1982) and *Corruption* (1983), as among the finest serious fuck films to hit the road running. Samantha Fox and Vanessa Del Rio star in a story of junkie hell. The contrast between west coast fluff and New York grit has never been clearer.

Sensational Janine is Austrian (not German) in origin and features the erotic charms of Patricia Rhomberg. Rank her as one of the all-time one shot wonders (at least in America) and rank the film among the handful of best foreign entries. Speaking of cult stars, Nancy Suiter's biggest box office hit was *Taxi Girls*, which became even more notorious for the lawsuit filed over the Cheryl Ladd look alike ad campaign. Nancy rates as perhaps the single most adored cult female, of those appearing in less than ten flicks.

Henri Pachard made *Babylon Pink–* in 1979, the first of his long string of superlative films and to this day, *Pink* remains the prototype for vignette porn movies. There is a difference between vignette films and loop-carriers.

In the adult world, comebacks are usually much over hyped and bally-hooed, but turn out to be ultimate disappointments and wastes of time. Babes always fail to realize that they have to cash in while they can. 1980's *Insatiable–* was a glaring exception to that rule. The advance video sales have still not been equaled, tons of publicity and a year of hyping the return of Marilyn Chambers to feature films, her first ever coupling with John C. Holmes (anal at that), etc. This Godfrey Daniels classic turned out to be one of the best ever; fast paced, breezy and hot. Most rate the pool table number with David Morris among the ten most memorable scenes.

Equally brilliant was Anthony Spinelli's *Talk Dirty to Me–*. He and others prefers the sequel, but few can match this jewel for wit, spark and wall-to-wall heat. Passion and prolonged eroticism is enhanced by the dirty talking–an element missing from much of the video dreck found today. John Leslie and Jesie St. James bring comparisons to the Hollywood romantic couplings of the Capra, Lubitsch and Preston Sturges years.

European star Bridgette Lahaye made *Education of the Baroness* on of the five hottest French films and the most erotically kinky bondage effort from overseas. Wesley Emerson's *Exposed* featured John Leslie and Sharon Kane as newlyweds, with John trying to hide his porn star past from her. Oft used premise, perfectly executed here by first time director Jeff Fairbanks. Billy Thornberg (the late Chris Warfield) provided high classed heat with the stylish *Champagne for Breakfast* with (John) Leslie and Lesllie (Bovee). Her double L first name was indicative of the flower power era. Another Bay Area cult classic featured Desiree Cousteau as *Randy (The Electric Lady)*.

On the east coast, Cecil Howard and Henri Pachard continued charting winners. Howard with *Platinum Paradise*, a candidate for best vignette movie ever, and Pachard with *The Budding of Brie*. The husband/wife team of David I. Frazer and Svetlana created multiple babe epics with "F" (a.k.a. *The Dream Girls of F*, *Dream Girl* [singular] or *Cannonball*) and *Sex Boat*. Gosh, guess what Hollywood premise the latter came from? Both films featured a bevy of sun drenched California beach honeys. *Inside Seka* was only natural, from director Eric Andersson, the "all about" movie with the newest platinum bombshell to hit porn.

Kirdy Stevens made the first of his infamous *Taboo* films, with Kay Parker as mom and Mike Ranger as son in this daring, ground breaking movie that was more believable than expected.

By the time the decade was over, Stevens and others had rung the double digit bell on sequels to this landmark monster seller. In my opinion 1980 was the second best year for great porn cinema.

The year 1981 saw a wide variety of great films, beginning with the Rinse Dream's bizarre *Nightdreams*, one of those rare movies that dared to break new ground. It must be scene to be believed, and the reason it is so much hotter than the *Cafe Flesh* follow-up is that Dorothy LeMay gave the performance of her career. A mainstream film book referred to Rinse Dream and Abe Snake as the hippest porn pseudonyms. For good reason, since Dream is known as Steven Sayadian in Hollywood (*Dr. Caligari*) and Snake is none other than horrormeister Wes Craven, despite what you may read elsewhere.

*Bad Girls–** was Svetlana's landmark "brand new fresh babes" epic, *Outlaw Ladies* was a sizzling and often seamy vignette film from Henri Pachard, Robert McCallum's *Amanda By Night–** rates as a top three porn mystery suspense classic, showcases the acting talents of Veronica Hart, R. (for Robert not Richard) Bolla, Samantha Fox, Jamie Gillis and the whole cast, and Philip Drexler's *A Scent of Heather* ventured into modern Victorian romance. *The Dancers–** was Anthony Spinelli's ultimate road stud/guys on the road/male bonding striptease switcheroo.

Perhaps the best of all was director Spinelli's sequel to *Talk Dirty to Me–**, made for another film company than the original. Called *Nothing to Hide–** and featuring John Leslie and Richard Pacheco reprising their Jack and Lenny roles, it was a much better overall movie than the producer's sequel the following year–*Talk Dirty to Me Part 2*. Raincoaters, however, would prefer Bridgette Monet in the latter. Leslie was the lead but Blair Harris replaced Pacheco.

Back then it was only a hunch, but now from a distance it can be clearly pointed out that 1982 marked the beginning of a downward spiral trend in terms of number of great productions being produced each year. Clearly a peak had been reached and there would be no looking back to the previous level of excellence throughout the industry. Bill Eagle's *All American Girls* proved that the fresh faced all star female laden bonanza would sell, *Cafe Flesh–** proved to be the best adult film ever made that is not the least bit erotic. Two superbly constructed and acted movies, *Irresistible* and *In Love*, lacked the raunch found in earlier classics.

The final year of the Golden Age fought the good fight, with *Devil in Miss Jones II* taking Damiano's serious classic and updating it into an hilarious Henri Pachard sex comedy. Gerard Damiano made the splendid *Night Hunger*, shot in three different styles, B&W, Sepia and Color. Anthony Spinelli's *Dixie Ray Hollywood Star* is heaven for pot boiler fans.

Henri Pachard's other outstanding film that year was *Sexcapades*. The next Marilyn Chambers vehicle was Godfrey Daniels' *Up 'n' Coming*, allowing Marilyn to use her vocal chords in a tale about a country singer.

Two west coast standouts top off 1983. Bob Chinn's *The Young Like It Hot* (credited at the time to Gail Palmer) introduced future hall-of-famers Hyapatia Lee and the late Shauna Grant.

Robert McCallum's *Suzie Superstar* provided all the proof needed to show that Shauna Grant, had she not committed suicide, would have rivaled Ginger Lynn as the all time "girl-next-door" type. The film demonstrated his superiority over the fun and fluff (but still raunchy) genre. It's a hell of a good film as well, with one of the outstanding musical scores ever.

THE DEATH OF THEATERS, THE VIDEO BOOM, GLUT CITY & GONZO

Clearly the heyday of great porn was passing, due in large part to the dwindling number of adult theaters and the growing number of in-home VCRs. From an all time high of nearly one thousand theaters were closing down, transitioning back to peep show houses or being zoned out. The video boom begun in the late 1970s was catching on. Adult pioneered the turf and paved the way for mainstream Hollywood studios to release features on tape, and anyone denying that fact is writing revisionist history to suit his or her agenda.

In 1985 The Meese Commission arrived at their predetermined outcome that porn was harmful, despite the academic and research testimony to the contrary. I had the opportunity to testify but passed. Why aid a witchhunt? Could some of you help me with one piece of research? Which group of people contains more convicted same sex pedophiles? Members of the Meese Commission, Televangelists or the Porno Directors I've known for over twenty years? In this case, two out of three is bad and the good guys are the hunted.

In 1985, according to Paul Fishbein, publisher of *Adult Video News*, the leading porn trade magazine, the number of films and the number of shot-on-video productions most closely approximated a 50/50 split. By 1986 video had taken oven the numbers game and would never be challenged again, yet alone relinquish the widening numerical advantage.

For the purposes of the World Pornography Conference, only five films were selected after the Golden Age and only one from the 1990s. Part of it involves using that historian's pretend theory that you need time to properly assess more recent material. Mostly, it's just that the recent movies don't hold up as well as the classics, despite what magazines trying to hype and shill the new films may tell you.

In 1984, Edwin Durell and Sandra Winters, who'd been making movies since 1974's *China Girl,* nailed their masterpiece down with *Every Woman Has a Fantasy–*. John Leslie and Rachel Ashley swept the awards and the film deserves status among the ten best ever. Unfortunately, an underage Kristara Barrington has resulted in a recut, so the original has lost its impact.

Cecil Howard's crowning achievement also came in 1984 with *Firestorm,* an epic erotic flick with Joanna Storm and Eric Edwards. Gregory Dark made his directorial debut that same year with *New Wave Hookers–*, the first film to explore and satisfactorily stake out wacky new ground since *Nightdreams.* The film established Ginger Lynn as the then current queen of adult cinema. The following year Dark followed up with a third interpretation of *Devil in Miss Jones 3–The New Beginning,* featuring an outrageous approach to fuck films aimed at the heart of Generation X.

The final entry comes from 1992, *The Chameleons–Not the Sequel.* This is John Leslie's film debut as a director using a premise he first developed on video. Ashlyn Gere, Diedre Holland and the Italian actor Rocco Siffredi prove that talented sexual actors can still be found. Now that some best selling titles have been shot on film some times and on video other times, it signals all too clearly the lack of care and concern for projects compared to the best return for the budget dollar.

The glut of product on the market could be signaling the beginning of the end. Less than 1 percent of new releases are shot on film. Shot on video and harder edged sex scenes are another matter. I would agree that video allows for more graphic pictures and is certainly the choice for members of the so-called raincoat brigade. Heat wise, the sex is both hotter and raunchier. Shot on video is a whole different area from landmark films. But all of these gonzo geniuses who think they've invented something revolutionary are merely returning to the loop shooting days of twenty years ago, linking unconnected, unrelated sex into something they pass off as a plotless feature.

What is the future of porn and where is it headed is one of the three most asked questions I've ever gotten from fans. Up until the 1990s I always had an answer. I no longer do, other than an educated guess. Anyone with $10,000 and a cheapo video camera is now a director and a distributor, competing with the majors for shelf space in video stores. No longer do people care for quality, but rather price breaks and pretty box covers. Perhaps they can no longer judge good porn from bad. Only time will tell whether this is a video boom or a disaster.

29

Going Gonzo!:
The American Flaneur,
the Eastern European On/Scene,
and the Pleasures of Implausibility

Jay Kent Lorenz

The documentary film movement was from the beginning an adventure in public observation.

–John Grierson

Baudelaire goes to the marketplace as a flaneur, supposedly to take a look at it, but in reality to find a buyer.

–Walter Benjamin

DESPITE THE ACADEMIC TURN TO THE BRACKETING, IF NOT THE OUTright discrediting, of "experience," I begin this overview of the gonzo phenomenon with a somewhat lurid confession: the first time that I crossed the border into hardcore was also the first time that I knowingly broke the law. It was the early 1980s, and the end of the *Boogie Nights* era. My girlfriend and I thought it would be a bit of a lark to take in an X-rated movie at Milwaukee's infamous Pussycat Theater. I being the minor, she purchased the tickets. The two most vivid particulars that I recollect about our excursion are seeing a performer named Veronica Hart–it seemed wonderful to me that this "girl next door" seemingly enjoyed sex, especially as I was literally dating the girl from next door–and the young woman and myself being too excited to observe proper rules of decorum. A partially cracked Trans Am window assisted in turning what had been intended as a private act into an unwitting public display. That night was the first and only time that I have been arrested; however, my memory of the experience retains an aura of innocence.

Despite the sensory overload of that evening, I did manage to note a few other features about that Veronica Hart film. One aspect, a formal element that I found quite baffling at the time, was what I would later recognize as a generic convention: the money shot. On the surface, the money shot, or the visual display of the male orgasm, is easily read as the porno-graphic film or video's overinvestment in realism. I do not wish to interro-gate this ritual of visual hardcore today, but Linda Williams has written per-suasively of the jarring displacement and fetishism that is occurring in a (het-erosexual) genre dedicated to discovering the "truth" of women's pleasures.[1] And yet if the Veronica Hart film wished to convince us that we were indeed watching the real thing, in all elements, including the sexual, the movie seemed quite removed, insurmountably distant. The huge screen that we viewed the film on certainly created a border, but the glossy, well-produced tale of single women making it (and making it) in Manhattan—Burt Reynolds's Jack Horner was definitely not directing—erected another bar-rier: we were excluded by virtue of the film's structure as a seamless, closed narrative in which we played our roles as ideal, unacknowledged voyeurs.

The overwhelming instance of this brand of narrative model, a model riffed from classical Hollywood cinema, is what typifies the feature-length hardcore of the 1970s and the 1980s. A conventional storyline consisting of rising action, climax (pun intended), and denouement, all punctuated by spectacular "numbers," was essential for a genre born in the early 1970s, a genre aiming for a "porno chic" legitimacy partly through appropriation of existing, respected frameworks.[2] This bid for approbation not only upheld the filmic fourth wall, but also pillaged the plots and the iconography of estab-lished Hollywood genres, oddly enough from the western to, and more often and more appropriately, the detective film, in the quest for boxoffice dollars.

But genres, and moving image porn is no exception, are never stable and always subject to extinction, morphing, rebirth. Their survival depends on technological innovations, the socioeconomic conditions of production, and the shifting cultural terrain that regulates what the consumer is willing (or legally able) to purchase at a given moment. In this paper I wish to dis-cuss a relatively new, very commercially viable pornographic genre, or sub-genre, if you will, that eschews narrative in favor of spectacle, that abandons a constructed pornotopia in pursuit of an ostensibly "real" erotic city, and that dispenses with characterization, instead often favoring an investigatory format to arrive at the "truth" of female pleasures. I propose an elaboration on the phenomenon of gonzo, a look at the genre's mid to late-nineteenth-century antecedents—the figure of the flaneur and the conventions of early cinema—and the possibility that gonzo may be depicting some epistemolog-ical slippage, namely the erosion of the once secure border distinctions between the private and the public spheres.

Just what exactly is gonzo? Well, it's an adult video that *appears* docu-mentary in nature, that features a male narrator-cum-host who usually dou-bles as the videographer and is often involved in the video's sexual activity. This narrator/host—whether he is John "Buttman" Stagliano, Ed Powers, Gre-gory Dark, or Max Hardcore—begins either by asking women questions about their sexuality—employing a standard talking-head interview format with min-imal editing—or by stumbling upon unusually gregarious women while he is engaged in a leisure activity, usually that of sightseeing. If the gonzo video unwinds in the talking-head style, as in the several video series' created by Ed Powers, then, after the Q&A session, the interviewee is shown in a sexual scenario, presumably enhanced by what she has revealed on the audio. If the gonzo is more along the lines of the exotic travelogue, which is my focus in this paper, then a wildly implausible setpiece ensues in which the pursued woman is more than happy to engage in sex with a stranger. Most germane for both of these gonzo subsets is the attempt to break the border of the video monitor: the presence of the point-of-view camera is directly acknowledged by all of the participants. And, in tandem with a genre film, each release is the same but different. For example, it's another "Buttman" movie, but this time the sights (predominately female) are in Barcelona rather than in Budapest.

What are the origins of pornographic gonzo? As with any genealogy, foundations are slippery but it appears that Jamie Gillis started experimenting with the docuform around 1989, toting his camera around southern California for a series entitled *On the Prowl.* Around the same time, Powers was popularizing the sit-down interview strand with *Bus Stop Tales,* while Stagliano's peripatetic alter ego, Buttman, began wandering the globe about a year later. An adult industry trade publication, without making any direct link between Hunter Thompson's brand of gonzo journalism and guerrilla filmmaking, reputedly coined the term "Gonzo" in an effort to label the emerging genre of direct-address docuporn. But according to Jeff Marton of Stagliano's Evil Angel Productions, no one set out to create a genre; they never do. Partially as a response to economic conditions—it is fiscally dangerous attempting to create a big-budget adult release in the Hollywood tradition, especially with an average of 650 X-rated video titles saturating the market each month. And the portability of videocameras, Marton says that the company decided to experiment with something along the lines of the ironic docudrama that had surfaced on the big screen in Errol Morris's *The Thin Blue Line* and was beginning to appear on television. Stagliano cites no influences and contends that he was searching for a visual style which would render porn more up-close, more virtual. But while the then-burgeoning docudrama may be a possible influence, conscious or not, I am more fascinated with the prototype of Buttman and company, the mid-nineteenth-century flaneur as described by poet and critic Charles Baudelaire. Similarly, I am intrigued by gonzo's affinities with early cinema, its links to a late-nineteenth-century moving-picture show that offered, as film scholar Tom Gunning notes, a steady stream of startling sensations.[3]

While it initially may appear to be a bit of a leap locating the etiology of the gonzo narrator in the figure of the European flaneur, circa 1850, the two are bound by gender, the power of the gaze, and the imperative to record that which the eye encounters. As Baudelaire, fittingly in his role as cultural observer, defined the flaneur—from the verb flanerie, meaning to stroll, to walk, to saunter—he, and the flaneur of mid-nineteenth-century Paris was most definitely male, was an appreciative spectator. He was a member of the upper or expanding middle classes who possessed the luxury of leisure and the desire to bear witness, the first of his kind. The flaneur made his way through the delights of the Parisian cityscape with the intoxication of a gleeful tourist. This man surveying and reporting upon the urban panorama was no mere voyeur but, as Baudelaire insists in his classic essay of 1859, "The Painter of Modern Life," an impassioned observer:

> He marvels at the eternal beauty and the amazing harmony of life in the capital cities. . . . He gazes upon the landscape of the great city. . . . He delights in fine carriages and proud horses, the dazzling smartness of the grooms . . . the sinuous gate of the women . . . in a word, he delights in universal life.[4]

In relation to the above passage, the most obvious difference between Buttman and his compatriots is the market imperative to wrack focus on the sinuous female flesh, all else is relegated to exotic local color and functions more often as prelude to sexual congress.

In a 1997 gonzo release directed by one Lee Nover, perhaps a cousin of the ubiquitous Ben,[5] the filmmaker/narrator does indeed function as Baudelaire's impassioned observer, as he first takes us on a virtual tour of some of London's most popular tourist attractions. We are shown the tower where Joel McCrea struggled with an enemy secret agent in Hitchcock's classic tale of intrigue, *Foreign Correspondent.* We then get a view and some history surrounding Big Ben, followed by a brief glimpse of the Thames. When we arrive in front of Buckingham Palace, Lee and his cameraman spot a buxom blonde behind the palace gates. As she departs what could only have been a tourist excursion, Lee introduces himself to her, admiring her beauty and dress. But in the geoporn "documentary," introductions and small talk are quickly dispensed with. Soon, we are at the blonde's flat, witnessing, along with Lee and his trusty camera operator, the woman's sexual congress with a purported boyfriend. The travelogue has morphed into a tour of bodies in pleasure.

To digress briefly, in a marvelous 1844 lithograph from a series by Ignace Isidore Gerard Grandville, "The Flaneur of the Universe," a tiny dandy, complete with top hat and walking stick, strolls across a vast iron bridge supported by several planets, anticipating the vast spaces for perusal in the late twentieth century. If the flaneur of the midnineteenth century was restricted to playing the role of observer-essayist in the urban environment of Paris, of perhaps any other cosmopolitan European city, such as the London that Lee Nover encounters at a later stage of modernity, then the gonzo filmmaker possesses the world as his oyster. Though not yet capable of interplanetary flanerie, unlike the little figure in Grandville's lithograph, this new incarnation of the impassioned observer records sexual sights and sounds on a global scale. Once forbidden territory, such as the former Soviet Bloc nations, is even available for tourism. As such, and because the figure of the flaneur is so tightly bound, courtesy of Walter Benjamin among others, to a specific place and time, it is prudent to confer a title upon our gonzo filmmaker other than flaneur. Let us refer to him then as a spectator-recorder, observing and preserving the sexual through a cyborgian vision that unmoors him from the triangular geographic of Chatsworth, Van Nuys, and Sherman Oaks, California.

When touring the diverse territories available to the gonzo spectator-recorder, we note that our host is not haughty and removed, never merely a passive voyeur–criticisms later leveled at Baudelaire's concept of the flaneur–but possesses an intense sense of wonder, aided by a frenzied, mobile, POV camera keeping the mostly female sight in a constant state of flux. While the gonzo filmmaker is guilty of the flaneur's penchant for hedonism, for aesthetic excess, the two also share a salutary dose of the wry, the ironic. Perhaps these playful qualities, so detectable in Baudelaire's celebratory essay, have allowed numerous scholars to dismiss the flaneur as a silly fop, an impotent Beau Brummel. Sociologist Chris Jenks locates the source for such hostilities in the flaneur's inability to be pinned down.[6] It is in their constant movement that Baudelaire's flaneur and the gonzo spectator-recorder are most alike.

Employing his patented frenetic camera in one of a handful of "chance" seductions from *Buttman in Barcelona* (1997), Stagliano as spectator-recorder videotapes a pickup in a town square under the noonday sun. In this sequence, so typical of Stagliano's rudimentary narrative framing and his playful habit of "privatizing" public space, Buttman's sidekick, Hatman, complete in the flaneur's top hat and tails, is first glimpsed in the square doing a soft shoe shuffle. As Hatman begins conversing with the man behind the lens, a long-tressed Parisian wanders into the frame; immediately, Stagliano's camera becomes kamikaze, first focusing on the woman's face and then zooming in on various body parts. The camera remains in flux, roaming over the woman, even during minor sexual foreplay between Hatman and the object of Stagliano's attention, until the scene cuts to a hotel interior.

This is a marvelous example of the gliding, zooming, hand-held camera movements that render the Buttman videos something akin to an assault on the visual. If we consider early feminist theories of moving image spectatorship, this frantic POV sequence seems an almost ideal reification of one feature of Laura Mulvey's seminal psychoanalytic work on visual pleasure: the female filmic body exists merely as a sight of erotic contemplation relayed through three circuits: the (presumably) male director, the male protagonist/performer, and the (ostensibly) male viewer.[7] While Mulvey was writing about classical Hollywood product (roughly films produced from the late 1920s to the mid 1960s), her theory still seems especially applicable to a genre such as hardcore porn. This scene from the Buttman series appears to follow what Mulvey terms the "sadistic" model of pleasure, and yet the gaze hardly seems stable here–the director/protagonist/spectator alignment just lacks that smooth Hollywood polish. The "I" of the camera seems in crisis, as if attempting to locate the source of women's pleasure is an impossible task, with the wild camera movement becoming indicative of that impossibility. Of course, the female body is still the genre's *raison d'etre*, but Buttman's kamikaze camera sabotages any tempered circuit relay.

A strong dose of irony is also discernible in that "Buttman" clip. While the flaneur projected irony through what might first be taken for aloofness but was in actuality engagement, the gonzo spectator-recorder inhabits the ironic through the employment of a cinema verite format that is in reality a bare-bones narrative. And "narrative" is the operative term here. Unless one is the most naive of viewers, it must be obvious that Buttman's chance encounters are tongue-in cheek staged scenarios. Just how many times does one need to hear performer Rocco Siffredi tell the camera that what is happening to him in a public square in Budapest is "too fantastic, too unbelievable" before agreeing with that statement? Usually, just once. While the sex we are witnessing is real, it is realism linked to narrative but more indebted to spectacle. In this aspect, gonzo pornography has less in common with late-twentieth-century television documentary than with early cinema. The aforementioned Tom Gunning's seminal work on the first ten years of the moving image explains these early screenings as providing a "cinema of attractions." An exhibition of usually one-shot shorts screened between approximately 1895-1905 might allow the viewer to witness a kiss, an execution of an elephant, and a risque belly dance—all these visceral shocks to the system available in one evening.[8] If a rudimentary narrative creeps into these early silents, it is often by accident. While this is in contrast to the gonzo video, in which narrative *appears* to creep in accidentally, both historical moments provide a moving image with the same goal: providing an array of thrills.[9]

As regards the thrills on view in the gonzo video, I would like to look briefly at the possible epistemological slippage that these images encourage, chiefly the assist of the binary collapse of the ostensibly separate spheres of public and private space. It must be first stated that the public and the private are never secure borders; they are legal creations of the state, determined through statute or case law. These zones are subject to whimsical redefinitions and geo realignments, often in an effort to codify sexual behaviors "appropriate" for citizenship. For example, in the infamous Supreme Court decision in the case of Bowers vs. Hardwick, antiquated notions of the "private" served to embrace only heterosexual activity behind closed doors. On a more recent front, in an well-publicized campaign to put Manhattan sex industry workers out of jobs, adult businesses are being forced out of the more public commercial zones—the sites where one would indeed expect to encounter a "business"—and into the less visible, far less public, and potentially dangerous industrial sections of the city. Thus, secure, reasonable, "public" access to adult materials becomes quite limited.

Just where does gonzo come into play over all this contested space? Well, the genre scandalously refuses to obey legal sanctions against the "proper" use of public space, while also sexualizing both the private and the public realms. Thus, gonzo helps to accentuate the private/public distinction as arbitrary, if not downright meaningless. This is evident in many of the genre's releases. For example, in *Buttman in Budapest* (1987), the ubiquitous Rocco Siffredi meets a woman near an historic statue, and they then indulge in acts of fellatio and intercourse in a nearby park under the noon sun. Such a scene is even more transgressive because it is set in a former Communist nation-state, behind a once secure geopolitical border in which great efforts were made to keep the sexual out of the public purview. Even more destabilizing is a video such as *Prague by Night* (Siffredi, 1997), an excursion into

Buda's burgeoning sex clubs that vacillates between the public and the private, often moving the sexual back and forth in one amazingly long take. We go from sex in the stairwell of a disco, to sex in a limousine, to sex in an apartment, and then return to the club—all without the use of video edits. Notions of the public and the private collide and collapse during such an excursion; however, capitalism has also effectively commodified Eastern European bodies *and* images in its global search for new buyers.

The gonzo director can depict such "scandalous" activity, can ignore rules of public decorum, can indeed exploit other nations-states because of advances in technology. He and the performers can quickly enter an area, film an activity, and leave just as quickly because no heavy film equipment is required, just a light-weight Betacam. This spectator-recorder has no need for shooting permits, can hightail it if anyone complains, and can return to the location at a later time if asked to leave. No border is secure.

NOTES

1. See *Hardcore: Power, Pleasure, and the "Frenzy of the Visible"* (Berkeley: University of California Press, 1989), 93-119 Despite the erasure of the money shot, as in the "couples friendly erotica" created by Candida Royalle, or the visual proof of female ejaculation, on display in a video magazine series such as *Rainwoman*, the convention still survives. Note that this conference devoted an entire panel to the problematic money shot.

2. Williams perceives structural similarities between the Hollywood musical and the feature-length filmic hardcore produced in the 1970s and the 1980s in their narrative reliance upon (musical or sexual) numbers. See pp. 120-52.

3. See Tom Gunning, "An Aesthetic of Astonishment: Early Film and the (In)Credulous Spectator," *Viewing Positions: Ways of Seeing Film*, ed Linda Williams (New Brunswick: Rutgers University Press, 1995), pp. 114-33.

4. Charles Baudelaire, *The Painter of Modern Life and Other Essays*, ed. and trans. Jonathan Mayne (New York: De Capo, 1964), p. 11.

5. For a wonderful look at porn's indebtedness to a history of bawdy low culture, see Constance Penley, "Crackers and Whackers: The White Trashing of Porn," *White Trash: Race and Class in America*, ed. Matt Wray and Annalee Newitz (New York: Routledge, 1997), pp. 89-112.

6. See Chris Jenks, "Watching Your Step: The History and Practice of the Flaneur," *Visual Culture*, ed. Jenks (New York: Routledge, 1995), pp. 142-60.

7. See Laura Mulvey, "Visual Pleasure and Narrative Cinema," *Film Theory and Criticism*, eds Gerald Mast and Marshall Cohen, 3rd ed. (New York: Oxford University Press, 1985) 803-16. It should be noted that Mulvey's smart 1975 essay was a starting point for considerations of the intersection between film and gender. It has been expanded upon, refuted, and even amended by Mulvey herself.

8. See Gunning, pp. 121-24.

9. This accent on spectacle is also evident in contemporary mainstream films. Releases such as *Speed* (Jan DeBont, 1994) and *Eraser* (Charles Russell, 1996) exhibit little plot and virtually no characterization, preferring instead to concentrate on outrageously implausible set pieces.

30

Ed Powers and the
Fantasy of Documenting Sex

Peter Lehman

V IDEO PORN IS MUCH MORE THAN THE "ENEMY" OF A ROMANTICIZED
notion of theatrical film porn as suggested both in the film *Boogie Nights* and in interviews by its director, Paul Thomas Anderson.[1] Indeed, such video porn *auteurs* as John Stagliano and Ed Powers who come to prominence in the 1990s are as creative in their accomplishments as the Mitchell Brothers, Alex de Renzy, Henry Paris or any of the theatrical porn *auteurs* were in the 1970s. Powers, Stagliano and others didn't just make cheaper copies of narrative theatrical porn with lower production values; they innovated entire new forms more closely linked to documentary than fictional narrative traditions.

Powers, in such series as *More Dirty Debutantes* and *Deep Inside Dirty Debutantes* brought entirely new erotic elements into play via the interview technique. Ironically, the lengthy interviews Powers frequently conducts with the women with whom he is about to have sex place much more emphasis on dialogue than 1970s theatrical porn, in the process contributing a psychological erotic dimension totally absent from the narratives. For this reason, Powers most recent series *Global Warming Debutantes: The Ed House Effect* is considerably less erotic than his other series, even though visually it looks much the same. *Global Warming Debutantes Vol. 2* (1997) is shot in Russian with women who speak little or no English, so Powers bypasses the usual interviews.

My point is not that these interviews are simply "real" or "true," but rather that they document some psychological interaction between the participants. The women (some of whom admit it on camera) may not be using their own names, may have a history of working in the adult entertainment industry as, for example, dancers, and may even have agents and be starting porn careers. Nevertheless, something about them as actual people is documented. Similarly, Powers even constructs a comic Woody Allen type Jewish persona for himself, acknowledging insecurities such as worrying about the size of his penis. In *More Dirty Debutantes #72* (1997), for example, he tells a woman, "Hey, I'm small. I'm only five inches." In another segment of the same tape, he tells a different woman he is about to have sex with that his penis is "only five-and-a-half inches" long and asked if that "scares" her. In *Deep Inside Dirty Debutantes #2* (1993), Powers brings up his smallness while he is still dressed and the woman tells him penis size doesn't matter. Yet, a few minutes later, he persists and brings it up again, this time when his genitals are visible. Again, she shows no interest in the topic but when he persists, she simply looks and tells him "it doesn't matter."

Powers helped break the oppressive domination of limited female body types in porn. At a time when nearly all porn stars in narratives had silicon breast enlargements, nearly all of the women in Powers's tapes did not. Women with small and average size breasts are common in Powers's tapes. Powers also features women of color and diverse ethnic backgrounds much more than was the case in the 1970s. Significantly, however, himself excluded, Powers maintains the emphasis on big penises. Indeed, he frequently revels in how the women respond to Jake Steed, a star of several of the tapes in the series. Steed is a black man with an exceptionally large penis, a point to which I will return.

Stylistically, Powers frequently is innovative with hand-held video cameras, employing mirrors and monitors as stylistic devices which, among other things, reveal the production process and apparatus. Similarly, he brings attention to the camera by at times holding it himself while engaging in sexual activity or, at other times, putting it on a tripod and re-entering the scene. Some of his sequences are shot entirely by himself with his sexual partner being the only other participant in the taping. At other time, he talks to the camera person, asking what is included in the composition, or uses a camera to reveal the camera person who has been shooting the footage we have just seen of the sexual partners whom we then see again through that person's camera. At still other times, he surprisingly reveals the presence of others on the set. All of the above listed techniques can be found on *Deep Inside Dirty Debutantes No. 2, No. 14* (1997), *More Dirty Debutantes No. 27* (1994) and *No. 72.* Perhaps most importantly, Powers displaces the monotonous emphasis on the meat shot that had come to characterize theatrical and video narrative porn and he eliminates the ever-present generic music audio track intermingled with dubbed moans. Most of Powers' work involves live, unadorned soundtracks which include actually dialogue with the participants and the sounds (and silences) of their sex. The work of video porn makers such as Powers deserve the kind of analysis Linda Williams brings to 1970s 35mm theatrical porn features.

Williams' model for studying the history of porn in her justly influential book, *Hard Core*, bears an uncanny resemblance to that of such film historians as David Bordwell, Janet Staiger and Kristin Thompson who have analyzed the classical style of film making.[2] What Williams terms the stag film is equivalent to what many film historians now term the primitive cinema and what she terms the hard-core feature is equivalent to what historians term the classical style which also involved an expansion to feature-length narration. Indeed, her analysis of the centrality of such devices as the "meat shot" and the "money shot" bear comparison with the manner in which historians have identified central stylistic devices such as shot-reverse-shot editing in the classical cinema. From this perspective, which seems to me valid, the history of pornography recapitulates the history of cinema in general, moving from a primitive mode in one exhibition context to a classical mode within a changing exhibition context. The stag smoker, for example, would compare with the nickelodeon and the theatrical hard-core feature with the classical feature exhibited in legitimate theaters. The analogy may, however, only work so far.

Once the classical Hollywood style was established it maintained a remarkable dominance, especially in regards to such aspects of narration as feature-length and the dominance of narrative within the style. But something much different may be happening in pornography. The development in the 1980s of porn made on video and aimed directly at the home market obviously was shaped by technology, economics, and exhibition. Using video equipment, these tapes are produced much more cheaply and quickly than their 35 mm theatrical precedents. If one measures them against the hard-core feature, they show a loss of both production values (e.g., lighting) and narrative development—that is, even by the limited standards of narrative development in the theatrical features, many of the videos are less developed. Rather than reify a golden age of theatrical 35mm porn as, incidentally, many of the 1970s porn *auteurs* have done by abandoning the form altogether and attempting to move into legitimate film making, perhaps we need to consider the less developed video forms as moving porn back into a format which is more closely aligned with many of its heterogeneous and fleeting moments of pleasure.

Tom Gunning has distinguished between the cinema of attractions and the development of narrative in early film history. Something of the unusual nature of the hard-core feature emerges if we consider it from this perspective. The cinema of attractions was one of display rather than storytelling. Attractions acknowledge the spectator in a manner that makes cinema more exhibitionistic than voyeuristic, and offer visual curiosity rather than interest in narrative enigmas. Attractions also have a different sense of time than narratives do since they do not build temporal patterns so much as display and then remove what has been seen: "rather than a development which links the past with the present in such a way as to define a specific anticipation of the future (as an unfolding narrative does), the attraction seems limited to a sudden burst of presence" (Gunning, 1993, p. 6). As such, attractions are characteristically brief and do not develop expectations based upon patterning. The suspense of the attraction is not how but when it will occur: "The act of display on which the cinema of attractions is founded presents itself as a temporal irruption rather than a temporal development" (Gunning, 1993, p. 7).

At first glance, it might seem that porn is just another form of the cinema of attractions; it is highly exhibitionist in its display of the body and shamelessly acknowledges in spirit, if not always in technique, what the spectator is there for. From theater advertising to video boxes to reviews, the makers, exhibitors and critics of porn all openly acknowledge its sexually arousing and even masturbatory function. It is all perhaps summarized by the manner in which magazines replace the usual ratings categories such as one to four stars and thumbs up or down with such things as penises ranging from limp to fully erect or a range of one to four erect penises. The institution of porn openly revels in what it is about.

In the hard-core feature, however, sexual display is anything but brief and it is strongly linked to patterns based upon expectation. Indeed, perhaps nothing in cinema is more ritualistically patterned and less full of surprises than the hard-core number with its predictable "meat shots" (close-ups of the penis thrusting in and out of the vagina) and "money shots" (visible ejaculation, frequently on the body of the woman). This type of patterning, however, is not like the patterning that Gunning attributes to the narrative. Although the lengthy sexual numbers typical of the hard-core feature include arousal, various types of sexual activity (e.g., anal and oral) and various positions (e.g., woman on top, rear entry) all of which culminate in the money shot, the patterning has little or nothing to do with narrative or character. Time is connected into a past, present, and future but it is not the enigmatic time of narrative. What lies at the center of the hard-core feature is a hybrid whereby the attraction, which is still based upon the exhibitionist display of the body and taboo subjects, is both extended and patterned, but within a pattern of curiosity, display, arousal, and satisfaction rather than one within a diegetic framework. The hard-core feature's diegesis has little or nothing to do with its display of sexual attractions. To put it another way, Gunning notes that the distinction between the cinema of attractions and the narrative cinema is not total; the former includes narrative elements and the latter found a place for attractions within it. The place of the attraction within the hard-core feature, however, is distinctly different than its place within the classical narrative.

In a sense, the hard-core narrative feature has always been a kind of documentary. Narrative and character development have always occupied a much less significant place in the films than in the classical Hollywood style. Acting and the star system are also different—porn stars really display their own bodies and their own style of fucking rather than believably act out a fictional role. This is manifest in the name confusion surrounding porn stars: some use their own name in the films (e.g., Marilyn Chambers *Private Fantasies* series) and some become known by the character's names (e.g., John Holmes a.k.a. Johnny Wadd). What little characterization there is in the porn film quickly falls by the way when the fucking starts; we watch the actors fuck, not their characters.

In this regard, watching Ed Powers may not be all that different form watching Jami Gillis. Indeed, the partnership between Gillis and Powers,

"The Nasty Bros," and the appearance of Gillis and Randy West in some of the tapes are a testament to this. Rather than switching porn from fictional features to documentary, Powers perhaps inflects and extends the implicit documentary component of the hard-core feature—documenting actual sex taking place. What does it mean to document "actual sex?" What then are the primary differences between Powers' brand of pro/am and the hard-core fictional feature? Part of the answer lies in the very name of the genre "pro/am." There is a "pro" (in this series, usually Powers though sometimes Jamie Gillis, Randy West, or Jake Steed) and there is an "amateur," nearly always a woman, though in a few episodes both the man and the woman are "real life" amateur couples.

The term "pro/am" actually raises more issues than the genre title designates. Stated bluntly, what is a sexual "pro"? At the intended level, the answer is simple enough: someone who works professionally in these tapes to make a living. Similarly, the term amateur is intended to simply designate a first time performer, though on occasion Powers invites them back for encores, thus blurring the line even further. But both terms "professional" and "amateur" imply something else. The "pros" either have bodies and/or fuck in a manner that approaches the norm for the porn genre, a norm that the hard-core feature played no small role in establishing. Presumably, then, the amateurs fuck like they do in their real lives, including "authentic" sounds, facial expressions, etc. But this documentary notion of authenticity is, we shall see, a mere illusion.

The whole notion of styles of fucking is something to which, as far as I know, no one has paid any attention—as if sex were just that, sex. But I would argue that in the hard-core feature sex of a very limited kind is performed over and over, as if it were synonymous with sex itself. The hard-core feature thus shows little imagination about the range of erotic possibilities, almost always concluding with what a female colleague of mine calls "pound pound pound" sex. In this form of sex, the male, who nearly always has a large penis, performs vigorous forms of penetration sex, lasting a long time and involving many positions, concluding, of course, with the inevitable money shot. The narratives of these films in various ways, including dialogue, moans, facial expressions, etc., all imply that this is what women want to be satisfied. When the man comes on her face and/or body, she is as satisfied as he and the scene is over.

There is what I will call, for lack of a better term, an ideology of sex implicit in this dominant notion of what constitutes good sex in porn. This form of sex becomes a performance whereby the male performs his masculinity on the woman, proving his virility and her dependence on it for pleasure. Within the world of hard-core porn films, women want long-lasting men with big cocks pounding on them until they have a blissful orgasm. This explains why Powers has not been innovative in the representation of men and why a porn star like Randy West easily segued into this market with his own pro/am series, *Up and Cummers*. No doubt such a fantasy of performed masculinity is appealing to many men but many women have actually told me that it looks painful and unpleasant to them in porn and that sexual pleasure in their lives also has nothing to do with either big cocks or "pound pound pound" sex. In short, the representation of good or ideal sex in porn has nothing to do with either fantasy or reality for them.

In many ways, however, Ed Powers, "the pro," performs precisely this kind of "I'll prove to you I'm a man" sex. As I've indicated above, he makes much of the fact that his penis is small by porn norms but he proves that he can compensate for this with his superhuman performing style. Many of his segments end with him asking the women how they feel, eliciting an answer that affirms his performance. And they nearly always give it. Yes, they feel wonderful; yes, he is wonderful, etc. One actually volunteers that he may have a small penis but he sure knows how to use it. Powers' segments all end with the money shot, another carry-over from the hard-core feature which "proves" that the man has actually performed to orgasm and which makes a spectacle out of his orgasm.[3]

If Powers then clearly performs sex within the hard-core narrative tradition, what about his partner? Although she is seeming the amateur, in fact, most of the women are directed to perform or attempt to perform sex in a manner like that of porn starlets. They may look into the cameras, throw back their heads, pull back their hair, moan and groan, etc., in a way they think will turn men on and perhaps enable them to use this as a springboard to become "pros." Within such a context they will take the cue from Powers (or whomever) as to what kind of sex it should appear they like. None of them ever stop him from doing what he wants to do by saying they don't like it or it is painful. But not all of them are equally good actors and some look bored, uncomfortable, nervous, or even pained. Some, for example, do not actively participate in the sex, simply lying there while Powers pounds away on them. Others at times acknowledge they are playing a role. In one tape, Powers complains when one of the women removes her clothes and reveals that she has shaved her pubic region. He asks whether she was told to do that the previous day when meeting with people in his company, and she answers in the affirmative, adding that she dislikes it as much as Powers does. Before they even begin to have sex, then, we might pose the question, "In what sense is this woman even an amateur?" She shaved her pubic hair just for her "performance" and she was hiding her dislike of it until Powers indicated he felt the same way. Without him eliciting her response, there is no reason to believe that she would have acted anything but "natural" and happy with her shaved pubic hair.

From time to time, the veneer breaks in such a manner. At the end of a segment in *Deep Inside Dirty Debutantes #2*, Powers asks the woman he has just finished fucking after replacing another man, whether she feels "fucked." Interestingly, she thinks for a moment and a bemused look comes over her face as she realizes the answer he is looking for and she replies "Sure" with a paper-thin "whatever" attitude. If that's what you want to hear, she implies, I'll be happy to say it to you. As a woman who worked in the sex industry as a masseuse told me, this was one of the first things she learned on her own at the age of seventeen!

Paradoxically then, if the hard-core narrative feature contains a somewhat hidden documentary function that acknowledges that the stories and character are minimal and not to be believed, Ed Powers' brand of video documentary contains a hidden, fictional performance element. The sex is not simply "authentic" but is rather shaped at many levels to conform to the limited hard-core notion and fantasy of what constitutes good sex. This is particularly the case with Powers, Steed, Gillis, and West, all of whom always perform up to snuff. If an occasional woman seems uncomfortable, that doesn't really matter since it is masculinity that is being performed as an impressive spectacle, not femininity. Women don't need to prove they're women in the way that Powers needs to prove he is a man, though many of these women are directed by Powers and/or themselves to display their bodies and sexual response in a manner that conforms to the porn norm of women in the throes of orgasmic pleasure.

Godard once remarked that the history of cinema was indeed that of the pole of documentary and the pole of fiction as summarized in the early days of the invention by Lumière and Méliès. His famous twist, of course, was that we got Lumière and Méliès confused: Lumière with his seeming presentation of reality was participating in a fiction that denied the actual representational practices of cinema while Méliès with his magic tricks and impossible stories of trips to the moon, was the true documentary film maker since his fantasies were recognized as just that by the spectators–they knew that they were really watching a fiction. *That* was the reality, not the illusion on the screen.

The ultimate illusion of Powers' brand of video porn is that it is somehow "real." It, like the hard-core theatrical feature before it, is a performed fiction and one that presents a similar fantasy of seeing "real sex." But with porn it seem to me that neither the pole of fiction nor documentary was ever as secure as that in the history of mainstream cinema. The 1970s hard-core features acknowledged their documentary fascination with watching the sex act just as surely as Powers' 1990s documentaries acknowledge their performance element. The two forms are not as far apart as they may at first seem. Henry Paris and Ed Powers are not as far apart as Lumière and Méliès.

NOTES

I wish to thank Melanie Nagisos for her help in revising this article.

1. For an analysis of this aspect of *Boogie Nights*, see my article "Will the Real Dirk Diggler Please Stand Up."

2. The following discussion of William's work and Gunning's work is drawn from my article, "Revelations about Pornography."

3. Powers' interviews with the women with whom he is about to have sex, discussed above, also conform to what Williams identifies as a major component of the hard-core feature: The drive to learn the "truth" about female sexuality. Powers

probes the sex lives of the women, asking them when they first had sex, how many lovers they have, what kind of sex they like, whether they also like sex with women, etc. The interviews are constructed almost entirely around the quest for the verbal "truth" of the subject's "hidden" sexuality.

WORKS CITED

Bordwell, David, Thompson, Kristin, & Staiger, Janet. (1985). *The Classical Hollywood Cinema: Film & Mode of Production to 1960.* New York: Columbia University Press.

Gunning, Tom (1993). "'Now You See it, Now You Don't': The Temporality of the Cinema of Attractions." *The Velvet Light Tap* 32 (Fall): 3-12.

Lehman, Peter. (1998). "Will the Real Diggler Please Stand Up?" *Jump Cut*, pp. 32–38.

———. (1995-96). "Revelations about Pornography." *Film Criticism* 20, no. 1-2: 3-16.

Williams, Linda (1989). *Hard Core: Power, Pleasure and the "Frenzy of the Visible."* Berkeley: University of California Press.

SECTION 8

OUR EROTIC HERITAGE: FROM LITERATURE TO TOYS TO COMIC BOOKS

W HEN AND WHERE DID MODERN PORNOGRAPHY BEGIN? THIS IS THE subject of Marianna Beck's chapter. She argues that the main purpose of pornography has been to shock, and in societies where the role of women was severely restricted, pornography transgressed social boundaries by often depicting female characters as self-empowered, sexual beings. In the twentieth century, pornography has carved out a literary and artistic niche all its own, functioning less as a political tool and more as genre devoted exclusively to the depiction of sexuality. Jack Hafferkamp examines how the courts have treated pornography beginning with the nineteenth century opinions in England and carrying through to the present day. He feels that the hard-won freedom to read pornography is threatened at the end of the twentieth century by quest for "decency."

As part of the new freedom for erotic and pornographic works which came about in the 1960s, there was a rise and flourishing of genitally explicit and sexually explicit heterosexually oriented photographic magazines and books. Louis H. Swartz examines this phenomenon including the type of sex depicted and the ambivalent feeling that many reporters of the phenomenon had. He believes that the availability of erotic materials led to many readers and users feeling a call to experience a different way of being, a "new light" within themselves.

But even before the courts grew more lenient toward pornography, there was a widespread circulation of underground materials One of the most widespread forms of such materials was what came to be called "Tijuana Bibles," illustrated sex comic books, usually between eight and sixteen pages. The booklets were not printed in Tijuana and they had nothing to do with religion, but this is the term that came to be applied to them. Dwight Dixon and Joan K. Dixon describe the phenomenon. All the comic

367

books heroes of the 1920s through the 1940s were subjects, from Lil Abner to Joe Palooka to Blondie and Dagwood Bumstead. The drawings were realistic facsimiles of the actual comic characters while the sex was direct and to the point. In fact, many people born before 1940 often learned about sexual matters through such books which somehow ended up on middle school or junior high school grounds.

Sex toys are part of the erotic tradition as well, and Herbert Otto gives a brief overview of this phenomenon and concentrates on the current generation of sex toys. While some of the "toys" are quire expensive, Otto feels that in general there has been a democratization of the phenomenon and they have been increasingly accepted as an important part of expanding an individual's sexual self development.

31

The Pornographic Tradition: Formative Influences in Sixteenth- to Nineteenth-Century European Literature

Marianna Beck

WHAT ARE THE ORIGINS OF MODERN PORNOGRAPHY? WHAT WERE some of the major works between the sixteenth and nineteenth centuries, as well as the major influences in the formation of the pornographic tradition? This survey traces the progression of pornography's development from its earliest manifestations in Italy, to its role in revolutionary France and through its golden age in Victorian England.

I

Pornography as a distinct literary category is a relatively modern concept. While sex has been depicted in many forms and in many cultures over thousands of years, the idea of creating images and text solely for the purposes of arousal is primarily a product of Western culture in the last five hundred years. The invention of the printing press, the emergence of the novel, and the creation of an entrepreneurial middle class along with the enormous changes wrought by the Renaissance, the Enlightenment and the French Revolution, all contributed to its development.

For the purposes of this discussion, pornography is defined at two levels: first, as text or images focusing on either genitals or acts of sexuality with the intention of violating social boundaries; second, as text or images designed to arouse. The balance between the political and sexual components of pornography has fluctuated over time. In sixteenth-century Italy, politics played a far greater role in its formation that it did in nineteenth-century England, when its major impetus was arousal. In its earliest incarnation in sixteenth- and seventeenth-century European literature, pornography's primary goal was subversion, developing largely out of a need for artists and writers to push political boundaries. What better way to draw attention to a

The burgeoning eroticism of the Renaissance could be found in religious paintings, including those of the Madonna and Child. (Jean Fouquet, portrait of Charles VII's mistress painted as the Madonna.)

corrupt church official or politician than to show him in an erect state, about to have sex with a nun? During the French Revolution, a pamphlet depicting Queen Marie-Antoinette in an orgy setting was a powerful, if not misogynistic, way to incite a starving mob already enraged over aristocratic excess. Pornography did not develop into a commercially oriented category of literature until well into the nineteenth century.

Pornography's main purpose has always been to shock. In societies where the role of women was severely restricted, pornography transgressed social boundaries by often depicting female characters as self-empowered, sexual beings. Granted that these early characterizations were always the expressions of male writers, they nonetheless underscore pornography's role of inverting social norms and toying with established social order.

In the twentieth century, pornography has carved out a literary and artistic niche all its own, and it functions less as a political tool and more as a genre devoted exclusively to the depiction of sexuality. But true to its subversive genre, it continues to inspire fear and loathing. To wit: the word "pornography" itself has become a handy epithet, a term hurled indiscriminately at any explicit image or text deemed sexually offensive. Politicians and religious leaders decry the loss of family values and hold the dreaded *P-word* responsible for everything from sex crimes to STDs to teenage pregnancy, as well as for a multitude of fill-in-the-blank social problems.

A quick review of the last few hundred years would indicate that pornography has had an extremely important, if thankless role, in questioning authority and reflecting social angst about established sex roles, as well as other unsanctioned activities. The best part about analyzing pornography from a historical perspective is discovering material that seems challenging (and occasionally shocking) even by contemporary standards.

If anyone can be called the originator of European pornography, it is Pietro Aretino, the man responsible for what has been called the premier stroke book of the Western world: *I modi* (or "The Ways," after a descriptive phrase of the historian Giorgio Vasari, who described the positions as "the ways in which low women lie with men.")[1] Aretino's work combined sixteen sexually explicit sonnets with sixteen engravings of couples having sex in varying positions.

Aretino, born in 1492, was one of the first writers to produce forbidden works for the emerging print culture. He was a resident of the Republic of Venice, a journalist, publicist, entrepreneur, and art dealer who made a living writing political tracts and essays. The fact that Aretino managed to create *and* circulate *I modi* had as much to do with the social and political conditions of Renaissance Italy as it did with an increasingly literate audience. Privately printed texts were less

Figures from pagan myths provided an endless excuse to depict erotic scenes. While the portrayal of nude bodies was generally off-limits, depictions of naked satyrs and nymphs were not. (Agostino Carraci, Satyr copulating with a nymph, circa 1584.)

and less the sole province of a small circumscribed group of aristocrats.

The new interest in humanism during the Renaissance inspired an endless fascination with classical antiquity. Intellectuals, schooled in Latin and Greek, read Cicero and Virgil, as well as the bawdy tales of Ovid and Catullus. For artists, figures from pagan myths provided an endless excuse to paint nudes or depict erotic scenes. While the portrayal of nude bodies involving contemporary individuals was certainly off-limits, depictions of naked gods and goddesses, satyrs and nymphs were not. Even in religious paintings, images of the Madonna and Child, as well as scenes from the Bible, were greatly eroticized. Given this general climate, Aretino had a built-in audience for material with a sexual theme.

The production of *I modi* involved three major artists of the Renaissance: Aretino, Giulio Romano and Marcantonio Raimondi. In 1524, Romano, the great Mannerist painter and former pupil of Raphael, drew sixteen scenes of copulating couples on some walls in the Vatican. One theory is that he was angry over the fact that Pope Clement VII had been late in paying for some

While these sixteenth-century images were not intended to elicit any feelings of eroticism whatsoever, the sexuality of Christ, as manifested by the shroud covering an erect penis, represented the ultimate symbol in the power of the Resurrection—the triumph in Christian belief of the flesh prevailing over mortality. In Renaissance art it was not unusual to focus on all aspects of Christ's life and death—even If it included tumescence. (Above: Martin van Heemskerck, Man of Sorrows, c. 1550. Below: Willem Key, Pietà, c. 1530.)

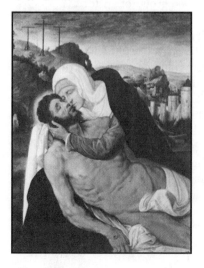

work.[2] (It is, however, conceivable that Romano had been commissioned to do this as his teacher, Raphael, had himself once been hired to paint erotic scenes in the bathroom of a cardinal at the Vatican.)

Raimondi, one of the foremost engravers of the time, made copper plates of Romano's *I modi* (literally, "postures"), printed copies and circulated them among the higher echelons of Roman society. The Pope, clearly outraged, ordered all prints and copper plates destroyed and made reprinting of *I modi* punishable by death. Romano fled town, while Raimondi was arrested and left to languish in the Vatican prison—until the intervention of a powerful Medici and Pietro Aretino.

It isn't clear whether Aretino wrote his piquant sonnets when he heard about Raimondi's arrest or whether he penned them *after* Raimondi's release. Whatever the case, the second edition of *I modi*, containing Raimondi's engravings and embellished by Aretino's sixteen sonnets, was meant to bait the authorities at the papal court. Aretino had already established a reputation as a free-lance journalist critical of certain politicians, and *I modi* provided an excellent venue for targeting his enemies. The new edition of *I modi* was ordered destroyed as well, and to date all that survives are a few fragments of the presumed original engravings in the British Museum, as well as one subsequent sixteenth-century imitation printed very soon after the first one, possibly in the same year—1527.[3]

Aretino's purpose in publishing *I modi* was certainly twofold: to depict earthy sex in vivid and colloquial terms, but also to mock the papal court as a repository of corruption. Some of those named in the sonnets, for instance, are thought to have been prominent courtesans as well as noteworthy figures of the day.[4] Ultimately, what made Aretino's work so reprehensible in the eyes of the Catholic Church was that he used sex to expose the corruption of the elite and worse, in doing so, informed a much broader audience about papal corruption as well.

Aretino also played with another radical concept by evoking an earthly utopia–a world of limitless sex and possibility, in which women expressed their desires as vociferously as men.[5] His work is a paean to sex, a celebration of eros, and reflects a powerful reaction against centuries of Church repression. Much of this is also evident in his violation of linguistic taboos: he pushed boundaries by employing the most colloquial language possible. He avoided euphemisms and used words like *cazzo, potta,* and *fottere*– "prick," "cunt," and "fuck." (See excerpt on page 376.)

Aretino's influence on the development of pornography did not end with *I modi.* In a work called *Ragionamenti,* or *Discussions,* which he published in 1539, two Roman courtesans discuss what goes on among whores, housewives and nuns (the conclusion: very much the same–"they all have sex."). While the dialogue form is a literary genre with precedents in Greek literature, it was Aretino's *Ragionamenti* that most profoundly influenced the proliferation of this genre over the next two centuries. These dialogues, which often involved talk about sex between an older woman and a younger one, weren't necessarily written for the purposes of arousal but rather as an excuse to convey information about sex–as bluntly as possible.

Artists and writers borrowed heavily from the Aretinian tradition long after his death in 1556. (Even the term "Aretinian postures" became synonymous all over Europe with the depiction of acrobatic sex.) In effect, Aretino helped to create a new marketplace for sexually explicit material. With works like *I modi* and those following, pornography became closely linked to political and religious subversion.

II

The growth of pornographic literature in seventeenth-century Europe can certainly be linked to the beginning of the Enlightenment, when basic attitudes about authority, religion, and science began to change. In some ways, the defining paradigm of porn literature in the Enlightenment was the propagation of sexual pleasure as a new religion. There was greater emphasis on the value of science–hence interest in the mechanics of conception and contraception. Condoms, for instance, were available in London in the 1660s, along with Italian-made dildos.[6]

In the evolution of pornography's revolutionary roots, France provided fertile soil for subversive literature. It became a primary function of libertine*

---

*In terms of the late seventeenth and eighteenth centuries, libertine meant someone who had lax morals, a debaucher, someone who went out of his way to defy traditional values. The origin of the word, however, is from the Latin libertinus which meant a "freed man"–as in a former slave. Gradually, libertine took on the meaning of someone who deviated from moral and religious principles. Before the seventeenth- and eighteenth-centuries, the term did not have a sexual connotation. It applied, rather, to those people who questioned the prevailing religious and scientific dogmas of the time.

From Aretino's I modi—c. 1527. Posture #4.

philosophy to attack the bastions of sexual repression, which were embodied, above all, by the moral teachings of the Catholic Church. Much libertine porn literature is set in churches and monasteries—one sure way to break moral, religious and sexual taboos all at the same time.

One of the most striking aspects of seventeenth- and eighteenth-century "Europorn" is the preponderance of female characters. Two early French works, *L'Ecole des Filles*, published in the late 1650s, and *L'Academie des Dames* (1680), were written in the Aretinian tradition as female dialogue—a literary device that was to repeat itself many times over the next century, in works such as John Cleland's *Fanny Hill* and the Marquis de Sade's *Juliette*.

Creating female narrators who were essentially the intellectual equals of men and as capable of, if not eager for, sexual pleasure, was certainly a transgression of expected female roles, and underscored, once again, pornography's subversive function. A courtesan or prostitute could not only convey sexual information but also act as a kind of social barometer. While courtesans, in some cases, wielded enormous power and influence, women in society were generally powerless. In large part, the character of the autonomous woman, sophisticated in the ways of the world, was a fictional creation because her powers generally weren't reflected in social reality.

L'Ecole des Filles' anarchistic message was the idealization of sex. While it by no means resembled the dark and more politically subversive works that made the Marquis de Sade notorious more than one hundred years later, *L'Ecole des Filles* is considered by scholars as the origin of pornography in France.[7] The book was severely criticized for celebrating a libertine lifestyle of decadence and debauchery despite the fact that the dialogue between two young women, sixteen-year-old Fanny and Suzanne, her older, more experienced cousin, is more ribald than subversive. (See excerpt on pages 378-79.) Largely, *L'Ecole des Filles* offended because it represented a gross undermining of the moral teachings of both parents and religion. Its language is explicit and the characters relate their sexual encounters with great enthusiasm.

The accused authors of the book, Michel Millot and Jean L'Ange, were given light jail sentences, suggesting that the true author might have been someone higher up and more politically connected. Several authors have been linked to *L'Ecole des Filles*, including Louis XIV's mistress, Madame de

Maintenon, and his finance minister, Nicholas Fouquet.[8]

Given the climate of political repression during the reign of Louis XIV, *L'Ecole des Filles* symbolized the fusion between sexual explicitness and political dissidence. Writing about the female body was perceived as writing about the body politic.[9] This connection between debauchery and tyranny is a theme that played out frequently in the seventeenth and eighteenth centuries, and it assumed an enormously pivotal role in the years leading up to the French Revolution in 1789.

From Aretino's I modi. *Posture #7.*

The spread of literacy in the eighteenth century triggered even greater concern over pornography's supposed power to corrupt and undermine society. Traditionally, its consumption had always been in the hands of the male ruling elite, but a burgeoning middle class whose moral attitudes weren't as easily patrolled, was increasingly challenging the power of the ruling classes. Anxiety centered on the growing belief that while erotic literature might not necessarily corrupt educated men, it threatened the morals of women and servants. Mothers were viewed as the family guardians of morality and therefore in need of special protection from vulgar and salacious representations of sex. This middle-class fear of porn's potentially deleterious effect on women was largely the same as earlier concerns of aristocrats, who feared the dissemination of incendiary material among the lower classes.

The belief in the power of pornography to deprave and corrupt (which remains the official motive for censorship even in the twentieth century) continued to fuel fear in the causal connection between sexual immorality and political subversion. The English, in particular, viewed the anti-clericalism of French libertine literature as a political threat, believing that exposing a population to blasphemous works would inevitably encourage political insurrection. The English feared the French for both their radical politics and their literature: France, after all, produced books like *L'Ecole des Filles* and, later, Laclos' *Les Liaisons Dangeureuses* (1782)—a manual of seduction.

By 1748, however, the British had their own erotic classic to contend with: John Cleland's *Memoirs of a Woman of Pleasure*, later known as *Fanny Hill*, which is among the most frequently reprinted, translated and illustrated of all English novels in history. (It has only been legally available in the U.S. since 1963 and in England since 1970.[10]) Cleland was no doubt very much influenced by

ARETINO'S *I MODI*—c. 1527

Aretino's purpose in publishing *I modi* was twofold: to depict earthy sex in vivid terms but also to mock the Papal court as a repository of corruption. His work is a paean to sex, a celebration of Eros, and reflects a powerful reaction against centuries of Church repression. What made his use of language consistent with pornography's role of violating taboos was the use of the most colloquial language possible. He avoided euphemisms and used words like *culo, cazzo, potta,* and *fottere* ("ass," "prick," "cunt," and "fuck").

Non tirar futtutelo di Cupido
La carriola, firmati bifmul o
Ch'io uó fotter in potta,e non in culo
Coftei,che mi to'l cazzo,e me ne rido;
E ne le braccia,e ne le gambe mi fido,
E fi difconcio fto, e non t'adulo,
Che ci morrebbe a ftarci un'hora un mulo,
E però tanto co'l cul foffio e grido;
E fe uoi Beatrice ftentar faccio
Perdonar mi douste,perch'io moftro
Che fottendo a disfaggio mi disfaccio,
E fe non,ch'io mi fpecchio nel cul uoftro
Stando fofpefo in l'uno ç'nl'altro braccio
Mai non fi fruirebbe il fatto noftro,
 O, cul di latte,e d'oftro
Se non ch'io fon per mirarti di uena,
Non mi ftarebbe il cazzo dritto à pena;

Sonnet #14

You little prick! Don't keep pulling the cart.
Cupid, you bastard, stop it!
I want to *fottere* her in the *potta* not in the *culo.*
She lets the *cazzo* slip and makes me laugh.

Forced to lean on my arms and legs,
I curse you for this clumsy position.
A mule would conk over after an hour of it.
That's why you hear me farting thunderously.

As for you, Beatrice, if you're uncomfortable,
Forgive me. You ought to be able to tell
How this crazy posture is killing me.

If I didn't mirror myself in your ass,
Lifted up, as I am, on both my arms,
We'd never get to the end of this act.

O milky, rosy *culo,*
If I didn't gaze voluptuously at you,
My *cazzo* would hardly stand up straight.

the French libertine novels that had found their way into England. Based on the adventures of its eponymous character, *Fanny Hill* is a wonderful window into the sexual mores and social customs of eighteenth-century life.

Cleland quit school early, went to India as a foot soldier and rose up through the ranks of the East India Company. When he returned to England and his fortunes declined, Cleland found himself in debtors' prison. He is thought to have revised and rewritten a draft of *Memoirs of a Woman of Pleasure* while still in jail. Some scholars think Cleland wrote *Fanny Hill* (as he later called the abridged version) as a way to get out of debtors' prison, but the consensus is that he began an early draft of the novel sometime in the 1730s.[11]

When the book first appeared in 1748-49, Cleland and his publisher experienced little trouble—despite the fact that the Bishop of London blamed it for two minor London earthquakes and wanted to have the book prosecuted, calling it "a vile Book, which is an open insult upon Religion and good manners, and a reproach to the Honour of government and the Law of the Country."[12]

Within several months, however, a warrant was issued for the arrest of Cleland and his publisher, partly as a result of the above letter but more likely because Cleland had produced an anonymously written pamphlet critical of the government. They were released shortly after their arrest and Cleland proceeded to rewrite *Memoirs of a Woman of Pleasure*, reducing it by one-third and omitting the sexually explicit portions, including one homosexual scene that had resulted in enormous criticism, and renamed it *Fanny Hill*. Cleland broke a major eighteenth-century taboo by the very act of including a homosexual encounter—a scene which Fanny describes in great detail and then proceeds to condemn. This cleaned-up version of *Fanny Hill* resulted in Cleland's arrest again, but no legal action appears to have been taken. Oddly enough, Cleland might even have profited from the experience. After being arraigned before the Privy Council, he secured a benefactor: a certain John Earl Granville stepped forward and arranged for Cleland to receive a small annual pension in return for not penning any more bawdy works (but more likely to ensure that Cleland wrote articles in favor of the government).[13] His publisher continued selling the expurgated version, but pirated editions of the longer, more explicit version were much more in demand all over Europe and the book enjoyed a vigorous underground existence for decades.

In many ways, John Cleland's work was a celebration of human sexuality and a reaction against the asceticism imposed by the Church. *Memoirs*, for instance, parodies the whole notion of Christian confession.[14] The novel is structured in the form of a series of first-person letters addressed to an unnamed "Madam," wherein Fanny sets out to confess all the "scandalous stages of my life." But rather than portraying her adventures negatively (as might be expected by this confessional track), she instead delights in titillating and arousing the reader. With its emphasis on sexual pleasure, *Memoirs* also echoes Aretino's *Ragionamenti*, in that it's another version of the whore dialogue—this time cast into novel form.[15]

What made Cleland's work revolutionary—and therefore dangerous in his time—was his sex-positive attitudes and characterizations. At a time when novels were filled with characters who, when they morally transgressed, almost always suffered dire consequences, Cleland's heroine, Fanny, settles into middle-class respectability after a life of sexual adventure. In *Memoirs*, both women and men feel sexual desire: an anarchistic message at a time when "virtuous" women were supposed to be repelled by such thoughts.

Cleland's use of language is also unusual for an erotic novel, since he employs no obscene or objectionable words. While he may have broken societal taboos with his novel, he clearly avoided breaking linguistic ones and in doing so became the master of the sexual metaphor. One rumor has

L'Ecole des Filles *(c.1650s) by Michel Millot was written in the Aretinian tradition as female dialogue—a literary device that was to repeat itself many times over the next century, including John Cleland's* Fanny Hill *and the Marquis de Sade's* Juliette. *L'Ecole des Filles had all the characteristics that link pornography with revolution, in that its anarchistic message was the idealization and celebration of sex.*

FANNY: But when he comes to you, what does he say, and what does he do?

SUZANNE: Usually he sets about it something like this. To start with, he comes at night by a little hidden staircase, when everybody's in bed, and he usually finds me in bed, tucked up for the night, and sometimes even asleep. He wastes no time; he gets undressed, puts a lighted candle by the bedside and then stretches out beside me. He takes a few minutes to get warmed up and then he has a drink and says: "Are you asleep, my love?"— and stretches his hand out over my belly—"I've had such a wearying day I can hardly move." So saying, he tells me all his troubles and puts his hand on my breast and fondles both breasts to his heart's content, telling me what he's being doing all day. He goes on and on at my tits, when he's done with one, he goes to the other, then he does both, and sometimes he says: "God, love, I'm lucky to get this served up every day." Then I can feel him turning onto his side as the fancy suddenly takes him, and sometimes I say: "Oh, love, leave me alone, I want to go to sleep." He doesn't seem to hear me, he puts his hand on my belly, and when he finds my nightdress he pulls it up and puts his hand on my mound and twists and pinches it for a while with his fingers. Then he puts his mouth on mine and slips in his tongue, then he goes and touches my buttocks and my thighs, and then he goes back to my belly, or sucks one of my tits. Then to have his fill of pleasure, because he likes looking, he throws off the sheet and the blanket, and if my nightdress is in the way he makes me take it off, and then he takes the candle and looks me all over. Then he makes me take hold of his thing, and it's all stiff, and sometimes he grabs right hold of me and rolls me all over him, first on top and then underneath, and makes me touch his prick, and between his thighs, and then his buttocks, then comes back again kissing my eyes and my mouth and calling me his dear love, his dear heart.

it that Cleland may have written *Memoirs* to prove that he could produce a book about sex without including an offending word. Thus, in circumventing colloquial terms like "cunt" and "prick," Cleland came up with wonderful euphemisms: over 50 metaphors for penis, such as "master member of the revels," "instrument of pleasure," "picklock," and, oddly, "nipple of Love." For vagina, he invented "soft laboratory of love," "pleasurethirsty channel," "embowered bottom cavity," and "abyss of joy." (See excerpt on pages 382–83.)

Unfortunately, Cleland never made any money from the publication of *Fanny Hill* or from any of the pirated editions. Although he went on to write other novels, including a sequel to *Fanny Hill, Memoirs of a Coxcomb*, he failed to gain much literary attention. He died in 1789.

After that he gets on top of me, puts his great stiff prick in my cunt and rides me till his spunk runs down in my womb.

FANNY: What was that other word besides "ride"? I've forgotten it.

SUZANNE: You say, he fucks me.

FANNY: Do you like it?

SUZANNE: What do you think! Now there are several different ways of putting this thing of his in mine, as I've found out going with him. Sometimes he does me underneath, sometimes on top, or else on my side, or across, or in front, kneeling, or from behind, like taking an enema, sometimes standing up, sometimes sitting down. Sometimes when he's in a hurry he throws me on a form or a chair or a mattress, or whatever he gets to first. Every way of doing it gives him a different kind of pleasure: the different positions he puts me in make his thing go in further, or not so far, or it sits at different angles inside mine. The fuss and bother isn't always so bad, and to be honest it's what makes the fun. Sometimes, if we meet in the daytime and there's no one else there, he makes me rest my hands on a form and bend over, and pulls my dress up behind, right over my head. When I'm like that he can look and gaze to his heart's content, and in case anyone comes in unexpectedly he doesn't take down his breeches, he just pulls his prick out of his fly, comes and shows me and then goes to the door to listen if anyone's coming, and then signals me not to move, comes over and shoves it round by my bum and into my cunt. He's told me Lord knows how many times that he likes it better doing me on the sly like that than any other way.

FANNY: Well, cousin, there must be a lot of pleasure in this, with so many different ways to do it. I can already picture all the ones you've told me, and if it's just a case of finding different ways of putting a prick in a cunt for the pleasure to be got out of it, I think I could soon think up others besides what you've told me, anyone at all could dream up new ones.

Prosecutions against pornography were largely haphazard in England during the eighteenth century, although the publication of pornography was judicially declared to be an offense of common law.[16] As noted, *Fanny Hill* was successfully driven underground without any legal prosecution and, generally speaking, there seems to have been little government interference in regard to publications described as bawdy or licentious. The main exception, of course, was if sexual activity found itself mixed in with politics and/ or blasphemy. Although the major campaigns against obscenity didn't start taking shape until the beginning of the nineteenth century, it was clear that the winds of tolerance were shifting. One of the more perceptible changes occurred in 1787, when King George III issued a proclamation against vice, exhorting the public to "suppress all loose and licentious prints, books, and

One of the reasons Fanny Hill *was dis-*
missed and labeled pornographic is
that many of the pirated editions con-
tained illustrations like this one by Borel
and Elluin from 1776.

publications dispensing poison to the minds of the young and the unwary, and to punish publishers and vendors thereof."[17]

Many of these "licentious" materials were coming in from France and highlighting England's angst over the consequences of politically subversive literature. France was on the brink of revolution, and its preoccupation with "immoral" and "blasphemous" libertine materials was, in the English view, fanning the flames of political insurrection.

III

In the years leading up to the French Revolution, politically motivated pornography increased steadily, reaching a fevered pitch in both volume and vitriol after the presses were freed in 1789. The prime targets were the aristocracy and the clergy, and both groups were frequently depicted as impotent, disease ridden and morally corrupt. Paradoxically, sexually oriented materials, which had once been the sole domain of the upper classes, now became the weapon used by the lower classes against the despised aristocrats.

No one connected with the aristocracy was immune to attack, including King Louis XVI and Queen Marie-Antoinette. Some of the most vicious attacks were leveled at the Queen. Pamphlets questioning the paternity of her children, her wild orgies and presumed lesbian activities circulated for the first time to large numbers of the bourgeoisie and working class.[18] These misogynistic attacks continued even after she was imprisoned, at which point materials were circulated accusing her of having an incestuous relationship with her young son.[19]

The purpose for these vicious assaults was to undermine royal authority; if the king couldn't control his wife or know for certain whether he was the father of his children, then how could he possibly demand obedience from his subjects?[20] Another possible reason for the extreme viciousness may center on the underlying anxiety about the role of women and the issue of delineating clear gender boundaries.[21] Degrading the queen had a kind of leveling, democratizing effect, particularly when she was depicted having sex with members of the lower classes. In other words, her body, especially when portrayed as a prostitute, made her ostensibly available to every man. These attacks continued until she was beheaded in 1793.

The Marquis de Sade's novels marked a major transition in the 1790s. After the French Revolution, pornography lost its political overtones and gradually began to be replaced by material that pushed more generalized social boundaries. Rather than targeting political figures, Sade attacked every aspect of conventional morality.

In many of his works, Sade focused primarily on the complete annihilation of the body in the pursuit of pleasure, and in doing so, he has been characterized as everything from a raving lunatic to the embodiment of the devil to a brilliant philosopher and prophet of disorder. Many of the themes in modern pornography were touched on in Sade's novels. He fixated on exploding bourgeois sensibilities and fantasized about a total inversion of all values—social and sexual. Many of Sade's inverted expressions and ideas detailed in novels like *Justine* and *Juliette* have been perceived as an embryonic form of twentieth-century existentialism and nihilism. (See excerpts on pages 388–89.)

Donatien Alphonse François Sade was born in 1740 to an aristocratic family. In his early years, he lived the life of a debauching aristocrat—until his powerful, politically connected mother-in-law made an arrangement with the government to have him imprisoned. Sade's incarceration gave him the isolation he needed to vent whatever anger he had against God, the state, women, his relatives—all the forces that had conspired to send him to prison. In all, he was incarcerated for twenty-seven years, first under the old regime and then at the hands of the revolutionaries who forced him to spend his declining years in an insane asylum.

Sade can really never be condemned for writing material that arouses. In fact, his obsession with blasphemy would indicate that his greatest mania was religious rather than sexual. The violence aside, his works are hard to read: they're didactic, repetitious and obsessive. It is, however, important to look at how Sade's work plays with gender. In his novels, he scoped out a polymorphous world—one in which sexual differences tended to blur and disappear. It is a world divided not into men and women, but rather slaves and masters. In orgy scenes described in *Juliette*, for example, there is often a switching of roles: females become aggressive and predatory, and males often have sex by penetrating one another. Bestiality, anal intercourse—anything other than ordinary heterosexual sex is presented as being preferable.

Sade's Juliette has a taste for torture and orgies that she shares with such figures as the Pope. She goes from whore to teacher to the complete embodiment of Sade's philosophy. In many ways, Juliette is also a send-up, a parody of the virtuous maiden who zealously guards her virginity (a popular theme in mainstream novels of the day).

The Misfortunes of Virtue, which is considered Sade's greatest contribution to eighteenth-century fiction, was originally written in two weeks. It was later revised as the *New Justine* in 1797, prefacing *Juliette*, and is a bizarre

In many ways, John Cleland's Memoirs of a Woman of Pleasure *(1748–49), aka* Fanny Hill, *was a reaction against the asceticism imposed by the Church. With its emphasis on sexual pleasure,* Fanny Hill *also echoes Aretino's* Ragionamenti *in that it's another version of the whore dialogue. While Cleland may have broken societal taboos with his novel, he clearly avoided breaking linguistic ones and in doing so became the master of the sexual metaphor.*

Here began the usual tender preliminaries, as delicious perhaps as the crowning act of enjoyment itself; which they often beget an impatience of that makes pleasure destructive of itself by hurrying on the final period, and closing that scene of bliss, in which the actors are generally too well pleased with their parts not to wish them an eternity of duration.

When we had sufficiently graduated our advances towards the main point, by toying, kissing, clipping, feeling my breasts, now round and plump, feeling that part of me I might call a furnace-mouth, from the prodigious intense heat his fiery touches had rekindled there, my young sportsman, emboldened by every freedom he could wish, wantonly takes my hand and carries it to that enormous machine of his that stood with a stiffness! a hardness! an upward bent of erection! and which, together with its bottom dependence, the inestimable burse of lady's jewels, formed a grand show out of goods indeed! Then its dimensions, mocking either grasp or span, almost renewed my terrors. I could not conceive how, or by what means, I could take or put such a bulk out of sight. I stroked it gently, on which the mutinous rogue seemed to swell and gather a new degree of fierceness and insolence; so that finding it grew not to be trifled with any longer, I prepared for rubbers in good earnest.

Slipping then a pillow under me, that I might give him the fairest play, I guided officiously with my hand this furious battering-ram whose ruby head, presenting nearest the resemblance of a heart, I applied to its proper mark, which lay as finely elevated as we could wish, my hips being born up and my thighs at their utmost extension; the gleamy warmth that shot from it made him feel that he was at the mouth of the indraught, and driving foreright, the powerfully divided lips of that pleasure-thirsty channel received him. He hesitated a little; then, settled well in the passage, he makes his way up the straights of it, with a difficulty nothing more than pleasing, widening as he went, so as to distend and smooth each soft furrow: our pleasure increasing deliciously, in proportion as our points of mutual touch increased in that so vital part of me in which I had now taken him, all indriven and completely sheathed, and which, crammed as it was, stretched splitting ripe, gave it so gratefully straight an accommodation! so strict a fold! a suction so fierce, that gave and took unutterable delight! We had now reached the closest point of union; but when he backened to come on the fiercer, as if I had been actuated by a fear of losing him, in the height of my fury, I twisted my legs round his naked loins, the flesh of which, so firm, so springy to the touch, quivered again under the pressure; and now I had him every way encircled and begirt; and having drawn him home to me, I kept him fast there, as if I had sought to unite bodies with him at that point. This bred a pause of action, a pleasure stop; whilst that delicate glutton, my nethermouth, as full as it could hold, kept palating, with exquisite relish, the morsel that so deliciously engorged it. But nature could not long endure a pleasure that so highly provoked without satisfying it; pursuing then its darling end, the battery recommenced with redoubled exertion; nor lay I inactive on my side, but encountering him with all the impetuosity of motion I was mistress of, the downy clothing of our meeting mounts was now of real use to break the violence of the tilt and soon, too soon indeed! the high-wrought agitation, the sweet urgency of this to-and-fro friction, raised the titillation on me to its height, so that, finding myself on the point of going, and loath to leave the tender partner of my joys behind me, I employed all the forwarding motions and arts my experience suggested to me to promote his keeping me company to our journey's end. I not only then tightened the pleasure-girth round my restless inmate, by a secret spring of suction and compression that obeys the will in those parts, but stole my hand softly to that store-bag of nature's prime sweets which is so pleasingly attached to its conduit-pipe, from which we receive them; there feeling, and most gently indeed, squeezing those tender globular reservoirs, the magic touch took instant effect, quickened, and brought on upon the spur the symptoms of that sweet agony, the melting moment of dissolution, when pleasure dies by pleasure, and the mysterious engine of it overcomes the titillation it has raised in those parts by plying them with the stream of a warm liquid, that is itself the highest of all titillations, and which they thirstily express and draw in like the hot-natured leech, which, to cool itself, tenaciously attracts all the moisture within its sphere of exsuction: chiming then to me, with exquisite consent, as I melted away, his oily balsamic injection mixing deliciously with the sluices in flow from me, sheathed and blunted all the stings of pleasure, whilst it flung us into an ecstasy that extended us fainting, breathless, entranced.

Between the 1740s and 1790s, pornography in France turned increasingly political, and the use of sexual imagery to underscore political tyranny reached a fevered pitch during the French Revolution. Hundreds of pamphlets were circulated that attacked the aristocracy, most notably King Louis XVI and Queen Marie-Antoinette. The purpose of the image above—which depicts Queen Marie-Antoinette and General Lafayette (the same Lafayette who aided in the American War of Independence)—was to underscore that "degenerate" sexual activities could not be separated from political corruption.

mixture of lust and brutality–the story of a virtuous girl who suffers under the whips and branding irons of her persecutors. The destruction of innocence, particularly if the victim was a young, beautiful female, was a favorite theme of Sade's and gave him endless opportunity to pillory religion and celebrate his belief in a godless universe, where the only "heroes" were those who tortured and murdered their victims.

Philosophy in the Bedroom, which is the shortest and perhaps least sadistic of Sade's novels, traces the gradual sexual initiation and corruption of a fifteen-year-old girl by several male libertines and one woman. The book is divided into seven dialogues in which Eugénie a young innocent, is given information about truth, politics and the world. The truth, of course, is imparted with violence and cruelty, but Eugénie responds with great enthusiasm to her sex education, and by the end of the story, she sees to it that her own mother suffers sexual violence as well. In true Sadian fashion, virtue and religion are described as despicable, while evil and cruelty are celebrated as the true laws of nature. It is important (but difficult) to read Sade with a sense of irony and attempt to view his extreme philosophy as a twisted parody of life. This begins to make greater sense when taking into account that *Philosophy in the Bedroom* was begun when Sade was incarcerated during the Reign of Terror in 1794, and was jailed within view of a guillotine used to execute over 1,800 men and women.[22]

Much like Aretino, Sade used pornography as a way to violate established social codes, but he pushed boundaries unlike anyone before him. His works evoked such fear that the majority were unavailable for public consumption until well into the twentieth century. At the British Museum, for example, where forbidden and "dangerous books" have been collected for well over a century, it was rumored that anyone wishing to read books of the Marquis de Sade would have to do so "in the presence of two museum trustees and the Archbishop of Canterbury."[23]

IV

During the nineteenth century, the traffic in pornography grew at an enormous rate and shifted from France, where it had been dramatically shaped by Sade, to England, where it would become highly commercialized. Ironically, the morally severe Victorian Age yielded some of pornography's most popular classics: *The Romance of Lust*, *The Amatory Experiences of a Sur-*

The major purpose behind politically motivated pornography during the French Revolution was to undermine the old regime. Many of the attacks were leveled at Queen Marie-Antoinette. Misogynistic pamphlets circulated questioning the paternity of her children, her presumed orgies and other sexual transgressions. (From a pamphlet attacking the Queen.)

geon, and *The Autobiography of a Flea*, to name just a few titles. In a century characterized by its rigid moral codes and authoritarian controls, pornography evolved into a genre whose sole *raison d'être* was sexual arousal.

With the French Revolution having sent shock waves throughout Europe, there was greater policing of potentially subversive materials. One major outward sign of changing attitudes in England was the formation in 1802 of the Society for the Suppression of Vice. It sought to get rid of bordellos, as well as to eliminate what it considered obscene, particularly the traffic in salacious materials from Paris. Based on what had happened in France, there was also a lingering fear of political subversion. In 1819, for instance, the Society for the Suppression of Vice successfully prosecuted publisher Richard Carlile for publishing, of all things, Thomas Paine's *Age of Reason*, in which he criticized Christianity and the morality of the Bible. (For this, the publisher spent two years in prison.) This proved to be one of many examples in which obscenity prosecution was used by government as a weapon to silence critics.[24]

Nineteenth-century social reformers were especially mindful of keeping incendiary literature suppressed—and especially out of the hands of women.

From a 1789 Dutch edition of Juliette.

Stricter moral standards evolved and every effort was made to eradicate sexual materials. Greater emphasis was placed on the modesty of women who it was thought, were biologically inferior and hence more impressionable to carnal influences. No longer was porn solely viewed with alarm for its social and political criticism, but for its potential harm in subverting established sexual differences and worst of all, corrupting the innocent.

Just as there was a growing distinction made between chaste women and sinful ones, books began to be classified as either morally uplifting or degrading. An instructional example of the tenor of the times was Dr. Thomas Bowdler, a well-to-do middle-class physician, who in 1818 produced *The Family Shakespeare.* What he did was to "purify" Shakespeare's plays by removing all the offending parts, so that "a man could read aloud to his daughters with complete confidence."[25] *The Family Shakespeare* was a great success. Hence the term "bowdlerize," which means to cleanse a literary work of anything offensive.

While women were protected from anything that might cause a blush to rise in their cheeks, pornography for men in England began to flourish. An official statistic of the Society for the Suppression of Vice indicates that by 1834, there were fifty-seven porn shops on one street in London alone.[26] One popular novel in this period was *The Lustful Turk* by the prolific author, Anonymous. Although it's considered a pre-Victorian novel with its narrative mode and prose style, its themes played out in much of the pornography that was to follow. *The Lustful Turk* is a good example of nineteenth-century pornography with Sadian overtones, particularly in its depiction of violent, aggressive sexuality. (See excerpt on page 392.) The plot of *The Lustful Turk*, as that of many other later works, was largely concerned with this sexuality of domination accompanied by elements of sadism: a reluctant virgin is raped and then herself becomes obsessed with sex. This particular fascination with deflowering virgins permeated much of nineteenth-century Victorian pornography, and was an all-consuming passion in an enormous work called *My Secret Life.*

This recurring theme of the virgin who metamorphoses into a sexually driven character is especially revealing, given the widely held perception of women as sexually pure creatures who, according to Dr. William Acton, a leading physician of the day, were "happily not much troubled with sexual feeling of any kind." Acton further asserted that "love of home, children and domestic duties are the only passions they feel."[27] Pornography's function has often been to mirror the opposite of standardized social behavior, so it seems no surprise that in a society that did not accord women sexual feelings, female porn characters would be portrayed as aggressive and highly sexed.

One of the prominent characteristics of Victorian porn is its almost burlesque quality, and its skewering of family values and institutions at almost every turn. Much like Sade, who excelled at mocking morality, Victorian pornography sought to create moral anarchy whenever possible. In a society that publicly refused to accept homosexuality or any other activity outside the bounds of heterosexual sex, pornography was filled with every possible kind of sex. It seems hardly a coincidence that the golden age of repression gave birth to the golden age of stroke literature. One of pornography's tenets has always been that its characterizations tend to lampoon, if not portray, society's opposites. The powerless morph into the powerful. Pornography becomes a kind of Rorschach test reflecting not only political and social discontent, but central cultural taboos.

Regardless of the increased availability of works with a sexual theme both from French imports and a flourishing underground press, the Society for the Suppression of Vice kept up a steady fight and, over the course of fifty-five years managed a successful prosecution rate of 97 percent.[28] In 1853 the English Parliament passed its first legislation on obscenity, which authorized customs to seize "indecent or obscene prints, paintings, books, cards, engravings or articles." It was regarded as the best way to stem the flow of Parisian etchings, books and the new daguerreotypes, but in reality only served to make everything more expensive.

The underground trade in pornography thrived in spite of the new restrictions, although smaller dealers and street traders who sold cheap prints, books and pamphlets were more vulnerable to the agents of the Society for the Suppression of Vice than booksellers who attempted to screen their clients more carefully. Nevertheless, publishers like William Dugdale, who produced huge amounts of material in the mid-nineteenth century, served at least nine prison sentences for publishing obscene books and prints.[29] Since there were generally no named authors to pay—besides the famed Anonymous or authors like "D. Cameron" (a playful twist on Boccaccio's fourteenh-century collection of bawdy tales entitled *The Decameron*)—publishers made a lot of their money re-printing old works like Sade's. Books like *Fanny Hill* had a rebirth with dozens of re-prints, some of which were enlivened with new chapters or with words altered to make the characters sound more crude and contemporary.

By the early 1850s, a plethora of magazines had emerged, some of them focusing on what Alfred Lord Douglas would later describe as "the love that

The works of the Marquis de Sade marked a major transition in the 1790s. Rather than using graphic sexual depictions for subversive political reasons, he fantasized about a total inversion of all values–social and sexual. In effect, one of his major "sins" lay in libeling bourgeois sensibilities. Much like Aretino, Sade used pornography as a way to violate established social codes.

From *Justine*:

"'Tis not man's election of Virtue which brings him happiness, dear girl, for Virtue, like vice, is nothing beyond a scheme of getting along in the world . . . ; in an entirely virtuous world, I would recommend Virtue to you, because worldly rewards being associated therewith, happiness would infallibly be connected with it too; in a totally corrupt world I would never advise anything but vice. . . . While the general interest of mankind drives it to corruption, he who does not wish to be corrupted with the rest will therefore be fighting against the general interest; well, what happiness can he expect who is in perpetual conflict with the interest of everyone else?"

From *Juliette*:

"The strong individual . . . when he despoils the weak . . . the more atrocious the hurt he inflicts upon the helpless, the greater shall be the voluptuous vibrations in him; injustice is his delectation, he glories in the tears his heavy hand wrings from the unlucky. . . . The more he crushes his woe-ridden prey, the more extreme he renders the contrast and the more rewarding the comparison; and the more, consequently, he adds fuel to the fire of his lust."

From *Juliette* (continued):

Pope Pius VI depicts the joys of slaughter with Juliette:

"In a word, murder is a passion, like gaming, wine, boys and women; never is it got rid of, once it has anchored in habit. No activity irritates as does this one, none prepares so much delight; it is impossible to weary of it; obstacles sharpen its flavor, and the relish for it we have in our heart goes to the point of fanaticism. . . . It exerts a puissant influence at once upon the

dare not speak its name"–homosexuality. Part of this was encouraged by an almost reverential attitude toward Classical Greek art and architecture and by the view that male friendship was somehow a purer expression of love than that between men and women. The contradiction, of course, was that the conventional Victorian view saw homosexuality as completely unacceptable.

In 1868, one of the tightest gags ever imposed on English writers–namely, the Hicklin rule–was to have profound effects on both sides of the Atlantic for decades to come. It established that the test for obscenity was whether or not material could corrupt those whose minds were open to immoral influences. If the answer was yes, the material was suppressed. The rule was applied not only to literary works but to materials like sex education pamphlets.

mind and the body; it inflames all the senses, it enchants, it dazzles. Its impact upon the nervous system, the commotion it produces there is greater by far than that of any other voluptuous agent; one is never fond of this one save inordinately, furiously, one never indulges in it save ecstatically. The plotting of it titillates, the executor electrifies, the remembrance inspires, the temptation to repeat it is enormous, the desire to do this and nothing else, constantly, is overwhelming."

Juliette attends an orgy given by King Ferdinand of Naples:

Dinner was magnificent in the extreme; four girls waited upon us at table, and four pregnant women, lying on the floor beneath our feet, were the targets of all kinds of hard treatment. . . . Electrified by the delicate fare and the exquisite wines, we removed, tipsily, to a superb hall. . . .

Thereupon, in the most anarchical fashion, we fling ourselves at the nearest object to hand: we fuck, have fucked, are fucked; but cruelty always presides over lewd doings as disorderly as ours. Here, breasts were being kneaded and wrung; there, asses were being lashed; to the right cunts were being stretched, gravid women were being martyrized to the left, and moans and sighs of pain or of pleasure, mingled with lamentations to one side, with awful blasphemies to the other side, were . . . the only sounds to be heard. . . .

La Riccia dons a pair of hobnailed boots, places his hands on the shoulders of two men and catapults himself feet first at the belly of the would-be mother who, her seams split, rent, bloodied, faints in her bonds and looses her worthless fruit, upon which the lustful nobleman straightway sprays his foaming seed. Very close to the spot where this occurred, being fucked at once frontwise and from behind, sucking the device of a youth who chose this moment to discharge into my mouth, frigging a cunt with either hand, I could not help but share the Prince's pleasures, and after his example I surrendered my sperm.

From *120 Days of Sodom*:

He binds the girl belly down upon a dining table and eats a piping hot omelette served upon her buttocks. He uses an exceedingly sharp fork.

The Hicklin rule, while a serious deterrent, simply made underground publishers more vigilant.[30] Booksellers kept secretly printed texts and magazines stashed away for only a select and trusted clientele—magazines with rather sophisticated titles like *The English Woman's Domestic Magazine, The Pearl,* and *The Exquisite*—one of the first to feature "pin-ups."[31] Others sounded a bit more suggestive: *The Boudoir, Glee, Pleasure, The Annals of Gallantry.* In short, magazines attempted to cater to every possible taste.

The Pearl (published between 1879 and 1880) contained serialized novels, short stories, poems, songs, jokes, limericks, letters, and gossip with a heavy interest in flagellation, as well as homosexuality and bisexuality. At one point, the entire collection was sold in a three-volume set for the sum

LYSISTRATA.

Social reformers were mindful of keeping incendiary literature suppressed—and especially out of the hands of women. Stricter moral codes evolved and greater emphasis was placed on the modesty of women. But as has often been the case, pornography functioned as a reflection of society's opposites. Much like Sade, who was a master at mocking morality, much nineteenth-century pornography was consumed with characters who embraced the opposite of "family values." (Drawing by Aubrey Beardsley.)

of twenty-five pounds–roughly the annual salary of the average worker of the time.[32]

Aside from the well-worn theme of the reluctant virgin, references to flagellation were ubiquitous in English pornography. judging from titles like *The Curiosities of Flagellation, The Whippingham Papers,* and *The Romance of Chastisement,* among dozens of other works, there was a clear and abiding fascination with it. The possible reasons for this consuming interest in the pleasure of whipping reflect the eroticization of a social reality. Corporal punishment had been an integral part of English culture for hundreds of years, and was more or less institutionalized in schools, the military and the penal system. The predominantly upper-class male audience interested in the flagellation genre would most likely have experienced it as children, where it was an ever-present component of boarding school life. One theory set forth regarding the Victorian fascination with flagellation literature centers on the notion of the buttocks replacing the genitals as the primary erotic zone. This becomes clearer when one analyzes this literature and noting that although it was designed to arouse, the genitals are almost never mentioned.[33]

No study of late-Victorian erotica would be complete without mentioning *My Secret Life,* a four-thousand-page, fact-crammed, first-hand portrait of Victorian sexuality written by "Walter"–presumably an Englishman of some means. Experts disagree on whether or not Walter was, in reality, Sir Henry Spencer Ashbee, a well-known collector of erotic books who ultimately donated his enormous collection to the British Library. Born somewhere between 1820 and 1825, Walter's memoirs essentially span the Victorian era, ending when he is in his mid-sixties. *My Secret Life* details Walter's sexual exploits with over twelve hundred women, recording dress, manners, social customs, and Victorian lifestyle. The book serves as an important document, in that it reveals more of London's lowlife and the exploitation of women and girls, including the massive trade in child prostitution, than any book Charles Dickens might have written. It is an extraordinary example of the thriving sexual subculture that existed in spite of Victorian efforts to eradicate the existence of sex through collective amnesia. (See excerpt on p. 393.)

Fin-de-siècle themes in both art and pornography played with a whole spectrum of ideas, including hermaphroditism, transvestitism, bisexuality, and homosexual love. The sexually provocative drawings of Aubrey Beardsley, for instance, were filled with both hugely erect and sexually ambiguous figures, and *Teleny*, a novel published in 1893 and to which Oscar Wilde is thought to have contributed, is considered to be the first modern

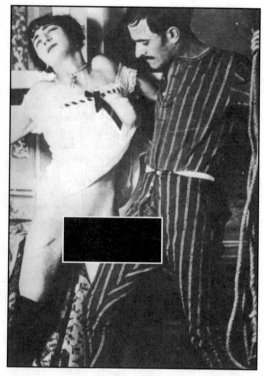

By the end of the nineteenth century, the invention of photography made it possible to disseminate sexual images to an evergrowing middle-class audience. While the 1890s produced some of the more interesting and sophisticated expressions of erotica, it was also the decade in which Oscar Wilde was sent to prison for being homosexual. (Victorian photograph c. 1890s.)

homosexual novel. While the 1890s produced some of the more interesting and sophisticated expressions of erotica, it was also the decade in which Oscar Wilde was sentenced to prison for being homosexual. At his arrest, Wilde was reported to have been carrying a copy of *The Yellow Book*, a controversial magazine that Aubrey Beardsley had helped found. As a consequence, Beardsley lost his job.[34]

Toward the end of the nineteenth century, the production of pornography in England subsided dramatically and shifted again to France, where several London publishers were forced to relocate.[35] In the early part of the century, as well as in the years following the First World War, France would become a publishing epicenter, nurturing writers of literary porn like Henry Miller and Anaïs Nin. It also became the arena for major censorship battles and home to Maurice Girodias' Olympia Press, a publishing house devoted

The Lustful Turk is a pre-Victorian novel, but its themes played out in much of the pornography that was to follow. Its point of view is utterly phallocentric and its depiction of sex is violent and aggressive.

I quickly felt his finger again introducing the head of that terrible engine I had before felt, and which now felt like a pillar of ivory entering me. . . . My petitions, supplications and tears were of no use. I was on the altar, and, butcher-like, he was determined to complete the sacrifice; indeed, my cries seemed only to excite him to the finishing of my ruin, and sucking my lips and breasts with fury, he unrelentingly rooted up all obstacles my virginity offered, tearing and cutting me to pieces, until the complete junction of our bodies announced that the whole of his terrible shaft was buried within me. I could bear the dreadful torment no longer, but uttering a piercing cry sunk insensible in the arms of my cruel ravisher.

Never, oh never shall I forget the delicious transports that followed the stiff insertion; and then, A me!, by what thrilling degrees did he, by his luxurious movements, fiery kisses, and strange touches of his hand to the most crimson parts of my body, reduce me to a voluptuous state of insensibility. I blush to say so powerfully did his ravishing instrument stir up nature within me, that by mere instinct I returned him kiss for kiss, responsively meeting his fierce thrusts, until the fury of the pleasure and ravishment became so overpowering that, unable longer to support the excitement I so luxuriously felt, I fainted in his arms with pleasure. . . . So lively, so repeated were the enjoyments that the Dey caused me to participate with him, I wondered how nature could have slumbered so long within me. I was lost in astonishment that in all the caresses I received from Ludovico he had not contrived to give the slightest alarm or feeling to nature.

almost exclusively to the production of porn novels. In 1947, French publisher Jean-Jacques Pauvert dared to publish the works of the Marquis de Sade, and then proceeded to fight a protracted legal battle in which it was ruled in 1958 that four of Sade's works—*120 Days of Sodom, The New Justine, Juliette,* and *Philosophy in the Boudoir*—would continue to be suppressed. A few years later, however, new publication freedoms made it possible for these works to appear in mass-market paperback editions. Similarly, it wasn't until the 1960s and the defeat of prosecutions against books like *Memoirs of a Woman of Pleasure*—a work written over two hundred years before—that the Western world would finally choose to recognize its erotic masterpieces.

As pornography has been shaped by historical forces, the battle over its existence has most often come down to issues of control: the right of the individual to read, view or produce it versus the right of society to control its consumption. In spite of this culture's heavy sex-negative mantle,

My Secret Life *is a 4,000-page, fact-crammed autobiography detailing one man's exploits with over 1,200 women. It is an enormously valuable document of Victorian-era sex practices, as well as a grim portrait of London's lowlife and the exploitation of women and girls.*

Her tears ran down. If I had not committed a rape, it looked uncommonly like one. . . .

I got off her, saw for an instant her legs wide open, cunt and thighs wet and bloody, she crying, sobbing, rubbing her eyes. I was now in a complete funk; I had heard fieldwomen so lightly spoken of that I expected only to go up a road that had often been travelled. This resistance and crying upset me, the more so when at length rising she said, "I'll tell my sister, and go to the magistrate, and tell how you have served me out."

I really had violated her, saw that it would bear that complexion before a magistrate, so would not let her go, but retained her, coaxed, begged, and promised her money. I would love her, longed for her again, would take her from the fields, and every other sort of nonsense a man would utter under the circumstances. She ceased crying, and stood in sullen mood as I held her asking me to let her go. I took out my purse and offered her money, which she would not take, but eyed wishfully as I kept chinking the gold in my hand. What a temptation bright sovereigns must have been to a girl who earned ninepence a day, and often was without work at all. . . .

wrought by its Judeo-Christian heritage, no Western society has yet been successful at purging sexual expression.

What the last few hundred years *do* seem to reveal is that suppression provides an effective, and often welcome springboard—to *more* sexual expression. In fact, the more a government attempts to squeeze erotic expression out of people, the more new ways it finds to raise its priapic head. Twentieth-century philosopher Herbert Marcuse recognized the potentially revolutionary aspects of pornography in political terms, applauding its subversive function in rigidly ruled societies. Those conforming to the status quo in a sexually repressed culture cannot tolerate pornography because, Marcuse explained: "The unsublimated, unrationalized release of sexual relations would mean the most emphatic release of pleasure as such and the total devaluation of work for work's sake. The tension between the innate value of work and the freedom of pleasure could not be tolerated by the individual; the hopelessness and injustice of working conditions would strikingly penetrate the consciousness of individuals and render impossible their peaceable regimentation in the social system of the bourgeois world."[36]

A concept that Aretino would have heartily endorsed.

NOTES

1. Wayland Young, *Eros Denied* (Brattleboro, Vt.: The Book Press, 1964), p. 94.

2. Lynne Lawner, *I Modi: The Sixteen Pleasures—An Erotic Album of the Italian Renaissance* (Evanston, Ill.: Northwestern University Press, 1988), p. 4.

3. Ibid., p. 15.

4. Ibid., p. 26.

5. Ibid., p. 36.

6. *The Invention of Pornography*, edited by Lynn Hunt (Zone Books, 1993), p. 30.

7. Ibid., Essay: "The Politics of Pornography," by Joan Dejean, p. 110.

8. Ibid., p. 113.

9. Ibid., p. 122.

10. Introduction by Peter Sabor to *Memoirs of a Woman of Pleasure* by John Cleland (Oxford University Press, 1985), p. vii.

11. Introduction by Peter Wagner to *Fanny Hill*, by John Cleland (Penguin Books, 1985), p. 11.

12. Ibid., p. 14.

13. Ibid., p. 14.

14. Ibid., p. 2 1.

15. Ibid., p. 25.

16. H. Montgomery Hyde, *History of Pornography* (London: Heinemann, 1964), p. 163.

17. Ibid. p. 164.

18. Op. cit., *The Invention of Pornography* essay: "Pornography and the French Revolution," by Lynn Hunt, p. 305.

19. Ibid., p. 325.

20. Ibid., p. 306.

21. Ibid., pp. 324-25.

22. Donald Thomas, *The Marquis de Sade* (London: Black Swan, 1993), p. 221.

23. Ibid., p. 16.

24. David Loth, *The Erotic in Literature* (London: Secker & Warburg, 1962), p. 107.

25. Ibid., p. 112.

26. Ibid., p. 113.

27. Steven Marcus, *The Other Victorians* (New York: Basic Books, Inc., 1966), p. 31.

28. Op. cit., *The Erotic in Literature*, p. 118.

29. Donald Thomas, *A Long Time Burning. A History of Literary Censorship in England* (New York: Frederick A. Praeger, 1969), pp. 280-82.

30. The explorer and writer, Sir Richard Burton, who translated the *Kama Sutra* as well as other erotic texts from the East, got away with having his works labeled obscene by publishing them for a very small, scholarly audience. Ibid., p. 259.

31. Peter Webb, *The Erotic Arts* (Boston: Little, Brown and Company, 1975), p. 196.

32. Op. cit., *A Long Time Burning: A History of Literary Censorship in England*, p. 275.

33. Op. cit., *The Other Victorians*, p. 260.

34. Charlotte Hill and William Wallace, *Erotica III. An Illustrated Anthology of Sexual Art and Literature* (New York: Carroll & Graf, 1996), p. 79.

35. Patrick Kearney, *A History of Erotic Literature* (Parragon Book Service, 1982), p. 120.

36. Herbert Marcuse, Zur Kritik des Hedonismus, cited by Robinson in *The*

Sexual Radicals (London: Paladin, 1972); quoted in *The Erotic Arts* by Peter Webb (Boston: Little, Brown and Company, 1975), p. 176.

PHOTOS AND ILLUSTRATIONS

Page 370: Marilyn Yalom, *A History of the Breast* (New York: Alfred A. Knopf, 1997), p. 50.

Page 371: Peter Webb, *The Erotic Arts* (Boston: Little, Brown and Company, 1975), p. 119.

Page 372: Leo Steinberg, *The Sexuality of Christ in Renaissance Art and Modem Oblivion* (The University of Chicago Press, 1996), pp. 88 and 84.

Page 374: Lynne Lawner, *I Modi: The Sixteen Pleasures—An Erotic Album of the Renaissance* (Northwestern University Press, 1988), p. 67.

Page 375: Ibid., p. 73.

Page 376: Ibid., pp. 86-87.

Page 380: *Erotica Universalis*, edited by Gilles Neret (Germany: Benedikt Taschen, 1994), p. 248.

Page 384: Ibid., p. 347.

Page 385: Patrick J. Kearney, *A History of Erotic Literature* (Parragon Book Service, 1982), p. 92.

Page 386: *Erotica Universalis*, p. 320.

Page 390: Ibid., p. 488.

Page 391: Peter Webb, *The Erotic Arts* (Boston: Little, Brown and Company, 1975), p. 199.

BIBLIOGRAPHY

Birkett, Jennifer, trans. *The Body and the Dream: French Erotic Fiction 1464–1900* (London: Quartet Books Ltd., 1983).

Cleland, John. *Fanny Hill* (Penguin Books, 1985).

———. *Memoirs of Woman of Pleasure* (Oxford University Press, 1985).

Hill, Charlotte, and William Wallace. *Erotica III: An Illustrated Anthology of Sexual Art and Literature* (New York: Carroll & Graf, 1996).

Hunt, Lynn, ed. *The Invention of Pornography* (Zone Books, 1993).

Hyde, H. Montgomery. *History of Pornography* (London: Heinemann, 1964).

Kearney. Patrick *A History of Erotic Literature* (Parragon Book Service, 1982).

Lawner, Lynne. *I Modi: The Sixteen Pleasures—An Erotic Album of the Italian Renaissance* (Evanston, Ill.: Northwestern University Press, 1988).

Loth, David. *The Erotic in Literature* (London: Secker & Warburg, 1962).

Marcus, Steven. *The Other Victorians* (New York: Basic Books, Inc., 1966).

Neret, Gilles, ed. *Erotica Universalis* (Germany: Benedikt Taschen, 1994).

Steinberg, Leo. *The Sexuality of Christ in Renaissance Art and Modem Oblivion* (Chicago: The University of Chicago Press, 1996).

Thomas, Donald. *A Long Time Burning: A History of Literary Censorship in England* (New York: Frederick A. Praeger, 1969).

———. *The Marquis de Sade* (London: Black Swan, 1993).

Webb, Peter. *The Erotic Arts* (Boston: Little, Brown and Company, 1975).

Yalom, Marilyn. *A History of the Breast* (New York: Alfred A. Knopf, 1997).

Young, Wayland. *Eros Denied* (Brattleboro, Vt.: The Book Press, 1964).

32

Un-Banning Books:
How the Courts of the United States
Came to Extend First Amendment
Guarantees to Include Pornography

Jack Hafferkamp

IN THE UNITED STATES THE AVERAGE INTERESTED PERSON OF AGE, IS ABLE today, legally, to read and view a wide and deep range of sexually-charged materials because of the evolution of opinion on obscenity issued by the courts of the United States. Mostly this is because of changes that took place in the courts from the 1950s to the 1970s.

The process of reform crested under that most liberal of Supreme Courts, the Earl Warren Supreme Court of 1953 to 1969. The process basically plateaued under Warren E. Burger's tenure as chief justice from 1969–1986. Under Chief Justice William Rehnquist, there has been an uneasy stasis in obscenity law. In 1996, the Supreme Court turned back the Communications Decency Act of 1996, which was about halting porn on the internet. But the freedom to read–to have a conference such as this–is under threat from a new direction, namely the quest for so-called decency.

In June 1998 the Supreme Court upheld a "decency standard" for federal grants to the arts through the National Endowment for the Arts. The context is not quite the same as our specific area for discussion, but the impetus, fueled by a conservative-based effort to limit freedom of expression in sexual matters, cuts across a number of contexts and must be seen as a clear danger to a range of First Amendment freedoms.

The complete history of the evolution of First Amendment privileges is long and complex, going back to the adoption of the Constitution and worthy of a career in its study. I am not a lawyer. I study this subject as an erotologist, the field I have my Ph.D. in. Erotology is an interdisciplinary study of the things a society holds to be erotic. It's a study of the sexual material culture of a society–from the highest art to the lowest trash.

I'm interested for a variety of reasons, not the least of which is that some of the most important court cases involved works that today we celebrate and study as major works of literature in English. These include James Joyce's *Ulysses*, D. H. Lawrence's *Lady Chatterley's Lover*, Henry Miller's *Tropic of Cancer*, John Cleland's *Memoirs of a Woman of Pleasure*, and William Burroughs's *Naked Lunch.*

I'm also interested in the people who stand out as heroes in this history: Margaret Sanger, Margaret Anderson and Jane Heap of *The Little Review*, Bennet Cerf of Random House, Barney Rosset of Grove Press, First Amendment attorneys Charles Rembar and Edward de Grazia and Supreme Court Justices Potter Steward and William Brennan, Jr.

My brief survey puts these cases into a context that better helps to understand where we are today, and why.

DEFINITIONS

Let us begin by defining six terms of primary importance: pornography, obscenity, hardcore, prurience, erotica and decency.

Pornography—from the Greek, is literally "the writing of or about prostitutes." In common American usage it broadly has come to mean any writing or images—either still or moving—or combinations of writing and images that are meant to arouse sexually.

A student of the term's meaning soon learns that its use and misuse frequently cloud public discussions and debates of porn and morality, porn and the law, porn and religion, porn and women, etc. You need to know that legally, the term pornography has meaning only in so far as it relates to obscenity.

Obscenity—from the Latin, meaning "dirty" or "containing filth or excrement." Obscenity is the legally significant term used in discussions of pornography. Only "hardcore pornography" can be banned obscene. The trick, of course, is in determining what is hardcore. For some *Playboy* magazine is hardcore pornography.

Until the 1960s, freedom of expression in America did not generally extend to any sexually related matter. There were some exceptions, usually related to patent medicines and birth control and contraception information, but in general we can say that before the 1960s, sexually-related material, no matter how beautifully written was, by definition, "obscene" expression. The only literary exception was James Joyce's novel *Ulysses*. And it was a special case.

Since 1973 we have lived under what is known as the "Miller Standard" for determining obscenity. It consists of three tests. To be obscene, a work's dominant theme must be prurient, it must offend contemporary community standards and it must lack serious literary, artistic, political or scientific value. This is known as the "three-pronged approach" to determining obscenity.

To be obscene a work must fail all three of the tests. This means that a work may be sexual in theme and offensive to some people, but if it has "serious" literary, artistic, political or scientific value it can not be banned. In her book *Defending Pornography*, American Civil Liberties Union President Nadine Strossen notes, with some ironic humor in her book *Defending Pornography* that lawyers refer to the last point as "SLAPS test."[1]

Hardcore–is the kind of pornography that, according to the Courts, appeals to "sick and morbid" interests, is patently offensive according to community standards and has no serious value.

The concept was re-animated by Chief Justice Warren Burger in the early days of his attempted "counter-revolution" in the 1970s when he was quite open about his efforts to put a cork in what conservatives saw as the rising tide of pornography floated by the Warren Court. In current usage the term "hardcore" has many meanings, each with its own political overtones, depending on who is using it.

Prurience–From the Victorian Era to the Vietnam Era, the U.S. Supreme Court defined as prurient any material that tended to excite lustful thoughts. If it turned you on, it was prurient. And that is the way most people continue to think of prurience.

In the *Lady Chatterley's Lover* case in the 1960s, the court made an important distinction between a normal, healthy expression of sexuality, and material that appeals to a "sick and morbid" interest. For social conservatives, hardcore pornography is bannable because it appeals to a sick and morbid interest. The trick bag in this is that one person's morbid interest is another person's light recreation.

Erotica–At this moment at the end of the twentieth century there is a profusion of "erotica." A question often asked is "What's the difference between pornography and erotica?

The term "erotica" has no meaning legally. But popularly it means "high class" pornography. For some, at both ends of the porn-debate, there is no difference between pornography and erotica. However, I believe the term can usefully be used to differentiate between demeaning, misogynistic, misleading and emotionally numbing types of pornography and a more enlightened, celebratory, tolerant and educational approach to sexual depictions. In this sense erotica at its best provides insight and inspiration.

Decency and indecency–are terms that comes up a lot today–especially in terms of the internet, where the battle lines formed around banning so-called "indecent" material that is taken to be dangerous because it is harmful to children.

In general, indecency has to do with not conforming to a community standard of propriety or modesty. Procensorship activists use the term as an alternate to obscenity, because they can't budge the courts on obscenity grounds. So decency was a term used specifically in the late Communications Decency Act of 1996, which set severe penalties for first-time offenses, including prison terms.

The CDA defined indecency as "any comment, request, suggestion, proposal, image or other communication that, in context, depicts or describes, in terms patently offensive as measured by contemporary community standards, sexual or excretory activities or organs."

The CDA was–as you'll see–a very loud echo of the nineteenth century. The Supreme Court voided the Communications Decency Act in 1997, but that it got as far as it did, shows just who is on the offensive when it comes to First Amendment Freedoms. Decency is at the heart of New York Mayor Rudolph Giuliani's campaign to close the city's sex stores.

FROM HICKLIN TO MARGARET SANGER

American law on the subject of obscenity and pornography came straight from British law. English law was based on what came to be known as the "Hicklin Act."

In 1857, the Lord Chief Justice of England introduced into the House of Lords the Obscene Publications Act, a bill he melodramatically claimed would eliminate the "sale of poison more deadly than prussic acid, strychnine or arsenic."[2] This was prurient materials that would corrupt the morals of innocent children, women and the "weak of mind." This act, he assured members, would not harm literature.

The case testing the act was the prosecution in the 1860s of a militant Protestant. His crime was publishing an anti-Catholic pamphlet that denounced the "depravity" of the confessional booth. Its full title was "The Confessional Unmasked: Shewing the Depravity of the Romanish Priesthood, the Iniquity of the Confessional and the Questions Put to Females in Confession."[3]

This particular fundamentalist was outraged by the things priests supposedly asked young women in the confessional, which he enumerated in his tract. The pamphlets were ordered seized by Benjamin Hicklin, a Wolverhampton magistrate, and the case was decided in 1868. Since then the Obscene Publications Act has popularly been known as the Hicklin Act.

From Hicklin, we get the idea that the test for obscenity should reside in any material's "tendency . . . to deprave and corrupt those whose minds are open to such immoral influences and into whose hands a publication of this sort may fall."[4] Porn's supposed ability to corrupt the naive, that is children and/or women and/or the weak of mind, is a continuing theme, and indeed is today at the heart of the battle over sex in the Internet, on TV, in movies, books and magazines.

Hicklin provided that a search warrant could be issued on sworn information–by anyone–that obscene publications were kept for sale or distribution on any premises, and that the owner of these materials had to show cause why they should not be destroyed. Under Hicklin, then, the burden of proof was on the owner of "obscene material" not the person making the charge. This approach carried over to the United States.

While Hicklin's supporters may have meant well, the act itself left the determination of obscenity up to the people with the narrowest possible interpretation. The result was that under Hicklin, all readers were reduced to what could safely be read by children, women and the "mentally weak." Hicklin not only hobbled literature, it prevented the dissemination of useful information, specifically scientific work and information on birth control and contraception.

So, for example, the findings of serious researchers such as the pioneering sexologist Havelock Ellis were banned. He was prosecuted in England in 1898 for publishing his study on homosexuality called "Sexual Inversions," the first part of his classic *Psychology of Sex*.

Yet instead of stamping out prurient books, Hicklin did just the opposite. It fed the fire for a thriving pornography market in Victorian England and to a lesser extent in he United States. Cheap novels, many of them printed in France and the Low Countries for export to English and American markets, flourished. In London, there also were a number of underground periodicals such as *The Pearl*, which was reprinted to wonder and acclaim by Grove Press nearly a century later.

In the United States, the towering figure of Victorian censorship was Anthony Comstock, who lived from 1844–1915. In granting Comstock the power to censor anything he didn't care for, the United States Congress stunted the American discussion of sexuality and reproduction for nearly a hundred years.

Let me tell you a little about Anthony Comstock. Much like J. Edgar Hoover at the FBI, Comstock in his heyday was able to do pretty much as he pleased. After serving in the Civil War, where *Fanny Hill* was particularly popular among the troops, former grocery clerk Comstock took it upon himself to be the guardian of public morals. His hysterical message found influential backers, including such Victorian magnates as banker J. Pierpont Morgan and Samuel Colgate. Even the *New York Times* praised Comstock for "protecting society from a detestable and dangerous group of enemies."[5]

In 1868 Comstock wrote New York state's law forbidding "immoral" works, and then he took on Washington, D.C. In 1873 he convinced the U.S. Congress to pass the Comstock Act. It not only established stranglingly strict national postal regulations, it gave Comstock the power to use them against any materials he personally considered obscene.

In the first six months of national operation, Comstock seized what he reckoned to be 194,000 obscene pictures and photographs, 134,000 pounds of books, 14,200 stereopticon plates, 60,300 rubber articles, 5,500 sets of playing cards and 31,500 boxes of "aphrodisiacs."[6]

One particular subject Comstock thought obscene was contraception. In fact the first American work on birth control to run afoul of the Comstock law was a pamphlet for married couples by Edward Bliss Foote, inventor of the rubber diaphragm. Comstock saw to it that in 1876 Foote was fined $3,000 for publishing his pamphlet.[7] The result was that birth-control information went underground.

Also in Comstock's very busy decade of the 1870s, he organized the New York Society for the Suppression of Vice. He remained its secretary until his death 42 years later. This organization inspired Boston's Watch and Ward Society and similar organizations in most of America's larger cities. These groups, usually religious and commercial people with strong ties to conservative political leaders, felt quite comfortable dictating what their neighbors could read, and they were remarkably successful. In Chicago, where I'm from, our censors worked their magic until the late 1960s.

Comstock and his supporters did have their critics. George Bernard Shaw, for instance, coined a pejorative term, "comstockery," for self-righteous censors. But Comstock was little troubled by it. During the course of his long career, Comstock claims to have convicted of obscenity "enough persons to fill a passenger train of 61 coaches—60 coaches containing 60 passengers and the 61st not quite full."[8] That's over 3,600 people.

Today we still feel echoes of Comstock in columnists like George Will, publicity seekers such as Donna Rice Hughes and in groups such as the Christian Coalition, the American Family Association, Citizens for Community Values and others that would like to control, in the name of decency, what people can and cannot read and see.

In the face of great social pressure of the Victorian era, one person standing for apart from the fanatics, hucksters, and cynical politicians was Margaret Sanger, who lived from 1883 to 1966. Her experience as a public health nurse in New York's tenements in the early twentieth century and her study with Havelock Ellis in London convinced her that family limitation was a necessary step in social progress, especially where poverty was a factor.

Sanger probably coined the term "birth control" in 1914, and in the same year she began publishing in a magazine called *The Woman Rebel*. Its goal was to get working women to think for themselves. In 1915, Sanger was indicted under the Comstock Act for sending birth control information through the mail. In 1916 she was arrested for conducting America's first birth-control clinic in Brooklyn.

Before her trial Sanger fled to Europe. But her husband, William Sanger, was arrested after he was tricked into giving a copy of her pamphlet, titled "Family Limitation," to a Comstock agent. Partly as a result of this situation, women formed the National Birth Control League in 1915 to demand changes in the law.

Sanger returned to America vowing to keep speaking up, and the government—partly because of the death of Comstock in 1915, and partly because of a new wave of pressure on Sanger's behalf, refused to prosecute. The result was that birth control information became more widely disseminated. However, it was not until 1965 that the U.S. Supreme Court removed the last obstacles in the case of *Griswald* v. *Connecticut* that birth control information could be given out freely in all 50 states.[10]

JAMES JOYCE'S *ULYSSES*

At Comstock's death in 1915, John Sumner took over as the nation's chief censor. Sumner was not the towering figure Comstock was, but he was not without influence. One of his earliest "successes" was in prosecuting two feminists who ran the Washington Square Bookstore in Greenwich Village where they published *The Little Review,* Jane Heap and Margaret Anderson

Anderson was quite an original. A writer, she started *The Little Review* in 1914 in Chicago as an avant garde literary journal that tackled whatever interested her: feminism, Emma Goldman, dadaism and on. She was also drawn to the "experimentalism" of a novel by a young Irish writer named James Joyce.

The novel, of course, was *Ulysses,* which has recently been chosen as the most important novel of the twentieth century in the English language. The *Little Review* began publishing excerpts of *Ulysses* in 1918. In 1920, at about half-way through the novel, Anderson and Heap were brought to trial for publishing in their July/August issue the episode culminating in Leopold Bloom's orgasm while looking up a young woman's skirt as she leans back to look at a fireworks display.

Ulysses is not a casual read. Joyce's novel is constructed as a modern retelling of Homer's *Odyssey.* All the action takes place on a single day, June 16, 1904, in Dublin, Ireland. Probably the most challenging aspect for first-time readers is Joyce's use of complex stream-of-consciousness interior monologues. That is, Joyce writes from inside his characters heads. Molly Bloom's soliloquy at the end of the book is one famous example. So is the "Nausicaa" section, which caused so much trouble for *The Little Review.*

Anderson and Heap were fined $100 for publishing their excerpt and John Sumner had made his point. After the case was lost, James Joyce could not find a publisher in the U.S. or England who would touch *Ulysses* until 1931. In Europe, it was another woman who finally took the plunge. From her famous Paris bookstore, Shakespeare and Co., Sylvia Beach put out an edition in 1922.

When *Ulysses* finally was published in the U.S. in 1932 by Random House, it was still risky for the publisher. According to First Amendment attorney and author Edward de Grazia, who goes over this case in great detail in his highly recommended book *Girls Lean Back Everywhere,* to get the rights Random House had not only to offer more money than other potential publishers, it had to conspire to arrange a favorable court hearing of its case.

The plan of Random House's young boss, Bennet Cerf, was to go to federal court to have the book declared not obscene. He arranged to have a copy of the Sylvia Beach publication confiscated by customs. Then to better their odds, Cerf and his attorney timed the proceedings to come up when a "liberal" federal judge, John M. Woolsey, was sitting.

It worked. Woolsey ruled in 1933 that the work as a whole had literary merit but would not arouse the average person—that is, it was not prurient—and thus should not be held as obscene.

Ulysses, however, was not a complete victory for the freedom to read, because it simply said that this book was not obscene even though it had some sexy parts. The *Ulysses* Standard for judging obscenity still held that obscene literature could be banned. It took another quarter century for works such as D. H. Lawrence's *Lady Chatterley's Lover*, Henry Miller's *Tropic of Cancer*, or even Erskine Caldwell's *God's Little Acre*, or Edmund Wilson's *Memories of Hecate County* to be cleared by the courts.

SAMUEL ROTH TO HENRY MILLER

The next important case did not occur until the 1950s. At that time the Hays Code still applied to films and local censor boards could stop any book they chose.

Samuel Roth was a New York writer and publisher who had gotten into trouble in the 1930s for selling *Ulysses*, among other books. In 1955, Roth was indicted for distributing magazines titled *American Aphrodite, Photo and Body* and *Good Times*. He was prosecuted in New York under the Comstock Act, and the U.S. Supreme Court upheld his conviction for sending obscene materials through the mail. But in reaching that decision in 1957, the court's majority opinion further changed the American standard for obscenity.

In *Roth* v. *U.S.* the Supreme Court spoke directly to the question of whether literature dealing with sex was meant to be protected by the First Amendment. The majority opinion, written by Justice William J. Brennan, Jr., with a look over its shoulder at *Ulysses*, concluded that obscenity was not protected by the First Amendment, but literature was. Brennan, who retired from the court in 1990, passed away last summer (1997).

At the time it was issued, Brennan's *Roth* decision was widely accepted as giving constitutional approval to the established law of obscenity. But in the hands of some very skillful First Amendment lawyers, especially Edward de Grazia and Charles Rembar, the Roth case provided the wedge for opening up the definition of obscenity and extending First Amendment protections.

The next significant case came in 1960, over the U.S. Postal Ban on *Lady Chatterley's Lover*, which had been published by Grove Press. This case did not have to go as far as the U.S. Supreme Court to make impact.

In case you don't know the book, *Lady Chatterley's Lover* was D. H. Lawrence's last novel. It revolves around Lawrence's belief that men and women must overcome the deadening squeeze of industrialized society and follow their natural instincts to passionate love. Lady Chatterley is married, unhappily, to a wealthy but paralyzed landowner. She turns to Mellors, her husband's groundskeeper and a symbol of natural man, to find passionate love, which Lawrence describes in a literal, photographic fashion—albeit often in difficult reading dialect.

The publisher of the American edition of *Lady Chatterley's Lover* was Grove Press, owned by Barney Rosset. Postal authorities seized Rosset's edition under the Comstock Act. Rosset's attorney, Charles Rembar, argued in federal district court that the book deserves First Amendment protections for two reasons:

1) It has literary merit.

2) There is a distinction between prurience and a "normal sexual interest." Rembar argued successfully that the book dealt in a normal, healthy sexual interest, which was not at all the same as a sick or morbid prurient interest.[11]

Rembar prevailed and *Lady Chatterley* then paved the way for the really big case that started in 1961 and involved Henry Miller's autobiographical novel *Tropic of Cancer*.

Miller's style in *Tropic of Cancer* and his other best known works is explicit but not erotic. The book is offhandedly funny, crude, rude and perceptive. It offers a mirror-like insight into the bohemian life of Paris in the 1930s. It is definitely worth reading again if you haven't in a while—if for no other reason to see just how politically incorrect it is.

It was Barney Rosset's Grove Press that published the first aboveground American edition of *Tropic of Cancer*, along with *Lady Chatterley's Lover*, *Naked Lunch*, *The Story of O*, and, really, a store full of books that grabbed America's attention. If there is a single hero in the history of unbanning books in America, it probably is Barney Rosset. He may be a flawed hero, but it was Rosset who determined to end censorship in America and he pretty much got it.

Rosset bought Grove Press for $3,000 after the end of World War II. In the 1950s he turned it into America's most exciting publishing house. He brought the European avant-garde to America: Samuel Beckett, Jean Genet, Marguerite Duras, and Alain Robbe-Grillet. He also published Jack Kerouac and Allen Ginsberg.

In the 1960s Rosset shifted to the work of the "Anglo-American sex radicals," including D. H. Lawrence, Henry Miller, John Rechy, William Burroughs, and third-world political radicals, including Frantz Fanon, Che Guevara and Malcolm X. Grove Press still exists, but Barney Rosset is no longer associated. A few years ago, in a money squeeze, he was forced out. Rosset now operates Blue Moon Books.

Rosset very consciously chose *Lady Chatterley's Lover* as his first tool for tackling American censorship. It's success emboldened him to take another step. His next case involved *Tropic of Cancer*, which, Grove Published in 1961, the year after litigation on *Lady Chatterley's Lover* ended.

It wasn't the hardback version of the *Tropic of Cancer* that was taken off bookstore shelves. It was the paperback edition, starting in Chicago and suburbs, where the hardcover had been selling peacefully for some while. The problem, as the censors saw it, was that because paperbacks are cheap and sold in drug and small variety stores they were more "available" to minors, and therefore should be suppressed. This reasoning, please note, is pure Hicklin.

Eventually there were cases against the book all over the country, perhaps 60 or so, in all and there was much jockeying for position among attorneys concerning whose case would find its way to the U.S. Supreme Court. It wound up being the Florida case, and the lead attorney was Edward de Grazia. The case, which was settled in 1964, is known as *Grove Press, Inc.* v. *Gerstein.*

At the time, the United States Supreme Court had a decided liberal majority, including Justice Brennan, Hugo Black, William O. Douglas, Arthur Goldberg, and Potter Stewart and Chief Justice Earl Warren. The *Tropic of Cancer* case wasn't the only case dealing with obscenity on the court's docket in that year, and it was joined with a case against *The Lovers,* a film by the late Louis Malle, starring Jeanne Moreau.

Given the court's composition, de Grazia's strategy for freeing *Tropic of Cancer* and *The Lovers* was to convince the court that valued cultural expression is at least as important as a work's sexual content for determining if it deserves First Amendment protection. In his petition to the court de Grazia wrote "regardless of its 'prurient appeal' or 'patent offensiveness,' *Tropic of Cancer* has obvious literary and social importance, which entitle it to full [First Amendment] protection."[12]

THE "BRENNAN DOCTRINE"

According to de Grazia, the pivotal figure in the court's *Tropic of Cancer* decision was Justice Brennan. His opinion elucidated what de Grazia calls The Brennan Doctrine. It essentially turned the established notions of book banning on their head because it accepted de Grazia's argument, declaring that instead of banning books because they have things in them that offend some people, no book should be banned unless it is utterly without value.

The key word in Brennan's opinion was "utterly." In Brennan's view obscenity did not enjoy First Amendment protections, but only work "utterly without social importance" could be branded obscene.

What the Brennan Doctrine meant was that it was now very difficult for prosecutors to prove works obscene, but easy for defense lawyers to demonstrate that the works of their clients should be entitled to First Amendment protection.

To this day, pro-censorship forces argue that the *Tropic of Cancer* decision mocked the founding father's intentions with regard to freedom of the press. They still bash Brennan and his colleagues for unleashing the "tides of pornography" that were washing over the American democracy.

Certainly the momentum of the Brennan doctrine did not stop with *Tropic of Cancer.* In fact, its concept of "social value" was clarified and expanded in the 1966 case against *John Cleland's Memoirs of a Woman of Pleasure* v. *Massachusetts*—otherwise known as the *Fanny Hill* case.

Actually 1966 was a big year for obscenity cases in the Supreme Court. There were three major decisions to know about. They involved *Fanny Hill,* three publications by Ralph Ginzburg, and a group of fetish, bondage and S/M booklets commissioned and published by Samuel Mishkin. Taken together these decisions demonstrated that while the Supreme Court was open to allowing "literature" to flourish, it had no problem setting limits on other so-called obscene works.

In the *Fanny Hill* case the big question for the court was "Does this book have any literary merit? Even Brennan, de Grazia concludes, wasn't certain it did.

It was attorney Charles Rembar who tried to convince the Supreme Court that *Fanny Hill* had "literary merit, historical significance and psychological values." He argued that there could be no such thing as "well-written pornography." If a work was well-written, Rembar pleaded, it could not be considered "pornography."

Rembar carried the day; the vote was six to three in favor of Fanny Hill. And more importantly, the case established a new Supreme Court standard for obscenity, the Memoirs Standard. This is the three-pronged approach mentioned at the outset. For a work to be judged obscene, "Three elements must coalesce, it must be established that:

a) the dominant theme of the material taken as a whole appeals to the prurient interest in sex ;
b) the material is patently offensive because it affronts contemporary community standards relating to the description or representation of sexual matters; and
c) the material is utterly without redeeming social value.

Each of these three criteria was to be applied independently; the social value of a book, for example, cannot be weighed against or canceled out by its prurient appeal or patent offensiveness.[13]

This Memoirs Standard decision was a great advance in opening America to legitimate literature that happens to deal with sexuality. Because of it books like Vladimir Nabokov's *Lolita*, Terry Southern and Mason Hofenberg's *Candy*, and Pauline Réage's *The Story of O* became readily available, and shows like *Marat/Sade*, *Hair*, and *Oh, Calcutta!* could appear on Broadway.

But as is often the case when the Supreme Court justices are asked to a dance, one big step forward is followed by a step to the side and a step back. The other two big cases of March 21, 1966, show that the Court was not throwing the door open to everyone and everything. The Ginzburg and Mishkin cases had quite different outcomes—even though they, too, were authored chiefly by Justice Brennan.

Samuel Mishkin was on trial under New York state's anti-obscenity statutes for publishing pulp fetish/porn books. Their themes involved fetishism, sadism, masochism and homosexuality. Mishkin's titles included *Mistress of Leather*, *The Whipping Chorus Girls*, *Swish Bottom* and *So Firm and Fully Packed.*

The case against Mishkin was based on his books supposed prurient interest and lack of redeeming literary or social value. The final vote was six to three against and Mishkin's conviction and three-year sentence was upheld. His books, it was concluded, had no literary value, offended community standards, and were purely prurient.

More interestingly was the case against Ralph Ginzburg. It was Attorney General Robert Kennedy who went after Ginzburg for violating the Comstock Act with three publications, his lovely hard-cover magazine *Eros*, a newsletter called *Liaison* and the whimsically titled book the *Housewife's Guide to Selected Promiscuity*. Thanks to federal efforts, Ginzburg had been convicted, sentenced to five years, and fined $42,000 for essentially what was a bad joke.

Ginzburg's problem was different from Mishkin's. His difficulty wasn't with what he was selling so much as the way he sold it. What was on trial was Ginzburg's blatancy in exploiting the new freedoms granted by the courts. His marketing of *Eros*, for example, was not subtle. Ginzburg wanted to mail promo materials from the Pennsylvania Amish towns of Blue Ball, and Intercourse. Refused there, he finally succeeded in mailing it from Middlesex, New Jersey. Postal authorities then arrested him for pandering to the prurient interest.

While the justices agreed that his publications had "marginal" social value, the court as a whole didn't at all care for his promotional methods. Many people, including some on the court, thought he had gone too far in flaunting a full-color interracial photo spread. Today, the spread looks–to me at least–quite lovely, very soft by even the standards of today's mainstream ads–think no farther than the Calvin Klein ads appearing on busses a couple of years back. But in the days of the rising tide of the Civil Rights Movement, these photos were the icing on Ginzburg's cake. Politically, Ginzburg pushed all the wrong buttons, and the court voted five to four against him.

In the end, Ginzburg actually served eight months and then was quietly released. He's been quiet ever since.

Taken together, what the three 1966 cases came to was ambiguity. *Fanny Hill* was okay because it was literature. *Swish Bottom* was not because it wasn't. But where, exactly was the line between them? And darn that Ginzburg, he was the wild hair in the formula. His conviction didn't go down so easily among the justices.

The case that pushed the concept of literature to a new extreme involved yet another Grove Press edition, this time of William Burroughs's very strange and difficult book *Naked Lunch*. As you know, Burroughs was another death last year, along with his friend and "editor," Allen Ginsberg.

Naked Lunch is a nightmarish plunge into the world of a boundary-pushing gay junkie. It is unlike typical novels in that it has no apparent structure, and in fact was created by cutting and pasting bits and pieces of writing. Many readers find it almost impossible to read, because while it is sometimes very funny, it is also by turns ugly, tedious, and annoying. It is a challenge.

Grove Press set about publishing *Naked Lunch* in 1959. But once he had copies printed, Barney Rosset put them in a warehouse until 1963, when he decided time was right for putting this particular book out. The case resulted from a bust in Boston. It reached the Massachusetts Supreme Judicial Court in 1966. Grove's trial strategy was simply to show that the book had undeniable "social importance."

It was to be a test of the Brennan doctrine based on a book that had something to offend everyone. Edward de Grazia used his literary big guns to defend the book: novelist Norman Mailer and poets Allen Ginsberg and John Ciardi as well as others, were called to testify on the book's value. The Boston trial judge didn't buy it, but the appeal to the Massachusetts Supreme Judicial Court on the basis of social importance got a reversal. *Naked Lunch* was thus the last undisputed work of literature censored by the United States Post Office, customs or state government.

And if *Naked Lunch* was literature, who then could say what was not? The case that really threw open the flood gates came in 1967. It was *Redrup v. New York.* Robert Redrup was a Times Square newsstand clerk who sold two pulp sex novels, *Lust Pool* and *Shame Agent* to plainclothes police. He was tried and convicted in 1965. The books were published by William Hamling and he paid Redrup's legal bills to the Supreme Court.[14]

According to de Grazia, Hamling firmly believed that he was not selling—as was said about his books—"commercialized obscenity," nor would he admit to "titillating the prurient interests of people with a weakness for such expression." Hamling felt his books were giving people who would never have the skills to read and enjoy *Ulysses* or *Fanny Hill* or *Naked Lunch* what they wanted. De Grazia also says that the judicial spearhead of Redrup was Justice Potter Stewart.

It was Stewart, of course, who in an earlier case wrote the famous line about not being able to define pornography, but knowing it when he sees it. In Redrup, Stewart went far beyond his established just-left-of-center position on obscenity to the most radical of outlooks. Apparently the vote to affirm Ralph Ginzburg's conviction was his personal wake-up call. In his *Ginzburg* dissent Stewart wrote:

> Censorship reflects a society's lack of confidence in itself. It is a hallmark of an authoritarian regime. Long ago those who wrote our First Amendment charted a different course. They believed a society can be truly strong only when it is truly free. In the realm of expression they put their faith, for better or worse, in the enlightened choice of the people, free from the interference of a policeman's intrusive thumb or a judge's heavy hand. So it is that the Constitution protects coarse expression as well as refined, and vulgarity no less than of elegance. A book worthless to me may convey something of value to my neighbor. In the free society to which our Constitution has committed us, it is for each to choose for himself.[15]

Stewart's arguments were persuasive enough to convince the court to reverse Redrup's conviction by seven to two. This was the decision by the

United States Supreme Court to affirm that consenting adults in the U.S. ought to be constitutionally entitled to acquire and read any publication that they wish—including concededly obscene or pornographic ones—without governmental interference.

Under this guiding principle, the Supreme Court systematically and summarily reversed without further opinion scores of obscenity rulings involving paperback sex books, girlie magazines and peep shows. Redrup became a descriptive term. To Redrup a case meant to dismiss it out of hand.

This practice lasted until 1973, when Justice Byron White changed sides to join the emerging new conservative majority in the Warren burger-led court.[16]

WARREN BURGER AND THE MILLER STANDARD

The highwater mark of the Supreme Court's liberalization involving freedom of individual choice in sexually related matters came in 1973 with *Roe* v. *Wade*, which made abortion a legal choice in the United States. But even before *Roe* changes were afoot in the court's momentum. When Warren Burger replaced Earl Warren as Chief Justice in 1969, he came in making it known that he very much wanted to reverse the process that had redefined obscenity and opened America's door to people reading whatever they wanted.

In 1973, the same year as *Roe*, the court experienced a sea change on the question of obscenity. The Supreme Court rejected the Memoirs Standard in favor of the more restrictive Miller Standard we now live under. As ACLU President Nadine Strossen puts it, in the swing year of 1973, taking Roe and Miller together ". . . the court decreased the government's power to curb sexual conduct but it increased the government's power to curb sexual expression."[17]

The Miller case, *Miller* v. *California*, was not about Henry Miller; it was about Marvin Miller, a California publisher who put out four illustrated books titled *Man-Woman, Intercourse, Sex Orgies Illustrated and An Illustrated History of Pornography* and a film, *Marital Intercourse*. He was arrested for violating California's anti-obscenity law. Under the new court majority Miller's conviction was upheld. In his majority opinion Burger redefined obscenity in terms of work without serious literary, artistic, political or scientific value. Instead of having to be *utterly without redeeming value*, to be protected under Burger's reinterpretation, a work had to have *serious value*.

By limiting the power of the "without redeeming value" aspect of the three-pronged test, the Miller guidelines gave more power to the other two prongs of the three pronged test: contemporary community standards and prurience. It is through these two "windows" that the decency argument has entered the obscenity equation.

Justice Burger's stated aim in *Miller* was to dismantle the notion of a single permissive national standard and to open the door to "contemporary community standards." It was, in effect, Burger's end-around the court's Redrup policy. His *Miller* decision was crafted to provide local community censors with the tools to prohibit works they do not want people seeing.

Burger was quite explicit about having this exact goal in mind. For example, he noted that while it was not the court's function to "propose regulatory schemes" regarding obscenity, he, as Chief Justice, was perfectly willing to offer some "plain examples" of what a state could define for regulation. These included "patently offensive representations or descriptions of ultimate sexual acts, normal or perverted, actual or simulated, including patently offensive representations or descriptions of masturbation, excretory functions, and lewd exhibition of the genitals." This kind of material, Burger concluded, was "hard-core pornography." That is, pornography that goes beyond merely being arousing to appeal to the morbid or sick interest.[18]

Burger's notion of community standards allowed Harry Reams, co-star of *Deep Throat* to be convicted of obscenity in Memphis even though he had never been to Memphis. Burger's approach allowed Al Goldstein, publisher of *Screw* to be prosecuted in Wichita, Kansas, even though his magazine was not sold on Wichita newsstands. And so, too, did this approach make possible for Larry Flynt, publisher of *Hustler*, to be convicted in Cincinnati of engaging in organized crime and pandering obscenity.

Fortunately, Burger's counterrevolution was cut short by *Jenkins* v. *Georgia* in 1974. This case concerned the Mike Nichols-directed film *Carnal Knowledge*, which starred Jack Nicholson, Candice Bergen, Ann-Margret, and Art Garfunkle. It is a very good, artistically serious film about the sexual attitudes of two men who come to symbolize the generation that came of age at the end of World War II. A community in Georgia decided it didn't care for the film's morals and moved to have it banned as obscene.

In a sense the case was a replay of *Ulysses* because it involved an artistic work that included sexual elements in its elucidation of character. To vote to uphold the conviction would be to unplug the three-pronged approach to First Amendment Freedoms and allow community standards to become the primary criterion for determining obscenity. And on this point Burger's majority faltered. A strict local standards policy, the court realized, would essentially allow the least tolerant local community to decide national standards.

Instead of promoting many independent local standards of obscenity—as Burger had claimed he was in favor of—this approach would reimpose a national standard—one that would be drastically restrictive. Even conservative justices were not willing to go that far, because it would have time-warped America directly back to the Comstock era.

TODAY

Since then, even as the chief justice chair passed to William Rehnquist in 1986, the Supreme Court has been in a kind of uneasy stasis on the question of obscenity, stuck between rules for obscenity law that are quite liberal and a Congress that is much more conservative and increasingly restive.

We have come to take the Miller Standard's relatively liberal freedoms for granted because after twenty-five years they seem so familiar and easy. We can read pretty much what we want, buy condoms and other birth-control supplies freely, we can see sexy stuff on our cable TV, we can dial up 900 numbers for phone sex or we can call up live companions from the pages of escort ads in the Yellow Pages. We can order up dildos and vibrators from mail order houses. We can look at pictures of naked people on the Internet.

But of course, none of this means we have these rights in perpetuity. There are plenty of people out there who think we were better off with Comstockery—neo-Victorian feminists, the religious right, politicians eager for an emotional issue, and even middle-class parents who are confused and afraid of exposing their children to harmful material. They are a powerful voice.

And their current tool of choice for dismantling the three-pronged approach is to move forward a "decency standard" for determining what work should be banned. As noted, in 1997 they got as far as the Supreme Court with the Communications Decency Act. Which is essentially the same old Hicklin act dressed up in another format. This time it was about limiting communication on the world wide web to what the most conservative communities in the country deem to be ok.

The CDA's framers realized that by attacking obscenity head on they were fighting a losing battle. So they substituted the concept of decency, which like Chief Justice Burger's concept of community standards, has a nice warm and fuzzy ring.

One bombshell in the CDA was that it did not stop with images. It included "indecent" written text by itself—something that has not been an issue in books since *Naked Lunch.*

And that's not the end of the nineteenth-century echoes in the CDA. According to the *New York Times:* "In a move that appeared to surprise many House and Senate members who voted for the legislation, Representative Henry J. Hyde of Illinois, a Republican and longtime abortion opponent, successfully added an amendment that would extend into the electronic age a 123-year-old legal prohibition, the Comstock Act of 1873, against disseminating abortion information."[19]

Sounding exactly like the Lord Chief Justice of England in 1857, Hyde, chairman of the House Judiciary Committee, "denied that his intent was to halt discussion of abortion on the Internet or on-line services." It was merely to prevent the passing along of information on how to do it and where.[20]

The Supreme Court's decision to shortcircuit the restrictions of the CDA was good news. But it certainly was not be the end of the story. This summer the Supreme Court established that there is, indeed, a decency standard—at least as far as grants from the National Endowment for the Arts is concerned. And the majority opinion underscored the court's position that "decency is a permissible factor where 'educational suitability' motivates . . ." the NEA's grants.

The court also clearly noted that the legislation in question in this case doesn't force the NEA to give or not give grants, but it does admonish the agency to take both "decency" and "respect" for community standards into consideration when making decisions.

Does this mean the door is now open a little wider for diminishing freedom through decency standards. I don't know the answer. But I do know that as long as sexuality is a hot-button issue; as long as people are afraid of it.; as long as people are abused sexually; as long as people exploit sex for political ends, any freedom in this area is not guaranteed.

Nadine Srossen of the ACLU says it best: "Sexually oriented expression long has been relegated to the bottom of the (Supreme) Court's First Amendment pecking order."[21]

You have been warned.

UNITED STATES OBSCENITY STANDARDS SINCE THE CIVIL WAR

- Hicklin Standard: obscenity is defined as the tendency to corrupt—that is arouse sexually—those whose minds are vulnerable, including women, children, and the weak of mind. (Midnineteenth century to 1932)
- *Ulysses* Standard: Obscenity is defined as work that would tend to arouse the average person. (1932 to 1957)
- Roth Standard: If, to the average person, applying contemporary community standards, the dominant theme of the material taken as a whole appeals to the prurient interest, it is defined as obscene. (1957 to 1964)
- Memoirs Standard: For a work to be judged obscene, three elements must coalesce: it must be established that a) the dominant theme of the material taken as a whole appeals to the prurient interest in sex; b) the material is patently offensive because it affronts contemporary community standards relating to the description or representation of sexual matters; and c) the material is *utterly* without redeeming social value. Each of the three criteria is to be applied independently. So, for example, the social value of a book cannot be canceled out because of prurient appeal or patent offensiveness. (1964 to 1973)
- Miller Standard: It is the current test for obscenity. It deleted the "utterly without redeeming social value" criterion from the Memoirs standard and substituted the notion of whether the work taken as a whole lacks serious literary, artistic, political or scientific value. The Miller standard also allows the jury to measure prurient appeal and patent offensiveness by the standard that prevails in the local or regional community. (1973 to present)

NOTES:

1. Nadine Strossen, *Defending Pornography* (Scribner, 1995), p. 52.

2. Quoted in *Sin, Sickness and Sanity: A History of Sexual Attitudes* by Vern Bullough and Bonnie Bullough (New American Library, 1997), p. 169.

3. Richard F. Hixson, *Pornography and the Justices* (Southern Illinois University Press, 1996), p. 7.

4. Quoted in *Sin, Sickness and Sanity: A History of Sexual Attitudes* by Vern Bullough and Bonnie Bullough (New American Library, 1997), p. 170.

5. Quoted in *Girls Lean Back Everywhere: The Law of Obscenity and the Assault on Genius* by Edward de Grazia (Random House, 1992), p. 6.

6. Ibid., p. 4.

7. Bullough, p. 109.

8. De Grazia, p. 4.

9. *1000 Makers of the Twentieth Century*, edited by Godfrey Smith (Times Newspapers Limited, 1971), Alphabetical listing.

10. Bullough, p. 110.

11. Charles Rembar, *The End of Obscenity: The Trials of* Lady Chatterley, Tropic of Cancer *and* Fanny Hill (Harper & Row, 1968), p. 119.

12. See de Grazia for a more detailed history of the case.

13. Leon Hurwitz, *The Historical Dictionary of Censorship in the United States* (Greenwood Press, 1985), p. 223.

14. De Grazia, p. 513.

15. De Grazia, p. 516.

16. For a concise summary see de Grazia.

17. Stossen, p. 52

18. As quoted in de Grazia, pp. 566–67.

19. *New York Times*, Feb. 8, 1996.

20. Later in the summer of 1998, Henry J. Hyde drew national attention as his committee, with a Republican majority, voted to send Congressional impeachment proceedings to the full House.

21. Strossen, p. 51.

33

Erotic Witness: The Rise and Flourishing of Genitally Explicit and Sex Act Explicit Heterosexually Oriented Photographic Magazines in the U.S., 1965–1985

Louis H. Swartz

> To see a world in a grain of sand
> And a heaven in a wild flower,
> Hold infinity in the palm of your hand
> And eternity in an hour.
>
> Blake, *Auguries of Innocence*

> The task of the artist is to sense more keenly than others the harmony of the world, the beauty and the outrage of what man has done to it, and poignantly to let people know.
>
> Solzhenitsyn, Nobel Lecture

M Y OBSERVATIONS HERE BUILD UPON SEVERAL RICH TRADITIONS, among them two which deserve special emphasis. One is the tradition of a free society. The other is the much less well understood tradition of erotology. As in the American case, the two may be intimately related. In a free society, what is freedom for? I agree with those who say that it is for the purpose of individuals and groups questing after the ideals of truth, beauty, the good, and the ideal of mutual tolerance (Swartz 1998). For me erotology, about which I will say more later, is inspired by these same ideals as they relate to erotic aspects of our being. I take such terms as erotic delight and erotic transcendence to refer to some of these matters in a poetic appreciative language. (See also McIlvenna 1997; Ricoeur 1971; Swartz 1994b.) In this paper I attempt to establish a framework for further scholarship and further discussion concerning certain erotic photographic magazines, including their meaning and social significance. I give priority to the enormously important theme of visual meaning. That is where understanding has been lacking.

TREASURE TROVE IN POPULAR CULTURE

A flowering of erotic heterosexually oriented, genitally explicit and sex act explicit adult photographic magazines took place in the United States during the period 1965–1985. Although we have literature dealing with erotic films and videos, and some so-called men's magazines which sought mainstream attention, we have had almost no journalistic or scholarly comment about the magazines discussed here. They constitute a wonderful, unrecognized treasure trove within American popular culture.

Far from degrading women and sexuality, this material most often tended to celebrate both in a positive way. As opposed to more recently prevalent erotic photographic magazines, if this material was transgressive it was so mainly within a framework inspired by ideals of the day concerning the delightfulness, the goodness and the beauty of ordinary women and men as genitally embodied sexually active people. Titles of series in the genitally explicit category include Film and Figure; publishers include Tudor House and Parliament Publications. In the sex act explicit class Academy Press was a leader, and high quality work under other imprints included Let's Pretend, Bon Vivant series, Connoisseur, Gourmet Edition, American Erotica, It's a Knockout, Le Baron, and (selectively) some of the Swedish Erotica series.

Because of legal and social campaigns against so-called pornography which can be expected to continue, we may never know many of the details of how this material was designed, produced and distributed. It came about when there was a favorable concurrence of several factors. These included strong protection of freedom of expression grounded in U.S. constitutional law plus the electrifying influence of elimination of sex censorship in Denmark, technological developments in color photography and high quality color reproduction, affluence, leisure, and on the social scene a confidence and zest with respect to what was enthusiastically greeted as sexual freedom and sexual liberation. Medically there was recent widespread availability of highly effective contraception, and the illusion of freedom from sexually transmitted diseases not readily curable had not yet been effectively dispelled. Of central importance was an erotic adventurousness of many women, and a drastic reduction in social stigmatization of sexually joyful women.

Magazine categories include (in the genitally explicit class), figure model, nudist transitional, and genital display, and (in the sex act explicit class), educational format, and sex act narrative and fantasy.

Existing Literature and Magazine Classification

Very little published literature deals directly and specifically with the magazines discussed here. The main sources of descriptive information are, in chronological order, the Report of the United States Commission on Obscenity and Pornography (1970) [the Lockhart Commission], sections of the Technical Report of the Commission (Sampson, 1971), Hebditch and Anning's book (1988) mostly emphasizing Europe and Asia, the Meese Commission and work done for that Commission (United States. Attorney General's Commission on Pornography 1986; Dietz and Sears 1987-1988; Linz and Donnerstein 1987-1988), and "The Business of Porn" articles in *U.S. News & World Report*, February 10, 1997. Much attention has been paid in one way or another, however, to erotic films and videotapes. In addition to works cited in the preceding sentence see the following, as a small sample: Hoffman 1965, 1973; Knight and Alpert 1967; Lasano 1973, 1975; Turan and Zito 1974; Williams 1989. Mainstream "men's magazines" (e.g., Hall 1982; Laner 1976; Riemschneider 1997) have been much discussed. Other literature deals with earlier printed visual material, e.g., Adelman 1997; Batters 1995, 1997; Gabor 1973 [republished 1996]; Server 1994; Stein 1994. Still other literature includes the following: gay male visual erotica (Waugh 1996); general reviews of erotica and sexuality in the U. S. at various times since 1950 (Chapple and Talbot 1989; Heidenry 1997; Talese 1980), the history of eros in Western civilization (e.g., Young 1964), and the history of photography, including nude photography (e.g., Pultz 1995). Crucial to an understanding of the joyful climate of the late 1960s and early 1970s are two beautiful books by Alex Comfort (1972, 1974), and Howard's (1970) book is useful. Sexological literature generally dealing with pornography and the erotic is extensive and I have not attempted to cite those works here. Finally, and of great importance, we have literature upholding legal freedom of expression, and describing the struggle to maintain such freedom (e.g., Brigman 1983; Grazia 1992; Grazia and Newman 1982; Heins 1993; Henkin 1963; Strossen 1995; see also Swartz 1994a).

Hartman, et al. (1970: 407-419) lists nudist magazines including some, such as three different *Jaybird* titles plus *Film and Figure*, which were "largely devoted to the activities of people in the nude who are not necessarily nudists."

An important group of magazines not focused upon here, but very familiar to the public in terms of the gay male and lesbian rights movement, concerns same-sex sexual intimacy. Nevertheless, in the sex act explicit category, some of the educational magazines referred to here, and a smaller number in the photo narrative and fantasy category, include these encounters within a context emphasizing mainly heterosexual interactions.

I think that the classification used by the Lockhart Commission is as good as any. It distinguishes two large categories based on where the magazines are usually sold. One category is "The Mass Market," which contains many subcategories. The other is "The Secondary or 'Adults Only' Market," referring to material sold in what we now call adult stores or adult bookstores. "Mail Order" overlaps with both of these, but I leave that to one side here. Within the mass market is the "under-the-counter" category. (U.S. Commission, etc. 1970: 12-17). In this paper I omit almost all of the Mass Market Magazines. This includes *Playboy*, *Penthouse*, and *Hustler*. It also includes other periodicals at the fringe of the mainstream market, featuring "raunchy" photographs, available perhaps only in what used to be called smoke shops or at highly cosmopolitan newsstands in large cities. Here we might sometimes find *Screw*, an erotic newspaper which I do not include in my discussion. With two possible exceptions, all of the magazines I speak of would probably have been sold only in adult stores. The two exceptions are the 1968-1970 version of art model studies, such as by Tudor House Press, plus what I call the nudist transitional category, which includes the Elysium publications of Ed Lange such as *Nude Living* and *Ankh*, as well as the Jaybird Enterprises publications.

WITNESS TO A REVITALIZATION MOVEMENT

Beginning in the 1960s, but building upon historical developments which go back much earlier, the United States began to experience a profound cultural ferment and realignment of values and social arrangements, here called a great awakening, or revitalization movement, or shift in the tectonic plates of our culture (McLoughlin 1978; Yankelovich 1981) which is still under way and whose eventual profound effects or lack thereof remain unclear.

Yankelovich (1981), a sociologist and pollster, tells of "Searching for Self-Fulfillment in a World Turned Upside Down" during the 1960's through the 1970's. Two of his central concepts are "the giving/getting compact" and "the relationship of the sacred to the instrumental" (id.: 13), with sacred defined very broadly. "People and objects are sacred in the sociological sense when, apart from what instrumental use they serve, they are valued for themselves (id.: 7)." The search creates predicaments for the individual and the nation (id.: xviii), as the book explains in its examination of individual lives as well as systematic survey data. "What is extraordinary about the search for self-fulfillment in contemporary America," Yankelovich says, "is that it is not confined to a few bold spirits or a privileged class. . . . [It] is instead an outpouring of popular sentiment and experimentation, an authentic grass roots phenomenon involving, in one way or another, perhaps as many as 80 percent of all adult Americans (id.: 3)." His book is a rich source of information focusing especially on the 1970s. "The self-fulfillment search is a more complex, fateful, and irreversible phenomenon than simply the by-product of affluence or a shift in the national character toward narcissism. It is nothing less than the search for a new American philosophy of life (id.: xix)."

William McLoughlin (1978) speaks of revitalization movements, previously called great awakenings, as "periods of fundamental ideological transformation necessary to the dynamic growth of the nation in adapting to basic social, ecological, psychological, and economic changes (id.: 8)." "Awakenings—the most vital and yet most mysterious of all folk arts—are periods of cultural revitalization that begin in a general crisis of beliefs and values and extend over a period of a generation or so, during which time a profound reorientation in beliefs and values takes place (id.: xiii)."

McLoughlin suggests "that, since 1960, we have been in the process of what may well be the most traumatic and drastic transformation of our ideology that has yet occurred (id. 1978: xv)." Elsewhere he says "The old lights never disappear; no new-light consensus is ever complete (id.: 180)." I find the "old light" and "new light" terminology helpful and I use it in this paper.

Loosening of Reason: Changes in Valuings

People cannot live by critical rationality (radical philosophical doubt) alone. That is one of the major routes to modern nihilistic despair. (See, e.g., Krutch 1929; see generally, Swartz 1998, and what Michael Polanyi calls modern nihilism.) In the 1960s and 1970s we saw in the U. S. a great and diverse cultural churning. What will become of the various components of that ferment over time, and whether some of those components will coalesce so as to constitute a fundamental revitalization, time will tell.

Part of the ferment of the 1960s and 1970s had to do with a flowering, for a while, on the part of some, of spontaneous new attitudes toward the goodness of our naked bodies, the goodness and the beauty of our genitals, and the goodness of women and men being joyfully sexual together. I think that the rationality of science and some of the teachings of medicine had influences here, but just as a matter of fact approach to botany cannot in itself make us feel that flowers are beautiful, even awe-inspiring, neither can science and medicine as conventionally understood teach us that our bodies are beautiful, delightful to behold.

Part of what went on in this period, or was greatly accelerated in this period, may be regarded as widely diverse consequences of a retreat from reason and reasonableness, as these had previously been conventionally understood. I argue that the photographic magazines which I discuss are a reflection of aspects of that ferment which certainly were part of an incipient revitalization movement, and which contributed to the richness of that movement. I argue further that these magazines are a treasure trove of a different way of both literally and metaphorically "seeing" ourselves as beautiful, sexually active, genitally endowed, embodied persons.

The loosening of the grip of conventional reason and reasonableness, and the rebellions against conventional reason and reasonableness, which, among many other things helped produce these pictures, helped bring about many other consequences which can be evaluated as good, bad or indifferent. These include important things still with us, namely, academic rebellions against reason and rationality, the emergence of a complex politics of identity involving race and gender, a revaluing of the natural environment, plus freshly energized religious fundamentalisms.

New Vision of Sexuality and Embodiment

The magazines under consideration bear visual witness to a central aspect of the ferment; bear witness far too clearly for some conventional tastes, as well as for some nominally radical tastes. The message of these magazines was not the old words, whether colloquial or medical. The powerfully persuasive "new light" message was in images. Inadequately translated into words which I will put forth here, that message asserted the beauty and goodness of our embodiedness, the beauty and goodness of our genitals, the beauty, goodness and delight of our erotic sexuality. That message denied the proposition that these things are incompatible with personal goodness and with a good society. That was the "revelation" contained in these magazines. They contained no specific blueprint, however, as to how this new vision might on a durable basis be translated into the American way of life.

Based upon the fact that the individuals in many of these images looked like the young mother next door, the counter attendant at a local store or diner, and the man you see working at the local auto repair shop or riding a motorcycle around town—they appeared to say that a fabulous beauty is all around us if only we were willing to see it—and ourselves—anew. That was a powerfully inspiring message, as well as a powerfully disturbing one. That was an American revitalization movement's augury of erotic innocence.

Profound Change Is Not an Easy Matter

Gay Talese (1980) starts his narrative of the sexual revolution with Diane Webber who posed nude for various photographers in the 1950s and 1960s, including especially Ed Lange. (See also Goodson 1991). Her "photographs began to be seen in nudist and camera magazines all over the country" by 1954 (id.: 24). Specifically, Talese tells of one Harold Rubin, in wintry Chicago in 1957, who masturbates while looking at a nude magazine photograph of Diane Webber, pictured on a California beach, whom he had seen before in other magazines, magazines usually purchased from "under the counter." "It was not only her beauty that had attracted him, the classic lines of her body or the wholesome features of her face, but the entire aura that accompanied each picture, a feeling of her being completely free with nature and herself as she walked along the seashore . . . or sat on a rocky cliff with waves splashing below" (id.: 2-3).

As he makes clear in the concluding pages of a book which includes bits of his own personal odyssey, Talese eventually takes a jaundiced view of much of the ferment which I have described here. He doesn't see in its sexual and erotic aspects anything resembling a "revitalization movement" (McLoughlin 1978) or a searching for a "new American philosophy of life" (Yankelovich 1981). He tracked down Diane Webber, who clothed, now in her forties and asserting a claim to privacy, did not look glamorous to him. She spoke of her posing nude as "art," but he doubted it. "As erotic and free-spirited as she appeared to be in the old photographs, she projected none of this in person, and Talese guessed that this was probably just as true when she had posed years ago" (Talese 1980: 537). Although he himself repeatedly crossed the line of the old rules, Talese remained, at heart, loyal to the "old light."

Masturbation, one of the elements in the Talese story, remains a difficult subject for many Americans. Shamefulness of masturbation, powerfully instilled in early childhood, continues to be a strong ally of traditional morality. If erotic magazines enhance masturbation experience, or erotic arousal, as they sometimes do, this proves that the magazines are evil. In recent memory we have had a Surgeon General of the United States who spoke openly and in accepting terms about masturbation, surely a distinguished person moving in the direction of what I here call the "new light," but nevertheless a high official who was fired from her job because she shocked and offended "old light" constituencies. As our revitalization movement continues, this political incident dramatizes what are by now massively conflicting interpretations of an almost universal activity, which some say is condemned by the Bible and must necessarily be wrong.

EROTOLOGY, CONNOISSEURSHIP AND FURTHER RESEARCH

In spite of the efforts of a small number of people in recent times, especially Ted McIlvenna, the tradition of appreciative erotology and connoisseurship of the erotic (e.g., Anand 1962; Crump 1994; Etimble 1970; Forberg 1966; Grant 1975; Grosbois 1966; Hoyle 1965; Marcade 1962, 1965; Rawson 1968; Surieu 1967; Tucci 1969) does not seem familiar to scholars who have confined themselves to a natural sciences model for understanding the richness of our sexuality.

An erotic connoisseurship would involve–as other connoisseurships do–development of a taste for certain standards of quality, a delight in and relishing of fine details, and a patronage and support for the art or craft involved, for those who carry it on and for those who share an appreciation of it. A tall order, but well worth thinking and writing about.

Even in viewing works of "high" art, convention inhibits candid expression of emotions and thoughts evoked by images (Freedberg 1989). Needless to say, those problems are greatly enhanced with respect to images which social convention, law and religious doctrine say must necessarily produce shame among persons claiming to be worthy of our respect.

Many important aspects of these magazines warrant an analysis for which I do not have space here. Discussion of the similarities and contrasts between still photographs and sequences of photographs, especially those on the printed page, on the one hand, and moving pictures, whether in the mode of film in a theater, or videotape, broadcast television, or internet transmission to personal computer, is a very large and important subject. I merely emphasize–without elaborating here–that moving pictures and printed still pictures will often be profoundly different in their qualities.

Other comparisons and contrasts I must leave to one side here are those between mainstream or mass market publications, within which I have included *Playboy, Penthouse, Hustler*, plus *Screw* which is in a special adult newspaper category, on the one hand, and the particular kinds of adult publications I mention here. Further distinctions should be drawn within the adult market.

All too quickly, and as only a sampling, I mention for further consideration with respect to these magazines: the great role of oral sex in erotic play; the fantasied (and actual) magic of the California scene (York 1984); all the themes—e.g., plot, locales, etc.—which have been studied in Hollywood films (Loukides and Fuller 1990-1996) and which are relevant in these sets of images; the relative absence of classical themes of evil (Losano 1973, 1975) in these magazines; body hair and personal grooming (Cooper 1971; Hope 1982; Lewis 1987); tattoos (Grovenar 1982, and much other literature); and the extent to which the standards of fashion photography (Hall-Duncan 1979) seem to have guided the choice of fine California homes whose interiors, shown in some of these photographs, provide settings that contribute to an impression of a sensuous joy of living.

CONCLUDING REMARKS

We have lived for a long time with great ambivalence about our sexuality, our eroticism, our genitals and our bodies. Our religiously grounded culture, our law, our vocabularies, have very strongly entrenched this ambivalence involving good and bad, seen and unseen, talked about and not talked about, higher and lower, clean and dirty, beautiful and disgusting. Our genitally endowed sexual selves have always been on the negative side of these dichotomies. Established religion says this must be so (Henkin 1963), as does our law (which says that communication "improperly" challenging these entrenched valuations, is not entitled to ordinary free speech protections), as does our language.

Images Say What Words Cannot Say

Our shared vocabulary here is either colloquial speech, that is to say "dirty" words which we try to reclaim but can't because of their historical "gutter" connotations, or a medical and scientific terminology. In what other area of our lives must we think and speak only in a denatured technical vocabulary designed for the clinic and the laboratory? Much that ordinary people experience, from childhood on, can't be translated into this language. The other alternatives are personal vocabularies such as loving couples sometimes invent, or special poetic appreciative erotic vocabularies, which we don't have in our culture, or the use of no words at all, the language of gestures, actions, and the nonverbal device of images. It is this last that sighted people use to an enormous degree in every aspect of their lives, not just the sexual. The device of images bypasses the iron grip, the current limitations, of our language.

The device of images, aided by camera, high quality full color or black and white printing, and so on, was the great device or medium used by these magazines. Through photographic images we could see the hereto unseen. As a matter of fact through high quality photographic images, split seconds frozen in time, printed on a page which we can take with us to view, study and even immerse ourselves in at our leisure, we can see far more than the unaided eye could have seen and the unaided mind could have remembered. (On the related example of strobe photography, see Edgerton 1994; Edgerton and Killian 1979). We have through the aid of photography an enormous extension and expansion of our ability to behold, to make a silent visual communion with, our fellow human beings. The photograph—especially, I would assert, the high quality image printed on a page—enables us, if we choose, to be more aware, more mindful, about visual aspects of human beings, their bodies, their emotions, their genitals, their sexuality, than we have ever been before.

Toward a New American Philosophy for Living

Even at their important and beautiful best these magazines present only fragments of a new vision, a new philosophy for living. They aim at a basic "change of heart" concerning who we are and what we are. No matter what the secular or religious background or inclination of the viewer and of the reader, reclaiming or not reclaiming, revaluing or not revaluing, our bodies and our eroticism surely must be seen by all of us as a locus of profound importance, and by many of us as a matter of powerful concern.

The cost of social respectability has been to pledge allegiance to the sex and genital negative creed, or at least not clearly and openly challenge that creed. During the intense ferment of our revitalization movement, a substantial number of ordinary people, including adventurous women and men such as we see in more conventional modes all around us today, suddenly, and for a brief window in time, felt a call to experience a different way of being. Term it a carelessness concerning the "old light," if you will. They felt a "new light" within themselves. Some were willing (as a few still are today) to share that "new light" vision of themselves with the camera and with a public out there consisting almost entirely of men. They did not wear masks, or dark glasses, cover their faces, or turn their heads. They dared to look straight at you, for those instants in time, and have you look at them. They, and the photographers and publishers dared to challenge the old mold directly, in a way that only images can do, bypassing the vocabularies which are servants of the "old light." To be sure, the old colloquial terminology is all over these publications. People who are in business in a mass society can't be mute and still sell their product.

Did the publishers and clerks in "adult bookstores" know that they were selling a pictorial witness to a "new light"? What their highly varied individual levels of awareness, or lack of awareness, were is hard to say. Somewhere, however, in the complex processes which resulted in publication of these images, there were many individuals who had inspiration, creativity, were "just being themselves," or had an intuitive positive feeling for the great new erotic ferment which was going on around them.

It may be that this revitalization movement, when it settles down, will not include the "new light" I have spoken of. Our faith has to be that even if it doesn't happen now, it will happen someday. That makes especially important a First Amendment freedom of expression which can nurture, preserve and further cultivate for the benefit of ourselves and posterity, images which are erotic witnesses to what I have here called a "new light." Perhaps that new vision is destined always to inspire only a small minority of persons. Even more crucial, in that case, will be a strong First Amendment which protects against majoritarian censorship.

NOTE

For their assistance I wish to thank Dr. Ted McIlvenna of the Institute for Advanced Study of Human Sexuality, San Francisco, CA, members of the staff of the Kinsey Institute, Bloomington, IN, and a number of individuals who have helped me have access to magazines considered here, or with whom I have discussed this subject. Mine, however, is the responsibility for whatever shortcomings are present in this paper.

REFERENCES

Adelman, Bob. 1997. *Tijuana Bibles: Art and Wit in America's Forbidden Funnies, 1930s–1950s.* Introductory Essay by Art Spiegelman. Commentary by Richard Merkin. Essay by Madeline Kripke. New York: Simon & Schuster Editions.

Anand, Mulk Raj. 1962. *Kama Kala: Some Notes on the Philosophical Basis of Hindu Erotic Sculpture.* Geneva, Switzerland: Nagel.

Batters, Elmer. 1995. *Elmer Batters: From the Tip of the Toes to the Top of the Hose.* Edited by Eric Kroll. Köln, Germany: Taschen.

———. 1997. *Elmer Batters: Legs That Dance to Elmer's Tune.* Köln, Germany: Taschen.

Blake, William. 1989. *Blake: The Complete Poems.* 2nd ed. Edited by W. H. Stevenson. Longman Annotated English Poets: General Editors, F. W. Bateson & John Barnard. London: Longman.

Brigman, William E. 1983. "Pornography as Political Expression." *Journal of Popular Culture* 17, no. 2 (Fall):129–134.

Chapple, Steve, and David Talbot. 1989. *Burning Desires: Sex in America, A Report from the Field.* New York: Doubleday.

Comfort, Alex, ed. 1972. *The Joy of Sex: A Cordon Bleu Guide to Lovemaking.* New York: Crown.

———. ed. 1974. *More Joy: A Lovemaking Companion to The Joy of Sex.* New York: Crown.

Cooper, Wendy. 1971. *Hair: Sex, Society, Symbolism.* New York: Stein and Day.

Crump, James. 1994. "The Kinsey Institute Archive: A Taxonomy of Erotic Photography." *History of Photography* 18, no. 1 (Spring):1–12.

Dietz, Park Elliot, and Alan E. Sears. 1987-1988. "Pornography and Obscenity Sold In 'Adult Bookstores': A survey of 5132 Books, Magazines, and Films in Four American Cities." *University of Michigan Journal of Law Reform* 21:7–46.

Edgerton, Harold E. 1994. *Seeing the Unseen: Dr. Harold E. Edgerton and the Wonders of Strobe Alley.* Introduction by James L. Enyeart. Biographical Essay by Douglas Collins. Historical Notes by Joyce E. Bedi. Edited by Roger R. Bruce. Rochester, NY: The Publishing Trust of George Eastman House; Distributed by MIT Press.

Edgerton, Harold E., and James R. Killian, Jr. 1979. *Moments of Vision: The Stroboscopic Revolution in Photography.* Cambridge, MA: MIT Press.

Etiemble. 1970. *Yun Yu: An Essay on Eroticism and Love in Ancient China.* Geneva, Switzerland: Nagel.

Forberg, Fred. Chas. [Friedrich Karl]. 1966. *Manual of Classical Erotology (De figuris Veneris).* [Translated by Viscount Julian Smithson, M.A., for whom it was privately printed in Manchester, England, in 1884.] Two Volumes in One. Latin Text and English Translation. New York: Grove Press. [The translator states, p. xiv, that he has given this work its new title.]

Freedberg, David. 1989. *The Power of Images: Studies in the History and Theory of Response.* Chicago, IL: University of Chicago Press.

Gabor, Mark. 1973. *The Pin-Up: A Modest History.* 2nd edition. New York: Universe Books. [Republished, 1996, by Taschen.]

Goodson, Aileen. 1991. *Therapy, Nudity & Joy: The Therapeutic Use of Nudity Through the Ages, from Ancient Ritual to Modern Psychology.* Los Angeles, CA: Elysium Growth Press.

Grant, Michael. 1975. *Eros in Pompeii: The Secret Rooms of the National Museum of Naples.* With photographs by Antonia Mulas and a description of the collection by Antonio De Simone and Maria Teresa Merella. New York: William Morrow.

Grazia, Edward, de. 1992. *Girls Lean Back Everywhere: The Law of Obscenity and the Assault on Genius.* New York: Random House.

Grazia, Edward, de and Roger K. Newman. 1982. *Banned Films: Movies, Censors and the First Amendment.* New York: Bowker.

Grosbois, Charles. 1966. *Shunga: Images of Spring; Essay on Erotic Elements in Japanese Art.* Geneva, Switzerland: Nagel.

Grovenar, Alan B. 1982. "The Changing Image of Tattooing in American Culture." *Journal of American Culture* 5, no. 1 (Spring): 30–37.

Hall, Dennis R. 1982. "A Note on Erotic Imagination: *Hustler* as a Secondary Carrier of Working-Class Consciousness." *Journal of Popular Culture* 15, no. 4 (Spring):150–156.

Hall-Duncan, Nancy. 1979. *The History of Fashion Photography.* With a Preface by Yves Saint Laurent and a Forward by Robert Riley. International Museum of Photography. Chanticleer Press edition. New York. Alpine Book Company.

Hartman, William E., Marilyn Fithian and Donald Johnson. 1970. *Nudist Society: An Authoritative, Complete Study of Nudism in America.* Illustrated. New York: Crown.

Hebditch, David, and Nick Anning. 1988. *Porn Gold: Inside the Pornography Business.* London: Faber and Faber.

Heidenry, John. 1997. *What Wild Ecstacy: The Rise and Fall of the Sexual Revolution.* New York: Simon & Schuster.

Heins, Marjorie. 1993. *Sex, Sin, and Blasphemy: A Guide to America's Censorship Wars.* New York: New Press.

Henkin, Louis. 1963. "Morals and the Constitution: The Sin of Obscenity." *Columbia Law Review* 63:391–414.

Hoffman, Frank A. 1965. "Prolegomena to a Study of Traditional Elements in the Erotic Film." *Journal of American Folklore* 78:143–148.

——. 1973. *Analytic Survey of Anglo-American Traditional Erotica.* Bowling Green, OH: Bowling Green University Popular Press.

Hope, Christine. 1982. "Caucasian Female Body Hair and American Culture." *Journal of American Culture* 5, no. 1 (Spring):93–99.

Howard, Jane. 1970. *Please Touch: A Guided Tour of the Human Potential Movement.* New York: McGraw-Hill.

Hoyle, Rafael Larco. 1965. *Checan: Essay on Erotic Elements in Peruvian Art.* Geneva, Switzerland: Nagel.

Knight, Arthur, and Hollis Alpert. 1967. "The History of Sex in Cinema. Part Seventeen. The Stag Film." *Playboy* 14, no. 11 (November):154–158, 170, 172, 174–176, 178, 180, 182–184, 186, 188–189.

Krutch, Joseph Wood. 1929. *The Modern Temper: A Study and a Confession.* New York: Harcourt, Brace.

Laner, Mary Riege. 1976. "Make-Believe Mistresses: Photo-Essay Models in Candy Sex Magazines." *Sociological Symposium* no. 15 (Spring):81–98.

Lewis, J. M. 1987. "Caucasian Body Hair Management: A Key to Gender and Species Identification in U.S. Culture?" *Journal of American Culture* 10, no. 1 (Spring):7–14.

Linz, Daniel, and Edward Donnerstein. 1987-1988. "Methodological Issues in the Content Analysis of Pornography." *University of Michigan Journal of Law Reform* 21:47–53.

Losano, Wayne A. 1973. "The Death of the Flesh Film." Pp. 17–25 in *Movies & Sexuality,* edited by Thomas R. Atkins. Hollins College, VA: The Film Journal.

———. 1975. "The Sex Genre: Traditional and Modern Variations on the Flesh Film." Pp. 132–144 in *Sexuality in the Movies,* edited by Thomas A. Atkins. Bloomington, IN: Indiana University Press.

Loukides, Paul, and Linda K. Fuller, eds. 1990-1996. *Beyond the Stars.* Vols. 1–5. (*Beyond the Stars: Stock Characters in American Popular Film,* 1990; *Beyond the Stars II: Plot Conventions in American Popular Film,* 1991; *Beyond the Stars III: The Material World in American Popular Film,* 1993; *Beyond the Stars: Studies in American Popular Film,* Volume 4—*Locales in American Popular Film,* 1993; *Beyond the Stars 5: Themes and Ideologies in American Popular Film,* 1996.) Bowling Green, OH: Bowling Green University Popular Press.

Marcade, Jean. 1962. *Eros Kalos: Essay on Erotic Elements in Greek Art.* Geneva, Switzerland: Nagel.

———. 1965. *Roma Amor: Essay on Erotic Elements in Etruscan and Roman Art.* Geneva, Switzerland: Nagel.

McIlvenna, Ted. 1997. "Finding God in Sex." Pp. 267–277 in *How I Got Into Sex: Personal Stories of Leading Researchers, Sex Therapists, Educators, Prostitutes, Sex Toy Designers, Sex Surrogates, Transsexuals, Criminologists, Clergy, and more . . . ,* edited by Bonnie Bullough, Vern L. Bullough, Marilyn A. Fithian, William E. Hartman, and Randy Sue Klein. Amherst, NY: Prometheus.

McLoughlin, William G. 1978. *Revivals, Awakenings, and Reform: An Essay on Religion and Social Change in America, 1607–1977.* Chicago History of American Religion: A Series Edited by Martin E. Marty. Chicago, IL: University of Chicago Press.

Pultz, John. 1995. *The Body and the Lens: Photography 1839 to the Present. Perspectives Series.* New York: Harry N. Abrams.

Rawson, Philip. 1968. *Erotic Art of the East: The Sexual Theme in Oriental Painting and Sculpture.* Introduction by Alex Comfort. New York: G. P. Putnam's Sons.

Ricoeur, Paul. 1971. "Wonder, Eroticism, and Enigma." Pp. 13–24 in *Sexuality and Identity,* edited by Hendrik M. Ruitenbeek. New York: Dell; Delta Book. [Reprinted from *Cross Currents* 14, no. 2 (Spring 1964):133–141].

Riemschneider, Burkhard, ed. 1997. *The Best of American Girlie Magazines.* Text by

Harold Hellmann. English translation by Christian Goodden. French translation by Catherine Henry. Köln, Germany: Taschen.

Sampson, John J. 1971. "Commercial Traffic in Sexually Oriented Materials in the United States (1969–1970)." Pp. 3–208 in *Technical Report of The Commission on Obscenity and Pornography*. Vol. 3. *The Marketplace: The Industry*. Washington, D.C.: U.S. Government Printing Office.

Server, Lee. 1994. *Over My Dead Body: The Sensational Age of the American Paperback, 1945–1955*. San Francisco: Chronicle Books.

Solzhenitsyn, Alexander. 1972. *Nobel Lecture*. Translated from the Russian by F. D. Reeve. New York: Farrar, Straus and Giroux.

Stein, Ralph. 1974. *The Pin-Up: From 1852 to Now*. Chicago, IL: Playboy Press; Ridge Press Book.

Strossen, Nadine. 1995. *Defending Pornography: Free Speech, Sex, and the Fight for Women's Rights*. New York: Scribner.

Surieu, Robert. 1967. *Sarv e' Naz: An Essay on Love and the Representation of Erotic Themes in Ancient Iran*. Geneva, Switzerland: Nagel.

Swartz, Louis H. 1994a. "Laws and Sex." Pp. 347-354 in *Human Sexuality: An Encyclopedia*, edited by Vern L. Bullough and Bonnie Bullough. New York: Garland.

———. 1994b. "Unification and Transcendence in Sexual Experience." Presented at the Western Regional Conference, Society for the Scientific Study of Sex, April 21-24, San Diego, CA.

———. 1998. "Michael Polanyi and the Sociology of a Free Society. *The American Sociologist* 29:59–70.

Talese, Gay. 1980. *Thy Neighbor's Wife*. Garden City, N.Y.: Doubleday.

Tucci, Guiseppe. 1969. *Rati-Lila: An Interpretation of the Tantric Imagery of the Temples of Nepal*. Geneva, Switzerland: Nagel.

Turan, Kenneth, and Stephen E. Zito. 1974. *Sinema: American Pornographic Films and the People Who Make Them*. New York: Praeger.

United States. Attorney General's Commission on Pornography. 1986. *Attorney General's Commission on Pornography: Final Report*. Washington, DC: U.S. Government Printing Office.

United States. Commission on Obscenity and Pornography. 1970. *Report of the Commission on Obscenity and Pornography*. Washington, D.C.: Government Printing Office.

U.S. News & World Report. 1997 (Feb. 10). "The Business of Porn: Special Report." (James Fallows, "Editor's Note: Why Write About the Porn Industry?" p. 9; Eric Schlosser, "Cover Story: The Business of Pornography" pp. 42–50; Eric Schlosser, "The Bill Gates of Porn: How Reuben Sturman Shaped the Sex Industry," pp. 51–52.)

Waugh, Thomas. 1996. *Hard to Imagine: Gay Male Eroticism in Photography and Film from Their Beginnings to Stonewall*. New York: Columbia University Press.

Williams, Linda. 1989. *Hard Core: Power, Pleasure, and the "Frenzy of the Visible."* Berkeley, CA: University of California Press.

Yankelovich, Daniel. 1981. *New Rules: Searching for Self-Fulfillment in a World Turned Upside Down*. New York: Random House.

York, Neil L. 1984. "California Girls and the American Eden." *Journal of American Culture* 7, no. 4 (Winter):33–43.

Young, Wayland. 1964. *Eros Denied: Sex in Western Society*. New York: Grove Press.

34

A Serious Look at the Amazing Phenomenon of Erotic Comic Books

Dwight Dixon and Joan K. Dixon

I N ORDER TO DISCUSS EROTIC COMIC BOOKS ONE HAS TO FIRST HAVE AN understanding of comic strips in general. When the authors were children, many years ago–before television–the Sunday comic section, which almost every major newspaper contained on that day, was practically devoured by most adults and children. It was not uncommon for young and old alike to scheme to be the first one in the family to get possession of that most prized item. Retributions were on occasion threatened against a spouse, child, or sibling who was suspect of misplacing a Sunday comic section before the aggrieved one could read it.

People of all ages and walks of life and both sexes had their own favorite comic strip or strips and favorite comic characters which they avidly followed. They were every bit as loyal to them as viewers are today of their favorite TV shows and characters. The much loved Mickey Mouse, after all, launched a global entertainment and financial powerhouse. One thinks of such perennial favorites as Superman and Batman. Then there are the modern TV versions of newly created animated comic characters. *Doonesbury* and *Dilbert* are two current comic strips which daily influence millions of readers with their creators' take on current events and the vicissitudes of daily life. *The 1996 Comic Book Index*, by Johnny Lauck and John R. G. Barrett, lists some 15,000 creative professionals, 350,000 credits, and 3,500 comic characters covering the previous thirty years.

As every one knows who has ever been exposed to comics, the term "comics" is very misleading. Although many characters and situations depicted in comics are indeed funny, perhaps just as many are not funny or humorous at all. Many deal straight away with crime, war, and various other kinds of violence against people, animals, inanimate objects, and institutions. So what is this strange, misnamed, journalistic creation known as a comic strip that has such a history of creating a loyal following and being entertaining while at the same time being capable of influencing people's thoughts and perhaps actions?

The best definition we've seen is offered by Roger Sabin in his book *Adult Comics: An Introduction* (1993). His definition covers several pages, so we'll briefly summarize his main points. He says that to define comics one has to work backward. The first element he says is the "comic strip," a narrative in the form of a sequence of pictures; often, but not always with a text. The "strip" may contain anywhere from a single image to thousands of images. Strips may be published in booklet, tabloid, or magazine form, or as a book containing one or more strips. They may be published at regular intervals (e.g., weekly, monthly, quarterly), irregular intervals, or only once.

They share certain common conventions of graphics and text; bordered panels, which are like windows through which actions or events are seen; speed-lines; speech-balloons; think-balloons; and various types of graphic symbolism, like hair standing on end to register fright.

The three basic types of language one finds in comics are narrative, dialogue, and sound effects. Narrative text, when used, may be found in a box in some position in a panel to describe some element depicted therein. Dialogue is often placed in speech-balloons. Sound effects are often onomatopoetically presented: e.g., pow!, zap!, bong!, etc.; using a word whose sound represents the action depicted. The size of type used often indicates the strength of the action depicted.

Reading a comic strip is an active endeavor. The reader must often move his or her gaze rapidly back and forth between text and picture and back again. Traditionally strips are read left to right and from the top of the page to the bottom of the page. An exception is Japanese Manga (pronounced "mahngha") which we'll mention in more detail later, which is read from right to left on a page, from top to bottom, and moving from right page to left page, as though one were starting in a Western book on the last page and progressing page by page to the front.

Comic strips may depict fictional characters and fictional events or a real character and actual events or any combination of the above. In telling these stories strips use many techniques that are similar to the cinema. These include so-called establishing shots, close ups, panoramas, different angles, segueing, and jump cutting.

Comic strips are usually not produced by one person but by teams, often consisting of one or more writers and artists, and sometimes one or more inkers, colorists, and letterers, and perhaps an editor. For simplicity here we refer to them all as artists.

As Roger Sabin points out, there is no such thing as an archetype comic strip. Not only is the medium constantly evolving, there are exceptions to every rule. Still, in understanding comic books what has just been stated is as good a starting point as any.

Alan Moore, who as a writer quickly achieved international acclaim, explains that he chose to do his writing in a comic book format because it is the medium which has been least explored. As a creator, he said, you have complete control over the verbal track and the image track, which you don't have in any other medium, including film. Even more important, he said, is that you control what he calls the interplay between these two elements.

He talks about a kind of "under-language" at work in comics which is neither the "visual" nor the "verbal" but is the unique effect caused by the combination of the two. And he points out the perhaps primal roots of language which connect the sound of words with the images they represent; thus in ancient Chinese ideograms, the word for "hut" looked like a hut. Reading a Chinese sentence was almost like reading a comic strip.

Because this type of language has been accorded a low spot on the cultural totem pole, most serious artists and writers have avoided it.

In fact it is a common experience of almost every comic book artist who attended, or tried to get into, an art school and revealed a desire to create comic book art to have that desire strongly denounced and examples of their comic-style art ridiculed. One example is the negative response from the faculty of an art school and from fellow students experienced by Kevin Eastman who later became the co-creator of the mega-billion dollar, world block-buster *Teenage Mutant Ninja Turtles*. Some comic artists who revealed their interest early have been refused admission to a school. Others have been made so uncomfortable that they drop out. This is rather strange when one considers the contribution that such artists have made to a variety of media in our contemporary culture, as for example films like *Star Wars, Alien,* and *Blade Runner,* and multi-media characters like Popeye, Mickey Mouse, Beavis and Butthead, and of course, the TV series *The Simpsons,* which CBS and *Time* recently cited as among the most influential media characters of the century. Today comic-style drawn characters are ubiquitous in the TV and advertising industries and are often found gracing the pages of a variety of publications.

In reading interviews with some of the leading past and current comic strip creators the thought was often expressed that the most important element of a comic strip is the empty space between frames. Certainly this expresses the extreme importance of the active participation of the reader in the process. One must actively imagine the course of events which either do take place or do not take place between frames. The reader must become part of the creation process. This takes on added importance when contemplating erotic comic books.

But before we move there, let's take just a moment to scan a very brief rundown of the genesis and history of comic strips in general and then take a brief look at erotic comic strips.

There is a lot of disagreement about the beginning date of comic art. Artist Scott McCloud, who defines the comic strip as "juxtaposed pictorial and other icons in deliberate sequence," dates the beginning of that art form around thirty-four centuries ago. However, he admits that the conventional wisdom is that the medium generally thought of today as the comic strip dates from 1896 when strings of cartoons in a designed sequence began appearing in daily newspapers.

As previously mentioned, the "comics" as they were soon called became a huge popular hit with people of all ages. They were almost universally read by children in our country. A pre-World War II Gallup poll showed that 70 percent of adults read them every day.

Beginning sometime in the 1920s and continuing into the late 1940s a quite different type of comic literature appeared on the scene. It was known in different parts of the country by different names, but for now we'll refer to the genre by its most popular name—Tijuana Bibles. They are believed to have had no connection with the city of Tijuana, Mexico and were certainly not bibles. It is thought that somewhere between seven hundred and one thousand different titles were printed. It is not known who the artists or publishers or distributors were. Some believe that organized crime was behind it all. Others think that the style and general format were simply replicated at various times and places by a variety of people working independently or in independent groups.

Tijuana Bibles were typically small booklets of approximately 4" × 3" and usually eight pages, although a few did extend up to thirty-two pages. They were printed on cheap paper stock, with one frame per page. The subject of each Tijuana Bible is sex. The artists purloined as the characters depicted in the fictional, usually humorous, sex romps remarkably accurate images of historically as well as then currently famous people and characters (both human and animal) from mainstream comics and real life. Reputations and copyrights were cheerfully ignored. Production, distribution, and sales were clandestine. Laws didn't matter. Fun and titillation was the game. It was a thumbing of one's nose at the strictures of society and the oppression of the depression. They took the high and mighty and the sanctimonious down to the common man's level. It was blue collar sex all the way. The common denominator was insatiable sex—by both males and females.

The bibles were often misogynous, xenophobic, and racist, but all of that was packaged in a light hearted way. One commentator's reply to a complaint that the bibles insulted women was, "Sure they did, they insulted everyone—that was the fun of reading them." No artist or publisher was known to have been arrested in connection with the bibles. However, one authority reports that a few men were arrested for selling them.

During the lifetime of the Tijuana Bibles, a mainstream comic book industry developed and came to be dominated by some large publishers. Due to concerns about their economic survival in a rather puritanical age the mainstream comic book establishment adopted a Comic Code Authority which set forth rigid restrictions on the creative process and the approved content of comic books.

Ironically, restrictions or no, some of the mainstream comics had characters and themes that, even though overtly not sexual, were quite sensual and sexually suggestive. One only has to gaze upon the barely covered and hardly disguised voluptuousness of Al Capp's Daisy Mae and his Moonbeam McSwine or Tarzan and his Jane or some of the damsels in *Terry and the Pirates* to make the point. But to a free spirited artist, that was far from enough.

Comic artists whose fertile imaginations were being stifled under the yoke of the Establishment strictures finally began to break free in the early 1960s. A subgenre, the underground comix (with an "x") sprang to life, tentatively at first, but soon with vigor. The artist, Frank Stack, is credited with creating the first one with the publication in 1962 of his scathing attack on the New Testament version of the life of Christ titled *The Adventures of Jesus.*

The 1960s spawned a culture rupture across the fabric of American society so vast and so deep and encompassing that it has been declared not merely a revolt but a revolution. Centered in the adolescent and young adult generations (Don't trust anyone over thirty!), it gulped the potent fuel mixture of flower power, generational revolt against the frigid 1950s, a phalanx of psychoactive drugs, free sex, even freer expressions in general lifestyles, and of course, anti-Vietnam War sentiment. As noted, a key ingredient was free expression.

A principal reason the young comic strip artists had been shackled to the yoke of the Establishment was the death grip the established publishing houses had on distribution of comic books. An artist could dare to be independent and produce something that would strike at a raw nerve of society, give expression to a phobia, or generally antagonize the masses, but he couldn't get it to a market of readers. So what's the use?

But, the 1960s counterculture produced a perfect solution to the distribution problem—the head shop. To the delight of increasing numbers of eager comic strip artists the head shops provided a ready and growing market of approving readers, many of whom were likely to be high on the same chemicals that had stoked the inspiration of the artist. Whether or not in any particular case that were true, there was a powerful communication that often occurred between artist and reader. Underground comics had arrived.

They ranged on the artistic and intellectual scales all the way from excellent and inspired to lacking any known value. Practically all subjects were explored with absolutely no regard for society's conventions. The tail was wagging the dog; the serfs controlled the manor; the meek had inherited the printing machine and were taking no prisoners. And, whether the subject of the plot was sex, gore, sci-fi, anti-establishment, antiwar, religions, drugs, down with authority, or any combination of the above, readers ate it up.

In this mix of subject matter and levels of quality, sex received a variety of treatments ranging from brutal to beautiful and from tasteless to exquisite. One suspects that many of the depictions of sex were expressions of the artists' own demons. In the psychedelic 1960s there were certainly enough of those haunting creatures to go around. The one common characteristic concerning the treatment of sex that a reader of underground comics of that era comes away with is the notion that the artist was limited or restricted only by his or her own imagination and daring. As far as the market place was concerned, anything could, and sometimes did, go. Unfortunately some impressionable readers must have gotten some really warped ideas about sex from some really messed up artists. Whatever the quality of the message, underground comics certainly had an influence on a lot of readers in the 1960s and 1970s, and continues to do so today.

The early to mid-1970s brought a blossoming of the international comix medium. Generally, comic books had been thought of in other cultures as an unusual form of children's literature. The impact of the underground comix movement in the United States unleashed an eruption of similar work across South America, post-Franco Spain, France, and Germany. Japan was and is a special case. The comics of the United States and Japanese manga comprise the two predominant and distinct forms of the medium in the world today.

The manga can be traced back in Japan at least as far as some images produced in the twelfth century and to humorous woodblock picture books and scrolls of the eighteenth and early nineteenth centuries. The latter have been called the world's first comic books.

Besides being read in reverse direction to the way American comics are read, manga differ in some other obvious ways; one is size. American comic books usually consist of between thirty and fifty pages, usually contain one serialized story, and usually are published monthly. Manga typically have four hundred or more pages, contain around twenty serialized and continuing stories, and are published weekly. Some manga magazines have as many as one thousand pages and forty stories.

Manga artists tend to rely heavily on the subtleties of their visual depictions rather than text to convey a story line, a message, a mood, or an intended emotion. Sometimes one will find page after page of perhaps one repeated scene or frame with no text whatsoever; to convey emphasis or perhaps the passage of time or just to give the reader time to study and reflect upon what it is the artist intends one to perceive. At other times only slight changes may be detected in a series of frames; perhaps to reveal a slowly changing mood or emotion.

To a non-Japanese reader, this type of ongoing silent dialog can be somewhat disconcerting. But those used to reading manga know that it is to be leafed through quickly, sometimes as fast as one can turn a page, and disposed of when finished; perhaps at the end of one's train ride to work in the morning.

Manga is an enormously popular medium in Japan. Former Prime Minister Miyazawa began a serial of his opinions in a manga magazine in 1995. Former Prime Minister Hashimoto and his wife were said in 1996 to enjoy manga at home on quiet evenings. Manga comprised 40 percent of all books and magazines sold in Japan in 1995. That's 1.9 billion manga books, or fifteen for every man, woman, and child in Japan.

An exhibit hall at a comic book convention in the United States may have several score or several hundred vendors. This compares to a convention in Japan where there may be nearly 18,000 booths. Whereas by far most of the attendees at such a convention in this country are male, attendees at one in Japan are often upwards of 90 percent young females. These young women often mobilize in an organized unit with specific individual assigned areas of the exhibit hall to cover and specific purchases to be made before supplies of desired titles are exhausted. Organized units of young men may use electronic communication to coordinate purchases.

But manga is not just for the young crowd. Japanese people of all ages and economic levels and in sizeable numbers are regular manga readers. Some manga is published in other languages outside of Japan. This has spawned groups of manga readers in several countries. The vast majority of manga is non-erotic and poorly done. One expert even calls most of it trash.

But manga is famous for that portion of it that is about sex, and often sex combined with violence. For such a nonviolent society this is a paradox that perplexes many people. For not only is the violent crime rate and sex crime rate lower than in the United States, it dropped substantially during the time when manga was growing most in popularity.

In a book, whose English title is *Manga and the Japanese: Dissecting the Myth of Harmful Comics Ruining the Nation* (1992), the author, a prominent Japanese psychiatrist and writer, used an extensive examination of statistics and surveys to explain this phenomenon. He first observed that despite the amount and explicitness of the sexual material to which young Japanese are exposed, and contrary to common perception, they are as a group highly repressed and late to develop sexually compared to their counterparts in other nations. He found that exposure to sexual material did not result in increased sex crimes or even sex activity. Then he concluded: (1) "The amount of sexual information that a people have access to is inversely proportional to the number of sex crimes in any country," and (2) "Sexual information can substitute for actual sexual activity."

Restraints on the degrees of sexuality to be overtly visually depicted in manga fluctuated somewhat in earlier periods, but generally until the 1980s manga had observed restrictions on the depiction of explicit sexual intercourse and adult genitalia. As more and more sexually explicit manga began appearing the national mood began to swing toward artistic censorship. Regressive organizations were formed against pornography in the early days of the 1990s. Laws were passed, and many arrests were made of publishers, store owners, and artists for possessing obscene material with intent to sell. In 1992 some of the top artists in Japan formed the Association to Protect Freedom of Expression in Comics to counter the censorship movement.

The national debate which followed that period is seen as being a good exercise of popular democracy in a country that is still rather new at it and had no history of freedom of the press until after the Allied Occupation began at the end of World War II.

There developed a general consensus that manga for children should not contain explicit sex. However, erotic material in adult manga became even more explicit. Nineteen ninety-three brought the end of the prohibition against depiction of pubic hair and adult sex organs. By 1995 some of the raciest material was to be found in manga for women drawn by women.

There isn't sufficient space here to examine in much detail the subtleties of differences in the erotic comics of other nations outside of the United States. However, a quick survey of examples of erotic and non-erotic comics of other countries shows that they draw heavily on their counterparts in the United States and to a lesser extent on Japanese manga. That said, some of the idiosyncrasies of the different national cultures naturally do find their way into their erotica.

While working our way through stacks of erotic comics from a variety of nations we became aware that, at least to us, there seemed to be more differences of concept and execution between artists as individuals than differences due to nationality.

Many foreign comics are produced with English language versions. A casual, non-expert reader of one in a typical case would not be likely to discern whether or not it was produced by an American artist.

After all, it is the reader who is a vital part of the creation process regardless of who the artist is or where the work is produced. In the end the final structure of the finished fantasy depends upon the foundation and complex individual experiential history of the reader.

Andrea Juno, editor of the book, *Dangerous Drawings* (1997), says in that book that in addition to the sex and subversion which she enjoyed finding in underground comics, what sustained her interest in them was "the exciting discovery of a medium that was able to formalistically distort perspectives and reinterpret time and space, creating a world close to what I'd experience in a dream, on an LSD trip or watching film." She brought along the unique, subjective experiences of her life to the process as a co-conspirator in the underground product.

The raw fodder for this process is the story line (if there is one) and the visual art of the erotic underground comix. They range in quality of conception and execution from top notch to forget it.

We'll defer on the question of quality of talent to an assessment made by Diane Noomin, one of the pioneer and most highly respected women artists of underground comix. In a published interview Diane states that she finds only about one out of fifty aspiring cartoonists to be good. She said they seem to think they only have to be good at writing and not drawing but that cartoonists must be good at both.

The subject matter of erotic comix literally cover the enormous range of human imagination. In some, sex is only suggested. In much of it the sex is as graphic and explicit as it's possible to present in the confines of the medium. And the degrees of explicitness of the rest fill the spectrum between those extremes. One can find erotic comix with only some nudity, and in some the characters are rarely clothed. Many very sensual comix have no total nudity or explicit sex, but some of the characters, especially the female ones, may just as well be nude. The effect is to some readers even more erotic and appealing than nudity would be. Naturally, the degrees of violence depicted also span a spectrum from none to "pardon-me-while-I-throw-up" bloody and gruesome.

Taken as a whole, erotic comix do not discriminate between the sexes. Women may be the victims but women may be the sadistic punishers or gory destroyers. Men may be murdered brutally and hideously, often in blood-splattered pieces, but it may be men who do the heartless dispatching. Evil at times triumphs, but often the good guy or gal does. Some characters are super humans, some just look gorgeous, some are weird alien forms of all descriptions, and some are just normal men and women. Some women are the seduced and some do the seducing. It's likewise for men.

Fortunately for the tastes of many readers, some erotic comix have no violence and some can be described as classically erotic, even a story of tender love.

As alluded to previously, one's responses to a particular presentation is entirely subjective. What repels one reader may be an erotic turn-on or perhaps merely a pleasant or interesting reading experience to another; or perhaps it's simply boring.

At bottom, this medium is intended to be contentious. The reader is not supposed to go away unmoved. If she or he does the underground artist has pretty much failed. This is, after all, like it or not, art. By its very nature art in many forms tends to be controversial and confrontative. And that is an apt description of the contents of a lot of comic (with a "c") and comix (with an "x") books. Often filled with violence or sex or both and often skewering, ridiculing, or gleefully ignoring the conventions of society, the latter are the epitome of political incorrectness.

When it comes to warding off the legal slings and arrows of a riled up community activist and a self-righteous, blood-thirsty prosecutor, the small artist or retailer of comic books is in a vulnerable position. To encourage retailers to continue to make a market for a genre that might otherwise just about disappear and to offer legal and financial aid to the publishers, retailers, artists, and others in the industry on the front lines of the continual battle against censorship, Denis Kitchen, a successful cartoonist and publisher of comics, established in 1988 the Comic Book Legal Defense Fund.

So far artists seem to be less vulnerable than others in the comix business. As far as we know, a Florida cartoonist, Michael Diana, who had self-published a small-press comic book, became in 1994 the first, and we think only, American cartoonist to be arrested and convicted of obscenity for art that he produced.

The hope for the future by some in the industry is for comic art and text to emerge from the pale of artistic disrespect and be received in the art and literary world as a legitimate art form and for comic books to take their place on the shelves and websites of ordinary booksellers, and libraries and museums.

REFERENCES

Adelman, B. 1997. *Tijuana Bibles*. New York: Simon & Schuster.

Blackbeard, B., ed. 1996. *The comic strip century*. Princeton, Wisconsin: Kitchen Sink Press.

Fukushima, A. 1992. *Manga and the Japanese: Dissecting the myth of harmful comics ruining the nation*. Tokyo: Nihon Bungeisha.

Gilmore, D. H. 1971. *Sex in comics: A history of eight pagers*. 4 vols. San Diego, California: Greenleaf Classics.

Groth, G., ed. March 1998. *The comics journal.* Seattle, Washington: Fantagraphics Books.

Horn, M., ed. 1980. *The world encyclopedia of cartoons.* New York: Chelsea House Publishers.

Juno, A., ed. 1997. *Dangerous drawings: Interviews with comix and graphix artists.* New York: Juno Books.

Lauck, J., and J. R. G. Barrett. 1996. *The 1996 comic book index.* New York: Alternate Concepts.

Sabin, R. 1993. *Adult comics: An introduction.* New York: Routledge.

Savage, Jr., W. 1990. *Comic books and America 1945–1954.* Norman, Oklahoma: University of Oklahoma.

Schodt, F. L. 1996. *Dreamland Japan: Writings on modern manga.* Berkeley, California: Stone Bridge Press.

Siden, H. 1972. *Sadomasochism in comics: A history of sex and violence in comic books.* San Diego, California: Greenleaf Classics.

Wiater, S., and S. R. Bissette. 1993. *Comic book rebels: Conversations with the creators of the new comics.* New York: Donald I. Fine, Inc.

Wood, A. 1987. *Great cartoonists and their art.* Gretna, Louisiana: Pelican Publishing Co.

35

A Short History of Sex Toys
with an Extrapolation
for the New Century

Herbert A. Otto

THIS CHAPTER HAS THREE PARTS. IT BEGINS WITH A SHORT HISTORICAL overview of the use of sex toys throughout human history. Included here are descriptions of the most popular contemporary erotic toys. Next, I will explore current social attitudes and trends vis-à-vis the use of sex toys in today's societies. I will also give a brief overview of my work and findings about the human orgasm and its relation to the use of sex toys. Finally, there is an extrapolation about the sex toys of tomorrow. The definitive book about the use of sex toys throughout human history remains to be written. I hope this report will stimulate work on such a project.

THE USE OF SEX TOYS IN WORLD HISTORY—AN OVERVIEW

Once humanity established towns, cities and particularly hierarchical social structures, sex toys came into use. Consistently, the use of sex toys was almost totally restricted to the nobility, moneyed classes or social elite. Regardless of the culture or state of "civilization," the so-called common people did not have the leisure time or means to play with such toys. All their energy went into the struggle for survival.

There were some exceptions to this. Primitive tribes, particularly those residing in areas of the Pacific, routinely used specific types of sex toys. This was also true of certain primitive peoples in other parts of the world. For the most part, these toys consisted of various additions and protuberances which added girth and textures to the penis. The use of sex toys by primitive women, exclusively for their own stimulation, was rare.

It is a fact that particularly in European but also in Asian cultures, the

437

use of sex toys was almost totally restricted to the nobility or social leadership as well as the moneyed classes who were in power positions. In the vast majority of instances, these users were also the most highly educated segment of their societies.

Throughout the history of most civilizations and cultures, the most often used sex toy continues to be the dildo or artificial penis. The popularity of this toy has persisted because women can use it to give themselves orgasms and men can use it with women as a sexual stimulant and also as a source of peak ecstasy. It has been the dominant sex toy from the beginning of human civilization. For instance, in the latter half of the eighteenth century, craftsmen perfected dildos which could yield an infusion of warmed milk to simulate the male orgasm. These toys tended to be very costly. They were much admired. Today, the variable speed vibrating dildo is about to replace any older versions.

The most popular contemporary female sex toy has its origin in the Orient, with its roots in China and Japan. In these two nations, women of the elite classes have used the so-called "ben-wa balls" for thousands of years. The ben-wa toy consists of one or two spherical (or oblong) balls made of bone, ivory or precious metal. The balls are connected by a short string. A longer string, about the length of a hand, is attached to one of the spheres to facilitate removal of the toy from the vagina.

One of the spheres is empty. The other is filled with mercury or some other heavy substance. To use this toy, the woman inserts the empty ben-wa ball into her vagina, placing it against her cervix. The filled ball is placed adjacent to and touching the empty one. With this placement, the slightest movement of the woman's hips produces a vibration which is transmitted to the cervix.

Numerous Asian erotic stories and pillow books describe the orgasm triggered by this toy as being exceptionally powerful and ecstatic. Very often, the Asian woman stretched out in a hammock with a maid present to get the hammock in motion. Modern ben-wa balls consist of one or two spheres or obloid cylinders with one or both containing small vibrators. The vibrational speed is controlled by a hand-held device which also contains the batteries.

This type of sex toy, also known as "love eggs," is now widely used by women in all parts of the world. One advantage of this toy is that it can be used by the woman while walking about or even while working. Today, placement directly on the cervix is not generally used to trigger a cervical orgasm, but rather to give a pleasurable sensation. There is also evidence that many if not most contemporary women have not deliberately experimented with the ben-wa balls to determine if they could trigger a cervical or G-spot climax.

Many women have not yet discovered that *orgasm discrimination* is a learned skill which can be acquired through practice. This involves directing one's consciousness into what exactly is taking place as one becomes stimulated and aroused. It is my observation that many women are still afraid of their own sexuality. They fear that it may overwhelm them or heighten their sexual needs to the point where a man will have a hard time satisfying them. It is very clear that, of the two genders, the woman is the more sexual member of the species.

The nation which has contributed most to the manufacture and distribution of sex toys is Japan. In the latter half of the twentieth century, the fashioning of sex toys has shifted from the craftsman to the factory. The variation in vibrators, erotic gadgets and dildos manufactured in Japan provided a significant momentum to the democratization of sex toys. Today, sex toys are known about, used and freely available to all classes of society, but the most intricate and thus most expensive toys remain out of the reach of many.

Both Germany and the United States have made a major contribution to the democratization of sex toys. Initially, the sales distribution pattern of sex toys in both nations showed unique differences. In Germany, the supermarket concept of sex toy sales was pioneered by Beate Uhse, who opened large shops in many of the major cities. The sex toys were readily available on shelves, with unwrapped samples provided to show the toy in action. In Beate Uhse's sex toy supermarkets, the customer took grocery baskets and went toy shopping. The percentage of women alone or shopping with men was almost twice to three times the ratio prevalent in this country. The U.S. ratio was about two women to eight men. This ratio has not changed.

In the United States, the initial tendency of "sex shops" was to display many if not most of the toys in display cases. The customer had to ask to examine a toy and samples were not readily available to show what the toy did. There was a heavy emphasis in these boutiques on the sale of porno videos and contemporary erotica, especially illustrated magazines and books. Over the years, U. S. sex shops have made more toys available to be handled, and the availability of working samples has shown a slight increase.

Beginning in the 1960s, with the onset of the sexual revolution and into the 1970s and 1980s, many variations of the old–and some new–sex toys have come along. For example, following the publication of the book, *The G-Spot*, the G-spot stimulator was introduced and is now increasingly used. Vibrators which can be attached to the female genitals by a harness and worn beneath ordinary street wear have proliferated. Both "Joanie's Butterfly" and the "Clitoral Kiss," as well as other clitoral stimulators, use a bullet-shaped vibrator. The latest version features a suction pump to facilitate attachment to a woman's genitals.

First to appear in a few sex shops about fifteen years ago, was the "double dildo" for women. It features two flexible shafts, one penis-sized, the other one a third that size, for simultaneous vaginal and anal stimulation. It has a built-in vibrator, adjustable for variable speeds, and is now selling well.

Over the last decade, there has been a marked increase in sex toys designed to facilitate an anal orgasm in both men and woman. Boxed *Back Door* Collections of sex toys are now readily available. They contain a variety of items for use by both genders. There is also the recently invented *Grape Jelly Bead Stick* featuring "Seven Inches for Posterior Pleasure. It contains five attached balls graduating in size from three-quarters of an inch to one and one-quarter inches in diameter. This unique toy stimulates the sphincter through a variety of 'grasp and release' maneuvers." There is also the six-inches long and one and one-half inch wide *Tail Twister.* Inside the Twister, the rotating mechanism activates dozens of pleasure beads for strong varied stimulation inside the anus or vagina."

There has also been a significant proliferation of masturbatory devices for men. Some of these toys consist of a vacuum chamber for the penis, in which a manual or electrical pump effectively sucks out the ejaculate. Also available are a variety of realistic-looking female sex organs which use vibrators and lubricants to induce male orgasm. Finally, there are inflatable full-size rubber replicas of women with vibrators which can be located in the mouth, vaginal and anal areas of the dolls to induce orgasm. Earlier variations of these dolls have been available since before World War II. They were bought from the Yokohama Sex Shop, principally by sailors from all over the world.

CONTEMPORARY CULTURES AND THE USE OF SEX TOYS

The democratization of sex toys referred to earlier has taken place, for the most part, in European countries as well as the United States and Canada. In underdeveloped or Third World countries, sex toys continue not to be readily available and are primarily used by the elite classes.

In the U. S., Canada (and seemingly to a lesser extent in European countries), the human sexual experience is affected by three major factors. These factors differentiate it from the sexual experiencing in the first half of the twentieth century. Today, more than ever before in history, a considerable number of people are involved in *sexploration.* They show a deliberate interest in trying out new sex positions and new sex experiences in general. The use of sex toys is becoming a way of having a new and different erotic experience. An increasing number of people appear to pursue sexploration on a planned basis.

Closely related to sexploration is sexual self-development. Through books, films and videos, people have become more and more aware that sex is a learned activity and that everyone is using only a small fraction of their sexual potential. Once this process is begun, it opens a lifetime of sexual adventuring. This is the best antidote to sexual routinization and habituation, which is so severely damaging to many long-term relationships. There is a growing recognition that one's sexual potential can be developed, actualized and used, extending the spectrum of erotic experiencing. My own estimate is that most people use less than 5 percent of their sexual potential.

Classes, workshops and many books (as well as some spiritual development programs) are now available to assist people with their sexual self-development. There is also a groundswell of individuals who pursue this on a systematic or planned basis. Sex toys have found growing acceptance and are used as an important part of expanding one's sexual self-development.

There is a third major factor which distinguishes sexual experiencing in the last quarter of this century–sex has increasingly become a form of *creative, playful togetherness.* The concept that "sex is serious business" and that it is an activity dominated by high performance anxiety is slowly being phased out. The erotic experience is becoming a way of having fun and engaging in a form of mutual play which welcomes the delights of humor. People are more able to joke while having sex and the use of sex toys has emerged as a distinct form of adult play.

It must also be mentioned that numerous restrictive religious doctrines which have repressed the European and American libido are gradually disappearing. *Our belief system about sex is undergoing a radical change.* It is becoming less dominated and handicapped by notions of "sin" and "guilt." This shift favors the rapidly expanding growth of sexual self-development.

Finally, particularly in the United States, open communication about sex has made rapid progress. Sex topics and sex jokes are now shared in numerous social gatherings with members of both genders present. A wide variety of sex subjects are openly discussed in popular magazines as well as films and videos.

Hardly any sex-related topic is excluded. For example, *Penthouse* is currently running "The Great American Pissing Contest." A series of photos have already appeared and readers are invited to send in photos of ladies urinating or ". . . doing what comes naturally. Our editors will select the best ones based on graphic excellence, volume, stream trajectory, distance and erotic appeal" (July 1998 issue). In America, it is obvious that not just attitudes about sex, but attitudes about natural body processes are in a profound state of change.

There has also been a marked increase in sadism and masochism (S & M) now re-labeled "D & S", or dominance and submission. D & S club membership is on the upswing. This may be due, at least in part, to the American media's pre-occupation with violence, murder and mayhem which is being successfully sold to the public as a form of entertainment. There is a conscious recognition by media moguls that "violence sells." As a nation, we have become addicted to the adrenaline kick triggered by violence.

However, there is also evidence that for many D & S devotees, this type of experiencing is a part of their sexploration and sexual self-development. For many, it appears to be a passing phase in their sex lives. They use D & S as a means of gaining increased self-knowledge and understanding. The routines, regalia and equipment of D & S can also be viewed from another perspective–it is a new playground with new sets of sex toys which yield very distinct and unique erotic experiences. A number of self-selected individuals use this type of erotic experiencing to expand their sexual horizons.

For more than a decade, I have been engaged in an exploratory research project focusing on the human climax. This work has yielded a new understanding of the dynamics and function of the human orgasm. There were a number of findings which can considerably enrich people's sexual experience.

There is a great deal of evidence–largely ignored–that the human orgasm can be developed or shaped. Orgasm shaping is a new discovery and a means of both exploring and enhancing the experience of peak ecstasy. By bringing conscious awareness to the climactic process, new erotic feeling tones and dimensions of experiencing become available.

A variety of effective methods have been developed to tailor an individual training program designed to intensify and enrich the orgasm. Over the past three decades, the thrust of human sexuality has been overwhelmingly in the direction of bringing increasing sophistication and massive enrichment to the erotic experience. Orgasm shaping offers a spectrum of new sexual horizons for people who are interested in increasing their sexual pleasure.

Among the findings from this project are the following:

A. Everyone capable of having an orgasm falls into one of the three basic climactic groups–they are either mono-orgasmic, poly-orgasmic or hetero-orgasmic. The *mono-orgasmic* person has an orgasm from the stimulation of one component of the sexual nervous system. The *poly-orgasmic* person is able to climax from stimulation of more than one component, yet all orgasms feel the same. The *hetero-orgasmic* person can climax from stimulation of more than one component of the sexual nervous system, yet each climax is experienced as having unique and distinct characteristics imparted by the component which triggers the orgasm.

B. Women have the ability to experience *seven* distinct types of orgasms–the clitoral orgasm, the vaginal/cervical orgasm, the breast orgasm, the mouth orgasm, the G-Spot orgasm, the anal orgasm, and the mental orgasm.

C. Men have the ability to experience *six* distinct types of orgasms–the penile orgasm, the anal orgasm, the prostate orgasm, the breast orgasm, the mouth orgasm, and the mental orgasm.

D. In addition to the preceding, both women and men are able to have a *fusion orgasm* as well as a *zone orgasm*.

E. A separate study revealed that the meanings which the sex act has for a person is known as the *intercourse and orgasm belief system*. This can have a marked effect on the coital experience.

F. The human climax is not a "monolithic event, solely under control of the autonomic nervous system," but is *capable of being shaped*. It can be lengthened and intensified. Creative processes can be used to shape and develop the nature of the orgasm resulting in new and different types of climaxes.

G. *The orgasmic states of being*, discovered during this study, furnish a map, or framework, for the exploration (and development) of the hidden aspects and dimensions of peak ecstasy.

H. For the first time, a comprehensive approach to the neglected art of *orgasm intensification* is offered, consisting of twenty-two distinct ways which can be utilized.

Finally, eight methods for *shaping or extending the liberated orgasm spectrum* have been developed or identified, and are already being used by some sexual sophisticates. These can be utilized to tailor individual sexual self-development programs.

This work is relevant vis-à-vis the use of sex toys. Findings have repeatedly indicated that the use of vibrators and other types of sex toys yield different types of climaxes for hetero-orgasmic people. Those acquainted with the findings from this exploratory research project will be interested in trying out various sex toys to see if they will expand their spectrum of orgasmic sexual experiencing.

THE SEX TOYS OF TOMORROW— AN EXTRAPOLATION

The years 1997 and 1998 have seen surprising advances in the invention of new sex toys. Almost a dozen new toys were invented and introduced in the latter half of the 1990s For example, there are several new combination kits which feature simultaneous clitoral and anal stimulation for the woman and which can also be used for anal stimulation of the man. In the area of providing anal pleasures for both genders, considerable innovation is taking place.

For example, there is now the first *Grape Jelly Double Header.* "This soft, squishy, super jelly dong measures a whopping fourteen inches in total length, but each side features delightfully different sensations for unlimited carnal combinations! One end is a slick, thick seven inch dong and the other is a perfectly proportioned seven inch long strand of balls. Just right for anal stimulation." Of all the mail order sex toy companies, Adam & Eve (website: www.adameve.com) is the most active and inventive in introducing new sex toys.

Also new is the *Rockin' Rabbit.* "Now both of you can have over-the-top orgasms with this double barrel vibrating pleasure toy. The double pronged "bunny ears" stimulate her clitoris with every thrust, while the second bullet pleases his balls for heightened orgasmic intensity."

Finally, the *Hustler Oriental Dragonfly* must be described. It provides the base structure for a new sex toy which will undoubtedly make its appearance in the next few years. The Dragonfly is designed to offer the woman simultaneous tri-sensual stimulation. " . . . there is a 'soft, velvety G-spot probe' with variable vibrator speed for the vagina. A similar vibrator provides simultaneous clitoral stimulation." Included is a "beaded tail for anal thrills." The beaded anal stimulator does *not* contain a vibrator.

In the very near future, or perhaps in the new millennium, the woman's ultimate sex toy will become available. This is the *Woman's Triple Super*

Orgasm Toy. It will have three variable-speed controls (including one fore the anus) to trigger a super fusion, or blended climax.

I would also extrapolate that a similar sex toy will be invented for the man. *The Man's Super Orgasm Toy* will provide simultaneous vibration for the penis while it is encased in a sleeve. The hand control unit will also feature controls for a separate vibrator designed for simultaneous prostate stimulation. Both vibrators will be the variable speed type.

About four years ago, I received a third hand report from a colleague that two sexologists in England were working on sex toys which used very low voltage electricity as the sole source of erotic stimulation. I immediately realized that t*his would be the major breakthrough in sex toys for the generations of the twenty-first century*. All efforts to locate the two British colleagues were unsuccessful. However, a year ago, when in Las Vegas, I saw an ad for the PES Sex Shop. I decided this would be another of the hundreds of sex shops I had visited in this country and abroad since 1962.

Much to my surprise, PES were the initials standing for the Paradise Electro Stimulations shop (website:www.peselectro.com). I subsequently made an appointment to meet and interview the owner, who goes by the name of Dante Amore. He is the world's foremost inventor in his field, and holds the patents on numerous erotic electro-stimulation toys.

Dante began his research and work in 1984 and opened the PES Shop four years ago. It has become a thriving business, with customers from all over the world. Dante's creations have already received considerable publicity—especially in Europe. A full length video entitled Electro Sex and featuring the PES product line is available. It made the top ten video rental list and became the Editors' Choice for ADULT VIDEO NEWS.

Electro-stimulation will play an important part in the sex toy wave of the future. Reportedly, these devices are capable of eliciting a surprising range of erotic sensations and are quite safe, with no injuries as yet reported. However, research is needed on the long term effects of consistent use. Finally, electro-stimulation toys have been used successfully in the sexual rehabilitation of paraplegics as well as others with major sex problems.

The citizen of tomorrow can be expected to make a much greater commitment to sexperimentation and sexual self-development than the generations of today. It will then be recognized and widely accepted that children lead their own sex lives and that this is normal. Conservative elements will no longer use the concept of protecting the sexual innocence of children as a means to censor and to repress human sexuality.

The conquest of the AIDS epidemic will trigger a sexual renaissance widely surpassing that of the sexual revolution in the sixties and seventies. Along with this, adult sex will become exponentially more playful. Sex toy use will also increase exponentially. In the new millennium, everyone will be aware that erotic experiencing basically nourishes and sustains health—SEX IS HEALTHY.

SECTION 9

"IN THEIR OWN WORDS": THE ACTORS AND ACTRESSES OF THE PORNOGRAPHY INDUSTRY

T HIS SECTION CONTAINS A PICTURE OF MANY OF THOSE FROM THE ADULT entertainment industry who attended the conference and the comments of a few about their participation. Their input provided insights and opportunities for an open dialogue; thus, a more accurate understanding of the area we call "pornography" was gained by those attending. It has been difficult for many in this industry, people who engage in X-rated behaviors, to open up and discuss with the clinicians and the academics their views about their "work." It is clear that the conference brought about significant further research and a better understanding of what goes on "behind the scenes."

36

All-Star Porn Panel

SELECTED EXCERPTS FROM THE CLOSING SESSION OF THE WORLD Pornography Conference. We apologize to those who were left out because of space limitations.)

Panelists: Annie Sprinkle, Vanessa Del Rio, Ron Jeremy, R. Bolla, Veronica Hart, Gloria Leonard, Juli Ashton, Nina Hartley, Dave Cummings, Howie Gordon (a.k.a. Richard Pacheco), Annabel Chong, Johnni Black, William Margold, Christi Lake, Gino Colbert, Meridian, Shayla Laveaux, Candida Royalle, Sharon Mitchell, and others

Moderator: Will Jarvis (a.k.a. Taliesin, the Bard)

Christi Lake: If you're out there and you've had sex on video for everyone to enjoy, get up here.

[The panel assembles]

Will Jarvis: I find myself, being an activist and advocate, usually looking out for the underdog, the unsung heroes. I want to say a tremendous "Thank you" and I think you should too, I'm telling you what to do, to the volunteer students from Cal. State Northridge for a fabulous job. They really deserve it.

Audience: (Applause)

Jarvis: Fourteen years ago I got into this business because of this fascination I had with human sexuality. And I saw it presented on the big screen and I said "Wow! This has got to be the most interesting business I could be in." What a fantasy to be. . . . I looked up to guys like R. Bolla and Richard Pacheco and Bobby Astyr, John Leslie, Paul Thomas and even that most humble of porn actors William Margold.

Audience/Panel: (Laughter)

Jarvis: I said "Wow! I want to do what they do." They get to have sex with all these great, sexy women like Vanessa Del Rio, Annie Sprinkle, Candida Royalle, Sharon Mitchell, Veronica Hart, and my fantasy girl Leslie Bovee.

And in my first movie I got to do sex with Vanessa Del Rio.

[Struts about with chest puffed out]

Audience: (Applause)

Jarvis: And they paid me.

William Margold: They paid her more.

Audience/Panel: (Laughter)

Jarvis: I'll be right back.

[Hangs head, sinks behind podium, comes back up]

Audience/Panel: (More laughter)

Jarvis: As with most porn productions we didn't rehearse what we're going to do here so I'm just going to let these terrific people share with you their lives, their experiences, what they want to say. I will just say this—I hope that if there is one thing you get from this conference is that the actors and actresses, and the crew, the producers and directors, are all professional people. There are so many women and men who've tried to be in our business and can't. The women lay there like dead fish, the men can't get erections. And to survive in this business you have to be professional at what you do and you have to be able to function sexually in a way that entertains an audience, not just pleases you. Some people think we're in this business because we can't do anything else. So okay you can at least fuck for a living. Uh uh. Too many people have tried to do what we do and not succeeded at it.

Now these people on the panel, who are much better performers, better actors and actresses than I, these wonderful people, I thank you for coming to see them.

*   *   *

Veronica Hart: I just want to tell you what a wonderful experience this has been for me. I'm at a time in my life when a lot of things in my business are not very much to my liking. I see a lot of negativity out there. I see a lot of bad images. I see a lot of stuff that really hurts me, and that I don't like, so to be involved in a situation like this that's so sex positive where people are open minded and obviously intelligent. It just makes me really very happy and very proud to be in pornography still. I just want to thank you very much for giving that to me.

*   *   *

Christi Lake: My name is Christi Lake. I have been in front of the cameras for the last three years for video, four for stills. I entered porn as something fun, interesting to do. Growing up in the mid-west I was a tomboy. I had good self-esteem about my person but I really didn't think I was the sexy, young kinda thing that guys wanted to watch having sex on camera. Boy, was I wrong.

[After a time] I realized I could do this for a living. And I enjoy it. And during this conference I'm finding out more and more stereotypes are getting crushed thanks to everyone here. We like what we do. We enjoy doing it for you. And most importantly we enjoy doing it for ourselves. We become better people, more open sexually and spiritually. And I want to thank you for letting us express that.

* * *

Miss Sharon Mitchell: Good morning. I'm very happy to be here with all my old buddies. I've had a great time for twenty-three years, through all my trials and tribulations, and there have been quite a few. This industry has always been a place to come back to. I've always had people who supported me. I look forward to the future and respect the past and the woman I am today.

* * *

Gloria Leonard: It's Sunday morning. I'm wearing. . . . Why don't you read the back of my shirt?

R. Bolla: In a society that is drug infested, violence wracked, and polluted by chemical greed, *no one* has ever died of an overdose of pornography.

Audience: (Applause)

Leonard: I think everybody who has attended this event over the last few days has nothing but really positive feelings about what has transpired here. I think this is truly historic in many ways. It's been an eye-opener to us, all of us. I'm very very pleased and very proud to have been a part of this whole event.

I just was in one of the other sessions prior to coming here and the gentleman who was conducing it somehow had a problem with the word "pornography." He felt it was pejorative, that in the future perhaps we should call it something else. Y'know what? It is what it is what it is. I think calling a rose a rose is the right thing to do and the right way to go. Somebody once said to me, what's the difference between erotica and pornography? In my opinion, it's the lighting.

Audience: (Uproarious Applause)

Leonard: You have the dim, mysterious lighting, that's erotic; you pump up the f-stop a couple of numbers, y'know, you get *Hustler*. It's the same material. It just looks a little different.

I have been in this business longer than I am willing to confess here today. There was an event a few months back where the audience was principally young talent, I think it was the XRCO Awards, and I got up there and I said, looking out at this very attractive young audience, "I have implants older than most of you."

Audience: (Laughter)

Leonard: It becomes sort of a generational thing, y'know there's the first tier, the second tier, the third tier of talent, so to speak, that have advanced this industry through its lifetime. . . . Through their fortitude, their perseverance, and their balls, to do what they do for a living. The technology may be a little different, nevertheless the end result is pretty much the same. What I think is most unusual in my view of what's happened with this industry, when I started in this business we made 8mm. It was called "loops." The ones that preceded us were the black and white variety where there was very little plot. The guy dressed up like a Chinese laundry guy to collect the bill from the woman and she couldn't pay the bill so he fucked her. That was how she paid the bill. There was really no rhyme or reason. . . .

Then technology progressed and it became 16mm then 35mm and the productions got more opulent and grandiose, a lot of production values. Very often they took the hard-core sex scenes out and you still had a watchable movie, during the 70s and early 80s. In my view however, although the technology has progressed now to video, the dynamic of the content is very much back to 8mm, there's no rhyme or reason very often for how these people got there or why they're having sex. But there's enough of a variety of material that I think can please all kinds of proclivities, fetishes and tastes.

*   *   *

[Audience member hands note to Jarvis]

Jarvis: A gentleman in the audience wants to know who the panelists are. Sir, you haven't been watching enough porn movies. So if everybody will introduce themselves when they come up the audience will know. . . .

Vanessa Del Rio: Hi. My name is Vanessa Del Rio.

Audience/Panel: (Applause)

Del Rio: I am so proud of my sister sluts. I've been out of the business for a while and I really didn't know what everybody was up to. I live in New York and I'm really pissed off. Guliani whipped the rug right out from under us. We were not paying attention, we were not looking, we were having too much fun and we were taking too much of our liberties for granted. And he did it in such a way that is making such an impact. It's like having an effect as you start to absorb it, you start to say "Holy shit!" He doesn't want people five-hundred feet from each other let alone everything else. . . .

I'm really proud of [my sister porn stars] that they have endured so long in fighting for our freedom and paving the way. I just want to give you guys a really big hand. I'm so proud of you. That's it. Thank you.

[Del Rio applauds panelists]

Audience: (Applause)

*   *   *

Gino Colbert: My name is Gino Colbert. It's nice to be here. It's actually an honor to be here.

My background is a little different, because when I was growing up my aunt ran a burlesque theater. And from the time I was five, six years old, I used to go there. My dad would drop me off, my mom would drop me off, my aunt would baby-sit me in the office. And as I grew up, this theater became the last of America's burlesque houses. I used to stand in the wings and catch the clothes of the strippers. I got to work with such greats as Blaize Star, Tempest Storm, Sally Rand. I used to hold the spotlight during her fan dance. I could go on and on with some of the names.

My aunt retired from burlesque in '58. She ran the theater up until I was fourteen years old. So basically I was brought up around a different branch of pornography, what used to be called burlesque, which is where our porn today comes from because the early porn movies were nothing more than loops filming the stripteasers doing their acts. So the early pornography was filming Lilly St. Cyr taking her bubble bath, filming Tempest Storm doing her strut. And Tempest is still working today at the age of seventy-three, still stripping, and she looks gorgeous.

Audience: (Applause)

Colbert: After my aunt died I ran the theater for a while. The comics died off, the three-piece band died off, and eventually we put up a screen. And you know the rest, it became a porn house.

*   *   *

Dave Cummings: Good morning. I'm Dave Cummings. I've been in the business bout three and a half years. I asked Will, I said, what do you want us to say up here? He says, tell everybody a little bit about yourself and what you think. So I jotted down five points.

The first one; I guess I'm proof that age is not a barrier. I'm fifty-eight years old. Point Number Two is, I don't know if you know it but I'm a retired Army Lieutenant Colonel. And I used to teach at West Point. And the reason I'm bringing that up is I find it very upsetting to see intrusive governmental legislation being proposed on all levels.

Audience: (Applause)

Cummings: It's happening terribly in Houston and New York. . . . We're constantly, a bunch of us on this panel are constantly up in Sacramento fighting for our rights. And I just see it as a big threat to our Constitution and our free speech. Point Three: This great nation of ours reaps great economic and social strengths from the impacts of the adult film industry. And it's not just in dollars. It's also in interpersonal relationships, human sexuality, and personal growth. Point Number Four: *Normal* people realize that it is absolutely okay and healthy to have and enjoy sexual cravings, harmless fantasy and pleasure. And the pleasure can be with another consenting adult or quite frankly it can be just with themselves, in self-gratification. I just wish that these normal people would not be so shy about speaking up and saying what they really think. Because certainly the very minor vocal people who are against us are out there speaking up. We all need to be voters. We can't just stand by and complain. We gotta get out there and vote.

Last point is, I'd like to close with kinda my favorite expression that indeed sex between consenting adults is natural, it's normal and it's healthy.

*   *   *

Ron Jeremy: They like me. They set up a buffet table. Hi. I'm Ron Jeremy.
Audience/Panel: (Applause)
Jeremy: You're way too kind. This is everything you wanted to know about adult film stars. I guess one thing you maybe might not know [about me] is that I did achieve a Master's Degree at Queens College, New York. I also got a BA in Theater, a BA in Education, and a Master's in Special Ed. Taught a year of elementary school. Pretty scary. You've heard of "Mothers Against Drunk Drivers." There's also "Fathers Against Ron Teaching," FART.
Audience: (Laughter)
Jeremy: I quit and went into acting, and adult acting. I still do lecture at Cal. State Fullerton every year, for the past eight years. Occasionally I lecture at other colleges. Thanks. It's great to be here.

*   *   *

Annie Sprinkle: Ahhhhh. . . .
[Breathes deeply for a minute, simulates a sexual climax]
Sprinkle: It's been so orgasmic being here.
Audience: (Applause)
Sprinkle: What a turn on. This is my idea of a good time. I guess I've always been in a kind of perpetual pursuit of ecstasy and pleasure, and that's been a lot of what my journey's been about. When I'm in a state of sexual ecstasy it's my most wonderful, special, delicious, precious part of life.

Thank you all. My mother was here. . . . I really want to thank you for giving her a lot of information, positive reinforcement, that was really important. And as a little token of my appreciation I would like to offer anyone who would like, a "public cervix" button.
Audience: (Laughter)
Sprinkle: It's a replica of a woman's cervix, the doorway to life itself. If you want to know about my journey, unfortunately I have to do some promotion to keep things going, to pay my bills . . .
[Holds up copy of *Post Porn Modernist*]
Sprinkle: So my book is out there. It's really lovely, it's a new edition. Support your local pornographer.

I'm aware that we're the happy pornographers, porn stars, but there are people who haven't had experiences as wonderful as we've had, like in any business, and I just want to, you know, acknowledge them for their part in the whole, the total picture of this vast, multifaceted, very fascinating business.

*   *   *

Candida Royalle: I'm Candida Royalle. Things are changing. I was talking with my father about censorship and the troubles the industry has had, and he said, "I don't understand it, all you're doing is bringing people pleasure." And that was my dad.

*   *   *

Johnni Black: Sitting next to some of these guys I sure feel young.
   Audience: (Laughter)
   Black: I'm Johnni Black. I have been in this industry for two years. I've done over two-hundred movies at this point. Before I came into this industry I was a Captain in the United States Army for six years and I very proudly served my country. But I can honestly say here I am so proud to be among this group of people and to finally be doing what it is that makes me happy, which is being a porn star.
   Thank you all for being here and for letting us express ourselves.

SECTION 10

GAY, BI, LESBIAN, AND TRANSGENDERED PORNOGRAPHY

SINCE EROTICISM IS IN THE EYES OF THE BEHOLDER, THERE ARE EROTIC or pornographic films, magazines, books, internet connections, and what have you, for every desire. This section concentrates on some of these specialized audiences. Henry Mach emphasizes some of the changes which have taken place and are taking place in the nature of pornography and the industry associated with it. He distinguished between two different kinds of porn aimed at gay male audiences, what he calls gay porn, X-rated adult material, and Queer Erotica, personal expressions of sexuality. He himself was deeply involved in what he calls chapbooks, magazines which concentrated on first hand experiences or alleged first hand experiences communicated to others through letters. For a time he edited *First Hand* which specialized in queer erotica, theoretically factual, although he himself believes that many of his articles were simply based on fantasy rather than reality. The audience for chapbooks declined in the 1990s as chat rooms and the internet sites became more popular, and Henry Mach moved into this new area of communication, although the competition for audiences was much greater than it was for publishers of chapbooks.

There is also a specialized gay video industry producing erotic films for a gay (and lesbian) audience. Joe Thomas writes that many of them can be defined as quite campy, but this is a different definition of camp than the older usage of the term which emphasized the trivial, trash, kitsch, and the not so terribly good in the cultural sphere. The new kind of camp is devoted to an emphasis on the Marlboro man and a highly masculinized persona. This is most evident in the gay porn movies, leather and S/M bars, and the male stripper. The new gay assertiveness of their manliness, he argues, led to open acceptance and celebration of homophobically dreaded sex acts, sexual intercourse between males, an emphasis on penis length, and ultra masculine characteristics. As gays gained freedom to see themselves in action, encouraging self identification so to speak, American porn became less European oriented, and became transnational in scope. Daniel C. Tsang examines some of the Asian gay male video porn as well as its appearance on the internet, CD-ROMs, and web sites.

One reason gays and others turn to various forms of pornography is because, Russell Wilcox claims, porn goes beyond giving us an ability to visualize ourselves in action by giving the users an opportunity to vicariously experience others. Male viewers, for example, can experience and identify with a female protagonist, and that the female viewer can do the same for a male. This means that the males, for example, might not be identifying with the machismo man dominating the weak female, as some of the Feminists Against Pornography seemed to imply, but with the female being portrayed. If Wilcox is correct, this makes it less likely, the man is less likely to rape because he identified with female victim rather than more likely. His arguments are not always easy to follow, but they offer a much more complex view of pornography than that which exists on the surface. Looking at this from a slightly different viewpoint, but emphasizing what Wilcox said, is Connie Shortes who believes that S/M gay porn, for example, played an affirming, celebratory, and mobilizing role for the 1970s leather community in the same way that gay porn did for the larger gay community. In a sense gayness had become accepted enough by the public, that gay porn could afford to be "politically incorrect" by going against the stereotypes and emphasize differences as does S/M porn.

37

Gay Porn/Queer Erotica

Henry Mach

INTRODUCTION

For the purpose of this chapter I am using these definitions:
Gay Porn: X-rated adult material marketed to gay men.
Queer Erotica: Personal expressions of sexuality.
- Gay Porn is defined by its business context;
- Queer Erotica may be seen as purgative confessional, or as communal sharing—sometimes both.
- They are not mutually exclusive. Much of the better Queer Erotica (personal expressions) has become successful Gay Porn (business ventures);
- most of the better Gay Porn is infused with a spirit of Queer Erotica. As with many fields, what we're talking about is
- the people who are in it for the Checkbook;
- and those who wish to express something from their Souls.

PUBLICATIONS BORN OF PASSION

THE IDEA THAT WRITING ABOUT SEX IS EXPRESSING SOMETHING FROM the soul has been embraced among gay men by Radical Faeries (going back to the 1970s), and now by a new generation of queer urban young men.

In the straight world, porno fanciers dream of "getting a letter into Penthouse Forum." Perhaps because the gay community welcomes it (certainly does not stigmatize it), many gay men have taken this a step further. A good example is the chapbook, "Straight to Hell" created by an editor named

Boyd McDonald. It is made up of letters from McDonald's correspondents. Some of these men talk about a special singular experience ("the first time a man ever . . ."); and many of the men write about sleazy, sequential sex in men's rooms or parks.

McDonald's slogan was, "Nothing is sexier than the truth."

There has been a boom in such chapbooks in the 1990s. Some of them have become full-fledged successful magazines and businesses–"Bound & Gagged," "Daddy," "Handjobs."

The two reasons for this growth are:

(1) Desktop Publishing has made the technology accessible to everyone;

(2) at the same time, mainstream publishers and newsstand distributors have gotten increasingly timid in the 1990s.

The subject matter dealt with in the 'zines I named–people tied up for sex; daddy-son fantasies; and intergenerational sex–these are exactly the topics that have been discarded by the newsstand publications.

CREATING FOR THE "NEWSSTAND" MARKET

Publications being sold at newsstands must be careful not to risk losing any potential markets. Iowa, for example, has a problem with handcuffs. Canada has a problem with incest.

This may be seen as an indicator of the New Puritanism of our times. Eighteen years ago and fifteen years ago in these same (or equivalent) publications, it was possible to have someone handcuffed during sex; it was also possible for someone to tell a story in flashback about a sexual experience that happened at age fifteen.

And, in point of fact, the publishers I went to work for in 1980 were (at that time) producing a very successful line of incest magazines: "Family Affairs," and its companion, "Family Letters."

In 1980, I had just spent the previous three years producing porno novels. I was hired by a group of New Jersey-based businesspeople to create a new gay men's magazine. They had gotten $100,000 from Kable News (at that time one of the larger magazine distributors in North America) based on one sentence: "To create a gay version of *Penthouse Forum.*"

I was handed five issues of *Penthouse Forum.* This would be the first gay men's magazine in digest format; the first gay men's magazine that wouldn't depend on glossy photos. (As I eventually said, "At least you have to be literate to jerk off to it.") I came up with one anchoring idea: The magazine would be entirely in the first person. Those glossy (color photo) sex magazines would often run articles about sexual kinks written in the third person, and those articles always sounded snide, even judgmental or mocking. This decision also meant *FirstHand,* as it came to be called, would not have any fiction.

I asked for articles rather than stories. My definition: a story simply chronicled a single incident; something like "The Night I Seduced My Neighbor's Husband." An article would have to include two or three stories, with some comments tying them together. So instead we'd have "FirstHand Encounters With Married Virgins."

Also the letters were very important to the magazine. Labeled "First-Hand Experiences." The first issues were peppered with "Tell Us FirstHand About . . ." and requests for people's first experiences, most memorable experiences, and fantasies. (These were actually just created as fillers to make page layout simpler.)

In the first issue of FirstHand, I had letters created by writers (including myself), plus a few bisexual letters referred from my publishers' other magazines. But by the time I got to the third issue, I had more letters than I could use; and that continued for the next three years.

Of course most of the stories in the letters never really happened. The ones that did happen had been elaborated outrageously out of proportion. I edited these letters for readability, and also for believability. I shortened penis size in the letters (12 inches became 8-1/2).

I also did serious cropping of storylines. The most common storyline in letters was:

- (1) big butch guy is mean and abusive (and may be straight-identified);
- (2) big butch guy makes tender love and becomes good provider; and, very often,
- (3) big butch guy dies when his tractor-trailer goes over a cliff.

Sometimes I would get a number of letters from one person, virtually repeating the same scenario. My job as editor was to change each of these letters just enough so it would sound different from the previous one.

Rather than Boyd McDonald's "Nothing Is Sexier Than the Truth," our slogan was "Talking About Sex Is Important."

- My goal was not to present the unvarnished truth;
- not even to permit our letter-writers to express their own truths;
- but to put together a well-packaged, well-edited, erotic finished product.

I believe there are three reasons why I had so many letters to the magazine:

- I edited to try to make the stories sound real.
- I treated all sexual variety with respect.
- But, MOST IMPORTANT, because there weren't other outlets at that time for people to share their sexual experiences and fantasies!!!

Today, the Internet has created more outlets for sexual expression and sexual sharing than we could've imagined eighteen years ago. But before I move to that, I'd like to focus on a few of the letterwriters: the things I learned from them, and the questions I still have about them.

THE LETTERWRITERS

Helena, Montana

There was an elderly man in Helena, Montana, whose letters were easily identifiable because he had no paragraph breaks, and he used ellipses between sentences. Even without that, his old manual typewriter became familiar. But even beyond that, every monthly letter told the same story.

Each of Montana's letters took place during the Depression. He identified himself as having been a teenager at that time, fourteen or fifteen. In each letter there was an older man, a Clint Eastwood type. In various letters the older man was the new assistant preacher at his church; his uncle's poker buddy; a bouncer at his aunt's brothel; or a friend of his father.

While the identity of the man changed, the scenario never did. In these letters, the teenage boy goes to the bathroom and the man steps in beside him. They urinate side-by-side. Then the man turns the youth's face to his, kisses him full on the lips, says, "Oh baby, I am hot for you," and invites the letter-writer to go for a ride in his car the next day. The following day the two of them go for a ride in the car and have sex.

I can only wonder: Perhaps this was the only same-sex experience in this man's life; if so, he romanticized it and recast for more than forty years. Maybe this was a total invention; but if so, what building blocks went into constructing such a specific sexual narrative.

When I spoke of "Expressing the Soul," this is the sort of thing I had in mind. Here was a scenario that was very likely in this man's thoughts everytime he masturbated. And yet, based on the evidence of those letters, I would suspect that he had never told that story out loud to anyone.

Western Canada

During my first year I was always trying to identify which letters were telling the truth, and which were invented. I remember that among the first letters I got was one postmarked from Western Canada. I remarked, "I know this letter is true. There are too many details."

Two years later I looked back at that letter. By then I had received six letters all postmarked from Western Canada; and each one, like that first letter, included detailed, complex scenarios which (somehow always) involved complete bodyshaving, a long overhanging foreskin, and rubber articles of clothing.

But that's not the weird part. Each of those six letters was on different stationery; was mailed from a different post office; and was either written by typewriter, or in a very careful, controlled handwriting.

There are two possible explanations: Either there are six men in Western Canada who really ought to get together and form a club; or, there is one man in Western Canada so fascinated (and yet frightened) by this combination of fetishes that he has devised complex scenarios in which they could co-exist, and then he is only comfortable communicating these to an anonymous editor three thousand miles away.

Toronto

The last letterwriter I want to talk about is the swimsuit man. I got five letters, each one handwritten on the same paper, each simply signed DOUG; all postmarked from Toronto; no return address. These five letters were mailed five days in a row. It appears that Doug had been writing a memoir, and mailing each chapter to me as it was done.

He discovered masturbation when he did exercises to build up his lanky upper body—doing chin-ups against the closet door. His favorite form of masturbation was wearing a tight swimsuit and chinning himself (rubbing his penis) against the closet door. He was capable of masturbating in bed; but only if he rubbed himself through a swimsuit or other appropriate fabric.

Doug's stories then involved encounters with other boys and young men (going on a hunting trip the next morning; sharing a bed after a late-night school event). These events all took place in high school and in his early-20s. At some point, Doug would demonstrate his favorite masturbation technique for his guest. His best nights were when the other boy or young man would try on a swimsuit and masturbate in the same way.

Actually, these letters led to the first conflict between myself and the publishers. The gay male art director had quit FirstHand. He had been replaced by a woman who preferred not to read the text. She had a bunch of black and white drawings to use as illustrations throughout the magazine. She chose to illustrate Doug's letters with a picture of a naked man in boots.

In the world of Gay Porn—the businessworld—why was I making a fuss about such an unimportant thing? The art director was being paid by the hour. Those pages were already pasted up. What did it matter?

If I had been dealing with people in Queer Erotica, they would have understood that this anonymous man in Toronto had shared something special. They would've understood that when you have such a unique and personal account, you don't illustrate a swimsuit fetishist's story with a picture of boots.

THE DESIRE TO COMMUNICATE

There are some questions I can't answer: What role did those "door-jacking" incidents play in Doug's sex life? And, what was going on during the five days when he wrote those letters?

I know that these men communicated with me, in large part, simply because I was there. As I said before, in 1998 there are many more options for expressing and sharing sexuality.

If the man in Helena, Montana, is still alive, what he would do in 1998:

- Get an anonymous email address at hotmail.com;
- write his story, and post it various places on newsgroups;
- ask people to email him with feedback to the story, or to share their own stories;
- maybe make contact with a few email buddies.

That sounds like a good thing to me. I address this to Dear Abby and Ann Landers, when I say that if I make it to age seventy, anything that might add a spark to my masturbatory fantasies (and which is safe, and not harming anyone) would be a great boon—and a positive thing.

The importance of communication within sexual minority communities shouldn't be underestimated. And the difference the internet has made in Queer Expression definitely should not be underestimated.

To put this in context:

George Mavety is a straight businessman in New York. His company publishes *Mandate, Honcho, Playguy,* and a slew of other gay titles (although the gay stuff is only a small part of his business).

Some of those magazines are monthly, some bi-monthly. Newsstand distributors probably want a print run of at least fifty thousand; for a title to continue being distributed, I'd guess at least 50 percent sales.

Do the math: Conservatively, George Mavety is overseeing the creation of 750,000 individual copies of gay publications in the course of a year.

I've never heard it described that way—speaking of each individual copy. But it's a valid way to speak of these. Sure, some of the magazines get tossed in the garbage before the month is out. But there are also copies that make their way around the world; fifteen years later still hidden under someone's mattress.

I don't know what the print run is on "Bound & Gagged." They're distributed in certain bookstores, some sex shops; then they have their subscription base (which is going to be faithful on a specialty title like this). I would be very surprised if the print run was more than ten thousand copies. If they produce six issues a year, that would mean sixty thousand (maximum number) individual copies produced by "Bound & Gagged" out there in the world.

What this says to me is that the power to communicate about sex to the widest audience of gay men was not in our hands.

Finally, with the Internet we can circumvent the filtering of publishers and distributors (though we don't know what Congress will do).

Will the Internet actually level the playing field between Gay Porn and Queer Erotica—creating opportunities for gay men to directly express and share their sexuality?

AND YET . . .

Between Gay Porn and Queer Erotica, it would seem I'm generally on the side of Queer Erotica (though I've often earned my living through the Gay Porn industry). So this level playing field, the rise of people working from the spirit of Queer Erotica, would appear to be a good thing.

But of course this new opportunity presents its own problems. And that leads me to talking about Badpuppy. Badpuppy is the most active gay sex membership site on the web. It's a gay-owned business, created by people who had a passion to do this.

My problem with Badpuppy is my problem with a lot of the internet. If I pick on Badpuppy it's because they claim to have 15,000 members (which means that at $10/month, they're grossing more than 1.5 million/year)

Badpuppy offers a number of services to its members. One of the important features: BP has software to filter the images out of online newsgroups.

A newsgroup is like a bulletin board. I may see a great Herb Ritts photo in a magazine, rip it out, and tack it to a bulletin board because I want to share it with other people.

When Badpuppy provides its service to its members (and filters the images from that online newsgroup), that Herb Ritts photo is now on the Badpuppy site.

Badpuppy also hosts "Contributor" sites.

Here is how I would explain contributor sites: Over the years I have known a few gay men who have created scrapbooks of their favorite centerfolds. And sometimes they will let you flip through their scrapbook. There were (of course) a number of gay men who created websites like that—men who even kept on updating their sites, scanning in pictures for their particular taste.

When concerns were raised about porn on the Internet, these websites suddenly needed firewalls, and some way to set up membership checks. Along came Badpuppy to the rescue: Badpuppy offered to host many of these sites; and those sites then became accessible through Badpuppy membership.

The images from newsgroups, and hosting the contributor sites—There are two ways of looking at this:

- (1) Badpuppy is doing a great service for its members (and for queer men who want to express themselves sexually); or
- (2) Badpuppy is raking in money for pictures without permission from the photographers and models (BP has not paid for the rights to those pictures).

If you ask a Badpuppy member, "What are you paying the $10/month for?" he's not going to say, "I'm paying for a service to extract blah-blah . . ." He's going to say, "I'm paying for the pictures." And I don't believe anyone would pay $100-$120/year for just the Badpuppy models.

The reason they can offer thousands and thousands of pictures is that they think they've found legal loopholes to get around copyright. I believe the reason they've gotten away with it for so long is—Who's gonna take them to court?

Bel Ami, the movies from Eastern Europe, demanded that Badpuppy remove all their images; Badpuppy complied. TITANMedia, a quality-oriented SF-based video company, recently got similar cooperation from Badpuppy.

For those Queer Erotica fans who would just like to share their personal scrapbooks on the internet, there's a Catch-22. The current rules require some sort of password protection to see adult material. Once you charge admission, then it's a business, it's not simply sharing your scrapbook with a friend.

And (leaving Herb Ritts aside for the moment), I know too many struggling queer photographers trying to make a living.

Is it possible for artists and models to be treated with respect? I ask that, of course, as a rhetorical question. The answer of course is: When hell freezes over.

For so many years, I have seen the world of Gay Porn (and Straight Porn for that matter) ripping off artists and models. The internet really has evened the playing field—now people producing Queer Erotica also get to rip off artists, models, and writers.

What I know is: The Internet is a wonderful opportunity for sexual expression and sexual communication. The way it gets defined, used, and legislated over the next few years will make a difference in a lot of (sex) lives.

38

Notes on the New Camp: Gay Video Pornography

Joe A. Thomas

I N THE SUMMER OF 1996 THE POPULAR AND GENERALLY HETEROSEXUALLY oriented Los Angeles magazine *Buzz* suggested that "camp is out, porn is in" (at least as far as gay life is concerned).[1] Although the writer was probably trying to put his finger on the pulse of the moment and "scoop" his fellow journalists by marking the latest trends, his observations were perhaps more penetrating than even he suspected. As traditional camp (represented by drag, the adoration of glamour, and the celebration of the marginal) has faded as an overriding cultural force in the gay subculture, gay video pornography has taken an increasingly prominent role. Coincidence? Or is pornography actually replacing camp because of their similar functions in gay life?

A history and definition of the camp sensibility seem as ephemeral and elusive as the sensibility itself. Reveling in anti-hierarchical thinking, camp does not willingly lend itself to scholarly dissection. Camp arose in the gay subculture of Europe and America primarily as a means to thwart the strict hierarchies of dominant, heterosexual society. Through camp an oppressed, often invisible minority could thumb its nose at the arbitrary standards of the "straight" culture that deemed gay men to be outcasts. Mark Booth has defined camp as being primarily involved with a way of self-presentation and a style of behavior. "To be camp is to present oneself as being committed to the marginal with a commitment greater than the marginal merits," he proclaimed.[2] While all sorts of things might fall into this category, it is in the broader cultural arena, especially arts and entertainment, that camp takes its primary stand. Booth elaborated further on the nature of camp:

465

. . . types of the marginal are the trivial, the trashy, the kitsch, and the not-terribly-good. Thus, in the cultural sphere, to be camp is to be perversely committed to the trash aesthetic or to a sort of "cultural slumming" . . . which, being in theory incomprehensible to non-camp people, becomes fashionably exclusive.[3]

In her famous 1964 article "Notes on Camp," the quintessential sixties essayist Susan Sontag tried to codify and explain camp thus: ". . . the experiences of Camp are based on the great discovery that the sensibility of high culture has no monopoly on refinement."[4] That is, what is marginal, or low culture, may be just as complex and fascinating as its high-cultural counterpart. Sontag argued that camp was style without substance,[5] thus unknowingly identifying camp as something that subverted modernism, which absolutely insisted upon having content with its style. The camp sensibility appreciated extremes of taste, from kitsch to the rarefied esthetics of fin-de-siécle decadents. The modernist tradition, on the other hand, had set up a strict hierarchy in which only elitist, "high" culture was worthy of consideration. Camp systematically destroyed these hierarchies by celebrating and glorifying all the things that modernist opinion despised. As Booth noted, the "traditionally feminine" has long been one of the most marginalized aspects of society[6]; drag can be seen as a campy parody of and identification with this other oppressed part of dominant culture. Ultimately, being a drag queen was an act of guerrilla warfare. Likewise, the idolization of strong women in films (such as Joan Crawford and Bette Davis) manifests a gay identification with the feminine struggle for power in a straight, patriarchal society.

By the 1960s, camp was a significant presence in the lives of many gay men, particularly urban American gay men. It was seen most stereotypically in the world of drag and in the tastes of many gay men for tragic camp figures such as Judy Garland or tasteless sub-divas such as Maria Montez. An appreciation for objects and art that were slightly out of style but not yet considered antiques was also supported by a camp sensibility (and by the pocketbooks of wealthy gay men in New York). By the time Susan Sontag wrote "Notes on Camp" in 1964 camp had thoroughly penetrated the public consciousness.[7] Cosmopolitan intellectuals such as Sontag—whether straight or gay—were clear enough about camp to codify it.

With the rise of Gay Liberation after the Stonewall riots in 1968, however, the mood in the gay community changed. We shouldn't forget that the initial public gathering of gays, lesbians, and drag queens in Greenwich Village that hot June night was partially due to the announcement of the death of camp diva Judy Garland. After Stonewall, seemingly overnight the male gay community's public image—especially in New York—changed from that of an effete interior decorator collecting antiques and adoring Marlene Dietrich to one of an angry, long-haired, political radical demanding social justice. And in fact, social changes came thick and fast. America was in the midst of a sexual revolution as well as political turmoil, and gays quickly became recognized as a new force to be reckoned with.

As the gay population came out of the closet and gained power, camp's secretive, coded slash-and-burn of straight hierarchies of taste was no longer necessary. In fact, in the context of the new radicalism, it might even be seen as a cowardly and backward "counter-revolutionary" move. As the political clout and public acceptance of gays gradually increased, the overt and stereotypical public association of gay men with camp seemed to wane. It's hard to imagine a gay man of the 1970s camping it up with friends watching Joan Crawford movies. Instead, the image of the Marlboro Man in his gay incarnation as the Castro Clone became the new stereotype, especially in San Francisco, the new gay mecca. This highly masculinized persona allowed little room for the sly, witty, ironic self-awareness of camp.

I would argue that camp began to disappear largely because it was a covert defensive strategy. Younger gay men, coming out well after the hard-fought gains of Gay Liberation, were less likely to care about the camp canon: Judy Garland, Talullah Bankhead, Victorian painters, or Joan Crawford (despite a brief, intense revival of interest after the outrageously camp movie *Mommie Dearest*). Camp was passed on as a process of social acculturation when gay men came out of the closet and joined others in the subculture. Younger generations, coming of age after Stonewall, had less need to use camp to assert their identity, since they were relatively free to be open about their sexuality as compared to earlier generations. Daniel Harris, in his recent book *The Rise and Fall of Gay Culture*, has also theorized that camp died as a result of greater gay visibility; camp had provided gay men with secret codes by which they could recognize each other. By the 1980s, according to Harris, camp's role had been usurped by a crass consumerism.[8] I would argue, however, that the mainstreaming of gay taste only minimally affected camp; rather, pornography moved to fill the void left by camp's waning in gay life.

Not coincidentally, during the early 1970s heterosexual hardcore pornography suddenly—and briefly—became highly fashionable. Trendy couples lined up around the block in 1972 and 1973 to see everyone's guilty pleasure: *Deep Throat*. A result of both the sexual revolution and of the sixties craze for underground films, the sudden popularity and easy availability of sex films extended to the gay community as well. Although gay stag films had been around almost as long as film itself, they were hard to find for most consumers. After the success of *The Boys in the Sand* (gay porn legend Casey Donovan's 1971 hardcore debut) short sex films and longer epics such as Donovan's became more readily available in specialized hardcore theaters. From there, all it took was the advent of the home video recorder in the eighties to put hardcore, XXX features in the hands of an adoring public.

Initially gay porno videos were collections of the earlier stag films or video versions of hardcore feature films. Anthologies such as the Falcon Videopacs brought together some of the popular, usually silent, short features from the seventies and early eighties. As prices of home VCRs fell during the 1980s, the market became increasingly lucrative and producers began shooting films directly on video, aimed at the domestic market of home viewers. More and more VCRs led to more and more videos and more and more viewers.

A similar phenomenon happened in the straight world. However, an interesting divergence took place. While straight porn lost the chic appeal it had with early hits such as *Deep Throat* and *Behind the Green Door* and returned to the marginalized realm of trash culture, gay videos achieved an almost respectable position in gay life. Trading and swapping of gay porno videos became common, and rental outlets began to move beyond the sleazy adult bookstores and arcades that were the initial forum for videos. Legitimate gay bookstores such as the Lobo chain in Texas or Gay Pleasures in New York began to rent and sell porno videos alongside pride flags and *New York Times* bestsellers. It was not uncommon by the mid-1980s to hear gay men discussing a particularly sexy video at bars, parties, or even at work (I myself eavesdropped on such a conversation in the front office of a major Dallas hotel in 1985). While one might easily hear two gay men discussing at a cocktail party, "Rick Donovan has the biggest dick I've ever seen," it seems highly unlikely to hear any kind of straight corollary outside of a specialized social group. Where might one hear, "Man, Kasha's tits looked great in that last movie"? While straight men might conceivably say this, they're unlikely to want to reveal publicly that they view pornography; to do so would suggest unfulfilled sexual needs and threaten their "macho" image.

Accompanying the popularization of gay pornography was the decline of feminized forms of camp, particularly drag. During the 1980s, drag shows (once ubiquitous in many gay bars) became increasingly rare. One began to hear stories of drag queens refused entrance to gay bars—and not just the leather and S/M bars where they had never been welcome anyhow. By the late 1980s, the favored form of entertainment in gay bars was the male stripper.

Go-go boys had been around for years, but in the late 1980s, following the lead of the popular Chippendale's dancers for women, roving troupes of muscular male dancers began making the circuits of America's gay bars. Most men's bars seemed to have dancers on the menu at least once a week by the early 1990's.[9] These dancing boys represented the same peak of physical perfection that one found in contemporary porno videos. A new gay ideal of masculine beauty had been born: muscular, smooth, and young. In the 1990s many gay porn performers use their video work primarily as a means to make a name for themselves to obtain work on the dance circuit in gay bars, where they can make much more money.[10]

Recently, gay writers such as Michelangelo Signorile and Daniel Harris have vilified gay porn and its muscular bodies as presenting destructive and impossible models of beauty and sexuality that have ravaged contemporary gay culture.[11] Their complaints, however, smack of the "pornophobia" of many radical right-wing and feminist groups. They assume, just as the doctrinal members of Women Against Pornography do, that people are unable to distinguish fantasy from reality, and that viewers mindlessly ape the images and activities that porn presents. Pornography, in fact, is just as artificial as camp, and few psychologically stable gay men would mistake it for reality.

Why did porno become so popular just as camp began its decline? With the post-Stonewall rise of gay liberation gays were able to critique the dominant culture overtly, and camp's more oblique attacks gradually assumed less and less importance. During the 1980s, however, the gay community fell under renewed attack both by AIDS and by a right-wing political backlash. The political and social gains of the early 1970s began to fall to an assault led by songstress and orange-juice huckster Anita Bryant (herself worthy of camp idolization due to her "almost-been" status). A new mechanism for flouting status-quo standards was needed. Camp and drag queens were part of the old guard. The masculinization of gay culture that took place alongside the development of hardcore porn in the 1970s demanded a different model. Conveniently, home VCRs and video pornography were right at hand, presenting a sleek, highly sexed, masculine version of gay identity. I would argue that the stylized masculinity of porno models and nightclub strippers was substituted for the bitter irony of camp and the exaggerated femininity of drag to produce a new weapon against the straight hegemony. Video pornography and its complex, interactive array of businessmen, directors, performers, and consumers, has reincarnated–if not replaced–the camp sensibility of earlier generations.

As Michael Bronski has pointed out, straight culture generally considers pornography to be highly dangerous, and gay pornography doubly so.[12] Despite the changes wrought by the sexual revolution mainstream America remains highly discomfited by the open display of sexuality, even heterosexuality. What better way to assert a gay identity than by the open, casual acceptance and celebration of homophobically dreaded sex acts? Charles Isherwood has written that porno came "out of the closet" in the late 1980s in conjunction with a politicization of the gay community that found a vehicle in groups such as ACT-UP; porno became a personal assertion of gay identity.[13] Heterosexual society's continued discomfort with sexuality in general and pornography in particular meant that gay men's casual acceptance of pornography provides another tool for thwarting the arbitrary standards of the dominant culture. Just as camp was a medium for the smirking derision of straight taste, the celebration of pornography, marginalized in both medium and message, confronted straight culture head-on with one of its most dreaded repressions.

By the 1990s video pornography exploded in popularity. It now includes an array of celebrity directors such as Chi Chi Larue; influential critics such as Mickey Skee; a variety of industry magazines and websites; and famous, popular performers who make profitable appearances as featured strip acts in gay clubs. Gay porn is thoroughly integrated into gay life in a way not seen with heterosexual porn and to a degree that recalls the importance of camp decades ago. The videos themselves often demonstrate the intimate connection between porn and gay life. In *Show Your Pride* (Chi Chi Larue, 1997) scenes from a gay pride parade center around the float of

Chi Chi Larue, who is surrounded by hordes of scantily-clad muscular porn models dancing to the disco beat, much as they might during their frequent club performances. This montage plays out against the sound of a plaintive voice wailing "Show your pride" to a simple disco tune. This scene, sandwiched in the middle of the video, segues abruptly to a massive orgy, completely without transition. This video not only illustrates the exalted position of porn stars in gay life through their prominent position on a float in a pride parade; it is also a metaphor for the casual ease that many gay men today demonstrate when dealing with pornography.

It would be a mistake, however, to think that porn has completely eliminated camp. In fact gay porn currently incorporates elements of traditional camp within a new, masculinized and sexualized context. Perhaps the best example is the above-mentioned director Chi Chi Larue. A drag queen originally from Minnesota, Larue appeared on the porno scene in the late eighties and quickly rose to *auteur* status while amassing a prolific and respectable body of work.[14] Larue freely incorporates drag into his public persona, appearing with his considerable retinue of buff performers as the emcee during their club dates. Larue has accrued remarkable influence as one of the few directors who consistently works with a variety of the top gay porn production companies. While the quality of his work remains somewhat uneven, at his best Larue is one of the premier producers of hardcore gay porn. His subversive use of a drag persona in this highly masculine arena is itself a successful use of camp; in addition he sometimes incorporates camp into his videos. In *The Hung Riders* (Chi Chi Larue, 1994) Larue himself plays the role of Miss Clitty, the saloon proprietor, and does a hysterical and typically campy job of overacting. In the narrative parts of this video Larue has given the actors free reign to ham it up to their heart's content, following his own lead. Especially notable is twenty-year porn veteran Sharon Kane dressed in male drag as one of the supporting cast. She provides yet another bit of gender-bending camp, as well as some arch overacting. Kane has become something of a fixture in gay porno films of the nineties. Her appearance in 1997's epic *Family Values* by Jerry Douglas—as a homophobic ex-wife of a homosexual who discovers her son, too, is gay—includes a spluttering, shrieking slapfest during a confrontation with her son that is worthy of Joan Crawford. Gay porn has also overtly parodied camp masterpieces. *Sunsex Boulevard* (Gino Colbert, 1994) is loosely based on the famous fifties movie *Sunset Boulevard,* and even includes a dramatic entrance down a grand staircase.

Such camp references allude to the close connections between camp and porn in gay culture. Gay porn's thorough penetration of contemporary gay life parallels camp's presence in earlier generations. Robert Hofler reports that porn stars are regularly seen at disco openings and various public and private parties. Porn work can even provide an entry into influential West Hollywood circles—ones available to those with the proper abs and pecs but without other credentials.[15] Like camp, porn defies the arbitrary standards of compulsory heterosexuality. As AIDS and the radical religious right have threatened the existence of gay sexuality, it is that sexuality itself that has been turned to use as a strategy for cultural survival.

Traditional camp, of course, is not dead. While writing this paper I visited a gay bar in Texas. I was surprised and amused to see on the video monitors a montage of famous scenes from *Mommy Dearest*, with Faye Dunaway at her over-the-top best, uttering her classic lines such as "Tina, bring me the axe!" Partway through the video, Dunaway's voice was replaced by music: "Mama Mia" by Abba. The bar-goers were a rapt and enthralled audience. While porno may be the new camp, the old camp sensibility still manages to make itself heard.

NOTES

My thanks to Bruce Kelton for kindly keeping me up to date on the latest videos and helping to make this paper possible. I am also grateful to the contributors to the ATKOL Forums website (www.atkol.com/forums) for their many helpful comments and criticisms on my abstract.

1. Robert Hofler, "The Men of Koo Koo Roo," *Buzz* (January 1998), p. 62.
2. Mark Booth, *Camp* (New York: Quartet Books, 1983): 17–18, 179.
3. Ibid., 19.
4. Susan Sontag, "Notes on 'Camp,'" *Partisan Review* 31 (Fall 1964): 530.
5. Ibid., 527.
6. Booth, 18.
7. For a detailed description of this phenomenon as it expressed itself in the art world, see Joe Thomas, "What's Queer About Pop Art?" *Decorum* [Leiden] 14 (December 1996): 43–48.
8. Daniel Harris, *The Rise and Fall of Gay Culture* (New York: Hyperion, 1997): 8-39.
9. Some documentary evidence does support this assertion, in addition to the anecdotal evidence. For instance, in the free Texas gay weekly *This Week in Texas*, commonly known as TWT, the issue of 15-21 October 1982 featured 61 bar ads, none of which mentioned male dancers. In the issue of 24-30 July 1998, almost half mentioned male dancers, although the total number of bar ads had diminished to 20. Ads including drag shows were at 40 percent in 1982, and, surprisingly, increased to 48 percent in 1998. However, the dwindling number of ads overall corresponds to the increasingly less important role of this periodical as others have surfaced to compete with it. In addition, drag shows, as special entertainment, are much more likely to be heavily advertised. The actual total number of drag ads went from 25 in 1982 to 9 in 1998.
10. In Ronnie Larsen's 1997 documentary film *Shooting Porn* a number of performers interviewed explained that video rarely paid the bills, but rather established a reputation for them to build on as escorts and dancers. According to Blue Blake, as an escort he made "more money than God."
11. Harris, 124–28, excoriates contemporary porn and compares it unfavorably with older pornography from the seventies. Michelangelo Signorile, *Life Outside–The Signorile Report on Gay Men: Sex Drugs, Muscles and the Passages of Life* (New York: HarperCollins, 1997): 145–46, points out the elevated status of porn stars and their

ideal physiques and connects it to gay men's use (abuse in Signorile's mind) of steroids and plastic surgery. They echo their condemnation in Hofler's article, p. 78.

12. Michael Bronski, *Culture Clash: The Making of Gay Sensibility* (Boston: South End Press, 1984): 165-66.

13. Charles Isherwood, *Wonder Bread and Ecstasy: The Life and Death of Joey Stefano* (Los Angeles: Alyson Publications, 1996): 62.

14. See Chi Chi Larue [Larry Paciotti] with John Erich, *Making It Big: Sex Stars, Porn Films, and Me* (Los Angeles: Alyson Books, 1997) for the story of the rise of Chi Chi Larue as well as other industry information.

15. Hofler, 65.

39

Beyond "Looking for My Penis": Reflections on Asian Gay Male Video Porn

Daniel C. Tsang

S INCE RICHARD FUNG'S PIONEERING ANALYSIS OF RACE AND SEXUALITY in gay Asian video porn (Fung, 1991), the genre has been transformed. No longer is white sexuality the dominant paradigm in Asian porn. Instead, the predominant image now being offered is sexuality between and among Asians. Numerous videos present Asians of various ethnicities getting it on with their fellow Asians. At times, in line with the influx of transnational capital into porn production, it is difficult to ascertain where (in Asia) the film was made; the packaging merely indicates it is "produced" in the U.S. (Some packages tout, however, that it is filmed on location in Thailand, for example.) Much of what is available on video store shelves in the U.S. (and online) appears filmed in Asia rather than in the U.S. Asian American gay male porn then, as a genre does not contain much content that is made in America even though it is distributed here. In addition, the Internet and digitalization has made such images accessible to a world-wide audience, with the click of a mouse. CD-ROMs, Web-sites, and adult pay-for-view digital photos and videos, are now the rage.

This essay looks at a subset of what's out there: Asian American gay male porn on video, and how it has changed since Richard Fung first looked at it.

Why the transition since Fung to a focus on Asian-Asian sex? (For a discussion of whether or not what Fung described still exists, see the round table discussion in Yung, 1998 and Fung's own reflections in Fung, 1998).

There are two alternative explanations for this. The first, more generous explanation, credits the emergence of the open queer Asians and the proliferation of support groups for Asian queers in north America for having a salutory effect on commercial gay porn, including gay Asian porn. In an arena where the quest for the Great White Knight appears increasingly displaced (as evidenced by personal ads that more and more seek same-race partners) in real life, it is not surprising that commercial porn producers are following suit and making films where the white guy is no longer the dominant figure, or even present!

Another, more plausible if darker explanation, credits not the gay movement but market forces for the shift. Asians remain marketable objects of desire and delicacies to be consumed, and porn producers, who undoubtedly make more money marketing white porn stars have decided that there is nonetheless a niche market that caters to non-white depictions. Hence a visit to any adult video store will see boxes and boxes of mainstream porn videos (featuring the latest Great White find), but also specialty shelves, where the nonwhite actors are shelved. On the one hand, such segregation means that those seeking white meat need never encounter anything different; on the other, those with special tastes can easily find the few videos that cater to their special needs. Indeed, the success of high quality print erotica featuring Asian youth (such as those put out in the OG "Oriental Guy" series), underlines the existence of a specialty market for such gay male Asian images.

Indeed, the marketing for these videos suggests that it is still the allure of the exotic, erotic Oriental that still underlies much advertising of gay Asian male porn in North America. In Fung's analysis, he focused on the work of an actor with the stage name of Sumyong Mahn, in fact a Vietnamese American from Orange County, California (see Tsang, 1996, p. 161). Mahn is featured on the cover of his most famous video, *Asian Knights*, but he is not alone. His naked torso is right next to an inset photo of a white actor. The cover plugs the video as a feature where the sensuous East meets the erotic West.

The sensuality of the East is what is stressed in today's adult video box covers aimed at highlighting Asian gay sex, with dreamy-eyed, languous, and boyish models featured. But the potential video buyer or renter is reminded that one can see "sweet smooth hairless buns with lots of action" (cover for *Asian Dreams, Vol. 2* or for *Asian Cuties*), or "smooth hairless buns with lots of action" (School Ties in Asian cover). Not a lot of originality, of course, but it does evoke a boyish image, even if the models portrayed look older. Other videos promote a remote land where you are encouraged to venture: Oriental Islanders has wordy text on the back cover amidst a collage of photos: "A group of adventurous oriental men are out exploring a junge island when they decide to make their trip hot and steamy . . . This is one adventure you don't want to miss."

This focus on lands far away from urban life (where presumably the audience with a VCR lives) suggests that the intended audience for Asian-Asian gay male videos is the sex tourist, whether in fact or vicarious. It also suggests that the audience is not necessarily just rice queens (those whites attracted to Asians), but also sticky rice—Asians who prefer other Asians. In fact, while almost every rice queen I've encountered has his own collection of Asian gay porn, I'm finding, increasingly, Asians who have watched Asian-Asian porn, even if their collection cannot match a rice queen's.

I would venture that for an increasing number of Asian queers in North America, their first exposure to porn may well be Asian-Asian porn—in fact some of my Asian friends specifically ask for such tapes. Hence, in contrast to videos like *Asian Knights* which were criticized by Richard Fung for its portrayal of Asian sexuality subjected to a white man's sexual dominance, videos today present more democratized sex play, in which no one necessarily plays the dominant role. There is clearly democratic sexual exchange among the Asian partners. In fact, what distinguishes above all the videos of today from those of Richard Fung's period are the amount of time practically all of these Asian-Asian videos spend on foreplay. There is a lot of nurturing, kissing, and licking, especially of the nipples and chest area. In contrast to what one expects from hardcore gay (white) porn, there is no rush to the "money shot"—these videos, like anything in Asia, take their time. It's not wham, bang and that's it. No, there's no rush; it's the Asian way, the video seems to say.

The filmmakers (and they invariably are still white, even if the actors are Asian) seem to think that the audience is not ready for anything very kinky. In most of the videos, the guys do nothing more exciting than vanilla sex; there is not even much S&M. Lack of variety in sexual repertoire is duplicated by lack of variety in the setting: Many of these videos are filmed inside hotel rooms in unnamed cities or countries.

(This suggests that the actors in these videos are probably underpaid for what they could get if they appeared in a video made in the U.S.) While the actors do talk with each other, the audience can't hear anything, presumably because the actors are not speaking English. Instead, some god-awful orientalist music is played in the background. Among the current batch of actors, two stand out. The buff Brandon Lee is specificially profiled on many videos, while the biracial (white/ Korean) Jordan Young with his boyish looks and lean body is easily marketable as a porn star with cross-over potential.

Among all the current batch of videos, one stands out: *Shanghai Meat Company* (HIS Video, 1991). Although he is not on the list of credits, its main star is none other than Quentin Lee, an independent film director, later to win fame for *Shopping for Fangs*, a cross-over Asian American youth feature film. Set in San Francisco's Chinatown, the video opens as if it were a travelogue, but this is a place where "Asian fantasies" are realized, and where "hot Oriental guys know how to have sex." These words appear on the screen as a black actor makes out with an Asian, a rare and transgressive scene in Asian gay cinema.

Eventually both blow each other and each jerk each other off. This famous director, whose face and torso decorate the box cover, eventually shows up as Peekay Chan, who's addicted to sex. His dad owns the Meat Company, "so he can do anything he wants." As the words on the screen state: "If he wants to fuck, he fucks." Chan engages in mutual fellatio with a Japanese guy, while looking bored. Eventually both come. There is no dialogue, just words on the screen describing certain characters, as in a silent movie. But the movie is not silent, with music playing throughout. By including actors of all shapes, *Shanghai Meat Company* appears to be challenging conventional norms of beauty. Chan himself is no hunk, but looks boyishly cute. Quentin Lee himself appears in Ming-Yuen S. Ma's artistic look at Asian gay porn, *Slanted Visions* (1995).

Asian gay porn rarely make any "best of" lists, but three did in "The Best of Gay Adult Video 1999": Far East Features' *Asian Persuasion* was cited (because of actors Brandon Lee and Brad Davis Mikado); Men of Odyssey Video's *Bangkok Boys Town*, and Sex Video's *K-Waikiki*.

Beyond commercial porn, among the more interesting of those video artists who have incorporated erotica into their shots have been a group of young Asian American filmmakers. Among them is Nguyen Tan Hoang. When an MFA student at University of California, Irvine, Nguyen made "7 Steps to Sticky Heaven," a creative blend of racial politics and erotica. In one scene, he films himself eating rice, in the next he's sucking cock. Its the penultimate Asian-Asian sex film, with all the fun that is missing in commercial porn. He even films himself fucking with his friends.

Nguyen's 24-minute film (made in 1995) is more interesting than all the adult gay Asian films put together. And Fung himself tried his hand (in "Chinese Characters") at safe sex videos, but found it ultimately inadequate as pedagogy (Fung, 1993).

The future of this genre, as an art form if nothing else, belongs to the independent filmmaker. The commercial porn scene remains, ultimately, boring and unsatisfying, quite unlike the spurt in queer films from Asia that have captivated the festival circuit (Berry, 1997). Unlike the commercial filmmaker whose main goal is market penetration (for want of a better word), independent filmmakers seem to film because they have fun and have something to say. And their videos show it.

REFERENCES

Berry, C. (1997). Globalisation and localisation: Queer films from Asia, in C. Jackson and P. Tapp, eds., *The bent lens: A world fuide to gay & lesbian film*. St. Kilda, Victoria: Australian Catalogue Company, pp. 14-17.

Fung, R. (1991). Looking for my penis: The eroticized Asian in gay video porn, in Bad Object-Choices, ed., *How do I look? Queer film and video*. Seattle: Bay Press, pp. 145–68.

——. (1993). Shortcomings: Questions about pornography as pedagogy, in M. Gever, J. Greyson, and P. Parma, eds., *Queer looks: Perspectives on lesbian and gay film and video*. New York: Routledge, pp. 355–67.

——. (1998). Interview with Richard Fung, in Song Cho, ed., *Rice: Explorations into gay Asian culture + politics*. Toronto: Queer Press, pp. 51–56.

Nguyen, T. H. (1998). 7 steps to sticky heaven, in Nguyen Tan Hoang [video-recording] / [produced, directed, and edited by Nguyen Tan Hoang], Durham, N.C.: Mr. Lady Records + Videos.

Skee, M. (1999). *The gest of gay adult video 1999.* Laguna Hills, Calif.: Companion.

Tsang, D. C. (1996). Notes on queer 'n Asian virtual sex, in R. Leong, ed., *Asian American sexualities: Dimensions of the gay & lesbian experience.* New York: Routledge, pp. 153–62.

Yung, W., Ma, M.Y.S., Xin, W., & Cho, S. (1998). Racy, sexy. Roundtable discussion, Vancouver 1995. In Cho, S., ed., *Rice: Explorations into gay Asian culture + politics.* Toronto: Queer Press, pp. 59–67.

APPENDIX

Asian Gay Male Erotic Videos (Commercially available):

Ambush
Asian Body Builders In Hot Core, 1
Asian Body Builders In Hot Core, 2
Asian Cuties Vol. 1
Asian Dreams Vol. 1
Asian Dreams Vol. 2
Asian Dreams, Vol. 3
Asian Force
Asian Knights
Asian Pesuasion
Asian Persuasion #2
Asian Sex Odyssey
Asian Studs Vol. #1
Asian Studs Vol. #2
Asian Studs Vol. #3
Asian Studs Vol. #4
Asian Studs Vol. #5
Asian Studs Vol. #6
Asian Studs Vol. #7
Bangkok Boys Town
The Best of Exotic Collection Vol. #1
The Best of Exotic Colleciton Vol. #2
Boys of Bankok
The Boys of Pattaya
Crem of the Coconuts
Deja Vu
Entering the Dragon
Fortune Nookie
Geisha Boys Vol. # 1
Geisha Boys Vol. #2
Geisha Boys Vol. #3
K-Waikiki
Lust at First Sight
Oriental Island
Memories of Bamboo Island
Men of Tokyo

Pacific Rim
The Penetrator
Red Hot Beaux Thai
Room Service
School Ties in Asian
Sextasy in Thaialnd
Sexual Healing
Shanghai Meat Company
Thai Boxer in Fighting & in Loving
Thai Erotica

40

Cross-Gender Identification in Commercial Pornographic Films

Russell Wilcox

SUMMARY

Pornographic movies are a tool for examining important issues in sexuality. This is true in an academic sense (as an intellectual tool, to impart ideas) and in an artistic sense (as an intuitive tool, to impart insights). One interesting phenomenon that illustrates this is cross-gender identification, which I will explain. I offer examples from some artistically acclaimed movies. These movies are good examples because the directors play with representation, and therefore also with identification. Because of their inventive construction, these movies offer more angles from which we can investigate the identification question.

It is important to note (though I don't prove this here) that the processes revealed in the example films carry over to more ordinary pornographic movies. I am describing phenomena that are common, though not universal.

WHAT IS IDENTIFICATION?

IDENTIFICATION IS A BASIC PSYCHOLOGICAL PROCESS. WE RECOGNIZE OUR-selves as individuals (primary identification) or recognize ourselves in others (secondary identification). To see others as like ourselves is the basis for social feeling, and may be necessary for person-to-person communication. Without this identification process, the motivations behind people's actions (in life or film) would be incomprehensible. In making a direct comparison between others' feelings and ours, we essentially make a model of the other person's mind in our own, to imagine their thoughts.

In cinema, identification is used as a process whereby the spectator is placed into the space of the film. This "subject position" can be created because we have more fun when we are deeply involved with the emotions of the characters. When we participate in films in this way, we derive benefit in a number of ways. It's a lazy way to experience the excitement of the film characters' lives. Most films provide the main character with an emotional journey, which we can happily ride along with. Besides, it's fun just to be someone else for a while, and we can explore these new experiences by proxy, in complete safety.

Additionally, the deeper we are into the world of the narrative, the stronger are the films effects on us. These can be effects developed over time, like the protagonist's emotional journey, or immediate effects like shock and fear.

SOME FORMAL AND NARRATIVE ELEMENTS USED TO CREATE IDENTIFICATION

A number of techniques are used to promote the viewer's identification with characters in movies, all of which are employed in pornographic movies as well as mainstream film and television. The most common device is the Point-of-View (POV) shot. This is a shot from the approximate view from the location of the character with whom you are to identify. This is the primary way of facilitating identification, but not absolutely necessary.

Another way of facilitating identification is to reproduce the viewer's immediate experience by putting screens in the movie, which are watched by the characters . The screen in the film then becomes the viewer's screen, and he is experiencing the same view as the movie character.

Alternatively, the script can state explicitly that a sequence represents the thoughts of a character, so that their thoughts are now the viewer's (sometimes preceded by a kind of POV shot).

In narrative films, there is usually a protagonist, who carries most of the emotional development in the movie. Following the main character around on their emotional "journey" is the trip the viewer expects to take. To do this, the viewer must identify with the main character, and empathize with that character's emotions. Very often, in porno, this protagonist is a woman. I am going to speculate without content analysis statistics, that this is *more often* the case in porno than it is in mainstream movies.

WHAT IS CROSS-GENDER IDENTIFICATION ("XGI")

If a male viewer does in fact identify with a female protagonist, this is identification that crosses gender lines, and can be called "cross-gender identification (hereafter referred to as XGI). Simply, it is when a viewer of one gender identifies with a character of another. Here, I am mainly talking about heterosexual male viewers and female characters in mainstream hetero movies and audiences, but the same reasoning can be applied to female viewers and male characters.

Identification works where the characters are animals (in cartoons), aliens (in science fiction), and machines (sympathetic robots, androids etc.). Why have some film theorists rejected the idea that men can identify with women? Most early feminist theories of film have assumed men can only identify with men. This naturally results in a negative evaluation, especially in "low" or "shocking" genres such as horror and porno. If anything bad happens to a female character at the hands of a male character, the male audience is assumed to be culpable. The assumed subtext "revealed" by such critiques of porno (i.e., woman-hating) tends to deny more obvious readings of the movie, which may reveal the opposite message.

Based on such analyses, there has been an erroneous attribution of the functions of porno (e.g., as propaganda for rape). The error in these critiques is to assume that the (male) spectator is only looking *at* the woman. In fact, he is often looking *from* (*within*) her.

If we include XGI in analysis of pornography, we can achieve new results. This opens up new avenues for film scholarship. Porno movies can be categorized in a new way, based on the degree to which they encourage same-gender or cross-gender identification. The complexity of some of the best movies can be appreciated. The functions and effects of porno in society and on the individual can be reevaluated; specifically there are important implications for understanding male sexuality.

Carol Clover has analyzed Horror and Slasher films, assuming XGI. In her book *Men, Women and Chainsaws*, she can explain the development of the genre, its appeal, and the structure of many of the films in very coherent terms. Linda Williams also mentions the possibility of porno XGI in her book *Hard Core*, but only briefly. In this paper I am trying to lay the groundwork for further exploration of this phenomenon.

THE CONCEPT OF "CHAINS OF IDENTIFICATION"

Identification with oneself has been called "primary" and with an onscreen character "secondary," but the situation is clearly more complex. This complexity, and chains of identification, were mentioned by Christian Metz in *The Imaginary Signifier*, but not developed fully.

The following is a list of possible subject positions in order of distance from the viewer:

Ourselves looking
The camera
The camera operator (usually offscreen)
Characters in the narrative

Figure 1. *A metaphor for serial identification*

Other characters seen or imagined by those characters (accessed through real or virtual screens)

The list can be seen as a series, or chain of spectator positions, making it possible for us to identify with different characters at different times. This has been called "oscillation," but it is not just a random or binary process. In a complex film, he structure of the film's formal elements leads the viewer into various identifications, to maximize emotional impact or pleasure.

A metaphor for this process of serial identification is that the viewer moves his "spectator position" game piece from one square to the next, as the possible positions are revealed in the film (figure 1). The film cues him to assume different positions (squares) in order to get maximum pleasure from viewing. If the viewer doesn't like the film, it "doesn't work" for him, and he remains at square one (self, or primary identification). This is called "lack of involvement," where pleasure is minimal.

In developing a picture of identification in cinema, it is interesting to note that identification and representation are almost reverse processes. Representation takes an artist's (writer or director or actor's) internal concept of a character and transfers it to external reality (the film). Identification on the other hand, takes a representation in external reality and internalizes it so it can be experienced and understood by the viewer.

Interestingly, when you identify with a character in a scene, that character "represents" you in that scene (by proxy), in another, related sense of "represent."

Since these processes are similar opposites, we can use diagrams as a tool for keeping track of "chains" of both identification and representation, as the spectator position moves in a path through them. This is important in understanding the example porno films I present, because these works play with both representation and identification simultaneously. Figure 2 is an example of a scene from one of the films reduced to a chain diagram, which is formed according to the following rules:

The eye symbol represents a real or imagined human being (that the viewer can identify with the camera is always assumed, not represented).

The eyes look at other characters in the movie, and see through windows, screens, and mental images to ever more distant orders of reality within the film.

The path of the viewer's subject position through the film is indicated by a line that passes through eye characters.

When it goes through a "mind's eye," that is a virtual screen of imagination.

Physical spaces in the film are separated by real or virtual screens.

Figure 2 below is an example of a chain diagram of a scene in the pornographic video *Latex*, directed by Michael Ninn (1995).

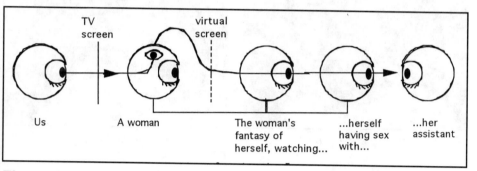

Figure 2: *The structure of identification in* Latex

In this video, a man in an insane asylum in a totalitarian, fascist society of the future, has the power to reveal people's secret sexual fantasies to himself and them (and the viewer) simply by touching them. Here he is being interviewed by a psychiatrist, and touches her. Figure 3 shows selected frames from the scene, in the form of a storyboard.

The structure of this scene is such as to encourage XGI in the (assumed) male viewer, as can be seen from several of its elements. The psychiatrist woman is the only character in the sex scene who previously had lines. Therefore the narrative elements favor her as the object of XGI. The fantasy (revelation of desire) we see is hers, and therefore we are inside her head, identifying with her experience of effectively realizing her fantasy. (We might identify with the magical man, because he too can see the sex scene, but he serves more as a metaphor for the filmmaker, by creating the scene for the woman to watch.)

Most important in terms of the chain structure is that we are watching the porno movie hoping to see our own fantasies played out. The woman is watching a scene where her fantasies are being played out. Her experience therefore mirrors ours. She is like the porno viewer—like us—and therefore we identify with her. When there is a situation in a film which looks structurally like the viewer's experience, the spectator position is rapidly moved into that situation.

Another example of a film's structure encouraging XGI is the first scene in *Night Dreams*, directed by Rinse Dream (1981).

Figure 4: structure of identification in *Night Dreams*

Figure 5: frame storyboard

A woman in an insane asylum is having sexual thoughts that she verbalizes, while two doctors monitor her via closed-circuit TV. She then fan-

Figure 3

"See the moving picture of desire and fantasy . . ."

"It's time we sent you back . . ." says the psychiatrist.

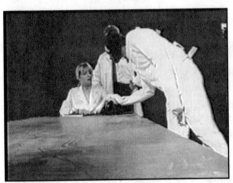

He touches her.

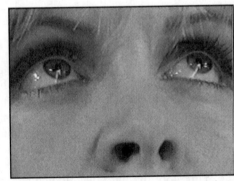

(his voice) "This is what I wanted to show you. Look familiar?"

She watches herself . . . having sex with her assistant.

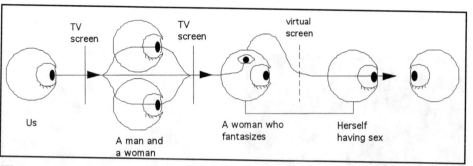

Figure 4: *The structure of identification in* Night Dreams

tasizes she is in a child's playroom, having sex with the Jack-in-the-box. Figure 5 shows some selected frames from this scene. It's interesting to note that in this and the previous film, inmates in the mental hospitals are there because of sexual mania. The sexually motivated person may find themselves ostracized socially, and this finds expression in this kind of scenario.

The act of watching facilitates our identification with the doctors initially. They may represent the "couples" audience which is more likely to watch this kind of sophisticated film. The doctors admit that they don't know what the patient is thinking, so when her fantasies become visible, we must stop identifying with the doctors.

We know the (female) patient's fantasies, and the camera is very close to her, so we tend to then identify with her. Since we watch this video in order to become aroused, we want the video to illustrate our fantasies. When it illustrates a character's fantasies, that character is like us, and we identify with them. They are a porno viewer within a porno movie.

The third example film is *The Opening of Misty Beethoven,* directed by Radley Metzger (1976). This film is essentially the story of *My Fair Lady* translated to the world of porno. In the selected scene, Misty (the Eliza Doolittle character) is to be tested for her newly learned seductive powers, by attempting to seduce and have sex with an "impotent" man (who actually looks effeminate, possibly gay). Her prerecorded, transmitted audio instructions are from a rehearsal where two other women played the parts of Misty and the (gay?) man. Figure 6 shows a chain diagram, and figure 7 a frame storyboard.

Figure 6: structure of identification in *The Opening of Misty Beethoven*

Misty is the film's protagonist, more than Eliza was in *My Fair Lady.* We have been identifying with her emotions and experience throughout the film, thus there is narrative XGI, although there are not a lot of POV shots for her.

The chain of identification is moved further by the fact that in the training session, she was to identify with the woman who played her in the mock seduction scene.

The gay man was also represented by a woman, although there was a

Figure 5

"I know you're watching me."

"Well, Mrs. Van Houten seems to be on fire today."

"Like the time the TV face caught me and it was so mad and I couldn't stop rubbing my pussy . . ."

"I wonder what she's going through," they muse.

She looks over her shoulder.

In a playroom, the Jack-in-the-box has sex with her.

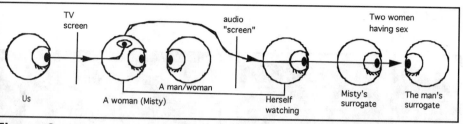

Figure 6: *The structure of identification in* The Opening of Misty Beethoven

need to translate the language of the homosexual scene into the eventual heterosexual scene, and that translation fails significantly at a certain point because of the actual dimorphism (the "ripe mango" simile). The viewer could also identify with this man, but then the viewer would be imagining himself a homosexual. If the viewer imagines himself a woman having sex with a man, is he then also homosexual?

Finally, by learning from the male sexologist, Misty is expected to internalize his way of thinking, which is a form of identification as well.

A final example is the first scene from *Fresh Meat: A Ghost Story*, directed by John Leslie (1995). Here, an effeminate man is putting on makeup at a bar, and two soldiers come in and harass him. A woman appears and insults the soldiers, knees one of them in the groin, slams him against a door, and forces both of them to watch as she has sex with the effeminate man (who she later identifies as her "wife"). Figure 8 shows the storyboard of selected frames.

In this video, John Leslie plays with the elements of identification so that he challenges gender identity on multiple levels. The scene is almost a visual metaphor for the porno making and viewing process. The soldiers are the viewers, who watch sex scenes and masturbate while they are manipulated by the producers of the video, who create the scene for them to watch. We therefore can easily identify with them initially.

If we are to identify with either of the performers, as the soldiers might be doing since they are like typical viewers, the choices are made difficult. We could identify with the man, but he is effeminate, even though he has sex in the usual hetero way. Alternatively, we could identify with the woman, since she is more masculine, even though she is having sex in the usual hetero way for a woman. Either way, we need to cross lines of either gender or sex, which are made *explicitly independent* here through *reversals*.

Let's assume one of the soldiers is identifying with the woman. When he says "fuck me up the ass" he might as well be saying "fuck the character that represents me [i.e., that I identify with] up the ass," because that's what happens. If the soldier's request is taken literally (which is what the director actually intended), the scene indicates one possible reason XGI is pleasurable to male viewers, i.e., latent homosexuality. I disagree with this interpretation in general, because it oversimplifies a phenomenon that could be a key to deeper understanding.

Figure 7

Misty is to seduce a gay gallery owner

Tape recorded instructions from a sex expert . . .

. . . to two women playing the roles of Misty and the gay man . . .

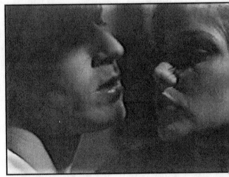

. . . are followed by Misty who listens through an earphone.

"I'm going to suck your cock . . ."

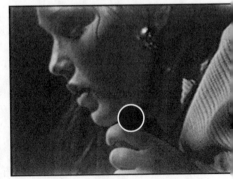

". . . like the inside of a ripe mango."

IMPLICATIONS OF XGI

What can we learn from having identified XGI in porno that we can apply to analysis of porno and to film in general? Obviously, analytical viewpoints assuming that men only identify with other men have to be completely rethought This is the case with many theories from the 1970s and 1980s, early feminist theories in particular.

Further, the place of the female spectator has to be reevaluated. Even though in the foregoing discussion, I have focused on male spectators, women watch porno also. With XGI, their experience can be much the same as men's. This has implications for how porno films can be made for both men and women.

With regard to content, the functions of various characters in the narrative must be evaluated based on the possibility of their being objects of identification or not, irrespective of gender.

Ultimately, porno cannot be assumed to exclusively reflect the "dominant ideology," because the breaking of gender boundaries in the genre is so prevalent. Mainstream heterosexuality would supposedly prohibit this, yet heterosexual porno does not.

The phenomenon of XGI also leads us to some challenging implications regarding male sexuality in the real world. Sex and gender appear to be separate in men's minds, even in a male-dominated, traditional sexuality-oriented genre like porno. This gender fluidity is widespread, as indicated by the popularity of movies with lots of XGI built in, a fact that does not bode well for those who would try to assert that gender is fixed and innate. This is maybe why conservatives of various kinds are afraid of it, and is one more indication of the anarchic nature of sex.

We need to understand why there is pleasure in XGI. There must be, because it is so common in popular movies. Latent homosexuality has been offered as an explanation, but that may be too facile, and misses a more interesting possible reason.

Let us assume that gender is most likely due to both innate tendencies and learned behavior. (This is supported by recent research and thought on the nature/nurture question.) Some of human learned behavior may be men's orientation toward expressing and experiencing pleasure. Culturally, it is male to be stoic and tough and inexpressive, even when you are having an orgasm. It is therefore female to be the opposite.

This is what we see in porno movies. Men grunt and wince a little, but women writhe and scream. It is they who express what ever pleasure there is to be expressed.

We know that in order to fully experience sexual pleasure, it is usually necessary to express it somehow. This is what is taught in classes for inorgasmic women. They are taught to give vent to their expression of the orgasm before it actually happens, and thus it is facilitated. Therefore it may be that to experience more pleasure, a man may have to

Figure 8

Two soldiers harass an effeminate man at a bar.

A leather-clad woman insults the soldiers: "Fuck your mother!"

She kicks him in the balls and slams him against a door.

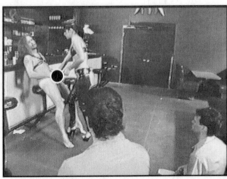

And forces them to watch her have sex with the effeminate man.

One soldier says, "Please, fuck me up the ass."

But she's the one who gets it.

momentarily become more "feminine" in behavior, or fully identify with someone who is.

This can be expressed as a two-step process:

1. Become a woman in your imagination
2. Experience pleasure fully, without the constraints of masculinity

Therefore XGI gives men an opportunity to have more pleasure, because they don't have to be themselves or even be their gender, but whatever gender expresses pleasure most easily (female).

Certainly this and other assertions in this paper will require more work to conclusively verify, but I offer them as suggestions to indicate the richness of the implications of XGI. By acknowledging the existence of this phenomenon, I have shown it is possible to gain insight into the formal structure of pornographic movies, and to derive messages that may be communicated to the viewer more or less obliquely, but are certainly contrary to what one would expect from stereotypic male heterosexuality. The existence of these messages implies a range of functions of porno in society that are not generally recognized or acknowledged.

41

Representations of S/M in the Gay Community: The Radical 1970s

Connie Shortes

G AY PORNOGRAPHY, AS THOMAS WAUGH POINTED OUT, IS ONE OF THE community's privileged cultural forms, since it is the expression of those qualities for which we are stigmatized" (1996, p. 6). His research suggests how the impulse to represent one's forbidden desire has connected and motivated even the most embryonic gay communities over the last century, and other gay scholars have documented ways in which gay pornography for the last thirty years has had a distinct communal function as "a medium of subcultural socialization, valorization, and networking" (1996, p. 26). Any discussion of gay pornography lacks meaning if it does not take place within an accompanying memoir of the gay community and its cultural debates. In this paper, I will investigate the relationship between a sub-genre of gay porn: "S/M gayporn," (as the late John Rowberry referred to it) and the leather sub-culture of the 1970s. I am less interested in what these images of S/M "mean," (for example, what they might mean about the gay psyche) than I am in how the films signified culturally and politically within their historical context. Did S/M gayporn play an affirming, celebratory and mobilizing role for the 1970s leather community in the same way that gay porn did for the larger gay community?

My analysis begins after Stonewall, when gay communities surfaced in society and gay porn became less a subterranean network of images and more of an above ground, albeit still disorganized industry, one that eventually took its place within and alongside the emerging heterosexual porn industry. I will, however, backtrack briefly into pre-Stonewall territory, in order to present what is generally considered the groundwork for explicit representations of radical, leather sexuality. I must emphasize again how indebted we are to Waugh's book *Hard to Imagine* for finding, organizing, enlivening and explicating the body/bodies of pre-Stonewall gay erotica, a portion of which clearly suggests the attraction to images of S/M, dominance and submission, gay martyrdom, bondage, etc. It wasn't until the 1960s, however, that these desires crystallized into a visible, identity-based sub-group of the larger gay community, and later still before an associated and coherent sub-genre of commercial, moving-image, pornographic representations emerged. Such representations are thematically preceded by Kenneth Anger's *Fireworks* (1947) which depicts a masochistic fantasy of a young gay man who encounters a group of sailors, and *Scorpio Rising* (1961), a film about some bike boys Anger met in the Tenderloin district of New York. According to Anger, an illicit print circulated and was screened in leather bars on the West Coast (Landis, 1995, p. 117). In fact, Anger captured this proto-sub-culture in all its thanatic glory, with images so powerful and a sexual energy so fascinating that the censors took notice, too. Upon its entry in 1964 into more public venues such as the Cinema Theater in Hollywood, it was busted for obscenity.

While Anger was considered an "underground" filmmaker, an even deeper underground existed in the form of privately produced 16mm loops of S/M activity available through mail order or circulated through private collections. Some were commercial, and some simply satisfied the desires of their creators to "see themselves" in action home movies. In the 1967 California case *People* v. *Samuels*, Dr. Samuels was convicted for aggravated assault on the basis of home movies he made of himself "whipping a naked man gagged and suspended from the ceiling."[1] Eastman Kodak turned the film over to the police, who transformed the work from a home movie into a surveillance film, and evidence of felony assault. Remember that before the advent of video, one assumed a great deal of risk recording one's kinky habits on celluloid. Dr. Samuels' predicament speaks to the power of the desire to see one's darkest and most taboo fantasies unfold before one's eyes. While the man being whipped in this particular film did not testify, Dr. Samuels claimed that he had the man's consent, but the court held that, under the law, one cannot consent to assault, a position similar to the one arrived at by the European Court of Human Rights in 1997 with regard to England's Spanner case.

If only Dr. Samuels had asserted, not a consent alibi, but an empirical one, that is, had he *distributed* the film as an educational, historical documentary, with an appropriate disclaimer and some "voice of god" narration, the outcome might have been different. He had a precedent, after all. Dr. Alfred Kinsey did as much in the 1950s when he solicited two of his male subjects (Charles Renslow and Sam Steward) to stage an S/M scene for him, which he filmed, for research purposes.[2] And in 1964, a *Life* magazine article had leeringly identified the newest social problem as the "far-out fringe of the 'gay' world," those "obsessively masculine men" with sadistic tendencies who gather at leather bars (Welch, 1964, p. 69).[3] Dr. Samuels probably could have gotten a grant. If he had represented himself as a performer or a documentarian, as opposed to a attacker who had been given consent, it would certainly have changed the legal context in which the case was tried.

Only four years later, Signature Films, one of the early gay production companies, produced *Black and Blue* (1971). It purports to present a history of the gay S/M lifestyle. But its creator, Tom Desimone, an early gay pornographer, gives us much more. The film is subtitled: *A Hard Look at Sado-Masochism on the Gold Coast*, and includes some real S/M action. It may not look that different than Dr. Samuels' home movies, but *Black and Blue* had an advantage in that it purported to document the activities of a subculture, as opposed to revealing the secret felonies of an isolated pervert—similar content, but vastly different context. *Black and Blue* as enunciation was made possible by, and at the same time announced the existence of, a *community*, one that had begun the necessary process of representing itself and announcing itself. It sought to contact those "Dr. Samuels," who had heretofore only fantasized and acted out in private, and at great risk, as well as those who sought a liberated state in which to experience the gamut of sexual variation. *Black and Blue* marks a moment of transition from the 1960s to the 1970s where "[p]eace, love, and granola gave way to leather, drugs, and performance-art sex" (Fritscher, 1978, p. 154).

   Black and Blue is no longer commercially available, pulled from circulation because it includes a "watersports" (urination) and a fisting scene, or at least, the original cut of the film did. I was able to screen a complete version of the film on video at The Kinsey Institute. Consistent with its documentary pretensions, the film begins with artists' renditions of ancient Roman and Egyptian cultures. The narrator, in serious, journalistic tones, discusses the "inception of sadism and sexual bondage in antiquity," accompanied by a three-toned tympanic drum beat. The narrator assumes a warning tone: "Some of these [ancient] practices are taking place in the homes of the modern gay male . . . S/M bars, leather dress, nude bartenders, raffling off young boys, orgy rooms . . ." The infamous "ranch scene," filmed at the Hanging Tree Ranch near San Diego, ensues. A cowboy, introduced as "the Master," rigs a young man up in some horse tack that has been cleverly modified for humans. It goes around the man's head and neck and attaches from the top of his head to a chain hanging from the ceiling. The man appears to be calm and compliant; however, at one point, the Master straps on a rather large dildo, and at the point he tries to force the dildo into the man's ass, the man faints, almost hanging himself. An extraordinary moment follows where frantic camera movement indicates the operator's distress, and the narrator explains, "Our cameraman had to discontinue filming to assist the Master." Filming resumes with a low angle shot of the Master calmly working to bring the man around. He is, to our relief, successful. Some additional context for the scene is provided in an interview contained in an unpublished dissertation by Paul Alcuin Siebenand 1975. Here, Desimone refers to *Black and Blue* as the film in which an actor "almost died on us." Apparently, Desimone recruited an actor who agreed to appear with the ranch owner for this scene, and otherwise had no prior knowledge of, or relationship, with him (Siebenand, 1975, p. 103).

   The next segment of the film attempts to present another "you are there" scenario set in a San Francisco club. A man is abducted by two other men and a chaotic rape scene ensues. He is subjected to clothespins on his nipples, hot candlewax and a sound strapping. The scene concludes with some watersports: one of the abductors urinates in the man's mouth. The cinema verité style accomplished in the ranch scene and suggested by the "you are there" narration and the documentary look of the film is belied by deftly edited cutaways from the wide shots to show close-ups of insertions and tortured flesh from seemingly impossible angles. That is, while the obligatory money shot is missing, the editing is worthy of any good porn movie.

The final scene has a special place in gay porn history. There, bigger than life, was the first filmic (and extremely indelicate) evidence that "fistfuckers" existed, something that before had only been represented in Polaroids kept in the kind of private collections Waugh discusses. As the scene commences, the sound of a heartbeat reverberates, and the screams of the man being fisted over a bathtub end the film. For those who might have previously considered a fisting only a mythological sexual possibility, *Black and Blue* had an educational function with regard to sexual variation. And least the viewer might still consider the practice somewhat exotic. The narrator informs that this is a practice "gaining popularity." The ranch scene, the club scene and the fisting scene present the staged, anonymous, and high-risk quality of S/M action which will prove to be a characteristic of other popular gay S/M films of the decade. The qualities of a good S/M film or video were in place by the mid-1970s, however. The participants convincingly embody their roles (tops appear masterful, bottoms are able to convey the experience of pain/fear), the action is well-paced (although regular cum shots obligatory for "straight" porn are not required), *authentic* and intense (physical limits are played with, if not breeched).

The "hanging" story at Hanging Tree Ranch becomes part of leatherlore, but in time, this type of action also becomes the subject of some controversy and conflict within a more evolved and self-conscious leather community desiring to communicate the mutual pleasure derived from S/M sexuality, as well as a concern for safety. In the early 1970s, however, complex struggles over the representation of such radical sex had not yet fully unfolded, and gay S/M available on film was raw, raunchy, brutal, authenticCand the focus was not on genital sex. This was in stark contrast to most "vanilla" gay porn being produced in the 1970s, which were all about sex (like heterosexual porn, the money shot was the ultimate point), and populated by "interchangeable blond twits or coltish modelles" (Fritscher, 1990, p. 114). For example, *Black and Blue* was released the same year as *Bijou,* Wakefield Poole's graceful classic about gay male sexual awakening featuring a gentle and inquisitive Bill Harrison, whose smile, Poole asserts, is the ultimate orgasm (Fritscher, 1978, p. 18).

The leather and S/M community was already defined by its hostility to the stereotype of the effeminate gay man and indeed, any gay man who displayed any "feminine" characteristics. In the 1964 Life article referred to above, Bill Ruquy, part owner of the Tool Box, a San Francisco "S&M bar," announces: "This is the antifeminine side of homosexuality. . . . We throw out anybody who is too swishy. If one is going to be homosexual, why have anything to do with women of either sex? We don't go for giddy kids" (Welch, 68). Leathermen felt that they had an obligation to get the word out to young, middle-American gay boys that one could be gay and manly at the same time, to destroy the "nelly-gay" stereotype held by many Americans.

A film which captures the polarity at this time of gay styles, sensibility and popular culture, and perhaps even presages the future conflicts, is Fred Halsted's *L.A. Plays Itself* (1972). Following closely upon *Black and Blue*, Halsted's bifurcated film became a gay classic.[5] The first half of the film takes place in an "enchanted forest" outside L.A. in which two beautiful young men find each other. Between artfully composed shots of wild flowers, bees buzzing, water flowing and dappled sunshine on the forest floor, the men engage in ecstatic, sumptuously filmed sex. There is no dialog, simply the merry strains of a baroque guitar piece. Panoramic scenes of bulldozers and acres of leveled, treeless landscape serve as a transition to scenes of inner-city L.A., billboards, movie marquees, and crowded streets viewed from inside a car being driven by Halsted. He picks up a hitchhiker, played by Joey Yale, Halsted's real-life lover. In the film, they perform an S/M scene that eerily mirrors the first half of the film, except that the garden of paradise is replaced by a gritty L.A. apartment, the grass by a bare mattress on springs in a small bedroom, and the butterflies dancing around the flowers by static shots of framed, glass cases filled with butterflies impaled on pins. Halsted beats Yale with a belt, ties him to the bed and ultimately, fists him. (Note that this scene has been cut from the video copy of the film commercially available today, but is included in MOMA's print.) The fisting scene which ends this film is much more dramatic than that in *Black and Blue*, which was somewhat perfunctory and frantic. Suspense and visceral fascination is solicited by a shot of Halsted's right arm filling the screen as his left hand greases it up to the elbow.

In those early, heady days after Stonewall, Halsted himself embodied the sort of gay man the leather community modeled itself after: a hardened, muscular, hyper-masculine male capable of intense brutality, the very epitome of machismo, but with a perverse, perhaps revolutionary irony: such a man desires other males. In his role as anti-hero, he did not exactly function as the spokesperson for the S/M-leather community, as much as ideal image. Nevertheless, in the decade which Jonathan Dollimore characterizes of "tension between . . . two strands of liberation: anarchic desire and political engagement" (1991, p. 213), Halsted was decidedly and vocally anarchist. He believed that gay porn was one of the most important agents of change available, and dismissed political activists' attempts to change discriminatory laws, claiming that even to change laws that have oppressed you is to buy into the oppressor's system. Halsted's idea of public demonstration was a giant orgy, "100,000 faggots around City Hall in a suck-and-fuck-in, and that would settle things once and for all" (Berlandt, 1975, p. 20).

In *L.A. Plays Itself*, a utopian segment depicting the kind of mutual pleasure men can afford each other co-exists along with the corresponding dystopia containing the brutality they can inflict. Unlike the gay community, however, the two halves of the film do not interrogate or critique each other. They simply exist benignly side by side, connected by the destructive/constructive movement of progress and urbanization. Halsted shows that in the matter of gay popular culture that would become increasingly factionalized, he could do both with style.

Completing the body of films that became part of the mythical framework around which the community formed was *Born To Raise Hell* (1975), directed by Roger Earl and produced by Terry Le Grand. Filmed in three parts: the backroom of an LA leatherbar, a private dungeon and the great outdoors, the film consolidated the fetishistic, visual code of the community, the ritual atmosphere of leather bars and the celebration of primal, unleashed masculine brutality. The action is non-stop, relentless, raw, sweaty, gritty and largely plot-less, proceeding from scene to scene. Hand held cameras capture the faces of the tops (the men who dominate), which signify no emotion or affectation, only grim determination. The faces of the bottoms (the men who submit) slide between expression of pain and amyl-coated vacuousness. Anticipating censorship problems, the film begins with a disclaimer which states that it is a study of sadomasochism using professional actors and that the filmmakers are not responsible for its effect on viewers. Then the phrase, "Psycho Films Presents" studded on the back of a leather jacket pays homage to leather forefather Anger's *Scorpio Rising.* Perhaps as if to signify that the intensity and viscerality were to be raised several degrees from that earlier film, the remainder of the opening credits are written on the skin of various men hanging out in the club.

Between frequent hits of amyl-nitrite (poppers), administered by the tops to their bound bottoms, we are treated to a veritable cornucopia of S/M action including watersports (the first scene of the film is of a kneeling man gulping what seems to be an endless stream of his master's urine), beatings with various objects, fistings, numerous styles of cock and ball torture, shaving (with a straight edge, of course), some skillful suspension and various bondage scenarios. It is also important to note what is not included: genital sex. In fact, there is nary a sign of tumescence anywhere in the film.

Born to Raise Hell became the standard, reigned supreme. In the leather press, writers longed for something as good, as mesmerizing, as hot as this film, and never seemed to find it. They regularly featured advertisements and photo essays for *Black and Blue* and *Born to Raise Hell,* almost as if viewing the films itself constituted a necessary ritual for sub-cultural membership. The world changed in the 1980s, however. Gay porn film and video production began to transform itself into an industry organized around detailed erotic specializations, something that would be completed with the conversion to video, accomplished about 1985. But more than technology and commercial imperative were changing the representation of gay S/M. As political gains for the gay community mounted after Stonewall, a somewhat less disenfranchised future could be imagined, a code of "normalcy" began to emerge, and the stakes for deviance and taboo breaking were raised. The phrase "politically correct" was not in full force yet, but the template for the community's increasing uneasiness with its own diversity that would fully unfold in the 1980s was already there, reflected in gay pornography as well.

Factionalized conflicts between the S/M sub-culture and the larger gay community would come to head with the release of the 1980 Hollywood film, *Cruising*, a police drama which used the New York leather community as its sensational backdrop. The film's exploitation of the gay community's kinky corners caused much discomfort in the "vanilla" gay world, and a few demonstrations. AIDS was on the horizon and the whole sexual ethos of the gay community and its leather sub-culture was about to radically change. The 1980s were marked by decisive battles over sexually explicit representations within the gay community, but that is another story.

REFERENCES

Berlandt, Konstantin. "An S&M Film the Whole Family Can Enjoy." *The Village Voice* 20, no. 120 (June 2, 1975): 21.

Dollimore, Jonathan. *Sexual Dissidence: Augustine to Wilde, Freud to Foucault.* Oxford: Clarendon Press, 1991.

Fritscher, Jack. "Dirty Poole: Everything You Fantasized About Wakefield Poole, but Were Too Wrecked to Ask," in *Drummer* 4, no. 27 (1978): 14–22.

———. *Some Dance to Remember.* Stamford, Connecticut: Knights Press, 1990.

Landis, Bill. *Anger: An Unauthorized Biography of Kenneth Anger.* New York: Harper-Collins, 1995.

Siebenand, Paul Alcuin, *The Beginnings of Gay Cinema in Los Angeles: The Industry and the Audience.* Unpublished Dissertation, University of Southern California, 1975.

Waugh, Thomas. *Hard to Imagine: Gay Male Eroticism in Photography and Film from Their Beginnings to Stonewall.* New York: Columbia University Press, 1996.

Welch, Paul. "Homosexuality in America." *Life* (June 26, 1964): 67–75.

NOTES

1. *Harvard Law Review*, 1968, vol. 81, p. 1339.

2. Sam Steward discusses this "documentary" film in "Dr. Kinsey takes a peek at S/M: A reminiscence," in Mark Thompson, ed. *Leather folk: Radical Sex, People, Politics, and Practice* (Boston: Alyson Publications, Inc., 1991), 81–90. Waugh also mentions the film in *Hard to Imagine*, 394.

3. Fritscher discusses the effect of this article on the gay community in *Some Dance* and his essay "Artist Chuck Arnett: His life/our times" in *Leatherfolk*, 107.

4. According to Rowberry's account, various versions circulated depending on the city in which it was playing, and the film was frequently busted. See "A Personal View of the History of Sadomasochism in Film and Video," *Drummer* 102 (January 1987): 31.

5. Original prints of the film are now part of MOMA's permanent collection, along with *Sex Garage*, another Halsted classic.

SECTION 11

CHILD PORNOGRAPHY: FORBIDDEN THOUGHTS AND IMAGES IN AN EROTIC LANDSCAPE

ONE OF THE MOST RADICAL CHANGES IN ATTITUDES IN THE LAST PART of the twentieth century has been in our views of child pornography. Photographs or artistic representations of children which were was regarded as innocent and tolerated throughout much of the nineteenth and most of the twentieth century are now illegal. Courts which have generally been tolerant towards adult erotic and pornographic images have become ever more rigid in outlawing images of nude children of any age, and even the traditional baby pictures of boys and girls playing in the nude have been forbidden and the owners of such photographs prosecuted. What started out as an effort to deal with battered children came to be a campaign against child abuse, and as increasing number of parents rebelled against state interference with children in a family setting, child abuse came to be synonymous with sexual abuse. The age of children in terms of child abuse laws now extends to eighteen, even though we know that young people are sexually active before then. It is even possible for a person of twenty who is sexually involved with a seventeen-year-old to be accused of child abuse. Harris Mirkin examines and explains these developments. To do so in this day and age takes considerable courage since those who criticize what can only be called "hysteria" over child sexual abuse are themselves likely to be accused of being involved in child abuse, their homes searched, and even the most innocent-seeming materials seized. At the World Pornography Conference, the session which Mirkin had chaired and organized received the most virulent press reaction as if merely talking about the issues was the same as engaging in sexual activity with children.

As a result of such hysterical reactions, we have a great deal of difficulty in examining childhood sexuality in any form. Ralph Underwager and Hollida Wakefield describe this as resulting from the Comstock syndrome, where a fascination and prurient interest in childhood sexuality and a fear of such sexuality is represented as a crusade against sexual pornography. The result is that the attacks on pornography became a means of power, power theoretically in terms of a noble goal, namely the protection and safety of the powerless children. Because the goal is so noble, the end justifies the means, even the suspension of constitutional safeguards. Because it is important for children to testify, tactics used to gain such testimony (whether reality based or not) have the potential of making innocent childhood activity a fearsome crime, setting back the sexual development of children, and making them troubled adults.

David Sonenschein describes the reaction to a set of four black and white photos dealing with a boy, about five, looking at the penis of an adult male, then looking and examining his own, and looking again at the adult's organ with an indecipherable but thoughtful look. The pictures were accepted by a gallery and initially there was a sympathetic and amused reaction to the series until a television station labeled the pictures pornographic. The reaction did not end there but continued at the conference where Sonenschein circulated the photos to the audience. One of the press representatives in attendance felt the photos were pornographic and obscene and questioned whether "pedophiles" should be allowed to exist. In sum, even the reader of this section could be labeled a pedophile by some Comstock cowboy for trying to find out something about the nature of child porn.

42

The Prohibited Image: Child Pornography and the First Amendment

Harris Mirkin

BEFORE WORLD WAR II MANY EROTIC IMAGES THAT WOULD BE COMMON today were illegal, and books like Joyce's *Ulysses* and Miller's *Tropic of Cancer* could not be published in England or the U.S. At the end of the century the scene is very different. We have explicit sexual images on the Internet, cable TV and in magazines. Explicit sexual scenes are in popular television shows, and ads for escort services and phone sex are common. High art is in a persistent dialogue with the erotic, as are advertisements. In most western countries the only significant restrictions on adult sexual material are on government funding and on where, when and how it is displayed. There have been some successful attempts to restrict the wide circulation of erotic images and to limit their display in the workplace, but the central direction is clear.

When children are involved, however, policy has moved in the opposite direction. In the 1920s, at a time when adult swimmers had to be very clothed, naked boys swam in the Serpentine in London's Hyde Park. Pictures of naked children and youths that used to be considered images of innocence are now seen as pornographic. In the United States it is usually illegal to merely possess an erotic photograph of a nude youth or young teen (a unique restriction in the speech area) or even to have a clothed picture in which the focus is thought to be on the genital area, and it is always illegal to take, distribute or possess pictures of natural and common acts like youth masturbation or boys with erections. England, which is generally far more permissive about public sexual images and speech than the United States, is even more restrictive of representations of child/youth sexuality. Canada restricts words as well as images. Even the sexually permissive Scandinavian countries and the Netherlands have tightened laws about nude and erotic photographs of children. Only Japan, among the major countries, is relatively permissive about nude photographs of girls (but not boys).

This two-tiered attitude towards nude images of children and adults needs to be examined. A comprehensive treatment requires a comparative study, but this article will focus on the United States. Its dominance in communications makes its policies especially influential, and it has been a lobbyist for international restrictions in this area, just as it was a force for restrictions on gay pornography in the post-WWII period. The country's strong First Amendment free speech tradition and conflicting moral attitudes set up a sharp conflict. Most important, the necessity of defending restrictions on free speech before the Supreme Court produces policy rationales that can be closely analyzed.

At the outset it is necessary to emphasize that child pornography is a form of speech, even though political arguments against it often equate it with the act of child molestation. This, therefore, is an article about speech. It may be speech that records or symbolizes real actions that are illegal, or images might be electronically manipulated. It is possible (though doubtful) that pornography causes sex crimes, and if a tight link could be shown that might provide constitutional grounds for limiting pornographic speech—whether in regard to children or adults. Many find the content of child pornography repulsive, just as some are repulsed by adult pornography, or by racist or sexist or blasphemous speech. It might not be a type of speech the founders wished to protect. It might be speech that some people believe that others shouldn't see or hear. All these issues need to be examined. But words and images are still speech, not actions. Though they disagree in most areas, many feminist and fundamentalist Christian theorists come together on sexual issues. Both deny the importance of the speech/action distinction in the sexual area, but—except when children are involved—the arguments have not been widely accepted. Usually it is permissible to represent the forbidden, and it is legal to have shows in which actors are cut up by chain saws or terrorists blow up buildings, while it is illegal to actually do these things.

Pornographic images are sometimes treated differently than other speech, and there is an important debate about whether they should be allowed, forbidden or restricted. But this article will not center on the general debate about pornography. Rather the focus is on whether child pornography should be treated differently than adult pornography, and I will argue that there is no justification for doing so. If adult pornography is permitted, child pornography should be permitted; if it is forbidden, child pornography should be forbidden. It is possible to both dislike child pornography and believe it should be permitted, just as it is possible to think racists and sexists should be allowed to speak while disagreeing with the content of their messages.

The justification for the child pornography laws has several prongs which need to be examined. The usual justification is that they protect the young but, as will be shown, that rationale doesn't hold up to analysis. An additional argument, used primarily in regard to sex and belied by beliefs and actions in other areas, is that youths are incapable of giving consent, or of resisting adult authority. Finally, essentialist conceptions of the innocent, non-sexual youth underlying these justifications conflict with the simultaneous belief that these same youths will seek out pornography if they have the opportunity. The contradictions are teleologically resolved: all of these beliefs justify censorship, and lead to laws restricting the behavior of the young. In fact, I will argue, the laws seemingly designed for the protection of the young are really intended to control them.

Definitions in the area of child pornography are (purposely) muddy, and the blurring of categories allows mild and common activities to be equated with rare and hurtful ones. After discussing definitions, and briefly examining the growth of the current, almost unquestioned, conception of the proper relationship between kids and sex, an examination of policy rationales will be made. If it can be shown that the policies cannot be justified with the arguments used to defend them, and can only be defended with arguments that are explicitly rejected, it becomes legitimate to try to uncover the forces behind the policies and to ask what, and whose, purposes they serve.

AN IMPRECISE (AND ALWAYS CHANGING) DICTIONARY

Like all politics, sexual politics is largely controlled by words and concepts. These define and classify, create and obfuscate differences, and forge associations. It is especially important to examine the vocabulary in an explosive area like child pornography.

Child: In discussions of child pornography the word "child" is used to refer all people under eighteen. This is contrary to normal usage, where we use "kids," "pre-teens," "teenagers" and "adolescents" to refer to older youths. When the news refers to child pornography it is natural to imagine small children, though most of the images referred to actually involve adolescents and pubescent youths. This has important consequences. For example, when we argue that children can't give consent to be photographed because they are easily controlled by adults we probably don't have the image of the rebellious adolescent in mind. Also, major differences in physical development and sexual attitudes are obscured by the blanket use of "child." Since most people don't have direct knowledge of child pornography, it is the phrase itself, combined with the images put forth by its opponents, that have created their impression of it. Of course the arguments had to resonate with other elements of the American tradition, specifically with the image of the innocent child that is discussed below.

Pornography and obscenity: Since the 1930s the Supreme Court has slowly widened protection of sexual speech, differentiating (permitted) pornographic from (forbidden) obscene expression. Though there are battles over the standards that should be applied, pornography is protected unless it is without literary, artistic, political, or scientific value and appeals dominantly to prurient interests. Material that only appeals to prurient interests is considered obscene and is not protected.

One important feature of pornography or obscenity is that the representation of an act is often more illegal than the action itself. The crucial element seems to be that they make a public display of things, like sex acts or nudity, which normally can only be done in private. For this reason pornography is more acceptable if it is in a magazine or book, and has to be consciously sought, than if it is on a billboard or prime time TV.

Child pornography: Child pornography is treated differently than adult pornography. The Supreme Court explicitly separated the two categories, so that while only adult obscenity can be forbidden, child pornography can be prohibited even if it has artistic, political, educational or scientific value. The Court argued that the government had a special interest in the protection of children. Also, the judges did not believe that child pornography could ever have any real value.

The concern about children and pornography moves down two tracks, though the meanings slide into and reinforce each other. Sometimes the concern is about pornographic images that children might see,[1] and at other times it is about sexual or erotic images of children. The common denominator is the association of children and sex, and each category justifies its own restrictive legislation. The concept of child pornography covers a broader range of material today than it did in earlier periods, and there has been a sexualization of images that would previously have been considered non-sexual. In the nineteenth century pictures of naked children, as angels and cherubs, were viewed as images of innocence. It was the display of pubic or body hair that was forbidden. These attitudes have now been reversed, and adult nudity is more acceptable than unclothed youths.[2,3]

Child Abuse: Unlike adult pornography, which is treated as speech, child pornography is equated with the act of hurting a child. Arguments against these acts are then used to justify restrictions on pornographic speech. Child abuse is the concept used to link violence, pedophilia and pornography. It is a new social construction. Prior to the 1960s there was no general category of child abuse, only individual types of cruelty to children. In 1962 "The Battered Child Syndrome," was published.[4] The article was about child beating, and the concept was associated with the term "abuse." The ensuing discussions led to the original legislation in this area, which was designed to protect children from poverty and from being harshly whipped by their parents. Some conservatives objected to the legislation since it restricted the power of the family over the child. The concept of child abuse became associated with sexual offenses in the 1970s.[5] And it was the use of child models and actors in photos and films which led to control of the distribution of child pornography. Congress first outlawed images of children under sixteen engaging or assisting in sexually explicit conduct, and in 1984 it criminalized non-commercial activity and the reproduction of existing child pornography and raised the age to eighteen. The law was amended to include computers, and in 1991 was expanded to include possession. In 1995 Congress passed the Communications Decency Act (CDA) which banned sexual images that might be accessible to children, but this bill has fared poorly in the courts. In 1996 legislation making it illegal to transmit or possess visual depictions "created, adapted, or modified to appear that an identifiable minor is engaged in sexually explicit conduct" was included in the Budget Bill and signed by the President. Several states have also passed legislation in this area.[6]

It is worth underlining the changes in this area. Originally the concept of child abuse was not connected with sex, and the laws limited the family's power over the child. Current policy focuses largely on sexual issues, and because of perceived problems in this area the family's power to control the child has been legally reinforced. The policies link pornographic images with sexual acts and sexual violence; forbidden images are equated with forbidden acts.

In order to understand current public policy towards child pornography it is necessary to briefly examine the changing social constructions of the relationship between youth and sex. The following section is a brief historical detour to examine some of the issues.

THE ASEXUAL CHILD IN CONTEXT (A HISTORICAL DETOUR)

The courts have given the government a great deal of flexibility in dealing with the young, and have allowed children to be treated as a separate class toward which it is permissible to act in ways that would be forbidden in regard to other classes. For example, curfews are applied to the whole category of youth, while it would be impermissible to apply them to other groups, such as blacks, the poor, homosexuals, males or even people with a criminal record. Youth's privacy rights are different from those of adults, as are the limits on their speech and writing. These restrictions can be viewed as acts of control or as child protection. Special restrictions are applied in regard to sex. Visual images of nude youths are largely forbidden, as is showing sexual pictures to them. Totally forbidden are photographs of the young that portray them as sexual or erotic beings who masturbate, engage in sexual play with each other, or have erections. Since the majority of teenagers have intercourse before they are sixteen (males) or seventeen (females), engage in various types of sex play well before that, and start to masturbate before their twelfth birthday, the lack of representations distorts empirical reality, both reflecting and reinforcing a picture of youths as largely non-sexual beings.[7]

The image of the innocent child is culturally powerful. Even male teen hustlers are viewed as the victims of their customers, and it is assumed that the hustler has been coerced and victimized.[8] Similarly it is simply assumed that children who allow erotic pictures to be taken have been forced to pose, and will be hurt by the experience. This is true even if they are nudists, or hustlers, or have given consent, or are eager to be photographed in order to show off or get approval or money. Children are considered, by definition, to be incapable of giving consent in this area, so the assumption of coercion is not refutable. As was noted above, this view of children is allied with the contradictory premise that they are strongly attracted to representations of sex and will disobey adult prohibitions and seek them out and be corrupted by them. Thus MTV, music, comics and the Internet have to be monitored so that children do not see sexual images. There is a great deal of hypocrisy about sex in the dominant culture, and there are rarely public defenses of sexual liberation, though the society is awash in sexual images, pornography is a big business, and sex groups are the most popular groups on the Internet. Rather, unlike the 1960s when sexual freedom was publicly defended as the path to a better society,[9] there are ubiquitous public statements decrying moral decay. The most common political claim is that sexual freedom lies at the center of other social problems.

The negative attitude toward sexual freedom is especially evident when youth is discussed. About 80 percent of adults think teenage sex is wrong, even if they reported an early onset of sexual activity in their own lives.[10] Children are not supposed to be socialized into sex but protected from it, and as the physical age of puberty has gone down the legal age of consent has gone up. Few public spokespeople celebrate youth's sexual freedom, or urge that they be socialized to enjoy it or experiment with it. Instead, it is argued that the young are not ready for sex and will be hurt by it. They are innocents who are not supposed to see sex, do sex, want sex or be desired as sexual objects.

Americans think this view is natural, but concepts of childhood sexuality have varied widely. In many cultures, and in much of the western tradition, children and teens are seen as erotic. This is true of both sexes, though girls and boys are portrayed differently. The erotic vision of young males is common in Greek and Roman art, in the Davids of both Michelangelo and Donatello, and in many of the portrayals of youths in diverse traditions. There is not a large photographic tradition of nude boys, since such representations have largely been forbidden, though Weston's photograph of his young son Neil, and Sally Mann's photographs of her sons are famous.[11] Young male desirability is also a theme in many classic and contemporary novels, including Mann's *Death in Venice* and Gide's *Immoralist.* Youthfulness is often glorified in gay male culture, though styles vary and sometimes the mature muscular body is the ideal.

Nubile girls have been more prominent than boys in Western art, and young female nudes are a staple. However, contemporary artists and photographers that portray nude girls (like Ovenden, Mann, Hamilton and Sturges) are often under legal siege. Many Asian cultures also celebrate the erotic appeal of the young girl. In American popular culture the young cheerleader is a fixture, as are nubile gymnasts, actresses and fashion models. The sexuality of young girls is also glorified in many popular songs. All these images have an erotic, though not necessarily an explicitly sexual, component. Women's fashions currently glorify the youthful slim figure, though style varies and at times the mature woman has been the ideal.

American men spend a great deal of time thinking about sex, and fantasies that involve youth are common. Of course few of these fantasies are acted on, and recognition of the difference between fantasy and reality lies at the heart of the First Amendment. Many argue that the current construction of youth shows moral progress. It might. In this area, though, the distinction between action and representation has been erased. It is illegal to create, distribute or possess a visual image that expresses a different conception of youth, that visualizes the child as an erotic person. It is a forbidden image as well as a prohibited action. This is a sharp break with the way other subversive thoughts and ideas are treated. We now return to the examination of how that has happened.

CURRENT POLICY—FROM *STANLEY* TO *FERBER* TO *OSBORNE*

For most of American history there was little public dissent from official sexual policies that assumed the correctness of a biblical framework. Sex arose as an arena of public conflict in the early twentieth century, as southern and eastern European immigrants began arriving in large numbers and as artists pushed against acceptable sexual standards. It became an even more important issue with the widespread urbanization that occurred after WW II. Feminists, gays, lesbians and sexual liberationists argued that the dominant ideas about sex and gender were social and political constructions that repressed some groups and advantaged others. These claims met with a refusal to argue over what were seen as natural and true moral standards that should not be compromised. Psychiatrists agreed the dissidents were sick. Rebellious women were treated, and homosexuality was classified as a mental illness. Normal civil and political liberties weren't thought to apply since deviant groups were seen as evil and subversive, hidden corrupters of the moral order and the American family. Cameras in toilet stalls, censorship, ridicule, and moral outrage were the accepted tools of battle.

As dissidents began to be viewed as political groups expressing a different world view, their writings and graphics received protection. Even though the Court has hesitated to cover sexual speech and images with a full First Amendment umbrella, it has supported a wide area of freedom for them. In *Miller* v. *California* the Court ruled that sexual speech and images can be forbidden only when it lacks serious literary, artistic, political or scientific value, and is patently offensive to the values of the community.[12] However, sexual images that either involve youth or can be seen by them are treated very differently.

Both child pornography and adult obscenity are considered subversive of the moral order but when pornography uses child actors or models there are two additional factors. Adult obscenity is banned for the same reason public nudity is forbidden: because it would annoy and shock inadvertent viewers, and exert a bad influence on those with weak characters. In the case of child pornography the primary claim is that the depiction harms the child. It is the models and actors rather than the audience who are seen as needing protection. A second way in which pornographic images of children are treated differently than other obscene or subversive materials is that possession of the images is a crime. In other speech areas restrictions apply only to the production of the material, and sometimes to their distribution. The controlling Court cases in this area are *Stanley* v. *Georgia, New York* v. *Ferber* and *Osborne* v. *Ohio.*

In the *Stanley* case the Court reviewed a situation in which the police, searching the home of Robert Stanley for evidence of illegal bookmaking, found obscene movies and arrested him for possession of this material. Stanley argued that he had a right of privacy, and that the State should not punish possession. The Court unanimously agreed, arguing that the State could not tell a person in his house what books he could read or what films he could watch. State regulation of obscenity could only cover distribution.[13] *New York* v. *Ferber* blurs the line between speech and activity and creates a sharp distinction between adult pornography, which is protected by the First Amendment, and child pornography. At issue was a statute that prohibited persons from knowingly promoting a sexual performance by a child under sixteen by distributing material which depicted that performance. "Sexual performance" is defined as actual or simulated sexual intercourse, sexual bestiality, masturbation, sado-masochistic abuse or the lewd exhibition of genitals. The statute focused on the production of child pornography, and prohibited distribution as a means of controlling production. The majority opinion, written by Justice White, upheld the state. It argued that pornography is created for sale, and the selling of child pornography is a part of the process of creating it. The protection of children from sexual abuse and exploitation is a government objective of "surpassing importance" and the "distribution network for child pornography must be closed if the production of material which requires the sexual exploitation of children is to be effectively controlled."[14] Thus child pornography is categorized as part of the illegal act of producing it, rather than as speech. Once child pornography is defined primarily as a commercial product questions of freedom of speech become moot, and it is "permissible to consider these materials as without the protection of the First Amendment."[15]

Despite the rejection of a First Amendment test, the second part of the opinion treats child pornography as a speech product that can be forbidden because it is, in itself, damaging to the child participants. The "materials produced are a permanent record of the children's participation and the harm to the child is exacerbated by their circulation."[16] It is irrelevant to the child if the published product passes the Miller obscenity test and has literary, artistic, political or scientific value. It is unusual in a speech case to unquestioningly accept a legislative finding of harm, but in *Ferber* that is done. There is not even provision for a court trial to see if harm was actually done to the particular youth involved, or if s/he voluntarily or even eagerly participated.

The New York statute defined child pornography as centering around explicit sex acts. This definition was obviously in White's mind when he argued that even if child pornography is considered as speech it would not be protected by the First Amendment since the "value of permitting live performances and photographic reproductions of children engaged in lewd sexual conduct is exceedingly modest, if not *de minimis.*" It is unlikely that "visual depictions of children performing sexual acts or lewdly exhibiting their genitals would often constitute an important and necessary part of a literary performance or scientific or educational work." The opinion uses a variation of the reasonable alternative argument, and White writes that even if there is some value in sexual depictions of children, there are alternatives to the their use, since youthful looking older persons could be used.[17]

The political pressure to control child pornography is strong and these considerations obviously influenced Justice Brennan who used a First Amendment test, reluctantly concurring in the Court's decision only because the evilness of the explicit types of sexual acts with children that are defined in the statute outweighed any benefits gained by their depiction. He noted that the standard raised by the Court's opinion recognized that the limited classifications of speech that could be suppressed without raising First Amendment concerns have two attributes: "They are of exceedingly 'slight social value,' and the State has a compelling interest in their regulation." Brennan argued that this balancing test means that if the material is itself a serious contribution to art, literature or science it becomes protected speech.[18] He thus raises a much higher standard than that used by the Court majority, and will dissent in *Osborne.*

The explicit sexual performance criteria of the Ferber case are widened considerably in *Osborne* v. *Ohio.*[19] Justice White, again writing for the Court, upheld an Ohio statute that outlawed the *possession* of child pornography as part of the attempt to restrict its production. The rationale of the law was that it was impossible to restrict the production or distribution of child pornography if it could be sold at a profit—that it was necessary to restrict sales in order to prevent distribution, and sales could be limited only if possession was outlawed.

The *Osborne* decision expanded the *Ferber* decision in two ways: the definition of child pornography was broadened so that any pictures of naked children could now be considered pornography,[20] and possession and viewing, in addition to sale and distribution, were made illegal. As in the *Ferber* decision, White is not willing endorse the regulation of speech or thought. He claims to agree with the Court's statement in *Georgia* v. *Stanley* that "whatever the power of the state to control public dissemination of ideas inimical to the public morality, it cannot constitutionally premise legislation on the desirability of controlling a person's private thoughts." But in this case, he writes, the state was not trying to protect the minds of viewers but to protect the child actors by eliminating the market. Child pornography is viewed primarily an article of commerce rather than as speech and therefore First Amendment protections can be dismissed.[21]

The rationale for the harmful effect of the making of child pornography on the minor is similar to the *Ferber* case, and the legislature's finding of harm is unquestioningly accepted. Here White seems to use a variant of the grave and probable danger test used in the *Dennis* case,[22] claiming that if the danger is grave enough images lose their character as speech and become part of the forbidden action. The danger can be theoretical—it doesn't have to be proven by tight standards, since legislative findings are sufficient and the harm alleged does not have to be demonstrated in court. The child's guardian, parents or custodian can decide that photographing the minor in a state of nudity is not harmful to the minor, though this standard later changes. As in the *Ferber* case, White concedes that to the extent that child pornography is considered speech it merits some protection if it is used for a "bona fide artistic, medical, scientific, educational, religious, governmental, judicial, or other proper purpose" by a person that is qualified and has a "proper interest in the material or performance."[23] This section of the opinion has an elitist tinge that harks back to the idea that only the educated classes had the character to look at pornographic objects like those at Pompeii. It could be an interesting exception to the general claim that child pornography is not allowed, but the courts have not followed the argument and the exception has not been allowed in practice. Neither psychologists who deal with pedophiles, nor reporters dealing with the issue, nor the writer of this article could use professional interest as a defense for possessing or looking at child pornography.[24]

The definition of pornography, both in the statute and in the Court's decision, remains vague. The statute outlawed all depictions of nude children, but the Court tried to narrow this by arguing that the mindset of the viewer needed to be considered. It is permissible to view pictures of nude minors "when that conduct is morally innocent." Thus the Court only prohibits conduct which is not morally innocent, i.e., the possession or viewing of the described material for prurient purposes. So construed, the statute's proscription does not outlaw all depictions of nude minors, but only those which involve sexual interest on the part of the viewer.[25] Unfortunately this brings the Court back to the thought control issue that it explicitly rejected, since it is contending that it is impermissible to view children as sexual objects. By the Court's standard a lascivious viewer of Donatello's *David*, a Balthus painting, a Sally Mann photograph or a picture of a child's foot would transform them into child pornography. This argument that truth is relative to the perspective of the beholder might be good post-modernist theory, but since law requires uniformity and predictability it makes bad law.

The Court's assumptions about possession become even more troublesome in an age of electronic distribution.[26] It is claimed that the downloading or possession of images of nude youths is commercially tied to their production, and that the young models are harmed. The argument does not hold up to analysis.

* *The claim that child pornography is commerce rather than speech*: This argument is that the downloader of pornography is engaging in an act that is directly connected to its production and is therefore a proximate cause of harm to the child actors. But images distributed on Newsgroups are free and

distributed (uploaded) anonymously, so it is difficult to see how they can be defined as articles of commerce. The clandestine distributor gets little glory, except under a pseudonym, and scanning and uploading images costs both time and money. Sharing images seems to be a political or aesthetic act rather than a commercial one.

* *The claim that there is a direct connection between downloading and production:* Though some images on the Internet are original, most are repostings of previously uploaded or printed material. The link between those who upload images and those who produce them is tenuous. Even if the creator of the image is the distributor (e.g., if s/he took the photograph) it is not evident that the circulation of an image to anonymous downloaders is a major cause of its creation. Since neither profit nor prestige comes with anonymous distribution, it seems probable that the images are made primarily for personal enjoyment and only indirectly for circulation. The downloaders are part of the chain of distribution, but they are so removed from the images' creation that it is difficult to argue they are an important causal factor in their production.

* *The claim of harm to the child models:* It is not obvious that repostings of old pictures put the models in new danger. In fact, it would be a difficult argument to make. But the claim has simply been assumed, not argued.

Youths' looks change, and adults would not be easily recognized in pictures taken when they were young. It is also not certain that the models or actors would be ashamed, since they might view their past as something rather glorious or cool, or that the people who viewed the pictures would have a low opinion of the models. It is primarily people who are repelled by child pornography, and who believe that it is wrong, who make these claims. The contention of people involved in the porn area is that, just like in adult pornography, most of the youths participate eagerly and willingly, and want their pictures to be taken and shown.[27] Certainly some people have been hurt, but there has been little systematic effort to go beyond mere assertions of harm, and harm does not have to be shown in court. The Supreme Court and the various legislatures have simply accepted the claim and have made no serious attempt to examine it. The fact that a belief is strongly held by many does not mean that it is true.

Though there have been few public objections to them, the child pornography cases are an astonishing series of decisions. Even at the height of the Communist scare owning Marxist books was permissible—there was no equivalent of the possession of forbidden images. In the *Stanley* case the Court balked at outlawing possession, but in subsequent cases the representation of children in a forbidden way has become the equivalent of treating them in that way, and possession of pictures is linked to the process of their creation. Interestingly, the limit on images is even stricter than the limit on actions. It is legal in most states to have sex with a sixteen-year-old, but it is not legal to have an erotic picture of him or her.

A legal fortress has been built around the social construction of the sexually innocent child, and dissenting images are prohibited. Empirical evidence is no defense. Boys have erections and masturbate, but it is illegal to possess or display photographs of a boy or young teen with an erection or masturbating. Children are interested in their genitals, have sexual experiences and engage in sex play, but such images of childhood are not allowed. Free distribution via the Internet is equated with commerce, the distinction between representation and action has been obliterated, and questionable legislative assertions of fact are accepted at face value. The Court's decisions cannot be defended on the grounds the Court chooses, and cannot be defended on other grounds without running into overwhelming First Amendment problems.   .

CONCLUSION: FORBIDDEN IMAGES

Many people feel it is repugnant for someone to look at a picture of a nude woman, man or child with lustful enjoyment, or feel a sexual charge when looking at Donatello's *David* or Botticelli's *Venus*, or to view people in ordinary life as erotic objects. The erotic perspective is not ideologically sanctioned in the same way as envisioning people as consumers or producers or members of a hierarchy though, as a way of viewing adults, it has become more legitimate since the early twentieth century and erotic radicalism has been an important component of many dissident political movements. Despite attempts by diverse groups to censor speech and images, western democracies allow far more latitude to words, pictures and fantasies than actual behavior, and rarely punish people only for their ideas.

This article has argued that child pornography is treated differently than other speech, including pornographic speech, and that the distinction can only be defended as a form of thought control. However, that argument is so illegitimate that it is commonly denied. Instead it is asserted that children need special protection. The argument makes us feel good, though with a large number of children in poverty, attending inadequate schools, malnourished, without adequate medical care and emotionally neglected, it is not always easy to find evidence of special protection. In any case the argument would normally extend only to the actual treatment of children, not to the way in which they are imagined or imaged. It is important not to confuse speech and pictures with actual behavior.

The child pornography fear has components that involve different issues, but move towards a common policy of censorship and control. They are similar to ideologies that previously were used to control women, under the guise of protection. Like today's children, nineteenth- and early twentieth-century women were believed to need protection from images and words that were dangerous to their mental and physical health, and had to be prevented from engaging in behavior that was not suitable for them.

The first set of policies involves sexual images that children, youths and teens can see. In more liberal eras it was argued that children and teens should be encouraged to question and explore, using parents or teachers for guidance or as people to talk with if they saw things that were disturbing. Today the fear is that youth is bad and out of control (though we think that they are easy for adults to manipulate in the sexual area) so that there has to be state reinforcement of authority's power. Thus we have the legal enlargement of school's powers over student publications, state enforcement of parental power over abortion and other sexual issues, and the increasing trend to treat young lawbreakers as adults. The assumption seems to be that children will not listen to their parents or talk with them unless the law reinforces the parent's power, and that they will seek the forbidden and harmful. They have to be ruled, and censorship chips or programs are needed.

The second policy issue in the child pornography arena involves pornographic photographs of kids. Most are of adolescents and pre-adolescents rather than young children, and do not involve sexual acts though they often have an erotic component and glorify the bodies and sexuality of youth. In a strange way they are mostly celebrations of innocence. Though it embodies a perspective on life different than the normal commercial one, and like adult pornography can easily be construed as having social, educational or artistic value, this type of image has been forbidden. The photographs are defined as commercial products, even though they are rarely sold. It is asserted that posting and possession harm the photographed youth, even though the connection between production and myriad repostings on the Internet is very indirect. Moreover, it is not obvious that the models are harmed, but it is difficult to do research in the area. The argument of consent is also raised, but aside from the arguments raised earlier in this paper the objection that the models are unable to consent can only validly apply to the initial taking of the picture. It is difficult to see how consent issues would apply to the non-paying possession of a picture, downloaded years after it was taken.

Given the current social construction of childhood the pictures are ideologically repellent to many, but that is not a sufficient reason for the ban. We allow many repellent images. At a minimum there needs to be a clear demonstration of harm, or a trial court finding, rather than unsupported assertion. If pornography inspires action, or is a harmful in itself, that is an argument for banning all pornography rather than only child pornography. If erotic portrayals of youthful bodies are harmful then some of the art in museums should be banned. However considered, current policies are illogical.

There is no room in this article to explain the venom of the attack on child pornography, but some comments seem appropriate. Deviant groups serve an important social function, and sexual pariahs are especially enticing. They leave people with a feeling of moral rectitude and help to unite them by reinforcing the feelings of superiority and morality of the dominant group. If minority groups identify themselves with the issues it helps make them legitimate. Feminists, gays, lesbians, Christian conservatives, politicians and angry white men can prove their moral worth by attacking child pornography. Just as being against a lynchee unites the lynchers, allowing them to feel that they are protectors of the moral order, so this issue unites a fragmented community. As Sartre noted in his discussion of the anti-semite, "by valiantly struggling against the Other as Symbolic Offender, the Just Man validates himself as good."[28]

Child pornography policies equate representations of youth sexuality with sexual abuse, and reaffirm concepts of innocence. They probably reflect an ambivalent attitude about adult sexual behavior. In other noncriminal enjoyable areas we socialize children into adult life. But in the sexual area we try to protect children from adult behavior and ideas, insisting that they would be harmful. Perhaps we are really intent on preserving an innocent part of our own psyches.

The fear of child pornography has been used in attempts to control new media, like comic books, CDs, radio and the Internet–all media that were understood better by children than parents. Currently the fear is being used against the Internet, which stands as the antithesis to a highly structured hierarchical world. Many governments and organizations have sought to control the Internet and the Newsgroups. In some countries forbidden political ideas has been the reason. In the United States attempts at control have focused on sexual images, and the issue is being used to bring the structure of the new information technologies under the control of regulators.[29] The fear of pornography has justified increased surveillance by the established authorities. Possibly most important, the fear of child pornography has allowed authority to drastically increase its control, all in the name of youth protection. Since policies on child pornography serve many agendas so it is unlikely they will be revised soon. But social constructions shift, and what is constructed can be deconstructed. As women once served as a moral standard and a haven in a heartless world, with all the controls that came along with that role, so children are considered today. The attempt to control child porn serves to mute arguments about an erotic rather than an economic society, thereby helping to silence radical criticism of the dominant political and economic system.

NOTES

1. This goes back to the original legal concept of pornography. It is a relatively new construct, developed in the nineteenth century to prevent sexually explicit material from corrupting women and children and from exciting the emotions of depraved immigrants and males of the lower classes. It emerged because of the spread of mass literacy and cheap popular fiction. See Walter M. Kendrick, The Secret Museum: Pornography in Modern Culture (New York: Viking, 1987).

2. According to Ronald Pearsall (*The Worm in the Bud: The World of Victorian Sexuality* [London: Pimlico, 1969, 1993], p. 106) in the Victorian period nude adolescent girls were considered "less heinous than the nude woman, if only for the absence of voluptuousness and pubic hair, which was a constant cause of affront to the respectable. . . . Pubic hair was a constant reminder of the animal in man, the hairy beast brought to the knowledge of the shocked middle classes by Darwin."

Currently images of nude children are largely forbidden. London's Hayward

Gallery pulled a picture of a three-year-old girl sitting without underwear, so that her genitals were visible, from a major Mapplethorpe show after police said the image was pornographic. Also questioned, but not banned, was a picture of a nude boy. Robert Mapplethorpe's photographs portray genitalia and various sexual actions. The photograph is clearly (in this observer's opinion) a picture of innocence, and *The Independent* fumed that "the current sensitivity about images of children produces the bizarre situation in which there is no such thing as an innocent image of a child, where a graphic portrayal of 'fisting' is seen as less problematic." (Sept. 12, 1996, p. 1.) Arguments that pictures like this will haunt the "victims" portrayed is belied, in this case at least, since the girl is now 27 years old and wanted the picture shown. (Though publishers are wary of printing pictures of nude children the photo, Rosie, is in some of the Mapplethorpe books as is the picture of the boy, Jesse McBride.)

3. Even pictures of clothed youths can be considered child pornography. In *Knox* v. *U.S.*, the Supreme Court let stand an Appeals Court decision that applied federal child pornography statutes to clothed models. The case involved videotapes of girls in bathing suits, leotards and underwear. Court documents said the camera zoomed in on their genital areas and drew attention to them in sexually provocative ways. Calvin Klein was also threatened with suit for advertisements that showed clothed teens in provocative poses. The ads were withdrawn.

4. Kempe, C.H., et al., *The Journal of the American Medical Association*, July 7, 1962, 181, pp. 17–24.

5. Conservative campaigns against child molestation and abduction were reinforced by feminist campaigns on the same issues. See Ian Hacking in "The Making and Molding of Child Abuse," *Critical Inquiry* 17 (Winter 1961), pp. 253–288, for a good discussion of the construction of the child abuse concept. He argues that the evaluative power of the label results in part from the way in which "distinct types of harm have been brought together" (268–259). Joel Best, *Threatened Children: Rhetoric and Concern about Child-Victims* (Chicago: University of Chicago Press, 1990) is also an excellent treatment of the issues. The concepts of sexual abuse by outsiders, incest and child abuse were brought together in an article by Suzanne M. Sgroi, "Sexual Molestation of Children: The Last Frontier in Child Abuse," *Children Today* 4 (May-June 1975), pp. 18–21. The melding of the concepts was continued by "Incest Abuse Begins at Home" in the April 1977 issue of *Ms.*

6. The 1991 version of federal law [18 USCS 2252 (1991)] criminalizes the transport or reception of visual depictions of minors engaging in sexually explicit conduct. Also criminalized is the possession of three or more such depictions. Those found guilty of violating this law face up to 10 years in jail. "Sexually explicit conduct" means "actual or simulated" (A) sexual intercourse, including genital, oral-genital, anal-genital, or oral-anal, whether between persons of the same or opposite sex, (B) bestiality, (C) masturbation, (D) sadistic or masochistic abuse . . . or (E) lascivious exhibition of the genitals or pubic area of any person." As was noted previously, "lascivious exhibition" currently means almost any exhibition of the genitals of a minor. In 1996 the Child Pornography Prevention Act was passed. This law outlaws computer manipulated (morphed) images, and seems to preclude scenes in which an adult portraying a minor is engaged in sexual activity. It also expands the search power of the government.

7. Robert Sorenson, *Adolescent Sexuality in Contemporary America: Personal Values and Sexual Behavior* (New York: World, 1973), p. 130. See also Chapter 9 in Laumann et al., *The Social Organization of Sexuality: Sexual Practices in the United States* (Chicago: University of Chicago Press, 1994). The allowed image of childhood is a false

image–or at a minimum is the legal embodiment of only one vision of reality. See Larry L. Constantine and Floyd M. Martinson, eds., *Children and Sex: New Findings, New Perspectives* (Boston: Little, Brown, 1981). The editors note that sex is seen as an adult characteristic, and children are not viewed as sexual. "This is . . . surprising . . . in view of the long and steady history of accumulating evidence for the sexual and not-at-all innocent nature of childhood." p. ix. See Chris Jenks for an excellent discussion of the model of pure childhood. Jenks argues that as contemporary life has come to be seen as bleak and impure we have put our images of love, purity and naturalness upon the child. See especially chapters 3–5 in *Childhood* (London: Routledge, 1996).

8. See D. J. West in association with Buz DeVilliers, *Male Prostitution: Gay Sex Services in London* (London: Gerald Duckworth and Co., 1992). In a study of English male prostitutes they found that these men most enjoyed what they were doing and viewed themselves as dominant over the customers. Any coercion was related to social status, since hustlers chose among available options. A similar pattern exists among female prostitutes in the Netherlands according to sociologists who work with them (personal conversations). In America studies indicate that, though the dominant ideology views sex workers and porn stars as hapless victims, many like their work.

9. The popular slogan was "make love, not war." Herbert Marcuse, Norman O. Brown, Paul Goodman and others argued that sexual energy was captured by an economic system that used this energy to oppress people, giving them only unsatisfactory choices among economic goods. Today it is economic freedom that is publicly extolled. Though there are still sexual radicals like Pat Califia, who wrote *Public Sex: The Culture of Radical Sex* (Pittsburgh: Cleis Press, 1994) they do not get much attention. See also the fascinating book by Murray S. Davis, *Smut: Erotic Reality/Obscene Ideology* (Chicago: University of Chicago Press, 1983). Davis argues that popular interpretations of sex must be understood in terms of Gnostic and Jehovinist ideologies. Gnosticism disputes the universe the Jehovinists have created, and its sacred texts are pornographic. It has different concepts of time (erotic time is closely synchronized with partners), space (erotic space contracts), social dimensions (different people are important in the two realities) and physicality. The two world views are mortal enemies.

10. Laumann et al., *The Social Organization of Sexuality*, p. 322.

11. There are, of course, some nude boy photographs. The most commonly reprinted are Von Gloeden's classic (and usually rather ugly) photographs of nude Sicilian boys. These have circulated widely in the gay community, and one or two of his photographs sometimes appears in standard histories of photography. There is also a tradition of nudist photography. Most often, though, images are censored–either voluntarily or by law. Though Weston's photo of Neil is considered one of his best it is rarely reprinted. Sally Mann's photographs of her son have met strong objections. Most histories of photography do not include pictures of nude children and youths. Astonishingly, this is even true of histories of erotic and nude photography.

12. *Miller* v. *California*, 413 U.S. 5. The Burger Court's *Miller* standard was a weakening of an earlier standard developed by the Warren Court in *Roth* v. *United States*, 354 U.S. 76 (1957). Under the earlier test the work had to be "utterly without redeeming social importance" and had to violate national, rather than local standards. But even the conservative *Miller* decision affords a great deal of protection to sexual expression, and it is difficult to win an obscenity conviction.

13. *Stanley* v. *Georgia*, 394 U.S. 557 (1969)

14. 102 S.Ct. 3348, 3356 (1982)

15. 102 S.Ct. 3348, 3351

16. p. 3355. The Court's argument rests on unsupported psychological speculation. A footnote supporting the argument quotes "one authority" who argues that the "pornography may haunt him in future years, long after the original misdeed took place. A child who has posed for a camera must go through life knowing that the recording is circulating within the mass distribution system for child pornography." Other support focuses on the harm to the child caused by the need for keeping the act secret, claiming that the "victim's knowledge of publication of the visual material increases the emotional and psychic harm suffered by the child" (pp. 3355–3356, footnote 10).

17. *New York* v. *Ferber*, 102 S.Ct. 3348, 3357. As was noted previously, in 1966 Congress outlawed the use of adults acting as youths, and banned morphed images.

18. 102 S.Ct. 3348, 3365

19. 110 L Ed 2d 98 (1990).

20. The law outlawed the possession of any pictures of nude minors, but the courts tried to narrow this so it would not apply to innocuous photos of children made by parents, but only to the lascivious display of genitals. The Court has found it difficult to define this term.

21. *Osborne* v. *Ohio* 109 L. Ed 2d 98, 108-109 (1990) ". . . we find this case distinct from Stanley because the interests underlying child pornography prohibitions far exceed the interests justifying the Georgia law at issue in Stanley. . . . In Stanley, Georgia primarily sought to proscribe the private possession of obscenity because it was concerned that obscenity would poison the minds of its viewers. 394 US, at 565. . . . We responded that '[w]hatever the power of the state to control ideas inimicable to the public morality, it cannot constitutionally premise legislation on the desirability of controlling a person's private thoughts.' Id., at 566. . . . The difference here is obvious: [T]he State does not rely on a paternalistic interest in regulating Osborne's mind. Rather Ohio has enacted [the law] in order to protect the victims of child pornography; it hopes to destroy a market for the exploitative use of children."

22. The test is often called the "clear and probable danger test." Justice Vinson wrote that the Court had to decide "whether the gravity of the 'evil,' discounted by its improbability, justifies such an invasion of free speech as is necessary to avoid danger." *Dennis* v. *U.S.* 341 US 494 (1951). Developed at the height of the Communist scare it is one of the weakest of the speech tests.

23. 109 L Ed 2d at 107

24. Personal correspondence with a psychologist working extensively with pedophiles and active in the pedophile movement. He said that his house had been searched many times in a quest for pornographic pictures. Lawyers agreed that he could not claim any kind of professional privilege. In an important pending case Larry Matthews, a freelance reporter who often works for National Public Radio and public TV, has been charged with using his computer to trade images of under-age girls engaged in various sexual acts. Matthews claims that he was researching a story on child pornography, but the trial judge ruled that "a press pass is not a license to break the law" and claimed that Matthews could have gathered the information needed by other methods and by interviewing law-enforcement officials. Matthew's lawyers have argued that such a method would only provide a government approved version of the story. The trial judge's ruling will be appealed. (*The New York Times*, July 7, 1998)

25. 109 L Ed 2d at 112, footnote 10.

26. The major fear has been about child pornography in the Newsgroups. There has not been a good study of the types of images found in these groups, and most of what is called child pornography are simply pictures of naked youths. These are very different from the hard core pornography that is feared and imagined. It is rare that images of children are explicitly sexual, and the most common theme is of innocence and beauty. Images of explicit sexual acts are mostly reposts of 1960s Scandinavian pornography.

27. Many children have denied that they felt violated or harmed. These statements parallel claims about adult pornography actors and sex workers, but they are dismissed by assertions that children do not know what they want. That is a part of the current construction of childhood. The Court refers to scientific evidence showing that child actors are hurt by participation in the making of pornography, but really relies on popular perceptions rather than the weight of evidence.

There are no empirical studies of the child porn underground, but studies of adults in the sex business don't support the idea that people in the business are harmed. Other evidence comes from studies of children involved in erotic relations with adults. These indicate that children involved in consensual relationships are not hurt and may have very positive experiences. Some studies criticize the methodological and conceptual flaws of much of the literature in this area. Alayne Yates' "Sexual Abuse of Children," pp. 699–710 in *Textbook of Child and Adolescent Psychiatry* (2nd edition. American Psychiatric Press, 1997) edited by Jerry Wiener, notes that we know little about the sexual development of children partially because there are strong social sanctions about asking normal ("innocent") children about sex, so researchers only question youngsters who show bad symptoms. "This situation is analogous to the late nineteenth century, when many studies reported that masturbation caused mental and moral decay. These studies were solely based on interviews with inmates of insane asylums" and concluded that since they masturbated there was a causal relationship between masturbation and insanity. Yates discusses the methodological problems with research on child abuse, including use of atypical populations, inappropriate statistical analysis, and confusing the effects of the abuse with the effects of intervention. See also Paul Okami, "Sociopolitical Biases in the Contemporary Scientific Literature on Adult Sexual Behavior with Children and Adolescents," in Jay Feierman, ed., *Pedophilia: Biosocial Dimensions* (NY: Springer-Verlag, 1990), pp. 91–121. Okami argues that the literature assumes all sex is bad and coercive." In accord with Victorian tradition, adult females, adolescents, and children—children in particular—are painted in highly idealized hues. The Victorian idealization of children as sexless innocents is clearly apparent in . . . assertions that children are by definition incapable either of desiring or voluntarily cooperating in a sexual interaction with an adult" or even another child, pp. 96–97. See also Theo Sandfort, "Sex in Pedophiliac Relationships: An Empirical Investigation Among a Non-Representative Group of Boys," *Journal of Sex Research*, Vol. 20, No. 2 pp. 123–42 (May, 1984) which argues that negative outcomes are associated primarily with coercion, not with consensual relationships. See also West, D.J and Woodhouse, T.P., "Sexual Encounters Between Boys and Adults" in C.K. Li, D.J. West and T.P. Woodhouse (eds.), *Children's Sexual Encounters With Adults* (London: Duckworth, 1990). Edward Brongersma, *Loving Boys*, uses extensive interviews to question the model of harm. See also Laumann et.al., *The Social Organization of Sexuality*, op.cit., pp. 339–47. There are also testimonials in the Newsgroups by people who affirm the experience of being the child partner in sexual relationships. Many claim that they were the seducers.

28. From "The Childhood of a Leader." Quoted by Thomas S. Szasz in *The Manufacture of Madness: A Comparative Study of the Inquisition and the Mental Health Movement* (New York: Harper, 1970, 1977), p. 269. After discussing the widespread and intense nineteenth-century belief that masturbation caused madness, Szasz asked how the idea could have been so widely accepted. He attributed it to the "tendency to embrace collective error" and argued that people were more interested in "preserving popular explanations which tend to consolidate the group than in making accurate observations which tend to divide it." (p. 187) Writing in 1970 he observed that there was "no significant difference between the former persecution of masturbators and the present persecution of homosexuals. . . ." Both were exercises in power. (p. 193) The groups were scapegoats. "[B]oth the medieval witch and the modern mental patient are the scapegoats of society. By sacrificing some of its members, the community seeks to 'purify' itself and thus maintain its integrity and survival." (p. 260) Scapegoat rituals allow us to transfer our guilt and suffering to another being who will bear them for us. "The scapegoat is necessary as a symbol of evil which it is convenient to cast out of the social order and, which, through its very being, confirms the remaining members of the community as good." (p. 268). See also Hunter, op. cit., who argues that moral scapegoats serve to bring a community together. p. 156.

29. See Lee Tien, "Children's Sexuality and the New Information Technology," in *Social and Legal Studies,* vol. 3, pp. 121–47 (London: Sage, 1994). Tien argues that the construction of children's sexuality is "being used to regulate both the uses and the structure of electronic information technologies. . . ." (p. 121) The control moves towards both increased censorship and increased surveillance, and both are largely done by private information providers and universities who "feel pressure to restrict access, censor their users or monitor traffic . . . in case illicit material may be present." This leverages the law, and the "result is a reorganization or a disciplining of information space." The new forms of control tend to be subtle and are often not defined as surveillance. "Highly public instances of indecency and child pornography still function as public morality plays and ceremonial displays of power which both establish the credibility of surveillance and publicly affirm its legitimacy." (pp. 142–43)

43

Sexual Abuse, Anti-Sexuality, and the Pornography of Power

Ralph Underwager and Hollida Wakefield

W E UNDERSTAND PORNOGRAPHY TO BE THE DESCRIPTION OF socially unacceptable behavior for the purpose of generating personal fantasies that produce private enjoyment and delight. This definition was proposed by anthropologist Geoffrey Gorer in 1955 (Rubinoff, 1967). Pornography is not limited to sexual stimuli nor is a rational discussion of pornography confined to the speech or depiction of human sexual behaviors (Rubinoff, 1967). Any human activity that is tabooed by consensual validation can be an arena for pornography. There can be a pornography of death, a pornography of religion, a pornography of absolute principles, a pornography of power, as well as sexual pornography.

In this presentation we describe and discuss the pornography of power, both institutional and personal, that we observe in the policies, myths, and practices that have emerged around the tabooed topic of child sexual abuse. There are some elements of sexual pornography discernible and exercise of power for the purpose of personal gratification and pleasure.

In an era of egalitarian excesses, a shrill insistence upon abandonment of any position involving power, and denigration of persons or groups that wield power, fantasy about power functions as a substitute and an entry way for the imposition of power on others while calling it something else. An imagination that values, rehearses, and delights in having and using power inevitably leads to the behavior of pursuing and using power in a self-serving and self-deluding manner.

It is a characteristic of pornographic fantasy and behavior that it is represented as something other that what it is. In the Comstock Syndrome, a fascination and prurient interest in sexuality is represented as a crusade against sexual pornography. In the pornography of power, the exercise of power is represented as expediency, in service of a noble goal, or as necessary for the protection and safety of the powerless or some large, amorphous group of potential victims. Violence, the canceling of the essence of our human nature to love and seek community, is the ultimate irrationality. It is difficult to gainsay the assertion that to love is better than to hate. Yet violence is claimed to be rational, useful, or required.

No one admits willingly that his intentions and pursuits are dishonorable. We readily persuade ourselves that we are doing something else entirely. Seduction is transformed education. Cruelty becomes therapy through aversive conditioning. It was here in California in the early 1960s that a psychologist was finally expelled from the American Psychological Association for doing therapy by whacking people with a baseball bat while nude in the swimming pool with his patients. Bombing a village out of existence becomes necessary in order to save it. In the last one hundred years we have slaughtered millions of fellow human beings while calling it the Final Solution, Cultural Revolution, Ethnic Cleansing, and a just war.

At the very beginning of our Western civilization, Athenian democracy was presented by Pericles in 430 B.C. in these words. "We do not get into quarrels with our next door neighbor if he enjoys himself in his own way. . . . We make friends by doing good to them, not by receiving good from them. . . . I declare that our city is an education to Greece . . . and everywhere we have left behind us everlasting memorials of good to our friends. . . ." Less than two decades later, 416 B.C., when the island of Melos wanted simply to be neutral in the war between Athens and Sparta, the Athenians conquered Melos. They put every man to death and sold the women and children to slavery. The Athenians said "the standard of justice depends upon the equality of power to compel, and in fact the strong do what they have the power to do and the weak accept what they have to accept . . . it is a general and necessary law of nature to rule where one can." When it comes to human nature, there really is not much new under the sun, is there?

INVESTIGATION OF SEXUAL ABUSE ALLEGATIONS

In the investigation of allegations of child abuse, adults seek to extract information from children. Often these are very young children. Some children have even been preverbal, but the ones we see most often are between age three and puberty. The adults may be parents, relatives, neighbors, or child protection workers and/or law enforcement personnel. The interrogation begins with some demonstration of the power of the adult(s). This may be by having more than one adult in the interview or showing badges, handcuffs, or handguns. It may be include telling children the adult has the job to talk with children about things that discomfort them, beginning by asking questions to which the adult already knows the answer or telling the where to sit and what to do (draw, play with dolls, answer questions truthfully, etc.). During this allegedly rapport building period, at least one expert advises the adults to lie to children and tell them they are experienced in talking to lots of kids, ". . . even if you are not . . . [it] establishes your credibility" (Sgroi, 1982, pp. 58-59).

Adults frequently lie to children when they are trying to get information from them. In the Kelley Michael's preschool case in New Jersey, the social worker and police interrogator routinely lied to many of the children, telling them that other children had told them that Ms. Michaels had done things to them. The tapes of the other children showed there had been nothing of the sort. The same tactic was used by Kee MacFarlane in the McMartin case when she interrogated children. Children have even been told that they cannot go to the bathroom or have a drink of water until they tell about the abuse.

Our research interrogation of children by adults shows a high level of coercive, leading and suggestive questioning interview (Underwager & Wakefield, 1990). This been replicated and extended by many other studies (Cassel & Bjorklund 1995; Bruck & Ceci, 1994; Lamb et al., 1996; Meyer, 1997; Warren et al., 1996). There can be no doubt that adults interviewing children about sexual abuse allegations are an exercise of power by the adults.

The investigation of sexual abuse allegations is regularly represented as necessary, expedient, required, but more than anything else, as protecting children. Apologists for the present child abuse system regularly claim that in prior eras, there was a conspiracy to deny the reality of adult-child sexual contact. It was necessary for a courageous, embattled small band of people of noble and high purpose to break the veil of silence and denial and bring the tragedy of sexual abuse to the consciousness of a society that does not want to face it.

Historically, this self-aggrandizing claim is suspect. In the second century there was a lengthy and detailed theological discussion of incest, abandoned children, and the wickedness of sexual contact between children and adults. This was in response to practices in pagan temples and worship rituals. During the Children's Crusade there was much lamenting of the fate of the crusade children who were sold into slavery and used for sexual purposes. The Smithsonian Institute has a newspaper published in London in the 1640s with the front-page story concerning a case of father-daughter incest and the punishment to be meted out.

There is no evidence that the system, in fact, serves to protect children. There have been a number of court ordered evaluation of the foster care system that have concluded that far more children are damaged, harmed, and abused in foster care than had they remained in their own families (i.e., Court appointed expert's report on *B.H. et al.* v. *Gordon Johnson, Director of Illinois Department of Children and Family Services*). There is no convincing evidence that the state can adequately care for children. A recent analysis of the system concludes that it is in crisis and has no demonstrated effectiveness but rather is harmful to children (Costin, Karger, & Stoesz, 1996).

Since 1979 (Starr, 1979) every scientific study of the type and level of error committed by the system has concluded that the error is in the direction of an unconscionable false positive rate. The range is from three false positives for every one false negative (Melton, 1994) to two thousand to one (Horner, 1992). Our analysis (Wakefield & Underwager, 1988) found the most likely ration to be nine to one. Using Bayesian inference the scientific analyses of the errors committed by the system have included examination of medical, psychological, social work, and law enforcement procedures. The results are the same in all areas studied. Such unanimity of findings is rather unusual. It appears well supported that the most likely consequence of the child protection system, the policies and procedures in place and continuing today, is that more children are harmed than are helped (Wakefield & Underwager, 1994).

EROTICIZATION OF CHILDREN

One of the more basic and potentially damaging outcomes for children is the anti-sexuality inherent in the system. When a child becomes enmeshed in the system, depending upon the level and time of exposure to the system's sex negative concepts and behaviors, the capacity of the child to into a full orbed and rewarding adult sexuality is impeded and limited. We first testified to this potential for grave harm to children in a sexual abuse trial in Anchorage, Alaska, in 1985. There are two facets to the sex negative bias of the child protection system.

First, the focus on genitalia alone can only impact to produce what appears to be the root cause of sexual dysfunction, that is, the genitalization of human sexuality. When the perception of sexuality is limited to genital tissue, performance anxiety is inevitable. Ignoring or simply not being able to experience the fullness of emotional, spiritual, imaginative intimacy, unity, and wholeness possible for human beings is a tragic denial of our humanity.

Second, the message that sexual contact is harmful, shameful, and his lifelong destructive efforts so that the person who is touched on the genitals can never fully recover can only create intense internal conflict between normal, natural sexuality and learned anxiety, fear, and resistance. The experience of pleasure in stimulation of genital tissue cannot outweigh the negatives associated with sexuality. The new puritanism of the child protection system is far more destructive, oppressive, and intrusive than that of the seventeenth century. The first Puritans still had the concept that human sexuality is a gift of God even though it had been distorted by sinfulness. The neopuritanism of the child protection system has nothing than sex is associated with reproduction. Even reproduction no longer needs the participation of two people in sexual congress.

Consider the impact and meaning of a three- to four-year-old child being questioned repeatedly about Daddy putting his wiener in the child's vagina or anus, about Daddy forcing the child to lick or suck genitals, or Daddy hurting the child by touching her genitals. Consider the impact of being trained to respond to adult coercion and pressure by compliance and conformity. Consider the research evidence suggesting that exposing a child to anatomically detailed dolls leads to heightened sexual awareness and increased sexual behaviors by young children (Boat, Everson, & Holland, 1990). Not only is there no incremental validity (Wolfner, Faust, & Dawes, 1993) but this study suggests that interrogation of children with such dolls is like showing adolescents *Playboy* and *Penthouse.*

We have tried unsuccessfully for over twenty years to stop a pediatrician, Dr. Carolyn Levitt, in St. Paul from pursuing her methodology of examining and interrogating children. She puts her fingers in the vagina and rubs the clitoris and anus of a female child and touches the penis and anus of the male children while asking them if that is how it feels when the accused did it (Levitt, 1986; undated; Underwager & Wakefield, 1990). She has also testified about his technique and has described it on *Nightline* in 1984. She has also testified that she examines over two hundred children a year using this methodology. She claims that this procedure produces accurate and reliable memories and accounts of prior abuse because the procedure elicits memories of earlier abuse. She has received grants of federal money to teach this procedure to other pediatricians. Prosecutors still today refer children to her for examination and evaluation.

We believe and have testified that what she does is state sanctioned rapine.

When there is an allegation of child sexual abuse, often the child is immediately placed in therapy. This is done long before there is and adjunction or a finding of fact. The therapy given is invariably feeling-expressive, insight-oriented, psychoanalytic in nature. It may also be called play therapy, art therapy, or sand tray therapy. There is no scientific evidence supporting the efficacy or utility of this therapy for children (Campbell, 1992). In fact, meta-analysis of relevant research studies suggests it may even be harmful to children (Weisz & Weiss, 1993). The only evident benefit to anyone is that mental health professionals get paid for it. Other than that, it may teach a child the story adults want to have and persuade the child that she is a lifelong victim living in a world of terror where even the people who love her cannot be relied upon.

We have examined case notes and investigation reports in cases demonstrating that children are sometimes are sometimes eroticized by interviews and therapy. We have seen several cases where children began masturbating in inappropriate situations or initiating peer sex play. These behaviors did not occur until after the intervention. In one case, after a four-year-old boy was interviewed about abuse and asked to demonstrate it with anatomical dolls, he became agitated and remarked that his penis tingled. Another child was placed in a residential program for behavior disordered children with the goal of talking about the alleged sexual abuse in therapy. The case notes indicate that this resulted in increased sexual acting out.

CONCLUSION

The system we have constructed that involves children in responding to allegations of sexual abuse is an exercise of power by adults. It fits the definition of pornography of power. As such we consider it far more destructive, more demeaning to the human spirit, more dangerous, and more to be feared than anything which may be labeled sexual pornography.

REFERENCES

Boat, B. W., Everson, M. D., & Holland, J. (1990). Maternal perceptions of non-abused young children's behavior after the exposure to anatomical dolls. *Child Welfare* 69 (5): 389–400.

Bruck, M., & Ceci, S. J. (1994). *Amicus Brief for the case of NJ v. Kelly Michaels.*

Campbell, T. W. (1992). Promoting play therapy: Marketing dream or empirical nightmare? *Issues in Child Abuse Accusations* 4 (3): 111–17.

Cassel, W. S., & Bjorklund, D. F. (1995). Development patterns of eyewitness memory and suggestibility. *Law and Human Behavior* 19 (5): 507–532.

Ceci, S. J., & Bruck, M. (1995). *Jeopardy in the courtroom: A scientific analysis of children's testimony.* Washington, D.C.: American Psychological Association.

Costin, L., Karger, D., and Stoesz, H. J. (1996). *The politics of child abuse in America.* Cary, NC: Oxford University Press, Inc.

Horner, T. M. (1992). *Expertise in regard to determinations of child sexual abuse.* Unpublished manuscript.

Lamb, M. E., Hershkowitz, I., Sternberg, K. J., Hovav, M., Manor, T., Yidilevitch, L. (1996). Effects of investigate utterance types on Israeli children's responses. *International Journal of Behavioral Development* 19 (3): 627–37.

Levitt, C. J. (1986). Sexual abuse in children: A compassionate yet thorough approach to evaluation. *Postgraduate Medicine* 80 (2): 201–15.

———. (undated). The role of the medicinal professional as an expert witness. Unpublished manuscript.

Melton, G. B. (1994). Expert opinions: Not for cosmic understanding. In B. D. Sales & G. R. VandenBos (Eds.), Psychology *in litigation and legislation* (pp. 55–99). Washington, D.C.: American Psychological Association.

Meyer, J. F. (1997). *Inaccuracies in children's testimony: Memory, suggestibility, or obedience to authority?* New York: The Haworth Press.

Rubinoff, L. (1967). *The pornography of power.* New York: Ballantine Books, Inc.

Sgroi, S. M. (1982). *Handbook of clinical intervention in child sexual abuse.* Lexington, Massachusetts: Lexington Books.

Starr, R. H. (1979). Child abuse. *American Psychologist* 34 (10): 872–78.

Underwager, R., & Wakefield, H. (1990). *The real world of child interrogations.* Springfield, IL: C. C. Thomas.

Wakefield, H., & Underwager, R. (1988). *Accusations of child sexual abuse.* Springfield, IL: C. C. Thomas.

———. (1994). The alleged child victim and real victims of sexual misuse. In J. J. Krivacska & J. Money (Eds.), *The handbook of forensic sexology: Biomedical & criminological perspectives* (pp. 223–64), Amherst, NY: Prometheus Books.

Warren, A. R., Woodall, C. E., Hunt, J. S., & Perry, N. W. (1996). "It sounds good in theory, but...": Do investigate interviewers follow guidelines based on memory research? *Child Maltreatment* 1 (3): 23–245.

Weisz, J. R., & Weiss, B. (1993). *Effects of psychotherapy with children and adolescents.* Newbury Park: Sage.

Wolfner, G., Faust, D., & Dawes, R. M. (1993). The use of anatomically detailed dolls in sexual abuse evaluations: The state of the science. *Applied & Preventive Psychology* 2: 2–11.

Wood, J. M., McClure, K. A., & Birch, R. A. (1996). Suggestions for improving interviews in child protection agencies. *Child Maltreatment* 1 (3): 223–30.

44

Sources of Reaction to "Child Pornography"

David Sonenschein

INTRODUCTION

ALTHOUGH THE 1980S CONTAINED THE HEIGHT OF THE MEDIA-DRIVEN child sex abuse hysteria, the issues are still contentious, and "child pornography," though still ill-defined, is yet a highly dangerous topic as well as artifact. The organizers of this conference are to be congratulated on including a session on the subject, though a fuller and more thoroughly focused conference has yet even to be proposed.

I have recently completed a study of the hysteria, an examination of the period from a culture history point of view, focusing on the popular images of the actors and events in the abuse drama. As part of documenting attacks on more artistic works that featured youth such as the much publicized tribulations of Jock Sturges, Robert Mapplethorpe, Sally Mann, Alice Simms, and others, I had wanted to publish a set of photographs that were also attacked as "child pornography."

The pictures were a series of four black and white photos entitled "The Inevitable Comparison," taken in 1979 but not displayed until a multi-artist show in 1985. The photographer is a documentary photographer who, since the late 1960s, has been well-known for his people-centered photos of causes, issues, and political events. He does not do nudes as a genre, nor does his work reek as much with artistic pretension as do the works of Simms, Mapplethorpe, or Sturges; his emphasis is on the commonalties of everyday life, especially of people who receive little media notice of their existence. His excellent eye for "the moment" make his photos engaging, memorable, and important.

The set captures a moment of exploration and comparison in a young boy's life, of a kind not unusual for most individuals. In Figure 1, the boy, about age five, is shown nude on a bed next to the reclining nude figure of an adult male. The boy is pointing inquiringly at the man's penis. In Figure 2, the boy has taken hold of the man's penis and looks at it curiously. In Figure 3, the boy then examines–compares–his own penis. In Figure 4, he looks back at the man's organ with an indecipherable but thoughtful look.

The photos were accepted by the gallery, and initially there was sympathetic and amused reaction to the set as viewers understood the naturalness and humanity of the almost real-time series. But it was surprising to many that within a couple of days complaints were registered with the show coordinators and building owners, as well as letters written to the newspaper complaining of "having perversion forced down their throats." The set was labeled "child pornography" by some, and a local television station headlined their silly and indignant report, "Art or Pornography?–the thin line between child pornography and fine art." The police examined the set but did not arrest the photographer or seize the photos, and a city attorney declined prosecution under the already broad "child pornography" statutes. Complaints continued, and after two days, the photos were removed from the show.

IN THE NEXT DECADE

Already having some sense of the ignorance and insanity over this issue, I took the photos to a printer I wanted to do my book. She declined to print them, not because she had any trouble with the pictures themselves, but because should "child pornography" charges be filed against the book, statutes also make the printer liable to prosecution as well as any distributor, seller, and possessor, and on that basis she could have all of her business and personal property seized and held as state's evidence; in short, as the state intends, her business and personal status would be at risk of destruction, even if in the long run courts decided the photos were not "pornography." This has held true in the last couple of decades: contrary to claims of winning being the name of the game in law, the purpose now is to inflict as much damage–financial, personal, or physical–as possible on those the state decides to bring charges against–whether they are innocent or not, and regardless of whether the laws are constitutional or not.

I then went back to the photographer and reviewed the political changes in the country since the late 1970s. He too realized his personal and professional endeavors were in jeopardy. Since neither he nor I had anything to gain by doing more jail time for political issues, we mutually decided not to print the photos in the book.

The announcement of this conference brought the pictures and the reactions they stirred again to mind, and I was allowed time and space to present the topic in this session. I drafted an outline and took the 5 × 7 photos to a copy shop to make enlarged paper copies so an audience could better see them. As I started to copy, the manager, a young man in his late twenties, came over and asked what I was doing. I told him, though the idea of a scholarly presentation seemed somewhat beyond his grasp. Upon seeing the photos, he exclaimed, "these look like kiddie porn!" and he then threatened to call the police. By this time, I had had enough of this sort of stupidity and I urged him to do so, telling him how police had previously declined to prosecute these photos from an art exhibition. It was quite all right with me if he wanted to go to court, risking malicious prosecution suits against him and his company. He then just demanded that I leave, which I did. I have been thrown out of better places, I had other errands to run, and I was able to make presentable copies elsewhere with no trouble.

CONCLUSIONS

First of all, I wanted to use the photos to show how some people may bring sexual meanings to visual material. One element in the judgments is the background cultural and historical situation. The hysteria was at its height in 1984–85, and the country saturated with highly emotional and exploitative media presentations on "missing children," sexual abuse, Satanic cult conspiracies, and child murder, all conflated into the singular interest of the newly reconstructed and demonized "pedophile."[1] Critical voices were ignored or stigmatized to the point that the issue received no investigation or challenge whatsoever for popular audiences. The mid-1970s feminist anti-pornography movement had just crested, and despite receiving challenges by progressive feminists, the anti-erotica mentality was dominant. Child abuse had been (re)discovered in the late 1960s, and while initially focused on physical abuse, by the early 1980s "sexual abuse" was an uncritically accepted term applied to *any* adult-minor sexual situation; feminists had also attracted attention to incest and subsumed it under the sexual abuse concept.

Additionally, since the late 1970s there had been a virulent resurgence of homophobic sentiment that had been made even nastier by the attribution of AIDS to "the gay lifestyle." Then there was the ever-ongoing agitation against youth sex (usually disguised as campaigns against teen pregnancy); "abstinence" became official state policy in the 1980s. Conflicts over the choice of abortion heated up also, carrying as usual its implicit texts regarding sexual activity.[2]

Thus there was in place a heated, active, and violence prone condemnatory context in which sexual representations and sexual relations involving non-adults and adults were viewed and acted upon. For the latter, data on productive and neutral sexual contacts between adults and youth were ignored or denied. Individuals accused of such contact, or of producing or possessing "kiddie porn," were stigmatized by journalists, imprisoned, destroyed financially, beaten, and in not just a few cases, killed.

Added to this context, there were several factors in the photos themselves that allowed individuals to attach sexual meanings to the images. Most immediately apparent is the nudity of both the boy and the adult. The product of a long tradition of a body-hating religion and its secular equivalents, Americans often take nudity as a sign of sexual activity or intent. Secondly is the fact that the adult's genitalia are visible and become the focus of attention (it's not clear if the child's genitalia are visible), taking the meanings of nudity even further. Thirdly, and most significantly, the genitals are touched when child grasps the adult's penis and examines his own. Genital touching, whether by oneself or others, is also nearly always taken as a sign of sexual behavior in this culture. An added factor is that the two figures are male, allowing a target for any anti-homosexual attitudes.

The photos are not as explicitly "artsy" as is usually the case in such exhibitions, and hence do not overtly claim exemption on that basis from personal aesthetic and moral judgments; one is "allowed in" as it were, past the gate of cultural sanctity, and the viewer consequently is placed on a more equal level with the pictures. In the photos, the setting is a domestic one, inside a home. Further, domesticity is escalated by the scene being in a bedroom, a place of emotional and physical intimacy, and of privacy. The hysteria championed itself for exposing "secrets," and the photo setting is a direct visual recall of the textual claims of abuse hidden by the shields of domestic privacy and complicity. Finally, the last photo in the series is ambiguous, open, uncertain, and consequently inviting of speculation and fantasy. In short, the virtues of this documentary approach, obtaining an immediate and equal involvement in the pictures, at this particular historical point in time spelled trouble for any claims of common humanity.

More to the point

What I really like doing, especially since leaving the academia, is to *show* what a situation involves rather than merely to talk or write about it. While reduced to writing here, I'd like readers to notice two things. One is the trouble I went through simply to bring this paper to the conference on pornography. I mean this not in a self-sacrificing sense, but for you to take note of what, when, and how the impediments to bring data, artifacts, and ideas to a collective attention operate in the contemporary period. It is far more serious than any academic session could realize, has been so for some time, and in fact continues to worsen.

Secondly, despite the difficulties, many experts have in fact seen the pictures. But this is privileged space,[3] and most importantly, they are *absent* from places where they should also be: in galleries, books, or anywhere. Just as sensing the silences became analytically fashionable in the 1970s for textual work, so too must be the seeing of the disappeared. That which is prevented, that which is removed, leaves holes, and the taken and absent leave an unseen emptiness and incompleteness. Moreover, the vacancy is a damaged space, the consequences of which made more severe by its own invisibility. The act of taking has to begin with the visible and in that lies the chance for considered retention, but once gone, the moment is lost, for return never fully restores.

Many of us who have been in sex research for some years, even if aware of Weimar lessons, have been struck by how quickly gains in knowledge and research can be obliterated, and how much work has to be done over and from scratch merely to recover to a point achieved decades before. Some professionals, however, have actively participated and assisted the state in steering our return to the practices and mentalities of previous centuries. Such obtains today largely in the practices revolving around the sexualities of youth. The current research trend is toward that very area, and while there are signs of progressive and humane methodologies, the historical impasse of approaching youth with a prohibitionary orientation will be very hard to overcome. We already know that research on children in general is severely governed by restrictions placed by a few, although such resistances to institutional intervention are not always mistaken. The current prohibitive conception of "child pornography," with its justifying politicized ideology of child sexual abuse, interdicts more than mere visuals; its chilling effect on intellectual, artistic, and empirical work give the lie to a widely proclaimed self-serving posture of protecting the young and saving civilization. As they once said of psychiatry, it is the very disease for which it claims to be the cure.

NOTES

1. Crucial terms of the period's vocabulary were labels like "pedophile" and "pedophilia." Like the words "homosexual," "heterosexual," or "pornography," these are not empirical terms that describe stable, eternal, inherent, and universal entities. They are the names of culturally grounded Western nineteenth-century anxieties and aspirations for power, and are the results of a fledgling psychology trying to manage an increasing awareness of inner motives and aspirations against outward behavior in the late nineteenth century. The concept of "The Pedophile" remains suspicious. Since the objectivist or categorical approach has proven to be as embarrassing as it is destructive (it is ludicrous to try to speak of "The Heterosexual" or of any of the other old homogeneous simplicities as a unified and distinct configuration of motives and behaviors), the continued forced use of such language is based in other concerns, usually psychological, economic, or political.

2. Less direct but still supportive currents in the period (from 1975 on) need to be at least mentioned for they also legitimized certain views and behavior, and actively denigrated and punished others. The anti-drug wars, despite growing liberal and conservative criticism, continued its usual simplicities. Financial and military aggression in the 1980s was glorified and celebrated. Conservative politics ventured further afield, and liberalism was extensively ridiculed and continued its defensive retreat. Terrorism was cultivated by politicians and journalists to the level of a country-wide fear and related to a growing fear of crime and personal violence; both combined to strengthen the turn to retributive justice and the passage of severe and savage laws, most notably the "three-strikes-and-you're-out" variety.

Religious fundamentalism made a widespread comeback, carrying all its ideological accouterments. The mystical idea of "evil" returned to popular and professional discourse, with belief in the Christian deity Satan as an actual being and the existence of Satanic cults also being more widespread. Judeo-Christian ideas of gender were heavily promoted and influenced economic and sexual debates; similarly, a restricted idea of "family" was advanced as the only possible and permissible form. The religious conception of the child also took dominance, including radical ideas of purity and innocence with claims of divine connections.

The scientific world (including some social and sexual science) directed more effort toward the promotion of reductionistic causal biological factors in behavior, and as a part of this, tended to support popular prejudices, especially concerning the sexual villain; the possibilities of a sexual child were strenuously and shrilly denied. Causing some agitation also was the rise of "creationism," a religiously based façade of science used to promote Judeo-Christian myths as scientific fact; evolution was seriously challenged as a fact.

Journalism as an institution continued as it always had, that is, by the selective promotion and exploitation of issues, events, and personalities, using its traditional methods of omission, distortion, and fabrication. Journalists and others were excited by the intense promotion of heroism and victimage in the period such that vigilante activity was made easier by media exhibitions.

3. This, despite pre-session rumors that city prosecutors or police would be in attendance to monitor the presentations of the Child Pornography Panel. This turned out not to be true, or at least no one identified themselves as such, however several hostile journalists were there. Harris Mirkin reported to me that a correspondent from Fox News asked him, "Should pedophiles be allowed to exist?" Such a question profoundly offends me as a scientist, angers me as a Jew, and insults me as a human being. That a journalist asked such a question in all seriousness is to be expected of that profession, but it is a striking indicator of how debased the social field has become.

SECTION 12
HISTORICAL ASPECTS OF PORNOGRAPHY

THE INVENTION OF PRINTING AT THE END OF THE FIFTEENTH CENTURY IS perhaps the crucial factor in making possible a mass produced literary and visual pornographic corpus, but what Berte C. Verstraete calls "proto porn" with both erotic and obscene themes existed in the classical world of the Greeks and Romans. He surveys the literary works of the Greco Roman world beginning with the *Iliad* and the *Odyssey* and goes through to the end of the second century in the modern era. But the Greco-Roman world also had visual erotic and obscene images in their vase paintings, in wall paintings, and in sculpture to further emphasize the sexual and the erotic nature of their culture. Verstraete goes so far as to hold that the erotic and obscene enjoyed a centrality in classical roman society which has still not been equaled in the modern Western world.

Often in pornographic writing, which until the last part of the twentieth century, was almost totally a male prerogative, the picture of women's sexual response is distorted. This, as Thomas Albrecht makes clear, was particularly true of Victorian erotic writings. Women in a sense were portrayed as responding similar to men, including female ejaculation. Such portrayals might well protect the male subject against his perception of sexual difference by allowing him to believe in the fundamental sameness of men and women, but such portrayals also emphasize the difficulty male writers had with describing the female sexual response since so much of it takes place internally.

One of the classic authors of pornographic writings at the beginning of the nineteenth century was the Marquis de Sade. De Sade has become almost a literary industry and his name itself gave the term *sadism* and *sadistic* to the English language (and other languages as well).

Vida Pavesich examines his story of Juliette, the story of a young

533

woman's education in the ways of sex and vice. As she progresses, she becomes increasingly more powerful, wealthy and cruel. Pavesich argues that she represents the culmination of a tradition of male-created, female fantasy figures. But because of Sade's irreverence for gender roles, his refusal to see female sexuality defined simply in terms of the female reproductive function, he has become a "moral" pornographer for some feminists. Without attempting to justify or glorify de Sade, his writings emphasize that pornography might well contain a social revolutionary statement as well as an erotic one.

This theme is carried further by Christian Hite who argues for a total reconceptualization of pornography from a simple image ("I know it when I see it") to viewing it as a complex constellation of interrelations between viewers and their own bodies. She illustrates her argument by using the changes wrought in viewing bodies by the stereoscope (which allowed the viewer to see things in depth) in the nineteenth century. Lastly, and finally, Timothy Madigan sums up the debate over pornography by emphasizing why de Sade and pornography has meaning to us today.

45

Classical Roman Perspective on the Erotic, Obscenity, and Pornography

Beert C. Verstraete

I N HER INTRODUCTION TO THE 1993 BOOK (EDITED BY HERSELF) *THE Invention of Pornography: Obscenity and the Origins of Modernity, 1500-1800,* Lynn Hunt places, quite rightly, the genesis of pornography, "both as a literary and visual practice and as a category of understanding, at the same time—and concomitantly with—the long term emergence of Western Modernity" (Hunt, 10-11; and she links it to "most of the major moments in that emergence: the Renaissance, the Scientific Revolution, the Enlightenment and the French Revolution" (Hunt, 11). The invention of printing is, of course, one of the most crucial specific historical moments in that emergence—one that also made the genesis of pornography as a mass-produced literary and visual corpus and as a new category of human experience and culture possible. To speak, without far-reaching qualifications, of pornography in the pre-technological, pre-industrial Greco-Roman world would, therefore, be a serious anachronism and thus my use of the word "pornography" in the title of my paper is indeed a heavily qualified one. To the extent that the Greco-Roman world did allow for at least some limited mass-production of the written word and icon (and here I am thinking in particular of the mass-copying of papyrus texts that was carried on in the large slave-staffed scriptoria of the Hellenistic and Roman periods, and of the fact that these mass-copied texts could be bought at a relatively inexpensive cost by the relatively large minority—although, I emphasize, still a minority—of the population in the later Greco-Roman world who were literate) to this extent we can speak of a kind of proto-pornography. (1) Even so, I will not use "pornography" as a category of analysis since the terms "the erotic" and "obscenity" carry a much greater facticity in the historical context with which I am concerned. When placed under these two headings pre-Christian Greco-Roman civilization offers much that is salient and illuminating for us as we endeavor to arrive a better understanding of pornography as a unique product of the modern technocratic West and to appreciate how socially and culturally conditioned the conceptions of obscenity and the erotic are that are subsumed in modern pornography. In this paper I will call your attention to conceptions of obscenity and the erotic that were current especially among the elite, literate classes of the Roman half of the Greco-Roman world. My principal time-span will be roughly three centuries, the last century B.C.E. and the first two centuries C.E., an era when the *Pax Romana* created an unparalleled degree of cultural commonality between Greeks and Romans. I will confine myself largely to the literary evidence since this my area of scholarly expertise, but in the closing part I will also underline the important dimension for our understanding of the erotic and obscenity provided by Roman art and decoration.

The treatment of the erotic in both Greek and Roman literature, art, and music is dictated above all by genre. In literature which lent itself to elaborate classifications and typologies of genre, this was especially true, and the handling of a genre was in turn dictated by the expectations of listeners, audiences, and readers. Thus, in epic the treatment of the erotic must be subdued, with little or no explicit references to, let alone descriptions of, love-making. This is true of the *Iliad*, where the most detailed reference to the erotic, namely Zeus' recollection of book fourteen, of his wonderfully pleasurable love-making with various mortal women, has a highly comic ring to it and in fact occurs in the comic, domestic context of Zeus' troubles with his wife Hera. The relationship between Achilles and Patroclus is portrayed as an especially close friendship, but I agree with Kenneth Dover and other classicists that it not portrayed or even intimated as a sexual one, however later generation of Greeks might interpret it. (2) The *Odyssey* is similarly subdued, even though the erotic plays a larger role in it. It is not until the third century B.C.E. Hellenistic Greek epic, the *Argonautica*, of Apollonius of Rhodes, with the lengthy episode of Medea's falling in love with Jason, that the erotic moves to a central position. Greek tragedy, too, in general, maintained the decorum with respect to the erotic. Euripides, the last of the three great Athenian authors of classical tragedy, was seen, and at times reviled—think of Aristophanes' *Frogs*—for his intense portrayal of women deeply and desperately in love. The Roman Virgil, in his great national epic, the *Aeneid*, let the tragic love story of Dido and Aeneas stand our conspicuously, but his example was not followed by the Latin epic poets in the two centuries after him—with the exception of Ovid in the *Metamorphoses*, which, however, with its anti-heroic tenor and episodic, bricolage-like structure, and treatment of subjects such as incest and transsexualism, cannot be counted as a true epic.

It was the prose romances—all the fully or at least substantially extant ones of which date from the first three centuries C.E. and a few of which might be called in fact novels—that were the only large-scale literary works of Greco-Roman antiquity that made the erotic their central theme. The Greek romances tend to be idealizing and sentimental, although there are comic elements especially in *Daphnis and Chloe* and *Cleitophon and Leucippe*, which are also notable for their occasional frankness and explicitness about the details of love-making between a man and a woman. In addition, papyrus finds over the past few decades have brought to light fragments of Greek in which the comic and the grotesque may have figured very conspicuously. Heterosexual love stands at the center of the Greek prose romances, but also featured are subplots involving male same-sex lovers and, in *Cleitophon and Leucippe*, a lengthy discussion of sexual preference, i.e., man-woman love versus pederasty. The two greatest classical Roman novels, the *Satyricon* and *The Golden Ass*, of the first and second centuries C.E. Respectively, push the genre's potential for the comic and grotesque much further than the Greek prose romance. Irony, parody and near-parody, even elements of outright satire are prominent especially in Petronius' *Satyricon*, which has the distinction of being the most sexually explicit of all the surviving ancient Greek and Roman prose romances. Its title, containing the Greek *satyros* ("satyr"), with a hint also of the Latin *satura* ("satire"), would have more than alerted the prospective reader. You may be surprised I have placed the *Satyricon* under the rubric of the erotic rather than the obscene. The primary love-interest of *Satyricon* is male same-sex, but this is presented and pursued in the spirit of non-problematic bawdy humor and playful irony—the same generous spirit that characterizes the now famous Warren cup, which will be discussed later, with its depiction of two male same-sex couples making love. The element of outright shaming and befouling that is so essential to the obscene in Roman literature and probably in all cultures, is, I submit, completely lacking in both the cup and Petronius' comic masterpiece.

In Roman literature, following pretty well the Greek example, the erotic was very much within the domain of the genres of short poetry, especially lyric and elegiac poetry including the epigram. (Here we need to remind ourselves that the Greeks and the Romans classified their poetry formally on the basis of the meter used, rather than content: thus a lyric poem—which meant originally a song to be sung to the accompaniment of a lyre—is simply a poem using one of the many lyric metrical forms, often stanzaic in nature, developed principally by the Greeks over the centuries; and an elegiac poem is any poem composed in elegiac couplets.) The Romans developed a lyric and elegiac poetry of a richness and complexity that made it more than equal to its Greek counterpart; and indeed, the love poetry of the classical Romans is unmatched in depth and variety by that of any culture of the ancient world. Catullus wrote love poetry in both the lyric and elegiac forms, including a number of elegiac epigrams. Horace's love poetry is exclusively in the lyric form, whereas that of Propertius, Tibullus, and Ovid employed only the elegiac couplet; mention must also be made of the very small extant corpus of love poetry of Sulpicia, who flourished during the early Augustan period and who is the only female classical roman author of whose work more than a few snippets have survived. Towards to the end of the first century C.E., a century later, Martial used exclusively the epigrammatic form for his love poetry. Most of this love poetry is heterosexual, but pederasty enjoys a significant minority presence, in particular in the poetry of Catullus, Tibullus, Horace, and Martial. This poetry can be unabashedly sensual, although the descriptions of love-making, while often vivid, almost always avoid the extremely graphic. The following opening lines of a poem by Propertius (2.15) show Roman elegiac love poetry at its most lively (3):

> How I prosper! O shining night! And O
> You little bed made blest by my delights,
> How much we told each other by lamplight
> How great our strife when the light was removed!
> For now with bare nipples she wrestled me.
> And now procrastinated, tunic closed.
> She opened my rolling eyes from sleep
> With her lips and said, "Will you lie so sluggish?"
> What varied embraces shifted our arm! And how
> My kisses loitered on your lips!

Towards to the end of his *Art of Love*, his famous mock-didactic poem purveying to both male and female lovers advice on all matters of love and the erotic, Ovid daringly—he is blushing, so he claims tongue-in-cheek—recommends the different positions in love-making accommodated to the individual woman's body and build and other physical assets (4):

> What's left I blush to tell you; but kindly Venus
> Claims as uniquely hers
> All that raises a blush. Each woman should know herself,
> pick methods
> To suit her body: one fashion won't do for all.
> Let the girl with a pretty face lie supine, let the lady
> Who boast a good back be viewed
> From behind. Milanion bore Atalanta's legs on
> His shoulders: nice legs should always be used this way.
> The petite should ride horses (Andromache, Hector's Theban
> Bride was too tall for these games; no jockey she)...

The Greeks and Romans expected emotional stimulation from their poetry, as well as from their rhetoric, art, and music. All their literary criticism is premised on this fundamental expectation, which we find not only in the writings of Plato and Aristotle and the later authors of literary and rhetorical handbooks, but also long before these in Homeric epic. Poetry dealing with erotic subject matter was expected, therefore, to be erotically stimulating—hence Ovid's probably somewhat ironic warning at the beginning of the *Art of Love* that his work is not to be read by respectable Roman matrons. As it turned out, of course, Ovid's *Art,* earned him the displeasure of Augustus, and was, Ovid says, one of the two principal reasons (the other one, perhaps the real catalyst, a serious political indiscretion committed by the poet which he never dared to reveal) for his being banished to the outskirts of the Empire until his death. Ovid thus has the distinction of being the only author in Greco-Roman antiquity who was punished, severely punished in fact, and his works censored, for his writing of risque erotic literature. Ovid had indeed warned off some potential readers, so that he could not be accused of encouraging them to commit adultery–adultery, of course, as understood according the patriarchal Roman norms and first made a public criminal offense by Augustus–but the warning had sounded insincere, and was in fact contradicted by much of the poem's content.

So far I have dealt with literature that I would characterize only as erotic, that charts the vagaries of romantic love (which, I would emphasize is *not*, C. S. Lewis's *The Allegory of Love*, an invention of the West) and celebrates, but also agonizes over sexual passion. This literature is undoubtedly, almost without exception, premised on the patriarchal, androcentric norms of gender and sexuality that also prevailed in the Greco-Roman world, as Amy Richlin has well demonstrated in her groundbreaking *The Garden of Priapus: Sexuality and Aggression in Roman Humor*, but it is not characterized by the elements of shaming and befouling which are the crucial components of obscenity. Although there is certainly and inevitably a grey zone, so to speak, between the erotic and the obscene since both these fundamentals of human experience and culture are grounded in the social construction of gender and sexuality, as ideal-types they are easily distinguished; whatever its mode is–serious, tragic, didactic, comic, ironic, or even satiric–the erotic views and constructs sexuality positively as life-affirming; obscenity, by contrast, shames and befouls sexuality, and thus paradoxically, for all its graphic explicitness belittles *homo sexualis*, and beyond this, the human as a whole. I am well aware that humans can play ingenious complex games with sexuality, so that, for instance, in a sadomasochistic scenario the shamed partner is expected to experience erotic exhilaration–perhaps even exaltation. Think, for instance, of the sexuality depicted in Jean Genet's writings or, in a very different, humorous vein of the scene in the *Satyricon* (section 132) where Encolpius, confronted once more with his impotence, curses his limp penis but does so with an ironic and parodying playfulness that renders this episode comic rather than obscene; by contrast, an identical scenario is handled in a Priapean poem in the Tibullan Corpus (*Albi Tibulli Priapea 2*) with a crass obscenity that climaxes with a threat to the uncooperative penis that it will be buried in the vagina of an ugly, old woman–jokes about the non-appetizing sexuality of old women being a staple in obscene Roman literature. (5)

Obscenity in Roman literature has received two detailed, philologically oriented studies over the past twenty years: J. N. Adams's *The Latin Sexual Vocabulary* and Amy Richlin's *Sexual Terms and Themes in Roman Satire and Related Genres*. Richlin offers an extensive analysis, to which I am very much indebted, of what the Romans understood by obscenity and its propriety or impropriety, basing herself in particular on the pronouncements of Cicero, Seneca the Elder, Martial, and Pliny the Younger. A recent article, Holt N. Parker's "The Teratogenic Grid," which furnishes a novel, schematic overview and analysis of sexual acts according to the norms of what Jonathan

Grant, 1975, p. 52

Clarke, 1998, plate 2. Photo Michael Larvey   *Clarke, 1998, plate 1. Photo Michael Larvey*

Winters, in another article in the same collection, *Roman Sexualities*, calls the Roman "sex/gender system," is also most relevant to the study of obscenity in Roman literature. Together with the two earlier studies I have mentioned, it lays out the spectrum of sexual acts and dispositions that the Romans–the Roman male elites certainly, but probably most men and women of all social classes–regarded as "deviant" and "perverse" and that thus provided the perfect material for obscene discourse. Any sexual act or disposition– lesbian sexual acts and preferences of women, especially of the more "mannish" ones, the voracious sexuality of older women, the "passive" role enjoyed by some men in anal intercourse, any form of oral sex, especially cunnilingus and the "active" role in fellatio–that violated the traditional sex/gender norms was fair game for ridicule. What distinguishes classical Roman society from ours is its much greater readiness to resort to graphic

Clarke, 1998, figure 2, p. 221. Photo Michael Larvey

Grant, 1975, p. 109

Clarke, 1981, figure 44, p. 125. Photo Michael Larvey

obscenities even in elite cultural discourse, in order to pillory such perceived sexual deviations. The obscene epigrams of Catullus and Martial, and the *Priapea*, a collection of poems in which the phallic god Priapus is the speaker, are not the scribblings of marginal, quasi-bohemian figures in Roman society, but represent the discourse of the dominant male elites. Interestingly, Catullus (16), Martial (1.4), and Pliny (5.3) make it a point of dissociating their own personal lives from the risque sex they describe in some of their poetry—as Martial puts it, "My writing is salacious, but my life virtuous"—although one suspects that this is done only as a half-humorous tactical ploy against the common belief in Greco-Roman antiquity that there is a close moral and psychological connection between the character of an author and the subject matter he writes about.

Many classicists, including the aforementioned J. N. Adams and the art-historian John R. Clarke, have called attention to the all-important apotropaic (i.e., warding off, protective) function of obscenity in Roman culture: the laughter excited by an obscenity will give protection against bad luck or the "the evil eye"–such an important tenet of Mediterranean superstition; representations of the phallus, too, or of Priapus himself, his macrophallic statue standing guard in many a Roman guardian, afforded protection for the household. Verbal and visual obscenity was an integral part of the wedding ceremony, with the bride, among others, compelled to sit on the phallus of the ithyphallic ancient Roman deity (Priapus being of Greek provenance) Mutunus Tutunus; and obscene verses were sung, usually by the returning soldiers, in the triumphal processions honoring victorious generals. The apotropaic function of obscenity is a Roman-cultural corollary of its universally aggressive function, for obscenity as aggression clearly provides psychic release for the individual and the group. However, the psychic release provided by obscenity stems also from the thrill of handling forbidden things, the shaming and befouling words that speak of shaming and befouling acts. In this respect, Martial states (11.16), even the most prudish and respectable persons are vulnerable: as he puts it (in my own somewhat free translation which eliminates the, for us, obscure local references). "You, though you are more serious than a stern Roman of olden times, beat your coat all the time with your stiff prick, and you, small-town girl though you are, get all wet as you read through these naughty sex-games of mine." These lines come from book eleven of Martial's epigrams, which contains an especially large number of conspicuously obscene poems. Although he is obviously using comic exaggeration, Martial, the most variedly "obscene" of classical Roman poets, it is always useful to be reminded of John P. Sullivan's insight that Martial's handling of sexuality fits in perfectly with general Roman norms and expectations.

For a few decades, mainly in the sixties and seventies, the portrayal of sexuality in Roman and Greek art and decoration was the subject of coffeetable books, which tended to be sensationalist and short on providing cultural context; of these, Michael Grant's *Eros in Pompeii* was clearly the best. John R. Clarke's (1998) recent book-length study, *Looking at Lovemaking: Construction of Sexuality in Roman Art, 100 B.C.–A.D. 200*, has finally and most expertly filled the gap for Roman studies. According to Clarke, an examination of the erotic and the obscene in Roman art and decoration reveals less judgmental attitudes to what in the literature is usually pilloried as "deviant" and "perverse." There are certainly surprises. The frank portrayal of more or less "normal" man-woman sexual intercourse in a bedroom wall-painting in a Pompeian house (Grant, 1975, p. 52) should not be surprising, although even by the liberal standards of modern Western society it would still be considered most daring and improper. However, the now famous silver Warren cup, dating probably from the Augustan period, is problematic: the portrayal, on one half of the cup, of a man-boy couple engaging in sex (Clarke, 1998, plate 2) is just passable in the Roman "sex/gender system," but the scene of two adult men, on the other half, making love (Clarke, 1998, plate 1) is clearly in violation of fundamental Roman norms for gender and sexuality. However, when one considers, as Clarke himself recognizes, that the Warren cup, a luxury object, must have been commissioned by an upperclass Roman, a sophisticated person—maybe a woman, as I would in fact suggest (6)—of more liberal sexual views and tastes than the average Roman, and that this precious cup was probably not meant for general household use, but was to be admired and handled by a select, elite group, the surprise should not be as great. The depiction, brought forward by Clarke, of fellatio on a humble oil lamp (Clarke, 1998, figure 92, p. 221) is certainly grotesque even by the most liberal Wester standards, and reminds us once more of how visible and public the erotic and obscene were in Roman society, but it should be emphasized that his coarsely rendered portrayal of a woman, a prostitute probably, fellating a man is not in violation of the fundamental patriarchal, androcentric norms of the Roman "gender/sex system." In Roman art and decoration, we are also constantly reminded of the apotropaic function of the phallus as a visual icon (Grant, 1975, p. 109), although a more complex configuration of signs, well analyzed by Clarke, arises when phallic endowment is welded to perceptions of exotic ethnicity, as in many depictions of blacks (Clarke, 1998, figure 44, p. 125); but here we must be careful not to read these icons against the background of Western racism and sexual fantasies.

The erotic and the obscene clearly enjoyed a centrality in classical Roman society that has still not been equaled in the modern Western world, although, as I have emphasized at the beginning, to speak of a Roman pornography would be quite anachronistic. Even in today's so-called permissive society we find little in common with ancient Rome. Yet to characterize Roman society and culture as ultra-permissive in matters sexual would be another serious anachronism, for pre-Christian and relatively non-prudish as classical Rome was, its adherence to the patriarchal, androcentric "gender/sex system" and its quasi-erotic glamorization of the institutionalized violence of the arena (7)—a subject that time and space have not permitted me to explore in this paper—did not make for a truly liberal civilization.

NOTES

I have used these notes to give guidance for further reading or to provide references that are not contained in the *Bibliography*.

1. Holt N. Parker, "Love Body's Anatomized: The Ancient Erotic Handbooks and the Rhetoric Of Sexuality," *Pornography and Presentation in Greece and Rome*, edited by Amy Richlin, New York and Oxford: Oxford University Press, 1992,

90–111, singles out the Greek erotic manuals of antiquity as meeting his definitional criteria for pornography. However, I think Hunt's position is essentially right, so that we cannot speak of a true pornography in classical civilization; thus, the use of the term "pornography" in the collection edited by Richlin is anachronistic.

2. Kenneth J. Dover, *Greek Homosexuality*, London: Duckworth/Cambridge: Harvard University Press, 1978, 197; but cf. W. M. Clarke's exploration, both scholarly and sensitive, of the issue in "Achilles and Patrolcus in Love," *Hermes* 106 (1978): 381–96.

3. Translation from Propertius, *The Poems*, translated by W. G. Shepherd (Penguin Books, 1985), p. 73.

4. Translation from Ovid, *The Erotic Poems*, translated by Peter Green (Penguin Books, 1982), p. 237.

5. On this topic see Amy Richlin in ch. 5 of *The Garden of Priapus*.

6. My suggestion is based on Juvenal's complaint in *Satires* 6 (1-34), the notorious satire on women, that some women (the Roman counterpart of the modern "faghag?") enjoy the company of *cinaedi*–seemingly effeminate men with a taste for the passive "homosexual" role–far too much.

7. On this "quasi-erotic glamorization" of the Roman arena, in particular of the gladiatorial fighters, see Carlin A. Barton, *The Sorrows of the Ancient Romans: The Gladiator and the Monster* (Princeton: Princeton University Press, 1993).

REFERENCES

Adams, J. N., *The Latin Sexual Vocabulary*. Baltimore: John Hopkins University Press, 1982.

Clarke, John R., *Looking at Lovemaking: Construction of Sexuality in Roman Art, 100 B.C.-A. D. 200*. Berkeley, Los Angeles, and London: University of California Press, 1998.

Grant, Michael, *Eros in Pompeii*. New York: William Morrow and Company, Inc.: 1975.

Hunt, Lynn (ed.), *The Invention of Pornography: Obscenity and the Origins of Modernity, 1500–1800*. New York: Zone Books, 1993.

Parker, Holt N., "The Teratogenic Grid," *Roman Sexualities*, ed. Judith P. Hallett and Marilyn B. Skinner. Princeton: Princeton University Press, 1997, pp. 47–65.

Parker, W. H. (Ed and transl.), *Priapea: Poems for a Phallic God*, London an Sydney: Croom Helm, 1988.

Richlin, Amy, *Sexual Terms and Themes in Roman Satire and Related Genres*, Ph.D. Dissertation, Yale University, 1978 (Ann Arbor and London: University Microfilms).

Richlin, Amy, *The Garden of Priapus: Sexuality and Aggression in Roman Humor*, revised edition. New York and Oxford: Oxford University Press, 1992.

Sullivan, J. P., *Martial: The Unexpected Classic: A Literary and Historical Study*. Cambridge and New York: Cambridge University Press, 1991, esp. ch. 5, "Martial's Sexual Attitudes."

Walters, Jonathan, "Invading the Roman Body: Manliness and Impenetrability in Roman Thought," in *Roman Sexualities*, ed. Judith P. Hallett and Marilyn B. Skinner. Princeton: Princeton University Press, 1997, 29-43.

46

Same and Other Victorians

Thomas Albrecht

I SHOULD LIKE TO CONSIDER SOME OF THE DIFFICULTIES VICTORIAN LIT-
erary pornography associates with understanding female sexual pleasure.
More particularly, I would like to dwell on the relation between this pleasure and the various mechanisms of representation that come into play once
Victorian pornographic writing begins talking about female passion.

I'll begin with two exemplary representations of female sexual response, chosen from two serialized pornographic novels of 1879:

> My partner, who had been no ways backward in sustaining my fierce
> lunges and had returned them with thrusts and upheavings fully as
> amorous as my own, feeling the heat of the burning liquid I was ejecting
> into her, gave way at the same time, and dissolving her very soul into a
> flood of sperm, opened the gates of love's reservoir, and let flow such a
> stream of pearly essence as never came from a woman before.

> She clasps me in her arms, and throws her snowy thighs around my back,
> the bounces of her bottom fairly spring me off her. I feel she is coming. Ah,
> my god, she comes—she spends! The sperm comes from her in a shower.

While this bizarre figure of a woman ejaculating sperm may give
readers reason to pause, she is recognizable to anyone who has read even a
little Victorian pornography. She is a standard topos of the genre, ubiquitous
both in novels and in purportedly non-fictional writings like *My Secret Life.*
In the world of Victorian pornography, nearly all women visibly ejaculate
when they have sex, and like their male counterparts, they do so frequently
and reliably. This ability is treated like a biological fact, and is not something
that the characters ever remark upon or wonder about. I want to suggest that
the burden of this figure in Victorian pornographic texts is to reveal the

truth of female sexual pleasure, both to the other characters within the narrative as well as to us, the readers.

In *The Other Victorians*, his foundational 1966 study of Victorian sexuality and pornography, Steven Marcus understands the figure of the ejaculating woman as a male fantasy. This fantasy, he argues, is determined by the unconscious desires and fears of the men who wrote most Victorian pornography, men like "Walter," the narrator and pseudonymous author of *My Secret Life*. Marcus maintains that Walter's belief in–and experience of–the "reality" of female ejaculation is an unconscious defensive reaction against actual female sexuality. Female sexuality and female anatomy threaten Walter, Marcus suggests, because he unconsciously interprets their difference from his own sexuality and anatomy as castration. According to Freud's theory of castration anxiety, a man's seeing a woman as castrated necessarily also implies his own potential castration. To protect himself from this kind of threat, Walter projects a familiar male sexual response, ejaculation, onto the woman. Seeing the woman ejaculate then allows him to see her as ultimately identical to himself, thereby disavowing the threatening fact of her difference.

Marcus's Freudian interpretation is suggestive because it implicitly considers the ejaculating woman as a kind of protective fetish, in Freud's own sense of that term. In the essay "Fetishism," Freud narrates the traumatic moment when a little boy first perceives his mother's genitals and interprets what he sees as castrated. This sight is extremely traumatic because the boy has thus far assumed that all people are like him (i.e., have a penis); his "recognition" of the mother's castration, however, destroys this happy assumption and, moreover, implies that he too could lose his penis. According to Freud, the boy may respond to the sight of his mother's genitals by disavowing what he sees: by accepting the traumatic perception and simultaneously denying it. Such a disavowal is made possible, Freud explains, by the adoption of a fetish. A fetish is an object like fur or a shoe that functions for the boy as a symbolic substitute for the lost maternal penis in which he once believed and which he does not want to give up. Insofar as the fetish substitutes for the wished-for penis, it restores that penis but also signifies the recognition of its loss. In other words, the boy uses the fetish to sustain simultaneously his newly gained knowledge of castration's "reality" and his former belief in the maternal penis. This paradoxical split attitude is the fetishistic logic of disavowal, a compromise-formation through which the boy is able to reconcile two incompatible positions: his perception and his desire.

Steven Marcus implies that the fantasy of the ejaculating woman in Victorian pornography is such a fetish because it protects the male subject against his perception of sexual difference by allowing him to believe in the fundamental sameness of men and women. Even while Walter recognizes sexual difference each time he inspects a woman's vagina, for instance, he is also able to disavow this recognition through the reassuring fetish of female ejaculation. This is the double logic of disavowal: I know the woman does not have a penis, but she ejaculates as if she did, which means that she really is just like me, i.e., a reassuring mirror of myself.

I would like now to propose a complementary, though differently nuanced reading of the ejaculating woman. My approach will not focus on the figure's psychic function in the author's unconscious (as Marcus does), but on her generic function in the texts of Victorian pornography. From a literary point of view, I am interested in why these writings compulsively trot out the ejaculating woman, and why she is always the privileged, even the exclusive, representation of female *jouissance*.

In her book *Hard Core*, Linda Williams (1989) explains that since the nineteenth century, pornography, as a genre, has specifically sought to attain and to represent a knowledge of female sexual pleasure. Why would pornography, a genre exclusively concerned with eliciting sexual arousal, be interested in producing any kind of knowledge at all? Following Michel Foucault's *History of Sexuality*, Williams argues that Victorian pornography must be understood in the context of a whole series of medical, psychological, sociological, juridical, and artistic discourses emerging in mid-nineteenth-century Europe, whose aim was to construct a *scientia sexualis*, a scientific or pseudo-scientific knowledge of the mysterious truths of sex. This thematic emphasis on sexual knowledge is suggested, for example, by such Victorian pornographic titles as *Adventures of a School-Boy* and *Miss Coote's Confession*. Both these titles furthermore suggest a specific preoccupation with female sexuality, regardless of whether the story's narrator is male or female. One reason for pornography's particular emphasis on the truth of female pleasure, Williams suggests, is that until the 1980s, pornographic texts were almost exclusively produced by and for men. In these texts, the truth of male sexual pleasure is taken as unproblematically self-evident, mainly because male pleasure can, as it were, be seen and felt (i.e., it has visible, tangible evidence). Female pleasure, on the other hand, poses a problem in and for these pornographic texts, especially if it is measured on the same standard as male pleasure. This is because it takes place within the body, it cannot always be seen, so there is no visible, undisputable evidence for it (as there is, one might say, undisputable evidence for the truth of male pleasure in the ejaculation). This invisibility is particularly troubling for pornography, which, as Williams notes, is a form of representation dedicated to the principle of maximum visibility. For this reason, female pleasure remains both the privileged object and the perpetually elusive blind spot of the genre.

If the representation of female passion is pornography's main formal and epistemological problem, then the figure of the ejaculating woman may be understood as an obvious and facile solution. She reproduces an image of pleasure that is comfortably familiar to male writers and readers because it is analogous to the genre's representation of male pleasure. The woman's ejaculation rewrites female pleasure as something visible and tangible. A secret event that takes place inside the body and out of sight is thus displaced to the outside of the body, into view. Because this pleasure has been externalized, its truth is presumably undeniable. What is striking about this solution is not that it may be inconsistent with biological reality, for one because pornography has never aimed much for verisimilitude. It is rather the uncanny degree to which the woman's ejaculation directly, symmetrically mirrors the representation of the male character's ejaculation. Here is an example of this kind of mirroring, a scene from a pornographic novel in which two boys are each matched up with two girls:

> We could feel [the girls'] bodies quiver with emotion as they reclined upon our necks, their hands and ours groping under shirts . . . in every forbidden spot; each of us had two delicate hands caressing our cocks, two delicious arms around our necks, two faces laid cheek to cheek on either side, two sets of lips to kiss, two pairs of bright and humid eyes to return our glances; what wonder then that we flooded their hands with our spurting seed and felt their delicious spendings trickle over our busy fingers.

This passage achieves its poetic effect through a series of simultaneous specular relations; the two sets of lovers, the two boys, and the four girls are all mirror images of one another. The passage also constructs a symmetrical mirror between the boys and the girls, since each group comes at the same time on the hands of the other. This mirroring of male pleasure by female pleasure, which here is explicitly thematized in the image of all the lovers coming at once in exactly the same manner, recurs throughout Victorian pornographic writing, both on the level of plot and of diction. To take a different example than female ejaculation, two very standard desires associated with the male characters in Victorian pornography are voyeurism and rape. In both cases, the representation of female desire almost inevitably takes the form of a complementary response to male desire: the woman takes her pleasure in being looked at or in being raped. This symmetry between women and men is moreover reiterated in words and images like "sperm" and "spendings" that pornographic writing uses in equal parts to describe both female and male sexual responses. Usually the woman will come in response to, or in anticipation of, the man's orgasm, and the text will use the same word to describe their respective ejaculation. This gives the effect that the representation of the female orgasm is simply quoting the representation of the male orgasm. To borrow a standard metaphor from Victorian pornography, there is a mechanical element to female ejaculation, not only because it repeats again and again, but because it comes again and again in the same familiar words and phrases. (I want to add parenthetically that the same can of course be said of the male ejaculation in these texts, a point whose implications I will briefly revisit at the end of the paper).

Victorian pornography's representation of female passion as fundamentally the same as male passion, and, in that sense, of women as men, offers a solution to the genre's problem of representing sexual difference and the difference of female pleasure and desire from male pleasure and desire. Briefly put, that solution is to rewrite difference as sameness. But I would argue that this solution is precisely the occasion on which pornography also acknowledges its failure as a representation and as an epistemological form. This failure is not simply that Victorian pornography has a limited point of view, a limited imagination, or a limited vocabulary. It is rather pornography's lack of an engagement with a sexuality that is absolutely, radically heterogenous to phallic sexuality, that is truly pornography's other, and that cannot be understood and represented as identical or complementary to male sexuality. If Victorian pornography is written, as is said, from a male point of view, from the point of view of a phallic sexuality (assuming we know to what those names refer), then this other, whatever it is, may be called female sexuality and desire. Because the ejaculating woman implicitly points to the absence of precisely this female other, she is pornography's figure not only for a solution but also a problem.

Like the girl who is seen as a boy, this solution that also signifies the problem evokes the contradictory logic of fetishism. We should recall that fetishism is Freud's name for a logic that, on the one hand, acknowledges the truth of a traumatic absence, and, on the other hand, covers over this truth by way of a comforting fiction, namely the fetish. I would suggest that the ejaculating woman is not only Walter's fetish, as Steven Marcus proposes, but pornography's fetish. In and through this fetish, pornography acknowledges a traumatic lack: not the lack of a penis, but the lack of the other, the lack of any representational and epistemological engagement with a desire that is absolutely different from its own, namely female desire. This lack is traumatic to pornography because, as I said earlier, female sexuality is the genre's privileged object and elusive obsession. At the same time, however, pornography protects itself from its recognition of this lack with the fetish of female ejaculation. The fetishistic ejaculating woman is a rhetorical figure that restores the absent other to pornography, but at the expense of its otherness. She can represent female pleasure, but only in the terms of male pleasure, which are the terms of the phallus, of ejaculation, of externalization, of visibility, and so on. Briefly put, she can only represent female pleasure as same, not as other (this is analogous to how Walter and Freud's little boy can only see women as either castrated or not castrated, not as heterogenous to the entire economy of castration). Despite and because of this limitation, the fetish reassures pornography because it allows representation and cognition of female passion to take place. It solves the problem of representing the other, even while it also reminds us of the other's absence.

This crisis of representation has significant consequences for an evaluation of the ways Victorian pornography defines gender and sexuality. Victorian pornography is usually understood as a male genre in which male writers and male desires control, objectify, define, and possess women. It is assumed to insist on rigid gender and sexual definitions. I would argue, however, that Victorian pornography questions this understanding of itself in the crisis it associates with representing female passion. On the one hand, the writing certainly does strive to represent and to know female sexuality, and arguably it even strives to contain and control female sexuality by placing it within very narrow phallic parameters. But as I suggest in this paper, the latter is less a sign of mastery than of quandary. Victorian pornography always testifies to its own failure in its endeavor to contain female desire; my example of this kind of testimony is the fetish of the ejaculating woman. This figure, which perpetually undermines its own authority, signifies the limitations, not the extent, of the writing's power over, and control of, female sexuality.

If "women" and "female sexuality," as they are depicted in Victorian literary pornography, are the fetishes and rhetorical figures of the genre, there are at least two possible conclusions to be drawn from this. One is to say that this kind of pornography is a male genre whose false and limited representations of women are male fantasies or simply imitations of male sexuality. The other conclusion, however, is perhaps the more interesting. Because the tropes and fetishes that pornography calls "the woman" and "female pleasure" are both epistemologically unreliable and limited, we might then also question the self-evidence and reliability of labels like "male" and "male fantasies" that we use to describe the essence of Victorian pornography.

NOTES

1. *The Pearl*, 328, 477. The citations are taken from *La Rose d'Amour*, or *The Adventures of a Gentleman in Search of Pleasure*, a novel serialized in the pornographic periodical *The Pearl*.

2. This general assumption is suggestively complicated by Donald Hall's recent essay, "Graphic Sexuality and the Erasure of a Polymorphous Perversity."

BIBLIOGRAPHY

Foucault, M. (1984). *The History of Sexuality: An Introduction.* R. Hurley, trans. Harmondsworth: Penguin.

Freud, S. (1961). Fetishism. In J. Strachey et al. (Eds.), *The Standard Edition of the Complete Psychological Works of Sigmund Freud*, vol. 21. London: Hogarth Press (pp. 149–57).

Hall, D.E. (1996). *Graphic Sexuality and the Erasure of a Polymorphous Perversity.* In D. Hall & M. Pramaggiore (Eds.). Representing Bisexualities: Subjects and Cultures of Fluid Desire. New York: New York University Press (pp. 99–123).

Marcus, S. (1966). *The Other Victorians: A Study of Sexuality and Pornography in Mid-Nineteenth-Century England.* New York: Basic Books.

The Pearl: A Journal of Facetive and Voluptuous Reading. London, 1879–90. New York: Grove Press (1968).

Williams, L. (1989). *Hard Core: Power, Pleasure, and the "Frenzy of the Visible."* Berkeley: University of California Press.

47

The Pornography of Proximity: From the Nineteenth-Century Stereoscope to the Present

Christian Hite

IN HIS BOOK *TECHNIQUES OF THE OBSERVER: ON VISION AND MODERNITY IN the Nineteenh Century,* Jonathan Crary argues that a rupture occurred in the nineteenth century between a formerly dominant Renaissance, or classical, model of vision and a newly emerging modern, or modernist, model of vision, and that this rupture was largely articulated in and made possible by the emergence of new visual technologies in the mid-nineteenth century, one of these visual technologies being the stereoscope. For Crary, this rupture with the formerly dominant Renaissance model of vision not only constituted a new *regime of perception* in the nineteenth century, but more importantly affected a sweeping transformation in the way the modern observer, or *seeing subject,* was configured in a wide range of social practices and domains of knowledge (1994, p. 7). One question Crary does not ask, however, but which Linda Williams has taken up in her essay entitled "Corporealized Observers: Visual Pornographies and the 'Carnal Density of Vision,' " is the question of the *linkage* between the emergence of this new "modern" observer in the nineteenth century and the simultaneous emergence of modern visual "pornographies" in the same period. While I see my essay here as largely an extension of certain implications raised by Crary and Williams, I should point out, however, that when I use the term "pornography" throughout this essay, I will be placing it in quotation marks, as I will also be doing for the term "art." The reason for this is to make an explicit textual gesture to show that neither of these terms ("pornography" or "art") refer to things or objects in their own right. There is no *thing* or *object* innately "pornography" or "art." Rather, these two (increasingly endangered) terms have functioned together as historically specific concepts or categories of *cultural distinction* that have been deployed to regulate and control the circulation of certain images and objects, certain audiences, and certain modes of interaction or cultural consumption. But just as we do not recognize the "pornographic" objects of one hundred and fifty years ago as "pornography" today (which as Walter Kendrick points out, were originally quasi-scientific studies of prostitution carried out in the name of public hygiene in the mid-nineteenth century [11-32]), I doubt very much that any of us will be able to recognize the "pornography" of one hundred and fifty years in the future using the current "content"-orientated criteria that continues to dominate our contemporary debates, notoriously summed up in the phrase "I know it when I see it." What I want to argue here, consequently, by the way of the stereoscope, is for a total reconceptualization and continued problematization of "pornography," not as a distinct object, image, or content ("I know it when I see it"), but as a particular complex *constellation of interrelations* (an *ensemble of interactions* between subject and object, viewer and image, body and machine, and between viewers and their own bodies). I also want to suggest that this reconceptualization of "pornography" as a complex constellation of interrelations is also crucial for making sense of the current explosion of new digital media and telecommunication technologies, and particularly in speculating about "Virtual Reality," in which, significantly we see the (re)emergence of digital stereoscopic vision-machines.

Both Crary and Williams, as I said, point to the emergence of the stereoscope in the midnineteenth century (along with a slew of other optical machines) as constituting a new binocular model of vision and a new "modern" observer fundamentally different from a previous Renaissance or *monocular* model of vision. Albrecht Dürer's *Draughtman Drawing a Nude* shows, for example, how this previous Renaissance model of vision was based on the conventions of *monocular* perspective: a geometrically spatialized point of view centered on a detached, unitary, rational (and in this case male) seeing subject, whose integrity as a distinct and autonomous subject was maintained and reinscribed by a separation of subject and object, viewer and image. As John Berger states, "The convention of perspective, which is unique to European art and which was first established in the early Renaissance, centers everything on the eye of the beholder. It is like a beam from a lighthouse-only instead of flight traveling outwards, appearances travel in. . . . Everything converges on to the eye as to the vanishing point of infinity. The visible world is arranged for the spectator as the universe was once thought to be arranged for God. According to the convention of perspective there is no visual reciprocity" (1976, p. 16). For Crary, these conventions of Renaissance perspective as well as its detached seeing subject are perpetuated and reinforced throughout the seventeenth and eighteenth centuries with the invention of the *camera obscura* (which was basically a box with a small opening at one end which literally embodied the monocular model of vision in its *singular lens* which was believed to impassively and mechanically register images of an objectively distinct external world. For Crary, then:

> the camera obscura is inseparable from a certain metaphysics of interiority: it is a figure for both the observer who is nominally a free-sovereign indi-

vidual and a privatized subject ... *cut off* from a public exterior world. ...
At the same time, another ... function of the camera [obscura] was to
sunder the act of seeing from the physical body of the observer, *to decorpo-
realize vision.* (1994, p. 39; emphasis added)

While Crary goes on to trace this disembodied, decorporealized model of
vision of the *camera obscura* in the philosophies of Descartes and Locke, what
is important for my discussion is still another Enlightenment philosopher,
Immanuel Kant, who, as the father of modern western aesthetics, established a theory of "art" against which modern visual "pornography" continues to be defined. Remember, since neither "art" or "pornography" refer
to any *thing* or *object,* it is only against each other that "art" or "pornography"
continue to make sense, that they continue to mutually constitute each
other. Thus Kant is extremely important since his aesthetic theory is basically a *placing of values* upon this disembodied, decorporealized model of
vision made possible by monocular perspective. Since perspective is less
abut vision than it is about *position* of *locating* an object in a geometric grid
and, subsequently, *locating* the viewer's body at an "appropriate distance"
from that object or image, it is interesting to see how Kant takes this disembodied model of vision and its detached observer *as a given* in constructing
his aesthetic hierarchy between sensory and contemplative pleasure, a hierarchy that continues to function to this day in the very structure of the
modern museum as it regulates viewers and their interactions with objects
and images through this notion of "appropriate distance." This is why you're
not supposed to become physically aroused by object or images in a
museum: true "art" is not supposed to incite a physical response in the body
of viewer. To want to reach out and physically touch an object, or heaven
forbid, to want to want to touch yourself, would be to violate this "appropriate distance," this "sacred frontier." As Lynda Nead states, for Kant "aesthetic pleasure is thus more refined than physical forms of pleasure since it
necessarily involves the 'higher' faculty of contemplation. Perhaps one of
the most influential of Kant's ideas was the axiom that the individual object
is detached in aesthetic judgement and considered simply for 'its own sake.'
The art object serves no ulterior purpose, and aesthetic judgement itself
should be disinterested; the observer's desires and ambitions should be held
in abeyance in the act of pure contemplation" (1992, p. 24). The ultimate
violation of this Kantian aesthetic of disinterested contemplation, for
example, would be for me to go to the Getty Center and masturbate to a
Greek statue, which, of course, is unthinkable for us today, and yet the
ancient myths of Narcissus and Pygmalion point to this "other" mode of
interaction as a constant threat always already there. Thus, it is important to
notice the coincidence in the nineteenth century of not only the modern
emergence of "pornography" and new visual technologies, but also of the
Victorian hysteria over masturbation.

What happens in the mid-nineteenth century with the emergence of the
stereoscope, then, is a shift from a geometrical, monocular model of vision to

a *physiological, binocular* model of vision. People like Sir David Brewster
(inventor of the Refracting Stereoscope), working in a new scientific field of
optics, noticed, for example, that when you hold a finger close in front of
your face and close one eye, and then alternate back and forth between your
right and left eye, your finger will appear to jump. But which is the "real"
visual referent? It was experiments like these into the nature of binocular
vision that led not only to the invention of the stereoscope, but to a radical
reconceptualization of vision. Suddenly the old camera obscura model of
vision in which the eye is merely a passive window for a distinct and objective external referent was replaced by a subjective model of vision that
depended intimately on the physiology of the eyes' binocular vision and on
the body of the observing subject, which now had to be seen as actively
involved in constructing its visual field: an observing body completely
enmeshed in the physical world. The external object (or visual referent) was no
longer an unproblematic "out there" separate from a distance "in here," but
rather a kind of uncanny *composite.* The idea of a detached, disembodied, disinterested model of vision (the very cornerstone of Kantian aesthetics) was
not merely discredited in the esoteric theories of a handful of scientists however. The tangible and concrete experience of interacting with stereoscopes
became, for a while, an immensely popular form of visual entertainment for
Victorian mass culture. As a result, "the loss of [monocular] perspective of
the camera obscura model of vision [with the advent of the stereoscope]
plunged both the high-modern and the low-popular observer into a *newly corporealized* immediacy of sensation" (Williams 7). And this is a crucial point,
since, as Linda Williams argues, this new model of *corporealized* vision made
explicit the fact that the public's interaction with stereoscopes was more
about the *body's vulnerability to sensation* than it was about the referents causing
those sensations (1995, p. 9). That is, the significance of the stereoscope was
not the higher degree of photographic verisimilitude or "realism" of its stere-
ographic "content," but rather its newly corporealized constellation of inter-
relations-interrelations which in their dangerous, sensual proximity (between
viewer/image, body/machine, and viewers and their own bodies) radically
violated the notion of "appropriate distance" operating in the conventions of
both monocular perspective and Kantian aesthetics.

If monocular perspective and Kantian aesthetics help to constitute and
reinforce a detached, disembodied, rational, and unitary seeing subject (a
distanced and controlled *point of view*), the stereoscope, by contrast, promoted what Williams calls "a new masturbatory 'carnal density of vision' "
(1995, p. 11). With the stereoscopic apparatus, the practice of viewing stere-
ographs in public was akin to a kind of masturbatory aesthetic: it involved
a "public" indulgence in an intimate "private" experience with an image-
machine to the sensual gratification and engagement of the physical body.
Like masturbation, however, the stereoscope (and the constellation of interrelations it made explicit) was a threat to both the detached, disinterested
seeing subject of Kantian aesthetics and the self-possessed bourgeois individual of Victorian society. If to masturbate, as understood in the economic

metaphors of the nineteenth century, was to lose *possession* of oneself, to waste or *spend* one's precious resources unproductively, then to interact with a stereoscopic image-machine involved a similar recklessness with one's self-possession, with one's sense of being positioned in the world as an autonomous point of view. Indeed, the experience of the stereoscope is a kind of giddy *reverse vertigo*. It is not so much the anxiety of falling into distant space, but of the sudden *absence of distance*, a kind of *pornography of proximity*. If the disorientation of vertigo depends on maintaining one's sense of a bounded-"self" a falling into a void of spatial distance, then the stereoscope's *reverse-vertigo* involves the dissolution of that bounded "self" (of that self- possessed point of view) as the stereoscopic object appears to devour the space in between, to rush in *too close* and *freeze* in a kind of 3-D image of tangible proximity-in-depth: a *confusion* not only of one's geophysical *spatial coordinates* of "near" and "far," but also of one's geophysical coordinates of sequential time, or duration, as the composite 3-D image that appears in the stereoscope only exists in that *continuous moment* of interaction, in the *continuous present* of the confusion between viewer and image, body and machine in the private/public intimacy of an embodied "now," which in the language of contemporary digital computing is called the "real time" interface.

As Crary states:

> Some have speculated that the very close association of the stereoscope with pornography was in part responsible for its social demise as a mode of visual consumption. Around the turn of the century sales of the device supposedly dwindled because it became linked with "indecent" subject matter . . . [But] the reasons for the collapse of the stereoscope lie elsewhere, as . . . the simulation of tangible three-dimensionally hovers uneasily at the limits of acceptable verisimilitude. (1994, p. 127)

And yet, ironically, it is precisely the simulation of tangible three-dimensionality that we see re- emerging with new digital telecommunication technologies, particularly in those surrounding "Virtual Reality." Paul Virilio, for example, refers to the virtual-reality DataSuit as a kind of "static vehicle" in which the absolute speed of electronic telecommunications (the paradoxical interval of the speed of light) creates a seemingly new relation between viewer and image, body and machine, in which, much like the stereoscope, the geophysical coordinates of space and time are collapsed in the cybernetic experience of *presence at a distance*, or what Virilio calls the remote interaction of "tactile telepresence" (1997, p. 105). Interestingly, these new relations of digital telecommunications technology outlined by Virilio do not seem so new after all, in light of the nineteenth-century stereoscope (and the complex constellation of interrelations which it makes explicit), as once again we see the "appropriate distance" of the interval (the "sacred frontier") being violated by the tactile proximity of the digital (stereoscopic) interface—or what Virilio, in a moment of Kantian aesthetics, disparaging calls "remote-control masturbation" (1994, p. 104). The ease with which Virilio *disparages* new digital media (and particularly virtual-reality "teledildoincs") as "remote-control masturbation" (i.e., as a particular *mode of interaction*) points not only to the necessity of recognizing the continued co-existence and effects of a *residual* Kantian aesthetic based on "appropriate distance" (despite the nineteenth-century rupture outlined by Crary), but more importantly, points to how this residual Kantianism continues to shore-up an increasingly problematic dichotomy between "art" and pornography." What I've tried to suggest here, by way of the stereoscope, is that the continued problematization and deconstruction of this dichotomy must first begin with the *de-familiarization* and *reconceptualization* of "pornography"–not as a distinct object, image, content, or "subject matter"–but rather as a complex *constellation of interrelations* which, growing increasingly volatile and nomadic, can no longer be contained (if they ever could) under the terms "art" and "pornography."

REFERENCES

Berger, John. *Ways of Seeing.* New York, Penguin, 1972.

Crary, Jonathan. *Techniques of the Observer: On Vision and Modernity in the Nineteenth Century.* Cambridge: MIT Press, 1994.

Kendrick, Walter. *The Secret Museum: Pornography in Modern Culture.* Berkeley: University of California Press, 1996.

Nead, Lynda. *The Female Nude: Art, Obscenity and Sexuality.* London: Routledge, 1992.

Virilio, Paul. *Open Sky.* New York: Verso, 1997.

Williams, Linda. "Corporealized Observers: Visual Pornographies and the Carnal Density of Vision." *Fugitive Images: From Photography to Video.* Ed. Patrice Petro. Bloomington: Indiana University Press, 1995. 3–41.

48

The Marquis de Sade's *Juliette*: Libertinism, Female Agency, and Pornography

Vida Pavesich

*J*ULIETTE IS THE STORY OF A YOUNG WOMAN'S EDUCATION IN THE WAYS of vice. Accordingly, her success entails that she become progressively more powerful, wealthy, and cruel. Her erotic imagination is schooled to transgress all limits methodically, and she is taught to habituate the disavowal of empathy and remorse. Her rise from rags to riches puts her in league with powerful ministers, judges, and mafia-like pope—all of whom have the power and resources to act out their sexual fantasies with impunity. Juliette represents the culmination of a tradition of male-created, female fantasy figures specific to libertine literature and pornography as it developed in the seventeenth and eighteenth centuries in England and France. Because of Sade's irreverence for gender roles and his rejection of Rousseauist recommendations for the sanctification of female modesty, his texts have been reread in the idiom of contemporary concerns for women's economic, sexual, and reproductive independence. For example, Angela Carter in the 1970s in *The Sadeian Woman* discovered the possibility of a moral pornographer in Sade. Her argument is based on Sade's refusal to see female sexuality defined in terms of its reproductive function.[1]

Our current preoccupations with the female subjectivity and agency and the representation of women in cultural history are access points for the reception of such figures as Juliette. Given that successful women are creatures with great power and wealth in *Juliette*, her character invites renewed appraisal. This is not because Juliette exhibited agency in a modern sense, or because Sade was concerned with what we would view as female emancipation, or because the Sade's libertines should be role models. My topic is how Sade appropriates themes contemporary to him and how portions of the reception history of his work can add historical density to current disagreements about images of women in pornography. In order to appreciate what *Juliette* might contribute to these issues, it will be helpful to 1) sketch out general features of the contemporary pornography disagreements, and 2) explain what influenced Sade's presentation of female characters. The latter will include examining the following themes: a) how Sade represents the culmination of libertinism; b) how Sade appropriates the male-created fantasy figure of the female heroine/narrator conventionally found in pornographic and libertine literature that preceded him, and c) how eighteenth-century women authors supplied a model for the female narrators in Sade's fiction. But before going into the historical material I will clarify how my discussion is intended to be related to the contemporary issues that will be taken up again in the second half of the paper.

CONTEMPORARY PORNOGRAPHY ISSUES

The pornography disagreements overall are about agency because they reflect the broader effort of women to come to terms with conditions they did not initially or ever choose, namely, a male-authored literature and are that has tended to depict women primarily as sexual beings. The pornography debates are, in part, a continuation of themes that were part of the libertine ethos in the eighteenth century. I am not arguing that Sade or the libertine tradition that preceded him has directly influenced these debates except where Sadean ideas, scenarios, or the name of Sade are appropriated as tropes. I am isolating a specific theme that occurs in both contexts.

The power of Sade's name lives on in our word "sadism," which tends to connote male power. In current debates the word is shorthand for the fantasy of an individual incapable of reciprocity and who straddles the border between what we normally consider human and inhuman. The fruit of Sade's lucidity, conditioned by the age in which he lived, continues to haunt us and have meaning because he articulated, like no one else, the point at which the human becomes inhuman and the other become a thing. In *Must We Burn Sade?* Simone de Beauvoir draws attention to this when she describes Sade's libertines as a combination of passionate sexual appetites and emotional apartness.[2] Sade is the ultimate pimp because this emotionally separate individual finds its ultimate form in the figure of a woman who is nonetheless a male creation. Sade's theatricalizes gender roles—as for example in the transvestite marriage between Juliette and Noirceuil at the end of *Juliette* and the frequent switching between roles of aggressor and victim that occur between the libertines who are momentarily on a par with each other. This suggests a mobility of power that relies in part on a blurring of genders.

The anti-porn position generally rests on a traditional gendering on this refusal of the other and sees this refusal in terms of an either/or power situation. The type of psychosexual imagery that has come to symbolize most dramatically the rejection of the other, what we now call sadism, often focuses the selection of what counts as pornography. For example, both Andrea Dworkin and Catharine MacKinnon define pornography as sexually explicit material involving violence and degradation that violates women's rights because it creates and environment that is hostile to them. MacKinnon graphically describes pornography as sexual abuse and battering that is often filmed or photographed. "In pornography women are gang raped so they can be filmed," writes MacKinnon in *Only Words.*[3] Similar passages can be found in Dworkin's writings. In addition, Dworkin's essay "The Marquis de Sade," affirms an identity between the cruelty represented in Sade's fiction and biographical facts we have about Sade's life. She also states that Sade's importance is not as a deviant but as "Everyman." Sade treated the women in his life despicably but this treatment pales next to the fantasies contained in his novels. Both MacKinnon and Dworkin blur the distinction between fictional representations in pornography and real acts of degradation. Both writers focus on images that portray sadistic acts as a representation of the bulk of pornography. Rather than trying to simply refute their claims, I want to add another perspective to the conflicts between antiporn feminists and those who oppose censorship–at least as it turns on the issue of sadism.

My sketch of contemporary positions is in no way exhaustive, but will delineate the basic contours of the disagreements. MacKinnon and Dworkin are the most vocal spokespersons for the position that sees porn a blatant discrimination against women and as a perpetuation of rigid gender hierarchies that victimize women. But others see pornography and erotica as staging areas for exploring female sexuality and identity. For example, Nicola Pitchford, in a recent article about the cultural and political contestation over pornography, maintains that contemporary feminism has no choice but to function in "postmodern conditions." That is, she believes it is necessary to see representations as a "crucial political arena" just as the antiporn feminists believe, but that is not fruitful to maintain a rigid oppositional stance to an inherited position in the hope of being liberated into a "new conceptual space." In *Sade, Fourier, and Loyola*, Roland Barth first drew attention to the impossibility of a neutral vantage point when he stated that there is no language site outside bourgeois ideology. For women not to have a neutral vantage point means that there are no clear moral categories from which to judge that men are essentially the aggressors and women essentially the victims. We do not have the "luxury of a fixed identity," says Pitchford. We cannot step outside our history and thus we cannot step outside the fact of how we have been represented. But to see and accept this is not necessarily to deny agency, because the subject position is multiple and therefore admits of multiple readings of inherited texts. Arguing against Catharine MacKinnon, Pitchford states that by eliminating the sexual practices found in male representations of sexuality and also the representations themselves, women limit not only their idea of sexual pleasure but severely constrict a sense of what the concept "woman" can come to mean.[4]

Similarly, Drucilla Cornell advocates a new "representational politics" that affirms the exploration of new forms of sexually explicit material that challenges "the stereotypes of femininity governing the presentation of the female 'sex' in mainstream pornography."[5] Linda Williams, in *Hard Core*, also discusses the issue of multiple subject positions and an oscillation between sadistic and masochistic stances. Both Williams and Cornell cite examples related to the development of woman-produced pornography that will be considered toward the end of this paper. These disputes resonate with themes whose partial historical roots are in libertine fiction.

The idea of multiple subject positions and a consideration of gender orientation in relation to questions of agency are useful entry point for rereading a text insofar as rereading is considered a from of resistance by feminism. However, Sade's texts can be reread only up to a point. The fundamental issue is how Sade's libertines give voice to the fictional dissolution of all human categories. Postmodernism seems to echo and sometimes celebrate this dissolution, but for Sade what is at stake is the annihilation of the other for the sake of the libertine sovereignty of the individual. Insofar as relatedness in some sense is a necessary condition of what it means to be human, the libertine writings that culminated in Sade's fiction posed most dramatically the issue of the relation to the other. To analyze such texts from the perspective of gender is partly to articulate and seek to resist the obliteration of the other and all that this stands for.

SADE AND LIBERTINISM

Libertine literature, especially after 1740, was characterized by a blend of eroticism and philosophizing that Michel Foucault would describe as a "compulsion to pursue sex as knowledge." In Sade's work orgies alternate with metaphysical speculation plus parodies and criticisms of social mores, Christian dogma, and contemporaneous philosophical issues. Sex is thus linked to and is the vehicle for the dissolution of customs and beliefs that have provided human orientation. This procedure has literary and philosophical antecedents, although it must be stressed that even though Sade's heroines and heroes articulate philosophical positions, he was not writing philosophical treatises. Sade was a novelist; he was not Andrea Dworkin's advocate. This paper is not intended to be a "rehabilitation" of Sade so much as it is an attempt to understand his influence from a particular perspective. But first, what is libertinism?

The word "libertine," in early contexts, referred simply to freethinking, to a rejection of past customs and a general questioning of religious and political authority associated with the epochal change that ushered in the birth of modernity. As J. S. Spink argues in *French Free Thought from Gassendi to Voltaire*, this impulse later evolved into the modern tradition of skepticism in philosophy and had no connection with eroticism even though skeptics were often accused of having dissolute habits.[6] Early "libertine" writing was thus basically a critical stance toward orthodoxy, and eroticism was used as a means of attack not only against the freethinkers, but also to slander the Church and the Crown.

In addition to referring to early free-thinking, the word "libertine" also came to designate an erotic-philosophic tributary represented in the tradition of libertine fiction. Although there were a few female libertines, the usual scenario of the seventeenth and eighteenth centuries portrays the calculating male libertine's conquest of the sensitive female victim, as for example, in the "immortal"–as Sade calls him–Samuel Richardson's *Clarissa*. In the eighteenth-century, libertine fiction often involved the effort to dominate and humiliate one's erotic conquest. As in the case of Crebillon's Versac and Laclos' Valmont and Merteuil, the libertine scenario, according to Raymond Trousson, came to include "an eroticism in the service of a Nietzscheian will to power allied with a cerebral sadism that found cruel pleasure by observing the reaction of victims."[7] Following closely in the steps of Laclos, Sade–who oddly doesn't mention Laclos–constructs a universe in which both men and women can be either the cold perpetrators or the recipients of eroticized violence.

A set of conflicting themes emerges. Woman has great power in the Sadean universe, but at the price of dissolving the ties traditionally connecting her to the sphere of women. Women are no longer part of a repressive domestic economy in Sade; they leave home but they have nowhere to go–except to make their fortunes as prostitutes, thereby admitting themselves to the libertine male world of power, knowledge, and money. This acquisition takes place within the confines of a dissolving feudal and aristocratic world, one of isolated enclaves: chateaus, convents, monasteries, and dungeons. Even though the men had at least nominal social positions, all libertines, male and female, are set apart from the rest of society by these dramatic devices–devices that mirror the rigid psychological apartness of which Beauvoir and Klossowski first wrote and which ensures immunity from punishment for crimes.

JULIETTE AND THE LIBERTINE PROSTITUTE HEROINES

Sade's work is the culmination both of libertine fiction and of the pornographic tradition that developed into a genre during the period of his maturity. In *Juliette*, Sade looks back critically on specific landmarks of fiction as though all had led up to him. He focuses on the pornographic works. He cites a work attributed to Argens, *Thérèse philosophe* [1748], Chorier's *L'Academie des dames* [1680], Latouche's *Le Portier des Chartreux* [1743], and Mirabeau's *L'Education de Laure*. Only *Thérèse philosophe* came close to fulfilling his requirement that erotic discovery fuse with philosophic inquiry. The word philosophe stood for the Enlightenment, and the title *Thérèse philosophe* echoed an important anonymous work of the early enlightenment that was later published by Voltaire, *Le philosophe*. *Thérèse* was a witty, worldly freethinker–a philosophe–who held everything up to the light of reason. In doing so she finds that reason must be our guide in dispelling illu-

sions. One such illusion is that God gave us religion. Religion and morality
are merely human constructions designed to maintain social order. But she
also reasons that God gave us passions and therefore they are good. To
indulge them is good for us and for the greater good of mankind. Happiness
is based on a utilitarian calculus that weighs pleasure from the perspective
of a self-love that is the "motive force of all our actions," but one that necessarily brings more pleasure and therefore happiness into the world.[8]

Juliette's biography follows the trajectory of the libertine whore story
found in earlier literature. Like Thérèse she examines religious belief, the
role of sensual pleasure in procuring happiness, and she uses her wit to
advance herself. Like Fanny in Cleland's novel *Fanny Hill,* she marries a
respectable man, Monsieur de Lorsange. But the similarities stop here.
Although Juliette is schooled to place her pleasures first, she never considers
the "greater good." And once she discovers that religion is merely a local
custom, she rejects a belief in God. If religion and morality are merely local
customs, they have no binding force. So she is free to poison her husband,
take his money, and scoot off to Italy with her entourage for a season of art
appreciation and unbridled dissolution. Her story continues for several hundred pages of ever more elaborate debauchery. Juliette becomes a grandiose
figure who deals in poisons, establishes an exclusive gambling establishment
and bordello, and prostitutes herself to heads of state in order to abscond
with their treasuries. She stages the brutal murder of four hundred people
for the delectation and erotic stimulation of a jaded nobility. She participates
vicariously in the libertine Clairwil's dream of committing a crime so
heinous that it will continue after her death. According to Kathryn Norbert,
Juliette transcends the "whore biography"; Juliette becomes a true roué, a
teacher, and "the embodiment of Sade's materialist philosophy."[9] She fuses
the cerebral sadism of the Marquise de Merteuil with the mobility and cav-
alier attitude of the libertine whore. These genres supply the prototypes for
the male-authored, female fantasy figure whose intellectual and financial
independence is achieved through the development of her rational powers
and through prostitution. The social mobility accorded to her through prostitution affords her the opportunity to acquire the "education" that male libertines are assumed to have as a birthright.

WOMEN AUTHORS

There is another piece to the puzzle about how women achieved such narrative significance in Sade. This strand of the story concerns women's social
and artistic position at the time. It must be noted that the ingredients for
imagining women both with a certain amount of agency and as objects of
masculine fear can be found in the position and representation of women
generally in eighteenth-century society. Sade's creations as well as the backlash against women that followed the Revolution are thus made more intel-
ligible. Salon women had some power to set the parameters of social and

cultural tastes. But as Erica Harth reminds us, even though the "eighteenth-century salonniere was the indispensible social center of the group, [she] stood outside its discourse, monitoring and protecting her flock."[10]

Figures with less than noble origins such as Louis XV's mistress, Madame du Barry, attained positions of great wealth and influence. Coincident with this was a growing distress "over the loosening of familial connections" and the threat posed by women who rejected their "natural" maternal roles.[11] This was fueled by Rousseau's codification of the rules for the proper education and sphere for women in *Emile* and an increasing acceptance of the idea that women's supposedly more refined sensibility destined them for a restricted life.[12] In his discussion of the extent to which libertine fiction mirrors historical reality, Raymond Trousson suggests that libertine men also wanted to put women back in their place, although that "place" differs. Women were merely interchangeable objects of desire that covered up the libertine's terror of ennui in a world that had lost its values and any transcendent meaning.[13]

Furthermore, as mentioned, women are associated with the rise of the novel as a genre. The genre itself was attacked on both aesthetic and moral grounds according to Marcel Hénaff. The Church and moralists saw the novel as frivolous and as responsible for disseminating false ideas of virtue. And because women were particularly successful in developing this genre, they were accused by men such as Voltaire, Rousseau, and Diderot of rejecting their roles as "guardians of the family" by "demanding freedom of (public and published) speech and freedom in amorous relationships."[14] Others, including Prevost, Marivaux, Crebillon, Duclos, d'Alembert, and Laclos defended both the novel and women's participation in developing the form. Women were considered more knowledgeable and of greater sensibility than men—particularly in matters of love—and so more suited to observe and record the goings-on depicted in novels. As Hénaff points out, this amounts to nothing more than "favorable prejudice," but it does reveal something important about "women's privileged relationship to the novel, and to narrative discourse." The novel, says Hénaff, is connected to several contemporaneous changes. It represents "territory to be conquered" because it was a minor genre not governed by [male] canonical rules, and so women could enter freely into its construction.

Furthermore, this effort coincides with the demand for equality between the sexes and the bourgeois demand for equality between individuals. Thus, the novel, with women often at the helm, is connected to the rise of the bourgeoisie and the writing of stories of "the individual in search of power, money, recognition, and pleasure." The novel involves "the advent of subjective authority, the staging of individual destiny, the demand that the subject as such have a story, an that this story be the adventure of his desire."[15] If the novel involves this and women are also authors, they present a challenge to centuries-old conventions about the social order of things, an order in which women are everywhere viewed as naturally subservient to men. In addition, novels written by women were also criticized for dealing with sexual pleasure, which critics such as Rousseau maintained women should know nothing about. *Juliette* is most definitely a story about the adventure of an individual's desire and the acquisition of power and knowledge. Sade thus draws on the ambiguity of women's actual position in society and as authors in their own right—positions that challenge social and literary conventions. In addition, the feudal class and the bourgeoisie meet in Sade's fiction in a quest for power.

INTEGRATION OF LIBERTINE, PROSTITUTE, AND AUTHOR IN SADE

Sade synthesizes all the above factors: libertine literature, prostitute heroines, and female narrators. Sade went against the grain; he made no exception to his literary program of inverting all standards and mocking all customs. He constructed libertines who applaud and encourage women to develop their intelligence and free themselves from the slavery imposed by the "unnatural" roles determined by social mores and to learn everything about sex and power. These women occupy the place of the narrative "I," as Hénaff points out. Women carry the narrative along and men are contained within their stories. The libertine heroes such as Noirceuil, St. Fond, Brisatesta, and the Pope already have an identity, an identity to which Juliette gains access through her education or countereducation. By becoming the victimizer she removes any possibility of becoming victimized unless she freely chooses to do so in a scenario with another libertine.

Juliette's mentor Noirceuil, during a period of instruction, asks rhetorically whether it makes sense to be virtuous in a very corrupt age [147]. The women, and people generally, most victimized in Sade's work are those who do not develop their intelligence, or who—like Justine—attempt to live according to conventional notions of virtue, and who do not follow what Sade understands as their own desires. The cannibal giant Minski reasons that Juliette's coveted maid Augustine deserved to die and become part of Minski's repast because "she did as she was told but was far from doing what she wanted." [592][16] Sade was clearly not a feminist; Sade's work is filled with representations of gratuitous violence against both women and men, but Minski's logic is intended throughout as support for Sade's thought experiment.[17] Accordingly, Juliette is repeatedly praised not only for her beauty, but for her intelligence, learning, and cruelty. And she enters the society of the nobility as a prostitute wherein she learns to gain control of the parameters of her exchange.[18]

As in *Thérèse philosophe*, the education that fuses sex and philosophy involves clearing away prejudices that prevent "enlightenment," that is, that prevent deciding on and following the course that would lead to the greatest pleasure. At the outset Juliette, unlike the male characters, has everything to learn. Her adventure begins under the tutelage of the Abbess Delbène who urges Juliette to follow Nature's "single precept [which is] to enjoy oneself, at the expense of no matter whom," a recommendation that, if spoken by a woman, flies in the face of the male order [52]. She states: "manners and morals are an arbitrary affair, and can be nothing else. Nature prohibits nothing; but laws are dreamt up by men, and these petty regulations pretend to impose certain restraints upon people . . . [these laws] are not in any sense sacred, in any way legitimate from the viewpoint of philosophy." [51] Maximizing pleasure depends on the espousal of atheism and the deconstruction of social bonds. In this text it is a woman who first articulates the parameters of the philosophical basis of Sade's concept of solipsistic libertinage. It is also note worthy that Juliette's apprenticeship begins and ends in the company of women and that female libertinage, at least in Sade, does not necessarily require the company or support of men except as expedients.

Sade's philosophical female libertines emerged from the female-training-ground scenario that had been a stock item in modern erotic literature since Aretino, but with a twist. Juliette's predecessors in male-authored erotic fiction never really challenge the male order in spite of their independence. They are simply the speakers of sex, the voices of male desire. This inherited position becomes Juliette's staging ground.

The main characteristic of fictional libertine characters generally, whether they inhabit the pornographic works or the novels of Laclos and Richardson, is an exaggerated emphasis on intellectual control. Sade plays ventriloquist to the Abbess Delbène who states that "reason is nothing other than the scales we weigh objects in, and balancing those of those objects that are external to ourselves, the reasoning mechanism tells us what conclusions we are to come to: when the scales tip beneath what looks to be the greatest pleasure, it is to that side our judgement always inclines." [34] Once conventional morality has been disposed of, the libertines are free to pursue maximal sensation, which is the only true reality.

The Abbess exhibits vast learning, and she imparts this to her eager student Juliette. She compiles and comments on the epistemologies, metaphysics, and anthropologies of her day. For example, in a parody of the Cartesian method and the theological tradition to which it is heir, Delbène investigates what can be know by unaided reason, which she states has been given to her by nature. "For guide in the night I have none buy my reason, and directly I bring up its light to help me in the task of examining all these competing aspirants to my belief" [30]. The notion that our ideas prove the existence of the external world or anything else is dismissed as rubbish. Our imagination manufactures the reality of the external world as well as the existence of God, and thus she continues the intellectual fabrication of the philosophical and ethical foundations of the libertine's solipsistic world. She also inquires about the consequences of "the tendency most men still have of according the same degree of belief to a fable as to a geometrical proof" [29]. God is merely a "short cut of skipping in a single great leap back to a primary cause" that results from the weariness of seeking to find a "cause in every effect" [36]. She taps into the Bible criticism that was also part of the clandestine literature and examines the relativity of all religions, the implausibility of the Christian God (a "grandiose phantom"), and ridicules the notion of a chosen people. [37]. It is only on the basis of her inverted dogmatism–the assertion of the relativity of all morals and the illusoriness of all religious objects–that Delbène can maintain that no moral code is of worth.[19]

Sade refuses to operate in gray areas, even though much of life is lived in gray areas. Either there is a moral criterion or there isn't. For Sade, moral codes dissolve once reason focuses its intense beam of light on their flimsy support and on the futility of believing that salvation is the result of good works. Sade's characters deduce a moral nihilism from their first principles, and the logical outcome is a justification of the split between the libertine and the world conceived as a community of men. The libertine, sequestered away in chateaus and castles and bent on destroying the "absurd notion of fraternity," attempts to be impervious to the influence of society. The tension between the reactive discourse of libertinism and the interactive notion of the self that was appearing everywhere at the time [Rousseau, Diderot, Hume, and Marivaux] provides us a historical mirror for the conundrums about reconciling or not reconciling domination, intersubjectivity, power, and pleasure that fuel the censorship debates. Sade wrote fiction; there is no philosophical consideration of the functional necessity of human institutions that regulate the differences among men and how institutions are necessary for the continuance of the human species.

Libertinism emphasized a completely rational approach to passion, to sexual experience, and to relationships and hence contributes to the emotional apartness referred to earlier. For Sade the goal is the achievement of an absolute autonomy that parallels the quest for an equally absolute pleasure. However, Sade's notion of pleasure goes against the shifting historical grain by requiring equality of intelligence in both men and women and by portraying Juliette as escaping the slavery that is usually imposed by women's traditional roles. The libertine Noirceuil, Juliette's next major mentor, enjoys Juliette's company not only because she possesses "the world's most beautiful ass," but because of her wit. Juliette in turn, once she is opulently ensconced in Noirceuil's house as his mistress and procuress, muses on the reasons for her respect for such a villain "whose disorders were faultlessly systematized." . . . "I loved Noirceuil for his libertinage, for his mental qualities" [159]. The libertines respect each other's diamond-hard lucidity, the wit that Barthes says "is the value of sex," its effervescence, its guarantee of vice.[20] But Sade maintains that women possess greater sensibility. The ideology connected with this supposedly natural sensibility is women's role as guardian of the hearth. But when great sensibility is combined with intellectual control and a deadening of emotional responses, women become more vicious libertines than men.[21]

Nature had increasingly come to be seen by Enlightenment thinkers as a moral criterion. But since women had been closely identified with nature, nature was also the criterion used to justify woman's subservient and dependent position in the scheme of things. Sade turns this around. Nature is a source for him too; it offers models for libertine crimes. The Abbess Delbène and many others instruct Juliette to imitate Nature's ways in order to learn the infractions of her laws and see "the queen melt before your impulsive desires . . . crawling toward you, begging to be shackled by your irons" [19]. Nature's destructiveness as manifested in plagues, earthquakes, and natural disasters is the justification for libertinism. Delbène describes a "dialectic" in which the libertine battles for supremacy over Nature by purposely fusing with her. Delbène's methods include understanding Nature's ways and imitating her indifference to human existence by cultivating apathy in the perpetuation of ever greater crimes.[22] Nature is not the rational and meaningful order esteemed by tradition and touted as moral source." Nature is a chaotic and teeming morass of birth, death, and destruction that supplies an ironic countermoral criterion. Hénaff argues that Sade's proof that libertinism is natural is based on woman becoming libertine, "nature is not what she seems: not the ultimate referee of norms but their silence."

The upshot of this is that Sade's libertines demythologize the Enlightenment; both mainstream Enlightenment thinkers and Sade's libertines search for standards of truth in "the light of reason and experience" alone. But for Sade the vehicles of this search are a satirical and obscene social criticism mouthed by prostitutes, corrupt government officials, and corrupt clergy. From this seemingly postmodern novel with its demonstration of the relativity of all customs and standards and its rejection of legitimation for any particular standard, a situation emerges in which "Crime," according to the libertine Noirceuil, "is not in any sense real." In other words, there is a denial of any social bond, a reductio ad absurdum of the loss of the idea of God and monarch. The deconstruction of the phantasmatic Christian God along with notions of remorse and pity then legitimate only the reign of the pleasure principle. Anything goes, but this "anything" is achieved by careful calculation, not impulsive behavior. The pursuit of pleasure is buttressed by a proliferation of ever more intricate murderous orgies in which people are merely props for the libertine's imaginative excesses and his or her habituation to apathy and evil.

As a prostitute Juliette reinscribes the master/slave, masculine/feminine hierarchy that operates loosely in this text. Yet Juliette's powerful position bequeathes an ambiguity to later commentators in so far as a conceptual space has opened within that part of the masculine imaginary preoccupied with representations of prostitutes and his blurring of genders. Madame Durand's penis-like clitoris is only one indication that gender is in one sense relatively unimportant for Sade. Ideally gender would disappear, especially given how Sade's libertines regale the rectum as the democratic and gender-unspecific preferred site of sexual gratification. Furthermore, Juliette is not the unthreatening male fantasy of the sexual heroine tradition of which she is the successor. She soars above and crawls below the independent and immodest yet compliant prostitute who articulates and satisfies the erotic urges of elite men. This creature was little more than a mirror of male lust. Juliette is still in some sense a blank slate, as Jane Gallop has suggested, and certainly she is a male fantasy. And although she is one of many powerful female characters in the novel, she is not around merely to restore virility, unless she sees this as a stepping stone on her way to power, wealth, and independence. She is acquisitive and coldly rational beyond anything ever imagined in the earlier literature. Her apathy and cruelty led to Max Horkheimer and Theodor Adorno in *The Dialectic of Enlightenment* to find in her a template for their view of the nihilistic consequences of instrumental rationality in modernity.

As a model for female independence, there are obvious shortcomings. Furthermore, if the libertine whore is much more a male fantasy than a social reality and if the independent, free-thinking libertine whore disappeared as a literary figure after her absorption by Sade, why is it important to pay attention to her? Robert Darnton suggests that *Thérèse philosophe*, *Juliette*'s most immediate predecessor in pornographic libertine literature, be seen as a thought experiment and as a challenge to the accepted values of the Old Regime and to the shortcomings of the institutions of marriage and motherhood. But Thérèse is also important as a thought experiment because she presents the image of a financially and sexually independent, educated woman projected into a liminal space and thus available to the imagination at whatever point in history she might become an object of interest or even of need. Sade wrote that only Thérèse came close to being a libertine. She had the independence and wit that were ingredients in the character of Juliette, but she did not represent the serious challenge to the male order that Darnton suggests. She did not inflame subsequent commentators, and her author did not lend his name to a type of behavior that is widely reviled as antihuman.

James Turner's comments about male-authored female libertines in English literature suggest a way to approach the legacy of the female narrator. He writes that "such representations relate to the world rather than reflecting it or concealing it: to treat them as pure fantasy is to distance them from their own 'reality-effect'; to treat them as direct evidence of the condition of women is to ignore their ontological complexity, their Pygmalionesque status as ideology made flesh . . . they may embody pertinent criticism and valid psychological observation, and they may develop a certain animation and autonomy beyond what their author would license in 'real life.' "[23] To treat Sade's female libertines as direct evidence of historical female autonomy or to treat Sade as an advocate of libertine crimes on the scale represented in his novels is to miss the point. The animation and autonomy of these fictional characters has been projected into a liminal space and has become the myth-like material of reception. We are free to reread them through contemporary lenses, although it is important to maintain a distinction between the eighteenth and twentieth centuries. The autonomy of the fictional characters acquires a pregnant historical ambiguity; they entered a time-capsule and have been reborn at a later time in different rhetorical and historical circumstances, not as essences but as problems. Our intense focus on gender and our use of gender as an analytic tool select Juliette's sex as a theoretical object.

JULIETTE AND CONTEMPORARY
PORNOGRAPHY

The libertine/pornographic tradition culminating in Juliette should be an ingredient in a genealogy of the female sexual subject. This is not because Margot, Thérèse, or Juliette express agency in a modern sense, but because they are part of the historic/symbolic platform occasioning discussions about female agency,and such discussion can be enriched by including them. Sade's legacy is complicated. The sexologist Krafft-Ebing, who coined the terms "sadism" and "masochism" in the 1880s, helped make Sade's name central to psychoanalytic theory and hence to much film and culture theory. The early "compact libertines" such as Juliette, Fanny Hill, and Thérèse have been fragmented into parts, into fetishes and perversions.[24] Furthermore, sadism and masochism as currently understood are often the stumbling blocks for feminism as we have seen in MacKinnon's and Dworkin's writing. It is held that sadomasochistic practices and the representations of such practices suppress the possibility of true intersubjectivity in sexual relations and literally snuff out the agency of women in so far as one person is totally dominated by the other. Leaving aside the fact that male submissives predominate the world of consensual heterosexual S/M, and that these practices involve mutual agreements and play, nowhere does the feminist anti-porn case seem stronger than in that portion of pornography that represents women as victims of violence.

Pornography is said to involve the pursuit of pleasure. Linda Williams, historian of porn videos, argues that the "concentration camp orgasm," identified as such by Andrea Dworkin, is the pleasure from pure victimization that anti-porn feminists associate with S/M porn, is an impossible pleasure, because pleasure requires some "leeway for play within assigned sexual roles." She acknowledges that sadomasochistic fantasy seem regressive to feminism in that it obsessively repeats images of rigid, "non mutual forms of power and pleasure–the very same hierarchically based notions that have traditionally prevented women from actively seeking their pleasure or that have forced them to pay for it in advance." But is is important to view fantasy realistically. She suggest that sadomasochistic fantasy has important lessons to teach; it can reveal the necessity of power in sexual and gender relations and in the production of pleasure. The variations and permutations of these themes were endlessly elaborated by Sadeian characters who cultivate apathy and for the most part allow no leeway in their roles. The exceptions are those special situations between the libertines themselves–most notably the precarious leeway between Juliette and Clairwil or Juliette and Durand. "Leeway" would constitute a great threat to a world in which one is either a master or a victim.[25] Leeway would involve acknowledging the reality of the "other." But Williams, appreciating the complexities of sexuality and who, in a sense, is rereading the Sadean legacy in contemporary terms, stresses the importance of not viewing that power as fixed.[26]

Although Angela Carter's vision of Sade as posing the problem of the possibility of a "moral pornographer" may be inappropriate when considered in relation to the eighteenth century, she was not off base when seen in the light of Sade's legacy. Carter suggests that a moral pornographer might use pornography, with its "logic of a world of absolute sexual license for all genders . . . as a critique of current relations between the sexes."[27] This is precisely what Drucilla Cornell documents in her analysis of the works of Candida Royalle and Ona Zee, both of whom produce pornography that Cornell locates in the domain of feminist practice. For example, Ona Zee's film *Learning the Ropes*, is about a ritualistic sadomasochistic performance in which the viewer see both the performance, which is controlled by the woman, and the fantasy behind it. According to Cornell, the dominatrix is presented as a performance that undermines the reality of the scene because it is seen in relation to the actual relationship between Ona and her husband Frank rather than in terms of the mythologizing of the dominatrix as the Phallic Mother that normally occurs in porn.

It may be that anti-porn feminists are indirectly sensing the complicated legacy of libertinism with its reduction of personal relationships to power differentials. They may also be indirectly sensing the complicated position of women in libertine literature—their odd freedom and provocative challenge to the male order that is at the same time firmly rooted in that same order. They may also be sensing the ethical lacuna bequeathed by Enlightenment thought that is expressed by Thérèse's proclamation that an emphasis on individual pleasure would lead to utilitarian benevolence. This last assumption did not pass muster before the critical acumen of Sade's libertines.

That women writers, intellectuals, and artists have commandeered control of the debates about the significance of pornography in popular culture signifies the choice women now know they have in relation to conditions they did not choose.[28] Women are actively involved in shaping a discourse in which they have been mutely represented historically; and it is a tradition of enormous importance to how women are viewed and view themselves. Through their disagreements about the status and effects of pornography, women are rereading the historical subject position partially marked out by Thérèse and Juliette.

I will end this paper by noting that male-created sexual fantasies are not the only ingredients to be taken into account in formulating concepts of the female sexual subject. Nor is this essay intended to be part of the tradition of attempt to rehabilitate Sade.[29] Sade and his predecessors and successors are part of the collective past. Women and men may make history but perhaps not always in relation to condition of their own choice—to adapt a thought from Marx. There is a creative tension to be exploited in the distance between the historical Sade and the position of late twentieth-century interpreters. This plays itself out in part in the dilemmas that have emerged in relation to interiority and its denial. Questioning the authorities of the past is part of the original impulse of libertine thinking in modernity.

NOTES

1 *The Sadeian Woman and the Ideology of Pornography* (New York: Pantheon Books, 1978).

2. Beauvoir writes that the libertine "compensates for separateness by deliberate tyranny . . . and shrinks from the kind of equality which is created by mutual pleasure," in *The 120 Days of Sodom and Other Writings,* trans. Austryn Wainhouse and Richard Seaver (New York: Grove Weidenfeld, 1987), p. 22.

3. (Cambridge: Harvard University Press, 1993), p. 15.

4. "Reading Feminism's Pornography Conflict: Implications for Postmodernist Reading Strategies" in *Sex Positives? The Cultural Politics of Dissident Sexualities,* edited by Thomas Foster, Carol Siegel, and Ellen E. Berry [Genders 25] (New York: New York University Press, 1997), p. 5, *passim.*

5. *The Imaginary Domain: Abortion, Pornography, & Sexual Harassment* (New York and London: Routledge, 1995), p. 97.

6. (London: University of London, The Athlone Press, 1960), ch. 1. Spink also states that libertine philosophical texts were basically of two types and they were published clandestinely in France in the eighteenth century. One type was devoted to the history of religions and particularly to Christianity. The other consisted of "essays which were atheistic, deterministic, and materialistic" [282]. The clandestine tracts were anonymous, but some were attributed to erudites of the early part of the century, particularly to Nicolas Fréret, who is said to have written the *Histoire critique du Christianisme ou Examen de la religion chretienne* which criticizes the authenticity of the gospels and maintains that the success of the Christian church was primarily for political reasons.

7. *Préface,* p. xli.

8. *Thérèse philosophe, ou mémoires pour servir à l'histoire du P. Dirrag et de Mlle Eradice,* in *The Forbidden Best-Sellers of Pre-Revolutionary France,* Robert Darnton (New York: W. W. Norton & Co., 1995), p. 299, *passim.*

9. "The Libertine Whore: Prostitution in French Pornography from Margot to Juliette," in *The Invention of Pornography: Obscenity and the Origins of Modernity, 1500–1800,* ed. Lynn Hunt (New York: Zone Books, 1996), pp. 247–48.

10. In *Cartesian women: Versions and Subversions of Rational Discourse in the Old Regime* (Ithaca and London: Cornell University Press, 1992), p. 33.

11. In *The Twilight of the Goddesses: Women and Representation in the French Revolutionary Era* (New Brunswick N.J.: Rutgers University Press, 1992), Madelyn Gutwirth examines the changes that occurred in the representation of women as the rococo period came to a close and the ideal of domesticity and separate spheres for men and women became *de rigueur.* Gutwirth is not concerned with erotic literature, except for section on Laclos and a brief treatment of Sade's *Justine,* but her broad treatment of women's eclipse nonetheless indirectly substantiates a portion of my argument.

12. See Anne C. Vila, "Sex and Sensibility: Pierre Roussel's *Système physique et moral de la femme,*" in *Representations* 52 (Fall 1995): 76–93. Vila refers to Roussel's influential theories on sensibility as "a new biology of enlightenment" wherein perfectibility involved "typecasting men and women so as to insert them into a fixed hierarchy." She claims that Roussel's sexual divisions were undertaken primarily to save his theories form their own inconsistencies.

13. *Préface to Romans Libertins du XVIIIe Siècle* (Paris: Presses Universitaires de France, 1978), p. 288.

14. *Sade: l'invention du corps libertin* (Paris: Presses Universitaires de France, 1978, p. 288.

15. Hénaff, pp. 289–91.

16. All pagination in the text is from the Austryn Wainhouse translation of *Juliette* (New York: Grove Weidenfeld).

17. There is much gratuitous violence directed toward men as well. I am not arguing that conventional notions of virtue are worthless merely because they are socially constructed. Sade presents a limit condition, a situation devoid of taboos. Leszek Kolakowski isolates what he takes to be the most dangerous characteristic of modernity: "the disappearance of taboo." He goes to say: "Various traditional human bonds which make communal life possible, and without which our existence would be regulated only by greed and fear, are not likely to survive without a taboo system, and it is perhaps better to believe in the validity of even apparently silly taboos than to let them all vanish." He notes the disappearance of sexual taboos and slippage in the area of incest and pedophilia as well as loss of respect for the dead. In "On Modernity, Barbarity, and Intellectuals," *Modernity on Endless Trial* (Chicago: University of Chicago Press, 1990), p. 13.

18. See also, Lucienne Frappier-Mazur's book *Writing the Orgy: Power and Parody in Sade*, trans. By Gillian C. Gill (Philadelphia: University of Pennsylvania Press, 1996). Frappier-Mazur notes Juliette's freedom of movement and its inseparability from libertinism and transgression. She also draws attention to the threat posed by women during this period as well as an anxiety that led to the idea that "classes and groups needed to be separated by impassable barriers. . . . These social contradictions and upheavals–exacerbated, warped, and confused–structure Sade's novel. The male libertines' furious hostility to their female victims warns us that these women are symbolically representing something. Quoting Mary Douglas' book *Purity and Danger*, she notes that it suggests a parallel with the violent class rivalries that run through the whole of society–as if relations between the sexes 'had to bear the tensions of the strongly competitive social system,' and as if it became all the more necessary to reaffirm the superiority of the male principle because of its 'vulnerability to female influence,'" pp. 1, 59–60.

19. Charles Taylor notes the inconsistencies in enlightenment materialism and how "Sade's views bring out, as a foil . . . the invisible background of Enlightenment humanism. . . . Just to be a materialist is to have an undetermined ethical position." *Sources of the Self: The Making of the Modern Identity* (Cambridge: Harvard University Press, 1989), p. 336.

20. *Sade, Fourier, and Loyola*, trans. Richard Miller (Baltimore and London: The Johns Hopkins University Press, 1997), p. 170.

21. According to Anne Vila, Sade has provided "an intriguing counterpoint to the medical complementarianism that emerged in the late eighteenth century" associated with the enlightenment theory of sensibility articulated by medical anthropologists such as Pierre Roussel. She claims that Sade's work can be seen not only as an "ironic turn" on the novel of sensibility but also on the sexual complementarianism dictated by the bimorphic medical model that supports the position that women's sensibility was more refined. For Sade, the libertine's capacity for intense sensations–not gendered sex–determined whether he/she would be an enlightened master or a victim, "Sex and Sensibility," pp. 88–89.

22. Arnold Heumakers sees a tragic dimension to Sade's cosmology. Liberation from convention is only one side of the picture; the libertine's crimes cannot go against or control nature. "The libertine suddenly realizes his imprisonment in nature; he is a will-less part of the great mechanism that entirely transcends his individual powers." "De Sade: A Pessimistic Libertine," in *From Sappho to de Sade:*

Moments in the History of Sexuality, ed. Jan Bremmer (London and New York: Routledge, 1989), p. 115. The outcome of the libertine position is literally a no man's land.

23. "The Culture of Priapism," p. 21.

24. I borrowed this notion from Ian Hunter, David Saunders, and Dugald Williamson, *On Pornography: Literature, Sexuality Obscenity Law* (New York: St. Martin's, 1993).

25. Timo Airaksinen notes the libertine's resistance to acquiring a "conventional personality." During a moment of weakness, Juliette states that she is menstruating and feels a bit out of sorts. She becomes a person with whom the reader can identify; she deliberates. According to Airaksinen, who says that "Sadean heroes are not psychologically well-defined" and are approached "from the outside," this means that Juliette is in great danger of becoming a victim because she is behaving simply as a human being confronted with ordinary problems. She must quickly get into action and produce results—on others. See *The Philosophy of the Marquis de Sade*, (London: Routledge, 1995), p. 69.

26. *Hard Core*, ch. 7, esp. pp. 227–28.

27. P. 19.

28. See, for example, Linda Williams' important work *Hard Core: Power, Pleasure, and the "Frenzy of the Visible"* (Berkeley and Los Angeles: University of California Press, 1989). Williams' book is a history of porn videos as a film genre and includes much valuable information about changing representations of women in pornography as well as how women are contributing to the creation of the symbolic world by making videos. Along these lines, the work of Constance Penley and Laura Kipnis also explores the history and meaning of pornography and its representation of gender. Artists such as Sue Spade, Joanna Frueh, and Barbara de Genevieve, and, in a lighter vein, Annie Sprinkle, to mention just a few, also grapple with the tropes of pornography in their work as seen through the experience of women.

29. Roger Shattuck's new book *Forbidden Knowledge: From Prometheus to Pornography* (New York: St. Martin's Press, 1996) contains lengthy section on Sade. Shattuck is critical of those who would heroize Sade or place him in the "canon."

49

Should We Read de Sade?

Timothy J. Madigan

WARNING: Reading this essay may be dangerous to your moral sensibilities.

> To sympathize with Sade too readily is to betray him. For it is our misery, subjection, and death that he desires; and every time we side with a child whose throat has been slit by a sex maniac, we take a stand against him.
> —Simone de Beauvoir, "Must We Burn Sade?"[1]

Long after his death, Donatien Alphonse Francois, Marquis de Sade (1740-1814), continues to infuriate. Virtually unknown during his own lifetime, his writings have since become almost sacred texts for generations of individuals fascinated by his extremism, his outrageousness, and his provocativeness. In her 1952 essay "Must We Burn Sade?" Simone de Beauvoir praised his "stubborn sincerity." While admitting that Sade was neither a skillful artist nor a coherent philosopher, she nonetheless argued that he deserves to be acknowledged as a great moralist. For, with his unflinching honesty, and his attempt to describe nature as it really is, Sade is the ultimate un-Romantic, the dark Knight of the Enlightenment. His advocacy of strength as the ultimate moral virtue precedes that of Nietzsche, and his atheistic avowal that life has no meaning anticipates the Existentialism which Beauvoir herself was to embrace.

While his writings were banned for centuries, and not readily available until after the Second World War, in recent years Sade has become more and more respectable. Indeed, in her 1978 book *The Sadeian Woman*, the late Angela Carter goes so far as to argue that this supreme misogynist was one of the first to separate sexuality from gender, and provides an empowering model for feminists. Sade, she writes, "was unusual in his period for claiming rights of free sexuality for women, and in installing women as beings of power in his imaginary worlds. This sets him apart from all other pornographers at all times and most other writers of his period."[2] Going even further, the iconoclastic feminist writer Camille Paglia, in her break-through work *Sexual Personae* (1991), claims that Sade's works should be required reading in all higher educational institutions:

> The Marquis de Sade is a great writer and philosopher whose absence from university curricula illustrates the timidity and hypocrisy of the liberal humanities. No education in the western tradition is complete without Sade. He must be confronted, in all his ugliness. Properly read, he is funny. Satirizing Rousseau, point by point, he prefigures the theories of aggression in Darwin, Nietzsche, and Freud.[3]

One sees a quantum leap from Beauvoir's qualified position regarding Sade's writing abilities to Paglia's bold assertion that he is a "great writer and philosopher." But the times seem to favor Paglia's interpretation, as can be witnessed by the fact that in 1990 the respected French series *Bibliotheque de la Pleiade* issued a scholarly edition of Sade's complete work, encased in leather binding (being bound in leather, by the way, adds a nice if unantic-ipated Sadeian touch). The Marquis's scabrous writings now share space with the works of Balzac, Hugo, and other French "Immortals." After cen-turies of opprobrium, Sade seems to have finally become respectable.

Yet one major critic at least is unwilling to let this matter rest. Roger Shattuck, in his recent best-selling book *Forbidden Knowledge* (1996), argues that the effect of Sade's work on most readers is harmful, and access to his writings should be restricted. Shattuck spends a good seventy pages (out of a 350-page book) excoriating Sade and all he stands for. Rather than cele-brating the Marquis as a moral hero, Shattuck argues, we should see him for what he really is: a menace to society. In Shattuck's words: "The divine mar-quis represents forbidden knowledge that we may not forbid. Consequently, we should label his writings carefully: potential poison, polluting to our moral and intellectual environment."[4]

In discussing his own initial introduction to Sade's writings, Shattuck writes:

> At age twenty-three, I first read a small sample of Sade's works in a public reading room overseen by an elderly woman reference librarian while I was working on an undergraduate thesis on Appollinaire. Almost forty years elapsed before I read him systematically in editions purchased openly in France and the United States. Both times, the experience of entering Sade's universe bore no resemblance to my knowledge of love, passion, copulation, debauchery, and tenderness. Sade's narrative plunged me into feelings and reactions associated with two vividly familiar experi-ences of a very different kind: witnessing a major surgical operation for the first time and participating in wartime combat fighting at close range.[5]

I would imagine that Sade himself would be delighted by such a com-parison, far more than with the praise bestowed upon him by those who

claim him as a great writer. The works for which he is most famous–*Justine,*
Juliette, The 120 Days of Sodom–are overly long, repetitious, and ultimately
soporific. How many orgies can one read about, and how many meals of
human excrement can one contemplate, before the whole thing seems like a
big bore? The saving grace of Sade's writings is not the sexual passages,
which are more likely to nauseate than titillate, but rather the witty and often
incisive philosophical passages (usually put in the mouths of the most monstrous of characters), which all-too briefly pop up when one least expects
them. It is these nuggets that have been of more influence than the endless
descriptions of human degradation that consume so many of his pages.

One reason for Sade's initial influence was the very scarcity of these
novels. By prohibiting them, the censors of his time helped to perpetuate
what Shattuck–using a Chaucerian analogy–calls "The Wife of Bath effect,"
namely:

> Something disturbing happens . . . when any limit is imposed from outside
> or by apparently arbitrary prohibition. I have called this response the Wife
> of Bath effect: "Forbid us thing, and that desire we."[6]

Like Shattuck, my own discovery of Sade was a rather furtive one. It
was while a student at a Catholic High School, during a course in psychology, that I learned the word "sadist" had been named after a real life
human being, one whose life and influence were the epitome of scandal.
"The Wife of Bath" effect took hold of me. After class I went to the library
and read the entry on him in *The Catholic Encyclopedia,* which confirmed his
dissolute existence, in rather veiled terms. But none of his writings, not surprisingly, was available there. So I then went to the public library, where his
works *were* on the shelf–but all in *French,* a language I could not read. Foiled
in my attempt to read him, I went on a quest of used book stores, and finally
found the holy grail: the Grove Press editions of his works, first translated
into English and published in the early 1960s. Like so many others, I experienced the illicit thrill of opening the pages of a truly scandalous author.

To the best of my knowledge, I was not corrupted by this initiation into
Sade's worldview. I quickly became bored with the rather clinical sexual
passages. What marked me as a philosopher (as opposed to a mere degenerate) was the fact that, repelled though I was by Sade's *ad nauseum* depictions of rapes, mutilations, shit-eating, and incest, I actually enjoyed reading
the asides about the nature of the universe and the meaninglessness of our
existence. While these passages also suffered from the long-windedness
endemic to the more salacious passages (no one would have benefited more
from a good editor than Sade), they presented a point of view which I had
never before thought about. It is not surprisingly that, when shortly thereafter, I became acquainted with the writings of Friedrich Nietzsche, I had a
similar awakening experience. Both men, to use Nietzsche's phrase, "phi-
losophized with a hammer."

Camille Paglia is correct that no contemporary discussion of modern culture can omit reference to Sade. His direct influence can be seen on such crucial contemporary figures as the playwright Yukio Mishima, the experimental novelist Kathy Acker, the radical filmmaker Pier Paolo Pasolini, the poet Allen Ginsburg, the semiotician Roland Barthes, and the philosopher Michel Foucault, to name just a few. Sade, unlike God, is omnipresent.

Given the influence which Sade has had on so many of the seminal figures of the nineteenth and twentieth centuries, it is simply not possible to conceal his existence, or to deny access to his works. Yet, paradoxically, his influence may well have been greater when reading him *was* a clandestine affair. The delightful *frisson* of the forbidden is lost when his bilious vision is caught on dainty paper, bound inside a text with a sewn-in bookmark not unlike those found in expensive Bibles.

I can imagine that Sade, for all his desire for fame, might well agree with Shattuck that his writings should be placed not within the prestigious *Bibliothèque de la Pléiade* collection but rather in dark, hidden crevices. Or at least, to use Shattuck's poison analogy, a large skull-and-cross bones should be placed as a warning sign on the *Pléiade* covers. I suspect that it is the severe critic Shattuck, much more than the modern acolytes Beauvoir, Carter, and Paglia, who will pique the greatest interest in the Marquis's work. No doubt many of the readers of *Forbidden Knowledge,* upon seeing this warning on the flyleaf—"Parents and teachers should be aware that Chapter VII does not make appropriate reading for children and minors"—did exactly what I did: skip immediately to Chapter VII, and thereby fell once more into the spider's web. Perhaps the best thing Shattuck could have done to keep the Marquis in his proper place would have been to not mention him at all in *Forbidden Knowledge.* Shattuck should rejoice that Sade is now safely behind fancy covers, rather than only inside of the lurid Grove Press editions I so cherish.

One must also wonder about the following passage from Shattuck's book, in which he says: "Gradually, we have replaced the *Index [of Forbidden Books]* and other forms of censorship with the free marketplace of ideas and a liberal education. And we have almost forgotten how bold a social experiment we have undertaken and how much devotion will be required to make it work."[7] Is he actually implying we should return to the days of the *Index* and the Inquisition? The fight against censorship is indeed a bold experiment. It is only by confronting Sade, and trying to understand what he has to say, that such an experiment can prove successful. Certainly curiosity can be dangerous—but so can its stifling. Limiting access to information cannot work, as Shattuck himself understands. We cannot help but want to take a peek at the Wife in her Bath. And in his own way, Shattuck—by taking Sade seriously—has done his bit to prove that the Marquis remains important.

In his last will and testament, Sade demanded that his body be buried in an unmarked grave, with acorns planted within, so that a tree would grow upon the spot, completely obliterating his memory. Thanks to Roger Shattuck, as well as to his myriad admirers, Sade's ghost still walks the earth, and will continue to haunt us for ages to come.

NOTES

1. Simone de Beauvoir, "Must We Burn Sade?" in *The Marquis de Sade,* The 120 Days of Sodom *and Other Writings* (New York: The Grove Press, 1966), p. 61.

2. Angela Carter, *The Sadeian Woman and the Ideology of Pornography* (New York: Pantheon Books, 1978), p. 36.

3. Camille Paglia, *Sexual Personae* (New York: Vintage Books, 1991), p. 235.

4. Roger Shattuck, *Forbidden Knowledge* (New York: Harcourt Brace and Company, 1996), p. 299.

5. Ibid., p. 298.

6. Ibid., p. 166.

7. Ibid.

Appendix I

Authors and Their Affiliations

THOMAS ALBRECHT is an Andrew W. Mellon Fellow in the Humanities Consortium at the University of California, Los Angeles.

RAY ANDERSON, PH.D., is a graduate from the UCLA clinical psychology program. He has been involved in the assessment and treatment of sexual offenders since 1966. He is a member of the Center for Sex Research, CSUN.

DAVID F. AUSTIN is an Associate Professor of Philosophy and a philosopher of mind and language at North Carolina State University. His research concerns norms and intentionality in visual representation, including pictorial representation of sexualities. E-mail: david-austin@ncsu.edu.

MICHAEL BARRETT is a research librarian at California State University, Northridge, a member of the Center for Sex Research and the co-author of bibliographies on homosexuality and transvestism. His speciality is sociology, history, and the retrieval of electronic information.

MARIANNA BECK, PH.D., has been a co-editor and publisher of *LIBIDO: The Journal of Sex and Sensibility* since its founding in 1988. She holds a Ph.D. in erotology.

GWEN BREWER, PH.D., is Professor Emeritus of English at California State University, Northridge.

PATTI BRITTON, PH.D., is a Fellow of the American Academy of Clinical Sexologists; a Diplomate of the American Board of Sexology; a Certified Sex Educator by the American Association of Sex Educators, Counselors, and Therapists; a member of the American College of Sexologists; and serves as faculty for the Institute for Advanced Study of Human Sexuality. Her e-mail address is DrPattiXOX@aol.com.

VERN L. BULLOUGH, PH.D., R.N., is a visiting professor of nursing at the University of Southern California and holds the title of Distinguished Professor Emeritus at the State University of New York. Vern is the founding director of the Center for Sex Research at California State University, Northridge, and is the author, co-author, or editor of approximately fifty books in the field of sexuality.

JOY CHANG is a graduate student in the Department of Sociology at California State University, Northridge. Her undergraduate work in Psychology was completed at the University of California, Riverside.

YOLANDA CORDUFF works as a freelance journalist in Australia and is regularly published by *Australian Penthouse, Australian Hustler,* and *Australian Women's Forum,* among other publications.

MILTON DIAMOND, PH.D., has been conducting research in the field of sexology for forty years. He is at the University of Hawaii, John A. Burns School of Medicine, where he is the Director of the Pacific Center for Sex and Society. In addition to his work on pornography, Dr. Diamond is best known for his studies of sexual development.

DWIGHT DIXON, J.D., PH.D., is a research sexologist in San Diego, California.

JOAN DIXON, PH.D., is a research sexologist in San Diego, California.

JEFFREY J. DOUGLAS, J.D., is a California criminal defense attorney representing all segments of the adult entertainment industry since 1982. Mr Douglas' practice encompasses a diverse range of matters such as political prosecutions, and drug a child molestation cases. He is the Executive Director and Chair of the Board of Directors of the Free Speech Coalition, the trade association of the adult entertainment industry, and an officer of the First Amendment Lawyers Association.

JAMES E. ELIAS, PH.D., is the Director of the Center for Sex Research at California State University, Northridge, and a professor in the Department of Sociology. He is a Marriage, Family, and Child Therapist and the co-author of *Gender Blending and Prostitution: On Whores, Hustlers, and Johns.* His e-mail is: james.elias@csun.edu.

VERONICA DIEHL ELIAS, PH.D., is a Professor of Sociology and former Director of the Center for Sex Research at California State University,

Northridge. She is a Marriage, Family, and Child Therapist and co-author of *Prostitution: On Whores, Hustlers, and Johns* (1998). She is a past member of the Board and Foundation of the Society for the Scientific Study of Sexuality.

VIRGINIA ELWOOD-AKERS is a librarian and member of the Center for Sex Research at California State University, Northridge, where she has been a member of the faculty since 1972. E-mail: virginia.elwood@csun.edu.

MARILYN A. FITHIAN, D.A., PH.D., is a licensed Marriage and Child Therapist, a sex researcher, educator, and writer. E-mail: mafithian@aol.com.

STANLEY FLEISHMAN, J.D., devoted almost fifty years defending the First Amendment in the courts. In 1957 he argued the first case presented to the Supreme Court squarely raising the question of whether "obscenity"—offensive sex speech—is protected by the Free Speech provision of the First Amendment. He was the attorney of record in twenty-five Supreme Court cases protecting sexual expression in books, magazines, films, and video.

WILLIAM GRIFFITT, PH.D., is a professor in the Department of Psychology at Kansas State University.

RICHARD GREEN, M.D., J.D., FRCPSYCH., is a Senior Research Fellow at the Institute of Criminology, Cambridge University, England. He is a Visiting Professor, Department of Psychiatry, and head of the Gender Identity Clinic of the Imperial College, School of Medicine at Charing Cross, London. He is also an Emeritus Professor of Psychiatry at UCLA, Los Angeles, and a member of the Center for Sex Research, California State University, Northridge.

JACK HAFFERKAMP, PH.D., is the co-publisher and editor of *LIBIDO: The Journal of Sex and Sensibility*. His Ph.D. is in the evolving field of erotology.

NINA HARTLEY, R.N., is a sixteen-year veteran of adult videos. She produces/directs an explicit sex-positive video series designed to increase viewer sexual literacy and dispel sexual guilt/shame.

PHILIP D. HARVEY is President of PHE and a pioneer in the distribution and sale of condoms to Third World countries.

MARJORIE HEINS, J.D., was the founding director of the ACLU's Arts Censorship Project until 1998. She is currently an Open Society Institute Individual Project Fellow, working on a book exploring the widely accepted belief that censorship is necessary to protect minors from sexual information or ideas. A second edition of her book *Sex, Sin, and Blasphemy—A Guide to America's Censorship Wars* was published by the New Press in 1999.

CHRISTIAN HITE, is a Ph.D. candidate in the Film, Literature, and Culture Division of the English Department at the University of Southern California. His dissertation concerns the politics and history of technology, sexuality, and theories of spectatorship.

JIM HOLLIDAY is the preeminent adult film and video historian. Holliday has written three books and has authored dozens of articles and monographs on the people and films of this unique explicit cinematic genre. His 1986 book, *Only the Best*, is regarded as the signature work on classic adult movies. For the past ten years he has been writing and directing adult features..

WILL JARVIS (aka Taliesin, the Bard) has been a part of the industry for a number of years and has worked in nearly all areas—actor, writer, and activist. He is a member of PAW.

BURTON JOSEPH, J.D., is the senior partner of the Chicago law firm Joseph, Lichtenstein, and Levenson concentrating in media law and Special Counsel to Playboy Enterprises, Inc. A leading attorney in the area of First Amendment Media Law, Burton Joseph has served as attorney in numerous cases involving the protection of First Amendment rights, privacy, censorship, and other constitutional issues.

MARTY KLEIN, PH.D., is a sex therapist in Palo Alto, California. His award-winning website (www.SexEd.org) contains more of his articles and information about his three books.

MISS CHARLIE LATOUR is a graduate of the Pershing School with degrees in psychology and sociology with graduate training in social work administration. She served as executive director of several social welfare organizations. Miss Latour, as an adult film/video actress for over twenty years, produced and directed adult movies and starred in numerous productions. She publishes the Latour Letter and has been honored with the prestigious Lady Liberty Award. She maintains her commitment to her family, her community, and her faith.

PETER LEHMAN, PH.D., is a Professor at Arizona State in the Interdisciplinary Humanities Program and the Hispanic Research Center and is the author of *Running Scared: Masculinity and the Representation of the Male Body*.

GLORIA LEONARD, award-winning actress and director, is one of the adult entertainment community's most visible members. For fourteen years she was the publisher of the men's magazine *High Society*, and has served as president of the Adult Film Association of America and as administrative director of the Adult Video Association. She is currently president of the Free Speech Coalition, the adult industry's trade organization and anti-censorship arm.

JAY KENT LORENZ is a doctoral candidate in Visual Culture at the University of California, Irvine, and also teaches film and literature at Georgetown University. His writing has appeared in publications ranging from *Film Quarterly* to *Psychotronic*, and he is currently completing a book on Italian horror cinema. Mr. Lorenz is the video reviewer for Sinclair Intimacy Institute, the sex education division of PHE.

HENRY MACH, MFA, is author of the cult musical *Dirty Dreams of a Clean-Cut Kid*. His book *Education of a New York Jewish Homosexual Pornographer* will be published by Haworth Press.

TIMOTHY J. MADIGAN is an editor with the University of Rochester Press, and chair of the editorial board of *Free Inquiry* magazine.

MAUREEN MERCURY, MA, in Depth Psychology. She is a writer currently completing the book *Pagan Fleshworks* for Inner Traditions International. She is an expert in the psychology of body modification. E-mail: Maureen@mmercury.com.

MOLLY MERRYMAN, PH.D., is the Director of the Women's Resource Center and assistant professor affiliated with American Studies, History, Journalism, and Mass Communications, and Women's Studies at Kent State University. She has written *Clipped Wings: The Rise and Fall of the Women's Airforce Service Pilots of World War II* (New York University Press) and has published numerous journal articles and reviews on feminist scholarship, popular culture, cultural studies, and queer studies. She is also a published poet and an award-winning documentary filmmaker.

HARRIS MIRKIN, PH.D., is Co-Director of the Honors Program at the University of Missouri-Kansas City and is an Associate Professor of Political Science. He received his Ph.D. from Princeton and has focused on the area of sexual politics. He is interested in the politics of child pornography because it was considered to be so evil that it could not even be discussed.

VERONICA MONET is a prostitute, a producer, and performer of feminist porn. She is a contributing author for several books who has appeared on a multitude of television shows including ABC's *Politically Incorrect* and *20/20* and on CNN, Veronica Monet conducts lectures and seminars on the subject of sexuality and gender. URL: http://www.veronicamonet.com.

CARLOS MORALES, J.D., is an attorney recently graduated from Indiana University Law School and residing in Los Angeles.

LAURENCE O'TOOLE is an editor and book critic from London, England. He is the author of *Pornocopia: Porn, Sex, Technology, and Desire* (Serpent's Tail

Publisher, 1998). A newly updated and extended edition is due out in spring of 2000. E-mail: o'toole@alos.demon.co.uk.

HERBERT OTTO, PH.D., is a consultant, therapist, author, and has published fourteen articles and four books on human sexuality. His latest book is *Liberated Orgasm* (Liberating Creations, 1999).

VIDA PAVESICH teaches philosophy at Diablo Valley College in Pleasant Hill, California, and is a photographer and painter. Her e-mail address is vidaluna@silicon.com.

FIONA PATTEN is the President of Australia's national sex industry association–The Eros Foundation. She has been a spokesperson and political lobbyist for the industry for the last ten years and regularly appears in the national media commenting on prostitution, censorship, and morality issues.

BILL PAUL is a professor of Art at the University of Georgia and former head of the department.

STEPHEN F. ROHDE, J.D., is a Los Angeles attorney, writer, and lecturer specializing in First Amendment and intellectual property law. He is President of the ACLU of Southern California and co-author of *Foundations of Freedom*, published by the Constitutional Rights Foundation.

MARK ROYSNER, J.D., is a Los Angeles–based attorney. His practice focuses on the hotel and entertainment industries. He is the author of two books on hospitality and entertainment contracts. He is a staunch supporter of First Amendment Rights.

CONNIE SHORTES, PH.D., teaches at the University of Texas at Austin.

WILLIAM SIMON, PH.D., is a Professor of Sociology at the University of Houston. He has received the lifetime award for his work from the Society for the Scientific Study of Sexuality. He is a member of the Center for Sex Research, CSUN, and his latest book is entitled *Postmodern Sexuality.*

DAVID SONENSCHEIN is an anthropologist, an independent scholar, and has published or presented numerous papers on sexualities and on American culture.

NADINE STROSSEN, J.D., president of the American Civil Liberties Union and a professor at New York Law School, comments frequently on legal issues in the national media, and is a monthly columnist for the Webzine *Intellectual Capital.* Her book *Defending Pornography: Free Speech, Sex, and the Fight for Women's Rights* was named by the *New York Times* a "notable book" of 1995.

LOUIS H. SWARTZ, PH.D., L.L.M., R.N., is an associate professor of law and social work at the State University of New York in Buffalo.

JOE A. THOMAS is an Associate Professor of Art History and Chair of the Art Department at Clarion University of Pennsylvania. His research involves various aspects of sexuality and representation. E-mail: thomas@ mail.clarion.edu.

ESAU TOVAR is a graduate student in Counseling and is an associate member of the Center for Sex Research, Northridge.

DANIEL C. TSANG is the politics, economics, and Asian American Studies bibliographer at the University of California, Irvine. E-mail: dtang@uci.edu. URL: hattp://go.fast.to/ar.

RALPH UNDERWAGER, PH.D., a psychologist, is the director of a forensic clinic in Minnesota dealing with issues of child abuse. He is the co-author of *Accusations of Child Abuse* (1988), *The Real World of Child Interrogation* (1990), and *Return of the Furies: An Investigation into Recovered Memory Therapy* (1994).

BEERT C. VERSTRAETE, PH.D., received his doctorate in Classics at the University of Toronto; he is currently Professor of Classics and Head of the Department of Classics at Acadia University, Wolfville, Nova Scotia, Canada. E-mail: beert.verstraete@acadiau.ca.

HOLLIDA WAKEFIELD, PH.D., is a licensed psychologist in the state of Minnesota and co-author of *Accusations of Child Abuse* (1988), *The Real World of Child Interrogations* (1990), and *Return of the Furies: An Investigation into Recovered Memory Therapy* (1994).

JO WELDON has since 1980 participated in many forms of sex work, including stripping, centerfold modeling, and professional domination. She is the director of the Sex Workers' International Media Watch, a member of Feminists for Free Expression, and a member of the Society of Professional Journalists.

RUSSELL WILCOX lectures on pornography to sexuality classes at San Francisco State University. He also writes porno video reviews for *Spectator* magazine and shoots and edits experimental erotic video.

JENNIFER YAMASHIRO, PH.D., is an art historian whose speciality is the history of photography. She has been the curator of photography, art, and artifacts at the Kinsey Institute since 1995.

Appendix II

The Organizations of "X"

Will Jarvis, Jeffrey Douglas, and Gloria Leonard

O NE OF THE SIGNPOSTS THAT THE MODERN ADULT ENTERTAINMENT and information industry is maturing is the number of institutions that now exist to support "the business." Like the rest of Hollywood, organizations are required to represent the needs of all aspects of the adult industry. The recognition of these institutions, and their evolution, is a vital part of appreciating the business and art of "porn."

THE EARLY ORGANIZATIONS

New York City, mid-1970s! The disco decade has picked up steam as has the number of theatrical venues for adult motion pictures, and yes, they WERE film productions, sometimes 16mm but mostly, 35mm. This was the era fondly referred to as "B.V."–before video–when an adult feature ran for a week, or two, or longer if it appeared the marketplace demand was there. Most New York City newspapers even accepted discreet ads right alongside those for Radio City Music Hall. Screenings for reviewers were held at mainstream screening rooms, complete with food and drink to keep the critics' stomachs–and columns–filled with tasty tidbits. The arbiters of adult movie taste banded together into two groups: the X.R.C.O.–X-Rated Critics' Organization–and C.A.F.A.–Critics' Adult Film Association–both of which hosted annual parties to bestow their blessings on the good, the bad and occasionally, the extraordinary. *The Opening of Misty Beethoven*, a film by Henry Paris, was not only a benchmark of quality in the genre, but hosted its screening at the tony Four Seasons Restaurant in New York City. In attendance were such literary luminaries as Molly Haskell, Andrew Sarris and others. The X.R.C.O. is still watching and writing, however, as production companies moved West in greater numbers, the East Coast-based C.A.F.A. had less and less product to review and in 1987 disbanded.

Los Angeles, mid-1970s. The promise of balmy weather, fresh faces, great outdoor shooting locations and far more office/studio space for lots less money, brings forth a wave of cross-country migration not seen since the Gold Rush, giving established California producers considerable competition. The formation of the Adult Film Association of America is the first organization to unite the industry and while their most notable claim to fame is an annual gala honoring excellence within their ranks, they also take on some of the legal challenges confronting the business. As video begins to make technological and economic inroads, the name of the organization is changed to the Adult Film and Video Association of America.

Let us not forget that adult videos were the FIRST movies available on videotape, long before the big Hollywood studios got with the program. Naturally, it isn't much longer before the name is changed once more, this time to the Adult Video Association but this time, the players are much more politically motivated.

Spurring them on is the landmark 1988 case involving veteran adult producer, Hal Freeman, who is convicted on pandering charges. At that time, it was considered legal to view an adult film but actually making one, was another matter entirely. Freeman appealed to the California Supreme Court and in a unanimous decision, won his case.

In response to the Reagan/Bush administration's war on pornography, another organization is born in 1991, calling itself the Free Speech Legal Defense Fund. One year later, it merges with the Adult Video Association becoming, as we now know it, the

Free Speech Coalition. This organization, discussed in detail later, proves that government attempts to control thought by regulating communication always fail. The attempt to destroy the business of pornography just made it stronger.

America, turn of the twenty-first century. A business whose growth is now charted on Wall Street finds itself sharing not only in all that is problematic to any large industry, but must especially concern itself with the health and well-being of its members.

THE CURRENT ORGANIZATIONS OF "PORN"

The History of the Free Speech Coalition— The Adult Entertainment Industry's Trade Association

In 1987 and again in 1990, the Reagan/Bush administrations ran sting operations attempting to stop interstate distribution of sexually explicit materials. In response, the adult entertainment industry formed an organization to fight back. Ultimately called the Free Speech Coalition, this organization initially focused upon a media relations campaign alerting the public to this assault on individuals' First Amendment rights which the thirty threatened Federal prosecutions in 1990 represented. Civil litigation arising from one of the original cases established exactly what the adult industry had argued: Federal prosecuting agents did not limit themselves to prosecuting materials which they believed obscene, but were actually attempting to destroy the lawful businesses, because of their hostility to legal sexually oriented materials.

When the prosecutions arising from the 1990 sting were resolved, the Free Speech Coalition redefined itself as a trade organization. The mission statement of the organization was twofold: First, improve the quality of life for the people earning their living in the creation, distribution and sales of adult products and services. Second, improve the external environment through education, media relations, lobbying and, as a last resort, litigation.

Initially, much of the energy of the organization focused on the part of the industry perceived as the most vulnerable, the actors, actresses and models upon whose talent the industry depends. The FSC undertook the difficult task of getting cost efficient, quality health insurance for those individuals, previously unacceptable to insurers because of their employment as sex workers, with the attendant negative stereotypes. Similarly, improved working conditions, standardized contract terms, and safer sexual practices, including regular testing for HIV and sexually transmitted diseases were all undertaken by the fledgling organization.

Supported entirely by voluntary member dues and fundraising events, the organization went five years with only one paid employee, the office administrator.

In 1995, a comprehensive Federal scheme regulating in minute detail the creation and wholesale distribution of recorded images of sexual conduct went into effect. Purportedly aimed at detecting and deterring child pornography, the so-called "Federal Labeling Law" eliminated all privacy in the creation of sexual images. Any producers of, and performers in, such images were ordered to comply with detailed disclosure requirements. In order for the industry to comply, the FSC was essential. The Coalition conducted training seminars, prepared compliance documents and uniform exemption labels and negotiated with the Justice Department for relief from some of the more burdensome and unreasonable components of the law.

It was Free Speech Coalition's response to the "Federal Labeling Law" that established broadly throughout the industry the necessity of a functional trade organization to assist the industry.

It was ironic that this Federal legislation was justified as an anti-child pornography measure. For over twenty years, and certainly since the advent of videotape, the industry had successfully self-policed to prevent the use of minors. Despite a handful of performers who had defrauded the Federal and/or State governments into providing them with identification falsely representing themselves as being of age, the industry had never tolerated the presence of underage performers.

Even one of the industry's sworn opponents, an attorney-representative of the California Law Center for Family and Children, an anti-pornography organization, testified before the California Legislature that "the modern adult entertainment industry has no involvement with the distribution or creation of child pornography." Indeed one of the first acts of the Free Speech Coalition was to offer a reward of up to $10,000 for information leading to the arrest and conviction of manufacturers and/or distributors of child pornography.

Overcoming the extreme individualistic tendencies of business people in the adult entertainment industry, the Free Speech Coalition continued to expand it member services, as well as its external advocacy.

The Coalition trained speakers, expanded its insurance benefits and subsidized a database publication which tracked and analyzed obscenity prosecutions throughout the United States. This former publication, *Know Censorship*©, was essential in providing a reappraisal of the national climate and attitudes toward obscenity prosecutions. The study revealed how rarely and arbitrarily obscenity prosecutions were actually undertaken. It was the absence of discernable patterns that was so striking. The publication debunked the "common knowledge" that the so-called Bible Belt states were dangerous environments for sexually explicit material, and that gay, interracial, and soft core bondage materials were far riskier to sell than "straight" heterosexual titles. Thus, the FSC's funding of *Know Censorship*© improved industry and academic understanding of the actual commercial and politico-legal environment for sales of sexually oriented materials.

Within a year or so, the FSC decided to create a sister organization to provide direct services. That entity, Protecting Adult Welfare Foundation (PAW) (see detailed history below), took on the onus of assisting individual actors and actresses during times of personal crisis, as well as offering business skills training, since actors and actresses are in actuality small business owners.

When a series of HIV scares struck the industry in the early 1990s, FSC and PAW aggressively educated and established uniform systematic testing regimes. Working with leading HIV researchers, laboratories, and the Centers for Disease Control, as well as state and county authorities, PAW and FSC have established a model testing and reporting program which has dramatically reduced, if not eliminated altogether the threat of an epidemic to the industry. Furthermore, the Free Speech Coalition and PAW took the lead in persuading the industry leaders to adopt a "condom-only" policy. Arising therefrom was a medical and psycological services entity, subsequently spun off from its parent organization. That organization, AIM (Adult Industry Medical Health Care Foundation) (see detailed history below), achieved independent status in 1998.

The Free Speech Coalition entered the field of lobbying in earnest in 1994, with the retention of a lobbyist in Sacramento, California's State Capitol. After a year, the lobbying presence proved itself critical for the health of the national industry. A wildly unconstitutional tax bill was introduced, with the nominal purpose of assisting victims of domestic abuse and rape. An excise tax was proposed for all adult products and services, with the proceeds going to collection of the tax, law enforcement and, if any pennies remained, to rape counseling centers and battered victim shelters.

Constitutional law had long forbade the targeting of a content-defined tax, and this bill was the model of such a tax scheme. Traditionally, the industry had relied solely on the judiciary to protect itself against such intrusions, and legislatures across the country have become accustomed to regulating the adult industry without consultation with the parties to be regulated. Both patterns came to a halt with this proposed tax.

The Free Speech Coalition led a coalition of affected businesses and industry groups in fighting the tax. The FSC demonstrated that the tax was not only a dangerous, unconstitutional precedent, but that it would be bad for the state's economy. During the course of the ensuing debate, the economic influence of the adult entertainment industry was established in the minds of the legislators and staff. The bill was not only defeated at its first committee hearing, it received zero votes in support.

This remarkable victory was historic on several fronts. First, had the industry relied upon its old patterns, one or more companies would have spent scores of thousands of dollars on legal fees challenging the law in court. Meanwhile, the rest of the industry would have spent hundreds of thousands of dollars complying with the burdensome regulatory scheme, while the matter was in litigation.

More importantly, the adult entertainment industry, through the Free Speech Coalition, proved itself an effective "player" in the legislature. Adult entertainment was no longer an easy target for an ambitious legislator. It established that regulation of the adult industry without dialogue with its representatives was, as with all other industries, a foolish and dangerous undertaking.

As implied earlier, one of the Free Speech Coalition's tenets is that "adult" communication is exactly that: Material made by adults, for adults. Consistent with that principle is the Free Speech Coalition's offer (and awarding) of up to $10,000.00 annually for information leading to the arrest and conviction of producers or distributors of child pornography. The industry and the Free Speech Coalition were therefore placed in a difficult position by the amendment of the Federal Child Pornography laws in 1997, which included "simulated" child pornography within the definition of child pornography.

The redefinition of child pornography to include adults "appearing" to be minors, engaging in actual or simulated sexual activity was extremely controversial. The Senate Judiciary Committee (the committee of origin), never even held a vote on the bill, yet it was signed into law, following Senator Orrin Hatch (Rep., Utah) attaching it during the Conference Committee to the October 1997 Spending Bill. Under the extraordinarily all-encompassing definition, even mainstream films such as *Midnight Cowboy, Last Picture Show, Animal House, A Clockwork Orange, Halloween, Fast Times at Ridgemont High, Return to Blue Lagoon, The Exorcist, If . . . , Risky Business, Porky's, Bull Durham, Blow-Up, Dirty Dancing, Angel, Murmurs of the Heart, Pretty Maids All in a Row, The People vs. Larry Flynt, Sleepers,* and *Ripe* are now subject to prosecution, with the attendant five year mandatory minimum imprisonment. When these concerns were brought to Senator Hatch's staff, they responded by conceding that such films could be charged, but that "legitimate" movies need not fear prosecution.

No group, including those traditionally in the vanguard of First Amendment rights, was willing to challenge the constitutionality of the law. Finally, the Free Speech Coalition decided to take on the burden. For the first time since its own redefinition as a trade association, the Free Speech Coalition undertook litigation challenging the constitutionality of a Federal statute. That challenge, *Free Speech Coalition* v. *Reno* (No. 97-16536), is now pending before the Ninth Circuit Court of Appeals, with the ultimate determination likely to be before the United States Supreme Court.

The most recent milestone for the Free Speech Coalition coincides with the publication of this book. In keeping with the Coalition's mission to improve both the external and internal environment for "adult" products and services, in 1998, the Free Speech Coalition teamed with Center for Sex Research to sponsor the first World Pornography Conference. This extraordinary event reflected the complexity and depth of the issues that inform and impel the trade association. Bringing together the unlikely combination of academics, attorneys and pornographers increased understanding and appreciation for the genre of communication called pornography. The Conference embodied that which caused the Free Speech Coalition to re-form into a trade association—improvement of the quality of life for the people living and working in the world of pornography, and improvement of the external environment for the appreciation of its products and services.

The contradictions embodied by the multi-billion dollar pornography media industry are overwhelming. It is a creative, communicative industry, both reviled and adored by popular culture, protected by the First Amendment, yet systematically attacked by law enforcement. Commercial pornography appeals to individualists, attracted by the outlaw image and the promise of access to wealth. But the very existence of that industry depends on the ability to work collectively. The Free Speech Coalition lives on the sharp edge of those contradictions. We who have fought for the vitality of both the industry and its trade association feel that the publication of this book represents one of the finest hours of both.

Protecting Adult Welfare Foundation (PAW)

According to one of its organizers, PAW represents the soul of the industry, as AIM (see below) represents the heart. Established in 1994 by the Free Speech Coalition, PAW provides direct services to the talent; i.e., the actors, actresses and other creators of adult entertainment and information. Historically, the talent was underserved by the business.

The relationship between fan and star is unique to adult entertainment. There is not only an identification with the stars, as there is in mainstream Hollywood, but in the X Industry, there is a deeper bond. The actors and actresses are so much more accessible. They are, of course, more exposed, and the audience sees intimacies unimaginable in general audience material. But it is much more than that. Adult stars meet, mingle and form direct relationships with the fans.

This relationship increases the importance of the individual star, thus making the health and well-being of the talent important to the industry and institution of adult entertainment. The business side slowly recognized that their stars were not just fungible bodies. This understanding coincided with the explosion of demand for new titles and new stars. Thus the need for a Foundation to foster a support system for the creative side of the industry was finally acknowledged.

Arising in part from the tragic suicide of superstar Savannah, the PAW Foundation began providing direct services with a drop-in office, and a "peer counseling line" for industry talent. The office and peer counseling is staffed by industry veterans trained by a Clinical Psychologist and Marriage and Family Counselor. These trained and dedicated volunteers address the unique relationship and workplace issues which arise for sex workers, as well as the other kinds of problems everyone faces—substance abuse, financial stress, loneliness and family issues.

Having a drop-in office for the talent, centrally located near the primary placement agency for the industry, effectively serves the purpose of providing support. The office offers a free videotape, answering the questions that every new and potential industry entrant should know. Many people interested in becoming a "porn star" change their minds after understanding the demands and reality of being in the industry. This is as much of a PAW success as helping an artist prosper in the challenging world of X.

The Peer Counseling Helpline is available on a twenty-four-hour basis for people in the adult industry. While not providing psychotherapy, nor offering suicide prevention or other crisis counseling, the Helpline does offer caring advice, referrals to appropriate professionals and resources, and most importantly perhaps, the reminder that the caller is part of a community that cares.

PAW increasingly provides other assistance as well. From its inception, emergency funds were provided for housing, placements in appropriate shelters if needed, as well as substance abuse intervention. A limited loan program exists to assist in times of temporary financial crisis. Since its founding in 1994, there are countless people whose lives were transformed, or even literally saved, by the commitment and experience of the extraordinary people who make up PAW.

Adult Industry Medical Health Care Foundation (AIM)

The Adult Industry Medical Health Care Foundation (AIM) represents one of the most extraordinary achievements of the adult industry. When for the first time HIV positive tests were detected in the adult industry in early 1998, the Free Speech Coalition responded to the industry's outcry, and established a rigorous standard testing regimen. Previous scares regarding HIV had resulted in testing programs in the past, but as terror caused by the false positives subsided, compliance with previous programs slipped.

Initially organized as merely a reminder service to talent to keep their tests up to date, the unique medical, social and psychological needs of the adult industry talent caused a proliferation of services offered. By the end of 1998, it was clear that affiliation with the Free Speech Coalition and PAW was becoming a limitation rather than an asset.

The Adult Industry Medical (AIM) Health Care Foundation created by Sharon Mitchell is a non-profit corporation formed in 1998 to care for the health needs (in the term's most comprehensive sense) of sex workers and people who work in adult entertainment. Its mission is to provide health care for the body, mind, emotion and spirit, as well as to take a leadership position in promoting safe and responsible sexual behavior.

Cordial relationships with the CDC and pharmaceutical companies allow AIM to offer the absolute cutting edge information and technology. AIM engages in trials for pharmaceutical and medical devices and products. The finest physicians and other health-related service providers seek out AIM to associate themselves. Services offered include state of the art testing for HIV, and all sexually transmitted diseases. AIM also provides educational programs, individual and group counseling, twelve-step programs, condoms, pap smears, psychiatric assessment, drug and alcohol counseling, cosmetic surgery information, chiropractic healing and support groups pertaining to relationships, surviving abuse, and other special educational workshops.

Specifically for the adult entertainment community, AIM maintains the essential HIV test database that allows producers to confirm that the performers are compliant with the industry's testing program. Currently performers work only with a PCR-DNA test showing negative status within the last twenty-eight days. AIM's participation and assistance makes this testing regime the first successful program of its kind.

By addressing the community's health needs so comprehensively and with such dedication, the people of AIM represent the very best that adult entertainment, or any other industry could offer. The founder received "The Special Achievement Award" for her commitment to AIM and the ongoing crises in the adult business at the prestigious AVN Awards. "Rarely," wrote the publisher of the industry's trade magazine, "have we seen someone so dedicated, selfless and hard working . . . all for a common good. Your work has been an inspiration to everyone."

FOXE (Fans OF X-Rated Entertainment)

FOXE is the only fan-based organization in the adult entertainment and information industry. It serves a unique role, because of the contradictory nature of being a fan of pornography in this era. The incredible success of the pornography industry represents the power of the voyeuristic urge. Millions of people spend tens of billions of dollars annually on sexual entertainment and information. Yet, hand-in-hand with the voyeuristic urge is the very powerful social mandate that sex is exclusively a private matter.

FOXE provides a means for the consumer to escape the isolation that the sexual privacy compulsion imposes. In 1989, when the organization was formed, it was virtually unimaginable that tens of thousands of people from all over North America (and the world) would join an organization dedicated to their love of X-rated communication. Even more unimaginable would be that thousands of those would travel to an annual awards show and participate openly in such a celebration.

By facilitating the interaction between actors and actresses and their dedicated fans, FOXE encourages an immediate communications line between fan and star unheard of in any other segment of the entertainment industry. The performers in this industry need not wait for polls or box office numbers to find out what their fans love and do not like.

Perhaps more importantly, the existence of an organization devoted to "porn pride" helps break down the shame culturally imposed upon those who enjoy watching pretty people make love. It is a mystery why there is shame associated with loving films openly focussed on sex, while "mainstream" movies, no matter how sexually oriented or violent do not engender such a stigma. Nevertheless, FOXE represents part of the sex positive aspects of the culture, and embodies the revolutionary growth and development of the adult entertainment world.

Erotic Entertainers Guild

There have been several attempts over the years to unify the actors and actresses of the adult industry into an organization. Whether to deal with traditional workplace issues such as working conditions or benefits, or to provide support services, organization of X-rated talent has been a difficult undertaking. The talent pool is traditionally young and very independent, drawn to pornography, at least in part, because of the outlaw image. Like the manufacturers, the creative talents of the actors and actresses are not easily united.

In other words, X-rated talent are not, by instinct, "joiners." Yet the need for unity, education and support in such a demanding and stressful environment is great. Thus over the years the performers with vision have continued to try to organize and unite their brothers and sisters. The current attempt carries a great deal of promise.

The Erotic Entertainers Guild was established exclusively for the Talent: erotic film and video actresses and actors, nude models, exotic dancers, and other erotic performers.

The specific purposes of the Guild are to provide encouragement, training, technical support and education to those who are engaged in the field of erotic entertainment. Further, the Guild will establish standards of conduct and a code of ethics designed to encourage ethical, safe, and professional behavior. While PAW and AIM cover the personal aspects of being a performer in the adult entertainment field, the Guild concentrates its efforts on the professional aspects. This ranges from instructing the talent on how to read and understand typical contracts or model release agreements to helping them with the management of their money. The erotica industry is not noted for its professionalism, but by setting just a few minimum standards of professionalism, the quality and morale of the entire industry can be uplifted.

Bibliography of the Major First Amendment Cases and the Current State of Obscenity Law in America

Mark Roysner, Carlos L. Morales, and Michael Barrett

INTRODUCTION

"Congress shall make no law respecting an establishment of religion, or prohibiting the free exercise thereof; or abridging the freedom of speech, or of the press; or the right of the people to peacefully assemble, and to petition the Government for a redress of grievances." U.S. CONST. amend. I

THIS BIBLIOGRAPHY PROJECT WAS INITIALLY COMPILED FOR DISTRIBU-tion at the *World Pornography: Eroticism and the First Amendment* confer-ence. A national conference dealing with topics and concerns related to pornography and the First Amendment.

The conference was held at the Sheraton Universal Hotel, Universal City, California, on August 6-9, 1998. The conference was presented by The Center for Sex Research of California State University, Northridge, The Free Speech Coalition, and was co-sponsored by The Society for the Scientific Study of Sexuality and The American Association of Sex Educators and Counselors.

In light of the historically large number of legal cases, books, articles, essays and annotations addressing the topic of obscenity and the First Amendment, it was the intent of the authors of this bibliography not to produce an exhaustive listing of all the material currently published. Instead, it was decided that this work would serve as an easy to use reference source providing a "snapshot in time" of landmark United States Supreme Court Decisions, and selected literature focusing on recent developments in the area of obscenity and pornography, and its current legal interpretation by the courts.

It is our hope this document will stimulate the reader's interest in the important concerns and issues raised at the Conference. This document will assist attorneys, scholars, researchers, investigators, and conference attendees in quickly identifying those documents, which are pertinent to their area of interest, while at the same time lessening the chance of overlooking an important publication.

The majority of the documents cited are drawn from the last two decades, although to bridge some topical areas, especially case law, some earlier publications have been included. Furthermore, the authors when choosing citations for inclusion evaluated the likely availability of individual documents in academic and law library collections, through interlibrary loan, or over Internet on-line services.

This bibliography is divided into two major sections. Part I and II present primary and secondary legal authority. Parts III through XII present secondary sources, primarily journal articles, dealing with specialized subtopical areas. If the reader discovers additional pertinent citations, which have been inadvertently omitted from this bibliography, the authors invite and welcome submission of those references to be used in future revisions.

I. PRIMARY LEGAL AUTHORITY

A) Supreme Court Cases

United States Supreme Court Cases Discussing Obscenity

A Book Named "John Cleland's Memoirs of a Woman of Pleasure v. *Atty. Gen. of Mass,* 383 U.S. 413 (1966) (elaborating on the definition of obscenity as set forth in "Roth").

Brockett v. *Spokane Arcades, Inc.,* 472 U.S. 492 (1985) (explaining that material that provokes normal, healthy sexual desires is not obscene).

Freedman v. *Md.,* 380 U.S. 51 (1965) (explaining that motion pictures, though within the purview of the 1st and 14th Amendments, are not subject to the rules governing other modes of expression).

Jacobellis v. *Ohio,* 378 U.S. 184 (1964) (explaining that conviction for exhibiting a film abridges freedom of the press).

Jenkins v. *Georgia,* 418 U.S. 153 (1973) (holding that film "Carnal Knowledge" does not meet the "obscene" threshold).

Kaplan v. *California,* 413 U.S. 115 (1974) (explaining that words alone can meet the "obscene" threshold).

Kingsley Books, Inc. v. *Brown,* 354 U.S. 436 (1957) (explaining that manner of use, and not quality of art or literature should determine obscenity)

Manual Enter., Inc. v. *Day,* 370 U.S. 478 (1962) (explaining the "obscene" threshold).

Marcus v. *Search Warrant of Property,* 367 U.S. 717 (1961) (explaining that certain materials will lie in the gray area of obscenity).

Mishkin v. *N.Y.,* 383 U.S. 502 (1966) (explaining the parameters of the "prurient interest" element in the "Roth" test).

Paris Adult Theatre I v. *Slaton,* 413 U.S. 49 (1973) (explaining that obscene, pornographic materials exhibited to consenting adults is not afforded constitutional immunity).

Pinkus v. *U.S.*, 436 U.S. 293 (1978) (explaining that children are not part of the relevant "community" for purposes of prosecution under U.S.C.A. §1461).

Reno v. *American Civil Liberties Union*, 117 S.Ct. 2329 (1997) (explaining that sexual expression that is indecent, but not obscene is afforded First Amendment protection).

Roth v. *U.S.*, 354 U.S. 476 (1957) (explaining that standard for obscenity should safeguard freedom of speech and press for material that is not appealing to the prurient interest).

Smith v. *California*, 361 U.S. 147 (1959) (explaining that although trier of fact can be regarded as the embodiment of community standards, the community cannot condemn that which it generally accepts).

Stanley v. *Georgia*, 394 U.S. 557 (1969) (holding that the First Amendment prohibits making mere private possession of obscene material a crime).

Times Film Corp. v. *Chicago*, 365 U.S. 43 (1961) (explaining that there is no complete and absolute freedom to exhibit every kind of motion picture).

United States Supreme Courts Cases Discussing Obscenity in Relation to "Time, Place and Manner" Restrictions

F. C. C. v. *Pacifica Foundation*, 438 U.S. 726 (1978) (explaining that Commission's order that monologue was indecent did not violate broadcaster's First Amendment rights).

R.A.V. v. *City of St. Paul, Minn.*, 505 U.S. 377 (1992) (explaining that categories of speech such as obscenity, defamation, and "fighting words" can be regulated consistent with the First Amendment).

Reno v. *American Civil Liberties Union*, 117 S.Ct. 2329 (1997) (holding that challenged provisions of the CDA could not properly be analyzed as a time, place, and manner regulation).

Schad v. *Borough of Mount Ephraim*, 452 U.S. 61(1981) (holding that ban on nude dancing was not a reasonable time, place, and manner restriction).

Virginia v. *American Booksellers Ass'n.*, Inc., 484 U.S. 383 (1988) (holding that plaintiffs had standing to bring facial challenge of statute before enforcement).

United States Supreme Courts Cases Discussing Obscenity in Relation to "Zoning"

City of Renton v. Playtime Theatres, Inc., 475 U.S. 41 (1986) (holding that zoning ordinance that prohibited adult motion picture theaters from locating within 1,000 feet of any residential zone was valid).

Smith v. *U.S.*, 431 U.S. 291 (1977) (explaining that whether mailings in question are intrastate, for purposes of federal statute prohibiting mailing of obscene material, is immaterial).

United States Supreme Courts Cases Discussing Obscenity in Relation to "Rico" Statutes

Alexander v. *U.S.*, 509 U.S. 544 (1993) (holding that forfeiture of defendant's assets after having been convicted for racketeering activities in violation of RICO did not violate defendant's First Amendment rights).

Fort Wayne Books, Inc. v. *Indiana,* 489 U.S. 46 (1989) (holding that Indiana Rico statute was not unconstitutionally vague, but that seizure of books and films before a judicial determination that items seized were obscene, or that the RICO statute had been violated was a violation of the First Amendment).

United States Supreme Courts Cases Discussing Obscenity in Relation to "Freedom of Association"

FW/PBS, Inc. v. *City of Dallas,* 493 U.S. 215 (1990) (holding that determination that hotels which rent rooms for less than 10 hours are "sexually oriented businesses" did not impinge on the occupant's freedom of association rights).

United States Supreme Courts Cases Discussing Obscenity in Relation to "Freedom of Expression"

Barnes v. *Glen Theatre, Inc.,* 501 U.S. 560 (1991) (explaining that requiring adult entertainers to wear pasties and G-string does not violate the First Amendment's guarantee of freedom of expression).
Ginsberg v. *State of N.Y.,* 390 U.S. 629 (1968) (holding that challenged statute did not invade freedom of expression constitutionally guaranteed to minors).
U.S. v. *12 200-Foot Reels of Super 8mm. Film,* 413 U.S. 123 (1973) (holding that Congress can constitutionally proscribe the importation of obscene matter whether or not the material is for private, personal use and possession).

United States Supreme Courts Cases Discussing Obscenity in Relation to Overbreadth and Vagueness

Denver Area Educ. Telecommunications Consortium, Inc. v. *F.C.C.,* 518 U.S. 727 (1996) (holding that prohibition of patently offensive or indecent programming on public access channels violates the First Amendment).
Hamling v. *U.S.,* 418 U.S. 87 (1974) (explaining that statute containing generic term, such as "obscene," was not unconstitutionally vague).
Massachusetts v. *Oakes,* 491 U.S. 576 (1989) (holding that overbreadth challenge became moot when statute was amended).
Osborne v. *Ohio,* 495 U.S. 103, (1990) (holding that prohibition against possession and viewing of child pornography is constitutional and not overbroad).
Reno v. *American Civil Liberties Union,* 117 S.Ct. 2329 (1997) (holding that challenged provisions of the CDA were facially overbroad in violation of the First Amendment).
Smith v. *U.S.,* 431 U.S. 291 (1977) (holding that federal statute prohibiting mailing of obscene material is not unconstitutionally vague).
U.S. v. *X-Citement Video, Inc.,* 513 U.S. (1994) (holding that pornography statute was not vague and overbroad by making age of majority 18 years).

United States Supreme Courts Cases Discussing Obscenity in Relation to the Internet

Reno v. American Civil Liberties Union, 117 S.Ct. 2329 (1997) (holding that provisions of the CDA prohibiting transmission of obscene or indecent communications by means of interactive computer were content-based restrictions on speech).

United States Supreme Courts Cases Discussing Obscenity in Relation to Nudity

Barnes v. *Glen Theatre, Inc.*, 501 U.S. 560 (1991) (explaining that totally nude dancing as sought to be performed in adult bookstore was outside the purview of the First Amendment).

Erznoznick v. *City of Jacksonville*, 422 U.S. 205 (1975) (holding that an ordinance failing to distinguish movies containing nudity from all other movies is invalid as a permissible exercise of a state's police power).

Ginzburg v. *U.S.*, 383 U.S. 463 (1966) (holding that convictions for violation of federal obscenity statute could be sustained in view of defendant's pandering in production and sale of obscene publications).

Kingsley Intern. Pictures Corp. v. *Regents of University of State of N.Y.*, 360 U.S. 684 (1959) (holding that denial of license to exhibit motion pictures on the basis that the movie will condone adultery is a constitutional violation).

Miller v. *California*, 413 U.S. 15 (1973) (holding that a work can be regulated where the work, taken as a whole, appeals to the "prurient interest." The Court also discarded the "utterly without redeeming social value" as a constitutional standard).

New York v. *Ferber*, 458 U.S. 747(1982) (holding that child pornography is not protected under the First Amendment, providing conduct to be prohibited is adequately defined).

Osborne v. *Ohio*, 495 U.S. 103 (1990) (holding that prohibition against possession of nude photographs of minors does not violate the First Amendment).

Sable Communications of California, Inc. v. *F.C.C.*, 492 U.S. 115 (1989) (holding that prohibition of obscene telephone messages was constitutional).

II. SECONDARY LEGAL AUTHORITY

A) American Jurisprudence (AMJUR)

The American Jurisprudence is a legal encyclopedia. It provides an exhaustive list of legal topics. Within each topic there is a comprehensive summary of the law, and reference is also made to relevant case law and recent developments. The following American Jurisprudence (AMJUR) citations deal with topics that pertain to the First Amendment, obscenity, pornography and other related issues. For convenience, the titles to the referenced sections have been provided after each citation.

1) Constitutional Law, Volume 16A (1979). Cumulative Supplement current through April 1997.

1.1) 16A AM. JUR. 2D Constitutional Law § 499 (1979). § 499. GUARANTIES AS PROTECTING PUBLICATION, DISTRIBUTION, AND RECEIPT OF MATERIAL.

1.2) 16A AM. JUR. 2D Constitutional Law § 510 (1979). § 510. SUBJECT, SCOPE AND MANNER OF SPEECH; GENERALLY.

1.3) 16A AM. JUR. 2D Constitutional Law § 512 (1979). § 512. OBSCENE MATTER.

2) Customs Duties and Import Regulations, Volume 21A (1981). Cumulative Supplement current through April 1997.

2.1) 21A AM. JUR. 2D Customs § 23 (1981). § 23. IMMORAL OR OBSCENE ARTICLES OR PUBLICATIONS.

3) Entertainment and Sports Law, Volume 27A (1996).

3.1) 27A AM. JUR. 2D Entertainment § 4 (1996). § 4. GENERALLY.

3.2) 27A AM. JUR. 2D Entertainment § 18 (1996). § 18. THEATERS, CONCERTS, AND EXHIBITIONS.

4) Lewdness, Indecency, and Obscenity, Volume 50 (1995). Cumulative Supplement current through April 1997.

4.1) 50 AM. JUR. 2D Lewdness § 3 (1995). § 3. GENERALLY.

4.2) 50 AM. JUR. 2D Lewdness § 4 (1995). § 4. DEFINITION; MILLER TEST.

4.3) 50 AM. JUR. 2D Lewdness § 5 (1995). § 5. SEX AND OBSCENITY.

4.4) 50 AM. JUR. 2D Lewdness § 6 (1995). § 6. SPECIFIC ELEMENTS AND FACTORS DETERMINING OBSCENITY; JUDGING MATERIAL "AS A WHOLE."

4.5) 50 AM. JUR. 2D Lewdness § 10 (1995). § 10. INTENT OR MOTIVE AS ELEMENT.

4.6) 50 AM. JUR. 2D Lewdness § 12 (1995). §12. VALIDITY OF PROCEDURES DESIGNED TO PROTECT PUBLIC.

4.7) 50 AM. JUR. 2D Lewdness § 13 (1995). § 13. CRIMINAL STATUTES AND PROSECUTIONS.

4.8) 50 AM. JUR. 2D Lewdness § 14 (1995). § 14. SEARCH AND SEIZURE STATUTES AND PROCEEDINGS.

4.9) 50 AM. JUR. 2D Lewdness § 15 (1995). § 15. INJUNCTIONS.

4.10) 50 AM. JUR. 2D Lewdness § 18 (1995). § 18. TOPLESS, BOTTOMLESS, OR NUDE. DANCING OR SIMILAR CONDUCT.

4.11) 50 AM. JUR. 2D Lewdness § 21 (1995). § 21. BOOKS, MAGAZINES, PAMPHLETS.

4.12) 50 AM. JUR. 2D Lewdness § 24 (1995). § 24. MOTION PICTURES AND PLAYS.

4.13) 50 AM. JUR. 2D Lewdness § 27 (1995). § 27. CONDUCT INVOLVING CHILDREN; GENERALLY; CHILD PORNOGRAPHY.

4.14) 50 AM. JUR. 2D Lewdness § 31 (1995). § 31. CRIMINAL PROSECU-TIONS; GENERALLY.

5) Municipal Corporations, Counties, and Other Political Subdivisions, Volume 56 (1971). Cumulative Supplement current through April 1997.

5.1) 56 AM. JUR. 2D Municipal Corporations § 369 (1971). § 369. ORDI-NANCES VESTING DISCRETION IN MUNICIPAL OFFICERS OR BODIES.

6) Nuisances, Volume 58 (1989). Cumulative Supplement current through April 1997.

6.1) 58 AM. JUR. 2D Nuisances § 179 (1989). § 179. OBSCENITY AS BASIS OR REQUIREMENT FOR DETERMINATION OF NUISANCE.

6.2) 58 AM. JUR. 2D Nuisances § 427 (1989). § 427. NOTICE AND HEARING; SUFFICIENCY OF DETERMINATION BY MUNICIPAL AUTHORITIES.

7) Penal and Correctional Institutions, Volume 60 (1987) Cumulative Supplement current through April 1997.

7.1) 60 AM. JUR. 2D Penal and Correctional Institutions § 51 (1987). § 51. SEX-UALLY EXPLICIT MAIL.

8) Post Office, Volume 62 (1990). Cumulative Supplement current through April 1997.

8.1) 62 AM. JUR. 2D Post Office § 45 (1990). § 45. PARTICULAR TYPES OF NONMAILABLE MATTER; SEXUALLY ORIENTED MATTER.

8.2) 62 AM. JUR. 2D Post Office § 133 (1990). § 133. OFFENSES AGAINST POSTAL LAWS AND REGULATIONS; GENERALLY.

9) Telecommunications, Volume 74 (1974). Cumulative Supplement current through April 1997.

9.1) 74 AM. JUR. 2D Telecommunications § 157 (1974). § 157. MISCELLA-NEOUS REGULATIONS.

9.2) 74 AM. JUR. 2D Telecommunications § 186 (1974). § 186. STATE AND MUNICIPAL.

9.3) 74 AM. JUR. 2D Telecommunications § 204 (1974). § 204. CRIMINAL OFFENSES INVOLVING USE OR ABUSE OF COMMUNICATIONS FACILITIES; GENERALLY.

9.4) 74 AM. JUR. 2D Telecommunications § 206 (1974). § 206. CRIMINAL OFFENSES INVOLVING USE OR ABUSE OF COMMUNICATIONS FACILITIES; THREATS, HARASSMENT, AND USE OF OBSCENE LANGUAGE.

B) American Law Review (ALR)

The American Law Review is a legal encyclopedia. It provides an exhaustive list of legal topics. Within each topic there is a comprehensive summary of the law, and reference is also made to relevant case law and recent developments.

Annotation, *Construction and Application of Provision of Organized Crime Control Act of 1970 (18 U.S.C.A. § 1963(a). That Whoever Violated 18 U.S.C.A. § 1962 Shall Forfeit to United States Any Interest in Unlawful Enterprise* 61 A.L.R. Fed. 879 (1983).

Barbre, Erwin S., Annotation, *Operation of Nude-Model Photographic Studio as Offense* 48 A.L.R.3d 1313 (1973).

——, Annotation, *Topless or Bottomless Dancing or Similar Conduct as Offense* 49 A.L.R. 3d 1084 (1974).

Blum, George L., Annotation, *Obscenity Prosecutions: Statutory Exemption Based on Dissemination to Persons or Entities Having Scientific, Educational, or Similar Justification for Possession of Such Materials* 13 A.L.R. 5th 567 (1994).

Bockrath, Joseph T., Annotation, *Pornoshops or Similar Places Disseminating Obscene Materials as Nuisance* 58 A.L.R .3d 1134 (1975).

Crocca, Carol A., Annotation, *Validity of Ordinances Restricting Location of "Adult Entertainment" or Sex-Oriented Businesses* 10 A.L.R. 5th 538 (1993).

Dorr, Kathleen M., Annotation, *Validity and Construction of 18 U.S.C.A. §§ 371 and 2252(a). Penalizing Mailing or Receiving, or Conspiring to Mail or Receive, Child Pornography* 86 A.L.R. Fed. 359 (1988).

Dougherty, Francis M., Annotation, *Validity and Application of Statute Exempting Nonmanagerial, Nonfinancially Interested Employees from Obscenity Prosecution* 35 A.L.R. 4th 1237 (1981).

Duffala, Donald Paul, Annotation, *Validity and Application of Statute Authorizing Forfeiture of Use or Closure of Real Property From Which Obscene Materials Have Been Disseminated or Exhibited* 25 A.L.R. 4th 395 (1981).

Edwards, Joseph E., Annotation, *Validity, Construction, and Application of Federal Criminal Statute (18 U.S.C.A. § 1464). Punishing Utterance of Obscene, Indecent, or Profane, Language by Means of Radio Communication.* 17 A.L.R. Fed. 900 (1973).

Evans, J., Annotation, *Validity and Construction of Federal Statutes (18 U.S.C.A. §§ 1463, 1718). Which Declare Nonmailable Matter, Otherwise Mailable, Because of What Appears Upon Envelope, Outside Cover, Wrapper, or on Postal Card* 11 A.L.R. 3d 1276 (1967).

Foster, Wayne F., Annotation, *Validity, Construction, and Application of State Criminal Statute Forbidding Use of Telephone to Annoy or Harass* 95 A.L.R. 3d 411 (1980).

Harris, Deborah F., Annotation, *Immoral or Obscene Materials as Subject to Copyright Protection* 50 A.L.R. Fed. 805 (1980).

Hart, Kevin D., Annotation, *Sufficiency of Description of Business Records Under Fourth Amendment Requirement of Particularity in Federal Warrant Authorizing Search and Seizure* 53 A.L.R. Fed. 679 (1981).

Jacobius, Arleen, Annotation, *Admissibility of Evidence of Public-Opinion Polls or Surveys in Obscenity Prosecutions on Issue Whether Materials in Question are Obscene* 59 A.L.R. 5th 749 ().

Jones, Janet Boeth, Annotation, *Validity of Criminal Defamation Statutes* 68 A.L.R. 4th 1014 (1989).

Jovanovic, Teresia B., Annotation, *Propriety, Under First Amendment, of School Board's Censorship of Public School Libraries or Coursebooks* 64 A.L.R. Fed. 771 (1983).

Kramer, Donald T., Annotation, *Validity, Construction, and Application of Provisions of Postal Reorganization Act of 1970 (18 U.S.C.A. §§ 1735-1737; 39 U.S.C.A. §§ 3010, 3011) (so-called Goldwater amendment) prohibiting mailing of sexually oriented advertisements to persons who have notified postal service that . . .* 15 A.L.R. Fed. 488 (1973).

——, Annotation, *Validity, Under Federal Constitution, of Public School or State College Regulation of Student Newspapers, Magazines, or Other Publications—Federal Cases* 16 A.L.R. Fed. 182 (1973).

Littwin, Jack L., Annotation, *Validity and Construction of Statute or Ordinance Proscribing Solicitation For Purposes of Prostitution, Lewdness, or Assignation—Modern Cases* 77 A.L.R. 3d 519 (1977).

McDaniel, Bruce I., Annotation, *Prohibition of Obscene or Harassing Telephone Calls in Interstate or Foreign Communications Under 47 U.S.C.A. § 223* 50 A.L.R. Fed. 541 (1980).

Purver, Jonathan M., Annotation, *Validity and Construction of Municipal Ordinances Regulating Community Antenna Television Service (CATV).* 41 A.L.R. 3d 384 (1972).

Russ, Lee R., Annotation, *Validity of Statutes or Ordinances Requiring Sex-Oriented Businesses to Obtain Operating Licenses* 8 A.L.R. 4th 130 (1981).

Schopler, E. H., Annotation, *Comment Not.—Anticipatory Relief in Federal Courts Against State Criminal Prosecutions Growing Out of Civil Rights Activities* 8 A.L.R. 3d 301 (1967).

——, Annotation, *Comment Note.—Validity of Procedures Designed to Protect the Public Against Obscenity* 5 A.L.R. 3d 1214 (1966).

——, Annotation, *Modern Concept of Obscenity* 5 A.L.R. 3d 1158 (1966).

Seep, Ralph V., Annotation, *Validity, Construction, and Application of 18 U.S.C.A. § 2251, Penalizing Sexual Exploitation of Children* 99 A.L.R. Fed. 643 (1990).

Shaw, Jack W., Jr., Annotation, *Exhibition of Obscene Motion Pictures as Nuisance* 50 A.L.R. 3d 969 (1974).

Theuman, John E., Annotation, *Validity of Statute Making Sodomy a Criminal Offense* 20 A.L.R. 4th 1009 (1981).

Trenkner, Thomas R., Annotation, *Validity and Construction of Statutes or Ordinances Prohibiting Profanity or Profane Swearing or Cursing* 5 A.L.R. 4th 956 (1981).

Vernia, Benjamin J. Annotation, *Validity, Construction, and Application of State Statutes or Ordinances Regulating Sexual Performance by Child* 42 A.L.R. 5th 291 (1996).

Zelin, Judy E., Annotation, *Seizure of Books, Documents or Other Papers Under Search Warrant Not Describing Such Items* 54 A.L.R. 4th 391 (1988).

Zupanec, Donald M., Annotation, *Validity, Construction, and Effect of Statutes or Ordinances Prohibiting the Sale of Obscene Materials to Minors* 93 A.L.R. 3d 297 (1980).

III. SECONDARY SOURCES

A) SUPREME COURT

Atherton, John, "Speech, Act and the Right to Offend in Their First Amendment Context" *Revue Française d'Etudes Americain*, Ricaines [France] 1992.

Bickel, Alexander; Kauffmann, Stanley; Mcwilliams, Wilson Carey; Cohen, Marshall "On Pornography: II-Dissenting and Concurring Opinions" *The Public Interest*, v. 22 (Win) pp. 25–44, 1971.

Funston, Richard, "Pornography and the Politics: The Court, The Constitution, and the Commission" *Western Political Quarterly* 1971 v. 24 (4): 635–652.

Gest, Ted, "Where The New Court Is Heading" *U.S. News & World Report*, v. 109 (Aug 6 1990) pp. 20–21.

Hixson, Richard F., "Pornography and the Justices: The Supreme Court and the Intractable Obscenity Problem" *Southern Illinois University Press* (LC 95-42412) (ISBN 0-8093-2057-6) 1996 xiii+268p.

Lederer, Laura J., & Richard Delgado, Eds., "The Price We Pay: The Case Against Racist Speech, Hate Propaganda, and Pornography" Hill and Wang (LC 94-074512) (ISBN 0-8090-7883-X) Harper Collins (Can) 1995 xiv+380p.

Lerner, Ralph E., & JudithBresler, "Obscenity, What The Supreme Court Says. (Excerpt From Art Law) *Art News*, v. 88 (Oct. 1989), pp. 144–45.

Padgett, George E., "The Voting Record of Justice Stewart On First Amendment Cases" *Journalism Quarterly* 1982 v. 59 (4): 554–59.

Rezmierski, Virginia E., "Hurrah For The Wisdom of the Supreme Court" *EDUCOM Review*, v. 32 (Sept./Oct.1997) pp. 52-56.

Rogge, O. John, "The Obscenity Terms of the Court" *Villanova Law Review*, 1972, v.17 (3) Feb, pp. 393–462.

Sachs, Andrea, "A Victory For Integration" (Various Rulings) *Time*, v. 135 (Apr. 30 1990), p. 85.

Strossen, Nadine, "Academic and Artistic Freedom" (Academe) v. 78:8-15 N/D 1992.

B) LEGAL

"A Novel Crackdown On Porn Films in L.A." (H. Freeman Convicted of Pandering). *Newsweek*, v. 105 (June 3 1985), p. 61.

"Constitutional Law: Obscenity: Washington's Pornography and Moral Nuisance Act of 1982 Withstand First Amendment Challenge. Spokane Arcades v. Eikenberry, 544 F. Supp. 1034." *Gonzaga Law Review*, v. 18 (1982/1983), pp. 143–52.

"Cyberporn and Children: The Scope of the Problem, The State of the Technology, and the Need For Congressional Action: Hearing, July 24, 1995, On S. 892, A Bill to Amend Section 1464 of Title 18, United States Code, to Punish Transmission By Computer of Indecent Material to Minors" United States. Senate. Com. on the Judiciary. Supt. Docs (ISBN 0-16-052623-X) Pa 1996 iv+191p.

"Final Report, July 1986" United States. Dept. of Justice. Attorney Gen.'s Comm. On Pornography Supt Docs Pa 1986.

"Is First Amendment in Trouble?" (Views of Gary Colboth and George Heneghan) *USA Today* (Periodical) v. 116 (Aug. 1987), p. 101.

"Pornography and the First Amendment: American Booksellers v. Hudnut (598 F. Supp.1316)" *Harvard Women's Law Journal*, v. 9 (Spring 1986), pp. 153–72.

"The Civil Rights Pornography Ordinances–An Examination Under The First Amendment." *Kentucky Law Journal,* v. 73 (1984/1985), pp. 1081–1108.

Baird, Robert M., Ed. Rosenbaum, Stuart E., Ed., "Pornography: Private Right Or Public Menace?" Prometheus Bks (LC 91-29627) (ISBN 0-87975-690-X) 1991 p. 248.

Benson, Rebecca, "Pornography and the First Amendment: American Booksellers v. Hudnut" *Harvard Women's Law Journal,* v. 9 pp. 153–72 Spring 1986.

Bleifer, Craig B., "Looking At Pornography Through Rabeasian Lenses: Affirmative Action For Speech." *New York University Review of Law and Social Change,* v. 22 (1996), pp. 153–201.

Blim, John M., "Undoing Our Selves: The Error of Sacrificing Speech in the Quest For Equality." *Ohio State Law Journal,* v. 56: p.7-93 No. 2 1995 .

Butler, Judith P., "Sovereign Performatives in the Contemporary Scene of Utterance" *Critical Inquiry,* v. 23 (Winter 1997), pp. 350–77.

Chevigny, Paul, "Pornography and Cognition: A Reply to Cass Sunstein" (Discussion of Pornography and the First Amendment. C. Sunstein. *Duke Law Journal* p. 589–627 S 1986).

Delgato, Richard, & Stefancic, Jean, "Must We Defend Nazis? Hate Speech, Pornography, and the New First Amendment" *New York University Press* (LC 96-25368) (ISBN 0-8147-1858-2) 1997

Downs, Donald Alexander, "The New Politics of Pornography" *University of Chicago Press* (LC 89-34968) (ISBN 0-22616162-5) (ISBN 0-226-16163-3) 1989 xxiv+266p.

Duggan, Lisa, Hunter, Nan., & Vance, Carol S., "False Promises: New Antipornography Legislation in the U.S." *SIECUS Report,* v. 13 (May 1985) pp. 1–5.

Dworkin, Ronald Myles, "Liberty and Pornography" *The New York Review of Books,* v. 38 (Aug. 15, 1991), pp. 12–15. Includes bibliography.

Emerson, Thomas I. "Pornography and the First Amendment: A Reply to Professor Mackinnon. (Discussion of Not a Moral Issue. C.A. Mackinnon 2 Yale L. & Pol'y Rev. 321-45 Spr 1984) *Yale Law & Policy Review,* v. 3 (Fall 1984), pp. 130–43.

Fiss, Owen M., "Liberalism Divided: Freedom of Speech and the Many Uses of State Power" Westview (LC 95-46272) (ISBN 0-8133-2484-X) (ISBN 0-8133-2485-8) Pa 1996 vii+192p.

Gey, Steven G., "The Apologetics of Suppression: The Regulation of Pornography As Act and Idea" *Michigan Law Review* 86 p.1564-1634 Je 1988.

Giglio, Ernest, "Rights, Liberties and Public Policy" Ashgate (LC 95-79583) (ISBN 1-85972-045-5) 1995.

Haiman, Franklyn S., "Speech Acts and the First Amendment" *Southern Illinois University Press* (LC 92-21157) (ISBN 0-8093-1882-2) 1993 x+103p.

Haiman, Franklyn S., "Speech Acts and the First Amendment" *Southern Illinois University Press* (LC 92-21157) (ISBN 0-8093-1882-2) 1993.

Hefner, Christie, "The Meese Commission: Sex, Violence, and Censorship; The Meese Commission Report Poses a More Serious Threat to the First Amendment Than to Pornography." *Humanist,* v. 47:25-9+ Jan./Feb. 1987.

Henneberger, Melinda, "How Free Can Teachers' Speech Be?" *New York Times* (Late New York Edition) (Oct. 3 1993), p. 6.

Huttig, J. W., "Putting Porn in Its Place? Senator's Bill Targets Online Porn" (Work of J.J. Exon) *PC Novice,* v. 6 (July 1995), pp. 78–79.

Jaeger, Eric, "Obscenity and the Reasonable Person: Will He Know It When He Sees It?" *Boston College Law Review,* v. 30:823-60 May 1989.

Lederer, Laura J., & Delgado, Richard (Eds.), "The Price We Pay: The Case Against

Racist Speech, Hate Propaganda, and Pornography" Hill and Wang (LC 94-074512) (ISBN 0-8090-7883-X) Harper Collins (Can) 1995 xiv+380p.

Linz, Daniel, "Issues Bearing On The Legal Regulation of Violent and Sexually Violent Media" *Journal of Social Issues* 42:171–93 Fall 1986.

Loewy, Arnold H., "Obscenity, Pornography, and First Amendment Theory." *William and Mary Bill of Rights Journal*, v. 2 (Winter 1993), pp. 471–93.

Mahoney, Kathleen, "The Canadian Constitutional Approach to Freedom of Expression in Hate Propaganda and Pornography." *Law and Contemporary Problems*, v. 55 (Winter 1992), pp. 77–105.

Michelman, Frank I., "Conceptions of Democracy in American Constitutional Argument: The Case of Pornography Regulation." *Tennessee Law Review*, v. 56 no. 2 (Winter 1989), pp. 291–319.

Richards, David A.J., "Pornography Commissions and the First Amendment: On Constitutional Values and Constitutional Facts" *Maine Law Review*, v. 39 (1987), pp. 275–320.

Routledge, "Stripping Pornography of Constitutional Protection." *Harvard Law Review*, v. 107 (June 1994), pp. 2111–16.

Schachter, Hindy Lauer, "The Pornography Debate in the United States: Politics, Law and Justification" Gazette: *The International Journal For Mass Communication Studies* [Netherlands], v. 42(2): 93-104, 1988–89.

Strossen, Nadine, "Hate Speech and Pornography: Do We Have to Choose Between Freedom of Speech and Equality?" *Case Western Reserve Law Review*, v. 46 (Winter 1996), pp. 449–78.

Sunstein, Cass R., "The First Amendment and Cognition: A Response." (Discussion of Pornography and Cognition: A Reply to Case Sunstein. P. Chevigny. *Duke Law Journal* p. 420–32 (Apr. 1989).

Taub, Nadine, "A New View of Pornography, Speech, and Equality Or Only Words?" *Rutgers Law Review*, v. 46 (Fall 1993), pp. 595–607.

Vadas, Melinda, "The Pornography/Civil Rights Ordinance v. The BOG: And the Winner Is?" *Hypatia*, 1992, v.7 (3), (Summer), p. 94–109.

Whicher, Jane M., "Constitutional and Policy Implications of "Pornography Victim" Compensation Schemes." *Federal Bar News & Journal*, v. 40 (July 1993), pp. 360-67.

C) LIBRARIES

"Concerning The Obscene" *Wilson Library Bulletin* 1968, v. 42(9), pp. 896-929.

Anderson, A. J., "Compromising Position" *Library Journal*, v. 122 (Nov. 1 1997), pp. 56–57.

Berry, John N., "Policy, Politics, and the Internet" *Library Journal*, v. 121 (Apr. 1 1996), p. 6.

Eckl, Lisa L., "American Library Association V. Reno (33 F.3d 78 (D.C. Cir. 1994)): Protecting Producers Against Infringement" Or Children Against "Vulnerability?" First Amendment Issues Surrounding Child Pornography Law." *Villanova Sports & Entertainment Law Journal*, v. 3 (2) 1996 p.589–612.

Kniffel, Leonard, "ALA-Led Coalition Challenges Communications Decency Act" *American Libraries*, v. 27 (Apr. 1996), pp. 13–14.

Kuh, Richard H., "Obscenity, Censorship, and the Nondoctrinare Liberal" *Wilson Library Bulletin* 1968, v. 42 (9), pp. 902–909.

Nelson, W. Dale, Is "Lust" a Four-Letter Word? (In First Amendment Case) *Wilson Library Bulletin*, v. 59 (Jan. 1985), pp. 330–31.

Pitman, Randy, "Where's The Sex? Our Double Standards in Visual Media" *Library Journal,* v. 122 (Nov. 15 1997), pp. 31–33. Includes bibliography.

Rembar, Charles, "As Long As It Doesn't Offend Our Own Ideas" *Wilson Library Bulletin* 1968, v. 42(9), pp. 896–901.

St. Lifer, Evan, "Libraries Challenge NY's Ban On "Indecency" Online" *Library Journal,* v. 122 (Feb. 15 1997), pp. 90–91.

Trotter, Andrew, "Bill Would Pressure Schools to Filter Out On-Line Smut" *Education Week,* v. 17 (Feb. 18 1998), p. 28.

IV. CENSORSHIP

"A Novel Crackdown On Porn Films in L.A." (H. Freeman Convicted of Pandering) *Newsweek,* v. 105 (June 3 1985), p. 61.

"Outlawing Pornography: What We Gain, What We Lose/; E. Chemerinsky; P. J. Mcgeady" *Human Rights,* v. 12 (Spring 1985), pp. 24–26.

"The Right War" (G. Hawkins' Fight Against Censorship) *The Nation,* v. 241 (July 6-13 1985), pp. 4–5.

"Two Meese Commissioners Speak Out At NCAC Luncheon" *Library Journal,* v. 111 (Aug. 1986), pp. 23–24.

Adler, Amy, "What's Left? Hate Speech, Pornography, and the Problem For Artistic Expression" *California Law Review,* v. 84 p.1499–1572 D 1996.

Baird, Robert M., Ed. Rosenbaum, Stuart E., Ed., "Pornography: Private Right Or Public Manace?" Prometheus Bks (LC 91-29627) (ISBN 0-87975-690-X) 1991 248p..

Bergman, Brian; Kaihla, Paul, "The Battle Over Censorship: Who Defines Public Morality?" *Maclean's,* v. 107, 24, pp. 26–31, 1994.

Bernstein, Nina, "A Free Speech Hero? It's Not That Simple." (L. Flynt) *New York Times* (late New York Edition) (Dec. 22 1996), p. 1 (Sec 2).

Bob, Murray L., "The Right Questions About Obscenity: An Alternative to the Meese Commission Report" *Library Journal,* v. 111 (Oct. 15 1986), pp. 39-41.

Bretnor, Reginald, "A Plea For Censorship" *Modern Age* 1966/67, v. 11(1), pp. 35–44.

Butler, Judith P., "Sovereign Performatives in the Contemporary Scene of Utterance" *Critical Inquiry,* v. 23 (Winter 1997), pp. 350–77.

Campbell, Patty, ("An Official Government Agency For Censoring Books For Youth") *Wilson Library Bulletin,* v. 59 (Oct. 1984), pp. 130–31.

Clark, Charles S., "The Obscenity Debate: Crackdowns On Pornography and Lewdness Draw Cries of Censorship" *CQ Researcher,* v. 1 p.971–91 D 20 1991.

Demac, Donna A., "Liberty Denied: The Current Rise of Censorship in America; Foreword By Walter Karp" PEN American Center, 568 Broadway, New York, NY 10012 (LC 88-17941) (ISBN 0-934638-09-8) 1988.

Duggan, Lisa, Hunter, Nan, & Vance, Carol S., "False Promises: New Antipornography Legislation in the U.S." *SIECUS Report,* v. 13 (May 1985), pp. 1–5.

Follain, Mary, "Little Ones and Liberties" The Times Educational Supplement No. 3692 (Apr. 3 1987), p. 18.

Friedman, Jane M., "Erotica, Censorship, and the United States Post Office Department" *Michigan Academician* 1971, v. 4 (1), pp. 7-16.

Gracyk, Theodore A. "Pornography As Representation: Aesthetic Considerations" *The Journal of Aesthetic Education,* v. 21 (Winter 1987), pp. 103–21. Includes bibliography.

Gunther, Albert C., "Overrating The X-Rating: The Third-Person Perception and

Support For Censorship of Pornography" *Journal of Communication,* 1995 (Winter) v. 45(1), pp. 27–38.

Haiman, Franklyn S. "Speech Acts and the First Amendment" *Southern Illinois University Press* (LC 92-21157) (ISBN 0-8093-1882-2) 1993 x+103p.

Harvey, Philip D., "Federal Censorship and the War On Pornography" *SIECUS Report,* v. 20 (Feb./Mar. 1992), pp. 8–12.

Hefner, Christie, "The Meese Commission: Sex, Violence, and Censorship" *The Humanist,* 1987, v.47 (1) Jan-Feb, pp. 25–29.

Hefner, Christie, "The Meese Commission: Sex, Violence, and Censorship; The Meese Commission Report Poses a More Serious Threat to the First Amendment Than to Pornography" *Humanist,* v. 47 p.25–9+ Jan./Feb. 1987.

Heins, Marjorie, "A Tentaive Taste of Freedom" (Limits of Liberty Film Festival and Conference) *The Nation,* v. 257 (Sept. 20 1993), p. 278.

Henneberger, Melinda, "How Free Can Teachers' Speech Be?" *New York Times* (Late New York Edition) (Oct. 3 1993), p. 6.

Hentoff, Nat, "Free Speech For Me-But Not For Thee: How The American Left and Right Relentlessly Censor Each Other" HarperCollins (LC 92-52550) (ISBN 0-06- 019006-X) 1992 ix+405p.

Huttig, J. W., "Putting Porn in Its Place? Senator's Bill Targets Online Porn" (Work of J. J. Exon) *PC Novice,* v. 6 (July 1995), pp. 78–79.

Jacobson, Daniel, "Freedom of Speech Acts? A Response to Langton" *Philosophy & Public Affairs,* v. 24 (Winter 1995), pp. 64–79.

Johnson, Dirk, "Colorado Vote Will Test Law On Obscenity" (Ballot Issue) *New York Times* (Late New York Edition) (Oct. 9 1994), p. 20 (Sec 1).

Katz, Leanne, "Censorship Too Close to Home" *SIECUS Report,* v. 23 (Oct./Nov. 1994), pp. 15–18. Includes bibliography.

Kuh, Richard H., "Obscenity, Censorship, and the Nondoctrinare Liberal" *Wilson Library Bulletin,* 1968, v. 42 (9), pp. 902–909.

Langton, Rae, "Speech Acts and Unspeakable Acts" *Philosophy & Public Affairs,* v. 22 (Fall 1993), pp. 293–330.

Lewis, Anthony, "The First Amendment, Under Fire From The Left."(Interview With C. Mackinnon and F. Abrams) *The New York Times Magazine* (Mar. 13 1994), pp. 40–45.

Lynn, Barry, "The New Pornography Commission: Slouching Toward Censorship" *SIECUS Report,* v. 14 (May 1986), pp. 1–6.

Mccormack, Thelma, Ed., "Studies in Communications, 1990: A Research Annual; Censorship and Libel: The Chilling Effect" JAI Pr (ISBN 0-89232-761-8) 1990 x+163p.

Melichar, Don, "My Biggest Worry About Censorship" *English Journal,* v. 74 (Jan. 1985), p. 24.

Molz, Kathleen, "A Panel Discussion On Censorship and Pornography" *Wilson Library Bulletin* 1968 v.42 (9), pp. 926–29.

Pally, Marcia, "Out of Harm's Way: The Great Soothing Appeal of Censorship" *SIECUS Report,* v. 23 (Oct./Nov. 1994), pp. 3–9. Includes bibliography.

Rolph, C.H., "The Literary Censorship in England" *Wilson Library Bulletin* 1968 v.42(9), pp. 912–25.

Stein, Joel, "Larry Flint, The Sequel (Pornographer Tests Obscenity Exception to the First Amendment in Cincinnati)" *Time,* v. 151 No. 15 (Apr. 20 1998), pp. 64.

V. CHILDREN AND PORNOGRAPHY

"Constitutional Law–Child Pornography and the First Amendment: Abrogation of the Obscenity Doctrine in New York v. Ferber, 102 S.Ct. 3348" *Creighton Law Review*, v. 16 (1982/1983), pp. 509–31.

"Constitutional Law–Child Pornography Is Outside The Scope of First Amendment Protection" *Memphis State University Law Review*, v. 12 (Summer 1982), pp. 613–23.

"Constitutional Law–Child Pornography: A New Exception to the First Amendment–New York v. Ferber (102 S.Ct. 3348)" *Florida State University Law Review*, v. 10 (Winter 1983), pp. 684–701.

"Constitutional Law–First Amendment–Freedom of Speech–New York v. Ferber (102 S.Ct. 3348)." *New York Law School Law Review*, v. 29 (1984), pp. 469-89.

"Constitutional Law–First Amendment–New York Statute Proscribing Distribution of Nonobscene Materials Depicting Minors Engaged in Sexual Conduct Does Not Violate The First Amendment Because The Materials Are Outside First Amendment Protection and the Statute Is Not Substantially Overbroad. New York v. Ferber (102 S.Ct. 3348)" *Villanova Law Review*, v. 28 (Jan. 1983), pp. 416–33.

"Constitutional Law–First Amendment–Section 2907.323(A)(3) of the Ohio Code, Which Prohibits The Private Possession and Viewing of Child Pornography, Is Not Unconstitutional Given The Compelling State Interest in Protecting The Psychological and Physical Well-Being of Minors and Preventing Their Exploitation. Osborne v. Ohio, 110 S.Ct. 1691." *University of Detroit Law Review*, v. 68 (Spring 1991), pp. 427–39.

"Constitutional Law–First Amendment–States May Proscribe The Private Possession of Non-Obscene Child Pornography–Osborne v. Ohio, 110 S.Ct. 1691." *Seton Hall Law Review*, v. 21 (1991), pp. 410–44.

"Constitutional Law–Ohio Statute Prohibiting In-Home Possession of Child Pornography Upheld Against First Amendment Interest–Osborne v. Ohio, 110 S.Ct. 1691. *Suffolk University Law Review*, v. 25 (Spring 1991), pp. 262–69.

"First Amendment: Child Pornography; Access to the Courtroom; Access to Judicial Records" *Annual Survey of American Law*, v. 1983 (Feb. 1984), pp. 531–67.

"First Amendment–Freedom of Speech–Child Pornography, Obscene Or Not, Possesses No First Amendment Protection–New York v. Ferber, 102 S.Ct. 3348" *Santa Clara Law Review*, v. 23 (Spring 1983), pp. 675–84.

"New York v. Ferber (102 S.Ct. 3348): Compelling Extension of First Amendment Infringement" *Golden Gate University Law Review*, v. 13 (Spring 1983), pp. 475–94.

"No First Amendment Protection For The Sexploitation of Children" *Loyola Law Review*, v. 29 (Winter 1983), pp. 227–35.

"Proliferation of Child Pornography On The Internet: Special Hearing [April 8, 1997]" United States. Senate. Com. On Appropriations. Subcom. On Commer., Justice, and State, The Judiciary, and Related Agencies. 105th Cong., 1st Sess. S. Hearing 105-214. (SD Cat. No. Y4. Ap. 6/2:S.Hrg.105-214).

"The Child Protection Act of 1984: Child Pornography and the First Amendment" *Seton Hall Legislative Journal*, v. 9 (1985), pp. 327–53.

Brill, Ann M., & Packard, Ashley, "Children and Pornography Online: State v. Federal Regulation" *Law/Technology*, v. 29:1-15, A-1-A-5 No. 4, 1996.

Cleary, John C., "Telephone Pornography: First Amendment Constraints On Shielding Children From Dial-A-Porn" *Harvard Journal of Legislation*, v. 22, Summer 1985, pp. 503–50.

Douglass, Michael C., "Child Pornography, Obscenity Statutes and the Overbreadth Doctrine: An Interrelationship As Viewed Through The Lens of Osborne v. Ohio (110 S.Ct. 1691 [1990])." *Thurgood Marshall Law Review*, v. 17 (Spring 1992), pp. 465–83.

Eckl, Lisa L., "American Library Association v. Reno (33 F.3d 78 (D.C. Cir. 1994)): Protecting Producers Against Infringement" Or Children Against "Vulnerability?" First Amendment Issues Surrounding Child Pornography Law." *Villanova Sports & Entertainment Law Journal*, v. 3 (2) (1996) pp. 589–612.

Green, William, "Children and Pornography: An Interest Analysis in System Perspective [Statutes to Protect Children From Abuse in the Production of Pornography and From Harm in the Sale of Obscene Materials; Issues of Free Speech, Privacy and Due Process]" *Valparaiso University Law Review*, v. 19 (Winter 1985), pp. 441–70.

Mungovan, Timothy W., "Constitutional Law–Protection of Children Against Sexual, Exploitation Act Chills Constitutionally Protected Speech-United States v. X-Citement Video, Inc., 982 F.2d 1285 (1992)." *Suffolk University Law Review*, v. 27 (Spring 1993), pp. 221–30.

Pierce, Robert Lee, "Child Pornography: A Hidden Dimension of Child Abuse" *Child Abuse and Neglect*, 1984, v. 8 (4), pp. 483–93.

Schauer, Frederick F., "Codifying The First Amendment: New York v. Ferber (102 S.Ct. 3348)" *The Supreme Court Review*, v. 1982 (1982), pp. 285–317.

VI. EDUCATION AND PORNOGRAPHY

Campbell, Patty, ("An Official Government Agency For Censoring Books For Youth") *Wilson Library Bulletin*, v. 59 (Oct. 1984), pp. 130–31.

Cornwell, Tim, "Bible Belt Whipped Into Fury Over Sex" *The Times Higher Education Supplement* No. 1229 (May 24 1996), pp. 9.

Dworkin, Ronald Myles, "Liberty and Pornography" *The New York Review of Books*, v. 38 (Aug. 15 1991), pp. 12-15. Includes bibliography.

Gracyk, Theodore A., "Pornography As Representation: Aesthetic Considerations" *The Journal of Aesthetic Education*, v. 21 (Winter 1987), pp. 103–21. Includes bibliography.

Hevener, Fillmer, "College Students' Attitudes Toward Censorship of Sexual Explicitness" *College Student Journal*, v. 24 (June 1990), pp. 167–72.

Katz, Leanne, "Censorship Too Close to Home" *SIECUS Report*, v. 23 (Oct./Nov. 1994), pp. 15-18. Includes bibliography.

Pally, Marcia, "Out of Harm's Way: The Great Soothing Appeal of Censorship" *SIECUS Report*, v. 23 (Oct./Nov. 1994), pp. 3–9. Includes bibliography.

Rezmierski, Virginia E., "Hurrah For The Wisdom of the Supreme Court" *EDUCOM Review*, v. 32 (Sept./Oct.1997), pp. 52–56.

Young, Jeffrey R., "Federal Judge Upholds Limits By U. of Oklahoma On Sex-Related Internet Material" *The Chronicle of Higher Education*, v. 43 (Feb. 7 1997), p. A27.

Young, Jeffrey R., "From His Dorm Room, A Vanderbilt Junior Becomes a Force Against Internet Regulation" *The Chronicle of Higher Education*, v. 43 (Mar. 7 1997), p. A23.

VII. FEMINISM AND PORNOGRAPHY

"Feminism, Pornography, and the First Amendment: An Obscenity-Based Analysis of Proposed Antipornography Laws" *UCLA Law Review*, v. 34 (Apr. 1987), pp. 1265–1304.

"Is Pornography Dangerous to Women?" *Glamour*, v. 90 (Aug. 1992), p. 116.

"Pornography and the First Amendment: The Feminist Balance" *Arizona Law Review*, v. 27 (1985), pp. 415–35.

"Pornography: A Humanist Issue; It Is Agreed That Pornography Is a Symptom of a Sick Society; But What Does One Do About It?" *Humanist* v. 45 (July/Aug. 1985), pp. 23–31+ .

"Sex Discrimination and the First Amendment: Pornography and Free Speech" *Texas Tech Law Review*, v. 17 (June 1986), pp. 1577–1602.

"Symposium: The Sex Panic: Women, Censorship, and Pornography" *New York Law School Law Review*, v. 38 (1-4) (1993), pp. 1–399.

Benson, Rebecca, "Pornography and the First Amendment: American Booksellers v. Hudnut" *Harvard Women's Law Journal*, v. 9 (Spring 1986), pp. 153–72.

Berger, Ronald J.; Searles, Patricia; Cottle, Charles E., "Feminism and Pornography" New York, NY: Praeger Publishers.

Bosmajian, Haig A., "Obscenity, Sexism, and Freedom of Speech" *College English*, 1978, v. 39 (7) (Mar.), pp. 812–819.

Bruce, Teresa M., "Pornophobia, Pornophilia, and the Need For a Middle Path-A Review Essay of Nadine Strossen's Defending Pornography: Free Speech, Sex, and the Fight For Women's Rights." *American University Journal of Gender & The Law*, v. 5 (Spring 1997), pp. 393–406.

Carpenter, Ted Galen, "Porn Busters: Radical Feminists Are Turning Their Backs On The First Amendment in a Crusade to Clean Up America" *Reason*, v. 17 (1985), pp. 26–30.

Dworkin, Ronald Myles, "Liberty and Pornography" *The New York Review of Books*, v. 38 (Aug. 15 1991), pp. 12–15. Includes bibliography.

Dworkin, Ronald Myles, "Women and Pornography" *The New York Review of Books*, v. 40 (Oct. 21 1993), p. 36. Includes bibliography.

Easton, Susan M., "The Problem of Pornography: Regulation and the Right to Free Speech" Routledge (LC 93-37378) (ISBN 0-415-09182-9) (ISBN 0-415-09183-7) xviii+197p.

Gates, David, "Free Speech-Or a Hostile Act?" *Newsweek*, v. 123 (Jan. 17 1994), p. 53.

Gey, Steven G., "The Apologetics of Suppression: The Regulation of Pornography As Act and Idea" *Michigan Law Review*, v. 86 (June 1988), pp. 1564-1634.

Hentoff, Nat, "Mackinnon v. Free Speech" *The Progressive*, v. 56 (Sept. 1992), pp. 14–15.

Isaacs, Susan, "Why We Must Put Up With Porn: To Have Speech We Love, We Have to Defend Speech We Hate" *Redbook*, v. 181 (Aug. 1993), p. 46.

Jensen, Robert, U Texas, Austin 78712 "Pornography and Affirmative Conceptions of Freedom" 1995 *Women & Politics*, v. 15 (1), pp. 1–18.

Kole, Janet, "The Anti-Porn Alliance-Feminists and the Religious Right" *Vogue*, v. 174 (Dec. 1984), p. 194.

Lacayo, Richard, "Assault By Paragraph" *Time*, v. 143 (Jan. 17 1994), p. 62.

Lansberg, Michele, "Canada: Antipornography Breakthrough in the Law" *Ms.*, v. 2 (May/June 1992), pp. 14–15.

Mackinnon, Catharine A., "Pornography, Civil Rights, and Speech" *Harvard Civil Rights- Civil Liberties Law Review*, v. 20 (Winter 1985), pp. 1-70.

Mansbridge, Jane J., "Post ERA: Should Every Flower Bloom?" *Ms.*, v. 15 (July 1986), p. 46.

Margolick, David, "Catering to a Feminist Superstar, Judges Find Themselves Tangled in a Free-Speech Debate" *New York Times* (Late New York Edition) (Nov. 5 1993), p. B11.

Melichar, Don, "My Biggest Worry About Censorship" *English Journal*, v. 74 (Jan. 1985), p. 24.

Nunamaker, Anne W.; Beasley, Maurine H., "Women, The First Amendment, and Pornography: A Historical Perspective" *Studies in Communications*, v. 4 (1990), pp. 101–18.

Pilpel, Harriet Fleischl, "Porn Vigilantes-Are They Confusing Feminism with Censorship?" *Vogue*, v. 175 (Sept. 1985), p. 681.

Post, Robert C., "Cultural Heterogeneity and Law: Pornography, Blasphemy, and the First Amendment" *California Law Review*, v. 76 (Mar. 1988), pp. 29–335.

Quistgaard, Bettina, "Pornography, Harm, and Censorship: A Feminist (Re) Vision of the Right to Freedom of Expression." *University of Toronto Faculty of Law Review*, v. 52 (Winter 1993), pp. 132–69.

Strossen, Nadine, "A Feminist Critique of "The" Feminist Critique of Pornography" *Virginia Law Review*, v. 79 (Aug. 1993), pp. 1099–1190.

Strossen, Nadine, "Defending Pornography: Free Speech, Sex and the Fight For Women's Rights" Simon (LC 94-40372) (ISBN 0-684-19749-9) 1995 320p.

Taub, Nadine, "A New View of Pornography, Speech, and Equality Or Only Words?" *Rutgers Law Review*, v. 46 (Fall 1993), pp. 595–607.

Tyrrell, R. Emmett, "The Worst Book of the Year" (C. Mackinnon's Only Words) *The American Spectator*, v. 27 (Feb. 1994), pp. 20+.

Winkelman, Sheila J., "Making a Woman's Safety More Important Than Peep Shows: A Review of the Pornography Victims' Compensation Act." *Washington University Journal of Urban and Contemporary Law*, v. 44 (Summer/Fall 1993), pp. 237–63.

VIII. HISTORY OF PORNOGRAPHY

Alstyne, Arvo Van, "Obscenity and the Inspired Constitution: A Dilemma For Mormons" *Dialogue: A Journal of Mormon Thought* 1967, v. 2(2) p.75–89.

Bernstein, Nina, "A Free Speech Hero? It's Not That Simple." (L. Flynt) *New York Times* (late New York Edition) (Dec. 22 1996), p. 1 (Sec 2).

Cox, Phil, "Speech" and Some of Its Wounds *Diacritics*, 1994, v. 24 (1) Spring p. 63–77.

Gest, Ted, "Where The New Court Is Heading" *U.S. News & World Report*, v. 109 (Aug 6 1990), pp. 20–21.

Lombardi, John, "Porn Again" *Los Angeles*, v. 41 (Nov. 1996), pp. 102–107.

Rich, Frank, "Larry Flint, Patriot" (Movie The People Vs. Larry Flynt; Oped) *New York Times* (Late New York Edition) (Oct. 12 1996), p. 23.

Rolph, C.H., "The Literary Censorship in England" *Wilson Library Bulletin*, 1968, v. 42(9), pp. 912–925.

Stein, Joel, "Larry Flint, The Sequel (Pornographer Tests Obscenity Exception to the First Amendment in Cincinnati)" *Time*, v. 151, no. 15 (Apr. 20 1998), p. 64.

Wilson, W. Cody, "Pornography: The Emergence of a Social Issue and the Beginning of Psychological Study" *Journal of Social Issues* 1973, v. 29(3), pp. 7–18.

IX. RELIGION

Alstyne, Arvo Van, "Obscenity and the Inspired Constitution: A Dilemma For Mormons" *Dialogue: A Journal of Mormon Thought* 1967, v. 2(2), pp. 75–89.

Dougherty, Jude P., "What Was Religion: The Demise of a Prodigious Power" *Modern Age* 1990, v. 33(2), pp. 113–21.

Kantzer, Kenneth S., "The Power of Porn" *Christianity Today*, v. 30 (Feb. 7 1986), pp. 18–20.

Kole, Janet, "The Anti-Porn Alliance-Feminists and the Religious Right" *Vogue*, v. 174 (Dec. 1984), p. 194.

Minnery, Tom, "What It Takes to Fight Pornography" *Christianity Today*, v. 29 (Feb. 15 1985), pp. 10–11.

Swomley, John M., "Pat Robertson's Contract On America" *The Humanist*, v. 55 July/Aug. 1995), pp. 35–36.

X. SOCIOLOGY AND PORNOGRAPHY

Baird, Robert M., & Rosenbaum, Stuart E., "Pornography: Private Right Or Public Menace?" Prometheus Bks (LC 91-29627) (ISBN 0-87975-690-X) 1991 248p.

Bosmajian, Haig A., "Obscenity, Sexism, and Freedom of Speech" *College English*, 1978, v. 39(7) Mar pp. 812–19.

Childress, Steven Alan, "Reel "Rape Speech": Violent Pornography and the Politics of Harm" *Law and Society Review*, 1991, v. 25(1) p.177–214.

Douglas, Lawrence, "The Force of Words: Fish, Matsuda, Mackinnon, and the Theory of Discursive Violence" *Law and Society Review*, 1995, v. 29(1) Apr pp. 169–190.

Hefner, Christie, "The Meese Commission: Sex, Violence, and Censorship" *The Humanist*, 1987, v. 47(1) Jan-Feb pp. 25–29, 46.

Jaeger, Eric, "Obscenity and the Reasonable Person: Will He Know It When He Sees It?" *Boston College Law Review*, v. 30, May 1989 pp. 823–60.

Jensen, Robert, "Pornography and Affirmative Conceptions of Freedom" *Women & Politics*, 1995, v. 15(1), pp. 1–18.

Lee, Simon, "The Cost of Free Speech" Faber (ISBN 0-571-14447-0) Pa L4.99 1990 x+149p.

Linz, Daniel, "Issues Bearing On The Legal Regulation of Violent and Sexually Violent Media," *Social Issues*, v. 42 Fall 1986, pp. 171–93.

Malamuth, Neil M. [Ed] and Others, "Pornography and Sexual Aggression" AI&SI. Orlando, FL: Academic Press, Inc.

Nelson, W. Dale, "Is 'Lust' a Four-Letter Word?" (In First Amendment Case) *Wilson Library Bulletin*, v. 59 (Jan. 1985), pp. 330–31.

Ritts, Vicki; Engbretson, Robert O., "College Students Attitudes Toward Adult Materials and the Legal Rental of Adult Videos" *College Student Journal*, v. 25 (4) Dec 1991, pp. 440–50.

Sharp, Elaine B., "Culture Wars and City Politics: Local Government's Role in Social Conflict" Urban Affairs Review Urban Affairs R, v. 31p.738-58 J1 1996.

Strossen, Nadine, "Academic and Artistic Freedom" *Academe*, v. 78 pp. 8–15 N/D 1992

Wilson, W. Cody, "Pornography: The Emergence of a Social Issue and the Beginning of Psychological Study" *Journal of Social Issues*, 1973, v. 29 (3), pp. 7–18.

XI. THE INTERNET AND PORNOGRAPHY

"Cyberporn: Protecting Our Children From The Back Alleys of the Internet: Joint Hearing, July 26, 1995, Before The Subcommittee On Basic Research and the Subcommittee On Technology" United States. House. Com. On Sci Supt Docs (ISBN 0-16-047717-4) Pa 1995 v+130p.

"First Amendment Constraints On The Regulation of Telephone Pornography" *University of Cincinnati Law Review*, v. 55 (1986), pp. 237–55.

"Free Speech Online. (Pornography and Sex-Related Discussion Groups On Computer Networks)" *Newsletter On Intellectual Freedom*, v. 42 (May 1993), p. 63.

"Proliferation of Child Pornography On The Internet: Special Hearing [April 8, 1997]" United States. Senate. Com. On Appropriations. Subcom. On Commer., Justice, and State, The Judiciary, and Related Agencies. 105th Cong., 1st Sess..S. Hearing 105-214. (SD Cat. No Y 4.Ap 6/2:S.Hrg.105-214).

Adelman, Ronald W., "The Constitutionality of Congressional Efforts to Ban Computer-Generated Child Pornography: A First Amendment Assessment of S. 1237" *John Marshall Journal of Computer & Information Law*, v. 14 (Spring 1996), pp. 483–92.

Anderson, A.J. "Compromising Position" *Library Journal*, v. 122 (Nov. 1 1997), pp. 56–57.

Berry, John N., "Policy, Politics, and the Internet" *Library Journal*, v. 121 (Apr. 1 1996), p. 6.

Browning, Graeme, "Net Effects: Opponents of Legislation That Would Bar "Lewd Or Indecent" Material From An International Computer Network Have Orchestrated An Avalanche of Protests, Most of Them Delivered By Computer; The Campaign May Be a Preview of Things to Come" *National Journal*, v. 27 p. 1336-40 June 3 1995.

Cate, Fred H., "Cybersex: Regulating Sexually Explicit Expression On The Internet" *Behavioral Sciences & the Law*, Spr 1996, v. 14 (2), pp. 145–66 1996.

Cleary, John C., "Telephone Pornography: First Amendment Constraints On Shielding Children From Dial-A-Porn" *Harvard Journal of Legislation*, v. 22 p. 503–50 Summer 1985.

Corliss, Richard, "Turned On? Turn It Off: Switching Channels May Be One Cure For The Contagion of Porn." *Time*, v. 130 (July 6 1987), pp. 72–73.

Cornwell, Tim, "Bible Belt Whipped Into Fury Over Sex" The Times Higher Education Supplement No. 1229 (May 24 1996), p. 9.

Coy, Peter, & Galen, Michele, "Let's Not Let Phone Pollution Hang Up Free Speech" *Business Week* (Aug. 19 1991), p. 32.

Crews, Jennifer Q., "Regulating Pornography On The Internet: Cyberporn Reignites First Amendment Battles" *Law and Psychology Review*, v. 20 (Spring 1996), pp. 179–95.

Curtis, Sara, "Policing Cyberspace" (Programs to Block Out Pornography) *Maclean's*, v. 109 (Feb. 19 1996), pp. 56–57.

Diamond, Edwin, & Bates, Stephen, "Law and Order Comes to Cyberspace" *Technology Review*, v. 98 (Oct 1995), pp. 22-33.

Dworkin, Ronald Myles, "Liberty and Pornography" *The New York Review of Books*, v. 38 (Aug. 15 1991), pp. 12–15, includes bibliography.

Elmer-Dewitt, Philip, "Censoring Cyberspace" (Carnegie Mellon's Attempt to Ban Sex From Campus Computer Network) *Time*, v. 144 (Nov. 21 1994), pp. 102-104.

Freedman, Eric M., "A Lot More Comes Into Focus When You Remove The Lens Cap: Why Proliferating New Communications Technologies Make It Particularly Urgent For The Supreme Court to Abandon Its Inside-Out Approach to Freedom of Speech and Bring Obscenity, Fighting Words, and Group Libel Within The First Amendment" *Iowa Law Review*, v. 81 (May 1996), pp. 883–968.

Friedman, Meredith Leigh, "Keeping Sex Safe On The Information Superhighway: Computer Pornography and the First Amendment" *New York Law School Law Review*, v. 40 (1996), pp. 1025–56.

Healey, Jon, "Telecommunications: Exon Plan to Sweep Indecency From Superhighway Criticized: Amendment to Protect Children From Adult Material Intensifies Cacophony of Opposition to Rewrite of Communications Law" *Congressional Quarterly Weekly Report*, v. 52 (S 17 1994), pp. 2565–66.

Huber, Peter W., "Electronic Smut" *Forbes*, v. 156 (July 31 1995), p. 110.

Huttig, J.W., "Putting Porn in Its Place? Senator's Bill Targets Online Porn" (Work of J.J. Exon) *PC Novice*, v. 6 (July 1995), pp. 78–79.

Lasica, J.D. "Censorship Devices On The Internet" *American Journalism Review*, v. 19 (7) (Sept. 1997), p. 56.

Lassiter, Christo, "Cyberspace and the Battle For First Amendment" *Law/Technology*, v. 30 (First Quarter 1997), pp. 27-45.

Meyerson, Michael I., "The Right to Speak, The Right to Hear, and the Right Not to Hear: The Technological Resolution to the Cable/Pornography Debate" *University of Michigan Journal of Law Reform*, v. 21 (Fall 1987/Winter 1988), pp. 137–99.

Olson, Tod, "Freedom of Speech in Cyberspace?" (Supreme Court Decision On The Internet and Pornography) Scholastic. Update (Teachers' Edition), v. 130 (Nov. 3 1997), pp. 10–12.

Rich, Frank, "Newt to the Rescue" *New York Times* (late New York Edition) (July 1 1995), p. 19.

Rosen, Jeff, "Cheap Speech" *The New Yorker*, v. 71 (Aug. 7 1995), pp. 75-80.

Rosenberg, Richard S., "Free Speech, Pornography, Sexual Harassment, and Electronic Networks" *Information Society*, v. 9 (Oct./Dec. 1993), pp. 285–331.

Rosenberg, Richard S., "Free Speech, Pornography, Sexual Harassment, and Electronic Networks" *The Information Society*, 1993, v. 9 (4) (Oct-Dec), pp. 285–331.

Samarajiva, Rohan; Mukherjee, Roopali, "Regulation of 976 Services and Dial-A-Porn: Implications For The Intelligent Network" *Telecommunications Policy*, v. 15 (Apr. 1991), pp. 101-5.

Shapiro, Andrew L., "The Danger of Private Cybercops" *New York Times* (Late New York Edition) (Dec. 4 1997), p. A31.

St. Lifer, Evan, "Libraries Challenge NY's Ban On 'Indecency' Online" *Library Journal*, v. 122 (Feb. 15 1997), pp. 90–91.

Stepka, Donald T, "Obscenity On-Line: A Transactional Approach to Computer Transfers of Potentially Obscene Material" *Cornell Law Review*, v. 82 (May 1997), pp. 905–46.

Sussman, Vic S, "Policing Cyberspace" (Work of the Federal Law Enforcement Training Center; Cover Story) *U.S. News & World Report*, v. 118 (Jan. 23 1995), pp. 54–60.

Wallace, Jonathan Mangan, Mark, "Sex, Laws, and Cyberspace" Holt, Henry (LC 96-2668) (ISBN 0-8050-4767-0) Fitzhenry 1996 xv+304p.

Woolfall, Brian D., "Implications of a Bond Requirement For 900-Number Dial-A-

Porn Providers: Exploring The Need For Tighter Restrictions On Obscenity and Indecency" *California Western Law Review*, v. 30 (Spring 1994), pp. 297-311.

Young, Jeffrey R. "From His Dorm Room, a Vanderbilt Junior Becomes a Force Against Internet Regulation" *The Chronicle of Higher Education*, v. 43 (Mar. 7 1997), pp. A23, Il.

Young, Jeffrey R., "Federal Judge Upholds Limits By U. of Oklahoma On Sex-Related Internet Material" *The Chronicle of Higher Education*, v. 43 (Feb. 7 1997), p. A27.

XII. WORKPLACE PORNOGRAPHY

"Constitutional Law–First Amendment–Municipal Zoning–Pornography–The Supreme Court Has Held That a Municipal Zoning Ordinance Prohibiting Adult Motion Picture Theaters From Locating Within 1,000 Feet of Any Residential Zone Single–Or Multiple-Family Dwelling, Church, Park, Or School, Does Not Violate The First Amendment. City of Renton, v. Playtime Theaters, Inc. 106 S.Ct 925." *Duquesne Law Review*, v. 26 (Fall 1987), pp. 163–80.

"Porn At Work: Is It Legal?" Glamour, v. 90 (Apr. 1992), p. 130.

Bruggman, Peggy E., "Beyond Pinups: Workplace Restrictions On The Private Consumption of Pornography." *Hastings Constitutional Law Quarterly*, v. 23 (Fall 1995), pp. 271–311.

Freedman, Warren, "Freedom of Speech On Private Property" Quorum Bks (LC 87-32262) (ISBN 0-89930-323-4) 1988 vii+167p.

Rudoloph, Glenn, "RICO: The Predicate Offense of Obscenity, The Seizure of Adult Bookstore Assets, and the First Amendment" (Northern Ky Law R) v. 15, No 3 (1988), pp. 585–609.